The Philosophy of Free Will

The Philosophy
of Free Will

ESSENTIAL READINGS FROM THE CONTEMPORARY DEBATES

Edited by Paul Russell and Oisín Deery

OXFORD
UNIVERSITY PRESS

OXFORD
UNIVERSITY PRESS

Oxford University Press is a department of the University of Oxford.
It furthers the University's objective of excellence in research, scholarship,
and education by publishing worldwide.

Oxford   New York
Auckland   Cape Town   Dar es Salaam   Hong Kong   Karachi
Kuala Lumpur   Madrid   Melbourne   Mexico City   Nairobi
New Delhi   Shanghai   Taipei   Toronto

With offices in
Argentina   Austria   Brazil   Chile   Czech Republic   France   Greece
Guatemala   Hungary   Italy   Japan   Poland   Portugal   Singapore
South Korea   Switzerland   Thailand   Turkey   Ukraine   Vietnam

Oxford is a registered trademark of Oxford University Press in the UK and certain other
countries.

Published in the United States of America by
Oxford University Press
198 Madison Avenue, New York, NY 10016

Library of Congress Cataloging-in-Publication Data

The philosophy of free will: essential readings from the contemporary debates / edited
by Paul Russell and Oisín Deery.
       p. cm.
Includes bibliographical references and index.
ISBN 978-0-19-973339-2 (pbk.: alk. paper)—ISBN 978-0-19-987584-9 (e-book)
1. Free will and determinism.   I. Russell, Paul, 1955–   II. Deery, Oisín.
BJ1461.P53 2012
123'.5—dc23
2012023581

ISBN   978-0-19-973339-2

9 8 7 6 5 4 3 2 1
Printed in the United States of America
on acid-free paper

In memory of our friend and philosophical companion,
Jamie Avis (1949–2011)

CONTENTS

PART TEN **Optimism, Pessimism, and Their Modes**

PART ELEVEN **The Phenomenology of Agency and Experimental Philosophy**

ACKNOWLEDGMENTS

We would like to thank a number of friends and colleagues for comments, suggestions, and other forms of advice relating to this collection. These individuals include Jamie Avis, John Fischer, Michael McKenna, and Derk Pereboom. We are especially grateful to Peter Ohlin and Lucy Randall for their encouragement and support in the production of this work.

PUBLISHED WITH PERMISSION

CONTRIBUTORS

John Christman is Professor of Philosophy, Political Science, and Women's Studies at Pennsylvania State University.

Randolph Clarke is Professor of Philosophy at Florida State University.

Daniel Dennett is co-director of the Center for Cognitive Studies, the Austin B. Fletcher Professor of Philosophy, and a University Professor at Tufts University.

Richard Double was an Associate Professor at Edinboro University of Pennsylvania.

John Martin Fischer is a Distinguished Professor of Philosophy at the University of California at Riverside.

Harry Frankfurt is Professor Emeritus in Philosophy at Princeton University.

Robert Kane is University Distinguished Teaching Professor of Philosophy Emeritus and Professor of Law at the University of Texas at Austin.

Joshua Knobe is an Associate Professor in the Program in Cognitive Science and Department of Philosophy at Yale University.

Benjamin Libet was a Professor in the Department of Physiology at the University of California, San Francisco.

Michael McKenna is Professor of Philosophy and the Keith Lehrer Chair at the University of Arizona.

Stephen Morris is Assistant Professor in Political Science, Economics, and Philosophy at the College of Staten Island, City University of New York.

Thomas Nadelhoffer is Assistant Professor of Philosophy and affiliate member of the Psychology Department at the College of Charleston.

Thomas Nagel is University Professor of Philosophy and Law at New York University.

Eddy Nahmias is Associate Professor in the Philosophy Department and Neuroscience Institute at Georgia State University.

Dana Nelkin is Professor of Philosophy at the University of California at San Diego

Shaun Nichols is Professor of Philosophy at the University of Arizona.

Timothy O'Connor is Professor of Philosophy at Indiana University.

Michael Otsuka is Professor of Philosophy at London School of Economics.

Derk Pereboom is Professor of Philosophy at Cornell University.

Paul Russell is Professor of Philosophy at the University of British Columbia.

Saul Smilansky is Professor of Philosophy at the University of Haifa.

Galen Strawson is Professor of Philosophy at the University of Texas at Austin.

P.F. Strawson was Waynflete Professor of Metaphysics at Oxford University.

Jason Turner is a Senior Lecturer in Philosophy at the University of Leeds.

Manuel Vargas is Professor of Philosophy at the University of San Francisco.

Peter van Inwagen is John Cardinal O'Hara Professor of Philosophy at the University of Notre Dame.

Kadri Vihvelin is an Associate Professor of Philosophy at the University of Southern California.

Gary Watson is Provost Professor of Philosophy and Law at the University of Southern California.

Susan Wolf is the Edna J. Koury Professor of Philosophy at the University of North Carolina at Chapel Hill.

Introduction

...those soul-trying moments when fate's scales seem to quiver, and good snatches the victory from evil or shrinks nerveless from the fight...That is what gives the palpitating reality to our moral life and makes it tingle...

—WILLIAM JAMES, "THE DILEMMA OF DETERMINISM"

It is often said that while philosophers may be good at asking questions their success in answering them is less impressive. These doubts may seem particularly apt in the case of the free-will problem—an issue that has been debated for many centuries in one form or another. There is, nevertheless, good reason to look more favorably on the accomplishments of philosophy in light of recent developments in the free-will debate. Although it may be said with some justice that the free-will debate stalled and became stagnant for a long period of time, lasting well into the twentieth century, this cannot be accurately said of the debate over the past half-century. Any student studying the core philosophical literature in the period around the middle of the twentieth century would be immediately struck by the contrast in complexity and subtlety, as well as the variety, of positions now available to their contemporary counterpart. This is, moreover, not just a feature of one side or one party in the debate—it is true right across the board. All the major parties in the free-will debate, judged by any reasonable philosophical standard, have had to revise and amend their core positions and strategies with a view to meeting the more sophisticated and nuanced positions and arguments advanced by their philosophical critics and opponents. If progress in philosophy is measured only in terms of securing consensus and agreement, or finding a view or position which all philosophers have come to accept and acknowledge, then the free-will debate has not progressed a great deal, judged in these terms. However, if progress is to be measured by the philosophical quality of the positions offered, understood in terms of their flexibility and ingenuity in dealing with familiar objections and failings, as well as finding new ground on which to develop alternative positions and strategies that offer a way through or around these difficulties and objections, then considerable and significant progress has been made in this area during the past half-century. Indeed, the range and number of valuable and significant new initiatives and contributions is so extensive that it is proving hard for anthologies and collections to keep up-to-date and at the cutting edge of this debate. This volume has been gathered together with the aim of providing contemporary readers with a clearer view of the field as it has recently evolved, identifying particularly important issues and proposals that are currently under consideration.

Although it is our intention to allow the contributions in this volume to speak for themselves, it will be helpful, nevertheless, if we provide our readers with a brief overview of the background to the classical free-will debate, along with a sketch of the central themes and issues of the contemporary debate that we will use to structure and arrange the contributions we have included in this volume.

The Classical Free Will Debate

Over a period of many centuries the problem of free will has taken a variety of forms and raised a number of interconnected issues and difficulties. The fundamental question at issue is the extent to which human agents are in control of their own lives and destinies. In different historical and social contexts various aspects of this problem have proved to be more salient than others. For many centuries the central preoccupation of philosophers concerned the religious difficulties involved in explaining how human freedom and moral responsibility could be rendered consistent with established assumptions about divine foreknowledge and predestination. In the early modern period the focus of attention switched from these theological aspects of the free-will problem to issues arising from the advance of modern science and its metaphysical assumptions. More specifically, when the concepts and categories of natural science were extended to include human thought and action, viewed as part of the seamless natural order of things, skeptical problems were generated relating to our self-image as free and responsible beings.

One familiar way of presenting these problems, as formulated in classical free-will debate associated with early modern philosophy, is through the dilemma of determinism. The thesis of determinism has traditionally been broadly interpreted as the claim that everything that happens in the world, including human thought and action, is subject to causal laws. While the analysis of causal laws and causal relations may vary, it has been widely accepted that causation involves necessitation of effects by antecedent causal conditions. It follows from this that insofar as human action is caused it is thereby necessitated by causal antecedents in such a way that the action *must* follow, given the antecedent conditions. These assumptions are, according to some philosophers, *incompatible* with human freedom and moral responsibility.

One argument that classical incompatibilists have advanced in support of this claim concerns the issue of alternate possibilities and an agent's ability to act otherwise. It is argued that moral responsibility requires the sort of freedom which ensures that the agent could have acted otherwise. If an agent's actions are causally necessitated then there is no real open alternative available, given the actual conditions. It follows from this that determinism rules out the sort of freedom required for moral responsibility. Classical compatibilists reject this line of argument, in the first place, on the ground that the correct analysis of "could have done otherwise" is not categorical but hypothetical or conditional in nature. When we say that an agent "could have done otherwise" this means only that the agent would have done otherwise *if* he had chosen or willed differently. The crucial distinction we need to get clear about, they argue, is the difference between causal necessitation and coercion or compulsion of some kind. While it is true that freedom requires an absence of coercion and compulsion, causal necessity does not imply any form of coercion or compulsion. Conduct is compelled or coerced when it is *caused in a particular way*, when it is produced without or against the agent's will and desires. However, when action is caused by the agent's own will or desires then the agent can be said to act freely in the sense required for moral responsibility. Granted that the agent brings about the action through her own willings, the action is plainly attributable to her. Moreover, as long as action is produced by the agent's own will or desires we are in a position to (causally) influence the agent's future conduct by means of the motives of rewards and punishments. When an agent is free in this sense, these incentives will serve to guide and determine their conduct in socially desirable ways. Clearly, then, the only sort of freedom required for moral responsibility is a freedom to act according to the determination of our own will.

Classical incompatibilists reject this strategy and object, in particular, to its forward-looking, utilitarian understanding of moral responsibility. Children and animals, they argue, also act according to their own will and may also be influenced by rewards and punishments. They are, nevertheless, obviously not moral agents who can be properly held accountable for their actions. It is evident, therefore, that something crucial is missing from the classical compatibilist account of freedom and responsibility. According to incompatibilists, the crucial missing element is captured by the notion of *moral desert*, which requires that the agent is in some relevant sense the source or origin of her conduct. For an agent to be the originator or source of her conduct it will not suffice that she acts freely (i.e., without coercion, compulsion, etc.). It is also necessary that she was able to *choose* between genuinely open alternatives, and this requires the falsity of determinism and the absence of causal necessity. What is needed, on this analysis, is freedom to choose among alternative possibilities in a way in which the outcome depends solely on the agent and not on prior causal conditions. What is required is not simply free action but *freedom of choice or free will*. Those incompatibilists who believe that these metaphysical requirements can be met or satisfied are known as *libertarians*.

One common objection to libertarianism, from a classical compatibilist perspective, is that there is a significant difference between an action being free and an action being simply uncaused. If an action lacks any cause, critics argue, then it is merely a chance event that cannot be attributed to any agent. In order for libertarians to avoid the difficulties associated with the horn of chance— i.e., the other side of the dilemma of determinism—it is crucial that they provide some account of free will that goes beyond the simple negative claim that our (free) actions are not causally necessitated. That is to say, libertarians need to be able to provide some metaphysical content to their notion of free will, or genuinely open choice, that does not collapse into mere chance or capriciousness. According to their critics, when libertarians try to meet this challenge their metaphysical commitments inevitably take the form of anti-naturalistic accounts that are obscure and impossible to integrate into the natural order of events in the world. The costs of adopting "spooky metaphysics" of this kind— such as non-empirical selves, special modes of causation, and so on—are both unnecessary and unacceptable. In sum, there is no available solution to the free-will problem on this side of the dilemma of determinism.

The trajectory of the classical free-will debate, given the difficulties encountered on both sides of the dilemma of determinism, threaten to lead us directly to the skeptical conclusion that the sort of freedom required for moral responsibility is impossible. On the side of compatibilism, the theory of freedom provided is too thin and frail to secure the sorts of distinctions that we need. A mere ability to act according to the determination of our own will, or to be subject to the influence of motives such as rewards and punishments, cannot serve as a credible foundation for moral life. On the other hand, when libertarians undertake to describe alternative metaphysical foundations that involve the absence of determinism and causal necessity, their accounts are not only obscure in nature, they also encounter their own particular set of difficulties relating to chance and luck. The upshot of all this is that a general skepticism about human freedom and moral responsibility seems unavoidable. Free will, like the existence of God or the immortality of the soul, is a metaphysical illusion that we must now abandon.

It is a rather striking fact about the history of the classical free-will debate that the radical skeptical conclusion has found relatively few defenders or adherents (in contrast, it may be said, with skepticism about the existence of God or the immortality of the soul). The explanation for this is that a radical skepticism of this kind seems both intellectually incredible and humanly impossible for us to live with or accept in practice. At one level this raises the concern that our core self-image as free and responsible agents is an indispensable part of our natural human make-up, and as such is immune to any skeptical challenges presented on the basis of philosophical reflection (e.g., in much the same way as skeptical challenges relating to the existence of the external world or other minds may also fail to secure any sincere or consistent acceptance—however difficult the arguments advanced may be to refute). At another level, resistance to radical skepticism with respect to our self-image as free and responsible beings may reflect our *practical* interest in this matter. Viewing ourselves as beings incapable of genuinely free, moral agency would disturb so many features and aspects of our lives that we value and care about—for example, relating to dignity, self-respect, creativity, and human emotions and relationships—that a deep pessimism about the human predicament would fall upon us and become unbearable if we were to sincerely embrace such an outlook or attitude to life. As beings who must live and act in the world, a gloomy pessimism of this sort is one that we will naturally and reasonably resist, whatever philosophical arguments may be put to us by the skeptic. Nevertheless, be this as it may, these observations do not, in themselves, refute the skeptic, so much as invite us to *ignore* the skeptic—which is a different matter. As things stand with the classical debate, none of the available positions seem to be philosophically secure or comfortable. For a period of several centuries, stretching from the middle of the seventeenth century through to the middle of the twentieth century, these familiar arguments of compatibilists, libertarians, and skeptics have been repeated and revised. The key battle-lines of the debate have remained largely unchanged, with little movement or variation in the strategies on offer and no sight of some credible solution on the horizon.

The Contemporary Debate

The readings in this volume make clear that the free-will debate is no longer stalled or stagnant. These readings have been selected and arranged with a view to highlighting the main contours of the current discussion by identifying the key issues and more significant contributions. The remarks that follow provide a brief description of the contents of the eleven sections of this volume and explain how they are structured and related to each other.

I. THE FREE WILL PROBLEM—REAL OR ILLUSORY?

Classical compatibilists have often argued that the free-will problem is either merely "verbal" in nature or simply a "pseudo-problem." The general force of these claims was to show that the obscure metaphysics of libertarianism is largely motivated by incompatibilist confusions and muddles that generate artificial and groundless worries and anxieties about the implications of determinism. In reply to this, incompatibilists maintain that classical compatibilism fails to appreciate the genuine difficulties that deterministic assumptions pose and that the sort of easy solutions compatibilists have offered fail to address the real and substantial difficulties we encounter here. The selections by Daniel Dennett and Thomas Nagel fall on either side of this dispute. According to Dennett, the classical free-will problem is largely a product of "fearmongery" by philosophers. The worries and anxieties generated on this subject are produced by false and misleading analogies in respect of the implications of determinism for the human condition. Once these misleading analogies and "intuition pumps" are exposed and discredited, the free-will problem will simply evaporate.

In contrast with this, Nagel aims to show just how deep and perplexing the free-will problem is and the way in which it is systematically and intimately connected with many other fundamental problems of philosophy. Nagel approaches this task by way of considering various ways in which agents lack control over their conduct and character, leaving them vulnerable to the influence of fate and luck. The overall effect of these reflections on the limits of human agency is to erode our confidence that agents can ever be legitimately held morally responsible for anything that they do, as ultimately everything an agent does is a result of factors that she does not control. Nagel does not aim to solve this problem so much as to explain its roots in the split between our internal (subjective) experience of being agents and an external (objective) perspective which presents our actions as mere events that are part of the natural causal order. The intractable nature of the free-will problem, Nagel maintains, has its source in this clash of perspectives with respect to human agency.

II. NATURALISM AGAINST SKEPTICISM

Throughout much of the twentieth century, consistent with widely accepted views about the nature of philosophical methodology, it was assumed that the right approach for solving the free-will problem was to provide a logical or conceptual analysis of the key (problematic) terms in this debate. With this in mind, much of the relevant literature was devoted to arguments about how to analyze different senses of "freedom," "causation," and their relations with "moral responsibility" and other similar notions. For the most part this was seen as an a priori or "armchair" investigation, requiring the special gifts and training of the philosopher to spot philosophical ambiguity or confusion. This way of thinking about the free-will problem was challenged in a radical and innovative way by P.F. Strawson in his influential paper "Freedom and Resentment"—a contribution that has done much to stimulate the current debate. In this paper Strawson aims to find an acceptable middle-ground between classical compatibilists and their libertarian/incompatibilist opponents. Strawson invites us to begin our investigations, not with a priori analyses of the meanings of the key terms involved, but rather with a careful consideration of some familiar psychological facts about human nature and our social attitudes and practices. More specifically, his approach begins by drawing attention to our natural human "reactive attitudes" (i.e., moral senti-ments broadly conceived), understood as basic human responses to the atti-tudes and intentions of people we are dealing with in social life. On the basis of an analysis of the rationale of excusing considerations, Strawson goes on to argue that with respect to our reactive attitudes considerations of determin-ism do not engage or fall within the scope of any recognized excusing consid-erations. According to Strawson, moral responsibility has to be understood and interpreted in terms of this general psychological and normative frame-work, or "web" of our reactive attitudes. It follows from this that determinism poses no threat to our commitment to moral responsibility understood in these terms. While classical compatibilists were right about this issue, their incompatibilist critics were also correct in claiming that "something vital" is missing from classical compatibilist accounts. The vital element that is miss-ing, however, is not "contra-causal freedom" of the sort that libertarians are searching after but rather a proper appreciation of the role that reactive atti-tudes play in this sphere—something both sides of this debate have failed to recognize and give appropriate weight to. One particularly controversial fea-ture of Strawson's wider argument is his claim that a proper appreciation of these psychological facts regarding the place and role that reactive attitudes in human life suggests that we are immune to the force of all skeptical argu-ments insofar as they aim to discredit and systematically dislodge our (natu-ral) human commitment to the attitudes and practices associated with moral responsibility.

In the decades that have followed, Strawson's approach to the free-will problem through reactive attitudes or moral sentiments has generated a large volume of literature. One of the most engaging and insightful contributions to this literature is Gary Watson's "Responsibility and the Limits of Evil." Although Watson's discussion is highly sympathetic, he raises several "hard questions" for Strawson's (expressivist) theory of responsibility. One of these is how exactly we are to identify the boundaries of the moral community as constituted by those individuals who are appropriate targets of our reac-tive attitudes? What is needed here, Watson argues, is a more precise account of the nature of exempting conditions, whereby some individuals (e.g., the immature, the insane, etc.) are excluded as legitimate targets of our reac-tive attitudes. According to Watson, Strawson does not provide any full or adequate interpretation of this important aspect of the rationale of excuses. Watson presents a powerful example of the sort of difficulties we face by way of his detailed description of the disturbing case of Robert Harris, a convicted murder. Harris's extreme evil, Watson suggests, makes it hard to decide whether or not he is really a proper target for reactive attitudes, since he lacks any shared framework of values that make for conditions of "intelligible moral address." In relation to this case, Watson describes the tension that we experience when we reflect not only on Harris's crimes, but also on his horrific background of childhood abuse and deprivation. One general conclusion that Watson draws from his reflections on the case of Robert Harris is that, contrary to Strawson, it is not obvious that our reactive attitudes are immune to historical considerations in the way Strawson supposes. (Here there are obvious points of overlap with Nagel's discussion of moral luck that merit further consideration.)

III. THE CONSEQUENCE ARGUMENT

While it is Strawson's central aim in "Freedom and Resentment" to allay any concern that the thesis of determinism poses a threat to freedom and moral responsibility, his arguments have not persuaded incompatibilists. A fundamental and long-standing incompatibilist objection concerns how, on the assumption of determinism, events in the distant past along with the laws of nature are related to our actions and our ability to do otherwise. In his *An Essay on Free Will*, Peter van Inwagen aims to articulate and present these concerns in a more rigorous form. He begins with an informal statement of his argument.

> If determinism is true, then our acts are the consequences of the laws of nature and events in the remote past. But it is not up to us what went on before we were born, and neither is it up to us what the laws of nature are. Therefore, the consequences of these things (including our present acts) are not up to us.

The basic intuition lying behind this argument is that if we cannot change something, then we cannot change anything that is a necessary consequence of it. For example, if it is true that the sun will explode in 2020 and no one has any choice about this, and also true that if the sun explodes all life on earth will die out and no one has any choice about this either, then it follows that no one has any choice about whether all life on earth will die out in 2020. In cases of this kind there is a "transfer of powerlessness" from one state of affairs to another. According to the Consequence Argument, the thesis of determinism implies that everyone is powerless with respect to all our actions, insofar as they are understood to be the necessary consequences of prior conditions and laws that we cannot change and have no choice about.

Van Inwagen's more formal presentation of this argument relies upon some more technical apparatus. He begins by introducing the expression "Np"—where "p" represents any sentence, and "Np" is read as, "p and no one has, or ever had, any choice about whether p." To have a choice about p is to be able to render p false. Additionally, van Inwagen employs two inference rules. The first, Rule Alpha, states that if a proposition is logically necessary then no one has any choice about it (i.e., it cannot be rendered false). The second, Rule Beta, states that if no one has any choice about p, and no one has any choice about p logically implying q, then no one has any choice about q. Using this apparatus van Inwagen constructs a formal argument to show that if determinism is true, a proposition describing the state of the world in the remote past, in conjunction with a proposition describing the laws of nature, logically entails any true proposition, including all true propositions describing any actions we may perform. Granted we have no choice about the past and the laws of nature, and no choice about their consequences (i.e., what is logically implied by these propositions), it follows, by Rule Beta, that we have no choice about any of our actions (i.e., we cannot render false any of the propositions describing these actions). If this is the case, we cannot do otherwise and, assuming free will requires the power to do otherwise, it follows that no one has free will.

Much of the debate is in response to van Inwagen's statement of the Consequence Argument has turned on the validity of Rule Beta. In the reading that follows, Dana Nelkin, following up on some of the critical literature on this topic, considers a serious problem facing libertarians who want to rely on Rule Beta and the Consequence Argument. The difficulty they face is that Rule Beta also lends support to an argument for the incompatibility of freedom and indeterminism—the influential (anti-libertarian) Mind Argument, as it is known. The basic idea behind the Mind Argument is that in an indeterministic world our actions are caused but not determined by prior states of mind of the agent. However, as ultimately no one has a choice about the causes of these states of mind, and no one has a choice about whether these states of mind will have a particular result or not, it follows that no one has a choice about the actions that they may cause. If this is the case, then adopting Rule Beta leads to skepticism about the very possibility of freedom understood as the ability to do otherwise. This is, of course, a conclusion that both compatibilists and libertarians will want to avoid.

Nelkin's discussion of this issue examines various ways that compatibilists and libertarians have responded to the challenges presented by Rule Beta. Some compatibilists have argued that Rule Beta is false on the ground that it is vulnerable to counterexamples based on concerns about agglomeration. In reply, libertarian incompatibilists have proposed a revised version of Rule Beta—Beta 2—which, they argue, still serves the purposes of the Consequence Argument but is not consistent with the Mind argument. This way the Consequence Argument can be saved but the Mind Argument fails. In response to this, Nelkin argues that the Mind Argument can be reformulated using Beta 2 and, therefore, both arguments stand or fall together. She concludes by noting that while it may be true that we cannot ensure that we act other than we actually do, this may not be the freedom we care about. If we understand acting freely in terms of our states of mind causing our actions we can escape both incompatibilist and skeptical conclusions.

IV. RESPONSIBILITY AND ALTERNATIVE POSSIBILITIES

If moral responsibility requires free will, and free will requires being able to do otherwise, then moral responsibility requires being able to do otherwise. This view is formulated by Harry Frankfurt as the Principle of Alternate Possibilities (PAP) and it is a view that was once shared by all parties in the free-will debate, including compatibilists. As we have noted, one particularly influential compatibilist strategy was to interpret the claim that we could have done otherwise as meaning that *if* the agent chose or willed to do otherwise, he would have done so. This hypothetical analysis has not, however, convinced incompatibilist critics, who argue that we require a categorical analysis of this ability, one that does not suppose our choices or willings were different in the actual circumstances. Harry Frankfurt has suggested a way in which the difficulties relating to PAP may be side-stepped. He does this by describing a counter-example to PAP which establishes that to be responsible, it is not necessary that an agent be able to do otherwise. The example he describes involves a neurosurgeon (Black) who wants Jones to choose a certain way (A). Black is able to intervene to control Jones's brain processes should Jones be about to choose differently (B). Jones is unaware of Black's presence and Black waits to see how Jones will choose on his own, as Black will intervene only if he has to. Granted that Jones chooses A on his own, without any intervention by Black, it seems that he is morally responsible for his choice, even though he had no alternative possibility (as Black would have intervened had he decided to do otherwise). It follows from the analysis of this situation that PAP is false. To the extent that both traditional incompatibilism and classical compatibilism rely on PAP, they too are false.

In response to Frankfurt's attempt to discredit PAP there have been a variety of criticisms aiming to show that his example fails, as well as new Frankfurt-style examples devised to meet these objections. Michael Otsuka's paper serves as an incompatibilist response to Frankfurt's example. Otsuka accepts that Frankfurt's example is a genuine counterexample to PAP. His strategy is to argue that we should replace PAP in favor of a different incompatibilist principle, which he calls "The Principle of Avoidable Blame." According to this principle one is responsible for performing an act of a given type only if one could instead have behaved in a manner for which one would have been entirely blameless. Unlike the PAP, the Principle of Avoidable Blame is sensitive to the ethical quality (i.e., blameworthiness) of our alternatives. The Principle of Avoidable Blame, Otsuka argues, allows us to formulate a revised argument for incompatibilism in a way that does not leave it vulnerable to Frankfurt-style counter-examples. In further support of his alternate principle Otsuka also provides an account of blame as it relates to "reactive attitudes," as well as a discussion of the Principle of Avoidable Blame as it relates to tragic choices and moral luck.

In "Free Will Demystified: A Dispositional Account," Kadri Vihvelin argues—from the *compatibilist's* point of view—that Frankfurt's argument against PAP fails. First, she argues that even though the classical compatibilist analysis of the ability to do otherwise fails, there is a viable account of the ability to do otherwise available to the compatibilist. According to Vihvelin, an ability to act (or not to act, which is just to be able to act in another way) is analyzable along the following lines: an agent can do A at t_1 (say, raise her hand at t_1) just in case were she to choose to do A at t_2, and her body stayed working normally and nothing interfered with her, she would do A at t_2. In other words, Vihvelin holds that "persons have abilities by having intrinsic properties that are the causal basis of the ability." So Vihvelin thinks that an ability to act is a disposition, or a bundle of dispositions. And, as she points out, "no one denies that dispositions are compatible with determinism." After all, even if determinism is true, glass is still fragile—i.e., it has the disposition to break if struck.

If this account is right, then Vihvelin thinks that compatibilists *shouldn't* abandon PAP. After all, Frankfurt's argument is supposed to work no matter how we understand the ability to do otherwise. The crucial step in his argument is that Black's presence has the result that Jones is unable to do otherwise, since he lacks alternative possibilities. But on Vihvelin's account of the ability to do otherwise, Jones *is* able to do otherwise, even with Black on the scene. So on Vihvelin's compatibilist understanding of the ability to do otherwise, Frankfurt's argument fails. The conclusion Vihvelin wants us to draw is that compatibilists should retain their classical position: agents can do otherwise even if determinism is true, and this ability is required for moral responsibility.

V. LIBERTARIAN ALTERNATIVES—SOFT AND HARD

Libertarians are incompatibilists who reject skepticism about freedom and moral responsibility. On their account, the possibility of and existence of human freedom and moral responsibility depends on indeterministic metaphysics. With regard to this, as we have noted, libertarians face the challenge of fending off the objection that placing human freedom and moral responsibility on the metaphysical foundations of indeterminism serves only to generate problems of chance and luck, which erodes and diminishes rather than supports freedom and responsibility. Even if this is not the case, it may still be argued that indeterminism does not and cannot *enhance* or *expand* our freedom and responsibility. The basic problem for libertarians, therefore, is to explain how the absence of determinism contributes to human freedom and moral responsibility.

The traditional libertarian approach, reaching back to figures such as Thomas Reid and Immanuel Kant, has been some form of agent causation. Agent causation is understood to be distinct from event-causation and may also be regarded as the only genuine or real causation. Although the details vary, all forms of the traditional view hold that when an agent acts with free will the event that is directly agent-caused has no event-cause. The two crucial elements in this account are the conception of an agent as a substance (in earlier versions this is generally taken to be an immaterial, indivisible, intelligent substance—or a *soul*) that is not reducible to a series of events or states, and also a conception of causation such that something that is not an event (e.g., a substance) can bring about an event without there being any antecedent sufficient conditions that necessitate that event. Famously, the difficulty here is to avoid obscure or unintelligible metaphysical commitments that render libertarianism incoherent or inconsistent with the naturalism of modern science.

The three papers in this section each suggest a different way in which contemporary libertarians may attempt to meet this challenge. The first way, adopted by Robert Kane, is simply to abandon agent-causal accounts in favor of an event-causal account. A key feature of Kane's account is that he combines an event-causal theory of action with the view that causes need not necessitate their effects. This enables the libertarian to construct a theory of freedom and moral responsibility which turns on the notion of "self-forming actions" whereby an agent is presented with plural reasons for action such that the agent is not necessitated to act on any one of the available reasons and could act otherwise, on another available reason, in the same circumstances. However, when the agent acts on one or other of the available reasons the agent still acts voluntarily, intentionally, and for a reason, even though she could have done otherwise in the same circumstances. Moreover, whichever way she acts, Kane argues, it is the result of her choice and efforts. According to Kane, this model allows libertarians to reject the criticism that indeterminism introduces unacceptable, responsibility-eroding forms of luck into our moral life. Beyond this, Kane also argues that his event-causal model of free action and moral agency is consistent with and supported by recent developments in neuroscience (e.g., relating to neutral networks) along with our understanding of the brain as a parallel processor—and so libertarianism of this kind in no way depends on obscure or unscientific metaphysical assumptions.

Unlike Kane, Randolph Clarke does not entirely abandon agent-causation as a feature of his alternative account of libertarianism. Although he argues that agent-causation in its traditional or pure form is vulnerable to the charge of being mysterious if not incomprehensible, he nevertheless believes it can be resuscitated in another form, one that integrates agent-causation with universal event-causation. Whereas the traditional view maintains that the relevant event that is directly caused by the agent when she acts freely has no event-cause, on Clarke's "causal agent-causal view" this event is non-deterministically caused by prior events. On Clarke's account, "the agent's acting with free will consists (crucially but not wholly) in her actions being caused, in this way, by her and by her reasons." The agent's reasons are prior events that have a causal role to play but do not necessitate or determine the action. Crucially, the agent also has a role to play in determining which of the particular reasons available become the cause of her actions. When an agent acts freely, on this account, she exercises a power that influences which of the alternative actions left open by prior events will actually be performed. In this way, the causal agent-causal view "mixes event causation and agent causation in its account of the production of action." Since the agent exercises a further causal power of this kind she is, "in a strict and literal sense an originator of her action." This alternative account, Clarke maintains, avoids many of the difficulties of the traditional view and, in particular, it provides a more naturalistic view of free action while still providing a role for the causal activity of the agent herself.

In the third and final contribution in this section Timothy O'Connor seeks to provide a defense and explanation of the traditional agent-causal view. Contrary to the widely held view that agent-causal theories are incoherent or unintelligible, O'Connor aims to show that we can come to a clearer understanding of agent-causal power and the metaphysics of free will on the basis of a more general account of the metaphysics of causal powers. O'Connor provides a "structural tendency account" of agent causation. First, he assumes a metaphysical picture according to which the world is populated by primitive qualities whose nature is irreducibly dispositional. Such qualities involve "tendencies to interact with other qualities in producing some effect, or some range of possible effects." Importantly, such dispositionality need not be deterministic; there may be "objective probabilities less than one that a cause will produce its characteristic effect on a given occasion." O'Connor applies this metaphysics to agents. According to O'Connor, "[A]n adequate account of freedom requires...a notion of a distinctive variety of causal power, one which tradition dubs 'agent-causal power.'" Of course, O'Connor doesn't insist that any agent *actually* possesses such a power, only that some possible agents (perhaps us) *could* possess it. O'Connor's key requirements are that the agent's power be ontologically both *emergent* and *basic*: it must confer on the system that possesses it the power non-redundantly to contribute to that system's overall causal power. O'Connor thinks we can make sense of such emergent powers, "ones that are at once causally dependent on microphysically-based structural states and yet ontologically primitive." The sort of power he envisages here would confer upon any agent possessing it an ability to *cause an intention*, or—as he puts it—to cause "an event which is the coming to be of a state of an intention." The idea here is that reasons *causally structure* the agent-causal power by conferring continually varying objective probabilities on the agent's causing certain intentions. But the forming of intentions is (crucially) goal-directed. By acting *on* a given reason, an agent may also act *for* that reason, when she causes an intention to act for the purpose of realizing a goal, and she believes that so acting will help her to achieve it.

VI. COMPATIBILISM: HIERARCHICAL THEORIES
AND MANIPULATION PROBLEMS

According to standard classical compatibilist accounts, the freedom required for moral responsibility is simply the freedom to do as we want or please. There is no metaphysical freedom of will lying behind this. This account, as we have noted, is vulnerable to a number of obvious objections. The most important of these is that it fails to distinguish responsible agents from children, the insane, and animals— all of whom may enjoy freedom to act according to their desires. A plausible and satisfying account of freedom and responsibility requires something deeper than the classical compatibilist can provide us with. Harry Frankfurt aims to supply this missing depth by means of his alternative hierarchical account. Frankfurt's hierarchical account turns on several key distinctions. In the first place we need to distinguish between "persons," who are able to form preferences about the structure of their will, and "wantons," who lack any such capacity. Persons, unlike wantons, are able to form second-order volitions about which of their first-order desires will become their will or be effective in action. Wantons lack this capacity to reflect critically on their own will and for this reason freedom of the will, as opposed to freedom of action, is not a problem for them. In contrast with the wanton, persons may or may not reflectively identify with and endorse their own will. When a person's will is not in conformity with his second-order preferences then, Frankfurt suggests, we may say it is not truly his own. The apparatus of second-order reflection allows us to speak of a person having a "real self," as identified through their second-order preferences about the structure of their will. What is crucial for moral responsibility, on this view, is that the agent reflectively identifies with his own will. A person who has freedom of will is one who can reliably secure conformity of his will to his second-order volitions.

The most obvious objection to hierarchical or real self views of the kind that Frankfurt proposes is that a manipulator or "puppeteer" could insert or implant second-order preferences of the relevant kind, satisfying the conditions of responsibility or free agency as described by the hierarchical model. Intuitively, such an agent is neither free nor responsible. The model cannot, therefore, critics maintain, provide us with a way of identifying sufficient conditions for free or responsible decisions. Richard Double suggests two possible lines of reply. First, granted that in ordinary cases of determinism we are not controlled by nature (since nature is not another agent), we may simply add a further condition that "free decisions require a normal etiology that excludes being brought about by external agents." Second, we may also identify a set of characteristics (i.e., "autonomy variables") that ensure that our decisions are ours irrespective of whether the cause that produces these decisions is determined or even controlled by a puppeteer. According to Double, as long as the agent has self-knowledge, and her states of mind are subject to critical self-assessment that effectively govern the agent's will, then she has rational control, which is all that is needed with respect to free will.

VII. COMPATIBILISM: REASON-BASED ALTERNATIVES

Although Frankfurt maintains that the formation of second-order volitions requires rational capacities, he places no restriction on the causes or source of these preferences. Our second-order volitions (or even higher-order preferences) may be capricious and lacking any rational basis. What matters, for the purpose responsible agency, is simply that the person concerned *decisively* identifies himself with the relevant first-order desires. Double's elaboration and revision of this model by way of the suggested "autonomy variables," demands tighter control of our higher-order preferences by our rational capacities. From this perspective, what really matters for the purpose of freedom and responsibility is not a hierarchical structure to our will as such, but rather that our will is subject to rational control. The papers by Susan Wolf and John Fischer present more elaborate versions of this general model. What is crucial to their proposals is that responsible agency requires some form of rational self-control that may be satisfied within the limits of compatibilist commitments.

Wolf argues that hierarchical views such as Frankfurt's (what she refers to as broadly the "deep-self view") correctly identify a necessary condition for responsibility but fail to provide a sufficient condition of responsibility since it is not evident that even our deepest selves are up to us. While some may insist that what is required for responsibility is some form of self-creation, Wolf argues that all that is actually required, in addition to the original model, is that our deep-self be *sane.* In its essentials, what sanity requires is that we are able to understand and appreciate right and wrong, and to change our character and our actions accordingly. What the sane deep-self view presupposes is that responsible agents are able to *correct* or *improve* themselves. Individuals who come from deprived childhoods or are victims of corrupt societies and upbringings cannot help but be mistaken about their values, and for this reason, Wolf maintains, we do not blame them for their actions that flow from their values.

John Fischer aims to combine the best features of incompatibilism and compatibilism, arriving at a position he calls "semi-compatibilism." On the incompatibilist side of things, Fischer finds the Consequence Argument "highly plausible" and is disposed to accept its conclusion that determinism rules out freedom understood in terms of a capacity to select among open alternatives. On the other hand, Fischer is also persuaded by Frankfurt-style examples, which suggest that we do not require alternative possibilities (or any freedom of this kind) for moral responsibility. He makes his case for compatibilism with respect to moral responsibility primarily on the basis of a distinction between two kinds of control. What he describes as "regulative control," which requires alternate possibilities and the freedom to choose otherwise, is not required for moral responsibility. What is required is simply "guidance control," where this is understood as effectively governing your choices and actions by your own reasons (e.g., when an agent is directly in control of a car's movements). As long as the agent has this kind of control operating in the actual-sequence, the absence of regulative control does not undermine the agent's responsibility (as we find in Frankfurt-style cases). Fischer goes on to provide a general account of what is required for guidance control and moral responsibility. His account requires, first, that the agent can recognize reasons and, in particular, recognize moral reasons. Secondly, it also requires that the underlying "mechanism" or process of practical reasoning involved is in a relevant way the *agent's own*. Ownership of this kind is explained by Fischer as a matter of "taking responsibility," whereby the agent comes to see herself in a certain way—in a way that involves, among other things, seeing herself as a fair target of reactive attitudes based upon how she exercises her agency. When these two conditions are satisfied then our self-image as (robustly) responsible moral agents will be secured against any threat related to the truth of determinism.

VIII. AUTONOMY AND HISTORY

Both hierarchical and reason-responsive compatibilist theories have done much to address some basic weaknesses and shortcomings in classical compatibilist accounts. This includes efforts to provide greater "depth" and complexity for compatibilists in a manner that allows it to draw several key distinctions that earlier, cruder views could not make. Having said this, however, a familiar and fundamental objection of incompatibilism persists: the worry that the sorts of conditions required by hierarchical or reasons-responsive theories could be satisfied consistent with the fact that the agents concerned have their (structured) wills or set of values and preferences implanted or manipulated by another agent (e.g., an evil neurosurgeon, the Devil, etc.). This general problem, as discussed by Richard Double and John Fischer, raises worries about "ownership" or "autonomy"—where autonomy is understood in terms of an agent's ability to be truly "self-governing" and motivated by desires and preference that are properly her own or "authentic" (i.e., not "alien" or "external"). The question arises, therefore, how compatibilists can meet this challenge. The "soft compatibilist" response is to agree that conditions of manipulation or implantation, as described, are indeed inconsistent with freedom and responsibility but that compatibilists have a principled way of dealing with cases of this kind by appealing to relevant "historical" considerations.

How can agent autonomy be protected or preserved by way of relevant historical considerations? John Christman presents an important statement of this approach, one that has been further developed and refined in recent philosophical literature. What Christman suggests is that we should "focus on the manner which the agent *came to have* a set of desires rather than her attitude towards the desires at any one time." It is, he argues, the process of desire formation that is relevant to understanding the conditions of autonomy, and this must involve the agent's *participation* in the formation of her preferences. More specifically, autonomy is satisfied only when an agent is aware of changes and developments of her character and is in a position to *resist* such changes on the basis of her self-understanding. These requirements, Christman maintains, serve to exclude cases where a person is manipulated or subject to social conditioning that undermines her reflective capacities. In general, the relevance of history for assessing issues of autonomy and ownership is that it aims to provide a basis for identifying deviant causal origins of an agent's desires and preferences which undermine or erode freedom and responsibility. (One especially significant feature of Christman's account of autonomy is that it is relevant to problems of political as well as moral freedom.)

In contrast with Christman's approach, Michael McKenna aims to provide a "modest defense" of a nonhistorical compatibilist response to objections based on global manipulation (i.e., consistent with Frankfurt's "tough stand" on manipulation cases). McKenna's "hard compatibilist" strategy begins by assessing the case for (soft) historical compatibilism, giving particular attention to Alfred Mele's influential efforts to support the conclusion that at least one necessary condition of "compatibilist-friendly agential structure" must be an historical one. McKenna argues that manipulation examples can be extended to cover historical conditions (i.e., relating to the way an agent's values and attitudes have been produced) whereby even historical compatibilists, such as Mele, must accept that a manipulated agent may nevertheless be free and morally responsible for what she does. With this in mind, McKenna goes on to explain why we are reluctant to accept that a manipulated agent may be free and responsible. Two considerations are especially important according to McKenna's hard compatibilist analysis. First, it is important to recognize that even if an agent who has been globally manipulated is free and responsible for the actions that flow from her values and attitudes, unlike a non-manipulated agent she is not responsible for coming to be the sort of person she is. With respect to this dimension of her agency there is a significant gap between the globally manipulated and non-manipulated agent, which the hard compatibilist can and should recognize. Secondly, it is consistent with the hard, nonhistorical compatibilist outlook to acknowledge that in at least some cases the globally manipulated agent may be wronged and have her rights violated by the process of global manipulation, when another agent decides what sort of a person she will be. Recognizing these points and the distinctions they involve helps us to account for any intuitive resistance we may have to a "tough" or "hardline" stance on this issue.

IX. SKEPTICISM, ILLUSIONISM, AND REVISIONISM

Whatever their differences with respect to the issue of determinism, both compatibilists and libertarians believe that freedom and moral responsibility can be provided with philosophically-sound foundations. In contrast with this, the skeptic about free will believes that no such secure foundations can be provided. One version of this view is "hard determinism": the claim that determinism is true and that compatibilism cannot provide an adequate or satisfactory theory of freedom and moral responsibility. An even stronger version of this view, however, is that whether determinism or indeterminism is true, it is impossible to provide any credible theory of freedom of the kind required for (true or ultimate) moral responsibility. This strong version of the skeptical position is defended by Galen Strawson in "The Impossibility of Ultimate Moral Responsibility." The key to Strawson's skeptical position is what he calls the "Basic Argument." Strawson provides several versions of this argument, each giving various degrees of detail and complexity. The most simple version, slightly amended, has the following three steps:

1. Nothing can be cause of itself (i.e., *causa sui*).
2. True moral responsibility requires that the agent is cause of himself, at least in certain crucial mental respects.
3. Therefore, true moral responsibility is impossible.

Strawson, as noted, refines and explains each one of the core premises of this argument, and he defends them from various objections from both compatibilist and libertarian perspectives.

A crucial issue of interpretation with respect to the Basic Argument is *how skeptical* it is intended to be. In particular, is the argument skeptical about moral responsibility *tout court* or just *ultimate* moral responsibility (i.e., considered as *one interpretation* of moral responsibility)? On the stronger reading, Strawson's reference to ultimate moral responsibility as "true" or "real" may be taken to imply that any other accounts of moral responsibility fall short of the relevant standard of adequacy (e.g., they are shallow, superficial, etc.). The notion of "true moral responsibility" is one that involves a commitment to certain established assumptions about agency and retributive justice. These are assumptions that are not only ingrained in our Western (Judeo-Christian) ethical outlook, they are also part of universal human experience of the phenomenology of choice and action. In contrast with this, a weaker reading may take the Basic Argument to be more limited in its objectives, holding that while "true moral responsibility" is impossible, other (viable) forms may replace it without any catastrophic loss in our self-image as moral agents. (A weaker reading of this kind, limited in its skeptical ambitions, would bring the Basic Argument closer to the ground occupied by "revisionists" such as Manuel Vargas, as described below.)

A related but distinct position, building along the lines suggested by the skepticism of the basic argument, is presented by Saul Smilansky in "Free Will: From Nature to Illusion." Smilansky's analysis turns on three major questions. The first is whether libertarian free will actually exists, to which Smilansky answers in the negative. The second is whether moral responsibility and related notions are compatible with determinism, to which he gives a more qualified answer. While Smilansky acknowledges the "partial validity of compatibilism" with respect to a number of important distinctions that it identifies, he nevertheless finds it "shallow" on the grounds that it is unable to account for morally significant features of our lives. These morally significant features include, Smilansky argues, core values such as justice and desert as well as self-respect. Smilansky pays particular attention to the aims of (P.F. Strawson's) "naturalism," understood as an attempt to deflect and deflate the skeptical threat to our common-sense attitudes and practices in this sphere. His basic objection to the naturalist project, as he interprets it, is that the reactive attitudes, and the emotions they appeal to, themselves depend on a belief in libertarian free will which cannot be defended in light of critical reflection.

With these "pessimistic" answers to his first two questions in place, Smilansky goes on to consider the consequences and implications of the conclusions that he has reached. Much of his answer to this question consists of reviewing the extent and costs of our inability to defend any form of libertarian free will against skeptical critique. Smilansky suggests that when we consider the matter from "the ultimate perspective" we will find things are very bleak indeed. Compatibilist distinctions will provide only a small measure of support for our deepest values relating to our sense of self-worth and achievement, remorse and integrity, and so on. This leads us to the "grim" and "disheartening" conclusion that there is "no real substitute for the framework of achievement, desert and value based on free action." The only possible escape from this "darkness" is to take the path offered by *Ilusionism*.

The final sections of Smilansky's paper outline what the Illusionist path involves and what justifies it. Smilansky claims that illusory beliefs concerning free will are already in place and that they play a positive and necessary role in human life. (Here we may, of course, compare parallels with illusory beliefs about God or future state.) Although our belief that we possess libertarian free will is false, we nevertheless have overwhelming practical reason, Smilansky claims, to do what we can to retain and support it. We may do this by, for example, encouraging wishful thinking and self-deception as well as by discouraging all forms of critical reflection that are likely to undermine it. Without illusion of this kind, it is argued, not only will our sense of self-respect and our deeper moral values of justice be damaged, but we will not even be able to effectively maintain compatibilist distinctions that we also need for ordinary moral life and practice. Smilansky concludes his defense of Illusionism by claiming "that our priority should be to live with the assumption of libertarian free will although there is no basis for this other than our very need to live with this assumption."

In "How to Solve the Problem of Free Will," Manuel Vargas articulates an alternative way of approaching this issue. Like Galen Strawson and Saul

Smilansky, Vargas argues that both the standard solutions, as advanced by libertarians and compatibilists, are not satisfying. While libertarianism captures important aspects of our everyday thinking on this subject, it also involves problematic metaphysics and makes claims that are epistemologically impossible to ever verify. When we turn to compatibilism, familiar difficulties arise here as well. In particular, according to Vargas, compatibilist accounts of free will are plausible only to the extent that they ignore the very problematic commitments "that gave us a problem that needs solving." Whereas Galen Strawson's basic argument encourages the thought that we must "eliminate" or abandon responsibility in these circumstances, and Smilansky suggests that we should embrace illusion, Vargas charts another course.

Vargas's revisionist approach turns on a fundamental distinction between *diagnostic* and *prescriptive* theorizing. A diagnostic account is one that aims to describe our ordinary, everyday thinking, or established understanding of free will. In contrast with this, a revisionary account provides an interpretation of how we ought to think about these matters. Clearly it is possible for a gap to open up between these two distinct concerns, given that it may turn out, after philosophical reflection, that free will is not the sort of thing that we have hitherto supposed it to be. What we are looking for, from the prescriptive point of view, is a notion of responsible agency and a justifiable system of praising and blaming that "can adequately function without an incompatibilist metaphysics." This is all we need, Vargas maintains, to be revisionists and avoid the skeptical conclusion that we must "eliminate" or abandon our commitment to the attitudes and practices associated with moral responsibility. The goal of such a revisionist theory is to "identify features of agency that can play an appropriate role in explaining the justification of our practices of praising and blaming and that helps to explain how familiar judgments and attitudes about freedom and responsibility make sense in a framework that minimizes ad hoc metaphysical commitments."

What, then, could justify praise and blame, when they are not founded upon libertarian metaphysics? Vargas suggests that praise and blame can be justified in terms of the role that they play in fostering those forms of agency that involve our ability to respond to moral considerations. A notion of free will developed along these lines is compatible with what we know about our agency and the world. Although it may require us to abandon that part of our self-conception that presents us as capable of initiating causal chains, it nevertheless serves the purpose of making sense of our moral lives, and of leading us away from "responsibility nihilism." Understood in this way, revisionism claims to find a way of acknowledging incompatibilist concerns at the diagnostic level while at the same time developing a satisfactory compatibilist account of free will at the prescriptive level. In taking this approach we can avoid the perils and difficulties of both skepticism and illusionism.

X. OPTIMISM, PESSIMISM, AND THEIR MODES

Throughout the free-will literature there is a close relationship between the alternative positions on this subject and metaphysical attitudes of optimism and pessimism. More specifically, the shared ambition of libertarians and compatibilists to somehow justify or vindicate free will and moral responsibility is generally associated with an optimistic outlook that holds that we possess those powers and capacities relating to agency and moral life that we most care about. On the other hand, the skeptical position is closely allied with a pessimistic outlook which claims to unmask our illusions relating to our self-image as genuine moral agents—a process which is understood to be disturbing and damaging to our aspirations to view ourselves beings who uniquely govern nature without being governed by it. This simple dichotomy between free will optimists and skeptical pessimists is challenged in Derk Pereboom's "Optimistic Skepticism about Free Will."

Pereboom defends a position that he describes as "Hard Incompatibilism." There are two key elements to this position: first, it defends skepticism about free will and moral responsibility, and, second, it argues that "a conception of life without this type of free will would not be devastating to morality or to our sense of meaning in life, and in certain respects it may even be beneficial." The form of free will that Pereboom denies has any existence is the kind that is required for moral responsibility, where this is understood as involving being *deserving* of praise and blame. Pereboom directs his skeptical arguments at both compatibilist and libertarian accounts of free will. With regard to compatibilism, Pereboom opts for "source" as opposed to "leeway" incompatibilism. Pereboom's source incompatibilism is based on a version of the manipulation argument, whereby compatibilists are challenged to draw a principled distinction between four cases, beginning with a case of direct manipulation and extending to a case of simple determinism by causal processes with no manipulation involved. In all these cases, Pereboom argues, the source of an agent's action can be traced back to factors beyond his control. Even though all relevant compatibilist conditions of responsibility are met in these cases, the agent is not intuitively responsible and there is no principled distinction to be drawn between the cases involving manipulation and the case of simple causal determinism. At the same time, Pereboom also rejects any effort to defend incompatibilism on the basis of considerations of alternative possibilities because he believes it is possible to construct a plausible Frankfurt-style case where an agent has no alternative possibilities but is nevertheless intuitively morally responsible. With regard to libertarianism, Pereboom argues that event-causal libertarianism (e.g., as advanced by Kane) is vulnerable to the "luck objection," insofar as the agent lacks any control over whether a given decision occurs or not. On the other hand, agent-causal libertarian theories, although not vulnerable to the luck objection, are not credible. More specifically, while theories of this kind may be coherent they require us to accept that there is an incredible coincidence between what our best physical theories lead us to expect and what results from agent-caused free choices.

With the skeptical side of his argument in place, Pereboom then turns to the constructive side of the hard incompatibilist agenda. Contrary to the view that skepticism about free will and moral responsibility would be impossible to live with or accept in practice, Pereboom maintains that most of what we care about could be preserved and maintained. He begins by arguing that our basic moral distinctions between right and wrong could be preserved, as could the importance we attach to moral education and reform by means of "admonition and encouragement." Similarly, although we would have to give up a retributivist justification for criminal punishment, we might still justify punishment for criminal behavior in terms of moral education (although this form of punishment may be objectionable or problematic for other reasons). We may also justifiably "quarantine" those who we deem criminally dangerous, even though these individuals are not responsible for being dangerous to others. Going beyond the boundaries of morality and law, Pereboom argues that there is no basis supposing that our lives would lose meaning or purpose if we accept the truth of hard incompatibilism. Nor do we have reason to suppose that important interpersonal relations would be seriously damaged or threatened. While some of our reactive attitudes would need to be abandoned (e.g., resentment and indignation) others—or "analogues" of them—would survive this alteration in our self-image. This includes, Pereboom argues, important forms of love that do not depend or rely upon the assumption that the object of these emotions is in some way morally deserving of them. Pereboom concludes that while there is a range of (reactive) emotions that may be lost or unavailable to us if we became convinced that we do not have the sort of free will required for moral responsibility this may be, on balance, a good thing.

It is generally accepted by both compatibilist and incompatibilists that responsibility and fate exclude each other—in circumstances where an agent is subject to fate she cannot be responsible for her conduct. However, although the two opposing parties are agreed on this point, they understand fate, and its relation to determinism, in very different terms. Compatibilists standardly argue that fatalistic circumstances should be interpreted in terms of the causal inefficaciousness of an agent's deliberations and actions. An agent is fated when her deliberations and actions cannot change or alter the outcome. The thesis of determinism does not imply that all our actions are fated in this sense. Although a fatalism of this kind is incompatible with moral responsibility, since agents in these circumstances cannot influence or contribute to the course of events, there is no threat to moral responsibility on the ground that determinism implies fatalism understood in these terms. In contrast with this, incompatibilists understand fate in less restricted terms, taking it to include, in particular, our concern that an agent is not the real or true originator or source of her conduct. According to incompatibilists, fatalism of this kind is implied by the thesis of determinism, and, in consequence of this, determinism implies that all our actions are fated and so no one is morally responsible.

In "Compatibilist-Fatalism," Paul Russell challenges the orthodox compatibilist position on this issue and argues that a plausible compatibilism requires a richer conception of fatalistic concern, one that recognizes the legitimacy of (pessimistic) concerns about the origination of character and conduct. The position generated by these compatibilist concessions to incompatibilism is described as "compatibilist-fatalism" and involves two key claims. The first is the claim that determinism is compatible with moral responsibility and the second is that determinism implies conditions of fatalism, which serves as a genuine basis for pessimistic concern. With respect to the first claim, all compatibilists will agree that indeterministic metaphysics is not a necessary condition of moral responsibility and that a suitably "deep" account of moral responsibility can be provided within the constraints of compatibilist commitments. This is not, however, the focus of concern in this paper. The specific challenge for compatibilist-fatalism is to explain or account for the basis of pessimistic concern about origination where this does not involve worries about moral responsibility.

The independent source of pessimistic concern, Russell argues, should be understood in terms of the (Spinozistic) metaphor of our "sovereignty" over nature. More specifically, agents subject to origination-fate cannot conceive of themselves as (actively) ordering nature without being (passively) subject to its laws. Our self-image as possessing God-like powers to initiate a causal series, and to be something more than complex and sophisticated causal intermediaries, cannot be sustained in circumstances where origination-fate holds. While we may aspire to be able to intervene in the flow of natural events—and interrupt and redirect it—no compatibilist account of human agency can secure this view of ourselves. So considered, the exercise of our (moral) agency is itself, in the final analysis, subject to external or alien causal influences. Any form of compatibilism that seeks to evade these troubling or disconcerting features of origination-fatalism, as found in the thesis of determinism, must be judged shallow and superficial (a charge that certainly applies to the orthodox attempt to restrict all worries about fate to issues of contribution and not origination). A plausible compatibilism, Russell maintains, must accept the relevance and legitimacy of pessimistic worries about origination, even if these worries should not be interpreted, as incompatibilists would suggest, in terms of skepticism about moral responsibility. In this way, a sensible compatibilism must acknowledge these pessimistic implications of determinism as this concerns the finite and limited nature of human agents even in circumstances where their powers of rational self-control and moral freedom are operating and exercised. (Compatibilist-fatalism may be understood as taking a view that is the opposite of Pereboom's "hard incompatibilism," insofar as the latter combines incompatibilism with a broadly optimistic attitude to the implications of determinism for the human predicament.)

XI. THE PHENOMENOLOGY OF AGENCY AND EXPERIMENTAL PHILOSOPHY

Various experimental methods have recently been brought to bear on the free-will problem. For instance, in "Do we have free will?" neuroscientist Benjamin Libet describes the results of experiments he ran that show that a spike in cerebral neural activity—what he dubs the "readiness potential," or "RP" for short—occurs up to a third of a second before people become consciously aware of having "an urge" to act. In his experiment, subjects were asked to flick their wrist whenever they wanted, while looking at an oscilloscope "clock" made up of a rapidly revolving dot of light on a dial. Subjects were asked to report the position of this dot when they first became aware of forming an urge to flick their wrist. Using this method, Libet was able to measure to within a few milliseconds' accuracy the onset of the urge to act. Meanwhile, an EEG machine recorded brain activity and an EMG machine measured muscular activity in subjects' arms when they flicked their wrist. Libet's results show that subjects' reported awareness of feeling an urge to move their wrists occurred 200 ms. before the muscular activation recorded on the EMG. But the interesting result was that the RP measured by the EEG occurred earlier than this—550 ms. before the muscle activation and 350 ms. before subjects reported feeling the urge to move their wrist. In addition, such RPs were not recorded when subjects didn't report feeling an urge to move their wrist or in cases where subjects subsequently vetoed such an urge. Libet concludes that conscious control of our actions is limited to *vetoing* what the brain has already "decided" to do. A subject's flicking her wrist is caused not by her conscious urge but by the preceding RP.

Complementing the work being done on free will by social psychologists and neuroscientists, some pioneering philosophers have lately "gone empirical," by rolling up their sleeves and actually conducting empirical studies themselves. These philosophers now comprise a growing movement called *experimental philosophy*, or X-Phi, and much of the early work done by these philosophers has focused on free will.

Practitioners of X-Phi employ the methods of experimental psychology to probe folk intuitions about concepts like that of free will. Their aims include showing that a given view is more widely judged to be intuitive than another or developing error theories to explain away either a majority or a minority intuition by uncovering the mechanisms that generate it and showing these to be unreliable. Indeed, the primary focus of much X-Phi is on uncovering just these cognitive mechanisms.

Taking the last two readings in this section in reverse order, in "Moral Responsibility and Determinism: The Cognitive Science of Folk Intuitions," Shaun Nichols and Joshua Knobe investigate the psychological processes that generate competing compatibilist and incompatibilist judgments about responsibility. Their hypothesis is that people hold an incompatibilist theory of moral responsibility, yet possess psychological mechanisms that nonetheless produce compatibilist judgments in certain cases. By conducting survey-type experiments, Nichols and Knobe show that in *abstract* conditions, which were designed to elicit theoretical cognition, subjects tended to be incompatibilists about moral responsibility. Yet in *concrete* conditions, which were designed to elicit an affective response, subjects tended to be more strongly compatibilist. One of Nichols and Knobe's central claims is that the affective response induces an *affective performance error*—in other words, such responses interfere with subjects' ability to reason correctly. In this case, the error is just that subjects are unable to apply their incompatibilist theory of moral responsibility. Nichols and Knobe also show that whereas subjects' judgments in *high-affect* conditions are compatibilist, their judgments in *low-affect* conditions are incompatibilist, which further supports the hypothesis that affect plays a role in compatibilist judgments.

In "The Phenomenology of Free Will," Nahmias and colleagues investigate how people describe their experience of agency (what they call the *phenomenology of free will*). In one study, subjects were asked about their current experience in an imagined case of decision-making. They were given descriptions of three apartments and were asked to choose an apartment as though they were going to live there for the next year. Subjects were asked to verbalize any thoughts that came to mind while they deliberated. The results indicated that what was most salient for subjects were the features of the apartments. In particular, they "did not mention anything suggestive of a self that determines the outcome of an otherwise undetermined choice." Nahmias and colleagues conclude that this "supports the compatibilist description of the phenomenology more than the libertarian description." In another experiment, compatibilism was pitted against incompatibilism more directly. Subjects in this experiment were asked to imagine an experience of making a difficult choice and then to select which of two different (compatibilist and incompatibilist) descriptions of the ability to do otherwise best described their imagined experience. The result was that a majority of subjects selected the compatibilist description.

The Rationale of This Collection and Its Format

We have selected and arranged the contributions in this volume with a view to two particular audiences. The first is the expanding community of established scholars working in the area of free will who need a single collection where they can find the most indispensable and key contributions to the contemporary debate. Because the scope and volume of the philosophical literature on this topic is now so vast, it would be too much to claim that this collection is "comprehensive." Difficult choices have certainly had to be made and some valuable contributions and prominent figures in the field are unfortunately left out. Nevertheless, the collection as presented remains, in our judgment, reflective of many of the *core* contributions and discussions, and provides a clear and reasonably comprehensive picture of the current debate. The other audience this volume is directed at is that of undergraduate and graduate students who are being introduced to this field as part of their wider philosophical education. We have structured this collection with a particular view to engaging the interest of students (and the general philosophical reader) and providing them with a clear sense of the way in which the various topics and central issues are related to each other.

As the table of contents indicates, we have arranged and structured the readings in this volume by dividing them into sections, generally pairing them together around a particular issue and/or position. (A few sections are exceptions to this and contain three rather than two readings.) In our introductory remarks above we have already provided each section with a brief description, outlining the specific topic or problem at hand and the relevance of the readings to this topic. At the end of each section we have included a short list of "suggested further readings" relating to this topic or issue. By structuring things in this way, it is our intention that the anthology will introduce the various topics in the general form of a "dialogue" between alternative viewpoints. This format varies from being a direct confrontation between opposing views to a pairing of alternative accounts or models of a given strategy or approach. In general, it is our intention that both the teacher and the student will find that the paired readings serve to focus attention on a major issue and/or position as taken up in week-by-week stages in the classroom or seminar situation. We hope that this will make our anthology not only different from other anthologies currently available, but will also make it a particularly useful and effective way of introducing students and general readers to the study of the free-will problem.

Suggested Further Readings

Introduction

A good selection of readings relating to the classical background material—ranging from Aristotle to Kant and Reid—can be found in:

Pereboom, Derk, ed. 2009. *Free Will*, 2nd ed. Indianapolis: Hackett.

Other useful collections giving representative samples of the debate around the middle of the last century include:

Berofsky, Bernard. ed. 1966. *Free Will and Determinism*. New York: Harper & Row.
Hook, Sidney, ed. 1961. *Determinism and Freedom in the Age of Modern Science*. New York: Collier.

For an historically-oriented survey see:

Dilman, Ilham. 1999. *Free Will: An Historical and Philosophical Introduction*. London: Routledge.

The quotation from William James at the beginning of this Introduction is from:

James, William. 1897. "The dilemma of determinism," reprinted in *The Will to Believe and Other Essays* (New York: Dover, 1956).

PART ONE

The Free Will Problem—Real or illusory?

1

Moral Luck

Thomas Nagel

Kant believed that good or bad luck should influence neither our moral judgment of a person and his actions, nor his moral assessment of himself.

> The good will is not good because of what it effects or accomplishes or because of its adequacy to achieve some proposed end; it is good only because of its willing, i.e., it is good of itself And, regarded for itself, it is to be esteemed incomparably higher than anything which could be brought about by it in favor of any inclination or even of the sum total of all inclinations. Even if it should happen that, by a particularly unfortunate fate or by the niggardly provision of a step motherly nature, this will should be wholly lacking in power to accomplish its purpose, and if even the greatest effort should not avail it to achieve anything of its end, and if there remained only the good will (not as a mere wish but as the summoning of all the means in our power), it would sparkle like a jewel in its own right, as something that had its full worth in itself. Usefulness or fruitlessness can neither diminish nor augment this worth.[1]

[handwritten margin note: good + bad aren't determined by the outcome of the will. it's about the will to begin with. e thinking about killing someone is bad even if you don't do it]

He would presumably have said the same about a bad will: whether it accomplishes its evil purposes is morally irrelevant. And a course of action that would be condemned if it had a bad outcome cannot be vindicated if by luck it turns out well. There cannot be moral risk. This view seems to be wrong, but it arises in response to a fundamental problem about moral responsibility to which we possess no satisfactory solution.

The problem develops out of the ordinary conditions of moral judgment. Prior to reflection it is intuitively plausible that people cannot be morally assessed for what is not their fault, or for what is due to factors beyond their control. Such judgment is different from the evaluation of something as a good or bad thing, or state of affairs. The latter may be present in addition to moral judgment, but when we blame someone for his actions we are not merely saying it is bad that they happened, or bad that he exists: we are judging him, saying he is bad, which is different from his being a bad thing. This kind of judgment takes only a certain kind of object. Without being able to explain exactly why, we feel that the appropriateness of moral assessment is easily undermined by the discovery that the act or attribute, no matter how good or bad, is not under the person's control. While other evaluations remain, this one seems to lose its footing. So a clear absence of control, produced by involuntary movement, physical force, or ignorance of the circumstances, excuses what is done from moral judgment. But what we do depends in many more ways than these on what is not under our control—what is not produced by a good or a bad will, in Kant's phrase. And external influences in this broader range are not usually thought to excuse what is done from moral judgment, positive or negative.

Let me give a few examples, beginning with the type of case Kant has in mind. Whether we succeed or fail in what we try to do nearly always depends to some extent on factors beyond our control. This is true of murder, altruism, revolution, the sacrifice of certain interests for the sake of others—almost any morally important act. What has been done, and what is morally judged, is partly determined by external factors. However jewel-like the good will may be in its own right, there is a morally significant difference between rescuing someone from a burning building and dropping him from a twelfth-storey window while trying to rescue him. Similarly, there is a morally significant difference between reckless driving and manslaughter. But whether a reckless driver hits a pedestrian depends on the presence of the pedestrian at the point where he recklessly passes a red light. What we do is also limited by the opportunities and choices with which we are faced, and these are largely determined by factors beyond our control. Someone who was an officer in a concentration camp might have led a quiet and harmless life if the Nazis had never come to power in Germany. And someone who led a quiet and harmless life in Argentina might have become an officer in a concentration camp if he had not left Germany for business reasons in 1930.

I shall say more later about these and other examples. I introduce them here to illustrate a general point. Where a significant aspect of what someone does depends on factors beyond his control, yet we continue to treat him in that respect as an object of moral judgment, it can be called moral luck. Such luck can be good or bad. And the problem posed by this phenomenon, which led Kant to deny its possibility, is that the broad range of external influences here identified seems on close examination to undermine moral assessment as surely as does the narrower range of familiar excusing conditions. If the condition of control is consistently applied, it threatens to erode most of the moral assessments we find it natural to make. The things for which people are morally judged are determined in more ways than we at first realize by what is beyond their control. And when the seemingly natural requirement of fault or responsibility is applied in light of these facts, it leaves few pre-reflective moral judgments intact. Ultimately, nothing or almost nothing about what a person does seems to be under his control.

Why not conclude, then, that the condition of control is false—that it is an initially plausible hypothesis refuted by clear counter-examples? One could in that case look instead for a more refined condition which picked out the kinds of lack of control that really undermine certain moral judgments, without yielding the unacceptable conclusion derived from the broader condition, that most or all ordinary moral judgments are illegitimate.

What rules out this escape is that we are dealing not with a theoretical conjecture but with a philosophical problem. The condition of control does not suggest itself merely as a generalization from certain clear cases. It seems correct in the further cases to which it is extended beyond the original set. When we undermine moral assessment by considering new ways in which control is absent, we are not just discovering what *would* follow given the general hypothesis, but are actually being persuaded that in itself the absence of control is relevant in these cases too. The erosion of moral judgment emerges not as the absurd consequence of an over-simple theory, but as a natural consequence of the ordinary idea of moral assessment, when it is applied in view of a more complete and precise account of the facts. It would therefore be a mistake to argue from the unacceptability of the conclusions to the need for a different account of the conditions of moral responsibility. The view that moral luck is paradoxical is not a *mistake,* ethical or logical, but a perception of one of the ways in which the intuitively acceptable conditions of moral judgment threaten to undermine it all.

It resembles the situation in another area of philosophy, the theory of knowledge. There too conditions which seem perfectly natural, and which grow out of the ordinary procedures for challenging and defending claims to knowledge, threaten to undermine all such claims if consistently applied. Most skeptical arguments have this quality: they do not depend on the imposition of arbitrarily stringent standards of knowledge, arrived at by misunderstanding, but appear to grow inevitably from the consistent application of ordinary standards.[2] There is a substantive parallel as well, for epistemological skepticism arises from consideration of the respects in which our beliefs and their relation to reality depend on factors beyond our control. External and internal causes produce our beliefs. We may subject these processes to scrutiny in an effort to avoid error, but our conclusions at this next level also result, in part, from influences which we do not control directly. The same will be true no matter how far we carry the investigation. Our beliefs are always, ultimately, due to factors outside our control, and the impossibility of encompassing those factors without being at the mercy of others leads us to doubt whether we know anything. It looks as though, if any of our beliefs are true, it is pure biological luck rather than knowledge.

Moral luck is like this because while there are various respects in which the natural objects of moral assessment are out of our control or influenced by what is out of our control, we cannot reflect on these facts without losing our grip on the judgments.

There are roughly four ways in which the natural objects of moral assessment are disturbingly subject to luck. One is the phenomenon of constitutive luck—the kind of person you are, where this is not just a question of what you deliberately do, but of your inclinations, capacities, and temperament. Another category is luck in one's circumstances—the kind of problems and situations one faces. The other two have to do with the causes and effects of action: luck in how one is determined by antecedent circumstances, and luck in the way one's actions and projects turn out. All of them present a common problem. They are all opposed by the idea that one cannot be more culpable or estimable for anything than one is for that fraction of it which is under one's control. It seems irrational to take or dispense credit or blame for matters over which a person has no control, or for their influence on results over which he has partial control. Such things may create the conditions for action, but action can be judged only to the extent that it goes beyond these conditions and does not just result from them.

Let us first consider luck, good and bad, in the way things turn out. Kant, in the above-quoted passage, has one example of this in mind, but the category covers a wide range. It includes the truck driver who accidentally runs over a child, the artist who abandons his wife and five children to devote himself to painting,[3] and other cases in which the possibilities of success and failure are even greater. The driver, if he is entirely without fault, will feel terrible about his role in the event, but will not have to reproach himself. Therefore this example of agent-regret[4] is not yet a case of *moral* bad luck. However, if the driver was guilty of even a minor degree of negligence—failing to have his brakes checked recently, for example—then if that negligence contributes to the death of the child, he will not merely feel terrible. He will blame himself for the death. And what makes this an example of moral luck is that he would have to blame himself only slightly for the negligence itself if no situation arose which required him to brake suddenly and violently to avoid hitting a child. Yet the negligence is the same in both cases, and the driver has no control over whether a child will run into his path.

The same is true at higher levels of negligence. If someone has had too much to drink and his car swerves on to the sidewalk, he can count himself morally lucky if there are no pedestrians in its path. If there were, he would be to blame for their deaths, and would probably be prosecuted for manslaughter. But if he hurts no one, although his recklessness is exactly the same, he is guilty of a far less serious legal offence and will certainly reproach himself and be reproached by others much less severely. To take another legal example, the penalty for attempted murder is less than that for successful murder—however similar the intentions and motives of the assailant may be in the two cases. His degree of culpability can depend, it would seem, on whether the victim happened to be wearing a bullet-proof vest, or whether a bird flew into the path of the bullet—matters beyond his control.

Finally, there are cases of decision under uncertainty—common in public and in private life. Anna Karenina goes off with Vronsky, Gauguin leaves his family, Chamberlain signs the Munich agreement, the Decembrists persuade the troops under their command to revolt against the czar, the American colonies declare their independence from Britain, you introduce two people in an attempt at match-making. It is tempting in all such cases to feel that some decision must be possible, in the light of what is known at the time, which will make reproach unsuitable no matter how things turn out. But this is not true; when someone acts in such ways he takes his life, or his moral position, into his hands, because how things turn out determines what he has done. It is possible *also* to assess the decision from the point of view of what could be known at the time, but this is not the end of the story. If the Decembrists had succeeded in overthrowing Nicholas I in 1825 and establishing a constitutional regime, they would be heroes. As it is, not only did they fail and pay for it, but they bore some responsibility for the terrible punishments meted out to the troops who had been persuaded to follow them. If the American Revolution had been a bloody failure resulting in greater repression, then Jefferson, Franklin and Washington would still have made a noble attempt, and might not even have regretted it on their way to the scaffold, but they would also have had to blame themselves for what they had helped to bring on their compatriots. (Perhaps peaceful efforts at reform would eventually have succeeded.) If Hitler had not overrun Europe and exterminated millions, but instead had died of a heart attack after occupying the Sudetenland, Chamberlain's action at Munich would still have utterly betrayed the Czechs, but it would not be the great moral disaster that has made his name a household word.[5]

In many cases of difficult choice the outcome cannot be foreseen with certainty. One kind of assessment of the choice is possible in advance, but another kind must await the outcome, because the outcome determines what has been done. The same degree of culpability or estimability in intention, motive, or concern is compatible with a wide range of judgments, positive or negative, depending on what happened beyond the point of decision. The mens rea which could have existed in the absence of any consequences does not exhaust the grounds of moral judgment. Actual results influence culpability or esteem in a large class of unquestionably ethical cases ranging from negligence through political choice.

That these are genuine moral judgments rather than expressions of temporary attitude is evident from the fact that one can say in advance how the moral verdict will depend on the results. If one negligently leaves the bath running with the baby in it, one will realize, as one bounds up the stairs toward the bathroom, that if the baby has drowned one has done something awful, whereas if it has not one has merely been careless. Someone who launches a violent revolution against an authoritarian regime knows that if he fails he will be responsible for much suffering that is in vain, but if he succeeds he will be justified by the outcome. I do not mean that any action can be retroactively justified by history. Certain things are so bad in themselves, or so risky, that no results can make them all right. Nevertheless, when moral judgment does depend on the outcome, it is objective and timeless and not dependent on a change of standpoint produced by success or failure. The judgment after the fact follows from an hypothetical judgment that can be made beforehand, and it can be made as easily by someone else as by the agent.

From the point of view which makes responsibility dependent on control, all this seems absurd. How is it possible to be more or less culpable depending on whether a child gets into the path of one's car, or a bird into the path of one's bullet? Perhaps it is true that what is done depends on more than the agent's state of mind or intention. The problem then is, why is it not irrational to base moral assessment on what people do, in this broad sense? It amounts to holding them responsible for the contributions of fate as well as for their own— provided they have made some contribution to begin with. If we look at cases of negligence or attempt, the pattern seems to be that overall culpability corresponds to the product of mental or intentional fault and the seriousness of the outcome. Cases of decision under uncertainty are less easily explained in this way, for it seems that the overall judgment can even shift from positive to negative depending on the outcome. But here too it seems rational to subtract the effects of occurrences subsequent to the choice, that were merely possible at the time, and concentrate moral assessment on the actual decision in light of the probabilities. If the object of moral judgment is the person, then to hold him accountable for what he has done in the broader sense is akin to strict liability, which may have its legal uses but seems irrational as a moral position.

The result of such a line of thought is to pare down each act to its morally essential core, an inner act of pure will assessed by motive and intention. Adam Smith advocates such a position in *The Theory of Moral Sentiments*, but notes that it runs contrary our actual judgments.

> But how well soever we may seem to be persuaded of the truth of this equitable maxim, when we consider it after this manner, in abstract, yet when we come to particular cases, the actual consequences which happen to proceed from any action, have a very great effect upon our sentiments concerning its merit or demerit, and almost always either enhance or diminish our sense of both. Scarce, in any one instance, perhaps, will our sentiments be found, after examination, to be entirely regulated by this rule, which we all acknowledge ought entirely to regulate them.[6]

Joel Feinberg points out further that restricting the domain of moral responsibility to the inner world will not immunize it to luck. Factors beyond the
agent's control, like a coughing fit, can interfere with his decisions as surely
as they can with the path of a bullet from his gun.[7] Nevertheless the tendency
to cut down the scope of moral assessment is pervasive, and does not limit
itself to the influence of effects. It attempts to isolate the will from the other
direction, so to speak, by separating out constitutive luck. Let us consider that
next.

Factsrs can change both internal external outcomes

Kant was particularly insistent on the moral irrelevance of qualities of
temperament and personality that are not under the control of the will. Such
qualities as sympathy or coldness might provide the background against
which obedience to moral requirements is more or less difficult, but they could
not be objects of moral assessment themselves, and might well interfere with
confident assessment of its proper object—the determination of the will by
the motive of duty. This rules out moral judgment of many of the virtues and
vices, which are states of character that influence choice but are certainly not
exhausted by dispositions to act deliberately in certain ways. A person may
be greedy, envious, cowardly, cold, ungenerous, unkind, vain, or conceited,
but behave perfectly by a monumental effort of will. To possess these vices
is to be unable to help having certain feelings under certain circumstances,
and to have strong spontaneous impulses to act badly. Even if one controls the
impulses, one still has the vice. An envious person hates the greater success
of others. He can be morally condemned as envious even if he congratulates
them cordially and does nothing to denigrate or spoil their success. Conceit,
likewise, need not be displayed. It is fully present in someone who cannot help
dwelling with secret satisfaction on the superiority of his own achievements,
talents, beauty, intelligence, or virtue. To some extent such a quality may be
the product of earlier choices; to some extent it may be amenable to change by
current actions. But it is largely a matter of constitutive bad fortune. Yet people
are morally condemned for such qualities, and esteemed for others equally
beyond control of the will: they are assessed for what they are *like*.

You could be greedy + envious but have an incredibly strong will to keep it @ bay

To Kant this seems incoherent because virtue is enjoined on everyone
and therefore must in principle be possible for everyone. It may be easier for
some than for others, but it must be possible to achieve it by making the right
choices, against whatever temperamental background.[8] One may want to
have a generous spirit, or regret not having one, but it makes no sense to condemn oneself or anyone else for a quality which is not within the control of
the will. Condemnation implies that you should not be like that, not that it is
unfortunate that you are.

Nevertheless, Kant's conclusion remains intuitively unacceptable. We
may be persuaded that these moral judgments are rational, but they reappear
involuntarily as soon as the argument is over. This is the pattern throughout
the subject.

The third category to consider is luck in one's circumstances. I shall mention it briefly. The things we are called upon to do, the moral tests we face, are importantly determined by factors beyond our control. It may be true of someone that in a dangerous situation he would behave in a cowardly or heroic fashion, but if the situation never arises, he will never have the chance to distinguish or disgrace himself in this way, and his moral record will be different.[9]

A conspicuous example of this is political. Ordinary citizens of Nazi Germany had an opportunity to behave heroically by opposing the regime. They also had an opportunity to behave badly, and most of them are culpable for having failed this test. But it is a test to which the citizens of other countries were not subjected, with the result that even if they, or some of them, would have behaved as badly as the Germans in like circumstances, they simply did not and therefore are not similarly culpable. Here again one is morally at the mercy of fate, and it may seem irrational upon reflection, but our ordinary moral attitudes would be unrecognizable without it. We judge people for what they actually do or fail to do, not just for what they would have done if circumstances had been different.[10]

This form of moral determination by the actual is also paradoxical, but we can begin to see how deep in the concept of responsibility the paradox is embedded. A person can be morally responsible only for what he does; but what he does results from a great deal that he does not do; therefore he is not morally responsible for what he is and is not responsible for. (This is not a contradiction, but it is a paradox.)

It should be obvious that there is a connection between these problems about responsibility and control and an even more familiar problem, that of freedom of the will. That is the last type of moral luck I want to take up, though I can do no more within the scope of this essay than indicate its connection with the other types.

If one cannot be responsible for consequences of one's acts due to factors beyond one's control, or for antecedents of one's acts that are properties of temperament not subject to one's will, or for the circumstances that pose one's moral choices, then how can one be responsible even for the stripped-down acts of the will itself, if *they* are the product of antecedent circumstances outside of the will's control?

The area of genuine agency, and therefore of legitimate moral judgment, seems to shrink under this scrutiny to an extensionless point. Everything seems to result from the combined influence of factors, antecedent and posterior to action, that are not within the agent's control. Since he cannot be responsible for them, he cannot be responsible for their results—though it may remain possible to take up the aesthetic or other evaluative anacogues of the moral attitudes that are thus displaced.

It is also possible, of course, to brazen it out and refuse to accept the results, which indeed seem unacceptable as soon as we stop thinking about

How can we be responsible for anything?

the arguments. Admittedly, if certain surrounding circumstances had been different, then no unfortunate consequences would have followed from a wicked intention, and no seriously culpable act would have been performed; but since the circumstances were not different, and the agent in fact succeeded in perpetrating a particularly cruel murder, that is what he did, and that is what he is responsible for. Similarly, we may admit that if certain antecedent circumstances had been different, the agent would never have developed into the sort of person who would do such a thing; but since he *did* develop (as the inevitable result of those antecedent circumstances) into the sort of swine he is, and into the person who committed such a murder, that is what he is blameable for. In both cases one is responsible for what one actually does—even if what one actually does depends in important ways on what is not within one's control. This compatibilist account of our moral judgments would leave room for the ordinary conditions of responsibility—the absence of coercion, ignorance, or involuntary movement—as part of the determination of what someone has done—but it is understood not to exclude the influence of a great deal that he has not done.[11]

The only thing wrong with this solution is its failure to explain how skeptical problems arise. For they arise not from the imposition of an arbitrary external requirement, but from the nature of moral judgment itself. Something in the ordinary idea of what someone does must explain how it can seem necessary to subtract from it anything that merely happens—even though the ultimate consequence of such subtraction is that nothing remains. And something in the ordinary idea of knowledge must explain why it seems to be undermined by any influences on belief not within the control of the subject—so that knowledge seems impossible without an impossible foundation in autonomous reason. But let us leave epistemology aside and concentrate on action, character, and moral assessment.

The problem arises, I believe, because the self which acts and is the object of moral judgment is threatened with dissolution by the absorption of its acts and impulses into the class of events. Moral judgment of a person is judgment not of what happens to him, but of him. It does not say merely that a certain event or state of affairs is fortunate or unfortunate or even terrible. It is not an evaluation of a state of the world, or of an individual as part of the world. We are not thinking just that it would be better if he were different, or did not exist, or had not done some of the things he has done. We are judging *him,* rather than his existence or characteristics. The effect of concentrating on the influence of what is not under his control is to make this responsible self seem to disappear, swallowed up by the order of mere events.

What, however, do we have in mind that a person must *be* to be the object of these moral attitudes? While the concept of agency is easily undermined, it is very difficult to give it a positive characterization. This is familiar from the literature on free will.

I believe that in a sense the problem has no solution, because something in the idea of agency is incompatible with actions being events, or people being things. But as the external determinants of what someone has done are gradually exposed, in their effect on consequences, character, and choice itself, it becomes gradually clear that actions are events and people things. Eventually nothing remains which can be ascribed to the responsible self, and we are left with nothing but a portion of the larger sequence of events, which can be deplored or celebrated, but not blamed or praised.

Though I cannot define the idea of the active self that is thus undermined, it is possible to say something about its sources. There is a close connexion between our feelings about ourselves and our feelings about others. Guilt and indignation, shame and contempt, pride and admiration are internal and external sides of the same moral attitudes. We are unable to view ourselves simply as portions of the world, and from inside we have a rough idea of the boundary between what is us and what is not, what we do and what happens to us, what is our personality and what is an accidental handicap. We apply the same essentially internal conception of the self to others. About ourselves we feel pride, shame, guilt, remorse—and agent-regret. We do not regard our actions and our characters merely as fortunate or unfortunate episodes— though they may also be that. We cannot simply take an external evaluative view of ourselves—of what we most essentially are and what we do. And this remains true even when we have seen that we are not responsible for our own existence, or our nature, or the choices we have to make, or the circumstances that give our acts the consequences they have. Those acts remain ours and we remain ourselves, despite the persuasiveness of the reasons that seem to argue us out of existence.

It is this internal view that we extend to others in moral judgment— when we judge *them* rather than their desirability or utility. We extend to others the refusal to limit ourselves to external evaluation, and we accord to them selves like our own. But in both cases this comes up against the bru- tal inclusion of humans and everything about them in a world from which they cannot be separated and of which they are nothing but contents. The external view forces itself on us at the same time that we resist it. One way this occurs is through the gradual erosion of what we do by the subtraction of what happens.[12]

The inclusion of consequences in the conception of what we have done is an acknowledgment that we are parts of the world, but the paradoxical character of moral luck which emerges from this acknowledgment shows that we are unable to operate with such a view, for it leaves us with no one to be. The same thing is revealed in the appearance that determinism obliter- ates responsibility. Once we see an aspect of what we or someone else does as something that happens, we lose our grip on the idea that it has been done and that we can judge the doer and not just the happening. This explains why the absence of determinism is no more hospitable to the concept of agency than is its presence—a point that has been noticed often. Either way the act is viewed externally, as part of the course of events.

The problem of moral luck cannot be understood without an account of the internal conception of agency and its special connection with the moral attitudes as opposed to other types of value. I do not have such an account. The degree to which the problem has a solution can be determined only by seeing whether in some degree the incompatibility between this conception and the various ways in which we do not control what we do is only apparent. I have nothing to offer on that topic either. But it is not enough to say merely that our basic moral attitudes toward ourselves and others are determined by what is actual; for they are also threatened by the sources of that actuality, and by the external view of action which forces itself on us when we see how everything we do belongs to a world that we have not created.

Notes

1. *Foundations of the Metaphysics of Morals*, first section, third paragraph.

2. See Thompson Clarke, "The legacy of skepticism," *Journal of Philosophy*, LXIX, no. 20 (November 9, 1972): 754–69.

3. Such a case, modelled on the life of Gauguin, is discussed by Bernard Williams in "Moral luck," *Proceedings of the Aristotelian Society*, supplementary vol. L (1976): 115–35 (to which the original version of this essay was a reply). He points out that though success or failure cannot be predicted in advance, Gauguin's most basic retrospective feelings about the decision will be determined by the development of his talent. My disagreement with Williams is that his account fails to explain why such retrospective attitudes can be called moral. If success does not permit Gauguin to justify himself to others, but still determines his most basic feelings, that shows only that his most basic feelings need not be moral. It does not show that morality is subject to luck. If the retrospective judgment were moral, it would imply the truth of a hypothetical judgment made in advance, of the form "If I leave my family and become a great painter, I will be justified by success; if I don't become a great painter, the act will be unforgivable."

4. Williams' term (ibid.).

5. For a fascinating but morally repellent discussion of the topic of justification by history, see Maurice Merleau-Ponty, *Humanisme et Terreur* (Paris: Gallimard, 1947), translated as *Humanism and Terror* (Boston: Beacon Press, 1969).

6. Part II, sect. 3, Introduction, para. 5.

7. "Problematic responsibility in law and morals," in Joel Feinberg, *Doing and Deserving* (Princeton, NJ: Princeton University Press, 1970).

8. "if nature has put little sympathy in the heart of a man, and if he, though an honest man, is by temperament cold and indifferent to the sufferings of others, perhaps because he is provided with special gifts of patience and fortitude and expects or even requires that others should have the sameand such a man would certainly not be the meanest product of naturewould not he find in himself a source from which to give himself a far higher

worth than he could have got by having a good-natured temperament?" (Foundations of the Metaphysics of Morals, first section, para. 11), 33

9. Cf. Thomas Gray, 'Elegy Written in a Country Churchyard':

Some mute inglorious Milton here may rest,
Some Cromwell, guiltless of his country's blood.

An unusual example of circumstantial moral luck is provided by the kind of moral dilemma with which someone can be faced through no fault of his own, but which leaves him with nothing to do which is not wrong., See chapter 5; and Bernard Williams, "Ethical consistency," *Proceedings of the Aristotelian Society*, supplementary vol. XXXIX (1965), reprinted in *Problems of the Self* (Cambridge: Cambridge University Press, 1973), 166–86.

10. Circumstantial luck can extend to aspects of the situation other than individual behavior. For example, during the Vietnam War even U.S.. citizens who had opposed their country's actions vigorously from the start often felt compromised by its crimes. Here they were not even responsible; there was probably nothing they could do to stop what was happening, so the feeling of being implicated may seem unintelligible. But it is nearly impossible to view the crimes of one's own country in the same way that one views the crimes of another country, no matter how equal one's lack of power to stop them in the two cases. One is a citizen of one of them, and has a connexion with its actions (even if only through taxes that cannot be withheld)—that one does not have with the other's. This makes it possible to be ashamed of one's country, and to feel a victim of moral bad luck that one was an American in the 1960s.

11. The corresponding position in epistemology would be that knowledge consists of true beliefs formed in certain ways, and that it does not require all aspects of the process to be under the knower's control, actually or potentially. Both the correctness of these beliefs and the process by which they are arrived at would therefore be importantly subject to luck. The Nobel Prize is not awarded to people who turn out to be wrong, no matter how brilliant their reasoning.

12. See P. F. Strawson's discussion of the conflict between the objective attitude and personal reactive attitudes in "Freedom and resentment," *Proceedings of the British Academy* (1962), reprinted in *Studies in the Philosophy of Thought and Action*, ed. P. F. Strawson (London: Oxford University Press, 1968), and in P. F. Strawson, *Freedom and Resentment and Other Essays* (London: Methuen, 1974).

2

Please Don't Feed the Bugbears

Daniel C. Dennett

The philosopher is the one who will contribute a paper on the
hangman paradox to a symposium on capital punishment

—JAMES D. MCCAWLEY

1. The Perennial Gripping Problem

The idea of Fate is older than philosophy itself, and since the dawn of the
discipline philosophers have been trying to show what is wrong with the idea
that our fates are sealed before we are born. It has seemed very important to
demonstrate that we are not just acting out our destinies but somehow choosing our own courses, *making* decisions—not just having "decisions" occur
in us.

Ideas about causation were at the focus of attention in the early days of
Greek philosophy, and it occurred to some to wonder whether all physical
events are caused or determined by the sum total of all prior events. If they
are—if, as we say, *determinism* is true—then our actions, as physical events,
must themselves be determined. If determinism is true, then our every deed
and decision is the inexorable outcome, it seems, of the sum of physical forces
acting at the moment, which in turn is the inexorable outcome of the forces
acting an instant before, and so on, to the beginning of time.

How then could we be free? The Epicureans, who were surprisingly modern *materialists* (they believed that minds were composed of material atoms,
just like everything else), tried to extricate themselves from this nightmare
of predestined choice by breaking the fabric of universal causation here and
there. They postulated that atoms occasionally exhibit "random swerves."

> Again, if all movement is always interconnected, the new arising from
> the old in a determinate order—if the atoms never swerve so as to origi-
> nate some new movement that will snap the bonds of fate, the everlasting
> sequence of cause and effect—what is the source of the free will possessed   **43**

by living things throughout the earth? (Lucretius, *The Nature* of *the Universe*, 11, lines 250–255, Latham translation 1951)

The oft-recounted difficulty with this proposed solution (and its more modern variants) is that even if such random swerves happen, they don't seem able to give us the sort of free will we want. If an atom in my brain suddenly veers off with a random swerve, it must do so "for no reason at all," and if this causes me to choose or decide something important, I am completely at the mercy of these random swerves. Random choice, as blind and arbitrary as the throw of dice or the spin of a wheel of fortune, does not seem to be any more desirable than determined choice. Indeed many have thought that it was *less* desirable, and have gone on to propose alternative reconciliations of free will with determinism (different varieties of *reconciliationism* or, as it is more frequently called, *compatibilism).* Some of these attempted reconciliations are hardly more appealing than the dire prospect they are supposed to keep at bay.

The Stoics, for instance, urged that a certain sort of freedom could be found in not struggling against the inevitable but rather adjusting one's desires downward to meet one's circumstances. They encouraged adopting an attitude of wise resignation which they called *apatheia.* And while one should recognize that the concept got simplified and cheapened as it took the etymological journey to our present-day *apathy,* the fact remains that the Stoics liked to explain their doctrine with the help of some particularly depressing metaphors. Each of us is assigned a role to play in the tragedy of life, they suggested, and there is nothing for us to do but say our prescribed lines as best we can; there is no room to ad-lib. Or consider a dog on a leash being pulled behind a wagon; it can trot along peacefully, or it can resist. Either way it will end up at the same destination, but if it resigns itself to the destination and makes the most of the journey, it will enjoy a certain kind of freedom. Being led through life with a rope around one's neck—some freedom!

For more than two millennia philosophers have been trying to discover a doctrine about free will that is both more attractive and more rationally defensible than these dire and unappealing beginnings. It is often said (plausibly, but I wonder how accurately) that more has been written on free will than on any other philosophical topic. Any philosopher ought to feel at least a little embarrassed that with so much work so little progress has been made.

The trouble with philosophy, some say, is that it isn't Science; if it were more like Science it would solve its soluble problems and dissolve or discard the rest. The trouble with philosophy, others say, is that it has tried to be "scientific" about matters that can only be dealt with through Art. If it would give up its love affair with the Scientific Method, it would no longer have to cast its projects in terms that guaranteed failure. The trouble with philosophy, I think, is that it is much harder than it looks to either Scientists or Artists, for it shares—and must share—the aspirations and methods of both.

There are undismissable philosophical questions—"Do we have free will?" is one of them—that require clear, well-supported, soundly reasoned answers. We should not be bought off with allusive, impressionistic answers, however appealing or moving they may be. But most attempts to deal truly rigorously with philosophical questions—and questions about free will are no exception—run afoul of the problems of premature formalization. There is an abundance of self-consciously technical work by philosophers on the problem of free will that is, ironically, of only aesthetic interest (to connoisseurs of formula architecture or "logic chopping") because it simply fails to make contact with the real issues. Finding a method appropriate to the task is philosophy's perennial first problem, and there has never been much of a consensus about the right or best method. Any book on free will makes a declaration, *ipso facto,* about method, about how one ought to approach the problem. This book will more self-consciously address the issue of method, beginning now. My method, to be exhibited presently in action, takes science very seriously but its tactics more closely resemble those of art.

In my student days I thought I was going to be a sculptor, and I addressed myself more energetically to blocks of wood and stone than to either philosophy or science. It occurred to me while working on this book that I have never abandoned the methods I developed in the studio, but simply changed media. Unlike the draftsman, who must get each line just right with the first stroke of the pen, the sculptor has the luxury of nibbling and grinding away until the lines and surfaces look just right. First you rough out the block, standing back and squinting now and then to make sure you are closing in on the dimly seen final product. Only after the piece is bulked out in the right proportions do you return to each crude, rough surface and invest great labor in getting the fine details just so.

Some philosophers are very unsympathetic to this method when they encounter it in philosophy. They have no patience with roughed-in solutions and want to see nothing but hard, clean edges from the outset. I aspire to the same finished product that they do, but question their strategy. It is just too hard getting off on the right foot in philosophy, and nowhere are the risks of their strategy more evident than in the philosophical literature on free will, which is littered with brilliant but useless fragments. One of the themes of this book is that little progress has been made on the free will issue because philosophers, rushing in to deal definitively with what they consider to be the important parts of the free will issue and lavishing somewhat myopic attention on these topics, have simply failed to see the shape of the main body of the topic. Out of the opaque marble block of the problem emerge an exquisitely rendered face and some highly polished hands and feet—but no room has been left for the elbows. In this book most of the work will be on roughing out the shape of the parts philosophers usually rush past with a lick and a promise.

It is often remarked that the problem of free will is a uniquely engaging or even gripping philosophical problem: people who otherwise have no taste at all for philosophy can be brought to care quite deeply about the problem, and can be genuinely troubled by the prospect that the answers to the questions may turn out "the wrong way."

Why do people find the free will problem gripping? In part, surely, because it touches deep and central questions about our situation in the universe, about "the human condition," as one portentously says. But also, I will argue, because philosophers have conjured up a host of truly frightening bugbears[1] and then subliminally suggested, quite illicitly, that the question of free will is whether any of these bugbears actually exist.

This has contributed to the lack of progress on the problem, because philosophers, partly taken in by their own fearmongery and partly using that contrived urgency to "motivate" the elaboration of metaphysical systems and theories, have set themselves a variety of unattainable goals: the creation of impossible philosophical talismans to ward off nonexistent evils.

I do not mean to suggest that philosophers have deliberately and knowingly fanned the coals of anxiety, or that they have disingenuously exploited that anxiety to provide the spurious motivation for their metaphysical exercises. We philosophers are more the victims than the perpetrators of the induced illusions. After all, we are the main and intended readership of the literature that innocently conspires to engender the misapprehensions. And our complicity in protracting the lives of the errors arises in part from the natural and virtually universal desire to be engaged in a project whose importance can be made clear to bystanders. If this leads us to overdramatize things here and there, to heighten a few contrasts and sharpen a few boundaries, we are only doing what everyone else does in their own line of work.

Notice for instance that one of my initial premises—that people care deeply about free will—has already undergone a familiar exaggeration in my hands. It is not as if *everybody* cares about having free will in the same way that everybody cares about avoiding pain or finding love, for instance. We might remind ourselves of the luxury of our own participation in this exploration. Most people—99 percent and more, no doubt—have always been too busy staying alive and fending for themselves in difficult circumstances to have any time or taste for the question of free will. Political freedom, for many of them, has been a major concern, but metaphysical freedom has just not been worth worrying about. As Dewey once said, "What men have esteemed and fought for in the name of liberty is varied and complex—but certainly it has never been a metaphysical freedom of will" (Dewey 1922: 303).

Most other people, then, have not been worried about free will. But it is comfortable for us (gentle reader) to believe that thanks to our leisure and intellectual inclinations we have seen deeper into their predicaments than they have. This may be true. But we should be cautious about accepting at face value our quite spontaneous and mutually accepted intuition that the problem of free will is one of the Great Issues. For we are a self-selected group.

Note particularly that free will is an almost exclusively Western preoccupation. Could we be deluded? Could we only *think* that free will matters? Do we even think it matters? That is, outside the lecture hall, outside our professional activities or midnight bull sessions, does the question have much hold on us? As Ryle once noted, we all have our fatalistic moments: "Yet though we know what it is like to entertain this idea, still we are unimpassioned about it. We are not secret zealots for it or secret zealots against it" (Ryle 1954: 28). Fatalism, according to Ryle, "is not a burning issue," and the same can be said of the broader issue of free will. But it can certainly be made to seem a burning tissue.

If having free will matters, it must be because not having free will would be awful, and there must be some grounds for doubting that we have it. What are we afraid of? We are afraid of not having free will. But what exactly are we afraid of? And why? Anyone who dreads the prospect of not having free will must have some inkling about *what that terrible condition would be like.* And in fact there are a host of analogies to be found in the literature: not having free will would be somewhat like being in prison, or being hypnotized, or being paralyzed, or being a puppet, or . . . (the list continues).

I do not think these analogies are merely useful illustrations, merely graphic expository devices. I think they are at the very foundation of the problem. Without them to anchor the philosophical discussions, the free will problem would float away, at best a curious issue to bemuse metaphysicians and puzzlemongers. One aspect of this can be easily seen. Suppose a philosopher claims to have solved the problem of free will; a layman might say, "Well, does your 'solution' allay my worries? Because if it doesn't, then whatever else it may be, it is no solution to what I have been taught to call the free will problem." So if we let tradition be our guide, the free will problem is essentially one we care about. Problems about the will that are of merely esoteric interest are just not *the* free will problem, however fascinating they might be to some specialists.

But there is more to it than that. The fears not only anchor the problem of free will; they also provide its content and shape the dynamics of argument and exploration. One of my themes will be that the "classic," "traditional" free will problem of philosophy is far more an artifact of traditional methods and preoccupations of philosophers than has been recognized.

I propose to explore the role of these fears, and in so doing expose, and thus dissolve, some—but not quite all—of the worries and confusions that conspire to create "the free will problem." That problem will turn out to be a misnamed and misbegotten amalgam of overhasty problem *posing* and self-induced panic, the false pretext for much otherwise unmotivated system building and metaphysical tinkering.

There are some undeniably dreadful things in our experience, and when we fear that we don't have free will, it is always because we fear that something importantly like one of these dreadful things is our fate. It is only because we know these predicaments quite well, and hence abhor them for good reasons and fear that something similar might be our lot, that we care about free will at all.

I will present a catalogue of these bugbears and briefly analyze them. Each one drives a part of the traditional free will discussion. None of them is easily dismissed in all its forms, but investigating the fears first may permit some of them to vanish. That is (as Mother used to say), if we look them straight in the eye (and don't avert our eyes ever so slightly and make ourselves ever so busy devising theories) we may see that some of them are only figments of our imaginations. Having reminded ourselves of the bugbears at the outset, we will be able to discern their shadows in the explorations of further issues in subsequent chapters.

In *The Concept of Mind,* Ryle tried to shock us or shame us out of a bad habit of thought by adopting the tactic of referring to the view he was attacking "with deliberate abusiveness as 'the dogma of the Ghost in the Machine.'" I am similarly speaking with deliberate disrespect (and a smidgen of caricature in this first chapter) when I speak of these bugbears. For it is my view that these metaphors have done most of the work behind the scenes in propelling the free will problem, and that they do not in the slightest deserve the respect and influence they typically enjoy. So my point is to heighten sensitivity to them, and to undercut their traditional eminence with my pejorative characterizations. Once immobilized, they will be addressed in a more surgical spirit in subsequent chapters.

2. The Bogeymen

The first of the bugbears are quite literally bogey*men*—bogeypersons if you insist—for they are all conceived as *agents* who vie with us for control of our bodies, who compete against us, who have interests antithetical to or at least independent of our own. These fearsome fellows are often used by philosophers as reverse cheerleaders (gloomleaders, you might call them) ushered onto the stage whenever anxiety flags, whenever the urgency of the topic under discussion becomes doubtful. As intricacy piles on intricacy, the reader begins to yawn and fidget, but is quickly regalvanized by a nudging analogy: "But that would be like finding yourself in the clutches of...."

The Invisible Jailer: Prisons are dreadful. Prisons are to be shunned. Anyone who fails to understand this is not one of *us.* Well, if prison is bad, what does it contrast with? If one is not in prison, one is free (in one important sense), and each of us can reflect gratefully on how glad we are not to be in prison. "Aha!" says the fearmonger. "What makes you so sure you're not in prison?" Sometimes it's obvious when one is in prison, but sometimes it isn't.

A sly jailer may conceal the steel bars in the window mullions, and install dummy doors in the walls (if you opened one, you would see a brick wall behind it). It might be some time before a prisoner realized he was in prison.

Are you *sure* you're not in some sort of prison?[2] Here one is invited to consider a chain of transformations, taking us from obvious prisons to unobvious (but still dreadful) prisons, to utterly invisible and undetectable (but still dreadful?) prisons. Consider a deer in Magdalen College park. Is it imprisoned? Yes, but not much. The enclosure is quite large. Suppose we moved the deer to a larger enclosure—the New Forest with a fence around it. Would the deer still be imprisoned? In the State of Maine, I am told, deer almost never travel more than five miles from their birthplace during their lives. If an enclosure were located outside the normal unimpeded limits of a deer's lifetime wanderings would the deer enclosed be imprisoned? Perhaps, but note that it makes a difference to our intuitions whether some*one* installs the enclosure. Do you feel imprisoned on Planet Earth—the way Napoleon was stuck on Elba? It is one thing to be born and live on Elba, and another to be put and kept on Elba *by someone*. A jail without a jailer is not a jail. Whether or not it is an undesirable abode depends on other features; it depends on just how (if at all) it cramps the style of its inhabitants.

The Nefarious Neurosurgeon: How would you like to have someone strap you down and insert electrodes in your brain, and then control your every thought and deed by pushing buttons on the "master" console? Consider, for instance, the entirely typical invocation of this chap by Fischer (1982: 26): the ominous Dr. Black, who arranges things in poor Jones' brain so that Black can "control Jones' activities. Jones, meanwhile, knows nothing of this." First, we may ask—as we always should—why is this other, rival *agent* introduced? Why bring Dr. Black into it? Couldn't the example get off the ground just as well, for instance, if Jones had a brain tumor that produced odd results? What makes Fischer's version more dreadful is that Jones' control of his own activities has been usurped by another controller, Dr. Black. A tumor might cause this or that in someone's brain, and it would be terrible indeed to have a debilitating brain tumor, but it would take an awfully smart tumor to *control* someone's brain.

Variations on the Nefarious Neurosurgeon are the Hideous Hypnotist and the Peremptory Puppeteer. We all know about stage hypnotists (we think we do, in any case) and what is particularly chilling about them is that unlike the Nefarious Neurosurgeons, they may leave no physical trace of their influence. Recall that Jones was stipulated to know nothing of Dr. Black's intervention—an important point to which we will return in later chapters. But more insidious still, stage hypnotists display their victims before an audience: they hold you up to ridicule before people who are in more desirable circumstances. It "helps" if you imagine their laughter as your plight is demonstrated to them. The Peremptory Puppeteer is a bit different, for he can be imagined to control your coarse-grained *motions* in spite of your *efforts* and *desires*. In the clutches of the Peremptory Puppeteer you may struggle vainly, like the Stoic's dog, and may at least hope to reveal your conscientious objection to your audience by sneaking in a frown or a whimper, a consolation apparently unavailable to the Hypnotist's victims.

We have never seen an actual human puppet, but we know all about slavery, and know it is an abhorrent condition if anything imaginable is. Which would you rather be: the Zombie of Dr. Svengali, or the Pitiful Human Puppet? Would you rather be a slave or a prisoner? These are all somewhat different fates, each horrible in its own ways, but there are other villains to fear as well.

The Cosmic Child Whose Dolls We Are: Nozick writes "Without free will, we seem diminished, merely the playthings of external forces" (Nozick 1981: 291). How undignified to be a mere plaything, a toy! But how could one be the plaything of a mere impersonal force? There can be no playthings without players. And players aren't just agents; they are playful, childish agents. (It's nowhere near as demeaning to think of yourself as God's *tool*—as many an evangelist will tell you.)

Stanislaw Lem explores, and explodes, the familiar philosophical supposition that we might be mere playthings in his short story, "The Seventh Sally *or* How Trurl's Own Perfection Led to No Good" (Lem 1974), and a delicious parody of this classic philosophical horror story is found in Tom Robbins' novel, *Even Cowgirls Get the Blues:*

> For Christmas that year, Julian gave Sissy a miniature Tyrolean village. The craftsmanship was remarkable.
>
> There was a tiny cathedral whose stained-glass windows made fruit salad of sunlight. There was a plaza and *ein Biergarten*. The *Biergarten* got quite noisy on Saturday nights. There was a bakery that smelled always of hot bread and strudel. There was a town hall and a police station, with cutaway sections that revealed standard amounts of red tape and corruption. There were little Tyroleans in leather britches, intricately stitched, and, beneath the britches, genitalia of equally fine workmanship. There were ski shops and many other interesting things, including an orphanage. The orphanage was designed to catch fire and burn down every Christmas Eve. Orphans would dash into the snow with their nightgowns blazing. Terrible. Around the second week of January, a fire inspector would come and poke through the ruins, muttering, "If they had only listened to me, those children would be alive today." (Robbins 1976: 191–192)

The craftsmanship of this passage is itself remarkable. Notice how the repetition of the orphanage drama year after year (echoing Nietzsche's idea of eternal recurrence—that everything that has happened will happen again and again) seems to rob the little world of any real meaning. But why exactly should it be the repetition of the fire inspector's lament that makes it sound so hollow?

Perhaps if we looked closely at what that entails we would find the sleight of hand that makes the passage "work." Do the little Tyroleans rebuild the orphanage themselves or is there a 'RESET' button on this miniature village? Where do the new orphans come from? Or do the "dead" ones come back to "life"? As we shall see, a close inspection of such fantasies often reveals that the real work is being done by some tacit feature of the example that is strictly irrelevant to the philosophical thesis being presumably motivated by its invocation.

The Malevolent Mindreader: This agent is essentially an opponent, but he does not cause or control your moves; he just foresees them and stymies them. Playing "rock, paper, or scissors" against this fellow is hopeless, for since he knows exactly what rut you're in, what policy you're following, he can see in advance which move you intend to make and always counters successfully (Hofstadter 1982a). If only you could shield your mind from him! If only you could find a strategy of unpredictability that would be proof against his calculations! Then you wouldn't be so impotent, so vulnerable in the game of Life. Predictions matter in a special way when one has a stake in them, when they are not merely future tense statements but rather wagers which one might want to *make* come true and an opponent might want to make come false. In real life one often comes into competition with other people, and even with other organisms (outwitting the rat or mosquito, for instance), but in the cosmic game of Life against whom is one wagering?

I cannot prove that none of the bogeymen in this rogues' gallery really exist, any more than I can prove that the Devil, or Santa Claus, doesn't exist. But I am prepared to put on a sober face and assure anyone who needs assuring that there is absolutely no evidence to suggest that any of these horrible agents exists. But of course if any of them did, woe on us! A closet with a ghost in it is a terrible thing, but a closet that is just like a closet with a ghost in it (except for lacking the ghost) is nothing to fear, so we arrive at what may turn out to be a useful rule of thumb: whenever you spy a bogey*man* in a philosophical example, check to see if this scary agent, who is surely fictitious, is really doing all the work.

3. Sphexishness and Other Worries

There are other fears fueling the free will problem that do not have personified objects. It often seems to people that if determinism were true, there would have to be something "mechanical" about our processes of deliberation that we would regret. We could not be free agents, but only *automata*, insectlike in our behavior. Consider the digger wasp, *Sphex ichneumoneus:*

> When the time comes for egg laying, the wasp *Sphex* builds a burrow for the purpose and seeks out a cricket which she stings in such a way as to paralyze but not kill it. She drags the cricket into the burrow, lays her eggs alongside, closes the burrow, then flies away, never to return. In due course, the eggs hatch and the wasp grubs feed off the paralyzed cricket, which has not decayed, having been kept in the wasp equivalent of deep freeze. To the human mind, such an elaborately organized and seemingly purposeful routine conveys a convincing flavor of logic and thoughtfulness—until more details are examined. For example, the Wasp's routine is to bring the paralyzed cricket to the burrow, leave it on the threshold, go inside to see that all is well, emerge, and then drag the cricket in. If the cricket is moved a few inches away while the wasp is inside making her preliminary inspection, the wasp, on emerging from the burrow, will bring the cricket back to the threshold, but not inside, and will then repeat the preparatory procedure of entering the burrow to see that everything is all right. If again the cricket is removed a few inches while the wasp is inside, once again she will move the cricket up to the threshold and re-enter the burrow for a final check. The wasp never thinks of pulling the cricket straight in. On one occasion this procedure was repeated forty times, always with the same result. (Wooldridge 1963: 82)

The poor wasp is unmasked; she is not a free agent, but rather at the mercy of brute physical causation, driven inexorably into her states and activities by features of the environment outside her control. In "Can Creativity be Mechanized?" Hofstadter (1982b) has proposed that we call this unnerving property, so vividly manifested by the wasp, *sphexishness.* One of the most powerful undercurrents in the free will literature is fear of sphexishness.

We are a lot cleverer than *Sphex,* thank goodness, but just as we reflect gratefully on this, the fearmonger asks again: "What makes you so sure you're not sphexish—at least a little bit?" Wouldn't it simply follow from materialistic determinism that human beings, as physical organisms however fancy, must be just as much at the mercy of the environmental impingements raining down on them? The Godlike biologist reaches down and creates a slight dislocation in the wasp's world, revealing her essentially mindless mechanicity; could a superior intelligence, looking down on us, find a similar if more sophisticated trick that would unmask us? Even when we remind ourselves that so far as we know, there are no such superagents out there determined to thwart our lives, the mere possibility in principle that we are imperfect and vulnerable in this way is distinctly unsettling.

Notice the parallel between the fear of the Invisible Jailer and the fear of sphexishness. One starts with a simple, clear case of something awful (being literally imprisoned, or being *just* like the wasp), and then, letting that awfulness sink in, one grants that in one's own case, matters are much more complex—almost too complex to imagine—but still importantly similar. Presumably then, our own case inherits the awfulness thanks to the similarity chain. But is this really so?

Here I want to point to a dangerous philosophical practice that will receive considerable scrutiny in this book: the deliberate oversimplification of tasks to be performed by the philosopher's imagination. A popular strategy in philosophy is to construct a certain sort of thought experiment I call an *intuition pump* (Dennett 1980 and Hofstadter and Dennett 1981). Such thought experiments (unlike Galileo's or Einstein's, for instance) are *not* supposed to clothe strict arguments that prove conclusions from premises. Rather, their point is to entrain a family of imaginative reflections in the reader that ultimately yields not a formal conclusion but a dictate of "intuition." Intuition pumps are cunningly designed to focus the reader's attention on "the important" features, and to deflect the reader from bogging down in hard-to-follow details. There is nothing wrong with this in principle. Indeed one of philosophy's highest callings is finding ways of helping people see the forest and not just the trees. But intuition pumps are often abused, though seldom deliberately.

Perhaps the most frequent abuse is deriving a result—a heartfelt intuitive judgment—from the very simplicity of the imagined case, rather than from the actual content of the example portrayed so simply and clearly. Might it not be that what makes the wasp's fate so dreadful is not that her actions and "decisions" are *caused* but precisely that they are so *simply* caused? If so, then the acknowledged difference between the object of our intuition pump and ourselves—our complexity—may block our inheritance of the awfulness we see in the simple case. Perhaps we should laugh, not shudder; perhaps this intuition pump is like that nightmare snake who swallows his tail and keeps on going until he's completely eaten himself up.

But only a detailed examination will tell. Are we sphexish? Are we importantly sphexish? We certainly know some people who are: the radically insane, the retarded, the brain-damaged. (For instance, Whitaker (1976) describes a brain-damaged woman who could no longer comprehend any language at all, but who parroted back everything that was spoken to her exactly—except for grammatical errors, which she always corrected!) Many unsettling experiments by psychologists seem to reveal something about the dimensions of our sphexishness: Milgram's classic horror story about the obedient torturers (Milgram 1974), experiments on human irrationality by Kahneman, Tversky and many others (Kahneman, Slovic, and Tversky 1982), and of course the famous, if officially unsubstantiated, anecdotes about students using Skinner's operant conditioning techniques to get their psychology professors to scratch their ears while lecturing (Brewer 1974). The likely extent of our sphexishness will be a central topic in the second chapter.

The Disappearing Self: Another feature lurking in the tale of the wasp is that spooky sense one often gets when observing or learning about insects and other lower animals: all that bustling activity but *there's nobody home!* We are looking at a world that appears to have been cleverly designed but then deserted by its designer. The ants and bees, and even the fish and the birds, are just "going through the motions." *They* don't understand or appreciate what they are up to, and no other comprehending selves are to be found in the neighborhood. This is the fear of the incredible Disappearing Self.

Again, we seem to know of clearly intermediate cases between the insects, the fish, and ourselves. The insane and brain-damaged, for instance, often do seem to be quite appropriately described as having no selves, as being alive and animated, but having no *animae.* When we look "too closely" at our own mental activities, the same vanishing act often occurs. As Mozart once said of his musical ideas: "Whence and how do they come? I do not know and I *have nothing to do with it* [emphasis added]." If determinism is true, it seems, there is no elbow room left for our selves, and no work for our selves to do. Can we find our selves, or is science on the verge of showing that they *(we?)* are illusions—like the illusion that the wasp is (or has) a self?

Science takes us inside things, and the inner, detailed view of our brains that science provides is not likely to reveal to us any recognizable version of what Descartes called the *res cogitans* or thinking thing we know so well "by introspection." But if we lose our view of our selves as we gain in scientific objectivity, what will happen to love and gratitude (and hate and resentment)?

> But what can I do if I don't even feel resentment?...My anger, in consequence of the damned laws of consciousness, is subject to chemical decomposition. As you look its object vanishes into thin air, its reasons evaporate, the offender is nowhere to be found, the affront ceases to be an offense and becomes destiny, something like toothache, for which nobody is to blame. (Dostoevsky, *Notes from Underground,* quoted by Bennett 1980)

The Dread Secret: Science often seems to be on the verge of telling us too much, of opening Pandora's Box and revealing some Dread Secret or ocher; as soon as we hear it, it will paralyze us. It will paralyze us by shattering some illusion that is absolutely necessary for the maintenance of our lives as agents. Our own rationality will undo us, because once we've seen the truth, we will be unable to deceive ourselves any longer.

It is easy enough to see how the paralysis is presumably accomplished by the Dread Secret, for it is by analogy, once again, with something that often happens, and can indeed be paralyzing and often pathetic. Suppose, for instance, we spend the day in Oxford debating the relative merits of the restaurants in London, trying to decide which to try in the evening. Then we learn the trains are not running, or all restaurants are closed for the day, or we are locked in the room in Oxford, or it is simply too late to get to London. We have just learned that that particular exercise of deliberation was utterly futile. There was no real opportunity for us to act; there were no real alternatives to decide among. Now if science were to show us that there really aren't ever any opportunities, wouldn't that—shouldn't that—lead us to cease deliberation altogether?

As Tolstoy says in the last line of *War and Peace*, "It is necessary to renounce a freedom that does not exist and to recognize a dependence of which we are not personally conscious." But this would be awful, it seems, for wouldn't it lead to a truly pernicious and self-destructive resignation and apathy? Think, for instance, of the obscene resignation of those who see nuclear war as utterly inevitable and hence not worth trying to prevent. Shouldn't we deplore the promulgation of any claim (even if it is true—perhaps especially if it is true) that encourages this sort of attitude?

What is the Dread Secret supposed to be? Perhaps it is the fact of determinism. (Or the fact of indeterminism!) In any event, it seems that we should bring it out into the open very gingerly, since its implication is that freedom is an illusion. Note that the fear here is not that a certain proposition is true, but that true or false it may come to be believed. After all, if determinism is true now, it always has been true. While many people's lives in the past have been quite horrible, many others have led lives apparently well worth living—in spite of their living in a deterministic world. Modern science isn't *making* determinism true, even if it is discovering this fact, so things aren't going to get worse, unless it is believing in determinism rather than determinism itself that creates the catastrophe.[3]

Could the discovery of determinism not only ruin our own lives but reveal retrospectively that all those earlier good lives were not what they seemed to those who led them? Some of the most haunting images in the philosophical literature play on this worry. Anscombe (1957: 6) tells us of a lecture in which Wittgenstein invited his audience to consider autumn leaves floating down to the ground, saying to themselves "Now I'll go this way... now I'll go that way." Hobbes devised a similar fantasy:

> A wooden top that is lashed by the boys, and runs about sometimes to one wall, sometimes to another, sometimes spinning, sometimes hitting men on the shins, if it were sensible of its own motion, would think it proceeded from its own will, unless it felt what lashed it. And is a man any wiser, when he runs to one place for a benefice, to another for a bargain, and troubles the world with writing errors and requiring answers, because he thinks he doth it without other cause than his own will, and

seeth not what are the lashings that cause his will? (Hobbes, Molesworth, ed., 1841, Vol V: 55)

Some illusions are almost irresistible. The golfer is watching his putt curving slowly toward the cup. He squirms and twists and leans, as if to get the ball to alter its course, as if his gyrations could actually make a difference. But it's too late, of course. There is a term for such antics: *body English.* Body English is always futile, sometimes comical, sometimes pathetic, and often irresistible. What science threatens to show us is that all our striving is just so much body English. Wouldn't it be awful if all our mental gymnastics, our deliberations and strivings and resolutions and struggles were just so much body English? They would be, if they were (however irresistible) utterly incapable of making any real difference to the outcomes of the events that matter to us. This bugbear looms large in discussions of fatalism, but that is not its only hunting ground. For the moment it might be useful to contrast body English with something quite similar, for this might help save us from a fear.

Consider follow-through. The golfer has been told by the golf pro to *keep his head down* until he has completed his swing. But how can this be good advice? The ball leaves the club head in midswing, and after it has begun its trajectory, nothing that happens on the tee can alter that trajectory. Isn't the attention to details of the swing that occur after the ball leaves the club head just so much body English? Not necessarily. For it may be that the only way to get the right thing to happen up to the moment of impact is to look ahead and fix a more distant goal, counting on one's efforts to satisfy that goal to produce bodily motions that traverse just the right space at just the right speed. One would be foolish indeed to disregard the pro's advice on the basis of the argument given above that it couldn't make any difference. It could make all the difference. Sometimes the only way to get what you really want is to try to do something else.

So I am willing to fight fire with fire. The fearmonger calls up the everyday image of body English, and gets you to transport your shudder of embarrassment or anxiety into the metaphysical realm of free will. I counter with the everyday image of follow-through, and ask why you shouldn't just as well transport its more congenial moral to the high metaphysical ground. But there ought to be a better way of proceeding, and there is. The more or less traditional philosophical practice is to move briskly through the analogies to a conclusion which then becomes the starting point for exquisitely careful theory construction and argument. For instance, it is taken as "obvious" that the sort of free will we all want is such that one has free will only if one "could have done otherwise," and then great care and energy is taken to spell out the necessary and sufficient conditions for this sort of power or circumstance.

This then creates the curious desire in some people that it should turn out to be true of any of one's acts that if *exactly the same* physical state of affairs should obtain again, some other act could issue forth. Much ingenuity has been expended in trying to say what this thesis amounts to, and what its chances are of being true, but surprisingly little attention has been given to the question of why anyone should care about this metaphysical might-be—aside from "reminding" the reader that if it weren't true, why, that would be like being in prison, being paralyzed, hypnotized, a wasp, a puppet, a plaything. The allusions to the awful alternative are sometimes so swiftly traversed that quite obvious incoherence is overlooked—incoherence that would never survive the careful attention philosophers devote to their theorizing proper.

4. Overview

So far I have not tried to prove anything about free will. Instead, I have been circling the topic, roughing out our sense of the issues, drawing attention to a few curious features of the raw material—a tempting shape here, a vein in the marble there. I have been concerned to draw attention to ways in which the free will problem *may* be in large part an artifact of the methods typically used to study it, and this preliminary consciousness-raising will be useful in keeping us out of some perennial ruts as we traverse the traditional terrain. Before we are finished, we will cover virtually all of the traditional topics and arguments in the free will literature, but my method will be *to go slow where others go fast,* pausing over the familiar analogizing instead of rushing headlong into theory construction and refutation.

A fairly vigorous institution of professional repression has submerged for us the centrality and influence of intuition pumps in the development of philosophy. It is not just in the free will area that intuition pumps have been the dominant force. I suggest that reflection on the history of philosophy shows that the great intuition pumps have been the major movers all along.

One might say that these intuition pumps are the enduring melodies of philosophy, with the staying power that ensures that they will be remembered by our freshmen, quite vividly and accurately, years after they have forgotten the intricate contrapuntal surrounding argument and analysis. A good intuition pump is more robust than any one version of it. (How many variations have been trotted out on the themes of Rawls' Original Position or Putnam's Twin-Earth?)

Intuition pumps are powerful pedagogical devices. Descartes' "cogito ergo sum" thought experiment is generally agreed to be logically suspect, if not downright defective. It has inspired literally dozens of reinterpretations and defenses; many philosophy professors would dismiss all these commentaries while never dreaming of removing Descartes' dramatic idea from the syllabus. Even great intuition pumps can mislead as much as they instruct.

When we teach Descartes, for instance, we typically do not teach his thought experiment as revealing the truth—or even as leading to the truth—about knowledge. In fact, we typically blame Descartes and his seductive intuition pump for leading philosophers on a three-century wild goose chase. At best we are grateful to him in the same way we might be grateful to someone who gave us the wrong directions, but whose directions led us on a fascinating misadventure from which we happened to learn a great deal.

The central role of intuition pumps in philosophy shows that philosophy is not, and could not reasonably aspire to be, science. Philosophy without intuition pumps occasionally succeeds in purifying and regimenting a conceptual area sufficiently for science to take over, but these are not mainstream philosophical triumphs, by and large. Philosophy with intuition pumps is not science at all, but in its own informal way it is a valuable—even occasionally necessary—companion to science. It should not embarrass philosophers to acknowledge that intuition pumps do much of the enduring work of philosophy (for better and for worse). After all, an intuition pump should be the ideal tool in the philosopher's kit, if we take seriously one of the best-known visions of what philosophy is *for*. It is for enlarging our vision of the possible, for breaking bad habits of thought. As Wittgenstein said, "Philosophy is a battle against the bewitchment of our intelligence by means of language" (Wittgenstein 1953, sec. 109). For such tasks, the regimented marshalling of rigorous argument is seldom more than an insurance policy, a check on the freewheeling intuition mongering that has laid down the lines of some new vision.

Notes

1. "A sort of hobgoblin...supposed to devour naughty children; hence, generally, any imaginary being invoked by nurses to frighten children" *(Oxford Shorter English Dictionary)*.

2. Berlin (1954: 68) says that determinism, "for all that its chains are decked out with flowers, and despite its parade of noble stoicism and the splendour and vastness of its cosmic design, nevertheless represents the universe as a prison."

3. See, for instance, Strawson 1962: "What effect would, or should, the acceptance of the truth of a general thesis of determinism have upon these reactive attitudes [our normal, interpersonal 'participant' attitudes, such as gratitude and resentment]?"

References

Anscombe, G.E.M. 1957. *Intention*. Oxford: Blackwell.

Bennett, J. 1980. "Accountability," in Z. van Straaten, ed., *Philosophical Subjects: Essays Presented to P.F. Strawson*. Oxford: Oxford University Press.

Berlin, I. 1954. *Historical Inevitability*. Oxford: Oxford University Press.

Brewer, W.F. 1974. "There is no convincing evidence for operant or classical conditioning in adult humans," in W.B. Weimer, ed., *Cognition and the Symbolic Processes*. Hillsdale, NJ: Erlbaum.

Dennett, D. 1980. "The milk of human intentionality," *Behavioral and Brain Sciences*, 3. 428–430.

Dewey, J. 1922. *Human Nature and Conduct*. New York: Henry Holt.

Fischer, J. 1982. "Responsibility and control," *Journal of Philosophy*, Jan. 1982. 24–40.

Hobbes, Thomas. 1841. *The Questions Concerning Liberty, Necessity, and Chance*, in *The English Works of Thomas Hobbes*, Vol. V, edited by Sir W. Molesworth. London: John Bohn.

Hofstadter, D.R. 1982a. "Undercut, Flaut, Hruska, behavioral evolution and other games of strategy," *Scientific American*, 247, August 1982. 16–24.

Hofstadter, D.R. 1982b. "Can creativity be mechanized?" *Scientific American*, 247, September 1982. 20–29.

Hofstadter D.R. and D. Dennett. 1981. *The Mind's I: Fantasies and Reflections on Mind and Soul*. New York: Basic Books.

Kahneman, D., P. Slovic, and A. Tversky, eds. 1982. *Judgment under Uncertainty: Heuristics and Biases*. Cambridge: Cambridge University Press.

Lem, S. 1974. "The Seventh Sally *or* How Trurl's Own Perfection Led to No Good," in *The Cyberiad*, translated by M. Kandel. New York: Seabury Press. (Reprinted in Hofstadter and Dennett 1981.)

Lucretius. 1951. *The Nature of the Universe*, translated by R.E. Latham. Harmondsworth: Penguin.

Milgram, S. 1974. *Obedience to Authority: An Experimental View*. New York: Harper & Row.

Nozick, R. 1981. *Philosophical Explanations*. Cambridge, MA: Harvard University Press.

Robbins, T. 1976. *Even Cowgirls Get the Blues*. New York: Bantham Books.

Ryle, G. 1954. *Dilemmas*. Cambridge: Cambridge University Press.

Strawson, P. F. 1962. "Freedom and resentment," *Proceedings of the British Academy*, 1962.

Whitaker, H. 1976. "A case for the isolation of language function," in H. Whitaker and H. A. Whitaker, eds., *Studies in Neurolinguistics*, Vol II. New York: Academic Press.

Wittgenstein, L. 1953. *Philosophical Investigations*, translated by G.E.M. Anscombe. Oxford: Blackwell.

Wooldridge, D. 1963. *The Machinery of the Brain*. New York: McGraw Hill.

PART 1

Suggested Further Readings

I. The Free Will Problem—Real or illusory?

For influential classical discussions of this issue see:

Hume, David, 1999 [1748]. *An Enquiry concerning Human Understanding*, edited by T.L. Beauchamp. Oxford: Clarendon Press. Section 8: "Of Liberty and Necessity."

Schlick, Moritz. 1966 [1939]. "When is a man responsible?" reprinted in B. Berofsky, ed., *Free Will and Determinism*. New York: Harper & Row.

Campbell, C.A. 1951. "Is 'freewill' a pseudo-problem?" *Mind* 60: 441–465. (Reprinted in B. Berofsky, ed. *Free Will and Determinism*. New York: Harper & Row, 1966.)

Two more recent works involved in this general debate:

Nagel, Thomas. 1986. *The View from Nowhere*. New York: Oxford University Press.

Williams, Bernard. 1986. "How free does the will need to be?" reprinted in Bernard Williams, *Making Sense of Humanity*. Cambridge: Cambridge University Press.

On the problem of moral luck more generally see:

Levy, Neil. 2011. *Hard Luck*. Oxford: Oxford University Press.

Mele, Alfred. 2006. *Free Will and Luck*. New York: Oxford University Press.

Statman, Daniel, ed. 1993. *Moral Luck*. Albany: SUNY Press.

PART TWO

Naturalism Against Scepticism

3

Freedom and Resentment

Peter F. Strawson

I.

Some philosophers say they do not know what the thesis of determinism is. Others say, or imply, that they do know what it is. Of these, some—the pessimists perhaps—hold that if the thesis is true, then the concepts of moral obligation and responsibility really have no application, and the practices of punishing and blaming, of expressing moral condemnation and approval, are really unjustified. Others—the optimists perhaps—hold that these concepts and practices in no way lose their raison d'être if the thesis of determinism is true. Some hold even that the justification of these concepts and practices requires the truth of the thesis. There is another opinion which is less frequently voiced: the opinion, it might be said, of the genuine moral sceptic. This is that the notions of moral guilt, of blame, of moral responsibility are inherently confused and that we can see this to be so if we consider the consequences either of the truth of determinism or of its falsity. The holders of this opinion agree with the pessimists that these notions lack application if determinism is true, and add simply that they lack it if determinism is false. If I am asked which of these parties I belong to, I must say it is the first of all, the party of those who do not know what the thesis of determinism is. But this does not stop me from having some sympathy with the others, and a wish to reconcile them. Should not ignorance, rationally, inhibit such sympathies? Well, of course, though darkling, one has some inkling—some notion of what sort of thing is being talked about. This lecture is intended as a move towards reconciliation; so is likely to seem wrongheaded to everyone.

But can there be any possibility of reconciliation between such clearly opposed opinions as those of pessimists and optimists about determinism? Well, there might be a formal withdrawal on one side in return for a substantial concession on the other. Thus, suppose the optimist's position were put like this: (1) the facts as we know them do not show determinism to be false;

(2) the facts as we know them supply an adequate basis for the concepts and practices which the pessimist feels to be imperilled by the possibility of determinism's truth. Now it might be that the optimist is right in this, but is apt to give an inadequate account of the facts as we know them, and of how they constitute an adequate basis for the problematic concepts and practices; that the reasons he gives for the adequacy of the basis are themselves inadequate and leave out something vital. It might be that the pessimist is rightly anxious to get this vital thing back and, in the grip of his anxiety, feels he has to go beyond the facts as we know them; feels that the vital thing can be secure only if, beyond the facts as we know them, there is the further fact that determinism is false. Might *he* not be brought to make a formal withdrawal in return for a vital concession?

II.

Let me enlarge very briefly on this, by way of preliminary only. Some optimists about determinism point to the efficacy of the practices of punishment, and of moral condemnation and approval, in regulating behaviour in socially desirable ways.[1] In the fact of their efficacy, they suggest, is an adequate basis for these practices; and this fact certainly does not show determinism to be false. To this the pessimists reply, all in a rush, that *just* punishment and *moral* condemnation imply moral guilt and guilt implies moral responsibility and moral responsibility implies freedom and freedom implies the falsity of determinism. And to this the optimists are wont to reply in turn that it is true that these practices require freedom in a sense, and the existence of freedom in this sense is one of the facts as we know them. But what "freedom" means here is nothing but the absence of certain conditions the presence of which would make moral condemnation or punishment inappropriate. They have in mind conditions like compulsion by another, or innate incapacity, or insanity, or other less extreme forms of psychological disorder, or the existence of circumstances in which the making of any other choice would be morally inadmissible or would be too much to expect of any man. To this list they are constrained to add other factors which, without exactly being limitations of freedom, may also make moral condemnation or punishment inappropriate or mitigate their force: as some forms of ignorance, mistake, or accident. And the general reason why moral condemnation or punishment is inappropriate when these factors or conditions are present is held to be that the practices in question will be generally efficacious means of regulating behaviour in desirable ways only in cases where these factors are *not* present. Now the pessimist admits that the facts as we know them include the existence of freedom, the occurrence of cases of free action, in the negative sense which the optimist concedes; and admits, or rather insists, that the existence of freedom in this sense is compatible with the truth of determinism. Then what does the pessimist find missing? When he tries to answer this question, his language is apt to alternate between the very familiar and the very unfamiliar.[2] Thus he may say, familiarly enough, that the man who is the subject of justified punishment, blame or moral condemnation must really *deserve* it; and then add, perhaps, that, in the case at least where he is blamed for a positive act rather than an omission, the condition of his really deserving blame is something that goes beyond the negative freedoms that the optimist concedes. It is, say, a genuinely free identification of the will with the act. And this is the condition that is incompatible with the truth of determinism.

The conventional, but conciliatory, optimist need not give up yet. He may say: Well, people often decide to do things, really intend to do what they do, know just what they're doing in doing it: the reasons they think they have for doing what they do, often really are their reasons and not their rationalizations. These facts, too, are included in the facts as we know them. If this is what you mean by freedom—by the identification of the will with the act—then freedom may again be conceded. But again the concession is compatible with the truth of the determinist thesis. For it would not follow from that thesis that nobody decides to do anything; that nobody ever does anything intentionally; that it is false that people sometimes know perfectly well what they are doing. I tried to define freedom negatively. You want to give it a more positive look. But it comes to the same thing. Nobody denies freedom in this sense, or these senses, and nobody claims that the existence of freedom in these senses shows determinism to be false.

But it is here that the lacuna in the optimistic story can be made to show. For the pessimist may be supposed to ask: But *why* does freedom in this sense justify blame, etc.? You turn towards me first the negative, and then the positive, faces of a freedom which nobody challenges. But the only reason you have given for the practices of moral condemnation and punishment in cases where this freedom is present is the efficacy of these practices in regulating behaviour in socially desirable ways. But this is not a sufficient basis, it is not even the right *sort* of basis, for these practices as we understand them.

Now my optimist, being the sort of man he is, is not likely to invoke an intuition of fittingness at this point. So he really has no more to say. And my pessimist, being the sort of man he is, has only one more thing to say; and that is that the admissibility of these practices, as we understand them, demands another kind of freedom, the kind that in turn demands the falsity of the thesis of determinism. But might we not induce the pessimist to give up saying this by giving the optimist something more to say?

III.

I have mentioned punishing and moral condemnation and approval; and it is in connection with these practices or attitudes that the issue between optimists and pessimists—or, if one is a pessimist, the issue between determinists and libertarians—is felt to be particularly important. But it is not of these practices and attitudes that I propose, at first, to speak. These practices or attitudes permit where they do not imply, a certain detachment from the actions or agents which are their objects. I want to speak, at least at first, of something else: of the non-detached attitudes and reactions of people directly involved in transactions with each other; of the attitudes and reactions of offended parties and beneficiaries; of such things as gratitude, resentment, forgiveness, love, and hurt feelings. Perhaps something like the issue between optimists and pessimists arises in this neighbouring field too; and since this field is less crowded with disputants, the issue might here be easier to settle; and if it is settled here, then it might become easier to settle it in the disputant-crowded field.

What I have to say consists largely of commonplaces. So my language, like that of commonplace generally, will be quite unscientific and imprecise. The central commonplace that I want to insist on is the very great importance that we attach to the attitudes and intentions towards us of other human beings, and the great extent to which our personal feelings and reactions depend upon, or involve, our beliefs about these attitudes and intentions. I can give no simple description of the field of phenomena at the centre of which stands this commonplace truth; for the field is too complex. Much imaginative literature is devoted to exploring its complexities; and we have a large vocabulary for the purpose. There are simplifying styles of handling it in a general way. Thus we may, like La Rochfoucauld, put self-love or self-esteem or vanity at the centre of the picture and point out how it may be caressed by the esteem, or wounded by the indifference or contempt, of others. We might speak, in another jargon, of the need for love, and the loss of security which results from its withdrawal; or, in another, of human self-respect and its connection with the recognition of the individual's dignity. These simplifications are of use to me only if they help to emphasize how much we actually mind, how much it matters to us, whether the actions of other people—and particularly of *some* other people—reflect attitudes towards us of goodwill, affection, or esteem on the one hand or contempt, indifference, or malevolence on the other. If someone treads on my hand accidentally, while trying to help me, the pain may be no less acute than if he treads on it in contemptuous disregard of my existence or with a malevolent wish to injure me. But I shall generally feel in the second case a kind and degree of resentment that I shall not feel in the first. If someone's actions help me to some benefit I desire, then I am benefited in any case; but if he intended them so to benefit me because of his general goodwill towards me, I shall reasonably feel a gratitude which I should not feel at all if the benefit was an incidental consequence, unintended or even regretted by him, of some plan of action with a different aim.

These examples are of actions which confer benefits or inflict injuries over and above any conferred or inflicted by the mere manifestation of attitude and intention themselves. We should consider also in how much of our behaviour the benefit or injury resides mainly or entirely in the manifestation of attitude itself. So it is with good manners, and much of what we call kindness, on the one hand; with deliberate rudeness, studied indifference, or insult on the other.

Besides resentment and gratitude, I mentioned just now forgiveness. This is a rather unfashionable subject in moral philosophy at present; but to be forgiven is something we sometimes ask, and forgiving is something we sometimes say we do. To ask to be forgiven is in part to acknowledge that the attitude displayed in our actions was such as might properly be resented and in part to repudiate that attitude for the future (or at least for the immediate future); and to forgive is to accept the repudiation and to forswear the resentment.

We should think of the many different kinds of relationship which we can have with other people—as sharers of a common interest; as members of the same family; as colleagues; as friends; as lovers; as chance parties to an enormous range of transactions and encounters. Then we should think, in each of these connections in turn, and in others, of the kind of importance we attach to the attitudes and intentions towards us of those who stand in these relationships to us, and of the kinds of *reactive* attitudes and feelings to which we ourselves are prone. In general, we demand some degree of goodwill or regard on the part of those who stand in these relationships to us, though the forms we require it to take vary widely in different connections. The range and intensity of our *reactive* attitudes towards goodwill, its absence or its opposite vary no less widely. I have mentioned, specifically, resentment and gratitude; and they are a usefully opposed pair. But, of course, there is a whole continuum of reactive attitude and feeling stretching on both sides of these and—the most comfortable area—in between them.

The object of these commonplaces is to try to keep before our minds something it is easy to forget when we are engaged in philosophy, especially in our cool, contemporary style, viz. what it is actually like to be involved in ordinary interpersonal relationships, ranging from the most intimate to the most casual.

IV.

It is one thing to ask about the general causes of these reactive attitudes I have alluded to; it is another to ask about the variations to which they are subject, the particular conditions in which they do or do not seem natural or reasonable or appropriate; and it is a third thing to ask what it would be like, what it *is* like, not to suffer them. I am not much concerned with the first question; but I am with the second; and perhaps even more with the third.

Let us consider, then, occasions for resentment: situations in which one person is offended or injured by the action of another and in which—in the absence of special considerations—the offended person might naturally or normally be expected to feel resentment. Then let us consider what sorts of special considerations might be expected to modify or mollify this feeling or remove it altogether. It needs no saying now how multifarious these considerations are. But, for my purpose, I think they can be roughly divided into two kinds. To the first group belong all those which might give occasion for the employment of such expressions as "He didn't mean to," "He hadn't realized," "He didn't know," and also all those which might give occasion for the use of the phrase "He couldn't help it," when this is supported by such phrases as "He was pushed," "He had to do it," "It was the only way," "They left him no alternative," etc. Obviously these various pleas, and the kinds of situations in which they would be appropriate, differ from each other in striking and important ways. But for my present purpose they have something still more important in common. None of them invites us to suspend towards the agent, either at the time of his action or in general, our ordinary reactive attitudes. They do not invite us to view the *agent* as one in respect of whom these attitudes are in any way inappropriate. They invite us to view the *injury* as one in respect of which a particular one of these attitudes is inappropriate. They do not invite us to see the *agent* as other than a fully responsible agent. They invite us to see the *injury* as one for which he was not fully, or at all, responsible. They do not suggest that the agent is in any way an inappropriate object of that kind of demand for goodwill or regard which is reflected in our ordinary reactive attitudes. They suggest instead that the fact of injury was not in this case incompatible with that demand's being fulfilled, that the fact of injury was quite consistent with the agent's attitude and intentions being just what we demand they should be.[3] The agent was just ignorant of the injury he was causing, or had lost his balance through being pushed or had reluctantly to cause the injury for reasons which acceptably override his reluctance. The offering of such pleas by the agent and their acceptance by the sufferer is something in no way opposed to, or outside the context of, ordinary inter-personal relationships and the manifestation of ordinary reactive attitudes. Since things go wrong and situations are complicated, it is an essential and integral element in the transactions which are the life of these relationships.

The second group of considerations is very different. I shall take them in two sub-groups of which the first is far less important than the second. In connection with the first sub-group we may think of such statements as "He wasn't himself," "He has been under very great strain recently," "He was acting under post-hypnotic suggestion," in connection with the second, we may think of "He's only a child," "He's a hopeless schizophrenic," "His mind has been systematically perverted," "That's purely compulsive behaviour on his part." Such pleas as these do, as pleas of my first general group do not, invite us to suspend our ordinary reactive attitudes toward the agent, either at the time of his action or all the time. They do not invite us to see the agent's action in a way consistent with the full retention of ordinary interpersonal attitudes and merely inconsistent with one particular attitude. They invite us to view the agent himself in a different light from the light in which we should normally view one who has acted as he has acted. I shall not linger over the first subgroup of cases. Though they perhaps raise, in the short term, questions akin to those raised, in the long term, by the second subgroup, we may dismiss them without considering those questions by taking that admirably suggestive phrase, "He wasn't himself," with the seriousness that—for all its being logically comic—it deserves. We shall not feel resentment against the man he is for the action done by the man he is not; or at least we shall feel less. We normally have to deal with him under normal stresses; so we shall not feel towards him, when he acts as he does under abnormal stresses, as we should have felt towards him had he acted as he did under normal stresses.

The second and more important subgroup of cases allows that the circumstances were normal, but presents the agent as psychologically abnormal—or as morally undeveloped. The agent was himself; but he is warped or deranged, neurotic or just a child. When we see someone in such a light as this, all our reactive attitudes tend to be profoundly modified. I must deal here in crude dichotomies and ignore the ever-interesting and ever-illuminating varieties of case. What I want to contrast is the attitude (or range of attitudes) of involvement or participation in a human relationship, on the one hand, and what might be called the objective attitude (or range of attitudes) to another human being, on the other. Even in the same situation, I must add, they are not altogether *exclusive* of each other; but they are, profoundly, *opposed* to each other. To adopt the objective attitude to another human being is to see him, perhaps, as an object of social policy; as a subject for what, in a wide range of sense, might be called treatment; as something certainly to be taken account, perhaps precautionary account, of; to be managed or handled or cured or trained; perhaps simply to be avoided, though *this* gerundive is not peculiar to cases of objectivity of attitude. The objective attitude may be emotionally toned in many ways, but not in all ways: it may include repulsion or fear, it may include pity or even love, though not all kinds of love. But it cannot include the range of reactive feelings and attitudes which belong to involvement or participation with others in inter-personal human relationships; it cannot include resentment, gratitude, forgiveness, anger, or the sort of love which two adults can sometimes be said to feel reciprocally, for each other. If your attitude towards someone is wholly objective, then though you may fight him, you cannot quarrel with him, and though you may talk to him, even negotiate with him, you cannot reason with him. You can at most pretend to quarrel, or to reason, with him.

Seeing someone, then, as warped or deranged or compulsive in behaviour or peculiarly unfortunate in his formative circumstances—seeing someone so tends, at least to some extent, to set him apart from normal participant reactive attitudes on the part of one who sees him, tends to promote, at least in the civilized, objective attitudes. But there is something curious to add to this. The objective attitude is not only something we naturally tend to fall into in cases like these, where participant attitudes are partially or wholly inhibited by abnormalities or by immaturity. It is also something which is available as a resource in other cases too. We look with an objective eye on the compulsive behaviour of the neurotic or the tiresome behaviour of a very young child, thinking in terms of treatment or training. But we *can* sometimes look with something like the same eye on the behaviour of the normal and the mature. We *have* this resource and can sometimes use it: as a refuge, say, from the strains of involvement; or as an aid to policy; or simply out of intellectual curiosity. Being human, we cannot, in the normal case, do this for long, or altogether. If the strains of involvement, say, continue to be too great, then we have to do something else—like severing a relationship. But what is above all interesting is the tension there is, in us, between the participant attitude and the objective attitude. One is tempted to say: between our humanity and our intelligence. But to say this would be to distort both notions.

What I have called the participant reactive attitudes are essentially natural human reactions to the good or ill will or indifference of others towards us, as displayed in *their* attitudes and actions. The question we have to ask is: What effect would, or should, the acceptance of the truth of a general thesis of determinism have upon these reactive attitudes? More specifically would, or should, the acceptance of the truth of the thesis lead to the decay or the repudiation of all such attitudes? Would, or should, it mean the end of gratitude, resentment, and forgiveness; of all reciprocated adult loves; of all the essentially *personal* antagonisms?

But how can I answer, or even pose, this question without knowing *exactly* what the thesis of determinism is? Well, there is one thing we do know: that if there is a coherent thesis of determinism, then there must be a sense of "determined" such that, if that thesis is true, then all behaviour whatever is determined in that sense. Remembering this, we can consider at least what possibilities lie formally open; and then perhaps we shall see that the question can be answered *without* knowing exactly what the thesis of determinism is. We can consider what possibilities lie open because we have already before us an account of the ways in which particular reactive attitudes, or reactive attitudes in general, may be, and, sometimes, we judge, should be, inhibited. Thus I considered earlier a group of considerations which tend to inhibit, and, we judge, should inhibit, resentment, in particular cases of an agent causing an injury, without inhibiting reactive attitudes in general towards that agent. Obviously this group of considerations cannot strictly bear upon our question; for that question concerns reactive attitudes in general. But resentment has a particular interest; so it is worth adding that it has never been claimed as a consequence of the truth of determinism that one or another of *these* considerations was operative in every case of an injury being caused by an agent; that it would follow from the truth of determinism that anyone who caused an injury *either* was quite simply ignorant of causing it *or* had acceptably overriding reasons for acquiescing reluctantly in causing it *or* .... The prevalence of this happy state of affairs would not be a consequence of the reign of universal determinism, but of the reign of universal goodwill. We cannot, then, find here the possibility of an affirmative answer to our question, even for the particular case of resentment.

Next, I remarked that the participant attitude, and the personal reactive attitudes in general, tend to give place, and, it is judged by the civilized, should give place, to objective attitudes, just in so far as the agent is seen as excluded from ordinary adult human relationships by deep-rooted abnormality—or simply by being a child. But it cannot be a consequence of any thesis which is not itself self-contradictory that abnormality is the universal condition.

Now this dismissal might seem altogether too facile; and so, in a sense, it is. But whatever is too quickly dismissed in this dismissal is allowed for in the only possible form of affirmative answer that remains. We can sometimes, and in part, I have remarked, look on the normal (those we rate as "normal") in the objective way in which we have learned to look on certain classified cases of abnormality. And our question reduces to this: could, or should the acceptance of the determinist thesis lead us always to look on everyone exclusively in this way? For this is the only condition worth considering under which the acceptance of determinism could lead to the decay or repudiation of participant reactive attitudes.

It does not seem to be self-contradictory to suppose that this might happen. So I suppose we must say that it is not absolutely inconceivable that it should happen. But I am strongly inclined to think that it is, for us as we are, practically inconceivable. The human commitment to participation in ordinary inter-personal relationships is, I think, too thoroughgoing and deeply rooted for us to take seriously the thought that a general theoretical conviction might so change our world that, in it, there were no longer any such things as inter-personal relationships as we normally understand them; and being involved in inter-personal relationships as we normally understand them precisely is being exposed to the range of reactive attitudes and feelings that is in question.

This, then, is a part of the reply to our question. A sustained objectivity of interpersonal attitude, and the human isolation which that would entail, does not seem to be something of which human beings would be capable, even if some general truth were a theoretical ground for it. But this is not all. There is a further point, implicit in the foregoing, which must be made explicit. Exceptionally, I have said, we can have direct dealings with human beings without any degree of personal involvement, treating them simply as creatures to be handled in our own interests, or our side's, or society's—or even theirs. In the extreme case of the mentally deranged, it is easy to see the connection between the possibility of a wholly objective attitude and the impossibility of what we understand by ordinary inter-personal relationships. Given this latter impossibility, no other civilized attitude is available than that of viewing the deranged person simply as something to be understood and controlled in the most desirable fashion. To view him as outside the reach of personal relationships is already, for the civilized, to view him in this way. For reasons of policy or self-protection we may have occasion, perhaps temporary, to adopt a fundamentally similar attitude to a "normal" human being; to concentrate, that is, on understanding "how he works," with a view to determining our policy accordingly or to finding in that very understanding a relief from the strains of involvement. Now it is certainly true that in the case of the abnormal, though not in the case of the normal, our adoption of the objective attitude is a consequence of our viewing the agent as *incapacitated* in some or all respects for ordinary inter-personal relations. He is thus incapacitated, perhaps, by the fact that his picture of reality is pure fantasy, that he does not, in a sense, live in the real world at all; or by the fact that his behaviour is, in part, an unrealistic acting out of unconscious purposes; or by the fact that he is an idiot, or a moral idiot. But there is something else which, *because* this is true, is equally certainly *not* true. And that is that there is a sense of "determined" such that (1) if determinism is true, all behaviour is determined in this sense, and (2) determinism might be true, i.e., it is not inconsistent with the facts as we know them to suppose that all behaviour might be determined in this sense, and (3) our adoption of the objective attitude towards the abnormal is the result of prior embracing of the belief that the behaviour, or the relevant stretch of behaviour, of the human being in question *is* determined in this sense. Neither in the case of the normal, then, nor in the case of the abnormal is it true that, when we adopt an objective attitude, we do so *because* we hold such a belief. So my answer has two parts. The first is that we cannot, as we are, seriously envisage ourselves adopting a thoroughgoing objectivity of attitude to others as a result of theoretical conviction of the truth of determinism; and the second is that when we do in fact adopt such an attitude in a particular case, our doing so is not the consequence of a theoretical conviction which might be expressed as "Determinism in this case," but is a consequence of our abandoning, for different reasons in different cases, the ordinary inter-personal attitudes.

It might be said that all this leaves the real question unanswered, and that we cannot hope to answer it without knowing exactly what the thesis of determinism is. For the real question is not a question about what we actually do, or why we do it. It is not even a question about what we would *in fact* do if a certain theoretical conviction gained general acceptance. It is a question about what it would be *rational* to do if determinism were true, a question about the rational justification of ordinary inter-personal attitudes in general. To this I shall reply, first, that such a question could seem real only to one who had utterly failed to grasp the purport of the preceding answer, the fact of our natural human commitment to ordinary interpersonal attitudes. This commitment is part of the general framework of human life, not something that can come up for review as particular cases can come up for review within this general framework. And I shall reply, second, that if we could imagine what we cannot have, viz. a choice in this matter, then we could choose rationally only in the light of an assessment of the gains and losses to human life, its enrichment or impoverishment; and the truth or falsity of a general thesis of determinism would not bear on the rationality of *this* choice.[4]

V.

The point of this discussion of the reactive attitudes in their relation—or lack of it—to the thesis of determinism was to bring us, if possible, nearer to a position of compromise in a more usual area of debate. We are not now to discuss reactive attitudes which are essentially those of offended parties or beneficiaries. We are to discuss reactive attitudes which are essentially not those, or only incidentally are those, of offended parties or beneficiaries, but are nevertheless, I shall claim, kindred attitudes to those I have discussed. I put resentment in the centre of the previous discussion. I shall put moral indignation—or, more weakly, moral disapprobation—in the centre of this one.

The reactive attitudes I have so far discussed are essentially reactions to the quality of others' wills towards us, as manifested in their behaviour: to their good or ill will or indifference or lack of concern. Thus resentment, or what I have called resentment, is a reaction to injury or indifference. The reactive attitudes I have now to discuss might be described as the sympathetic or vicarious or impersonal or disinterested or generalized analogues of the reactive attitudes I have already discussed. They are reactions to the qualities of others' wills, not towards ourselves, but towards others. Because of this impersonal or vicarious character, we give them different names. Thus one who experiences the vicarious analogue of resentment is said to be indignant or disapproving, or morally indignant or disapproving. What we have here is, as it were, resentment on behalf of another, where one's own interest and dignity are not involved; and it is this impersonal or vicarious character of the attitude added to its others, which entitle it to the qualification "moral." Both my description of, and my name for, these attitudes are, in one important respect, a little misleading. It is not that these attitudes are essentially vicarious—one can feel indignation on one's own account—but that they are essentially capable of being vicarious. But I shall retain the name for the sake of its suggestiveness; and I hope that what is misleading about it will be corrected in what follows.

The personal reactive attitudes rest on, and reflect, an expectation of, and demand for, the manifestation of a certain degree of goodwill or regard on the part of other human beings towards ourselves; or at least on the expectation of, and demand for, an absence of the manifestation of active ill will or indifferent disregard. (What will, in particular cases, *count* as manifestations of good or ill will or disregard will vary in accordance with the particular relationship in which we stand to another human being.) The generalized or vicarious analogues of the personal reactive attitudes rest on, and reflect, exactly the same expectation or demand in a generalized form; they rest on, or reflect, that is, the demand for the manifestation of a reasonable degree of goodwill or regard, on the part of others, not simply towards oneself, but towards all those on whose behalf moral indignation may be felt, i.e., as we now think, towards all men. The generalized and non-generalized forms of demand and the vicarious and personal reactive attitudes which rest upon, and reflect, them are connected not merely logically. They are connected humanly; and not merely with each other. They are connected also with yet another set of attitudes which I must mention now in order to complete the picture. I have considered from two points of view the demands we make on others and our reactions to their possibly injurious actions. These were the points of view of one whose interest was directly involved (who suffers, say, the injury) and of others whose interest was not directly involved (who do not themselves suffer the injury). Thus I have spoken of personal reactive attitudes in the first connection and of their vicarious analogues in the second. But the picture is not complete unless we consider also the correlates of these attitudes on the part of those on whom the demands are made, on the part of the agents. Just as there are personal and vicarious reactive attitudes associated with demands on others for oneself and demands on others for others, so there are self-reactive attitudes associated with demands on oneself for others. And here we have to mention such phenomena as feeling bound or obliged (the "sense of obligation"); feeling compunction; feeling guilty or remorseful or at least responsible; and the more complicated phenomenon of shame.

All these three types of attitude are humanly connected. One who manifested the personal reactive attitudes in a high degree but showed no inclination at all to their vicarious analogues would appear as an abnormal case of moral egocentricity, as a kind of moral solipsist. Let him be supposed fully to acknowledge the claims to regard that others had on him, to be susceptible of the whole range of self-reactive attitudes. He would then see himself as unique both as one (*the* one) who had a general claim on human regard and as one (*the* one) on whom human beings in general had such a claim. This would be a kind of moral solipsism. But it is barely more than a conceptual possibility; if it is that. In general, though within varying limits, we demand of others for others, as well as of ourselves for others, something of the regard which we demand of others for ourselves. Can we imagine, besides that of the moral solipsist, any other case of one or two of these three types of attitude being fully developed, but quite unaccompanied by any trace, however slight, of the remaining two or one? If we can, then we imagine something far below or far above the level of our common humanity—a moral idiot or a saint. For all these types of attitude alike have common roots in our human nature and our membership of human communities.

Now, as of the personal reactive attitudes, so of their vicarious analogues, we must ask in what ways, and by what considerations, they tend to be inhibited. Both types of attitude involve, or express, a certain sort of demand for inter-personal regard. The fact of injury constitutes a prima-facie appearance of this demand's being flouted or unfulfilled. We saw, in the case of resentment, how one class of considerations may show this appearance to be mere appearance, and hence inhibit resentment, *without* inhibiting, or displacing, the sort of demand of which resentment can be an expression, without in any way tending to make us suspend our ordinary inter-personal attitudes to the agent. Considerations of this class operate in just the same way, for just the same reasons, in connection with moral disapprobation or indignation; they inhibit indignation without in any way inhibiting the sort of demand on the agent of which indignation can be an expression, the range of attitudes towards him to which it belongs. But in this connection we may express the facts with a new emphasis. We may say, stressing the moral, the generalized aspect of the demand, considerations of this group have no tendency to make us see the agent as other than a morally responsible agent; they simply make us see the injury as one for which he was not morally responsible. The offering and acceptance of such exculpatory pleas as are here in question in no way detract in our eyes from the agent's status as a term of moral relationships. On the contrary, since things go wrong and situations are complicated, it is an essential part of the life of such relationships.

But suppose we see the agent in a different light: as one whose picture of the world is an insane delusion; or as one whose behaviour, or a part of whose behaviour, is unintelligible to us, perhaps even to him, in terms of conscious purposes, and intelligible only in terms of unconscious purposes; or even, perhaps, as one wholly impervious to the self-reactive attitudes I spoke of, wholly lacking, as we say, in moral sense. Seeing an agent in such a light as this tends, I said, to inhibit resentment in a wholly different way. It tends to inhibit resentment because it tends to inhibit ordinary inter-personal attitudes in general, and the kind of demand and expectation which those attitudes involve; and tends to promote instead the purely objective view of the agent as one posing problems simply of intellectual understanding, management, treatment, and control. Again the parallel holds for those generalized or moral attitudes towards the agent which we are now concerned with. The same abnormal light which shows the agent to us as one in respect of whom the personal attitudes, the personal demand, are to be suspended, shows him to us also as one in respect of whom the impersonal attitudes, the generalized demand, are to be suspended. Only, abstracting now from direct personal interest, we may express the facts with a new emphasis. We may say: to the extent to which the agent is seen in this light, he is not seen as one on whom demands and expectations lie in that particular way in which we think of them as lying when we speak of moral obligation; he is not, to that extent, seen as a morally responsible agent, as a term of moral relationships, as a member of the moral community.

I remarked also that the suspension of ordinary inter-personal attitudes and the cultivation of a purely objective view is sometimes possible even when we have no such reasons for it as I have just mentioned. Is this possible also in the case of the moral reactive attitudes? I think so; and perhaps it is easier. But the motives for a total suspension of moral reactive attitudes are fewer, and perhaps weaker: fewer, because only where there is antecedent personal involvement can there be the motive of seeking refuge from the strains of such involvement; perhaps weaker, because the tension between objectivity of view and the moral reactive attitudes is perhaps less than the tension between objectivity of view and the personal reactive attitudes, so that we can in the case of the moral reactive attitudes more easily secure the speculative or political gains of objectivity of view by a kind of setting on one side, rather than a total suspension, of those attitudes.

These last remarks are uncertain; but also, for the present purpose, unimportant. What concerns us now is to inquire, as previously in connection with the personal reactive attitudes, what relevance any general thesis of determinism might have to their vicarious analogues. The answers once more are parallel; though I shall take them in a slightly different order. First, we must note, as before, that when the suspension of such an attitude or such attitudes occurs in a particular case, it is *never* the consequence of the belief that the piece of behaviour in question was determined in a sense such that all behaviour *might be*, and, if determinism is true, all behaviour *is*, determined in that sense. For it is not a consequence of any general thesis of determinism which might be true that nobody knows what he's doing or that everybody's behaviour is unintelligible in terms of conscious purposes or that everybody lives in a world of delusion or that nobody has a moral sense, i.e., is susceptible of self-reactive attitudes, etc. In fact no such sense of "determined" as would be required for a general thesis of determinism is ever relevant to our actual suspensions of moral reactive attitudes. Second, suppose it granted, as I have already argued, that we cannot take seriously the thought that theoretical conviction of such a general thesis would lead to the total decay of the personal reactive attitudes. Can we then take seriously the thought that such a conviction—a conviction, after all, that many have held or said they held—would nevertheless lead to the total decay or repudiation of the vicarious analogues of these attitudes? I think that the change in our social world which would leave us exposed to the personal reactive attitudes but not to all their vicarious analogues, the generalization of abnormal egocentricity which this would entail, is perhaps even harder for us to envisage as a real possibility than the decay of both kinds of attitude together. Though there are some necessary and some contingent differences between the ways and cases in which these two kinds of attitudes operate or are inhibited in their operation, yet, as general human capacities or proneness, they stand or lapse together. Finally, to the further question whether it would not be *rational*, given a general theoretical conviction of the truth of determinism, so to change our world that in it all these attitudes were wholly suspended, I must answer, as before, that one who presses this question has wholly failed to grasp the import of the preceding answer, the nature of the human commitment that is here involved: it is *useless* to ask whether it would not be rational for us to do what it is not in our nature to (be able to) do. To this I must add, as before, that if there were, say, for a moment open to us the possibility of such a godlike choice, the rationality of making or refusing it would be determined by quite other considerations than the truth or falsity of the general theoretical doctrine in question. The latter would be simply irrelevant; and this becomes ironically clear when we remember that for those convinced that the truth of determinism nevertheless really would make the one choice rational, there has always been the insuperable difficulty of explaining in intelligible terms how its falsity would make the opposite choice rational.

I am aware that in presenting the arguments as I have done, neglecting the ever-interesting varieties of case, I have presented nothing more than a schema, using sometimes a crude opposition of phrase where we have a great intricacy of phenomena. In particular the simple opposition of objective attitudes on the one hand and the various contrasted attitudes which I have opposed to them must seem as grossly crude as it is central. Let me pause to mitigate this crudity a little, and also to strengthen one of my central contentions, by mentioning some things which straddle these contrasted kinds of attitude. Thus parents and others concerned with the care and upbringing of young children cannot have to their charges either kind of attitude in a pure or unqualified form. They are dealing with creatures that are potentially and increasingly capable both of holding, and being objects of, the full range of human and moral attitudes, but are not yet truly capable of either. The treatment of such creatures must therefore represent a kind of compromise, constantly shifting in one direction, between objectivity of attitude and developed human attitudes. Rehearsals insensibly modulate towards true performances. The punishment of a child is both like and unlike the punishment of an adult. Suppose we try to relate this progressive emergence of the child as a responsible being, as an object of non-objective attitudes, to that sense of "determined" in which, if determinism is a possibly true thesis, all behaviour *may* be determined, and in which, if it is a true thesis, all behaviour *is* determined. What bearing *could* such a sense of "determined" have upon the progressive modification of attitudes towards the child? Would it not be grotesque to think of the development of the child as a progressive or patchy emergence from an area in which its behaviour is in this sense determined into an area in which it isn't? Whatever sense of "determined" is required for stating the thesis of determinism, it can scarcely be such as to allow of compromise, borderline-style answers to the question, "Is this bit of behaviour determined or isn't it?" But in this matter of young children, it is essentially a borderline, penumbral area that we move in. Again, consider—a very different matter—the strain in the attitude of a psychoanalyst to his patient. *His* objectivity of attitude, *his* suspension of ordinary moral reactive attitudes, is profoundly modified by the fact that the aim of the enterprise is to make such suspension unnecessary or less necessary. Here we may and do naturally speak of restoring the agent's freedom. But here the restoring of freedom means bringing it about that the agent's behaviour shall be intelligible in terms of conscious purposes rather than in terms only of unconscious purposes. *This* is the object of the enterprise; and it is in so far as *this* object is attained that the suspension, or half-suspension, of ordinary moral attitudes is deemed no longer necessary or appropriate. And in this we see once again the *irrelevance* of that concept of "being determined" which must be the central concept of determinism. For we cannot both agree that this object is attainable and that its attainment has this consequence and yet hold (1) that neurotic behaviour is determined in a sense in which, it may be, all behaviour is determined, and (2) that it is because neurotic behaviour is determined in this sense that objective attitudes are deemed appropriate to neurotic behaviour. Not, at least, without accusing ourselves of incoherence in our attitude to psychoanalytic treatment.

VI.

And now we can try to fill in the lacuna which the pessimist finds in the optimist's account of the concept of moral responsibility, and of the bases of moral condemnation and punishment; and to fill it in from the facts as we know them. For, as I have already remarked, when the pessimist himself seeks to fill it in, he rushes beyond the facts as we know them and proclaims that it cannot be filled in at all unless determinism is false.

Yet a partial sense of the facts as we know them is certainly present to the pessimist's mind. When his opponent, the optimist, undertakes to show that the truth of determinism would not shake the foundations of the concept of moral responsibility and of the practices of moral condemnation and punishment, he typically refers, in a more or less elaborated way, to the efficacy of these practices in regulating behaviour in socially desirable ways. These practices are represented solely as instruments of policy, as methods of individual treatment and social control. The pessimist recoils from this picture; and in his recoil there is, typically, an element of emotional shock. He is apt to say, among much else, that the humanity of the offender himself is offended by *this* picture of his condemnation and punishment.

The reasons for this recoil—the explanation of the sense of an emotional, as well as a conceptual, shock—we have already before us. The picture painted by the optimists is painted in a style appropriate to a situation envisaged as wholly dominated by objectivity of attitude. The only operative notions invoked in this picture are such as those of policy, treatment, control. But a thoroughgoing objectivity of attitude, excluding as it does the moral reactive attitudes, excludes at the same time essential elements in the concepts of *moral* condemnation and *moral* responsibility. This is the reason for the conceptual shock. The deeper emotional shock is a reaction, not simply to an inadequate conceptual analysis, but to the suggestion of a change in our world. I have remarked that it is possible to cultivate an exclusive objectivity of attitude in some cases, and for some reasons, where the object of the attitude is not set aside from developed inter-personal and moral attitudes by immaturity or abnormality. And the suggestion which seems to be contained in the optimist's account is that such attitude should be universally adopted to all offenders. This is shocking enough in the pessimist's eyes. But, sharpened by shock, his eyes see further. It would be hard to make *this* division in our natures. If to all offenders, then to all mankind. Moreover, to whom could this recommendation be, in any real sense, addressed? Only to the powerful, the authorities. So abysses seem to open.[5]

But we will confine our attention to the case of the offenders. The concepts we are concerned with are those of responsibility and guilt, qualified as "moral," on the one hand—together with that of membership of a moral community; of demand, indignation, disapprobation and condemnation, qualified as "moral," on the other hand—together with that of punishment. Indignation, disapprobation, like resentment, tend to inhibit or at least to limit our goodwill towards the object of these attitudes, tend to promote an at least partial and temporary withdrawal of goodwill; they do so in proportion as they are strong; and their strength is in general proportioned to what is felt to be the magnitude of the injury and to the degree to which the agent's will is identified with, or indifferent to, it. (These, of course, are not contingent connections.) But these attitudes of disapprobation and indignation are precisely the correlates of the moral demand in the case where the demand is felt to be disregarded. The making of the demand *is* the proneness to such attitudes. The holding of them does not, as the holding of objective attitudes does, involve as a part of itself viewing their object other than as a member of the moral community. The partial withdrawal of goodwill which *these* attitudes entail, the modification *they* entail of the general demand that another should, if possible, be spared suffering, is, rather, the consequence of *continuing* to view him as a member of the moral community; only as one who has offended against its demands. So the preparedness to acquiesce in that infliction of suffering on the offender which is an essential part of punishment is all of a piece with this whole range of attitudes of which I have been speaking. It is not only moral reactive attitudes towards the offender which are in question here. We must mention also the self-reactive attitudes of offenders themselves. Just as the other-reactive attitudes are associated with a readiness to acquiesce in the infliction of suffering on an offender, within the "institution" of punishment, so the self-reactive attitudes are associated with a readiness on the part of the offender to acquiesce in such infliction *without* developing the reactions (e.g. of resentment) which he would normally develop to the infliction of injury upon him; i.e. with a readiness, as we say, to accept punishment[6] as "his due" or as "just."

I am not in the least suggesting that these readinesses to acquiesce, either on the part of the offender himself or on the part of others, are always or commonly accompanied or preceded by indignant boiling or remorseful pangs; only that we have here a continuum of attitudes and feelings to which these readinesses to acquiesce themselves belong. Nor am I in the least suggesting that it belongs to this continuum of attitudes that we should be ready to acquiesce in the infliction of injury on offenders in a fashion which we saw to be quite indiscriminate or in accordance with procedures which we knew to be wholly useless. On the contrary, savage or civilized, we have some belief in the utility of practices of condemnation and punishment. But the social utility of these practices, on which the optimist lays such exclusive stress, is not what is now in question. What is in question is the pessimist's justified sense that to speak in terms of social utility alone is to leave out something vital in our conception of these practices. The vital thing can be restored by attending to that complicated web of attitudes and feelings which form an essential part of the moral life as we know it, and which are quite opposed to objectivity of attitude. Only by attending to this range of attitudes can we recover from the facts as we know them a sense of what we mean, i.e. of *all* we mean, when, speaking the language of morals, we speak of desert, responsibility, guilt, condemnation, and justice. But we *do* recover it from the facts as we know them. We do not have to go beyond them. Because the optimist neglects or misconstrues these attitudes, the pessimist rightly claims to find a lacuna in his account. We can fill the lacuna for him. But in return we must demand of the pessimist a surrender of his metaphysics.

Optimist and pessimist misconstrue the facts in very different styles. But in a profound sense there is something in common to their misunderstandings. Both seek, in different ways, to over-intellectualize the facts. Inside the general structure or web of human attitudes and feelings of which I have been speaking, there is endless room for modification, redirection, criticism, and justification. But questions of justification are internal to the structure or relate to modifications internal to it. The existence of the general framework of attitudes itself is something we are given with the fact of human society. As a whole, it neither calls for, nor permits, an external "rational" justification. Pessimist and optimist alike show themselves, in different ways, unable to accept this.[7] The optimist's style of over-intellectualizing the facts is that of a characteristically incomplete empiricism, a one-eyed utilitarianism. He seeks to find an adequate basis for certain social practices in calculated consequences, and loses sight (perhaps wishes to lose sight) of the human attitudes of which these practices are, in part, the expression. The pessimist does not lose sight of these attitudes, but is unable to accept the fact that it is just these attitudes themselves which fill the gap in the optimist's account. Because of this, he thinks the gap can be filled only if some general metaphysical proposition is repeatedly verified, verified in all cases where it is appropriate to attribute moral responsibility. This proposition he finds it as difficult to state coherently and with intelligible relevance as its determinist contradictory. Even when a formula has been found ("contra causal freedom" or something of the kind) there still seems to remain a gap between its applicability in particular cases and its supposed moral consequences. Sometimes he plugs this gap with an intuition of fittingness—a pitiful intellectualist trinket for a philosopher to wear as a charm against the recognition of his own humanity.

Even the moral sceptic is not immune from his own form of the wish to over-intellectualize such notions as those of moral responsibility, guilt, and blame. He sees that the optimist's account is inadequate and the pessimist's libertarian alternative inane; and finds no resource except to declare that the notions in question are inherently confused, that "blame is metaphysical." But the metaphysics was in the eye of the metaphysician. It is a pity that talk of the moral sentiments has fallen out of favour. The phrase would be quite a good name for that network of human attitudes in acknowledging the character and place of which we find, I suggest, the only possibility of reconciling these disputants to each other and the facts.

There are, at present, factors which add, in a slightly paradoxical way, to the difficulty of making this acknowledgment. These human attitudes themselves, in their development and in the variety of their manifestations, have to an increasing extent become objects of study in the social and psychological sciences; and this growth of human self-consciousness, which we might expect to reduce the difficulty of acceptance, in fact increases it in several ways. One factor of comparatively minor importance is an increased historical and anthropological awareness of the great variety of forms which these human attitudes may take at different times and in different cultures. This makes one rightly chary of claiming as essential features of the concept of morality in general, forms of these attitudes which may have a local and temporary prominence. No doubt to some extent my own descriptions of human attitudes have reflected local and temporary features of our own culture. But an awareness of variety of forms should not prevent us from acknowledging also that in the absence of *any* forms of these attitudes it is doubtful whether *we* should have anything that we could find intelligible as a system of human relationships, as human society. A quite different factor of greater importance is that psychological studies have made us rightly mistrustful of many particular manifestations of the attitudes I have spoken of. They are a prime realm of self-deception, of the ambiguous and the shady, of guilt-transference, unconscious sadism and the rest. But it is an exaggerated horror, itself suspect, which would make us unable to acknowledge the facts because of the seamy side of the facts. Finally, perhaps the most important factor of all is the prestige of these theoretical studies themselves. That prestige is great, and is apt to make us forget that in philosophy, though it also is a theoretical study, we have to take account of the facts in *all* their bearings; we are not to suppose that we are required, or permitted, as philosophers, to regard ourselves, as human beings, as detached from the attitudes which, as scientists, we study with detachment. This is in no way to deny the possibility and desirability of redirection and modification of our human attitudes in the light of these studies. But we may reasonably think it unlikely that our progressively greater understanding of certain aspects of ourselves will lead to the total disappearance of those aspects. Perhaps it is not inconceivable that it should; and perhaps, then, the dreams of some philosophers will be realized.

If we sufficiently, that is *radically*, modify the view of the optimist, his view is the right one. It is far from wrong to emphasize the efficacy of all those practices which express or manifest our moral attitudes, in regulating behaviour in ways considered desirable; or to add that when certain of our beliefs about the efficacy of some of these practices turns out to be false, then we may have good reason for dropping or modifying those practices. What *is* wrong is to forget that these practices, and their reception, the reactions to them, really *are* expressions of our moral attitudes and not merely devices we calculatingly employ for regulative purposes. Our practices do not merely exploit our natures, they express them. Indeed the very understanding of the kind of efficacy these expressions of our attitudes have turns on our remembering this. When we do remember this, and modify the optimist's position accordingly, we simultaneously correct its conceptual deficiencies and ward off the dangers it seems to entail, without recourse to the obscure and panicky metaphysics of libertarianism.

Notes

1. Cf. P.H. Nowell-Smith, "Freewill and moral responsibility," *Mind* (1948).

2. As Nowell-Smith pointed out in a later article: "Determinism and libertarians," *Mind* (1954).

3. Perhaps not in every case *just* what we demand they should be, but in any case *not* just what we demand they should not be. For my present purpose these differences do not matter.

4. The question, then, of the connection between rationality and the adoption of the objective attitude to others is misposed when it is made to seem dependent on the issue of determinism. But there is another question which should be raised, if only to distinguish it from the misposed question. Quite apart from the issue of determinism might it not be said that we should be nearer to being purely rational creatures in proportion as our relation to others was in fact dominated by the objective attitude? I think this might be said; only it would have to be added, once more, that if such a choice were possible, it would not necessarily be rational to choose to be more purely rational than we are.

5. See J. D. Mabbott's "Freewill and punishment," in *Contemporary British Philosophy*, 3rd ser. (London: Allen & Unwin, 1956).

6. Of course not *any* punishment for *anything* deemed an offence.

7. Compare the question of the justification of induction. The human commitment to inductive belief-formation is original, natural, non-rational (not *ir*rational), in no way something we choose or could give up. Yet rational criticism and reflection can refine standards and their application, supply "rules for judging of cause and effect." Ever since these facts were made clear by Hume, people have been resisting acceptance of them.

4

Responsibility and the Limits of Evil: Variations on a Strawsonian Theme

Gary Watson

> Responsibility is...one aspect of the identity of character and
> conduct. We are responsible for our conduct because that conduct is
> ourselves objectified in actions.
>
> —JOHN DEWEY, "OUTLINES OF A CRITICAL THEORY OF ETHICS"

> There is nothing regrettable about finding oneself, in the last
> analysis, left with something which one cannot choose to accept or
> reject. What one is left with is probably just oneself, a core without
> which there could be no choice belonging to the person at all. Some
> unchosen restrictions on choice are among the conditions of its
> possibility.
>
> —THOMAS NAGEL, THE POSSIBILITY OF ALTRUISM

> Our practices do not merely exploit our natures, they express them.
>
> —PETER STRAWSON, "FREEDOM AND RESENTMENT"

Introduction

Regarding people as responsible agents is evidently not just a matter of belief. So regarding them means something in practice. It is shown in an embrace or a thank you, in an act of reprisal or obscene gesture, in a feeling of resentment or sense of obligation, in an apology or demand for an apology. To regard people as responsible agents is to be ready to treat them in certain ways.

In "Freedom and Resentment,"[1] Peter Strawson is concerned to describe these forms of treatment and their presuppositions. As his title suggests, Strawson's focus is on such attitudes and responses as gratitude and resentment, indignation, approbation, guilt, shame, (some kinds of) pride, hurl feeling, (asking and giving) forgiveness, and (some kinds of) love. All traditional theories of moral responsibility acknowledge connections between these attitudes and holding one another responsible. What is original to Strawson is the way in which they are linked. Whereas traditional views have taken these attitudes to be secondary to seeing others as responsible, to be practical corollaries or emotional side effects of some independently comprehensible belief in responsibility. Strawson's radical claim is that these "reactive attitudes" (as he calls them) are *constitutive* of moral responsibility; to regard oneself or another as responsible just is the proneness to react to them in these kinds of ways under certain conditions. There is no more basic belief which provides the justification or rationale for these reactions. The practice does not rest on a theory at all, but rather on certain needs and aversions that are basic to our conception of being human. The idea that there is or needs to be such an independent basis is where traditional views, in Strawson's opinion, have gone badly astray.

For a long time, I have found Strawson's approach salutary and appealing. Here my aim is not to defend it as superior to its alternatives, but to do something more preliminary. A comparative assessment is not possible without a better grasp of what Strawson's theory (or a Strawsonian theory)[2] *is*. As Strawson presents it, the theory is incomplete in important respects. I will investigate whether and how the incompleteness can be remedied in Strawsonian ways. In the end, I find that certain features of our practice of holding responsible are rather resistant to such remedies, and that the practice is less philosophically innocent than Strawson supposes. I hope that the issues uncovered by this investigation will be of sufficient importance to interest even those who are not as initially sympathetic to Strawson's approach as I am.[3]

Strawson's theory

Strawson presents the rivals to his view as responses to a prima facie problem posed by determinism. One rival—consequentialism—holds that blaming and praising judgments and acts are to be understood, and justified, as forms of social regulation. Apart from the question of its extensional adequacy, consequentialism seems to many to leave out something vital in our practice. By emphasizing their instrumental efficacy, it distorts the fact that our responses are typically personal reactions to the individuals in question that we sometimes think of as eminently appropriate reactions quite aside from concern for effects. Rightly "recoiling" from the consequentialist picture, some philosophers have supposed that responsibility requires a libertarian foundation, that to bring the "vital thing" back in, we must embrace a certain metaphysics of human agency. This is the other rival.

What these otherwise very different views share is the assumption that our reactive attitudes commit us to the truth of some independently apprehensible proposition which gives the content of the belief in responsibility; and so either the search is on for the formulation of this proposition, or we must rest content with an intuition of its content. For the social-regulation theorist, this is a proposition about the standard effects of having and expressing reactive attitudes. For the libertarian, it is a proposition concerning metaphysical freedom. Since the truth of the former is consistent with the thesis of determinism, the consequential is a compatibilist; since the truth of the latter is shown or seen not to be, the libertarian is an incompatibilist.

In Strawson's view, there is no such independent notion of responsibility that explains the propriety of the reactive attitudes. The explanatory priority is the other way around: It is not that we hold people responsible because they *are* responsible; rather, the idea (*our* idea) that we are responsible is to be understood by the practice, which itself is not a matter of holding some propositions to be true, but of expressing our concerns and demands about our treatment of one another. These stances and responses are expressions of certain rudimentary needs and aversions: "It matters to us whether the actions of other people...reflect attitudes toward us of good will, affection, or esteem on the one hand or contempt, indifference, or malevolence on the other." Accordingly, the reactive attitudes are "natural human reactions to the good or ill will or indifference of others toward us [or toward those we care about] as displayed in *their* attitudes and actions" (67). Taken together, they express "the demand for the manifestation of a reasonable degree of good will or regard, on the part of others, not simply towards oneself, but towards all those on whose behalf moral indignation may be felt..." (71).

Hence, Strawson accuses rival conceptions of "overintellectualizing" our practices. In their emphasis on social regulation, consequentialists lose sight of sentiments these practices directly express, without which the notion of moral responsibility cannot be understood. Libertarians see the gaping hole in the consequentialist account, but rather than acknowledging that "it is just these attitudes themselves which fill the gap" (79), they seek to ground these attitudes in a metaphysical intuition—"a pitiful intellectualist trinket for a philosopher to wear as a charm against I he recognition of his own humanity" (79). Holding responsible is as natural and primitive in human life as friendship and animosity, sympathy and antipathy. It rests on needs and concerns that are not so much to be justified as acknowledged.

Excusing and exempting

To say that holding responsible is to be explained by the range of reactive attitudes, rather than by a commitment to some independently comprehensible proposition about responsibility, is not to deny that these reactions depend on a context of belief and perceptions in particular contexts. They are not mere effusions of feeling, unaffected by facts. In one way, Strawson is anxious to insist that these attitudes have no "rationale," that they neither require nor permit a "rational justification" of some general sort. Nevertheless, Strawson has a good deal to say about the particular perceptions that elicit and inhibit them. Reactive attitudes do have internal criteria, since they are reactions to the moral qualities exemplified by an individual's attitudes and conduct.[4]

Thus, reactive attitudes depend upon an interpretation of conduct. If you are resentful when jostled in a crowd, you will see the other's behavior as rude, contemptuous, disrespectful, self-preoccupied, or heedless: in short, as manifesting attitudes contrary to the basic demand for reasonable regard. Your resentment might be inhibited if you are too tired, or busy, or fearful, or simply inured to life in the big city. These are causal inhibitors. In contrast, you might think the other was pushed, didn't realize, didn't mean to.... These thoughts would provide reasons for the inhibition of resentment. What makes them reasons is, roughly, that they cancel or qualify the appearance of non-compliance with the basic demand.[5]

In this way, Strawson offers a plausible account of many of the "pleas" that in practice inhibit or modify negative reactive attitudes. One type of plea is exemplified by the aforementioned reasons for inhibited sentiments. This type of plea corresponds to standardly acknowledged *excusing* conditions. It works by denying the appearance that the other failed to fulfill the basic demand; when a valid excuse obtains, the internal criteria of the negative reactive attitudes are not satisfied. Of course, justification does this as well, but in a different way. "He realized what he was doing, but it was an emergency." In general, an excuse shows that *one* was not to blame, whereas a justification shows that one was not to *blame*.

Strawson distinguishes a second type of plea. These correspond roughly to standard *exempting* conditions. They show that the agent, temporarily or permanently, globally or locally, is appropriately exempted from the basic demand in the first place. Strawson's examples are being psychotic, being a child, being under great strain, being hypnotized, being a sociopath ("moral idiot"), and being "unfortunate in formative circumstances." His general characterization of pleas of type 2 is that they present the other either as acting uncharacteristically due to extraordinary circumstances, or as psychologically abnormal or morally undeveloped in such a way as to be incapacitated in some or all respects for "ordinary adult interpersonal relationships."

In sum, type-2 pleas bear upon the question of whether the agent is an appropriate "object of that kind of demand for goodwill or regard which is reflected in ordinary reactive attitudes" (65). If so, he or she is seen as a responsible agent, as a potential term in moral relationships, as a member (albeit, perhaps, in less than good standing) of the moral community. Assuming the absence of such exemptions, type-1 pleas bear upon the question of whether the basic demand has been met. These inhibit negative reactive attitudes because they give evidence that their internal criteria are not satisfied. In contrast, type-2 pleas inhibit reactive attitudes because they inhibit the demand those attitudes express (73).

When reactive attitudes are suspended on type-2 grounds, we tend to take what Strawson calls an "objective view." We see individuals not as ones to be resented or esteemed but as ones to be controlled, managed, manipulated, trained.... The objective view does not preclude all emotions: "It may include repulsion and fear, it may include pity or even love," though not reciprocal adult love. We have the capacity to adopt an objective view toward capable agents as well; for certain kinds of therapeutic relationship, or simply to relieve the "strains of involvement," we sometimes call upon this resource.

As we have seen, one of Strawson's concerns is to deny the relevance of any theoretical issue about determinism to moral responsibility. In effect, incompatibilists insist that the truth of determinism would require us to take the objective altitude universally. But in Strawson's view, when we adopt the objective attitude, it is never a result of a theoretical conviction in determinism, but either because one of the exempting pleas is accepted, or for external reasons—fatigue, for example, or relief from the strain of involvement. No coherent thesis of determinism entails that one or more of the pleas is always valid, that disrespect is never meant, or that we are all abnormal or undeveloped in the relevant ways. Holding responsible is an expression of the basic concern and the basic demand, whose "legitimacy" requires neither metaphysical freedom nor efficacy. The practice does not involve a commitment to anything with which determinism could conflict, or which considerations of utility could challenge.

Blaming and finding fault

This is the basic view as Strawson presents it. For convenience, we may call it the expressive theory of responsibility. With certain caveats,[6] the expressive theory may be called a nonconsequentialist form of compatibilism; but it is not the only such form. It can he clarified by contrasting it with another.

Consider the following common view of blame and praise: To blame someone morally for something is to attribute it to a moral fault, or "shortcoming," or defect of character, or vice,[7] and similarly for praise. Responsibility could be construed in terms of the propriety conditions of such judgments: that is, judgments to the effect that an action or attitude manifests a virtue or vice.[8]

As I understand the Strawsonian theory, such judgments are only part of the story. They indicate what reactive attitudes are reactions *to* (namely, to the quality of the other's moral self as exemplified in action and attitude), but they are not themselves such reactions. Merely to cite such judgments is to leave out something integral to the practice of holding responsible and to the concept of moral responsibility (of being one to whom it is appropriate to respond in certain ways). It is as though in blaming we were mainly moral clerks, record-ing moral faults, for whatever purposes (the Last Assizes?).[9] In a Strawsonian view, blaming is not merely a fault-finding appraisal—which could be made from a detached and austerely "objective" standpoint—but a range of responses to the agent on the basis of such appraisals.[10] These nonproposi-tional responses are constitutive of the practice of holding responsible.

I will have something to say later about the nature of these responses. Clearly they make up a wide spectrum. Negative reactive attitudes range from bombing Tripoli to thinking poorly of a person. But even those at the more covert and less retributive end of the spectrum involve more than attributions of defects or shortcomings of moral character. Thinking poorly (less well) of a person is a way of regarding him or her in view of those faults. It has subtle implications for one's way of treating and interacting with the other. (Where the other is dead or otherwise out of reach, these implications will be only hypothetical or potential.) It is the sort of attitude that is forsworn by forgive-ness, which itself presupposes the attribution of (former) fault.

Some critical questions

I turn now to certain hard questions for the expressive theory. It accounts nicely for "excusing conditions," pleas of type 1; but exactly—or even roughly—what is its account of type-2 pleas? The "participant" reactive attitudes are said to be "natural human reactions to the good or ill-will or indifference of oth-ers as displayed in their attitudes and actions" (67); but this characterization must be incomplete, for some agents who display such attitudes are neverthe-less exempted. A child can be malicious, a psychotic can be hostile, a socio-path indifferent, a person under great strain can be rude, a woman or man "unfortunate in formative circumstances" can be cruel. Evidently reactive attitudes are sensitive not only to the quality of others' wills, but depend as well upon a background of beliefs about the objects of those attitudes. What are those beliefs, and can they be accommodated without appealing to the rival accounts of responsibility that Strawson sets out to avoid?

Strawson says that type-2 pleas inhibit reactive attitudes not by providing an interpretation which shows that the other does not display the pertinent attitudes, but by "inhibiting" the basic demand. It would seem that many of the exemption conditions involve *explanations* of why the individuals display qualities to which the reactive attitudes are otherwise sensitive. So on the face of it, the reactive attitudes are also affected by these explanations. Strawson's essay does not provide an account of how this works or what kinds of expla-nations exempt.

The problem is not just that the theory is incomplete, but that what might be necessary to complete it will undermine the theory. Strawsonian rivals will rush to fill the gap with their own notions. So it will be said that what makes some of these explanations exempting is that they are deterministic; or it will be said that these conditions are exempting because they indicate conditions in which making the basic demand is inefficacious. To the extent that some such account seems necessary, our enterprise is doomed.

In the following sections, I investigate a Strawsonian alternative. Following Strawson's idea that type-2 pleas inhibit reactive attitudes *by* inhibiting the basic demand, I propose to construe the exempting conditions as indications of the constraints on intelligible moral demand or, put another way, of the constraints on moral address.

I shall not attempt anything like a comprehensive treatment of the type-2 pleas mentioned by Strawson. I discuss, first and rather briefly, the cases of being a child and being under great strain. I then turn to a more extended discussion of "being unfortunate in formative circumstances," for this looks to be entirely beyond the resources of the expressive theory.

Demanding and understanding

As Strawson is fully aware, being a child is not simply exempting. Children "are potentially and increasingly capable both of holding, and bring objects of, the full range of human and moral attitudes, but are not yet fully capable of either" (75). Children are gradually becoming responsible agents; but in virtue of what are they potentially and increasingly these things? A plausible partial answer to this question is "moral understanding." They do not yet (fully) grasp the moral concepts in such a way that they can (fully) engage in moral communication, and so be unqualified members of the moral community.

The relevance of moral understanding to the expressive theory is this: The negative reactive attitudes express a *moral* demand, a demand for reasonable regard. Now a very young child does not even have a clear sense of the reality of others; but even with this cognitive capacity, children may lack an understanding of the effects of their behavior on others. Even when they understand what it is to hurt another physically, they may lack a sense of what it is to hurt another's feelings, or of the various subtle ways in which that may be done; and even when these things are more or less mastered, they may lack the notion of *reasonable* regard, or of justification. The basic demand is, once more, a moral demand, a demand for reasonable regard, a demand addressed to a moral agent, to one who is capable of understanding the demand. Since the negative reactive attitudes involve this demand, they are not (as fully) appropriately directed to those who do not fully grasp the terms of the demand.

To be intelligible, demanding requires understanding on the part of the object of the demand. The reactive attitudes are incipiently forms of communication, which make sense only on the assumption that the other can comprehend the message.

No doubt common views about the moral capacities of children are open to challenge, and the appeal to the notion of understanding itself raises important issues.[11] However, what is important here is whether these views can be understood by the Strawsonian theory, and it seems the ordinary view that reactive attitudes make less sense in the case of children is intelligible in Strawsonian terms; this exemption condition reflects constraints arising from the notion of moral demand.

In a certain sense, blaming and praising those with diminished moral understanding loses its "point." This way of putting it smacks of conse-quentialism, but our discussion suggests a different construction. The reactive attitudes are incipient forms of communication, not in the sense that resentment et al. are usually communicated; very often, in fact, they are not. Rather, the most appropriate and direct expression of resentment is to address the other with a complaint and a demand. Being a child exempts, when it does, not because expressing resentment has no desirable effects; in fact, it often does. Rather the reactive attitudes lose their point as forms of moral address.[12]

Not being oneself

Let's consider whether this kind of explanation can be extended to another of Strawson's type-2 pleas: "being under great strain." Strawson includes this plea in a subgroup of exemptions that include "he wasn't himself" and "he was acting under posthypnotic suggestion." His statement of the rationale in the case of stress is somewhat cryptic:

> We shall not feel resentment against the man he is for the action done by the man he is not; or at least we shall feel less. We normally have to deal with him under normal stresses; so we shall not feel towards him, when he acts under abnormal stresses, as we should have felt towards him had he acted as he did under normal stresses. (65–6)

I take it that what leads Strawson to group these cases together is that in each case the agent, due to special circumstances, acts *uncharacteristically*.

When you learn that someone who has treated you extremely rudely has been under great strain lately, has lost a job, say, or is going through a divorce, you may reinterpret the behavior in such a way that your erstwhile resentment or hurt feelings are inhibited and now seem inappropriate. How does this reinterpretation work? Notice, again, that unlike type-1 pleas, the new interpretation does not contradict the *judgment* that the person treated you rudely; rather, it provides an explanation of the rudeness.

What Strawson says about this case seems plausible. What seems to affect your reactive attitudes is the thought that she's not herself, that the behavior does not reflect or fully reflect the person's moral "personality." The following remark indicates the same phenomena: "He was drunk when he said that; I wouldn't hold it against him." (There is room here for disagreement about the bounds of the moral self. Some parts of folk wisdom have it that one's "true self" is revealed when drunk. To my knowledge, this has never been claimed about stress.) Again, what is the Strawsonian rationale?

Perhaps this type of case can also be understood in terms of the conditions of intelligible moral address. Insofar as resentment is a form of reproach addressed to an agent, such an attitude loses much of its point here—not, as before, because the other does not fully understand the reproach, but because *he* or *she* (the true self) repudiates such conduct as well. Unlike the case in which the agent acts rudely in the absence of "strain," here the target of your resentment is not one who "really" endorses the behavior you are opposing. You see the behavior as not issuing from that person's moral self, and yet it is the person, qua moral self, that your resentment would address.

The point can be put more generally in this way: Insofar as the negative reactive attitudes express demands (or in some cases appeals) addressed to another moral self, they are conceptually conditioned in various ways. One condition is that, to be fully a moral self, the other must possess sufficient (for what?) moral understanding; another is that the conduct in question be seen as reflecting the moral self. Insofar as the person is subject to great stress, his or her conduct and attitudes fail to meet this latter condition.

I am unsure to what extent these remarks accord with Strawson's own views. They are in any case exceedingly sketchy, and raise problems I am unable to take up here. For one thing, the notion of moral address seems essentially interpersonal, and so would be unavailing in the self-reflexive case. We have negative reactive attitudes toward and make moral demands upon ourselves. To determine whether this is a fatal asymmetry, we would have to investigate the reflexive cases in detail. For another thing, the notion of moral self is certainly not altogether transparent. Why are our responses under stress not reflections of our moral selves—namely, reflections of the moral self under stress? Clearly then, the explanation requires development.

It will be recalled, however, that I am not trying to determine whether a Strawsonian account of the exemption conditions is the *best* account, but to indicate what such an account might be. It will be enough for my purposes here if we can be satisfied that a Strawsonian theory has the resources to provide *some* explanation.

To recapitulate, then, the thesis is this: First, type-2 pleas indicate in different ways limiting conditions on moral address. These are relevant to reactive attitudes because those attitudes are incipiently forms of moral address. This thesis makes sense of Strawson's remark that pleas of this type inhibit reactive attitudes by inhibiting moral demand. Second, given that those conditions are satisfied, type-1 pleas indicate that the basic demand has not been flouted, contrary to appearances (though here again, we must distinguish excuse from justification).

On this account, the practice of holding responsible does indeed seem metaphysically modest, in that it involves no commitments to which issues about determinism are relevant. In a subsequent section I will consider some more bothersome features of our practice; but first I want to call attention to some general issues raised by the account given so far.

Evil and the limits of moral community

To understand certain exempting and extenuating considerations, I have appealed to the notion of the conditions in which it makes sense morally to address another. I suggested that in different ways these conditions are not (fully) satisfied by the child and the person under severe stress. In the case of children, it seemed plausible to speak of a lack of understanding. What is involved in such understanding is a complex question. Obviously we do not want to make *compliance* with the basic demand a condition of moral understanding. (After all, for the most part, children *do* "comply," but without full understanding.) For the negative reactive attitudes come into play only when the basic demand has been flouted or rejected; and flouting and rejecting, strictly speaking, require understanding.

These remarks raise a very general issue about the limits of responsibility and the limits of evil. It is tempting to think that understanding requires a shared framework of values. At any rate, some of Strawson's remarks hint at such a requirement on moral address. He writes that the reactive attitudes essentially involve regarding the other as "a morally responsible agent, as a term of moral relationships, as a member of the moral community" (73). This last phrase suggests shared ends, at some level, or a shared framework for practical reasoning. Thus, comembers of the moral community are potential interlocutors. In his discussion of Strawson's essay, Lawrence Stern suggests this point:

> ...when one morally disapproves of another person, it is normal to believe that he is susceptible to the appeal of the principles from the standpoint of which one disapproves. He either shares these principles or can come to share them.[13]

Does morally addressing another make sense unless we suppose that the other can see some reason to take us seriously, to acknowledge our claims? Can we be in a moral community with those who reject the basic terms of moral community? Are the enemies of moral community themselves members? If we suppose that moral address requires moral community, then some forms of evil will be exempting conditions. If holding responsible requires the intelligibility of moral address, and if a condition of such address is that the other be seen as a potential moral interlocutor, then the paradox results that extreme evil disqualifies one for blame.

Consider the case of Robert Harris.

On the south tier of Death Row, in a section called "Peckerwood Flats" where the while inmates are housed, there will be a small celebration the day Robert Alton Harris dies.

A group of inmates on the row have pledged several dollars for candy, cookies and soda. At the moment they estimate that Harris has been executed, they will eat, drink and toast to his passing.

"The guy's a misery, a total scumbag; we're going to party when he goes," said Richard (Chic) Mroczko, who lived in the cell next to Harris on San Quentin Prison's Death Row for more than a year. "He doesn't care about life, he doesn't care about others, he doesn't care about himself.

"We're not a bunch of Boy Scouts around here, and you might think we're pretty cold-blooded about the whole thing. But then, you just don't know the dude."

San Diego County Assistant Dist. Atty. Richard Huffman, who prosecuted Harris, said, "If a person like Harris can't be executed under California law and federal procedure, then we should be honest and say we're incapable of handling capital punishment."

State Deputy Atty. Gen. Michael D. Wellington asked the court during an appeal hearing for Harris, "If this isn't the kind of defendant that justifies the death penalty, is there ever going to be one?"

What crime did Robert Harris commit to be considered the archetypal candidate for the death penalty? And what kind of man provokes such enmity that even those on Death Row...call for his execution?

On July 5, 1978, John Mayeski and Michael Baker had just driven through [a] fast-food restaurant and were sitting in the parking lot eating lunch. Mayeski and Baker...lived on the same street and were best friends. They were on their way to a nearby lake for a day of fishing.

At the other end of the parking lot, Robert Harris, 25, and his brother Daniel, 18, were trying to hotwire a [car] when they spotted the two boys. The Harris brothers were planning to rob a bank that afternoon and did not want to use their own car. When Robert Harris could not start the car, he pointed to the [car] where the 16-year-olds were eating and said to Daniel, "We'll take this one."

He pointed a...Luger at Mayeski, crawled into the back seat, and told him to drive east....

Daniel Harris followed in the Harrises' car. When they reached a canyon area.... Robert Harris told the youths he was going to use their car in a bank robbery and assured them that they would not be hurt. Robert Harris yelled to Daniel to get the .22 caliber rifle out of the back seat of their car.

"When I caught up," Daniel said in a recent interview, Robert was telling them about the bank robbery we were going to do. He was telling them that he would leave them some money in the car and all, for us using it. Both of them said that they would wait on top of this little hill until we were gone, and then walk into town and report the car stolen. Robert Harris agreed.

"Michael turned and went through some bushes. John said, 'Good luck,' and turned to leave."

As the two boys walked away, Harris slowly raised the Luger and shot Mayeski in the back, Daniel said. Mayeski yelled: "Oh, God," and slumped to the ground. Harris chased Baker down a hill into a little valley and shot him four times.

Mayeski was still alive when Harris climbed back up the hill, Daniel said. Harris walked over to the boy, knelt down, put the Luger to his head and fired.

"God, everything started to spin," Daniel said. "It was like slow motion. I saw the gun, and then his head exploded like a balloon,...I just started running and running....But I heard Robert and turned around.

"He was swinging the rifle and pistol in the air and laughing. God, that laugh made blood and bone freeze in me."

Harris drove [the] car to a friend's house where he and Daniel were staying. Harris walked into the house, carrying the weapons and the bag [containing] the remainder of the slain youths' lunch. Then, about 15 minutes after he had killed the two 16-year-old boys, Harris took the food out of the bag...and began eating a hamburger. He offered his brother an apple turnover, and Daniel became nauseated and ran to the bathroom.

"Robert laughed at me," Daniel said. "He said I was weak; he called me a sissy and said I didn't have the stomach for it."

Harris was in an almost lighthearted mood. He smiled and told Daniel that it would be amusing if the two of them were to pose as police officers and inform the parents that their sons were killed. Then, for the first time, he turned serious. He thought that somebody might have heard the shots and that police could be searching for the bodies. He told Daniel that they should begin cruising the street near the bodies, and possibly kill some police in the area.

[Later, as they prepared to rob the bank,] Harris pulled out the Luger, noticed blood stains and remnants of flesh on the barrel as a result of the point-blank shot, and said, "I really blew that guy's brains out." And then, again, he started laughing.

...Harris was given the death penalty. He has refused all requests for interviews since the conviction.

"He just doesn't see the point of talking," said a sister,...who has visited him three times since he has been on Death Row. "He told me he had his chance, he took the road to hell and there's nothing more to say."

...Few of Harris' friends or family were surprised that he ended up on Death Row. He had spent seven of the previous 10 years behind bars. Harris, who has an eighth-grade education, was convicted of car theft at 15 and was sentenced to a federal youth center. After being released, he was arrested twice for torturing animals and was convicted of manslaughter for beating a neighbor to death after a dispute.

Barbara Harris, another sister, talked to her brother at a family picnic on July 4, 1978. He had been out of prison less than six months, and his sister had not seen him in several years.

...Barbara Harris noticed his eyes, and she began to shudder.... "I thought, 'My God, what have they done to him?' He smiled, but his eyes were so cold, totally flat. It was like looking at a rattlesnake or a cobra ready to strike. They were hooded eyes, with nothing but meanness in them.

"He had the eyes of a killer. I told a friend that I knew someone else would die by his hand."

The next day, Robert Harris killed the two youths. Those familiar with the case were as mystified as they were outraged by Harris' actions. Most found it incomprehensible that a man could be so devoid of compassion and conscience that he could kill two youths, laugh about their deaths and then casually eat their hamburgers....

...Harris is a dangerous man on the streets and a dangerous man behind bars, said Mroczko, who spent more than a year in the cell next to Harris'....

"You don't want to deal with him out there," said Mroczko,.... "We don't want to deal with him in here."

During his first year on the row, Mroczko said, Harris was involved in several fights on the yard and was caught trying to supply a prisoner in an adjacent yard with a knife. During one fight, Harris was stabbed and the other prisoner was shot by a guard. He grated on people's nerves and one night he kept the whole cell block awake by banging his shoe on a steel water basin and laughing hysterically.

An encounter with Harris always resulted in a confrontation. If an inmate had cigarettes, or something else Harris wanted, and he did not think "you could hold your mud," Mroczko said, he would try to take them.

Harris was a man who just did not know "when to be cool." he said. He was an obnoxious presence in the yard and in his cell, and his behavior precipitated unwarned attention from the guards ....

He acted like a man who did not care about anything. His cell was filthy, Mroczko said, and clothes, trash, tobacco and magazines were scattered on the floor. He wore the same clothes every day and had little interest in showers. Harris spent his days watching television in his cell, occasionally reading a Western novel.[14]

On the face of it, Harris is an "archetypal candidate" for blame. We respond to his heartlessness and viciousness with moral outrage and loathing. Yet if reactive attitudes were implicitly "invitations to dialogue" (as Stern puts it), then Harris would be an inappropriate object of such attitudes. For he is hardly a potential moral interlocutor, "susceptible to the appeal of the principles from the standpoint of which one disapproves." In this instance, an invitation to dialogue would be met with icy silence (he has "nothing more to say") or murderous contempt.

However, not all communication is dialogue. Harris refuses dialogue, and this refusal is meant to make a point. It is in effect a repudiation of the moral community; he thereby declares himself a moral outlaw. Unlike the small child, or in a different way the psychopath, he exhibits an inversion of moral concern, not a lack of understanding. His ears are not deaf, but his heart is frozen. This characteristic, which makes him utterly unsuitable as a moral interlocutor, intensifies rather than inhibits the reactive attitudes. Harris's form of evil *consists* in part in being beyond the boundaries of moral community. Hence, if we are to appeal to the constraints on moral address to explain certain type-2 pleas, we must not include among these constraints comembership in the moral community or the significant possibility of dialogue – unless, that is, evil is to be its own exemption. At these outer limits, out reactive attitudes can be nothing more (or less) than a denunciation forlorn of the hope of an adequate reply.

The roots of evil

I said that Harris is an archetypal candidate for blame—so, at least, we react to him. Does it matter to our reactions how he came to be so? Strawson thinks so, for, among type-2 pleas, he includes "being unfortunate in formative circumstances." We must now investigate the relevance of such historical considerations to the reactive attitudes. As it happens, the case of Robert Harris is again a vivid illustration.

[During the interview] Barbara Harris put her palms over her eyes and said softly, "I saw every grain of sweetness, pity and goodness in him destroyed....It was a long and ugly journey before he reached that point."

Robert Harris' 29 years...have been dominated by incessant cruelty and profound suffering that he has both experienced and provoked. Violence presaged his birth, and a violent act is expected to end his life.

Harris was born Jan. 15, 1953, several hours after his mother was kicked in the stomach. She was 6½ months pregnant and her husband, an insanely jealous man,...came home drunk and accused her of infidelity. He claimed that the child was not his, threw her down and kicked her. She began hemorrhaging, and he took her to the hospital.

Robert was born that night. His heartbeat stopped at one point...but labor was induced and he was saved. Because of the premature birth, he was a tiny baby; he was kept alive in an incubator and spent months at the hospital.

His father was an alcoholic who was twice convicted of sexually molesting his daughters. He frequently beat his children...and often caused serious injury. Their mother also became an alcoholic and was arrested several times, once for bank robbery.

All of the children had monstrous childhoods. But even in the Harris family,...the abuse Robert was subjected to was unusual.

Before their mother died last year, Barbara Harris said, she talked incessantly about Robert's early years. She felt guilty that she was never able to love him; she felt partly responsible that he ended up on Death Row.

When Robert's father visited his wife in the hospital and saw his son for the first time,...the first thing he said was, "Who is the father of that bastard?" When his mother picked him up from the hospital...she said it was like taking a stranger's baby home.

The pain and permanent injury Robert's mother suffered as a result of the birth,...and the constant abuse she was subjected to by her husband, turned her against her son. Money was tight, she was overworked and he was her fifth child in just a few years. She began to blame all of her problems on Robert, and she grew to hate the child.

"I remember one time we were in the car and Mother was in the back seat with Robbie in her arms. He was crying and my father threw a glass bottle at him, but it hit my mother in the face. The glass shattered and Robbie started screaming. I'll never forget it," she said....

"Her face was all pink, from the mixture of blood and milk. She ended up blaming Robbie for all the hurt, all the things like that. She felt helpless and he was someone to vent her anger on."

...Harris had a learning disability and a speech problem, but there was no money for therapy. When he was at school he felt stupid and classmates teased him, his sister said, and when he was at home he was abused.

"He was the most beautiful of all my mother's children; he was an angel," she said. "He would just break your heart. He wanted love so bad he would beg for any kind of physical contact.

"He'd come up to my mother and just try to rub his little hands on her leg or her arm. He just never got touched at all. She'd just push him away or kick him. One time she bloodied his nose when he was trying to get close to her."

Barbara Harris put her head in her hands and cried softly. "One killer out of nine kids.... The sad thing is he was the most sensitive of all of us. When he was 10 and we all saw 'Bambi,' he cried and cried when Bambi's mother was shot. Everything was pretty to him as a child; he loved animals. But all that changed; it all changed so much."

...All nine children are psychologically crippled as a result of their father, she said, but most have been able to lead useful lives. But Robert was too young, and the abuse lasted too long, she said, for him ever to have had a chance to recover.

[At age 14] Harris was sentenced to a federal youth detention center [for car theft]. He was one of the youngest inmates there. Barbara Harris said, and he grew up "hard and fast."

...Harris was raped several times, his sister said, and he slashed his wrists twice in suicide attempts. He spent more than four years behind bars as a result of an escape, an attempted escape and a parole violation.

The centers were "gladiator schools," Barbara Harris said, and Harris learned to fight and be mean. By the time he was released from federal prison at 19, all his problems were accentuated. Everyone in the family knew that he needed psychiatric help.

The child who had cried at the movies when Bambi's mother dies had evolved into a man who was arrested several times for abusing animals. He killed cats and dogs, Daniel said, and laughed while torturing them with mop handles, darts and pellet guns. Once he stabbed a prize pig more than 1,000 times.

"The only way he could vent his feelings was to break or kill something." Barbara Harris said. "He took out all the frustrations of his life on animals. He had no feeling for life, no sense of remorse. He reached the point where there wasn't that much left of him."

...Harris' family is ambivalent about his death sentence. [Another sister said that] if she did not know her brother's past so intimately, she would support his execution without hesitation. Barbara has a 16-year-old son; she often imagines the horror of the slain boys' parents.

"If anyone killed my son, I'd try my damnedest, no matter what it took, to have my child revenged." Barbara Harris said. "I know how those parents must suffer every day.

"But Robbie in the gas chamber ...." She broke off in mid-sentence and stared out a window. "Well, I still remember the little boy who used to beg for love, for just one pat or word of kindness....No I can't say I want my brother to die."

...Since Harris has been on Death Row, he has made no demands of time or money on his family. Harris has made only one request; he wants a dignified and serene ceremony after he dies—a ceremony in marked contrast to his life.

He has asked his oldest brother to take his ashes, to drive to the Sierra, hike to a secluded spot and scatter his remains in the trees.[15]

No doubt this history gives pause to the reactive attitudes. Why does it do so? "No wonder Harris is as he is!" we think. What is the relevance of this thought?

Note, to begin with, that the story in no way undermines the judgments that he is brutal, vicious, heartless, mean.[16] Rather, it provides a kind of explanation for his being so. Can the expressive theory explain why the reactive attitudes should be sensitive to such an explanation?

Strawson's general rubric for type-2 pleas (or the subgroup in which this plea is classified) is "being incapacitated for ordinary interpersonal relationships." Does Harris have some independently identifiable incapacity for which his biography provides evidence? Apparently, he *is* incapacitated for such relationships—for example, for friendship, for sympathy, for being affected by moral considerations. To be homicidally hateful and callous in Harris's way is to lack moral concern, and to lack moral concern is to be incapacitated for moral community. However, to exempt Harris on these grounds is problematic. For then everyone who is evil in Harris's way will be exempt, independently of facts about their background. But we had ample evidence about *this* incapacity before we learned of his childhood misfortunes, and that did not affect the reactive attitudes. Those misfortunes affect our responses in a special and nonevidential way. The question is why this should be so.

This would seem to be a hard question for compatibilist views generally. What matters is whether, in one version, the practice of holding responsible can be efficacious as a means of social regulation, or whether, using the expressive theory, the conditions of moral address are met. These questions would seem to be settled by how individuals *are,* not by how they came to be. Facts about background would be, at most, evidence that some other plea is satisfied. In themselves, they would not seem to matter.

A plea of this kind is, on the other hand, grist for the incompatibilists' mill. For they will insist on an essential historical dimension to the concept of responsibility. Harris's history reveals him to be an inevitable product of his formative circumstances. And seeing him as a product is inconsistent with seeing him as a responsible agent. If his cruel attitudes and conduct are the inevitable result of his circumstances, then he is not responsible for them, unless he was responsible for those circumstances. It is this principle that gives the historical dimension of responsibility and of course entails the incompatibility of determinism and responsibility.

In this instance, however, an incompatibilist diagnosis seems doubtful. In the first place, our response to the case is not the simple suspension of reactive attitudes that this diagnosis would lead one to expect, bin ambivalence. In the second place, the force of the example does not depend on a belief in the *inevitability* of the upshot. Nothing in the story supports such a belief. The thought is not "It had to be!" but, again, "No wonder!"

Sympathy and antipathy

How and why, then, does this larger view of Harris's life in fact affect us? It is too simple to say that it leads us to suspend our reactive attitudes. Our response is too complicated and conflicted for that. What appears to happen is that we are unable to command an overall view of his life that permits the reactive attitudes to be sustained without ambivalence. That is because the biography forces us to see him as a *victim,* and so seeing him does not sit well with the reactive attitudes that are so strongly elicited by Harris's character and conduct. Seeing him as a victim does not totally dispel those attitudes. Rather, in light of the "whole" story, conflicting responses are evoked. The sympathy toward the boy he was is at odds with outrage toward the man he is. These responses conflict not in the way that fear dispels anger, but in the way that sympathy is opposed to antipathy. In fact, each of these responses is appropriate, but taken together they do not enable us to respond overall in a coherent way.

Harris both satisfies and violates the criteria of victimhood. His childhood abuse was a misfortune inflicted upon him against his will. But at the same time (and this is part of his very misfortune) he unambivalently endorses suffering, death, and destruction, and that is what (one form of) evil is. With this in focus, we see him as a victimizer and respond to him accordingly. The ambivalence results from the fact that an overall view simultaneously demands and precludes regarding him as a victim.

What we have here is not exactly a clash between what Thomas Nagel has called the objective and subjective standpoints.[17] It is not that from the more comprehensive viewpoint that reveals Harris as a victim, his responsibility is indiscernible. Rather, the clash occurs within a single point of view that reveals Harris as evil (and hence calling for enmity and moral opposition) and as one who is a victim (calling for sympathy and understanding). Harris's misfortune is such that scarcely a vestige remains of his earlier sensibilities. Hence, unless one knew Harris as a child or keeps his earlier self vividly in mind, sympathy can scarcely find a purchase.

Moral luck and moral equality

However, what is arresting about the Harris case is not just the clash between sympathy and antipathy. The case is troubling in a more personal way. The fact that Harris's cruelty is an intelligible response to his circumstances gives a foothold not only for sympathy, but for the thought that if *I* had been subjected to such circumstances, I might well have become as vile. What is unsettling is the thought that one's moral self is such a fragile thing. One tends to think of one's moral sensibilities as going deeper than that (though it is not clear what this means). This thought induces not only an ontological shudder, but a sense of equality with the other: I too am a potential sinner.[18]

This point is merely the obverse of the point about sympathy. Whereas the point about sympathy focuses on our empathetic response to the other, the thought about moral luck turns one's gaze inward. It makes one feel less in a position to cast blame. The fact that my potential for evil has not been nearly so fully actualized is, for all I know, something for which I cannot take credit. The awareness that, in this respect, the others are or may be like oneself clashes with the distancing effect of enmity.

Admittedly, it is hard to know what to do with this conclusion. Equality of moral potential does not, of course, mean that Harris is not actually a vile man; on the contrary, it means that in similar circumstances I would have become vile as well. Since he is an evil man, we cannot and should not treat him as we would a rabid dog. The awareness of moral luck, however, taints one's own view of one's moral self as an achievement, and infuses one's reactive attitudes with a sense of irony. Only those who have survived circumstances such as those that ravaged Harris are in a good position to know what they would have done. We lucky ones can only wonder. As a product of reflection, this attitude is, of course, easily lost when the knife is at one's own throat.

Determinism and ignorance

Nothing in the foregoing reflections is necessarily inconsistent with the expressive theory. The ways in which reactive attitudes are affected by sympathy and moral luck are intelligible without appealing to any of the conceptions of responsibility that Strawson eschews. Nevertheless, our attitudes remain puzzling in a number of respects.

Earlier we questioned an incompatibilist diagnosis of our example on the grounds that the historical explanation need not the construed as deterministic. Horrid backgrounds do not inevitably give rise to horrid people. Some manage somehow to survive a similar magnitude of misfortune, if not unscathed, at least as minimally decent human beings. Conversely, people are sometimes malicious despite a benign upbringing. What do we suppose makes the difference?

Strictly speaking, no one who is vicious in *just* the way we have interpreted Harris to be could fail to have had an abusive childhood. For our interpretation of who Harris is depends upon his biography, upon our interpretation of his life. Harris's cruelly is a response to the shattering abuse he suffered during the process of socialization. The objects of his hatred were not just the boys he so exultantly murdered, but the "moral order" that mauled and rejected him. (It is significant that Harris wanted to go out and kill some cops after the murder; he wanted not just to reject authority, but to confront it.) He defies the demand for human consideration because he has been denied this consideration himself. The mistreatment he received becomes a ground as well as a cause of the mistreatment he givers. It becomes part of the content of his "project."

Thus, someone who had a supportive and loving environment as a child, but who was devoted to dominating others, who killed for enjoyment, would not be vicious in the way Harris is, since he or she could not be seen as striking back at "society"; but such a person could be just *as* vicious. In common parlance, we sometimes call such people "bad apples," a phrase that marks a blank in our understanding. In contrast to Harris, whose malice is motivated, the conduct of "bad apples" seems inexplicable. So far, we cannot see them as victims, and there is no application for thoughts about sympathy and moral luck.

However, do we not suppose that *something* must have gone wrong in the developmental histories of these individuals, if not in their socialization, then "in them"—in their genes or brains? (Suppose a certain kind of tumor is such that its onset at an early age is known to be strongly correlated with the development of a malicious character. This supposition is no doubt bad science fiction; that a complex and articulated psychological structure could be caused by gross brain defect seems antecedently implausible.) Whatever "nonenvironmental" factors make the difference, will they not play the same role as Harris's bad upbringing – that is, will they not have victimized these individuals so that thoughts about sympathy and moral luck come into play? Or can evil be the object of unequivocal reactive attitudes only when it is inexplicable?

If determinism is true, then evil is a joint product of nature and nurture. If so, the difference between any evil person and oneself would seem to be a matter of moral luck. For determinism seems to entail that if one had been subjected to the internal and external conditions of some evil person, then one would have been evil as well. If that is so, then the reflections about moral luck seem to entail that the acceptance of determinism should affect our reactive attitudes in the same way as they are affected in Harris's case. In the account we have suggested, then, determinism seems to be relevant to reactive attitudes after all.

Actually, this conclusion does not follow without special metaphysical assumptions. For the counterfactuals that underlie thoughts about moral luck must be constrained by the conditions of personal identity. It may be that no one who had been exposed to just the internal and external conditions of some given individual could have been me. To make sense of a counterfactual of the form, "If i had been in C, then i would have become a person of type t," C must be supposed to be compatible with i's existence as an individual (i must exist in the possible world in which C obtains). For example, it is widely held that genetic origin is essential to an individual's identity. In that case, the counterfactual, "If I had had Harris's genetic origin and his upbringing, then I would have been as evil as he," will not make sense. Now it might be that Harris's genetic origins are among the determinants of his moral development. Thus, even if this is a deterministic world, there may be no true counterfactual that would support the thought that the difference between Harris and me is a matter of moral luck. There is room for the thought that there is something "in me" by virtue of which I would not have become a vicious person in Harris's circumstances. And if that factor were among my essential properties, so to speak, then that difference between Harris and me would not be a matter of moral luck on my part, but a matter of who we essentially were. That would not, of course, mean that I was essentially good or Harris essentially evil, but that I would not have been corrupted by the same circumstances as those that defeated Harris. To be sure, to suppose that this difference is in itself to my moral credit would be odd. To congratulate me on these grounds would be to congratulate me on being myself. Nevertheless, this difference still might explain what is to my credit, such moral virtues as I may possess. This will seem paradoxical only if we suppose that whatever is a ground of my moral credit must itself be to my credit. But I see no compelling reason to suppose this.

Historical responsibility

Libertarians believe that evil is the product neither of nature nor of nurture, but of free will. Do we understand what this might mean?

It is noteworthy that libertarians will be able to agree with much of what we have said about moral luck. Harris's history affects us because it makes us wonder how *we* would have responded, and thus shakes our confidence that we would have avoided a pernicious path in those circumstances. But this effect is perfectly compatible with Harris's responsibility for how he did respond, just us we would have been responsible for how we would have responded. The biography affects us not because it is deterministic, libertarians can say, but because it shakes our confidence that we would have exercised that freedom rightly in more dire straits. We are not, of course, responsible for our formative circumstances—and in this respect we are morally lucky and Harris is unlucky—but those circumstances do not determine our responses to them. It is the individual's own response that distinguishes those who become evil from those who do not.

This idea is nicely captured by Peter Abélard: "Nothing mars the soul except what is of its own nature, namely consent."[19] The idea is that one cannot simply be caused to be morally bad by the environment. So either Harris's soul is not (morally) marred, or he has been a willing accomplice to the malformation of the self. His evil means that he has consented to what he has become—namely, one who consents to cruelty. Thus, Abélardians try to fill the statistical cracks with the will. The development of the moral self, they will say, is mediated by consent.

We should be struck here by the a priori character of libertarian convictions. How is Harris's consent to be construed, and why *must* it have occurred? What evidence is there that it occurred? Why couldn't Harris just have become that way? What is the difference between his having acquiesced to what he became and his simply having become that way? The libertarian faces the following difficulty: If there is no such difference, then the view is vacuous, for consent was supposed to explain his becoming that way. If there is a difference, what evidence is there that it obtains in a particular case? Isn't there room for considerable doubt about this, and shouldn't libertarians, or we, insofar as we are libertarians, be very doubtful about Harris's responsibility—and indeed, on the Abélardian thesis, even about whether Harris is an evil man, whether his soul is morally marred? (Notice that the tumor case is a priori impossible on that thesis, unless we think of the tumor somehow as merely presenting an occasion for consent – as inclining without necessitating.) One suspects that the libertarian confidence in their attributions of historical responsibility is rooted in a picture according to which the fact that Harris became that way *proves* that he consented. Then, of course, the appeal to consent is explanatorily vacuous.

Epistemology apart, the attempt to trace the evil self to consent at an earlier stage is faced with familiar difficulties. If we suppose (fancifully) that Harris, earlier on, with full knowledge and deliberation, launched himself on his iniquitous career,[20] we would be merely postponing the inquiry, for the will which could fully and deliberately consent to such a career would have to have its roots in a self which is already morally marred – a self, therefore, which cannot itself be seen simply as a product of consent. Are we instead to suppose that at some earlier stage Harris slipped heedlessly or recklessly into patterns of thought and action which he ought to have known would eventuate in an evil character? (This seems to have been Aristotle's view in *Nicomachean Ethics,* Book III.5.) In that case, we would be tracing his present ways to the much less egregious faults of negligence.[21]

Responsibility for the self

Strawson and others often charge libertarians with a metaphysically dubious conception of the self. The foregoing reflections indicate a basis for this charge. Libertarianism combines the Abélardian view about consent (or something like it) with the principle (or something like it) that to be responsible for anything, one must be responsible for (some of) what produces it. If we think of agents as consenting to this or that *because* they are (or have?) selves of a certain character, then it looks as though they are responsible for so consenting only if they are responsible for the self in which that consent is rooted. To establish this in each case, we have to trace the character of the self to earlier acts of consent. This enterprise seems hopeless, since the trace continues interminably or leads to a self to which the individual did not consent. The libertarian seems committed, then, to bearing the unbearable burden of showing how we can be responsible for ourselves. This burden can seem bearable only in a view of the self as an entity that mysteriously both transcends and intervenes in the "causal nexus," because it is both product and author of its actions and attitudes.

Must libertarians try to bear this burden? Perhaps the idea that they must rests upon a view of the self to which libertarians need not be committed. Perhaps the trouble arises in the first place from viewing the self as a thing standing in causal relation to acts of consent. The libertarian might say that to talk about the (moral) self is not to talk about an entity which necessitates specific acts of consent but to talk about the sorts of things to which an individual tends to consent. To speak of Harris's moral self is not to explain his conduct, but to indicate the way he is morally. What we are responsible for are the particular things we consent to. We need not consider whether we are responsible for the genesis of the entity whose characteristics necessitate those acts of consent, for there is no such entity. In a way, of course, one is derivatively responsible for one's self, since one's moral self is constituted by the character of what one consents to, and one is responsible for what one consents to.[22]

The historical dimension of the concept of responsibility results from the principle that one is not responsible for one's conduct if that is necessitated by causes for which one is not responsible. This leads to a problematic requirement that one be responsible for one's self only if one thinks of the self as an entity that causes one's (its) actions and willings. Libertarians can reject this view. What they must affirm is that we are responsible for what we consent to, that consent is not necessitated by causes internal or external to the agent, and that if it were, we could not properly hold the individual responsible for what he or she consents to. These claims are far from self-evident. But they hardly amount to a "panicky metaphysics" (80).[23]

In the end, however, I do not think that libertarianism can be so readily domesticated. The idea that one is responsible for and only for what one consents to is not of course distinctive of libertarianism; that idea has no historical implications. What is distinctive is the further requirement that consent be undetermined. I do not think the idea that consent is undetermined is in itself particularly problematic. The trouble begins only when we ask why this is *required*. The ground of this requirement is the intuition that unless consent were undetermined, we would not truly be *originators* of our deeds. We would be merely products, and not, as it were, producers. It is this intuition to which the libertarian finds it so difficult to give content. "Being an originator" does not mean just "consenting to," for that is already covered by the first thesis. Nor is this notion captured simply by adding the requirement of indeterminism; that is a merely negative condition. Attempts to specify the condition in positive terms either cite something that could obtain in a deterministic world, or something obscurely transcendent.

I suspect, then, that any metaphysically innocuous version of libertarianism must leave its incompatibilist component unmotivated.

Ignorance and skepticism

I have been exploring some ways in which the expressive theory might explain the relevance of certain historical considerations. Whatever the best explanation may be, the remarkable fact is that we are, for the most part, quite ignorant of these considerations. Why does our ignorance not give us more pause? If, for whatever reason, reactive attitudes are sensitive to historical considerations, as Strawson acknowledges, and we are largely ignorant of these matters, then it would seem that most of our reactive attitudes are hasty, perhaps even benighted, as skeptics have long maintained. In this respect, our ordinary practices are not as unproblematic as Strawson supposes.

It might be thought that these suspicions about reactive attitudes have no bearing on responsibility, but with the expressive theory, that cannot be easily maintained. As we normally think of the matter, not all considerations that affect reactive attitudes are strictly relevant to responsibility. For example, if one shares a moral fault with another, one may feel it inappropriate to blame the other. Here the point is not that the other is not responsible or blameworthy, but that it is not *one's* business to blame. One should tend to one's own faults first.[24] Thoughts about moral luck seem to be continuous with this ordinary phenomenon. The thought is not that the other is not blameworthy, but that one may be no better, and that indignation on one's part would be self-righteous and indulgent. By calling our attention to our general ignorance of historical considerations, the skepticism we have just been considering is merely an extension of these reflections.

With an expressive theory, however, it is not clear that a general skepticism about the propriety of the reactive attitudes can be separated from skepticism about responsibility. For the latter concept *is* the concept of the conditions in which it is appropriate to respond to one another in reactive ways. In a Strawsonian view, there is no room for a wedge between the practices that evince the reactive attitudes and the belief in responsibility. In a particular case, one may believe another to be responsible without actually responding to him or her in reactive ways (due to strains of commitment and so on), because one may regard the other as blameworthy, as an appropriate object of the reactive altitudes by others in the moral community. But if one thinks that *none* of us mortals is in a position to blame, then it is doubtful that any sense can be given to the belief that the other is nonetheless blameworthy. One can still attribute cowardice, thoughtlessness, cruelty, and so on, to others; but as we have seen, these judgments are not sufficient in a Strawsonian view to characterize the practice of holding responsible. We might try to appeal to the reactive attitudes of a select group of actual or hypothetical judges (here is another job for God to do),[25] but then the connection to reactive attitudes becomes so tenuous or hypothetical that the attitudes lose the central role they are given in "Freedom and Resentment," and the expressive theory loses its distinctive character. It then collapses into the view discussed in the section called "Blaming and finding fault."

Objectivity and isolation

It remains unclear to what extent our ordinary practices involve dubious beliefs about ourselves and our histories. To acknowledge the relevance of historical considerations is, on any account, to acknowledge a potential source of skepticism about those practices; moreover, in a Strawsonian account (though not in a libertarian account), such skepticism cannot be readily separated from skepticism about responsibility itself. In this respect, Strawson is inordinately optimistic about our common ways.

However, these practices are vulnerable to a different kind of suspicion. This suspicion is related to Strawson's conception of the place of "retributive" sentiments in those practices, and to his claim that that practice, so conceived, is not something that is optional and open to radical criticism, but rather is part of the "framework" of our conception of human society. One could agree that the expressive theory best gives the basis and content of the practice of holding responsible and still maintain that abandoning this practice is not only conceivable but desirable, for what it expresses is itself destructive of human community. I conclude with some comments on this further issue.

Consider some remarks by Albert Einstein:

> I do not at all believe in human freedom in the philosophical sense. Everybody acts not only under external compulsion but also in accordance with inner necessity. Schopenhauer's saying, "A man can do what he wants, but not want what he wants," has been a very real inspiration to me since my youth; it has been a continual consolation in the face of life's hardships, my own and others', and an unfailing well-spring of tolerance. This realization mercifully mitigates the easily paralysing sense of responsibility and prevents us from taking ourselves and other people all too seriously; it is conducive to a view of life which, in particular, gives humor its due.[26]

Significantly, in the same place Einstein speaks of himself as a "lone traveler," with a "pronounced lack of need for direct contact with other human beings and human communities," who has

> never belonged to my country, my home, my friends, or even my immediate family, with my whole heart; in the face of all these ties, I have never lost a sense of distance and a need for solitude—feelings which increase with the years.

The point that interests me here is not that these remarks confute Strawson's claim that reactive attitudes are never in practice affected by an acceptance of determinism, but that they corroborate his central claim about the alternative to the reactive, participant stance. The "distance" of which Einstein speaks is just an aspect of the "detachment" Strawson thinks characterizes the objective stance. At its extremes, it takes the form of human isolation. What is absent from Einstein's outlook is something that. I suspect, Strawson cherishes: the attachment or commitment to the personal, as it might be called.[27]

Whatever its grounds, Einstein's outlook is not without its appeal. Perhaps part of its appeal can be attributed to a fear of the personal, but it is also appealing precisely on account of its repudiation of the retributive sentiments. In another place, Einstein salutes the person "to whom aggressiveness and resentment are alien."[28] Can such an ideal of the person be pursued only at the cost of the attachment to the personal? Must we choose between isolation and animosity?

Some of Strawson's remarks imply that we must:

> Indignation, disapprobation, like resentment, tend to inhibit or at least to limit our goodwill towards the object of these attitudes, tend to promote

at least partial and temporary withdrawal of goodwill.... (These are not contingent connections.) But these attitudes...are precisely the correlates of the moral demand in the case where the demand is felt to be disregarded. The making of the demand *is* the proneness to such attitudes.... The holding of them does not...involve...viewing their object other than as a member of the moral community. The partial withdrawal of goodwill which these attitudes entail, the modification they entail of the general demand that another should if possible be spared suffering, is...the consequence of *continuing* to view him as a member of the moral community: only as one who has offended against its demands. So the preparedness to acquiesce in that infliction of suffering on the offender which is an essential part of punishment is all of a piece with this whole range of attitudes... (77). [From *proceedings of the British Academy*, Vol. 48 (1962): 1–25. Reprinted by permission of the British Academy.]

This passage is troubling. Some have aspired to rid themselves of the readiness to limit goodwill and to acquiesce in the suffering of others not in order to relieve the strains of involvement, nor out of a conviction in determinism, but out of a certain ideal of human relationships, which they see as poisoned by the retributive sentiments. It is an ideal of human fellowship or love which embodies values that are arguably as historically important to our civilization as the notion of moral responsibility itself. The question here is not whether this aspiration is finally commendable, but whether it is compatible with holding one another morally responsible. The passage implies that it is not.

If holding one another responsible involves making the moral demand, and if the making of the demand is the proneness to such attitudes, and if such attitudes involve retributive sentiments and hence[29] a limitation of goodwill, then skepticism about retribution is skepticism about responsibility, and holding one another responsible is at odds with one historically important ideal of love.

Many who have this ideal, such as Gandhi or King,[30] do not seem to adopt an objective attitude in Strawson's sense. Unlike Einstein's, their lives do not seem characterized by human isolation: They are often intensely involved in the "fray" of interpersonal relations. Nor does it seem plausible to suppose that they do not hold themselves and others morally responsible: They *stand up* for themselves and others against their oppressors; they *confront* their oppressors with the fact of their misconduct, *urging* and even *demanding* consideration for themselves and others; but they manage, or come much closer than others to managing, to do such things without vindictiveness or malice.

Hence, Strawson's claims about the interpenetration of responsibility and the retributive sentiments must not be confused with the expressive theory itself. As these lives suggest, the retributive sentiments can in principle be stripped away from holding responsible and the demands and appeals in which this consists. What is left are various forms of reaction and appeal to others as moral agents. The boundaries of moral responsibility are the boundaries of intelligible moral address. To regard another as morally responsible is to react to him or her as a moral self.[31]

Notes

To Sally Haslanger and Brian Skyrms. I am grateful for discussing bits and pieces of this material with me; to Ferdinand Schoeman, for comments on an earlier draft.

1. *Proceedings of the British Academy*, 1962, reprinted in *Free Will*, edited by Gary Watson (Oxford University Press, 1982), 59–80. Hereafter, page references in the text will be to the latter edition.

2. My interpretation of Strawson's essay will be in many places very conjectural: and I will sometimes signal this fact by speaking of a "Strawsonian" theory.

3. I have learned much from the penetrating exploration of Strawson's essay by Jonathan Bennett: "Accountability," in *Philosophical Subjects*, edited by Zak van Straaten, (Oxford: Clarendon Press, 1980), 14–47.

4. Reactive attitudes thus permit a threefold classification. Personal reactive attitudes regarding others' treatment of one (resentment, gratitude, etc.); vicarious analogues of these, regarding others' treatment of others (indignation and approbation); self-reactive attitudes regarding one's own treatment of others (and oneself?) (guilt, shame, moral self-esteem, feeling obligated). Many of the reactive attitudes reflect the basis demand (on oneself and others, for oneself and others); whereas others (for example, gratitude) directly express the basic concern.

Contrary to some of Strawson's discussion, responsibility does not concern only other-regarding attitudes. Yon can hold yourself responsible for failing to live up to an ideal that has no particular bearing on the interests or feelings of others. It may be said that others cannot *blame* you for this failure; but that would be a moral claim.

5. Below, this remark is qualified significantly.

6. The term "compatibilism" denotes the view that determinism is compatible with responsibility. Hence it may presuppose that determinism is an intelligible thesis. Since Strawson seems skeptical about this presupposition, he might refuse this appellation.

7. See Robert Nozick, *Philosophical Explanations* (Harvard University Press, 1981), 224.

8. Such a view is hinted at by James Wallace: "Answers to [the question of when an action is fully characteristic of an excellence or a vice] are fundamental for an account of the conditions for the appropriateness of praise, blame, reward and punishment and for an account of the derivative notion of responsibility" (*Virtues and Vices*, Cornell University Press, 1986, 43). This also seems to be R. Milo's view in *Immorality* (Princeton University Press, 1984). I don't say that such a view is necessarily incompatibilist—it could be insisted that conduct fully exemplifies a virtue or a vice only if determinism is false (this is clearly the Abélardian view, discussed below)—but it is clear how a compatibilist version would go.

9. Consider Jonathan Glover's remark: "Involved in our present practice of blame is a kind of moral accounting, where a person's actions are recorded in an informal balance sheet, with the object of assessing his moral worth." (*Responsibility*, Routledge and Kegan Paul, 1970, 44.)

10. "Blaming is a type of response to faults in oneself or in others," Robert Adams, "Involuntary sin," *Philosophical Review*, January 1985: 21. Adams does not tell us what kind of response it is. Since he thinks that thinking poorly of someone *is* a form of unspoken blame (ibid.), he must think that thinking poorly of is more than noting a moral fault. I think this is correct.

11. Do *we adults* fully comprehend the notions of justification and reasonable regard? Does understanding presuppose a disputable cognitive view or morality? Certainly conceptions of children are subject to cultural variation. William Blackstone discusses the case of an 8-year old boy who was tried for setting fire to some barns. Because he was found to exhibit "malice, revenge, and cunning, he was found guilty, condemned and hanged accordingly." (In *Commentaries on the Laws of England (1765-7)*, as quoted by Jennifer Radden, *Madness and Reason*, George Allen and Unwin, 1985, 136.) It is doubtful that diminished moral understanding is the only relevant factor here. Surely various capacities of concentration and "volitional" control are relevant as well. I do not know how the expressive theory could take these into account.

12. Reactive attitudes are even more clearly pointless in the case of a radically disintegrated personality, one that has no coherent moral self to be addressed. The case of the sociopath is much more complicated, but arguably something similar may be said here. Those who deal with sociopaths often lose the sense that such characters have a moral self at all: despite appearances, there is "no one home."For case studies and psychiatric commentary, see Hervey Cleckley, *The Mask of Sanity* (C. V. Mosby, 1941). For philosophical discussion, see Herbert Fingarette, *On Responsibility*, Chap. 2: Vinit Haksar, "The responsibility of psychopaths," *The Philosophical Quarterly*, Vol. 15 (1965); M. S. Pritchard, "Responsibility, understanding, and psychopathology," *The Monist*, Vol. 58 (1974); Antony Duff, "Psychopathy and moral understanding," *American Philosophical Quarterly*, Vol. 14 (1977); and Jeffrie Murphy, "Moral death: a Kantian essay on psychopathy," *Ethics*, Vol. 82 (1972).

13. "Freedom, blame, and moral community," *Journal of Philosophy*, February 14, 1974: 78.

14. From Miles Corwin, "Icy killer's life steeped in violence," *Los Angeles Times*, May 16, 1982. Copyright. 1982, *Los Angeles Times*. Reprinted by permission. For the length of this and the next quotation, I ask for the reader's patience. It is very important here to work with realistic and detailed examples.

15. Miles Corwin, op. cit. Copyright, 1982, *Los Angeles Times*. Reprinted by permission.

16. Although, significantly, when his past is in focus, we are less inclined to use certain *reactive* epithets, such as "scumbag." This term is used to express an attitude about the appropriate treatment of the individual (that he is to be thrown in the garbage, flushed down the toilet, etc.). Some other reactive terms are "jerk," "creep," "son of a bitch."

17. In *The View from Nowhere* (Oxford University Press, 1985).

18. In "Determinism and moral perspectives," *Philosophy and Phenomenological Research*, September 1960, Elizabeth Beardsley calls attention to the perspective evoked

by such cases as Harris, though she links this perspective too closely, in my opinion, to the notion of determinism.

19. From "Intention and sin," reprinted in Herbert Morris (ed.), *Freedom and Responsibility* (Stanford University Press), 169.

20. If such a thing ever occurred, it must have occurred at a stage when Harris clearly would have fallen under the exemption condition of "being a child."

21. Adam makes this point, op. cit.

22. It is noteworthy that Harris himself seems to accept responsibility for his life: "He told me he had his chance, he took the road to hell and there's nothing more to say." (From the end of the first extract from the Corwin article.)

23. For an attempt at libertarianism without metaphysics, see David Wiggins, "Towards a credible form of libertarianism," in T. Honderich (ed.), *Essays on Freedom of Action* (Routledge and Kegan Paul, 1973).

24. Montaigne would not agree: "To censure my own faults in some other person seems to me no more incongruous than to censure, as I often do, another's in myself. They must be denounced everywhere, and be allowed no place of sanctuary." ("On the education of children," in *Essays*, Penguin Classics, 1971, 51.)

25. Just as Berkeley tried to save the thesis that material objects consist in ideas.

26. Albert Einstein, *Ideas and Opinions* (Crown Publishers, 1982) 8–9.

27. To what extent Einstein lived up to that outlook, I am not prepared to say. Some other writing suggest a different view: "External compulsion can...reduce but never cancel the responsibility of the individual. In the Nuremberg trials, this idea was considered to be self-evident....Institutions are in a moral sense impotent unless they are supported by the sense of responsibility of living individuals. An effort to arouse and strengthen this sense of responsibility of the individual is an important service to mankind" (op. cit., 27). Is Einstein taking a consequentialist stance here?

28. Ibid.

29. Rather than attempting to separate retribution from responsibility, one might try to harmonize retribution and goodwill. This possibility seems to me worth exploring.

30. For these examples, and the discussion in this section, I am indebted to Stern (op. cit.).

31. We have, of course, seen reasons why these boundaries require further delineations.

PART 2

Suggested Further Readings

II. Naturalism Against Scepticism

A number of the major contributions responding to Strawson's "Freedom and Resentment" can be found in:

McKenna, Michael and Paul Russell, eds. 2008. *Free Will and Reactive Attitudes*. Aldershot, UK: Ashgate Press.

See also:

Bennett, Jonathan. "Accountability (II)," included in McKenna & Russell, eds., cited above. (An earlier version of this paper appears in Zak van Straaten, ed., *Philosophical Subjects*. Oxford: Oxford University Press, 1980.)

Darwall, Stephen. 2006. *The Second-Person Standpoint: Morality, Respect and Accountability*. Cambridge, Mass. Harvard University Press.

Knobe, Joshua and John Doris. 2010. "Strawsonian variations: folk morality and the search for a unified theory," in John Doris *et al* eds., *The Oxford Handbook of Moral Psychology*. Oxford: Oxford University Press, 321–54.

Mackie, J. L. 1985. "Morality and the retributive emotions," reprinted in *Persons and Values: Selected Papers (Volume 2)*. Oxford: Clarendon Press.

McKenna, Michael. 1998. "The limits of evil and the role of moral address: a defence of Strawsonian compatibilism," *Journal of Ethics*, 2: 123–42. (Included in McKenna & Russell as cited above.)

McKenna, Michael. 2012. *Conversation & Responsibility*. New York: Oxford University Press.

Nichols, Shaun. 2007. "After incompatibilism: a naturalistic defense of the reactive attitudes," *Philosophical Perspectives* 21.1: 405–28.

Russell, Paul. 1992. "Strawson's way of naturalizing responsibility," *Ethics* 102/2: 287–302. (Included in McKenna & Russell as cited above.)

Russell, Paul. 2004. "Responsibility and the condition of moral sense," *Philosophical Topics* 32/1&2: 287–305.

Smith, Angela. 2007. "On being responsible and holding responsible," *Journal of Ethics*. 11: 465–84.

Shoemaker, David. 2007. "Moral address, moral responsibility, and the boundaries of the moral community," *Ethics* 118: 70–108.

Strawson, P.F. 1985. *Skepticism and Naturalism: Some Varieties*. London: Metheun.

Wallace, R.J. 1994. *Responsibility and the Moral Sentiments*. Cambridge, MA: Harvard University Press.

PART THREE

The Consequence Argument

5

A Modal Argument for Incompatibilism

Peter van Inwagen

The main contested question in current discussions of free will is not, as one might expect, whether we *have* free will. It is whether free will is compatible with determinism. It seems to me that free will and determinism are incompatible, and in this chapter I shall try to demonstrate this incompatibility.

Discussions of this question are usually not on a very high level. In the great majority of cases, they are the work of compatibilists and consist to a large degree in the ascription of some childish fallacy or other to incompatibilists (conflation of "descriptive" and "prescriptive" laws; failure to distinguish between causal necessity and compulsion; equation of freedom and mere randomness). Donald Davidson places himself in this tradition when he writes:

> I shall not be directly concerned with [arguments for the incompatibility of freedom and causal determination], since I know of none that is more than superficially plausible. Hobbes, Locke, Hume, Moore, Schlick, Ayer, · Stevenson, and a host of others have done what can be done, or ought ever to have been needed, to remove the confusions that can make determinism seem to oppose freedom.[1]

It is not my purpose in this book to defend any previous writer against a charge of fallacious argument. My own arguments will be explicit, and any fallacies they commit should be correspondingly visible...

In Chapter I, I mentioned the following simple argument for Incompatibilism, the Consequence Argument:

> If determinism is true, then our acts are the consequences of the laws of nature and events in the remote past. But it is not up to us what went on before we were born, and neither is it up to us what the laws of nature are. Therefore, the consequences of these things (including our present acts) are not up to us.

This, I think, is a *good* argument. But I must admit it's rather sketchy. The present chapter is an attempt to fill in the details of this sketch in three different ways. (I have called this chapter "Three Arguments for Incompatibilism," but the principle of individuation for arguments is far from clear; I might have called it "One Argument for Incompatibilism Done Three Ways".) These three arguments, or versions of one argument, or whatever they are, are intended to support one another. Though they have essentially the same point, they are very different in structure and vocabulary...

The Third Argument is a modal argument; that is, it involves a modal operator, an operator that attaches to sentences that have (or that express propositions that have) truth-values, to form sentences that have truth-values; and the truth-value of a sentence formed in this way is not in every case a function of the truth-value of the sentence to which the operator attaches. The operator is 'N'. For any sentence p, the result of prefixing p with 'N' may be regarded as an abbreviation for the result of flanking 'and no one has, or ever had, any choice about whether' with occurrences of p. Thus

N All men are mortal

is an abbreviation for

All men are mortal and no one has, or ever had, any choice about whether all men are mortal.

'N' is a very interesting operator, and the task of constructing a plausible and complete logic for 'N' would be an interesting one. It would be even more interesting if the vocabulary of this logic included the usual "alethic" modal operators. But it would not be necessary for our purposes actually to construct such a logic. I think the following two inference rules ought to be valid rules of this logic:

(α) $\Box\, p \vdash Np$
(β) $N(p \supset q), Np \vdash Nq$.

I shall require no formulae that contain 'N' to be logically true other than those that these two rules allow us to deduce from the empty set of premises. The operator '$\Box$' in Rule (α) represents "broadly logical necessity."

The Third Argument will have the following logical structure: from a logical consequence of determinism (determinism being conceived as in the First Argument)[2], we shall deduce that no one has any choice about anything whatever.

In the Third Argument we shall once more use the symbols 'P_o' and 'L,' which appeared in our statement of the First Argument. [Eds.: 'P_o' is an abbreviation for the sentence expressing the proposition that describes the state of the world at a particular instant in the remote past; 'L,' similarly represents a conjunction of all the laws of nature into a single proposition.]...

We shall once more use the letter 'P.' This letter will serve as a dummy for which one can substitute any sentence one likes, provided it expresses a true proposition—'Quine finds quantified modal logic puzzling,' say, or 'Paris is the capital of France'.

If determinism is true, then it follows that

(1) $\Box\, ((P_0 \,\&\, L) \supset P)$

is true. From (1) we may deduce

(2) $\Box\, (P_0 \supset (L \supset P))$

by elementary modal and sentential logic. Applying rule (α) to (2), we have:

(3) $N(P_0 \supset (L \supset P))$.

We now introduce a premiss:

(4) NP_0.

From (3) and (4) we have by Rule (β):

(5) $N(L \supset P)$.

We introduce a second premiss:

(6) NL.

Then, from (5) and (6) by (β):

(7) NP.

This deduction shows that if determinism is true, then no one ever has any choice about anything, since any sentence that expresses a truth may replace 'P' in it. Consider, for example, the question whether anyone had a choice about whether Richard Nixon would receive a pardon for any offences he committed while in office. Nixon did receive such a pardon. Therefore, if determinism is true,

$\Box\, (P_0 \,\&\, L. \supset$ Richard Nixon received a pardon for any offences he might have committed while in office).

Therefore, if (α) and (β) are valid rules, and if NL and NP_0, then we have:

No one had any choice about whether Richard Nixon received a pardon for any offences he might have committed while in office.

Most of us, I presume, think this conclusion is false. Most of us think Gerald Ford had a choice about whether Nixon would receive a pardon. (Even if someone thinks that Ford's actions were wholly controlled by some cabal, he none the less thinks *someone* had a choice about whether Nixon would receive a pardon.) But the above deduction (The Third Formal Argument) shows that if we wish to accept this conclusion we must reject one of the following five propositions:

Determinism is true;
NP_o;
NL;
Rule (α) is valid;
Rule (β) is valid.

My choice, of course, is to reject determinism. But let us examine the alternatives.

I do not see how anyone can reject 'NP_o' or 'NL'…The proposition that P_o is a proposition about the remote past. We could, if we like, stipulate that it is a proposition about the distribution and momenta of atoms and other particles in the inchoate, presiderial nebulae. Therefore, surely, no one has any choice about whether P_o. The proposition that L is a proposition that "records" the laws of nature. If it is a law of nature that angular momentum is conserved, then no one has any choice about whether angular momentum is conserved, and, more generally, since it is a law of nature that L, no one has any choice about whether L.

I do not see how anyone could reject Rule (α). If (α) is invalid, then it could be that someone has a choice about what is necessarily true. Hardly anyone besides Descartes has been willing to concede such a capability even to God. No one, so far as I know, has ever suggested that human beings could have a choice about what is necessarily true…

Only Rule (β) remains to be considered. The validity of (β) is, I think, the most difficult of the premises of the Third Argument to defend. How might one go about defending it?

…I must confess that my belief in the validity of (β) has only two sources, one incommunicable and the other inconclusive. The former source is what philosophers are pleased to call "intuition": when I carefully consider (β), it seems to be valid. But I can't expect anyone to be very impressed by this fact. People's intuitions, after all, have led them to accept all sorts of crazy propositions and many sane but false propositions. (The Unrestricted Comprehension Principle in set theory and the Galilean Law of the addition of Velocities in physics are good examples of propositions in the second category.) The latter source is the fact that I can think of no instances of (β) that have, or could possibly have, true premises and a false conclusion. Consider, for example, these two instances of (β):

Alice has asthma and no one has, or ever had, any choice about whether she has asthma;

If Alice has asthma, she sometimes has difficulty breathing, and no one has, or ever had, any choice about whether, if she has asthma, she sometimes has difficulty breathing;

hence, Alice sometimes has difficulty breathing, and no one has, or ever had, any choice about whether Alice sometimes has difficulty breathing.

The sun will explode in 2000 AD, and no one has, or ever had, any choice about whether the sun will explode in 2000 AD;

If the sun explodes in 2000 AD, all life on earth will end in 2000 AD, and no one has, or ever had, any choice about whether, if the sun explodes in AD, all life on earth will end in 2000 AD;

hence, All life on earth will end in 2000 AD, and no one has, or ever had, any choice about whether all life on earth will end in 2000 AD.

These arguments are clearly valid. There is simply no way things could be arranged that would suffice for the truth of their premisses and the falsity of their conclusions. Take the second. Conceivably we could do something to prevent the explosion of the sun. Then perhaps the conclusion of this argument would be false; but its first premiss would also be false. Perhaps we could erect an enormous shield that would protest the earth from the explosion of the sun; if we could do this, the conclusion would be false. But the second premiss would also be false. Perhaps we could spread a poison that would destroy all life on earth before 2000 AD; but in that case too the second premiss would be false. I cannot help feeling that the reader who makes a serious attempt at constructing a counterexample to (β) will begin to appreciate, even if he does not come to share, the intuition that I have expressed by saying, "when I carefully consider (β), it seems to be valid."

It is interesting to note that rule (β) seems to figure in recent discussions of the philosophical and social implications of socio-biology and the question whether certain widespread features of human social behaviour are genetically determined. Consider, for example, the proposition (P) that there are certain jobs (jobs that both sexes are physically capable of performing) such that, in every society, these jobs devolve almost entirely on women. Suppose a socio-biologist alleges that there is a certain fact or set of facts (F) about the evolutionary history of our species that explains why P is true. Anyone who says this is likely to be the target of some such criticism as this:

> What you are saying is that "women's role" is genetically determined, and thus that all attempts at changing the role of women in this or any other society are doomed by biology. This doctrine is pernicious. You are not a scientist but an ideologue, and the ideology you are peddling makes you a most useful prop for the existing system.

Anyone who is the target of such criticism is likely to defend himself in some way pretty much like this:

> Not so. While I believe that F explains why P is true, I do not say that F makes P *inevitably* true. Given F, there is a tendency for P to be true, but

tendencies can be resisted. I do not say that "biology is destiny". It may well be that we have a choice about whether we shall behave in accordance with this tendency that our evolutionary heritage has presented us with.

Now I am not so much interested about where the right lies in disputes that take this form—after all, where it lies may depend on what is substituted for 'F' and for 'P'—as I am in its underlying logic. I believe that the logical skeleton of this dispute looks something like this:

CRITIC: It follows from your position that the premises of the following valid argument are true:
                         N F obtains
                         N (F obtains ⊃ P is true)
                         hence, N P is true
SOCIO-BIOLOGIST: The first premiss is certainly true, but the second premiss does *not* follow from my position and may very well be false.

It would probably never occur to the socio-biologist to deny that the conclusion of the argument he has been charged with endorsing actually does not follow from its premises. And if he did deny this, then the critic would rightly charge him with sophistry, for if it is granted that no one has any choice about whether, given that our history is such-and-such, we do so-and-so, and if it is granted that our history *is* such-and-such and that we have no choice about this, then it just obviously does follow that no one has any choice about whether we do so-and-so. This does not, of course, entail that (β) is valid, for it may be that while this instance is valid, other instances of (β) are invalid. But I think that anyone who said that, while the argument the critic has formulated is valid, (β) is *not* valid, would be saying something that is not on the face of it very plausible. The validity of (β), in its full generality, certainly does seem to be part of the "common ground" in the socio-biological dispute I have imagined. (Despite the fact that I have imagined it, its logical structure is similar to disputes about biological determinism.); That is, (β) seems to be accepted, and properly so, by both sides in the dispute; the dispute seems to turn simply on *what*—according to socio-biology—we have a choice about, and not on any questions about the validity of inferences involving 'having a choice about.' People who accept, or are accused of accepting, "special determinisms"—that is, theories that say, or are sometimes interpreted as saying, that some important aspect of human behaviour is determined by this or that factor outside our control—tend to find themselves embroiled about disputes about the freedom of the will. I have used a socio-biologist as an example of such a person because I am writing now, but the "biology is destiny" debate is not the only one of its type. If I had been writing a few years ago, I should have constructed an example involving a Freudian or a Marxist and the point of my example would have been the same. Anyone who denies the validity of (β), it seems to me, must react to such disputes in one of two ways. He must either call them pseudo-disputes that arise because both parties to the dispute wrongly accept (β), or he must contend that the dispute does not really involve (β) after all. In the former case, he should recommend that the socio-biologist reply to his critic like this:

> I admit that F is a fact about the history of our species and that that's something no one has a choice about. I admit that *if* F is a fact about the history of a given species, then, in societies that comprise members of that species, certain jobs will devolve almost entirely upon women, and that no one has any choice about *that*. Still, we *do* have a choice about whether, in our society, these jobs will devolve almost entirely upon women.

I cannot imagine anyone saying this with a straight face. In the latter case, he owes us an account of these disputes that shows how the apparent acceptance of (β) by both parties is merely apparent.

The point of this discussion may be summed up in a question: Why is none of the participants in the debates about biological determinism a compatibilist? Perhaps the answer is that the participants in these debates take the idea of biological determinism much more seriously than philosophers are accustomed to take the idea of "universal" or "Laplacian" determinism, and that compatibilism with respect to a given type of determinism is possible only for people who do not take that type of determinism very seriously.

I said above that I could think of no instances of (β) that had, or could possibly have had, true premises and a false conclusion. I meant, of course, that I could think of no instances of (β) that could be seen to have true premises and a false conclusion independently of the question whether free will is compatible with determinism. If free will is compatible with determinism, and if determinism is true, then, presumably, at least one of the following two instances of (β) has true premises and a false conclusion:

$N (P_o \supset (L \supset \text{Nixon received a pardon}))$
$N P_o$
hence, $N (L \supset \text{Nixon received a pardon})$.

$N (L \supset \text{Nixon received a pardon})$
$N L$
hence, N Nixon received a pardon.

But it would be nice to see a counter-example to (β) that did not presuppose the compatibility of free will and determinism. After all, the examples I gave in support of (β) did not presuppose the *incompatibility* of free will and determinism. I should think that if there are *any* counter-examples to (β), then some of them, at least, could be shown to be such independently of the question whether free will and determinism are compatible...

Some compatibilists, when they are confronted with arguments for the incompatibility of free will and determinism, say something like this: "Your argument simply demonstrates that when you use phrases like 'could have done otherwise' or 'has a choice about,' you are giving them some meaning other than the meaning they have in our actual debates about moral responsibility." This criticism is equally applicable, *mutatis mutandis*, to all three of our arguments for incompatibilism. And my answer to it is essentially the same in each case. But this answer can be presented very compactly and efficiently in terms of the vocabulary employed in the Third Argument. Therefore, I shall answer only this charge: "When you use the phrase 'has a choice' you are giving it a meaning different from the meaning it has in our actual debates about moral responsibility," and I will leave to the reader the mechanical task of adapting this answer to the requirements of the First and Second Arguments. My answer consists simply in a reinterpretation of 'N':

$Np =_{df} p$ and, in just the sense of *having a choice* that is relevant in debates about moral responsibility, no one has, or ever had, any choice about whether p.

If there is anything to the objection we are considering, then at least one of the four propositions,

NP_o,
NL,
Rule (α) is valid,
Rule (β) is valid,

is false, given that 'N'—which occurs in (α) and (β)—is interpreted as above. But this does not seem to be the case. If one carefully retraces the steps of the Third Argument, one will find, I think, that no step becomes doubtful under our new interpretation of 'N.' The conclusion of the present chapter is, therefore, that if determinism is true, then no one has any choice about anything, in just that sense of *having a choice* that is relevant in debates about moral responsibility.

Notes

1. "Freedom to act," in Ted Honderich, ed., *Essays on Freedom of Action* (London: Routledge and Kegan Paul, 1973), 139.

2. [Eds.: van Inwagen's definition of determinism, from his First Argument, is as follows:]

We may now define 'determinism.' We shall apply this term to the conjunction of these two theses:

For every instant of time, there is a proposition that expresses the state of the world at that instant;

If p and q are any propositions that express the state of the world at some instants, then the conjunction of p with the laws of nature entails q.

This definition seems to me to capture at least one thesis that could properly be called 'determinism.' Determinism is, intuitively, the thesis that, given the past and the laws of nature, there is only one possible future.

6

The Consequence Argument and the *Mind* Argument

Dana K. Nelkin

The Consequence argument for the incompatibility of freedom and determinism is stated eloquently by Peter van Inwagen in his *Essay on Free Will*:

> If determinism is true, then our acts are the consequences of the laws of nature and events in the remote past. But it is not up to us what went on before we were born, and neither is it up to us what the laws of nature are. Therefore, the consequences of these things (including our present acts) are not up to us. (1983: 5)

Van Inwagen, like many other libertarians, is convinced by the argument. But there is a problem: one of the presuppositions of the Consequence argument seems to yield a powerful argument for the incompatibility of freedom and *in*determinism, an argument van Inwagen calls the *Mind* argument.[1] It seems, then, that what many have taken to provide the most powerful reason to reject compatibilism also provides reason to embrace scepticism about the very possibility of freedom. Since van Inwagen is a libertarian and would like to reject both compatibilism and scepticism, he recognizes the need to respond to this problem. His solution is to identify and reject a premiss of the *Mind* argument not shared by the Consequence argument, but he admits that he does not know "*how it could be*" that the premiss in question is false.

Recently, Alicia Finch and Ted A. Warfield (1998) have taken up the libertarian's conundrum and come to van Inwagen's aid in an ingenious and unexpected way: they argue that the common presupposition behind both arguments is indeed false, but that the Consequence argument can be reformulated so as to make it sound while the *Mind* argument cannot. In this paper, I argue that Finch and Warfield's strategy ultimately fails to save the libertarian position, and that van Inwagen is right to worry that the two arguments stand or fall together. Nevertheless, I argue that the implications of this conclusion for the freedom that we care about are much less threatening than has been thought.

1. The Consequence argument and the *Mind* argument

In setting out the Consequence and *Mind* arguments, I follow Finch and Warfield, who in turn follow van Inwagen, while making slight changes in the abbreviations and order of presentation.

Let me begin with the Consequence argument. Determinism is the thesis that the conjunction of the past and laws of nature fixes a unique possible future. More formally, let F be any truth, let P be a proposition expressing the complete state of the world at a time in the distant past, and let L be a conjunction of the laws of nature. Where '$\Box$' expresses broad logical necessity, it is a consequence of determinism that

$$\Box\{(P \,\&\, L) \to F\}$$

Now let 'Np' abbreviate 'p and no one ever has, or ever had, any choice about whether p,' and understand one's having a choice about whether a truth p as one's being able to act to ensure p's falsity.[2] Finally, the following inference rules are required:

Alpha: $\Box p$ implies Np
Beta: $\{Np \,\&\, N(p \to q)\}$ implies Nq.

The Consequence argument can now be stated as follows:

The Consequence argument
(1) $\Box\{(P \,\&\, L) \to F\}$ Consequence of Determinism
(2) $\Box\{P \to (L \to F)\}$ 1
(3) $N\{P \to (L \to F)\}$ 2, Alpha
(4) NP Premiss, fixity of the past
(5) $N(L \to F)$ 3, 4, Beta
(6) NL Premiss, fixity of the laws
(7) NF 5, 6, Beta

Each premiss seems difficult to deny, and both inference rules appear to be valid. The problem for libertarians is that Beta also seems to undergird the *Mind* argument. The basic idea behind the *Mind* argument is this:

In a world in which events relevant to the formation of free actions are undetermined, actions are caused by, but not determined by, the prior states of mind (e.g. desires and beliefs) of agents. But, in such an indeterministic world, no one has a choice about whether one's state of mind will have a particular result or not. Similarly, one's state of mind, being an ultimate result of earlier events over which one has no choice, is also not something one has a choice about. Thus, since one has no choice about anything that is relevant to the bringing about of one's actions, one has no choice about those actions themselves.[3]

To see just how the *Mind* argument is related to the Consequence argument, it will be helpful to turn to a more formal rendering of this basic idea. Suppose that we are in an indeterministic world and that actions are caused by, but not determined by, particular sets of agents' desires and beliefs.[4] Let '*DB*' represent the particular belief/desire complex of some agent, and let '*R*' represent an action brought about exclusively by *DB*. Thus, *DB* is the only thing causally relevant to the occurrence of *R*.

Now, since *R* is an indeterministic consequence of *DB*, it seems that no one has a choice about whether or not *R* follows *DB*. That is,

$N (DB \rightarrow R)$.

Similarly, since *DB* seems to be an indeterministic consequence of earlier facts over which the agent has no control, it seems that no one has a choice about having *DB*.[5] Thus,

$N(DB)$.

Now we have all that is needed to set out the *Mind* argument:

The Mind *argument*
(P1) $N(DB)$ Premiss
(P2) $N(DB \rightarrow R)$ Premiss
(C1) $N(R)$ P1, P2, Beta

Although (P1) and (P2) are represented as premisses, in a way parallel to the Consequence argument, they are intended to be seen as consequences of an agent's being situated in an indeterministic world.[6] Thus, if the reasoning behind the *Mind* argument is accepted, then the argument generalizes and it seems to follow that freedom is incompatible with indeterminism.

Once again, the premisses appear difficult to deny (on the assumption that the relevant agent inhabits an indeterministic world), and the inference rule appears valid. Further, libertarians who have embraced the Consequence argument will be particularly reluctant to reject Beta. Van Inwagen (1983: 147, 151), for one, chooses to reject (P2), but he cannot see any reason why (P2) should be false, and offers a positive reason in support of it.[7] He writes, 'I must choose between the puzzling [rejecting (P2)] and the inconceivable [rejecting Beta]. I choose the puzzling' (1983: 150).

Enter Finch and Warfield with their quite different libertarian solution.

2. A counter-example to Beta and a reformulated Consequence argument

Despite the intuitive appeal of Beta, McKay and Johnson (1996) offer a persuasive counter-example to it.[8] Their strategy is to show first that Alpha and Beta entail 'the principle of Agglomeration':

Np & Nq implies $N(p$ & $q)$.

They then offer a counter-example to this principle, and since they, like van Inwagen and Finch and Warfield, take Alpha to be 'beyond suspicion', they conclude that Beta is invalid.

The counter-example to Agglomeration is as follows: Suppose one does not toss a coin, but one could have. Let p = 'the coin does not land on heads' and q = 'the coin does not land on tails.' Now suppose also that no one can ensure that the coin lands on tails (or heads), so that Np and Nq are true. But, by hypothesis, one *could have* ensured that (p & q) is false, simply by flipping the coin. Thus, $N(p$ & $q)$ is false. It follows that Agglomeration is false, and Beta is the most likely culprit.

Does this leave the libertarian in the lurch? Finch and Warfield say 'no.' For there is an inference rule, closely related to Beta, that can do all the work required of Beta in the Consequence argument, namely:

Beta 2: $(Np$ & $\Box(p \to q))$ implies Nq.

Employing this new principle, Finch and Warfield propose the following revised Consequence argument:

The Improved Consequence argument
(P1) $\Box\{(P$ & $L) \to F\}$ Consequence of Determinism
(P2) $N(P$ & $L)$ Fixity of the past and laws
(C1) NF P1, P2, Beta 2[9]

Beta 2 claims only that 'one has no choice about the logical consequences of those truths one has no choice about' (1998: 522). In addition to its intuitive plausibility, Beta 2 avoids McKay and Johnson's counter-example to Beta. Thus, Beta 2 is extremely difficult to deny.

Finch and Warfield also persuasively defend the plausibility of (P2), which, as they acknowledge, is formally stronger than the conjunction of (4) and (6) in the original Consequence argument. They suggest that the conjunction of P and L 'offers a description of what might be called the 'broad past'—the complete state of the world at a time in the distant past including the laws of nature' (1998: 523). Intuitively, it seems that the broad past is fixed in just the way that the past is. We have no choice about either.

Given the plausibility of (P2) in the Improved Consequence argument and the strengths of Beta 2, Finch and Warfield have provided a powerful argument on behalf of libertarians. In addition, they claim to have offered in place of Beta an inference rule that works in a reformulated Consequence argument but does *not* work in a reformulated *Mind* argument. They reason that in order to employ Beta 2 in place of Beta and retain a valid argument, 'N' in (P2) must be replaced by '□.' But then (P2) would be false on the assumption of indeterminism, and the argument would be unsound.[10] They conclude that the Improved Consequence argument is sound, that the *Mind* argument cannot be revived, and that libertarianism is unthreatened by the worries that the two arguments stand or fall together.

3. Why the consequence and the *Mind* arguments stand or fall together

Despite the appeal of this solution for libertarians, it ultimately fails in its attempt to dissociate the Consequence argument from the *Mind* argument. For the *Mind* argument *can* be reformulated so as to employ Beta 2 instead of Beta. The key is that it must be reformulated in a way different from that envisioned by Finch and Warfield.

Let me begin by returning to the intuitions behind each argument. By focusing on their informal renderings, it is perhaps easier to see that there is indeed a common assumption driving them both. It is this: if we lack a choice about the things that constitute all that is relevant to bringing about our actions, then we lack a choice about our actions themselves. One way of capturing this is by means of Beta 2, which says that if we lack a choice about a total state of affairs that logically entails a second state of affairs, then we lack a choice about the second state of affairs.

I propose that we reformulate the *Mind* argument in a way exactly parallel to the Improved Consequence argument. Recall that the Improved Consequence argument rests on the plausibility of the claim that one lacks a choice about the conjunction of the past and the laws of nature (and not just about each individually). In a similar way, it is also plausible that, in an indeterministic world, one lacks a choice about the conjunction of the proposition specifying one's state of mind and the proposition that one's state of mind causes the actions it actually does (and not just about each individually). Thus, (P1) and (P2) in the *Mind* argument can be replaced by:

(P^*) N{DB & ($DB \to R$)}

With (P^*) in hand, here is a reformulated *Mind* argument:

Improved Mind *argument*
(P^*) N{DB & ($DB \to R$)}   Premiss
(P^{**}) □{(DB & ($DB \to R$)) $\to R$}   Premiss (logical truth)
$(C1)$ N(R) (P^*), (P^{**}), Beta 2

Is there reason to think that (P*) is true in an indeterministic world? In fact, there is exactly the same kind of reason as there is supporting (P2) in the Improved Consequence argument. Just as we can think of the conjunction of *P* and *L* as the 'broad past,' we can think of the conjunction of *DB* and (*DB* → *R*) as the 'broad nature of our mental states.' In other words, the conjunction of *DB* and (*DB* → *R*) represents the nature of an agent's mental states, including (some of) their causal properties. And, just as in a deterministic world the broad past is not up to us, in an indeterministic world it is not up to us what the nature of our mental states is.

In fact, the same reason why we accept that no one has any choice about the broad past applies equally to the broad nature of our mental states. Why are we inclined to accept (P2)? I believe that the reason we are inclined to accept (P2) is that no one has any choice about either part of the broad past, namely, the past or the laws of nature. This sounds like an implicit appeal to Agglomeration, but it need not be. For we cannot think of anything that anyone could possibly do (analogous to the flipping of a coin in McKay and Johnson's case) that would ensure the falsity of the conjunction of *P* and *L*, while lacking both the ability to ensure the falsity of *P* and the ability to ensure the falsity of *L*. Thus, it seems that we are implicitly appealing to a restricted version of Agglomeration when we accept (P2), even though we do not fully articulate it.

Now turn to (P*) in the Improved *Mind* argument. Similar reasoning is available in the case of the broad nature of our mental states. We have no choice about either *DB* or (*DB* → *R*). Further, we cannot think of anything one could do to ensure the falsity of the conjunction of *DB* and (*DB* → *R*) itself, while lacking the ability to falsify the first conjunct and the ability to falsify the second conjunct. Thus (P*) is just as plausible as (P2) in the Improved Consequence argument and, together with a logical truth and a single application of Beta 2, yields the conclusion of the *Mind* argument.

Now one might object that there is a unity to the broad past that is lacking in the broad nature of our mental states, and that as a result (P2) has stronger support than (P*). Indeed, Finch and Warfield suggest that there is more to the intuitiveness of (P2) than I have suggested. They claim that our acceptance of premiss (4) and our acceptance of (6) in the original Consequence argument are both motivated by the same core intuition, and that core intuition can also be used directly to motivate our acceptance of (P2). They describe the core intuition as that 'the past is fixed and beyond the power of human agents to affect in any way' (1998: 523). And, in a note, they explain that because we think of the laws of nature as unalterable and unchanging, we think of them, 'in a sense, as part of the past' (523, fn. 15). If we accept Finch and Warfield's claim here, (P2) might be thought to be more strongly supported than if it rested on the appeal of premisses (4) and (6), together with our inability to see (P2) as analogous to the McKay and Johnson case.

I believe that this is stretching our intuitive idea of the past too far. For, by parity of reasoning, mathematical truths, which are also unalterable and unchanging, should be counted as part of the past. Yet, this is unintuitive. Although I would accept that I have no choice about the truth of mathematical truths and the past, my reason is not simply that I find it intuitive that I have no choice about the past. This reply does not impugn Finch and Warfield's claim for the intuitive plausibility of (P2); rather it shows that there is no *more* reason to accept (P2) than to accept (P*).

4. Where we are

I conclude that if the core idea behind the Consequence argument is right, then so is the core idea behind the *Mind* argument. It is possible that both arguments fail. However, as long as we understand the ultimate conclusion in the way van Inwagen does, it is difficult to see *how* they could. For it is difficult to deny that if one cannot ensure the falsity of anything relevant to the bringing about of one's actual actions, then one cannot ensure the falsity of the proposition that one acts as one actually does. At the same time, it seems clear that whether the world is deterministic or indeterministic, one lacks the ability to *ensure* the falsity of true propositions, including those relevant to the bringing about of one's actual actions. Thus, we cannot ensure that we act other than we actually do.

But is the ability to ensure that one does other than what one does required for freedom, or, at any rate, the freedom we care about? I do not believe so. Compatibilists can certainly deny that the idea of having a choice about—cashed out as the ability to ensure that one does not act as one does—captures the sense of freedom that is required for moral responsibility and that we ultimately care about.[11]

There is also some room for libertarians to deny that freedom requires an ability to ensure that one acts differently from the way one does in fact. For it is strictly consistent with libertarianism that we act freely as long as our states of mind cause our actions and that indeterminism is true, even if we lack the ability to ensure that we do otherwise. However, libertarians face the challenge of explaining why the truth of indeterminism should endow someone with free agency. For, if indeterminism is unsupplemented by a story about the kind of control free agents have over their actions, then the mere fact of indeterminism would seem merely to *undermine* freedom by making our actions a matter of chance. In claiming that freedom requires the ability on the part of agents to ensure that they do other than they do, van Inwagen offers such a story, and addresses this difficult challenge for libertarians. Perhaps there is another way for libertarians to address this challenge, in which case they could also avoid embracing scepticism about the freedom that we care about. But if not, then it appears that the only way to reject compatibilism is to embrace scepticism, a price I believe it is not necessary to pay.[12]

Notes

1. Van Inwagen uses the name '*Mind* argument' because he finds it in a number of articles of that journal. Strictly speaking, the argument I discuss in this paper is what van Inwagen calls the "third strand" of the *Mind* argument. But he claims that the "point" of all three strands is basically the same and that they stand or fall together. For the sake of simplicity, I will refer to the "third strand" as the *Mind* argument in what follows.

2. This is the only place where a question might arise whether Finch and Warfield have precisely captured van Inwagen's intention, and they themselves acknowledge it. When van Inwagen introduces the 'N' operator, he says only that, "[f]or any sentence p, the result of prefixing p with 'N' may be regarded as an abbreviation for the result of flanking 'and no one has, or ever had, a choice about whether' with occurrences of p" (1983: 93). However, passages elsewhere in the same chapter clearly support Finch and Warfield's further cashing out of the lack of a choice about a (true) fact as the lack of an ability to ensure the falsity of the fact (1983: 67–68 and fn. 31, 233–34).

3. This passage is based on an informal reconstruction of van Inwagen 1983: 126–27 and 142–48.

4. It is important to note that van Inwagen (1983: 126–27) provides an argument that if indeterminism is to be relevant to the formation of free actions, it *must* be that actions are caused by, but not determined by, agents' mental states and deliberations. (It cannot be, for instance, that there is, say, a single undetermined particle in the universe that is unrelated to any rational agents, while the rest of the universe is governed by strict deterministic laws.) Mele (1995: 211–20 and 230) offers (although he does not endorse) an alternative point in the formation of free actions for events to be undetermined, but he suspects that many libertarians will find this "modest" alternative less than satisfying. I believe that Mele's suspicion is right, and that van Inwagen's position is one that libertarians should endorse. In what follows, then, I assume that van Inwagen's position on this point is correct.

5. As Finch and Warfield (1998: 518, fn. 6) argue, echoing van Inwagen, "one could have a choice about *DB* only if one had a choice about the earlier state of affairs from which *DB* followed, in which case proponents of the *Mind* argument will simply raise their worries about this earlier state until we reach an initial state about which the agent in question had no choice."

6. To be more precise, they are consequences of an agent's being situated in an indeterministic world in which there are undetermined events relevant to the formation of free actions (see fn. 4). In what follows, I will use 'indeterministic world' or 'indeterminism' as shorthand for 'indeterministic world in which there are undetermined events relevant to the formation of free actions.'

7. In fact, van Inwagen (1983: 149) explicitly rejects the conditional that "if an agent's act was caused but not determined by his prior inner state, and if nothing besides that inner state was causally relevant to the agent's act," then (P2). Since van Inwagen takes the antecedent to follow from the agent's being in an indeterministic world of the sort required by incompatibilism, this amounts to an implicit denial of (P2).

8. See O'Connor 1993 for an interesting discussion of previous attempts to provide counter-examples to Beta.

9. See also Widerker 1987 for a similar proposal. Unlike Finch and Warfield, Widerker does not defend (P2) or consider the implications of his discussion for the *Mind* argument.

10. Finch and Warfield (1998: 525–26) consider a number of alternative inference rules that might be used to try to preserve the core idea behind the *Mind* argument, but they rightly reject each attempt to use them in a reformulated *Mind* argument.

11. See, for example, Frankfurt 1969, Wolf 1990, Mele 1995, Fischer and Ravizza 1998. For a survey of the recent discussion of Frankfurt's argument, see Fischer 1999.

12. I would like to thank Michael Clark, Al Mele, Sam Rickless, Fritz Warfield, and an anonymous referee for very helpful comments.

References

Finch, A., and T. A. Warfield. 1998. "The *Mind* argument and libertarianism," *Mind* 107: 515–28.

Fischer, J. M. 1999. "Recent work on moral responsibility," *Ethics* 110: 93–139.

Fischer, J. M., and M. Ravizza. 1998. *Responsibility and Control: A Theory of Moral Responsibility*. New York: Cambridge University Press.

Frankfurt, H. 1969. "Alternate possibilities and moral responsibility," *Journal of Philosophy* 66: 829–39.

McKay, T., and D. Johnson. 1996. "A reconsideration of an argument against compatibilism," *Philosophical Topics* 24: 113–22.

Mele, A. 1995. *Autonomous Agents*. Oxford: Oxford University Press.

O'Connor, T. 1993. "On the transfer of necessity," *Noûs* 27: 204–18.

van Inwagen, P. 1983. *An Essay on Free Will*. Oxford: Oxford University Press.

Widerker, D. 1987. "On an argument for incompatibilism," *Analysis* 47: 37–41.

Wolf, S. 1990. *Freedom within Reason*. Oxford: Oxford University Press.

PART 3

Suggested Further Readings

III. The Consequence Argument

Campbell, Joseph. 2005. "Compatibilist alternatives," *Canadian Journal of Philosophy* 35: 387–406.

Foley, Richard. 1979. "Compatibilism and control over the past," *Analysis* 39.2: 70–74.

Finch, Alicia and Ted Warfield. 1998. "The Mind argument and libertarianism," *Mind* 107: 515–28.

Kapitan, Tomis. 2002. "A master argument for incompatibilism?" in R. Kane, ed., *The Oxford Handbook of Free Will*. Oxford: Oxford University Press.

Lewis, David. 2003. "Are we free to break the laws?" in Gary Watson, ed., *Free Will*. Oxford: Oxford University Press, 122–29.

Slote, Michael. 1982. "Selective necessity and the free will problem," *Journal of Philosophy* 79: 5–24.

Van Inwagen, P. 2000. "Free will remains a mystery," in J. Tomberlin, ed., *Philosophical Perspectives* 14 (*Action and Freedom*). Malden, MA: Blackwell Publishing, 1–19.

Widerker, David . 1987. "On an argument for incompatibilism," *Analysis* 47: 37–41.

Responsibility and Alternative Possibilities

7

Alternate Possibilities and Moral Responsibility

Harry G. Frankfurt

A dominant role in nearly all recent inquiries into the free-will problem has been played by a principle which I shall call "the principle of alternate possibilities." This principle states that a person is morally responsible for what he has done only if he could have done otherwise. Its exact meaning is a subject of controversy, particularly concerning whether someone who accepts it is thereby committed to believing that moral responsibility and determinism are incompatible. Practically no one, however, seems inclined to deny or even to question that the principle of alternate possibilities (construed in some way or other) is true. It has generally seemed so overwhelmingly plausible that some philosophers have even characterized it as an *a priori* truth. People whose accounts of free will or of moral responsibility are radically at odds evidently find in it a firm and convenient common ground upon which they can profitably take their opposing stands.

But the principle of alternate possibilities is false. A person may well be morally responsible for what he has done even though he could not have done otherwise. The principle's plausibility is an illusion, which can be made to vanish by bringing the relevant moral phenomena into sharper focus.

I.

In seeking illustrations of the principle of alternate possibilities, it is most natural to think of situations in which the same circumstances both bring it about that a person does something and make it impossible for him to avoid doing it. These include, for example, situations in which a person is coerced into doing something, or in which he is impelled to act by a hypnotic suggestion, or in which some inner compulsion drives him to do what he does. In situations of these kinds there are circumstances that make it impossible for the person to do otherwise, and these very circumstances also serve to bring it about that he does whatever it is that he does.

However, there may be circumstances that constitute sufficient conditions for a certain action to be performed by someone and that therefore make it impossible for the person to do otherwise, but that do not actually impel the person to act or in any way produce his action. A person may do something in circumstances that leave him no alternative to doing it, without these circumstances actually moving him or leading him to do it—without them playing any role, indeed, in bringing it about that he does what he does.

An examination of situations characterized by circumstances of this sort casts doubt, I believe, on the relevance to questions of moral responsibility of the fact that a person who has done something could not have done otherwise. I propose to develop some examples of this kind in the context of a discussion of coercion and to suggest that our moral intuitions concerning these examples tend to disconfirm the principle of alternate possibilities. Then I will discuss the principle in more general terms, explain what I think is wrong with it, and describe briefly and without argument how it might appropriately be revised.

II.

It is generally agreed that a person who has been coerced to do something did not do it freely and is not morally responsible for having done it. Now the doctrine that coercion and moral responsibility are mutually exclusive may appear to be no more than a somewhat particularized version of the principle of alternate possibilities. It is natural enough to say of a person who has been coerced to do something that he could not have done otherwise. And it may easily seem that being coerced deprives a person of freedom and of moral responsibility simply because it is a special case of being unable to do otherwise. The principle of alternate possibilities may in this way derive some credibility from its association with the very plausible proposition that moral responsibility is excluded by coercion.

It is not right, however, that it should do so. The fact that a person was coerced to act as he did may entail both that he could not have done otherwise and that he bears no moral responsibility for his action. But his lack of moral responsibility is not entailed by his having been unable to do otherwise. The doctrine that coercion excludes moral responsibility is not correctly understood, in other words, as a particularized version of the principle of alternate possibilities.

Let us suppose that someone is threatened convincingly with a penalty he finds unacceptable and that he then does what is required of him by the issuer of the threat. We can imagine details that would make it reasonable for us to think that the person was coerced to perform the action in question, that he could not have done otherwise, and that he bears no moral responsibility for having done what he did. But just what is it about situations of this kind that warrants the judgment that the threatened person is not morally responsible for his act?

This question may be approached by considering situations of the following kind. Jones decides for reasons of his own to do something, then someone threatens him with a very harsh penalty (so harsh that any reasonable person would submit to the threat) unless he does precisely that, and Jones does it. Will we hold Jones morally responsible for what he has done? I think this will depend on the roles we think were played, in leading him to act, by his original decision and by the threat.

One possibility is that Jones$_1$ is not a reasonable man: he is, rather, a man who does what he has once decided to do no matter what happens next and no matter what the cost. In that case, the threat actually exerted no effective force upon him. He acted without any regard to it, very much as if he were not aware that it had been made. If this is indeed the way it was, the situation did not involve coercion at all. The threat did not lead Jones$_1$ to do what he did. Nor was it in fact sufficient to have prevented him from doing otherwise: if his earlier decision had been to do something else, the threat would not have deterred him in the slightest. It seems evident that in these circumstances the fact that Jones$_1$ was threatened in no way reduces the moral responsibility he would otherwise bear for his act. This example, however, is not a counterexample either to the doctrine that coercion excuses or to the principle of alternate possibilities. For we have supposed that Jones$_1$ is a man upon whom the threat had no coercive effect and, hence, that it did not actually deprive him of alternatives to doing what he did.

Another possibility is that Jones$_2$ was stampeded by the threat. Given that threat, he would have performed that action regardless of what decision he had already made. The threat upset him so profoundly, moreover, that he completely forgot his own earlier decision and did what was demanded of him entirely because he was terrified of the penalty with which he was threatened. In this case, it is not relevant to his having performed the action that he had already decided on his own to perform it. When the chips were down he thought of nothing but the threat, and fear alone led him to act. The fact that at an earlier time Jones$_2$ had decided for his own reasons to act in just that way may be relevant to an evaluation of his character; he may bear full moral responsibility for having made *that* decision. But he can hardly be said to be morally responsible for his action. For he performed the action simply as a result of the coercion to which he was subjected. His earlier decision played no role in bringing it about that he did what he did, and it would therefore be gratuitous to assign it a role in the moral evaluation of his action.

Now consider a third possibility. Jones₃ was neither stampeded by the threat nor indifferent to it. The threat impressed him, as it would impress any reasonable man, and he would have submitted to it wholeheartedly if he had not already made a decision that coincided with the one demanded of him. In fact, however, he performed the action in question on the basis of the decision he had made before the threat was issued. When he acted, he was not actually motivated by the threat but solely by the considerations that had originally commended the action to him. It was not the threat that led him to act, though it would have done so if he had not already provided himself with a sufficient motive for performing the action in question.

No doubt it will be very difficult for anyone to know, in a case like this one, exactly what happened. Did Jones₃ perform the action because of the threat, or were his reasons for acting simply those which had already persuaded him to do so? Or did he act on the basis of two motives, each of which was sufficient for his action? It is not impossible, however, that the situation should be clearer than situations of this kind usually are. And suppose it is apparent to us that Jones₃ acted on the basis of his own decision and not because of the threat. Then I think we would be justified in regarding his moral responsibility for what he did as unaffected by the threat even though, since he would in any case have submitted to the threat, he could not have avoided doing what he did. It would be entirely reasonable for us to make the same judgment concerning his moral responsibility that we would have made if we had not known of the threat. For the threat did not in fact influence his performance of the action. He did what he did just as if the threat had not been made at all.

III.

The case of Jones₃ may appear at first glance to combine coercion and moral responsibility, and thus to provide a counterexample to the doctrine that coercion excuses. It is not really so certain that it does so, however, because it is unclear whether the example constitutes a genuine instance of coercion. Can we say of Jones₃ that he was coerced to do something, when he had already decided on his own to do it and when he did it entirely on the basis of that decision? Or would it be more correct to say that Jones₃ was not coerced to do what he did, even though he himself recognized that there was an irresistible force at work in virtue of which he had to do it? My own linguistic intuitions lead me toward the second alternative, but they are somewhat equivocal. Perhaps we can say either of these things, or perhaps we must add a qualifying explanation to whichever of them we say.

This murkiness, however, does not interfere with our drawing an important moral from an examination of the example. Suppose we decide to say that Jones₃ was *not* coerced. Our basis for saying this will clearly be that it is incorrect to regard a man as being coerced to do something unless he does it *because* of the coercive force exerted against him. The fact that an irresistible threat is made will not, then, entail that the person who receives it is coerced to do what he does. It will also be necessary that the threat is what actually accounts for his doing it. On the other hand, suppose we decide to say that Jones₃ *was* coerced. Then we will be bound to admit that being coerced does not exclude being morally responsible. And we will also surely be led to the view that coercion affects the judgment of a person's moral responsibility only when the person acts as he does because he is coerced to do so—i.e., when the fact that he is coerced is what accounts for his action.

Whichever we decide to say, then, we will recognize that the doctrine that coercion excludes moral responsibility is not a particularized version of the principle of alternate possibilities. Situations in which a person who does something cannot do otherwise because he is subject to coercive power are either not instances of coercion at all, or they are situations in which the person may still be morally responsible for what he does if it is not because of the coercion that he does it. When we excuse a person who has been coerced, we do not excuse him because he was unable to do otherwise. Even though a person is subject to a coercive force that precludes his performing any action but one, he may nonetheless bear full moral responsibility for performing that action.

IV.

To the extent that the principle of alternate possibilities derives its plausibility from association with the doctrine that coercion excludes moral responsibility, a clear understanding of the latter diminishes the appeal of the former. Indeed the case of Jones₃ may appear to do more than illuminate the relationship between the two doctrines. It may well seem to provide a decisive counterexample to the principle of alternate possibilities and thus to show that this principle is false. For the irresistibility of the threat to which Jones₃ is subjected might well be taken to mean that he cannot but perform the action he performs. And yet the threat, since Jones₃ performs the action without regard to it, does not reduce his moral responsibility for what he does.

The following objection will doubtless be raised against the suggestion that the case of Jones₃ is a counterexample to the principle of alternate possibilities. There is perhaps a sense in which Jones₃ cannot do otherwise than perform the action he performs, since he is a reasonable man and the threat he encounters is sufficient to move any reasonable man. But it is not this sense that is germane to the principle of alternate possibilities. His knowledge that he stands to suffer an intolerably harsh penalty does not mean that Jones₃, strictly speaking, *cannot* perform any action but the one he does perform. After all it is still open to him, and this is crucial, to defy the threat if he wishes to do so and to accept the penalty his action would bring down upon him. In the sense in which the principle of alternate possibilities employs the concept of "could have done otherwise," Jones$_3$'s inability to resist the threat does not mean that he cannot do otherwise than perform the action he performs. Hence the case of Jones$_3$ does not constitute an instance contrary to the principle.

I do not propose to consider in what sense the concept of "could have done otherwise" figures in the principle of alternate possibilities, nor will I attempt to measure the force of the objection I have just described.[1] For I believe that whatever force this objection may be thought to have can be deflected by altering the example in the following way.[2] Suppose someone— Black, let us say—wants Jones$_4$ to perform a certain action. Black is prepared to go to considerable lengths to get his way, but he prefers to avoid showing his hand unnecessarily. So he waits until Jones$_4$ is about to make up his mind what to do, and he does nothing unless it is clear to him (Black is an excellent judge of such things) that Jones$_4$ is going to decide to do something *other* than what he wants him to do. If it does become dear that Jones$_4$ is going to decide to do something else, Black takes effective steps to ensure that Jones$_4$ decides to do, and that he does do, what he wants him to do.[3] Whatever Jone$_4$'s initial preferences and inclinations, then, Black will have his way.

What steps will Black take, if he believes he must take steps, in order to ensure that Jones$_4$ decides and acts as he wishes? Anyone with a theory concerning what "could have done otherwise" means may answer this question for himself by describing whatever measures he would regard as sufficient to guarantee that, in the relevant sense, Jones$_4$ cannot do otherwise. Let Black pronounce a terrible threat, and in this way both force Jones$_4$ to perform the desired action and prevent him from performing a forbidden one. Let Black give Jones$_4$ a potion, or put him under hypnosis, and in some such way as these generate in Jones$_4$ an irresistible inner compulsion to perform the act Black wants performed and to avoid others. Or let Black manipulate the minute processes of Jones$_4$'s brain and nervous system in some more direct way, so that causal forces running in and out of his synapses and along the poor man's nerves determine that he chooses to act and that he does act in the one way and not in any other. Given any conditions under which it will be maintained that Jones$_4$ cannot do otherwise, in other words, let Black bring it about that those conditions prevail. The structure of the example is flexible enough, I think, to find a way around any charge of irrelevance by accommodating the doctrine on which the charge is based.[4]

Now suppose that Black never has to show his hand because Jones$_4$, for reasons of his own, decides to perform and does perform the very action Black wants him to perform. In that case, it seems clear, Jones$_4$ will bear precisely the same moral responsibility for what he does as he would have borne if Black had not been ready to take steps to ensure that he do it. It would be quite unreasonable to excuse Jones$_4$ for his action, or to withhold the praise to which it would normally entitle him, on the basis of the fact that he could not have done otherwise. This fact played no role at all in leading him to act as he did. He would have acted the same even if it had not been a fact. Indeed, everything happened just as it would have happened without Black's presence in the situation and without his readiness to intrude into it.

In this example there are sufficient conditions for Jones$_4$'s performing the action in question. What action he performs is not up to him. Of course it is in a way up to him whether he acts on his own or as a result of Black's intervention. That depends upon what action he himself is inclined to perform. But whether he finally acts on his own or as a result of Black's intervention, he performs the same action. He has no alternative but to do what Black wants him to do. If he does it on his own, however, his moral responsibility for doing it is not affected by the fact that Black was lurking in the background with sinister intent, since this intent never comes into play.

V.

The fact that a person could not have avoided doing something is a sufficient condition of his having done it. But, as some of my examples show, this fact may play no role whatever in the explanation of why he did it. It may not figure at all among the circumstances that actually brought it about that he did what he did, so that his action is to be accounted for on another basis entirely. Even though the person was unable to do otherwise, that is to say, it may not be the case that he acted as he did *because* he could not have done otherwise. Now if someone had no alternative to performing a certain action but did not perform it because he was unable to do otherwise, then he would have performed exactly the same action even if he *could* have done otherwise. The circumstances that made it impossible for him to do otherwise could have been subtracted from the situation without affecting what happened or why it happened in any way. Whatever it was that actually led the person to do what he did, or that made him do it, would have led him to do it or made him do it even if it had been possible for him to do something else instead.

Thus it would have made no difference, so far as concerns his action or how he came to perform it, if the circumstances that made it impossible for him to avoid performing it had not prevailed. The fact that he could not have done otherwise clearly provides no basis for supposing that he *might* have done otherwise if he had been able to do so. When a fact is in this way irrelevant to the problem of accounting for a person's action it seems quite gratuitous to assign it any weight in the assessment of his moral responsibility.

Why should the fact be considered in reaching a moral judgment concerning the person when it does not help in any way to understand either what made him act as he did or what, in other circumstances, he might have done?

This, then, is why the principle of alternate possibilities is mistaken. It asserts that a person bears no moral responsibility—that is, he is to be excused—for having performed an action if there were circumstances that made it impossible for him to avoid performing it. But there may be circumstances that make it impossible for a person to avoid performing some action without those circumstances in any way bringing it about that he performs that action. It would surely be no good for the person to refer to circumstances of this sort in an effort to absolve himself of moral responsibility for performing the action in question. For those circumstances, by hypothesis, actually had nothing to do with his having done what he did. He would have done precisely the same thing, and he would have been led or made in precisely the same way to do it, even if they had not prevailed.

We often do, to be sure, excuse people for what they have done when they tell us (and we believe them) that they could not have done otherwise. But this is because we assume that what they tell us serves to explain why they did what they did. We take it for granted that they are not being disingenuous, as a person would be who cited as an excuse the fact that he could not have avoided doing what he did but who knew full well that it was not at all because of this that he did it.

What I have said may suggest that the principle of alternate possibilities should be revised so as to assert that a person is not morally responsible for what he has done if he did it because he could not have done otherwise. It may be noted that this revision of the principle does not seriously affect the arguments of those who have relied on the original principle in their efforts to maintain that moral responsibility and determinism are incompatible. For if it was causally determined that a person perform a certain action, then it will be true that the person performed it because of those causal determinants. And if the fact that it was causally determined that a person perform a certain action means that the person could not have done otherwise, as philosophers who argue for the incompatibility thesis characteristically suppose, then the fact that it was causally determined that a person perform a certain action will mean that the person performed it because he could not have done otherwise. The revised principle of alternate possibilities will entail, on this assumption concerning the meaning of 'could have done otherwise,' that a person is not morally responsible for what he has done if it was causally determined that he do it. I do not believe, however, that this revision of the principle is acceptable.

Suppose a person tells us that he did what he did because he was unable to do otherwise; or suppose he makes the similar statement that he did what he did because he had to do it. We do often accept statements like these (if we believe them) as valid excuses, and such statements may well seem at first glance to invoke the revised principle of alternate possibilities. But I think that when we accept such statements as valid excuses it is because we assume that we are being told more than the statements strictly and literally convey. We understand the person who offers the excuse to mean that he did what he did *only because* he was unable to do otherwise, or *only because* he had to do it. And we understand him to mean, more particularly, that when he did what he did it was not because that was what he really wanted to do. The principle of alternate possibilities should thus be replaced, in my opinion, by the following principle: a person is not morally responsible for what he has done if he did it only because he could not have done otherwise. This principle does not appear to conflict with the view that moral responsibility is compatible with determinism.

The following may all be true: there were circumstances that made it impossible for a person to avoid doing something; these circumstances actually played a role in bringing it about that he did it, so that it is correct to say that he did it because he could not have done otherwise; the person really wanted to do what he did; he did it because it was what he really wanted to do, so that it is not correct to say that he did what he did only because he could not have done otherwise. Under these conditions, the person may well be morally responsible for what he has done. On the other hand, he will not be morally responsible for what he has done if he did it only because he could not have done otherwise, even if what he did was something he really wanted to do.

Notes

1. The two main concepts employed in the principle of alternate possibilities are "morally responsible" and "could have done otherwise." To discuss the principle without analyzing either of these concepts may well seem like an attempt at piracy. The reader should take notice that my Jolly Roger is now unfurled.

2. After thinking up the example that I am about to develop I learned that Robert Nozick, in lectures given several years ago, had formulated an example of the same general type and had proposed it as a counterexample to the principle of alternate possibilities.

3. The assumption that Black can predict what $Jones_4$ will decide to do does not beg the question of determinism. We can imagine that Jones, has often confronted the alternatives—A and B—that he now confronts, and that his face has invariably twitched when he was about to decide to do A and never when he was about to decide to do B. Knowing this, and observing the twitch, Black would have a basis for prediction. This does, to be sure, suppose that there is some sort of causal relation between $Jones_4$'s state at the time of the twitch and his subsequent states. But any plausible view of decision or of action will allow that reaching a decision and performing an action both involve earlier and later phases, with causal relations between them, and such that the earlier phases are not

themselves part of the decision or of the action. The example does not require that these earlier phases be deterministically related to still earlier events.

4. The example is also flexible enough to allow for the elimination of Black altogether. Anyone who thinks that the effectiveness of the example is undermined by its reliance on a human manipulator, who imposes his will on Jones$_4$, can substitute for Black a machine programmed to do what Black does. If this is still not good enough, forget both Black and the machine and suppose that their role is played by natural forces involving no will or design at all.

8

Incompatibilism and the Avoidability of Blame

Michael Otsuka

In this article I address a topic that is foundational to moral philosophy: that of the conditions that must obtain if human beings are to be worthy of blame for wrongdoing. My ambition is to provide one significant part of the explanation of why no one would be worthy of blame if the universe were causally determined.[1] The most familiar argument for the incompatibility of determinism and blameworthiness can be presented in roughly the following form:

> *Familiar argument for incompatibilism:*
> 1. One is blameworthy for performing an act of a given type only if one could have refrained from performing an act of that type. (I shall call this claim the "Principle of Alternate Possibilities.")[2]
> 2. If determinism is true, then one never could have refrained from performing acts of whatever types that one has performed.
> 3. Therefore, if determinism is true, then one is never blameworthy for performing an act of a given type.

The second premise of this argument is controversial. But I will not discuss it here. Rather, my focus will be on the first premise. The Principle of Alternate Possibilities that constitutes this premise went largely unchallenged before the publication nearly thirty years ago of Harry Frankfurt's "Alternate Possibilities and Moral Responsibility."[3] In that article Frankfurt presented an ingenious counterexample to this principle which, in the opinion of many, presents the most serious challenge to incompatibilism to date. Incompatibilists have responded to Frankfurt's challenge in a variety of ways. Some have tried to show that his example is not a genuine counterexample to the Principle of Alternate Possibilities. I do not pursue this strategy here, since I am inclined to believe that Frankfurt's example *is* a genuine counterexample to this principle. Rather, my strategy is to propose that the Principle of Alternate Possibilities be rejected in favor of a different incompatibilist principle that I call the 'Principle of Avoidable Blame.' This principle can be deployed in an argument for incompatibilism that is closely related to the familiar argument. In Section I, I demonstrate that the Principle of Avoidable Blame is resistant to counterexample of the sort that Frankfurt has shown to embarrass the Principle of Alternate Possibilities. In Section II, I present a positive argument for the Principle of Avoidable Blame that appeals to the relation of blame to the "reactive attitudes" of resentment and indignation. In Section III, I argue against the possibility of blamelessly stumbling into a "moral blind alley" where, contrary to the Principle of Avoidable Blame, one would be blameworthy for whatever one is capable of doing.

I assume throughout that, when we say that X is blameworthy for performing an act of a given type (e.g., for killing Y), we are saying that this person is blameworthy under a given description of what she has done, where this description specifies one of the types of thing that this act was.[4] Often the description under which a person is blameworthy refers to consequences that extend beyond the movements of her body. If, for example, X moved her trigger finger, we might justifiably blame her, not just for doing that, but also for pulling the trigger and for killing Y, where the latter types of act are specified by descriptions that refer to consequences that extend beyond the movements of her body. We might, of course, be justified in blaming X for killing Y even if such a killing was unintended—even if, for example, her only intention was to maim. But in such circumstances X need not be blameworthy under every description of what she has done that refers to an unintended consequence of the moving of her trigger finger. X's alerting her neighbor to her crime by the sound of gunshot involves an unintended consequence. But she is not blameworthy for alerting her neighbor.[5]

I.

Frankfurt's counterexample to the Principle of Alternate Possibilities runs as follow.[6] Suppose an indeterministic world in which people can normally do otherwise. Imagine that somebody in this world named Jones killed an innocent person named Smith, and that he killed him wholeheartedly, with premeditation, for selfish gain, and without any prompting.[7] According to Frankfurt, Jones might be blameworthy for killing Smith even if he could not have refrained from doing so. For we can imagine that Jones could not have refrained for the following reason: had it become clear to somebody named Black (who is an excellent judge of such things) that Jones was about to decide not to kill Smith, then Black would have intervened and forced him to do so.[8] But Black never had "to show his hand because Jones, for reasons of his own, decide[d] to perform, and [did] perform, the very action that Black want[ed] him to perform."[9] Moreover, Jones had no idea that Black would have intervened and forced him to kill Smith if he had not done so on his own. Given the nature of Jones's deed, it is hard to deny that he would have been blameworthy for killing Smith if, ceteris paribus, Black had been altogether absent from the scene and Jones had killed Smith even though he could easily have refrained from doing so and knew that he could have refrained. Moreover, Frankfurt contends that Black's presence should make no difference to whether or not Jones is worthy of blame. Even though Black's presence and his readiness to intervene were sufficient to ensure that Jones could not have refrained from performing an act of the type "killing Smith," this fact does not supply Jones with a legitimate excuse for what he has done. Frankfurt believes that this is so because Black in fact exerted no influence whatsoever on Jones's behavior even though he rendered it impossible for Jones to have refrained from killing Smith.

In the light of this counterexample, I propose that the Principle of Alternate Possibilities be replaced by a different incompatibilist principle— the aforementioned Principle of Avoidable Blame. Unlike the Principle of Alternate Possibilities, the Principle of Avoidable Blame is sensitive to the ethical quality of—that is, one's blameworthiness or blamelessness with respect to—one's alternatives. According to this principle:

> *Principle of Avoidable Blame*: [10] One is blameworthy for performing an act of a given type only if one could instead have behaved in a manner for which one would have been entirely blameless.

To clarify this principle: (1) It merely states a necessary condition, and not a partial definition, of blameworthiness. (2) When I say that one could instead have behaved in a manner for which one would have been entirely blameless, I mean that it was within one's voluntary control whether or not one ended up behaving that way.[11] But I need not claim that the behavior itself must have been voluntary. (3) I argue below that one would instead have been entirely blameless if one had behaved least badly in comparison with all of one's other options.[12] (4) By "entirely blameless," I mean "blameless under any description of what one has done." [13]

The Principle of Avoidable Blame can be deployed in the following revised version of the familiar argument for incompatibilism:

Revised argument for incompatibilism:
1′. One is blameworthy for performing an act of a given type only if one could instead have behaved in a manner for which one would have been entirely blameless (Principle of Avoidable Blame).
2′. If determinism is true, then one never could instead have behaved in a manner for which one would have been entirely blameless.
3. Therefore if determinism is true, then one is never blameworthy for performing an act of a given type.

The revised second premise follows from the conjunction of the second premise of the familiar argument[14] and the following claim: if one is blameworthy for performing an act of a given type, then one could instead have behaved in a manner for which one would have been entirely blameless only if one could have refrained from performing at least one type of act that one has performed. This claim is true for the following reason. Suppose that one is blameworthy for actually performing an act of a given type but would have been entirely blameless in a different scenario. It follows that one would in some respect have behaved less badly in this different scenario. This difference in behavior can be captured in terms of one's having refrained in this different scenario from performing at least one type of act (specified at some level of description) that one actually performed.[15]

Given the above claim, it is a consequence of the Principle of Avoidable Blame that if one is blameworthy for performing an act of a given type, then one must have been able to refrain from performing at least one type of act that one has performed. But unlike the Principle of Alternate Possibilities, the Principle of Avoidable Blame does not impose, as a requirement of blameworthiness for performing an act of a given type, that one have been capable of refraining from performing an act of the given type for which one is worthy of blame. So long as one could instead have been entirely blameless while performing an act of this type, one can be blameworthy for performing, even if one could not have refrained from performing, an act of this type.

Some have defended the Principle of Alternate Possibilities against Frankfurt's counterexample by arguing that Jones is not blameworthy for performing an act of the type "killing Smith *simpliciter*"; rather, he is blameworthy for performing an act of the type "killing Smith on *his own*." And even though Jones could not have refrained from killing Smith, he could have refrained from killing Smith on his own. He could instead have killed Smith as a result of compulsion.[16] This line of defense is controversial, since it is arguable that one needs to draw too fine a distinction in order to maintain that Jones is blameworthy for killing Smith on his own while at the same time denying that he is blameworthy for killing Smith. It is a virtue of the Principle of Avoidable Blame over the Principle of Alternate Possibilities that, even if Jones is blameworthy for killing Smith (and not merely for killing Smith on his own), Frankfurt's example does not refute the Principle of Avoidable Blame. It follows from what I say below that if Jones is indeed blameworthy for killing Smith, then he could have behaved in a manner for which he would have been entirely blameless. Jones could have behaved in such a manner even if Black's presence and readiness to intervene were enough to ensure that Jones could not have refrained from performing an act of the type "killing Smith." Hence delicate questions regarding the precise delineation of the type or types of act that Jones is really worthy of blame for performing—questions whose answers are crucial to a determination of whether Frankfurt's example refutes the Principle of Alternate Possibilities—are irrelevant to an assessment of whether Frankfurt's example refutes the Principle of Avoidable Blame.

I now explain why the Principle of Avoidable Blame is resistant to counterexample of the sort that Frankfurt has deployed against the Principle of Alternate Possibilities.

Frankfurt's counterexample to the Principle of Alternate Possibilities refutes the Principle of Avoidable Blame just in case it is an example in which Jones is blameworthy (under at least one description of what he has actually done) but could not instead have behaved in a manner for which he would have been entirely blameless. In Frankfurt's example Jones would have ended up behaving in a manner for which he would have been entirely blameless if, instead of doing what he did, he had entertained those thoughts that would have led Black to conclude that he was about to decide not to kill Smith. At this point Black would have stepped in and forced Jones to kill Smith. Recall that Frankfurt has suggested that he would have done so by pronouncing a terrible coercive threat, inducing an irresistible impulse by means of hypnosis or potion, or directly manipulating Jones's brain and nervous system. Compatibilists and incompatibilists alike would agree that each of these methods would be sufficient to absolve Jones of blame for killing Smith (and for whatever he would have done under any other level of description).[17] Jones therefore had an entirely blameless alternative.

But this still leaves open the question of whether Jones *could have* behaved in a manner for which he would have been entirely blameless—that is, whether it was within his *voluntary control* that he ended up behaving this way. Frankfurt has proposed that Black's intervention would have been triggered by an involuntary twitch that Jones would have registered if and only if he was about to decide to refrain from killing Smith.[18] We are to suppose that this twitch would have been caused by the sort of thought processes that would always and only have preceded a decision on the part of Jones to refrain from killing Smith.

Now the twitch would have been the result of thought processes over which Jones either had voluntary control or not.

Suppose, on the one hand, that these thought processes are something over which Jones had voluntary control. In this case Frankfurt's example would involve Jones's voluntary control over that which would have led to his doing something for which he would have been entirely blameless. The Principle of Avoidable Blame is therefore unrefuted, since Jones could have behaved in a manner for which he would have been entirely blameless.

Suppose, on the other hand, that Jones lacked voluntary control over the twitch-inducing thought processes that would have preceded any decision to refrain from killing Smith. In this case Jones would not have had voluntary control over whether, instead of doing what he did, he ended up behaving in a manner for which he would have been entirely blameless because of Black's intervention. Hence he could not have behaved in a manner for which he would have been entirely blameless because of Black's intervention.[19] Nevertheless Jones could have behaved less badly without provoking Black's intervention: he could have killed Smith from a nobler motive, or without premeditation, or less wholeheartedly. It follows from what I say in the next section that since Jones could have behaved less badly, he could have behaved in a manner for which he would have been entirely blameless. Hence, the Principle of Avoidable Blame is, once again, unrefuted.[20]

One might try to modify Frankfurt's counterexample to the Principle of Alternate Possibilities so that it is more closely tailored to refute the Principle of Avoidable Blame. I do not think that any such modification would give rise to an example that refutes this latter principle. Suppose once again, for the sake of trying to construct such an example, that Jones killed an innocent person named Smith, and that he killed him wholeheartedly, with premeditation, for selfish gain, and without any prompting. If Black had been entirely absent from the scene, then it would have been within Jones's voluntary control to behave less badly. But, as before, Black is lurking in the background and monitoring Jones's behavior. In order for this example to refute the Principle of Avoidable Blame, the following must be true: had it become clear to Black (who remains an excellent judge of such things) that Jones was about to decide to behave *any less badly* than the manner in which he actually ended up behaving, then Black would have intervened to ensure that Jones ended up behaving no less badly.

It is not clear how such intervention would have succeeded.

If, on the one hand, it would have involved the bringing to bear of pressure on Jones that is supposed to make it inevitable that he end up behaving no less badly, then it would have involved a scenario in which Jones would in fact have behaved less badly, indeed would have been excused from blame, on account of his having been irresistibly pressured into doing something. Each of the aforementioned methods of intervention that Frankfurt has suggested—coercive threat, potion or hypnosis, or direct neural manipulation—would have been sufficient to excuse Jones from blame for what he ended up doing.[21] Less intrusive means of bringing irresistible pressure to bear on Jones would also have been sufficient to excuse him. Suppose, for example, that, had it become clear to Black that Jones was about to decide to behave any less badly, then Black would have stepped in and tempted Jones to do something (that is at least prima facie) wrong and that Jones would not have been able to do other than succumb to this temptation.[22] This may appear to be a case in which Black is able to ensure that Jones behave in a blameworthy fashion. But this appearance is deceptive. When one says that one could not help but succumb to temptation, one typically says something that is not strictly speaking true: such temptation, however great, is rarely literally irresistible. When the temptation is not literally irresistible, we often hold the person blameworthy. But here the person could instead have behaved in a manner for which she would have been entirely blameless, and hence the Principle of Avoidable Blame is not called into question. Only in highly extreme and unusual cases is the temptation to do wrong literally irresistible. Such cases might, for example, involve the prospect of relief from excruciating torment.[23] But in these cases the person is excused on account of the severity of the pressure that was brought to bear.[24] We should therefore be careful not to export our intuitions regarding blame in more ordinary cases to these extraordinary cases.

If, on the other hand, Black's intervention would not have involved the exerting of literally irresistible pressure on Jones, then such intervention could not have ensured that Jones would have ended up behaving no less badly. Hence we do not have a counterexample to the Principle of Avoidable Blame in the absence of intervention that involves irresistible pressure.

Even if one manages to construct an example that overcomes these difficulties, I do not think that such an example would refute the Principle of Avoidable Blame. Let us assume, for the sake of argument, that it is somehow possible to construct an example in which, unbeknownst to Jones and without actually exerting any influence on him, Black (or someone or something else) closed all possibility that Jones have behaved any less badly than he actually behaved. It follows from what I say in the next section that, in this case, Jones would not be worthy of blame for what he has done. He would not be worthy of blame even if he would have been blameworthy if Black (or this other person or thing) had not closed all possibility that Jones have behaved less badly. It therefore follows from what I say in the next section that, contra Frankfurt, the closing of alternate possibilities can make a difference to whether or not someone is worthy of blame even if that person's behavior is entirely unaffected by the closing of these alternatives.

In the next section, I explain why I affirm the Principle of Avoidable Blame. Of particular relevance to the arguments I have advanced in this section, I argue that blaming someone for what she has done is warranted only if she could have behaved less badly and that if she could have behaved less badly, then she could have behaved in a manner for which she would have been entirely blameless. In order to do so, I first distinguish blame from something else that can genuinely be unavoidable and that others have mistaken for blame.

II.

Robert Adams has defended the thesis that one might legitimately be unavoidably blameworthy for one's attitudes, temperament, or character.[25] If such unavoidable blameworthiness for *the way one is* were warranted, then serious doubt would be cast on my thesis that one cannot be unavoidably to blame for *what one has done*. For we would have discovered that it is not a general fact about blame that it can never be both unavoidable and justifiable. I would, however, like to affirm this general fact about blame. I grant that one's arrogance, callousness, ingratitude, tendency toward *Schadenfreude,* and so on, may have been involuntarily formed and may remain beyond one's voluntary control. I also grant that these traits of character are nevertheless properly regarded as vices. According to Adams, the attribution of a vice to somebody can properly be construed as a form of justifiable blame even if the vice is involuntary. Moreover, the blame in question is, as he would describe it, "moral" blame insofar as it is condemnation for a moral failing. I agree with Adams that the attribution of a vice to somebody is the attribution of a bad-making property that is ethical in nature, unlike the nonethical bad-making properties of stupidity, athletic ineptitude, or ugliness. But the attribution of a vice does not necessarily involve blame. For one can properly regard somebody as nasty and cruel while still leaving open the question of whether that person is *blameworthy* for being the way she is. One does not withdraw these attributions of vices on concluding that the person is not to blame for being this way because she is a psychopath who was deprived of oxygen in the womb and severely abused as a child. Even in the light of these findings, she is still nasty and cruel, and these are still vices of character.

When one asks whether someone is blameworthy either for a vice of character or for what she has done, one wants to know whether something more than an attitude of horror, loathing, disgust, or pity, or a policy of avoidance, management, quarantine, or elimination, is called for. One wants to know whether, in addition or instead, a "reactive attitude" of a different sort is warranted. This attitude is aptly described as indignation.[26] I believe, and shall assume, that someone is blameworthy for the way she is or for what she has done if and only if indignation on account of the way she is or what she has done would warranted.[27] In the remainder of this section, I argue that indignation, and therefore blame, that is directed at someone for what she has done is warranted only if she could have behaved less badly.[28] The Principle of Avoidable Blame follows from this claim if we plausibly assume that (at least) one of the ways in which she could have behaved less badly is the least bad way that she could have behaved. She would have been blameless for what she has done if she had behaved in this way, since she could not have behaved less badly than it.

According to Peter Strawson: "If someone treads on my hand accidentally, while trying to help me, the pain may be no less acute than if he treads on it in contemptuous disregard of my existence or with a malevolent wish to injure me. But I shall generally feel in the second case a kind and degree of resentment that I shall not feel in the first."[29] I would qualify this observation by adding that indignation (of this personal sort) would be warranted in the second case only if the person did what he did even though he could have behaved less badly. Moreover, indignation would be warranted in the first case if the person, while wishing me no ill, had exercised far less caution than he could and should have. Any indignation should dissipate, not only if I discover that he trod on my hand accidentally while exercising due caution, but also if I discover that he did so malevolently, or in contemptuous disregard, but could not have behaved any less badly. A person would be worthy of indignation for malevolently inflicting pain only if such infliction was gratuitous—not in the sense that it was done for no reason (he could well have had ample selfish or malevolent reason), but—in the or sense that it was an expression of the agency of someone who was free, and knew (or ought to have known) that he was free, to behave less badly instead. It is the fact that such a person behaved so badly even though he knew (or ought to have known) that he didn't have to that makes his behavior galling and hence worthy of indignation.[30]

Take any imagined pair of individuals who have behaved badly (e.g., who have maliciously injured another) and hold everything constant except for the fact that the one could have behaved less badly, and knew that she could have, whereas the other could not have behaved less badly. The fact that the one person behaved as badly as she did even though she knew that she didn't have to provides sufficient grounds for indignation in her case that are lacking in the second case. Moreover, there are no other grounds that are sufficient for indignation in this second case. Such grounds are lacking no matter how malevolent or otherwise vicious this person might have been. But, one might ask, what if the second individual possessed the justified (but false) belief that she could have behaved less badly but nevertheless chose to behave badly in spite of this belief? Suppose that she could not have behaved less badly because everything about her was causally determined (assuming that determinism renders it impossible to have behaved less badly), but she didn't know this fact and didn't think for a minute that she had no option but to injure this person maliciously. Is it so clear that she is not to blame for what she has done just because (astonished as she would be to hear it) she could not actually have behaved any less badly?[31] Although I acknowledge the skeptical force of this question, I do not think she is to blame. One's knowledge that someone justifiably (albeit falsely) believes that she could instead have behaved less badly is not enough to justify indignation. The offense must genuinely be gratuitous in the sense offered in the previous paragraph, and not merely believed by the offender to be gratuitous. "How dare you treat me this badly when you didn't have to, and you knew you didn't have to." This objection carries force and provides grounds for indignation. But a victim is not entitled to such an objection when she knows that the aggressor was causally determined or otherwise incapable of behaving less badly. Rather, the most she is entitled to say is: "I realize that you could not have behaved any less badly. But how dare you treat me this badly when you had the justified but false belief that you didn't have to." This accusation lacks force.

We would, of course, have every reason to attribute a vicious character to this person who could neither have behaved less badly nor have been any better because everything about her was causally determined. She is a worse person for injuring another in spite of her belief that she didn't have to than she would have been if she injured others only when she believed that she could not help but do so. In holding her blameless both for her actions and for her character, I do not obliterate an important ethically relevant difference between the following two sorts of causally determined individuals: (1) someone who knew the difference between right and wrong and who possessed a general ability to control her actions but who wholeheartedly injured somebody else for the sadistic thrill of it in circumstances (which were unavoidable) in which she could not have behaved any less badly, and (2) someone who inflicted an equally severe injury on another as the result of something outside the boundaries of her rational agency (e.g., a seizure, an obsessive/compulsive disorder, or a slip and a fall). One might be tempted to say that this difference involves a difference in the blameworthiness of the person. One might argue that in the first case we are justified in blaming the person for what she did, since it was an act which flowed from a vicious character, and she wholeheartedly identified with both the act and the character from which it arose;[32] whereas, in the second case, the person is not to blame. Blame in the second case should be attributed, not to the person, but rather to her pathology or to her body qua physical object. But here one is employing a different and familiar nonmoral sense of blame—that of merely causal responsibility, which is the same sense we employ when we blame the faulty wiring for starting the fire. When that which irresistibly moves an agent to act is a vice of character with which (again, irresistibly) she identifies, it is easy to see how the attribution of causal responsibility might take on moral tones. But the morally relevant difference between the two cases is not a difference in moral blameworthiness. Rather the difference lies in the fact that the behavior was a manifestation of a vicious character in the one case but not the other. But, again, the presence or absence of a vicious character, even one that is causally efficacious, need not imply a difference in blameworthiness even if it implies a difference that is of an ethical nature.

III.

The Principle of Avoidable Blame has implications that reach beyond the problem of free will. It rules out predicaments in which a person is unavoidably blameworthy even though the freedom of her will is not at issue. It rules out a predicament in which a fully competent, undeceived, and strong-willed adult who has the ability and opportunity autonomously to perform any of a diverse range of activities faultlessly stumbles into a "moral blind alley" where each option is so ghastly, tragic, or otherwise unacceptable that she would be worthy of blame for performing it.[33] On some interpretations of the myth, Agamemnon is alleged to be blameworthy for sacrificing his daughter even though he would have been blameworthy if instead he had exercised his only other option of abandoning his responsibilities as the commander of his fleet. Yet Agamemnon's alleged unfreedom from unavoidable blameworthiness has nothing to do with the freedom of his will. The alleged unfreedom from unavoidable blameworthiness featured in many modern versions of moral blind alleys also has nothing to do with freedom of the will. One who must, for example, lie in order to maintain the secrecy of that which a friend has told one in strict confidence, or who must abandon a dependent mother in order to join the Resistance, or who must kill an innocent in order to prevent many more innocents from being killed, is not necessarily afflicted with any impairment of powers of agency that leaves untouched those who do not find themselves in such binds.

Since the Principle of Avoidable Blame cannot coexist with moral blind alleys, I would like in this section to cast doubt on the existence of the latter.

In making the case for moral blind alleys, philosophers often point to cases in which feelings of guilt for certain things that are unavoidable and outside of one's control appear to be justified. One cannot, however, always slide from claims about the justifiability of unavoidable guilt to claims about the justifiability of unavoidable blame. The following three cases illustrate this point.

1. One can feel guilt over the fact that one has survived and flourished even though others no less virtuous have suffered enormously. This guilt need not be over any failure to divest oneself of unjust riches. Rather, it might be traced to nothing other than the justified conviction that one is utterly undeserving of the good fortune that makes one's life much better than the lives of others who are utterly undeserving of their bad fortune. This guilt is not necessarily irrational; one really does not deserve one's good fortune. It would, however, be irrational to think that one must somehow be to blame for one's good fortune.[34]

2. It is also not necessarily irrational to feel guilt over the unforeseeable harm one has caused through one's actions. Imagine that I instruct a casual friend to switch to a later flight because it will be more convenient for me to pick her up from the airport after rush-hour traffic has thinned out. She switches, and it crashes. Here I will undoubtedly feel guilt owing to the fact that a free action of mine figured in the immediate causal chain leading to my friend's death. So long as my guilt is not entirely a reflection of feelings that I am *to blame* for what I have done, it should not immediately be dismissed as

irrational. Nevertheless, it is significant that, even though many believe that it would be perfectly natural for me to feel guilt, no reasonable person would think it justifiable to blame me.

3. Similar sorts of things can be said about the guilt one might feel over a choice that one has made even when, through no fault of one's own, every other available choice was as bad or worse. Many of the moral dilemmas discussed in the literature involve cases in which it is difficult for one to tell whether what one did was the best one could have done in a bad situation. It is easy to see how one might feel guilt in the face of such epistemic uncertainty, for here one can doubt that one has done the right thing. A better case for the opponent of the Principle of Avoidable Blame is one in which there is no question that one has done the right thing but nevertheless one feels guilt over what one has done. I am to imagine that I am the bystander at Judith Thomson's switch who has turned Philippa Foot's runaway trolley onto the one stranger instead of letting it run over five other strangers. If I were to come across the grief-stricken family of the one whom I killed, I am fairly certain that I would suffer feelings of guilt that would survive the thought that what I did was perfectly justifiable. Once again, such guilt, however natural and understandable, does not translate into the justified belief that I am to blame for what I have done.

An opponent of the Principle of Avoidable Blame might nevertheless insist that this principle should be rejected on the ground that its acceptance implies the repudiation of the undeniable fact of moral luck, by which one's degree of praise or blame may depend on factors beyond one's control. This objection can be met, since affirmation of the Principle of Avoidable Blame does not imply the wholesale repudiation of moral luck. The Principle of Avoidable Blame requires that whether or not one is blameworthy at all for what one has done be under one's control. But it does not require that the *degree* of one's blameworthiness be completely under one's control. It is consistent with this principle that one be more blameworthy if one's attempt at murder succeeds than if it fails, or if one's drunken driving results in the death of a pedestrian rather than not, even if luck is the only thing that makes the difference between one's killing someone or not.[35] In these cases, even though the degree of one's blameworthiness for one's actions may differ depending on external circumstances, whether or not one attempts murder or drinks and drives is still up to oneself. Hence, one could have behaved in a manner for which one would have been entirely blameless.

Evidence of moral luck is very strong in some cases, but not, I believe, in cases in which circumstances beyond one's control would make one unavoidably worthy of blame for what one has done. Consider the following case in which whether or not one is blameworthy *at all* partially depends on factors beyond one's control. Suppose that one would have become a Nazi collaborator rather than the innocent grocer that one is if one's parents had not emigrated from France to New York in 1938. I believe that one would have been worthy of blame for collaborating in France only if such collaboration were avoidable. Hence, this case does not cast doubt on the Principle of Avoidable Blame.

More troubling to my thesis are cases of the following sort: those in which it seems that one is morally compelled to take a risky course of action but in which one would also be worthy of blame if this gamble fails. One reaches the point, for example, at which it seems that one has no choice but to send in the commandos to try to free the hostages. Yet it also seems that one would be worthy of blame if the raid fails and all the hostages are killed (even though one would be worthy of praise if it succeeds). Thomas Nagel writes: "It is tempting in all such cases to feel that some decision must be possible, in the light of what is known at the time, which will make reproach unsuitable no matter how things turn out. But this is not true; when someone acts in such ways he takes his life, or his moral position, into his hands, because how things turn out determines what he has done." [36] A suppressed premise of Nagel's argument is that sometimes one has no viable option but to take such moral gambles. Contrary to Nagel, I maintain that if one believes that someone is blameworthy for taking a gamble that has failed, then one is committed to the claim that this person ought to have refrained from taking this gamble. She should have refrained, not given the knowledge of hindsight, but given the facts available to her at the time of her decision. But it is surely incorrect to maintain of every gamble that fails that it should not have been wagered, given the facts available at the time of the decision. If, however, one believes that, given the facts available at the time, she *ought* to have chosen to take a certain gamble, then the fact that this gamble is obligatory immunizes the gambler from blame for any bad consequences that ensue. I believe that the same holds for morally permissible but nonobligatory gambles. [37]

IV.

I hope through my articulation and defense of the Principle of Avoidable Blame to have identified and verified the authenticity of an overlooked but reputable source of the undeniable appeal of the claim that determinism is incompatible with blameworthiness.

Notes

I thank the following people who read and provided commentary on earlier drafts: R. Albritton, T. Burge, F. Bruno, G. A. Cohen, M. Della Rocca, C. Dingman, J. M. Fischer, S. Foran, T. Hall, S. Hansen-Castro, B. Herman, A. Hsü, S. L. Hurley, M. Lange, M. Mc- Kenna, A. Rajczi, S. Shiffrin, J. Tannenbaum, M. Thau, K. Vihvelin, G. Watson,

R. Wedgwood, an anonymous referee for and two anonymous editors of *Ethics*, and especially David Copp. I have also profited from discussion with members of the Law and Philosophy Discussion Group and those who attended talks at Yale; the University of California, Santa Barbara; the University of California, Irvine; the University of California, Davis; and the University of Colorado at Boulder.

1. I understand causal determinism to be the claim that "the prevailing laws of nature are such that there do not exist any two possible worlds which are exactly alike up to some time, which differ thereafter, and in which those laws are never violated." Here I follow David Lewis, "Causation," *Journal of Philosophy* 70 (1973): 556–67, 559.

2. Here I follow Harry Frankfurt's nomenclature. This claim is a narrower version of, and implied by, Frankfurt's unrevised version of the Principle of Alternate Possibilities, according to which one is *morally responsible* for performing an act of a given type only if one could have refrained from performing an act of that type. See Frankfurt, "Alternate possibilities and moral responsibility," *Journal of Philosophy* 66 (1969): 829–39. In Frankfurt's version, the requirement also applies to acts for which one is worthy of praise and those acts for which one is held morally accountable even though neither praise nor blame is appropriate (e.g., the signing of a contract that accompanies purchases made by credit card). In this article I limit myself to a discussion of acts for which one is blameworthy.

3. Ibid.

4. Here I follow Elizabeth Anscombe, who introduced the locution of an act's being intentional under one description but unintentional under another. She has also written of being obliged to do something under one description but not obliged under another. See Anscombe, *Intention* (Oxford: Blackwell, 1957), 11, and "'Under a description,'" *Noûs* 13 (1979): 219–33.

5. I believe that when X moves her trigger finger, she performs a single act of indefinitely many types (e.g., pulling the trigger, firing a bullet, killing Smith, killing a human being, killing before breakfast, alerting her neighbor, etc.) rather than many distinct acts of these different types. But nothing of substance in this article hangs on the correctness of the former rather than the latter view regarding the individuation of acts. I could reformulate, without diminishing the strength of, my argument in terms of this latter view.

6. Frankfurt credits Nozick for having made a similar point in earlier unpublished lectures. See Frankfurt, "Alternate possibilities," 835, n. 2. John Locke presented a similar counterexample to the claim that voluntariness requires ability to do otherwise. See Locke, *Essay Concerning Human Understanding*, bk. 2, chap. 21, sec. 10.

7. I have taken the liberty of adding a bit of detail to the example. Frankfurt does not himself specify the nature of Jones's deed.

8. Frankfurt proposes that we let "Black pronounce a terrible threat" and thereby coerce Jones into killing Smith. To those who maintain that it is impossible by such means literally to render it impossible that someone refrain from performing an action, Frankfurt proposes that we let "Black give Jones a potion, or put him under hypnosis, and in some such way as these generate in Jones an irresistible inner compulsion to perform the act Black wants performed and to avoid others. Or let Black manipulate the minute processes of Jones's brain and nervous system... so that causal forces running in and out of his synapses and along the poor man's nerves determine that he chooses to act and that he does act in the one way and not in any other" (Frankfurt, "Alternate

possibilities," 835–36). To those who maintain that such neural manipulation is not compatible with agency on the part of Jones, we can imagine, on Frankfurt's behalf, that Black is an omnipotent being who has the power to impose deterministic laws of physics that make it inevitable that Jones kill Smith. Frankfurt's opponent would not want to deny the compatibility of determinism and action, for such a denial would beg the question against Frankfurt, since then, a fortiori, determinism would have to be false for there to be action for which one could be blameworthy.

9. Ibid, 836.

10. A note on nomenclature: like the Principle of Alternate Possibilities, the Principle of Avoidable Blame states that the presence of an alternate possibility is a necessary condition of blameworthiness. Were it not for the fact that the Principle of Alternate Possibilities is already so well known by that name, I would have given it a name that differentiates it from the Principle of Avoidable Blame and subsumed both it and the Principle of Avoidable Blame under a genus by the name of 'Principles of Alternate Possibilities.'

11. Suppose that someone would have behaved in a manner for which she would have been entirely blameless if and only if she had had a totally unexpected, involuntary, and incapacitating seizure. Suppose that she could have had such a seizure insofar as this was a physiologically live possibility. There is perhaps a sense in which she could have behaved in a manner for which she would have been entirely blameless. But for the purpose of interpreting the Principle of Avoidable Blame, she could not have so behaved.

12. As I shall define the notion of "behaving less badly," one would behave less badly by X-ing rather than Y-ing if and only if, given one's factual knowledge of one's circumstances, one would have stronger moral reason to X rather than Y if one could do either. In order to determine the strength of one's moral reasons, one must consider such familiar morally relevant factors as the expected harmfulness of one's behavior, the extent to which such behavior would come into conflict with one's duties and obligations, the nature of one's intentions, one's motives, and so forth.

13. One further qualification: even if one found oneself in a predicament in which one is worthy of blame for what one has done and would have been worthy of blame for whatever else one could have done in this predicament, one nevertheless could have behaved in a manner for which one would have been entirely blameless if one landed in this predicament as the result of a previous choice for which one is worthy of blame. For example: one found oneself in a predicament in which one could not have prevented one's car from barreling through a crosswalk filled with schoolchildren. But one landed in this predicament because of a previous choice for which one is blameworthy to drive far in excess of the posted speed limit. The Principle of Avoidable Blame also applies to this previous choice: one is blameworthy for it only if one could instead have behaved in a manner for which one would have been entirely blameless.

14. Recall that this premise states that if determinism is true, then one never could have refrained from performing acts of whatever types that one has performed.

15. I am indebted to David Copp for the ideas in this paragraph.

16. Margery Bedford Naylor offers this criticism of Frankfurt's counterexample in "Frankfurt on the principle of alternate possibilities," *Philosophical Studies* 46 (1984): 249–58.

17. More precisely, they would agree if this claim is qualified in the manner indicated in n. 24 below.

18. Frankfurt, "Alternate possibilities," 835, n. 3.

19. See n. 11 above and accompanying text.

20. If, however, Jones could neither have behaved less badly in any fashion that would not have provoked Black's intervention nor have entertained those thoughts that would have triggered Black's intervention, then Frankfurt is not entitled to the claim that Jones is blameworthy for killing Smith. Such a claim would beg the question against the incompatibilist, since in this case Jones could not have done otherwise in any possibly morally relevant respect even if Black had been entirely absent from the scene.

21. It would make no difference if Black were replaced by an imperceptible, impenetrable "force field" that happens to contour itself perfectly to all of Jones's actual thoughts, choices, and actions without influencing them at all. It might appear that this force field rendered it impossible for Jones to have refrained from doing anything that he did and hence that it rendered it impossible for Jones to have behaved any less badly than he did. This appearance is deceptive since Jones could, instead of acting independently of the force field, have voluntarily (but unintentionally) run up against this field and consequently have been irresistibly forced to kill Smith. Hence, even though he is blameworthy (under at least one description of what he has actually done), he could have behaved in a manner for which he would, as the result of such force, have been entirely blameless. (I thank an anonymous referee for drawing my attention to this case.)

22. I am indebted to John Campbell for this example.

23. We can imagine that someone presents a heroin addict in the throes of withdrawal with the easy opportunity to steal some heroin from its rightful owner.

24. In cases in which one succumbs to temptation or other pressures that irresistibly move one to act, Frankfurt maintains that one is not blameworthy if one unwillingly succumbs but that one may be blameworthy if one willingly succumbs to this irresistible pressure. See Harry Frankfurt, "Freedom of the will and the concept of a person," *Journal of Philosophy* 68 (1971): 5–20, esp. sec. 4. I maintain that one is not blameworthy for anything at all in the latter case if one had no blameless alternative to willingly succumbing to this pressure (and was not at fault for having no such alternative). I stipulate, in the cases under discussion, that if one willingly succumbed to the irresistible pressure, then both the willingness and the succumbing were made irresistible by this pressure.

25. Robert Adams, "Involuntary sins," *Philosophical Review* 94 (1985): 3–31, 21–24.

26. Here I follow Peter Strawson, who regards indignation and resentment as impersonal and personal versions of the same attitude. On his account, indignation in response to the actions of others is a reaction "to the quality of others' wills, not towards ourselves, but towards others." Resentment, by contrast, is a reaction to the qualities of others' wills toward ourselves. Indignation is therefore the "vicarious analogue of resentment"; it is, in other words, "resentment on behalf of another, where one's own interest and dignity are not involved." See Strawson, "Freedom and resentment," *Proceedings of the British Academy* 48 (1962): 187–211, 199–200. I shall employ the term 'indignation' to encompass resentment as well as its impersonal analogue. (Strawson himself notes that his own restriction of 'indignation' to the impersonal is artificial, since "one can feel indignation on one's own account," and this is just another name for resentment [ibid., 200].)

27. Compare Allan Gibbard: "An observer thinks an act *blameworthy* ... if and only if he thinks it rational for the agent to feel guilty over the act, and for others to resent the agent for it" (Gibbard, *Wise Choices, Apt Feelings* [Cambridge, MA: Harvard University Press, 1990], 47).

28. I also affirm the analogous claim that indignation, and therefore blame, that is directed at someone for the way she is (i.e., for her character) would be warranted only if she could have had a better character.

29. Strawson, 191.

30. But if the cost of behaving less badly was so high that it would have been supererogatory to do so, then indignation is not warranted. I shall set this possibility aside in the following discussion.

31. Here I paraphrase an objection that Rogers Albritton has offered in correspondence with me. Albritton believes that the Principle of Avoidable Blame is more plausible in cases (unlike the above) in which someone saw no alternative to doing what she did that was less bad and was not at fault either for not seeing any such alternative or for there not being any (if indeed there was none).

32. Compare Frankfurt, "Freedom of the will and the concept of a person."

33. The phrase 'moral blind alley' is Thomas Nagel's. See Nagel, "War and massacre," *Philosophy and Public Affairs* 1 (1972): 123–44, 143–44.

34. Compare Herbert Morris, "Nonmoral guilt," in *Responsibility, Character, and the Emotions,* ed. Ferdinand Schoeman (New York: Cambridge University Press, 1987), 220–40, esp. 236–37.

35. These examples and those that I discuss below were drawn from or inspired by Nagel. See Thomas Nagel, "Moral luck," in his *Mortal Questions* (New York: Cambridge University Press, 1979), 24–38.

36. Ibid., 29–30.

37. More difficult are cases in which one cannot tell, at the time of choosing, whether the gamble is impermissible, permissible, or obligatory. I believe that in these cases the uncertainty should transfer to an assessment of blameworthiness in the event that the gamble turns out a failure.

9

Free Will Demystified: A Dispositional Account

Kadri Vihvelin

We believe that free will is or includes the ability to make choices on the basis of reasons, an ability that can be exercised in more than one way. You chose ice cream, but you could have had an apple instead. You chose to speak, but you could have remained silent. You chose selfishly, but you could have chosen to do the right thing, for the right reason.

From this common-sense belief about free will it is often only a short step to the incompatibilist view that free will requires the falsity of determinism. The short step consists in what looks like a natural way of spelling out what we mean when we say things like: "You didn't have to eat the ice cream; you could have chosen the apple." We mean, "You could have chosen the apple, *given the way things were right up to the point at which you chose the ice cream.*"

This short step is so natural that it's often thought to be part of common sense. But here is another short step (and this one will take us all the way): Part of what we mean when we say, "You could have chosen the apple," is: "Your choosing the apple is possible, given the laws of nature." If we add this assumption, then what we mean when we say, "You could have chosen the apple," is: "You could have chosen the apple, *given the laws and the past until just before you chose the ice cream.*" But if we grant this assumption, we have granted the key premise in the following argument for incompatibilism:

1. We have free will only if we can choose otherwise.
2. We can choose otherwise only if we can choose otherwise, *given the laws and the past until just before our choice.*
3. If determinism is true, we can *never* choose otherwise, given the laws and the past until just before our choice.
4. Therefore, if determinism is true, we can never choose otherwise.
5. Therefore, if determinism is true, we have no free will.

Since the key premise (2) is based on a claim about the meaning of 'can,' I will call this the "Meaning Argument" for incompatibilism. So far as I know, no incompatibilist has *officially and explicitly* argued for incompatibilism in this way. However, one often finds something like this argument lurking just below the surface of a philosopher's explicit argument for incompatibilism. I suspect that something like this argument is the real reason many people, including many philosophers, are incompatibilists.

Since the argument is deductively valid and premise 3 is entailed by the definition of determinism, there are only two ways to resist the conclusion of the argument—by rejecting premise 1 or by rejecting premise 2. I accept premise 1; that is, I agree that free will entails the ability to choose, and I agree that someone with the ability to choose must be able to choose otherwise. But I reject premise 2 and therefore reject the conclusion.

But how can I reject premise 2? Isn't it just *obvious* that what we mean when we say "You could have chosen the apple instead" is, "You could have chosen it given the laws and given all the facts about the past until just before your choice"?

I agree that it is easy to talk ourselves into accepting premise 2.[1] But if we accept premise 2, then we must accept incompatibilism. And incompatibilism is not so easy to accept. So we even if we are tempted to accept premise 2, we should not be too quick to accept it.

'Can,' like 'must,' can be used in many different ways. Sometimes when we say "I can do X," we mean that our doing X is morally permissible, sometimes we mean that it's technologically possible, sometimes we mean that it's physically possible. And so on. But that doesn't mean that 'can' is multiply ambiguous or that it changes meaning from context to context. As David Lewis has observed, 'can' has always and everywhere one meaning.[2] When we say "I can do X," we are saying that our doing X is compossible with certain other facts F. What varies—depending on the intentions of the speaker, the context of utterance, or some combination of the two—is what facts F are relevant. Thus, when we say that doing X is morally permissible, we mean that doing X is compossible with facts about what's morally permitted; when we say that doing X is physically possible we mean that doing X is compossible with facts about the laws, and so on. The 'can' relevant to free will is the 'can' that we have in mind in contexts in which we raise questions about moral responsibility, and, in particular, contexts in which we raise questions about the justification of choices and the evaluation of agents on the basis of their choices. We hold someone morally responsible for what she does only if we believe that she has free will, and we believe that someone has free will only if we believe that she has the ability to make choices on the basis of reasons. This suggests the following proposal: In these contexts, the relevant facts F are facts about the person's ability to choose for reasons. That is, when we say that someone could have chosen otherwise in contexts where questions of moral responsibility are being discussed, we mean that she could have chosen otherwise given the facts about her ability to choose on the basis of reasons. She in fact chose X, but she had "what it takes" to choose Y instead.[3]

Note that this proposal is neutral with respect to the debate between compatibilists and incompatiblists. The incompatibilist can argue that if determinism is true, then no person ever has the *genuine ability* (as opposed to some inferior, merely apparent "ability") to make choices on the basis of reasons. After all, the ability to make choices for reasons is an ability that can be exercised in more than one way, the incompatibilist might argue, and if determinism is true, then what actually happens is the only thing that can happen, thus no one can ever make any "choice" other than the "choice" she actually makes. So the proposal that the relevant facts F are facts about the ability to choose on the basis of reasons does not beg the question in favor of compatibilism. Nor do I offer it as a defense of compatibilism.

However, I do propose the following way of defending compatibilism. We have the ability to choose on the basis of reasons by having a bundle of capacities which differ in complexity but not in kind from the capacities of things like thermostats, cars, and computers. These capacities are either dispositions or bundles of dispositions, differing in complexity but not in kind from dispositions like fragility and solubility. So my view is that to have free will is to have a bundle of dispositions. Note that I do not say that to have free will is to "just have a disposition." To say this is to oversimplify free will in a crucial way.

Let's give a name to this proposal and define it as follows:

FWBD: To have free will is to have the ability to make choices on the basis of reasons and to have this ability is to have a bundle of dispositions.

If FWBD is true, then compatibilism is also true. For no one denies that dispositions are compatible with determinism. Indeed, it is precisely because dispositions are uncontroversially compatible with determinism that it has seemed obvious to some people that FWBD *cannot* be true. Despite this, I believe that FWBD is true. And I believe that compatibilists should accept FWBD.

FWBD consists of two claims—the claim that free will is the ability to make choices on the basis of reasons and the claim that we have this ability by having a bundle of dispositions. I take the first claim to be uncontroversial; insofar as there is any agreement about what free will is, it is agreement about this. It is the second claim that is controversial. Part of the controversy stems from controversy about the nature of reasons in general and practical reasoning in particular. In what follows, I hope to sidestep this controversy as much as possible. For disagreements about the nature of reasons and reasoning cut across the compatibilist/incompatibilist divide and there are objections to FWBD that have nothing to do with worries specific to reasons and reasoning.

Before we consider the objections, let's begin by noting some similarities between dispositions (of objects and persons) and the abilities of persons.

Dispositions and abilities

We believe that objects have dispositions (tendencies, causal powers, capacities). A lump of sugar is soluble. Coffee has the power to dissolve sugar. A rubber band is elastic. A thermostat has the capacity to regulate heat. We have empirical knowledge of the dispositions of objects, and we rely on this knowledge in our dealings with things. Avoid drinking arsenic; pack crystal carefully. In relying on this knowledge, we assume that dispositions are relatively stable characteristics of things that typically continue to exist even when they are not manifested. We also believe that something with the disposition to X *can* X even during times that it is not X-ing and even if it never X-s. A fragile glass is a glass that is liable to break; that is, it is a glass that *can* break, even if it never does.

We also believe that persons have dispositions (tendencies, causal powers, capacities). Some people are color-blind; others have normal color-vision; a lucky few can discriminate shades and hues the rest of us cannot see. Some people can understand French; others can't. Some people are easygoing, others are more easily provoked, and some are hot-tempered. We have empirical knowledge of the dispositions of persons, and we rely on this knowledge in our dealings with persons. Don't provoke Joe, especially when he's been drinking. If you need a cool head in a tough spot, you can count on Mary. In relying on this knowledge, we assume that dispositions are relatively stable features of persons that typically continue to exist even when they are not manifested. We also believe that if a person has a disposition then he *can* manifest it even when he is not doing so. Suppose that Joe quits drinking and learns to control his temper. He may still be disposed to lose his temper; insofar as we believe that this is true, we believe that he is someone who *can* lose his temper, even if he never does.

Philosophers don't dispute these common-sense claims. The philosophical questions concern the proper analysis of dispositions; not whether we speak truly when we say that objects and persons have dispositions.

We also believe that persons have abilities (or, as some philosophers prefer to say, "powers" or "agent-causal powers"). Here are some examples: the ability to speak French, to sing in tune, to do mental arithmetic, to take charge of situations and direct others, to deliberate for the purpose of figuring out what to do.[4]

There are some striking similarities between abilities and dispositions. We have empirical knowledge of both. Abilities, like dispositions, don't typically pop into existence only on the occasion of their exercise or manifestation. Nor do they go out of existence simply because a person is not exercising them. A person may lose her ability to speak French if she doesn't speak French for many years, but she does not lose this ability every time she stops speaking French. Finally, abilities, like dispositions, entail the corresponding 'can' claim. Someone with the ability to play piano is someone who can play piano even when she's not playing it; someone with the ability to speak French can speak French even when she's speaking English instead.

I think these similarities between abilities and dispositions are no coincidence. I think that these similarities exist because ABD is true:

> ABD: To have an ability is to have a disposition or a bundle of dispositions.

If ABD is true, this provides support for FWBD, since the ability to choose for reasons is just a special case of an ability. If other abilities, including mental abilities like the ability to add numbers in one's head and the ability to deliberate for the purpose of figuring out what to do, are dispositions or bundles of dispositions, then it's hard to see why we should deny that the ability to choose for reasons is a disposition or bundle of dispositions.

Is ABD true? Some say it isn't. Here, for instance, is Peter van Inwagen:

> For a man to have the capacity to understand French is for him to be such that if he were placed in certain circumstances, which wouldn't be very hard to delimit, and if he were to hear French spoken, then, willy-nilly, he would understand what was being said. But if a man can speak French, then it certainly does not follow that there are any circumstances in which he would, willy-nilly, speak French. The concept of a causal power or capacity would seem to be the concept of an invariable disposition to react to certain determinate changes in the environment in certain determinate ways, whereas the concept of an agent's power to act would seem not to be the concept of a power that is dispositional or reactive, but rather the concept of a power to *originate* changes in the environment.[5]

Van Inwagen appears to be claiming that the concept of an agent's ability ("power") is different from the concept of a disposition ("capacity") in the following way: the concept of a disposition is the concept of something that is compatible with determinism whereas the concept of an agent's ability is the concept of something that is incompatible with determinism—the ability to originate changes in the environment. If van Inwagen is right, and if determinism is true (or close enough to being true), then our common-sense beliefs about the abilities of agents are all mistaken.

Suppose that van Inwagen is wrong and ABD and FWBD are both true. If so, then we have the makings for a very robust compatibilism. In particular, we can respond to the charge that determinism robs us of free will by robbing us of the ability to choose and/or do otherwise by arguing as follows:

1. Dispositions are compatible with determinism.
2. Abilities are dispositions or bundles of dispositions. (ABD)
3. Therefore, the existence of abilities is compatible with determinism.

4. Free will is the ability to choose on the basis of reasons and we have this ability by having a bundle of dispositions. (FWBD)
5. Therefore free will (the ability to choose on the basis of reasons) is compatible with determinism.
6. Abilities (like other dispositions) typically continue to exist even when they are not being exercised or manifested.
7. Therefore, determinism is compatible with the existence of unexercised abilities, including the ability to choose on the basis of reasons.
8. Abilities are like dispositions with respect to the entailment from the claim that a person has the ability (disposition) to do X to the claim that the person can do X.
9. Therefore, determinism is compatible with the truth of the claim that persons can choose and do other than what they actually choose and do.

And if ABD and FWBD are true, then the compatibilist has what she needs to answer the argument for incompatibilism that is the most influential one these days—van Inwagen's Consequence Argument.[6]

The Consequence Argument goes something like this. Suppose, for the sake of argument that determinism is true. If so, there is some proposition P which is the conjunction of the laws of nature and facts about the remote past such that P entails every true proposition about the future, including propositions about my choices and actions. I cannot do anything that would make it false that P (since I lack causal power over the laws and the past). I cannot do anything that would make it false that P entails that I will choose and do what I will in fact do (since this entailment is a necessary truth and I lack the ability to bring it about that any necessarily true proposition is false). Therefore, I can neither choose nor do *anything* other than what I in fact choose and do.

But if our abilities, including the ability to choose on the basis of reasons, are dispositions, the conclusion of the Consequence Argument is false. Suppose that I am asked to raise my hand if I want to vote yes. I refrain from raising my hand. Assume normal circumstances—no broken bones, pathologies, or nefarious neurosurgeons manipulating my limbs or brain states. Could I have raised my hand? Yes, because my ability to raise my hand is one of my dispositions and my dispositions don't cease to exist *merely* because I am not exercising them. Could I have *chosen* to raise my hand? Yes. But note that there are two possible ways in which this might be true. I might have kept my hand down without going through any kind of reasoning process, perhaps without thinking about the matter at all. Even so, my ability to choose for reasons is one of my dispositions, and my dispositions don't cease to exist *merely* because I am not exercising them. On the other hand, I might have thought it over, and decided, for what seemed to me good reasons, to refrain from raising my hand. In that case, I exercised my ability to choose for reasons. But just as a malleable object that is bent can be bent in more than one way, the disposition to choose for reasons is a disposition that can be exercised in more than one way. So even though I in fact manifested my disposition to choose for reasons by choosing not to raise my hand, I could have manifested the very same disposition by choosing to raise my hand. The truth of determinism is not relevant to any of this. Therefore, even if the premises of the Consequence Argument are true, the conclusion is false.

So here are the makings for a compatibilist program. Why isn't anyone working on it?

There is a historical explanation.

Brief history

At one time, the debate between compatibilists and incompatibilists about free will and determinism was widely believed to turn on the question of whether 'could have done otherwise' is "categorical" or can be given a "hypothetical" or "conditional" analysis. Compatibilists argued that when we say things like "he could have done otherwise" (in contexts where questions of justification of action and moral responsibility are at stake), we mean something like "if he had wanted (or chosen, decided, willed, intended, or tried) to do otherwise, he would have done otherwise." This idea can be traced as far back as Hobbes and Hume, but it was first clearly proposed and defended by G. E. Moore,[7] who remarked that while in one sense of 'can' no one can do otherwise if determinism is true, in another sense—the sense in which a cat can climb a tree but a dog can't—we can often do otherwise even if determinism is true. Moore then proposed that this other sense of 'can' is equivalent in meaning to a conditional; he suggested that what we mean, when we say, "I could have done otherwise" is just "if I had chosen to do otherwise, I would have done otherwise."

What has not been noted is that Moore made two distinct and distinguishable proposals: The first was the proposal that the 'can' relevant to questions of free will and moral responsibility—let's call this "the agent ability 'can'"—is a kind of capacity or disposition, to be understood the same kind of way we understand capacities like the cat's capacity to climb a tree or a ship's capacity to steam twenty knots. The second was the proposal that the 'can' relevant to free will and moral responsibility is equivalent in meaning to a single and 'simple' conditional.[8]

These are different proposals, with independent motivations. The first might be true without the second being true, and vice versa. In the debate that followed, a debate which reached its peak in the middle years of the last century, the emphasis was on the second proposal. That is, the debate was generally taken to be over the question of whether the agent ability 'can' is equivalent in meaning to a single 'simple' conditional. By the mid-seventies everyone agreed that the compatibilists had lost this debate. It wasn't just that no satisfactory analysis of 'could have done otherwise' had been proposed. The consensus in the literature was that the very project of trying to give a Conditional Analysis of 'could have done otherwise' is mistaken in principle.[9]

This consensus about the failure of the Conditional Analysis is significant. Without this agreement, van Inwagen's Consequence Argument would not have enjoyed the success it did.[10] And without this agreement, compatibilists would not have been so ready to turn to other strategies for defending the claim that free will or at least the kind of free will worth wanting or at least moral responsibility can somehow be reconciled with determinism.[11]

I'm not saying that these philosophical investigations are not significant. But I think that the philosophical despair which motivated them was unfounded. The Strawsonian program can be endorsed by a hard determinist. The idea that free will can be understood in terms of higher-order desires or in terms of a "real" or "deep" self can also be endorsed by a hard determinist. In fact, the contemporary free will literature is such that it is very hard to see what the difference is supposed to be between a hard determinist and a compatibilist.[12]

I will argue that the despair was unfounded because Moore's original proposal—that agent abilities are capacities or dispositions—was not properly developed or defended. Given the time period in which these debates took place, this was inevitable. For at that time, everyone assumed that dispositions could be analyzed in terms of a single "simple" conditional about what an object or person would do given the appropriate conditions. We now know that this is not the case. Objects and persons have dispositions and capacities by having intrinsic properties that are the causal basis of the disposition. And some of the arguments that were made against the simple Conditional Analysis of agent ability count equally against a simple Conditional Analysis of dispositions.

Dispositions: why the simple conditional analysis is false

Consider the following proposal about the correct analysis of dispositions: O has the disposition at time t to X iff if Conditions C obtained at time t, O would X. Thus, O is fragile at time t iff if O were dropped or struck at t, O would break. Call this "the Simple Conditional Analysis" of disposition, for it says that the having of a disposition is equivalent to the truth of a counterfactual conditional.

At one time, it was widely assumed that the Simple Conditional Analysis is the correct analysis of disposition. But the current consensus in the literature is that the Simple Conditional Analysis of disposition has been decisively refuted. According to David Lewis, the refutation has been part of philosophical folklore since 1971 or earlier, but it did not appear in print until 1994.[13]

The refutation is due to C. B. Martin, who argued against the Simple Conditional Analysis by arguing that the truth of a counterfactual conditional is neither necessary nor sufficient for the truth of the claim that something has a disposition.[14] His argument was based on two kinds of counterexamples to the Simple Conditional Analysis, counterexamples that have come to be known in the literature as cases of 'finkish disposition' and 'finkish lack of disposition.' Here are examples of the two kinds of cases:

1. A sorcerer takes a liking to a fragile glass, one that is a perfect intrinsic duplicate of all the other fragile glasses off the same production line. He does nothing at all to change the intrinsic properties of the glass. He only watches and waits, resolved that if ever his glass is dropped or struck, he will quickly cast a spell that changes the glass, renders it no longer fragile, and thereby aborts the process of breaking.[15]

This is a case of a finkish disposition—a disposition which would vanish immediately, on being put to the test.

This case shows that the truth of 'if the glass were dropped or struck at time t, it would break' is not *necessary* for the truth of 'the glass is fragile at time t.'

2. Another sorcerer says: "I shall make the glass cease to be fragile, but if it is ever struck or dropped, I will make it fragile again." He melts the glass. I throw a stone at it, and, just before the impact, the glass cools and solidifies and the stone breaks the glass. Then the glass melts again. I do the experiment again, and the same thing happens.[16]

This is a case of a finkish lack of disposition—an object which gains a disposition when, and only when, it is put to the test.

This case shows that the truth of 'if the glass were dropped or struck at time t, it would break' is not *sufficient* for the truth of 'the glass is fragile at time t.'

There is nothing peculiar about fragility that makes it vulnerable to this kind of counterexample. Here is Lewis's argument for the possibility of finkish dispositions:

1. Dispositions are not permanent.
2. Anything can cause anything, so the conditions C in terms of which the disposition is defined might be the very thing that causes the disposition to go away.

3. If the disposition goes away quickly enough, it would not be manifested in Conditions C.
4. If so, then O has the disposition at time t to X but it's false that if C at time t, O would X.
5. Therefore, the truth of 'if C at time t, then O would X' is not *necessary* for the truth of 'O has the disposition at t to X.'[17]

And here is Lewis's argument for the possibility of a finkish lack of disposition:

1. Dispositions are not permanent.
2. Anything can cause anything, so the conditions C in terms of which the disposition is defined might be the very thing that causes the disposition to come into existence.
3. If the disposition comes into existence quickly enough, it would be manifested in conditions C.
4. If so, then it's true that if C at time t, O would X, but it's false that O at time t has the disposition to X.
5. Therefore, the truth of 'if C at time t, O would X' is not *sufficient* for the truth of 'O has the disposition at t to X.'[18]

These kinds of counterexamples refute the Simple Conditional Analysis of disposition. But they don't refute the claim that there are dispositions, nor do they refute a more complex Conditional Analysis of disposition. What these cases seem to show is that objects have dispositions by having intrinsic properties which are the causal basis of the disposition. An object loses or gains a disposition by changing with respect to these intrinsic properties.

Lewis proposes the following Revised Conditional Analysis of disposition:

> O has the disposition at time t to X iff, for some intrinsic property B that O has at t, for some time t' after t, if Condition C were to obtain at time t and O retained property B until t', C and O's having of B would jointly be an O-complete cause of O's X'ing.[19]

For the purposes of this paper, I will assume that Lewis's analysis of disposition, or something reasonably close to it, is correct.

If it isn't, some of my arguments will have to be reformulated, but the basic line of argument will be the same. For no one takes the failure of the Simple Conditional Analysis to show that there are no dispositions. Everyone agrees that dispositions are compatible with determinism and everyone agrees that dispositions are real properties of objects—as opposed to being what Gilbert Ryle used to call 'inference tickets.'[20] And while not everyone agrees that dispositions necessarily have an intrinsic causal basis, everyone agrees that the dispositions that interest us—the dispositions of persons and medium-sized objects—have an intrinsic causal basis.

Abilities: why the simple conditional analysis is false

Recall Moore's proposal about the correct analysis of ability: S has the ability at time t to do X just in case S has the capacity (disposition) at t to do X and S has the capacity at t to do X just in case it's true that if S chose at t to do X, S would do X. Call this "the Simple Conditional Analysis" of ability, for it says that the having of an ability is equivalent to the truth of a counterfactual conditional.

The Simple Conditional Analysis of ability is prima facie plausible for the same reason that the Simple Conditional Analysis of disposition is prima facie plausible. We typically test disposition and ability claims by observing what the object or person does in the specified conditions C. We test for fragility by dropping or striking the object; we test for water-solubility by immersing the object in water; we test for the capacity to understand a language by speaking to the person in that language. We test for the ability to do something (e.g., to speak a language; e.g., to move one's limbs) by seeing if the person succeeds in doing that thing if she decides, chooses, intends, or tries to do it.[21]

But despite the relevance of counterfactual conditionals to the *testing* of ability claims, the Simple Conditional Analysis does not provide the correct *analysis* of ability. Here are two counterexamples:

1. A sorcerer has a peculiar interest in J, who has the ability to speak French. He resolves to make sure that J never succeeds in speaking French. He does nothing at all to change any of J's intrinsic properties. He only watches and waits, resolved that if ever J chooses or tries to speak French he will quickly cast a spell that changes J, removing his ability to speak French before J succeeds in uttering a word of French.

This is a case of a finkish ability—an ability which would vanish immediately, on being put to the test.

This case shows that the truth of 'if S chose (decided, intended, or tried) at time t to do X, S would do X" is not *necessary* for the truth of 'S has the ability at t to do X.'

2. Another sorcerer has a peculiar interest in L. He resolves to make sure that L never moves his left hand absent-mindedly or involuntarily or in any way other than by choosing, deciding, intending, or trying to move it. He says: "I shall remove your ability to move your left hand, but if you ever choose, decide, intend, or try to move it; I will restore your ability." He paralyzes L's left hand. L decides to raise the hand; quick as

a flash, the sorcerer removes the paralysis. L puts the hand down; the sorcerer paralyzes it again.

This is a case of a finkish lack of ability—a person who gains an ability when, and only when, it is put to the test.

This case shows that the truth of 'if S chose (decided, intended, or tried) at time t to do X, S would do X' is not *sufficient* for the truth of 'S has the ability at t to do X.'

The lesson to be learned from these counterexamples appears to be the same as the lesson we learned from the parallel counterexamples to the Simple Conditional Analysis of disposition. The Simple Conditional Analysis of ability is false because it does not take into account the fact that persons have abilities *by having intrinsic properties that are the causal basis of the ability.* These intrinsic properties are what we gain when we acquire an ability and what we lose when we lose an ability; they are what persist during the times that the person does not exercise her ability. It is because we believe that J continues to have the intrinsic properties that are the causal basis of his ability to speak French that we believe that he continues to have this ability, even though the sorcerer's dispositions ensure that he *will not speak French.* And it is because we believe that L lacks some of the intrinsic properties that are the causal basis of his ability to move his left hand that we believe that he lacks the ability to move his left hand, even though the sorcerer's dispositions guarantee that it is always true that L *will move his left hand, if he chooses.*

Let's try revising the Simple Conditional Analysis of ability in the way that Lewis suggested we revise the Simple Conditional Analysis of disposition:

> *Revised Conditional Analysis of Ability*: S has the ability at time t to do X iff, for some intrinsic property or set of properties B[22] that S has at t, for some time t' after t, if S chose (decided, intended, or tried) at t to do X, and S were to retain B until t', S's choosing (deciding, intending, or trying) to do X and S's having of B would jointly be an S-complete cause of S's doing X.

The *Revised Conditional Analysis* gets the right results about the two cases that were counterexamples to the Simple Conditional Analysis of ability. J has the ability to speak French because he has some intrinsic property or set of properties B which is the causal basis of his ability to speak French and because it is true that if he both chose to speak French *and* retained B for the specified time interval (i.e., if the sorcerer does not interfere), then J's choosing to speak French, would, together with B, cause him to speak French and would be a J-complete cause of his speaking French. L lacks the ability to move his left hand because it is false that he has *any* intrinsic property or set of properties B such that if he chose to raise his left hand *and* retained B during the specified time interval, then B together with his choosing to raise his hand would be an L-complete cause of L's raising his hand.[23]

I have claimed that abilities, including the ability to make choices for reasons, are either dispositions or bundles of dispositions. If I am right about this, and if I am right in claiming that Lewis's Revised Conditional Analysis, or something reasonably close to it, is the correct analysis of dispositions, then the Revised Conditional Analysis of ability, or something reasonably close to it, is the correct analysis of those abilities—let's call them 'basic abilities'—which are dispositions.

Basic abilities are dispositions, but not all abilities are basic abilities. Complex abilities, including the ability to make choices for reasons, are not dispositions; they are *bundles of dispositions*.[24] Which dispositions are included in the bundle? This depends on your views about reasons and reasoning, but at least some elements of this package are relatively uncontroversial. A person has the ability to make choices for reasons only if she has the following dispositions (capacities, causal powers): the disposition to form and revise beliefs in response to evidence and argument; the disposition to form intentions (choose, try to act) in response to her desires (understood broadly as "pro-attitudes") and beliefs about how to achieve those desires; the disposition to engage in practical reasoning in response to her intention to make a rational (defensible, justifiable) decision about what to do and her belief that by engaging in practical reasoning she will succeed in making such a decision.

There is, of course, room for argument about what other items need to be added to the list, as well as argument about whether any bundle of dispositions can add up to the ability to choose for reasons. But much of this argument has nothing to do with the debate between compatibilists and incompatibilists. Compatibilists and incompatibilists agree that there are possible worlds where creatures like us have free will—and thus the ability to choose for reasons—in the sense relevant to moral responsibility.[25] Their disagreement concerns whether *determinism* robs us of this ability. That is, incompatibilists agree that there are possible worlds where we, or creatures much like us, have the ability to choose for reasons; their claim is that none of these possible worlds are deterministic worlds. It will be helpful to have a way of characterizing the common ground between compatibilists and their incompatibilist opponents. Earlier I suggested that the common ground lies in the idea that free will is the ability to make choices on the basis of reasons. I now propose that the common ground extends further. Incompatibilists and compatibilists should agree that the ability to choose on the basis of reasons is a complex ability constituted by simpler abilities. To put it more bluntly, the ability to choose for reasons is a bundle of simpler abilities. This gives us the following common ground between compatibilists and incompatibilists:

FWBA: Free will is the ability to make choices on the basis of reasons and to have this ability is to have a bundle of simpler abilities.[26]

An incompatibilist who accepts FWBA, has, it seems to me, only two ways of resisting my claim that abilities, including the ability to choose for reasons, are dispositions or bundles of dispositions:

She could stamp her feet and insist that *no* abilities are dispositions, that there is a sharp difference between the capacity (disposition) to understand a language, on the one hand, and the ability to speak a language, on the other. The ability to speak a language requires the falsity of determinism; the capacity (disposition) to understand a language does not. This seems implausible.

Alternatively, the incompatibilist could agree that *some* abilities are dispositions or bundles of dispositions, but insist that the bundle of abilities which constitute free will includes at least one ability which is not a disposition.[27] This is perhaps not as implausible but has an ad hoc look to it nevertheless.

Arguments against the conditional analysis of ability reconsidered

If what I have said so far is even roughly correct, compatibilists made a big mistake when they gave up on the idea of giving a Conditional Analysis of ability claims. In this section, I will take a look at the objections that were most influential in the literature. I will argue that these objections do not hold against my proposal that compatibilism be defended by ABD, FWBD, and the Revised Conditional Analysis of disposition and ability. But before I do this, I would like to make a few general observations which help explain why compatibilists gave up such a promising research program.

First, the debate was cast in terms of the question of whether attributions of agent ability are "categorical," on the one hand, or "hypothetical," "conditional," or "constitutionally iffy," on the other. We are now in a position to see that this was a false dilemma. The possibility of finkish abilities and finkish lack of ability shows us that persons have abilities by having intrinsic properties that are the causal basis of the ability. If the Revised Conditional Analysis is correct, then the correct analysis of ability quantifies over these intrinsic properties *and* uses an 'if' clause. So attributions of agent ability are both "categorical" and "iffy."

Second, the debate was conducted before the development of possible worlds semantics for counterfactual conditionals.[28] Most participants understood that these conditionals are not material conditionals, but the truth-conditions for subjunctive and counterfactual conditionals were not well understood. The prevailing view was that these conditionals are metalinguistic assertions in disguise. When we say something like "if I had sold those shares last week, I would be rich now" or "if I had struck that match, it would have lit" what we really mean must be filled out by something like "there is a valid argument from the antecedent and some other true statements to the consequent." But this left all sorts of things unclear, including the difference between the indicative conditional "if Oswald did not kill Kennedy, then someone else did" and the counterfactual conditional "if Oswald had not killed Kennedy, then someone else would have." In his seminal "The Problem of Counterfactual Conditionals,"[29] Goodman identified "the problem of cotenability" as an insoluble problem for the metalinguistic account, and this led to skepticism about the prospects of giving an account of objective truth-conditions for *any* counterfactuals.

Finally, defenders of the Conditional Analysis took the relevant analysandum to be "S could have done X" where "X" is an intentional action which S does by *moving her body*, and they assumed that the relevant ability is a single ability, definable in terms of a single conditional. This was due to the behaviorist and positivist climate of the times in which these debates were conducted; the idea was to reduce the (obscure and intractable) problem of free will and determinism to the (less obscure and hopefully tractable) problem of *freedom of action* and determinism. This wasn't a crazy strategy. After all, the incompatibilist is someone who believes that if determinism is true, we can neither choose nor *do* anything other than what we actually choose or do. If the Conditional Analysis of 'could have done otherwise' is correct, then the latter claim is false, and this is a significant victory for the compatibilist. But of course there is a difference between the abilities which constitute free will and the abilities which constitute freedom of action. In ignoring this difference, the defenders of the Conditional Analysis left themselves vulnerable to objections which can easily be avoided if we do not attempt this reductionist strategy.

Let's turn, finally, to the historical objections.

Some of the objections were curious, yet revealing. For instance, it was objected that the fact that S *does* A implies that S *can* do A, but doesn't imply any conditional statement and therefore "S can do A" cannot be equivalent in meaning to any conditional statement.[30] This objection is correct, but irrelevant. The truth of any proposition P entails that it is logically and metaphysically possible that P, so if S does A, this entails that it is logically and metaphysically possible that S does A. (That is, S's doing A is compossible with the truths of logic and metaphysics.) But this is obviously not the relevant 'can.' That S does A also entails that it is physically possible that S does A. But this is also not the 'can' relevant to free will and moral responsibility. What's needed for this to be an objection to the Conditional Analysis is that S's doing A entails that S has the *ability* to do A. But this entailment does not hold. There are many different ways to do something. One way is by having and exercising the ability. Another way is by accident or lucky fluke. Yet another way is by having one's brain and body moved, puppet-like, in the appropriate ways by a sorcerer. Doing something by accident or lucky fluke does not entail having the ability to do it; doing something due to direct manipulation by someone else does not entail having the ability to do it. This shows that the fact that S does A does not entail that S has the ability to do A.[31]

Another objection was that having the ability to do something is consistent with trying (choosing, deciding, etc.) and failing to do that thing, and therefore the truth of the conditional "if she had tried (chosen, decided, etc.) to do X, she would have done X" is not *necessary* for the truth of "she has the ability to do X."[32] The basic point made by this objection is correct. Just as we may get *lucky* and succeed in doing something we *don't* have the ability to do, we may also get *unlucky* and fail at something we *do* have the ability to do. This objection succeeds against the Simple Conditional Analysis of ability, but has no force against the claim that abilities are dispositions.[33] A fragile glass doesn't break *every* time it's dropped, even when it's dropped in the right kind of way, and even when no finking sorcerer is present. A flammable match may fail to light, even when struck in the presence of oxygen and without a finking sorcerer present. There is room for disagreement about how these sorts of cases should be handled, but for our purposes the point to be noted is just this: No one thinks that cases like this show that there are no dispositions.[34]

Another influential objection was the infinite regress objection. The objection was that while it is true that we often use conditionals like "if S had chosen to do X, S would have done X" as if they are equivalent to "S could have done X," this is because we are presupposing that S *could have chosen* to do X. But this means that our analysis is incomplete. To complete our analysis we have to provide a conditional that is equivalent in meaning to "S could have chosen to do X." And any attempt to provide a Conditional Analysis of "S could have chosen to do X" leads to a vicious infinite regress.[35]

The correct answer to this objection is, I think, this: Yes, when we say, of someone, "if she had chosen to do X, she would have done X," we usually assume that she could have chosen to do X. But that's not because we think that having the ability to do X *requires* having the ability to choose to do X but, rather, because we think that people typically have the *ability to choose* whether or not to do what they do *in addition to* having the *ability to do* what they do. That is, we assume that persons have the bundle of abilities which constitute the ability to make choices on the basis of reasons as well as abilities to do various things with their bodies (at 'will,' for no reason other than impulse or 'mere' desire). There is no regress because someone (an animal, a young child) may have abilities of the second kind without having any or many abilities of the first kind.

Another category of objections consisted in counterexamples to the claim that a particular Conditional Analysis succeeds in providing a *sufficient* condition for the truth of "S could have done X." There are many different sorts of cases, and not all cases work against every (Simple) Conditional Analysis, but the basic structure of these cases goes like this: A person suffers from some pathological condition which either impairs her capacity to make a rational decision concerning some particular kind of action (e.g., claustrophobia, e.g., a pianist overcome by stage-fright) or impairs her capacity to make *any* rational decision about what to do. But if she (somehow, miraculously) decided (or chose, formed the intention, etc.) to perform the relevant action, she would succeed. Susan Wolf offers the following example of the second sort of case: A person attacked on a dark street is too paralyzed by fear to consider, much less choose, whether to scream. But if she had chosen or tried to scream, she would have screamed.[36]

The intuition we are supposed to have about these cases is that, due to the psychological incapacity, the person *cannot* perform some bodily action X (e.g., go into a small enclosed space, play the piano, scream). According to the Conditional Analysis, however, the person can perform action X. So the Conditional Analysis is false.

I agree that there is a temptation to respond to these cases by agreeing that the person cannot do X. But if we succumb to this temptation, we will be vulnerable to the vicious infinite regress objection. So I think we had better avoid this temptation. I also think that there is a better answer. I think the better answer to the question, "Can the person do X?" is "Yes and no." Yes, she has the ability to go into the tiny enclosed space, play the piano, scream. (She knows how to walk; her legs aren't paralyzed. She knows how to play piano; her fingers aren't broken. She knows how to scream; she doesn't have laryngitis.) No, she lacks the ability to bring herself to do those things; she cannot use her reasoning ability to bring it about that she intentionally does these things. Due to her phobia (stage fright, panic, etc.), she is unable to choose or try to act according to her own conception of what counts as a good reason for acting.

These kinds of cases are significant, and they do show us something. They show that it was a mistake, on the part of the defenders of the Simple Conditional Analysis, to try to reduce or replace the question of free will with the question of freedom of action. They show that it's possible for someone to be unfree due to her inability to choose on the basis of reasons. But they don't show what the objector claims they show—that the ability to do X entails the ability to choose to do X (which in turn entails the ability to choose to choose to do X, and so on to infinity).

It may be instructive to compare these pathological cases with two different techniques doctors can use to ensure that the patient remains immobile after a delicate surgery. The first technique is by using drugs that work in the way that general anesthesia works—by depriving the person of the capacity for conscious thought. The second technique is by using drugs of the first kind together with drugs ("paralytics") that work by depriving the person of the ability to move her body. Regardless of which technique is used, we can be sure (so long as the drugs work) that the person *will not* raise her hand (or move any other part of her body). But in the first case, if the person became momentarily conscious, and chose or tried to raise her hand, she would. In the second case, even if the person became momentarily conscious and chose or tried to raise her hand, she would not. In the second case, there is an *additional* safeguard against movement.

Can the person in either of these cases raise her hand? I think that in the first kind of case, we should answer 'yes' and 'no.' Yes, because she's not paralyzed; she still has the *ability to raise her hand.* No, because she *lacks the ability to choose,* on the basis of reasons, to raise her hand; the general anesthesia is the functional equivalent of mental paralysis. (That is, the person retains reasoning and choosing skills, but these skills are temporarily impaired due to the general anesthesia.)

In the second case, however, I think we want to answer a flat "No." The unconscious paralyzed person cannot raise her hand for the same reason a conscious paralyzed person cannot. If she chose or tried to raise her hand, she would fail, no matter how hard she tried, no matter how many times she tried. And her failure would be due to a fault in her. Due to her paralysis, she no longer has some of the intrinsic properties which are the causal basis of the ability.

This brings us, finally, to the objection that in the end proved decisive against the Simple Conditional Analysis—Keith Lehrer's argument that "S can do X" cannot be equivalent to *any* conditional of the form "if Condition C, S will do X."[37]

His argument went like this: It is logically possible that the following are all true:

(i) if Condition C, S will do x;
(ii) not-Condition C;
(iii) if not-Condition C, S cannot do X.

(ii) and (iii) entail, by Modus Ponens, that S cannot do X. Therefore, Lehrer concluded, this logically possible case is a counterexample to any Conditional Analysis whatsoever.

Lehrer backed up his "consistent triad" argument with the following example:

It is logically possible that as a result of my not willing, not choosing, or not undertaking some action, I might lose any of my powers. Suppose that, unknown to myself, a small object has been implanted in my brain, and that when the button is pushed by a demonic being who implanted this object, I become temporarily paralysed and unable to act. My not choosing to perform an act might cause the button to be pushed and thereby render me unable to act.

If this story sounds familiar, it should. It is a story about a finkish lack of ability; it is, in all basic respects, the story I told earlier about L and the sorcerer.

In claiming that (i) to (iii) are a consistent set of propositions, Lehrer was, in effect (though he did not realize it), pointing out that a person may suffer from a "finkish lack of ability." The story he told is the story of someone who currently lacks the ability to move his arm (because he is paralyzed) but of whom it's true that if Condition C obtained (e.g., if he chose to move his arm) he would very quickly acquire the ability to move his arm and immediately exercise this ability.

Lehrer's case refutes the Simple Conditional Analysis of ability, but, as we have seen, it does not refute the claim that abilities are dispositions. Nor does it refute the Revised Conditional Analysis of ability.

Frankfurt's argument and the dispositional account of free will

The proposal that free will is the ability to make choices for reasons and that to have this ability is to have a bundle of dispositions (FWBD) can be used to shed light on a famous argument made by Harry Frankfurt in 1969,[38] during the last years of the debate about the Simple Conditional Analysis of 'could have done otherwise.' Frankfurt argued that this debate was *irrelevant* to the question of whether or not moral responsibility is compatible with determinism because it rested on a widely shared but false assumption. He called this assumption 'the Principle of Alternate Possibilities' and characterized it as follows:

> PAP: A person is morally responsible for what he has done only if he could have done otherwise.

Frankfurt's argument for the falsity of PAP was based on a simple thought experiment. You are invited to tell a story about a person, Jones, who chooses to do, and succeeds in doing, some action X. Tell the story in a way that convinces *you* that Jones is morally responsible for doing X. If you are an incompatibilist, you may specify that Jones is an indeterministic agent who can choose and do otherwise, given the actual past and the laws. If you are a compatibilist, you may specify that Jones has all the abilities you think are required for moral responsibility. Now add to your story the following facts: Standing in the wings is another person, Black, with mysterious powers. Black is interested in what Jones does. In particular, Black wants Jones to choose and to do X and Black has it in his power to prevent Jones from choosing or doing anything other than X. But due to a happy coincidence, Jones chooses and does exactly what Black wants him to do, and Black never intervenes.

According to Frankfurt, this story shows that someone may be morally responsible for what he has done even though he could not have done otherwise. The addition of Black to the story makes it true that Jones could not have done, or even chosen to do, anything other than X. But, Frankfurt argued, the addition of Black does not affect Jones's responsibility for his action. After all, though Black could have intervened, he didn't. Jones does X for his own reasons, exactly as he would have done had Black never existed. So this story shows that PAP is false.

If PAP is false, then, even if determinism robs us of the ability to do (and to choose to do) otherwise, it does not necessarily rob us of moral responsibility. So a great deal is at stake here. Many philosophers have been convinced by Frankfurt; others have not. A huge literature continues to discuss Frankfurt's thought experiment and argument; the debate about whether Frankfurt is right about the irrelevance of "alternate possibilities" to moral responsibility has displaced the older literature about the Conditional Analysis of 'could have done otherwise.'

Frankfurt's argument is supposed to show that someone may be morally responsible for what he did even if he could not have done (or chosen to do) otherwise. And it is supposed to show this no matter how we understand 'could have done otherwise.' Let's test his argument with FWBD.

Let's begin by spelling out Frankfurt's argument for the conclusion that Jones is morally responsible *even though he could not have done or chosen to do otherwise.*

1. In the first stage of the thought experiment, Jones chooses and does X and has whatever you think it takes to be morally responsible for doing X, including the ability to choose and/or do otherwise.
2. In the second stage of the thought experiment, Jones can neither choose nor do otherwise (due to Black).
3. Stage 1 Jones and Stage 2 Jones are alike with respect to all their intrinsic properties and they perform the same action for the same reasons (since Black never actually intervenes).
4. Two persons who are alike with respect to all their intrinsic properties and who perform the same action for the same reasons are alike with respect to their moral responsibility for their action.

Therefore Stage 2 Jones is morally responsible for doing X.

The first and third premises are entailed by the thought experiment. The fourth premise says that moral responsibility for action supervenes on the intrinsic properties of a person, her reasons, and her action; this is intuitively plausible.

The controversial premise is the second one. Can Black really make it true that Jones can neither choose nor do otherwise without ever laying a finger on him? In the literature it is usually assumed that Black can do this if determinism is true; the controversy lies in whether he can do it if determinism is false.

Since the thought experiment is supposed to work for all of us, we can stipulate that Stage 1 Jones has the ability to choose on the basis of reasons whether or not to do X, and that he has this ability by having a bundle of dispositions (FWBD). We learned, from our discussion of finkish cases, that objects and persons have dispositions by having intrinsic properties which are the causal basis of the disposition, and that dispositions are altered or removed by altering or removing the intrinsic properties that are the causal basis of the disposition. Since Black never actually intervenes, he does not tamper with any of Jones's intrinsic properties. It follows that Black does not tamper with any of Jones's dispositions, and thus also follows that Black does not tamper with or remove any of Jones's abilities. Since Stage 1 Jones has the ability to choose, on the basis of reasons, whether or not to do X, Stage 2 Jones has the same ability. And since Stage 1 Jones could have chosen otherwise, this is also true of Stage 2 Jones.

So if FWBD is true, Frankfurt's argument against the Principle of Alternate Possibilities fails. Indeed, the dispositional account of free will allows us to explain why Frankfurt's argument fails. Frankfurt's argument fails because Black is a fink—a superfink.[39] Black's presence makes it the case that *all* of Jones's abilities, including the abilities that constitute free will, are finkish. Black leaves all of Jones's abilities intact, but Black's power and intentions ensure that if Jones ever begins or tries to exercise any of his abilities in any way contrary to Black's intentions, he will immediately lose that ability. This is not a good thing. We would not want to live at a world where our abilities are vulnerable in this kind of way. But, it turns out, this way of being vulnerable does not rob us of our moral responsibility. This is a significant and interesting discovery; it shows that we are more willing to live with moral luck than some philosophers have thought. But to be *at risk* of losing our abilities is not the same thing as *actually* losing our abilities. And because of this difference, Frankfurt's argument fails.

Notes

I am grateful to Janet Levin, Terrance Tomkow, and the Philosophy Department of North Carolina State University for helpful discussion and comments.

1. See, for instance, John Searle, *Minds, Brains, and Science* (Cambridge, Mass.: Harvard University Press, 1984), 87–89; and Thomas Nagel, *What Does It All Mean? A Very Short Introduction to Philosophy* (Oxford: Oxford University Press, 1987), 47–51.

2. David Lewis, "Scorekeeping in a language game," *Philosophical Papers,* vol. 1 (Oxford: Oxford University Press, 1983), and "The paradoxes of time travel," *Philosophical Papers,* vol. 2 (Oxford: Oxford University Press, 1986).

3. In ordinary language, "ability" is used in two different ways. Does someone with a broken leg have the ability to ride a bike? That depends. Speaking one way, we might agree that she has the ability. (She took lessons, she knows how; she has the necessary skills and competence.) Speaking another way, we might deny that she has the ability. (Her leg is broken; her bike-riding skills are temporarily *impaired*). In what follows, I will use 'ability' in the second, stronger way and I will sometimes characterize it as "she has what it takes." (Where the intended contrast is with 'opportunity,' as in "she has the ability to ride a bike, but lacks the opportunity; her *bike* is broken.")

4. Some of these examples of abilities, together with the parallel examples of capacities, are taken from Peter van Inwagen, *An Essay on Free Will* (Oxford: Clarendon Press, 1983), 8–11.

5. Ibid., 11.

6. Ibid., chap. 3.

7. G. E. Moore, *Ethics* (Oxford: Oxford University Press, 1911), chap. 6.

8. By a 'single' conditional, I mean something like "if he had chosen to do X, he would have done X" (in contrast to something like: 'if he had chosen to do X, he would have done X and if he had had different beliefs or desires, he would have chosen to do X") as an analysis of "he could have done X." For the contrast between 'simple' conditionals and more complex conditionals, see the discussion, below, of finks and the contrast between the Simple and Revised Conditional Analysis of disposition and ability.

9. Keith Lehrer was, I believe, the first compatibilist to argue this in "Cans without ifs" in *Freedom and Determinism* (New York: Random House, 1968), reprinted in Gary Watson, ed., *Free Will* (Oxford: Oxford University Press, 1982). See also Susan Wolf, *Freedom within Reason* (Oxford: Oxford University Press, 1990); Bernard Berofsky, "Ifs, cans, and free will: the issues," in *The Oxford Handbook of Free Will,* ed. Robert Kane (Oxford: Oxford University Press, 2002); and Michael McKenna, "Compatibilism," *Stanford Encyclopedia of Philosophy,* http://plato.stanford.edu, among many others.

10. Van Inwagen was well aware of this: "If someone produced a simple, easily graspable conditional analysis of ability and if this analysis seemed right and if there were no known counterexamples to it, this would vitiate my argument. If someone produced a plausible argument for the correctness of some conditional analysis—however complex that analysis might be—this would vitiate my argument. But none of these things have ever been produced" (*Essay on Free Will,* 125).

11. See, for instance: P. F. Strawson, "Freedom and resentment," *Proceedings of the British Academy* 48 (1962): 1–25; Harry Frankfurt, "Alternate possibilities and moral responsibilty," *Journal of Philosophy* 46 (1969), and "Freedom of the will and the concept of a person," *Journal of Philosophy* 48 (1971); Daniel Dennett, *Elbow Room: The Varieties of Free Will Worth Wanting* (New York: Bradford Books, 1984); R. Jay Wallace, *Responsibility and the Moral Sentiments* (Cambridge, Mass.: Harvard University Press, 1994).

12. John Martin Fischer, who sees this point more clearly than most, has coined the term "semicompatibilist" to describe those who believe that determinism is incompatible with "alternative possibilities" and the "freedom to do otherwise" but is compatible with

moral responsibility (*The Metaphysics of Free Will*, Cambridge, MA: *Blackwell*, 1994). I suspect that many of the philosophers who call themselves "compatibilists" are in fact "semicompatibilists."

13. Lewis, "Finkish dispositions," *Philosophical Quarterly* 47 (1997): 143–158.

14. Martin, "Dispositions and Conditionals," *Philosophical Quarterly* 44 (1994): 1–8.

15. This example is from Lewis, "Finkish dispositions," 147.

16. This example is adapted from Martin, "Dispositions and conditionals," 2.

17. Lewis, "Finkish dispositions," 144.

18. Ibid.

19. Ibid., 157. I have replaced Lewis's "were to undergo stimulus s" and "to give response R" with "if Condition C were to obtain" and "to X."

20. Gilbert Ryle, *The Concept of Mind* (New York: Penguin, 1949), 112–30. For an excellent collection of some of the older literature on dispositions, see Raimo Tuomela, ed., *Dispositions* (Dordrecht, The Netherlands: D. Reidel, 1978).

21. There is, of course, a difference in the way in which we test ability claims, the difference to which van Inwagen alludes when he says that a person's ability to speak French does not entail that there are any circumstances in which he would "willy-nilly, speak French." We cannot test for ability simply by placing the person in some *external circumstance* and then watching to see if she exercises the ability. A person may have reasons for refusing to exercise an ability that she in fact has. However, it does not follow that abilities can't be defined in terms of what a person would do in response to some *internal* condition; for instance, in response to wanting or choosing or trying to do some action. And this seems right, as a general characterization of what distinguishes abilities from other dispositions.

22. Why "set of properties"? Because to have the ability to do X is to have not just the skills or competence required to do X, but for these skills to be in good working order, not impaired due to broken limbs, paralysis, laryngitis, and so on. (See note 3.)

23. Note that property set B includes all the properties that are the intrinsic causal basis of the capacity to understand French. You can't speak a language unless you can understand it, though you can understand a language without being able to speak it. Given this, we can test the ability to speak a language even in finkish cases, by testing to see if the person can understand the language. If she can understand it, this provides us with some evidence that she can also speak it. I believe that similar points can be made about other abilities and their corresponding capacities.

24. The bundles is not necessarily limited to basic abilities. Depending on how we draw the line between basic abilities and other dispositions, some elements in the bundle may be "mere" dispositions.

25. I argue this in "Compatibilism, incompatibilism, and impossibilism," in *Contemporary Debates in Metaphysics*, eds. John Hawthorne, Theodore Sider, and Dean Zimmerman (Blackwell, 2008, 303–318). I argue this by distinguishing between the incompatibilist (someone who thinks that *determinism* robs us of free will) and someone I call the "impossibilist" (someone who thinks that free will is impossible for creatures like us, regardless of whether determinism is true or false). I count Galen Strawson as an impossibilist. Galen Strawson, *Freedom and Belief* (Oxford: Clarendon Press, 1986).

26. Even the agent-causation theorist can agree with this.

27. Which ability? That depends on the incompatibilist. Traditional agent-causation incompatibilists will presumably insist on the ability to be a causal originator, where this is understood as the ability to be the irreducible substance-cause of events.

28. Possible worlds semantics for counterfactuals was developed independently by David Lewis and Robert Stalnaker in the late sixties and early seventies. David Lewis, *Counterfactuals* (Cambridge, Mass.: Harvard University Press, 1973); Robert Stalnaker, "A theory of conditionals," in *Studies in Logical Theory,* ed. N. Rescher (Blackwell, 1968); Robert Stalnaker, *Inquiry* (New York: Bradford Books, 1984).

29. *Journal of Philosophy* 44 (1947): 113–28.

30. This objection is reported by Bernard Berofsky, "Ifs, cans, and free will: the issues," in *The Oxford Handbook of Free Will,* ed. Robert Kane (Oxford: Oxford University Press, 2002), 184. Berofsky cites M. R. Ayers, *The Refutation of Determinism* (London: Methuen, 1968), as the source of the objection.

31. Compare dispositions. The fact that something broke entails that it is logically, metaphysically, and physically possible that it breaks, but it does not entail that it is fragile.

32. This point was most famously made by J. L. Austin, "Ifs and cans," in Austin, *Philosophical Papers* (Oxford: Oxford University Press, 1970), 218. Austin's example was a golfer who misses a very short putt and then kicks himself because "I could have holed it."

33. And whether it has force against the Revised Conditional Analysis of dispositions and abilities depends on how that analysis is spelled out. Lewis seems to think that it's not a problem; others disagree.

34. In the literature on dispositions, these kinds of cases are known as cases of "masking." For discussion, see Lewis, "Finkish dispositions," and also Mark Johnston, "How to speak of the colors," *Philosophical Studies* 68 (1992): 221–63.

35. R. M. Chisolm, "J. L. Austin's Philosophical Papers," in Bernard Berofsky, ed., *Free Will and Determinism* (New York: Harper and Row, 1966). See Berofsky, "Ifs, cans, and free will: the issues," 184–88, for discussion.

36. *Freedom within Reason,* 99.

37. "Cans without ifs."

38. "Alternate possibilities and moral responsibility," *Journal of Philosophy* 66 (1969): 829–39.

39. There are different ways of telling "Frankfurt-style" stories, as they have come to be known in the literature; I do not say that Black is a fink in all of them. However, if FWBD is true, then Black does not and cannot succeed in depriving Jones of the ability to choose otherwise while leaving his moral responsibility intact. For discussion and criticism of other kinds of Frankfurt-style stories and arguments, see my "Freedom, foreknowledge, and the principle of alternate possibilities," *Canadian Journal of Philosophy* 30 (2000): 1–23.

PART 4

Suggested Further Readings

IV. Responsibility and Alternative Possibilities

Many important papers relating to the debate about alternative possibilities can be found in:

Widerker, David, and Michael McKenna, eds. 2003. *Moral Responsibility and Alternative Possibilities*. Aldershot, UK: Ashgate Press.

Among the most influential classical discussions of the issue of alternative possibilities and "could have done otherwise" the following are particularly influential:

Austin, J. L. 1961. "Ifs and cans." In *Philosophical Papers*. J. O. Urmson and G. Warnock, eds. Oxford: Clarendon Press, 153–80. (Reprinted in B. Berofsky, ed., *Free Will*, 295–321.)

Moore, G. E. 1912. "Free will," in *Ethics*. Oxford: Oxford University Press, Chapter 6.

Important recent contributions include:

Adams, Robert. 1985. "Involuntary sins," *Philosophical Review*, 94: 3–31.

Berofsky, Bernard. 2002. "Ifs, cans, and free will: the issues," in R. Kane, ed., *The Oxford Handbook of Free Will*. New York: Oxford University Press.

Campbell, Joseph. 2005. "Compatibilist alternatives," *Canadian Journal of Philosophy* 35: 387–406.

Clarke, Randolph. 2009. "Dispositions, abilities to act, and free will: the new dispositionalism," *Mind* 118: 323–51.

Copp, David. 1997. "Defending the principle of alternative possibilities: blameworthiness and moral responsibility," *Nous* 31: 441–56.

Dennett, Daniel. 1984. "I could not have done otherwise—so what?" *Journal of Philosophy*. 81: 553–65. (Reprinted in R. Kane, ed., *Free Will*. Oxford: Blackwell, 2002.)

Fischer, John M., and Neal Tognazzini. 2010. "Blame and avoidability: a reply to Otsuka," *Journal of Ethics* 14 (1).

Hunt, David P. 2000. "Moral responsibility and unavoidable action," *Philosophical Studies* 97: 195–227.

Stump, Eleonore. 1996. "Libertarian freedom and the principle of alternative possibilities," in Howard-Snyder, Daniel, and Jeff Jordan, eds., *Faith, Freedom, and Rationality*. Lanham, MD: Rowman and Littlefield, 73–88.

Widerker, David. 1995. "Libertarianism and Frankfurt's attack on the principle of alternative possibilities," *Philosophical Review* 104: 247–61.

Libertarian Alternatives—Soft and Hard

10

Responsibility, Luck, and Chance: Reflections On Free Will and Indeterminism

Robert Kane

Ludwig Wittgenstein[1] once said that "to solve the problems of philosophers, you have to think even more crazily than they do" (*ibid.*, 75). This task (which became even more difficult after Wittgenstein than it was before him) is certainly required for the venerable problem of free will and determinism.

I. The luck principle

Consider the following principle:

> (LP) If an action is *undetermined* at a time *t*, then its happening rather than not happening at *t* would be a matter of *chance* or *luck,* and so it could not be a *free* and *responsible* action.

This principle (which we may call the *luck principle,* or simply LP) is false, as I shall explain shortly. Yet it seems true. LP and a related principle to be considered later in this paper are fueled by many of those "intuition pumps," in Daniel Dennett's[2] apt expression, which support common intuitions about freedom and responsibility. LP and related principles lie behind the widespread belief that indeterminism, so far from being required for free will and responsibility, would actually undermine free will and responsibility. Dennett does not dwell on the intuition pumps of this sort, as I shall do in this paper. As a compatibilist, he is more interested in criticizing intuition pumps that lead people to think (mistakenly, on his view) that freedom and responsibility are not compatible with determinism, whereas intuition pumps that support LP lead people to think freedom and responsibility are not compatible with indeterminism. Yet intuition pumps of the latter kind are every bit as pervasive and influential in free-will debates as those Dennett dwells upon; and they are as much in need of deconstruction, since they play a significant role in leading people to believe that freedom and responsibility must be compatible with determinism.

I think the modern route to compatibilism—which is the reigning view among contemporary philosophers—usually goes through principles like LP at some point or other. In my experience, most ordinary persons start out as natural incompatibilists. They believe there is some kind of conflict between freedom and determinism; and the idea that freedom and responsibility might be compatible with determinism looks to them at first like a "quagmire of evasion" (William James) or "a wretched subterfuge" (Immanuel Kant). Ordinary persons have to be talked out of this natural incompatibilism by the clever arguments of philosophers—who, in the manner of their mentor, Socrates, are only too happy to oblige. To weaken natural incompatibilist instincts, philosophers first argue that what we mean by freedom in everyday life is the power or ability to do whatever we choose or desire to do—in short, an absence of coercion, compulsion, oppression, and other impediments or constraints upon our behavior. They then point out that we can be free in these everyday senses to do what we choose or desire, even if our choices and desires are determined by causes that lie in our past.

But this line of argument does not usually dispose of incompatibilist intuitions by itself. Ordinary persons might grant that many everyday freedoms are compatible with determinism and still wonder if there is not also some deeper freedom—the freedom to have an *ultimate* say in what we choose or desire to do in the first place—that is incompatible with determinism. (I have argued elsewhere[3] that this deeper freedom is what was traditionally meant by "free *will*.") So the philosophers must add a second step to their case—an argument to the effect that any allegedly deeper freedom (of the will) that is not compatible with determinism is no intelligible freedom at all. And with this step, principles like LP come into the picture. For any freedom not compatible with determinism would require indeterminism; and what is undetermined, it seems, would happen by chance or luck and could not be a free and responsible action. This kind of argument is the one that usually puts the final nail in the coffin of incompatibilist instincts.

When philosophy professors go through this two-stage argument in the modern classroom, they are replicating the standard case against traditional (incompatibilist or libertarian) free will which is one of the defining characteristics of modernity. The goal is to consign incompatibilist freedom to the dustbin of history with other beliefs that a modern scientific age is encouraged to outgrow. Students and ordinary persons subjected to this argument may have an uneasy feeling they are being had by the clever arguments of philosophers. But, also seeing no obvious response, except an appeal to mystery, many of them become compatibilists.

II. Indeterminism, the bogeyman

The second stage of this two-stage argument in support of compatibilism will concern me here, the one that goes through LP and related principles in the attempt to show that indeterminism would not enhance, but in fact would undermine, freedom and responsibility. What is at stake here is not merely the clever arguments of philosophers; for it happens that the case for principles like LP is a powerful one. It *is* difficult to see how indeterminism and chance can be reconciled with freedom and responsibility. Philosophers have tried to bring this out in a number of ways which will be addressed here. We may think of these as the varied intuition pumps that support LP and principles like it.

(1) We are often asked to consider, for example, that whatever is undetermined or happens by chance is not under the *control* of anything, and so is not under the control of the agent. But an action that is not under the control of the agent could not be a free and responsible action. (Here it is evident that the notion of control is involved in the case for LP: indeterminism and chance imply lack of control to a degree that implies lack of freedom and responsibility.)

(2) Another line of argument often heard is this: suppose a choice occurred as the result of an undetermined event (say, a quantum jump) in one's brain. Would that be a free choice? Being undetermined, it would appear to be more of a fluke or accident than a free and responsible action. Some twentieth-century scientists and philosophers have suggested that free will might be rescued by supposing that undetermined quantum events in the brain could be amplified to have large-scale effects on choice or action.[4] Unfortunately, this modern version of the ancient Epicurean "swerve" of the atoms seems to be subject to the same criticisms as its ancient counterpart. It seems that undetermined events in the brain or body, whether amplified or not, would occur spontaneously and would be more of a nuisance—or perhaps a curse, like epilepsy—than an enhancement of freedom and responsibility.

(3) Nor would it help to suppose that the indeterminism or chance came *between* our choices (or intentions) and our actions. Imagine that you are intending to make a delicate cut in a fine piece of cloth, but because of an undetermined twitching in your arm, you make the wrong cut. Here, indeterminism is no enhancement of your freedom, but a *hindrance* or *obstacle* to your carrying out your purposes as intended. Critics of libertarian freedom[5] have often contended that this is what indeterminism would always be—a hindrance or impediment to one's freedom. It would get in the way, *diminishing* control, and hence responsibility, instead of enhancing them.

(4) Even more absurd consequences follow if we suppose that indeterminism or chance is involved in the initiation of overt actions. Arthur Schopenhauer[6] imagined the case of a man who suddenly found his legs start to move *by chance,* carrying him across the room against his wishes. Such caricatures are popular among critics of indeterminist freedom for obvious reasons: undetermined or chance-initiated overt actions would represent the opposite of controlled and responsible actions.

(5) Going a little deeper, one may also note that, if a choice or action is undetermined, it might occur otherwise *given exactly the same past and laws of nature* up to the moment when it does occurs. This means that, if Jane is deliberating about whether to vacation in Hawaii or Colorado, and gradually comes to favor and choose Hawaii, she might have chosen otherwise (chosen Colorado), given *exactly the same deliberation* up to the moment of choice that in fact led her to favor and choose Hawaii (exactly the same thoughts, reasonings, beliefs, desires, dispositions, and other characteristics—not a sliver of difference). It is difficult to make sense of this. The choice of Colorado in such circumstances would seem irrational and inexplicable, capricious and arbitrary.[7] If it came about by virtue of undetermined events in Jane's brain, this would not be an occasion for rejoicing in her freedom, but for consulting a neurologist about the waywardness of her neural processes.

(6) At this point, some defenders of incompatibilist freedom appeal to Gottfried Leibniz's[8] celebrated dictum that prior reasons or motives need not determine choice or action, they may merely "incline without necessitating"—that is, they may incline the agent toward one option without determining the choice of that option. This may indeed happen. But it will not solve the present problem; for it is precisely *because* Jane's prior reasons and motives (beliefs, desires, and the like) incline her toward the choice of Hawaii that choosing Colorado by chance at the end of exactly the same deliberation would be irrational and inexplicable. Similarly, if her reasons had inclined her toward Colorado, then choosing Hawaii by chance at the end of the same deliberation would have been irrational and inexplicable. And if prior reasons or motives had not inclined her either way (the celebrated medieval "liberty of indifference") and the choice was a matter of chance, then the choosing of one rather than the other would have been all the more a matter of luck and out of her control. (One can see why libertarian freedom has often been ridiculed as a mere "liberty of indifference.")

(7) Indeed, critics of indeterminist freedom have often argued that indeterminist free choices must always amount to *random* choices of

this sort and hence the outcomes would be matters of mere luck or chance—like spinning a wheel to select among a set of alternatives. Perhaps there is a role for such random choices in our lives when we are genuinely indifferent to outcomes.[9] But to suppose that *all* of our free and responsible choices—including momentous ones, like whether to act heroically or treacherously—had to be by random selection in this way has been regarded by many philosophers as a *reductio ad absurdum* of the view that free will and responsibility require indeterminism.

(8) Consider one final argument which cuts more deeply than the others and to which I shall devote considerable attention. This paper was in fact prompted by new versions of this argument advanced in recent years against my incompatibilist account of free will by Galen Strawson, Alfred Mele, Bernard Berofsky, Bruce Waller, Richard Double, Mark Bernstein, and Ishtiyaque Haji[10]—though the argument is meant to apply generally to any view requiring that free actions be undetermined up to the moment when they occur.

Suppose two agents had exactly the same pasts (as indeterminism requires) up to the point where they were faced with a choice between distorting the truth for selfish gain or telling the truth at great personal cost. One agent lies and the other tells the truth. As Waller puts it, if the pasts of these two agents "are really identical" in every way up to the moment of choice, "and the difference in their acts results from chance," would there "be any grounds for distinguishing between [them], for saying that one deserves censure for a selfish decision and the other deserves praise" (*op. cit.,* 151)? Mele poses the problem in terms of a single agent in different possible worlds. Suppose in the actual world, John fails to resist the temptation to do what he thinks he ought to do, arrive at a meeting on time. If he could have done otherwise given the same past, then his counterpart, John* in a nearby possible world, which is the same as the actual world up to the moment of choice, resists the temptation and arrives on time. Mele then argues that, "if there is nothing about the agents' powers, capacities, states of mind, moral character and the like that explains this difference in outcome, ... the difference is just a matter of luck" (*op. cit.,* 582–83). It would seem that John* got lucky in his attempt to overcome temptation, whereas John did not. Would it be just to reward the one and punish the other for what appears to be ultimately the luck of the draw?

Considerations such as (1)-(8) lie behind familiar and varied charges that undetermined choices or actions would be "arbitrary," "capricious," "random," "uncontrolled," "irrational," "inexplicable," or "matters of luck or chance," and hence not free and responsible actions. These are the charges which principles like LP are meant to express. Responses to them in the history of philosophy have been many; but none to my mind has been entirely convincing. The charges have often led libertarians—those who believe in an incompatibilist free will—to posit "extra factors" in the form of unusual species of agency or causation (such as noumenal selves, immaterial egos, or nonoccurrent agent causes) to account for what would otherwise be arbitrary, uncontrolled, inexplicable, or mere luck or chance. I do not propose to appeal to any such extra factors in defense of libertarian freedom. Such appeals introduce additional problems of their own without, in my view, directly confronting the deep problems about indeterminism, chance, and luck to which considerations (1)-(8) are pointing. To confront these deep problems directly, I believe one has to rethink issues about indeterminism and responsibility from the ground up, without relying on appeals to extracausal factors—a task to which I now turn.

III. Indeterminism and responsibility

First, one must question the intuitive connection in people's minds between "indeterminism's being involved in something's happening" and "its happening merely as a matter of chance or luck." 'Chance' and 'luck' are terms of ordinary language which carry the connotation of "its being out of my control" (as in (1) and (4) and above). So using them already begs certain questions, whereas 'indeterminism' is a technical term that merely precludes *deterministic* causation (though not causation altogether). Second, one must emphasize that indeterminism does not have to be involved in all free and responsible acts, even for incompatibilists or libertarians.[11] Frequently, we act from a will already formed; and it may well be that our actions are determined in such cases by our then existing characters and motives. On such occasions, to do otherwise by chance *would* be a fluke or accident, irrational and inexplicable, as critics of indeterminist freedom contend (in (3) and (4) above).

Incompatibilists about free will should not deny this. What they should rather say is that when we act from a will already formed (as we frequently do), it is "our own free will" by virtue of the fact that we formed it (at least in part) by earlier choices or actions which were not determined and for which we could have done otherwise voluntarily, not merely as a fluke or accident. I call these earlier undetermined actions *self-forming actions* or SFAs.[12] Undetermined SFAs are a subset of all of the actions done of our own free wills (many of which may be determined by our earlier formed character and motives). But if there were no such undetermined SFAs in our lifetimes, there would have been nothing we could have ever voluntarily done to make ourselves different than we are—a condition that I think is inconsistent with our having the kind of responsibility for being what we are which genuine free will requires.

Now, let us look more closely at these undetermined SFAs. As I see it, they occur at times in life when we are torn between competing visions of what we should do or become. Perhaps we are torn between doing the moral thing or acting from self-interest, or between present desires and long-term goals, or we are faced with difficult tasks for which we have aversions. In all such cases, we are faced with competing motivations and have to make an effort to overcome temptation to do something else we also strongly want. In the light of this picture, I suggest the following incompatibilist account of SFAs.[13] There is a tension and uncertainty in our minds at such times of inner conflict which are reflected in appropriate regions of our brains by movement away from thermodynamic equilibrium—in short, a kind of stirring up of chaos in the brain that makes it sensitive to micro-indeterminacies at the neuronal level. As a result, the uncertainty and inner tension we feel at such soul-searching moments of self-formation is reflected in the indeterminacy of our neural processes themselves. What is experienced phenomenologically as uncertainty corresponds physically to the opening of a window of opportunity that temporarily screens off complete determination by the past. (By contrast, when we act from predominant motives or settled dispositions, the uncertainty or indeterminism is muted. If it were involved then, it *would* be a mere nuisance or fluke, capricious or arbitrary, as critics contend (in (2), (5) and (6) above).)

When we do decide under such conditions of uncertainty, the outcome is not determined because of the preceding indeterminacy—and yet it can be willed (and hence rational and voluntary) either way owing to the fact that in such self-formation, the agents' prior wills are divided by conflicting motives. If we overcome temptation, it will be the result of our effort; and if we fail, it will be because we did not *allow* our effort to succeed. And this is owing to the fact that, while we wanted to overcome temptation, we also wanted to fail, for quite different and incommensurable reasons. When we decide in such circumstances, and the indeterminate efforts we are making become determinate choices, we *make* one set of competing reasons or motives prevail over the others then and there *by deciding*.

Return now to concerns about indeterminism and responsibility in the light of this picture. Consider a businesswoman who faces a conflict in her will of the kind typically involved in such SFAs. She is on the way to a meeting important to her career when she observes an assault in an alley. An inner struggle ensues between her moral conscience, to stop and call for help, and her career ambitions, which tell her she cannot miss this meeting—a struggle she eventually resolves by turning back to help the victim. Now suppose this woman visits some future neuroscientists the next day and they tell her a story about what was going on in her brain at the time she chose, not unlike the story just told. Prior to choice, there was some indeterminacy in her neural processes stirred up by the conflict in her will. The indeterminism made it uncertain (and undetermined) whether she would go back to help or press onward.

Suppose further that two recurrent and connected neural networks are involved in the neuroscientists' story. Such networks circulate impulses and information in feedback loops and generally play a role in complex cognitive processing in the brain of the kind that one would expect to be involved in human deliberation. Moreover, recurrent networks are nonlinear, thus allowing (as some recent research suggests) for the possibility of chaotic activity, which would contribute to the plasticity and flexibility human brains display in creative problem solving (of which practical deliberation is an example).[14] The input of one of these recurrent networks consists of the woman's moral motives, and its output the choice to go back; the input of the other, her career ambitions, and its output, the choice to go on to her meeting. The two networks are connected, so that the indeterminism that made it uncertain that she would do the moral thing was coming from her desire to do the opposite, and vice versa—the indeterminism thus arising, as we said, from a conflict in the will. When her effort to overcome self-interested desires succeeded, this corresponded to one of the neural pathways reaching an activation threshold, overcoming the indeterminism generated by the other.

To this picture, one might now pose the following objection: if it really was undetermined which choice the woman would make (in neural terms, which network would activate) right up to the moment when she chose, it seems that it would be a matter of luck or chance that one choice was made rather than the other, and so she could not be held responsible for the outcome. (Note that this is an expression of LP.) The first step in response is to recall a point made earlier: we must be wary of moving too hastily from 'indeterminism is involved in something's happening' to 'its happening merely as a matter of chance or luck.' 'Luck' and 'chance' have meanings in ordinary language that mere indeterminism may not have. The second step is to note that indeterminism of itself does not necessarily undermine control and responsibility.[15] Suppose you are trying to think through a difficult problem (say, a mathematical problem) and there is some indeterminacy in your neural processes complicating the task—a kind of chaotic background. It would be like trying to concentrate and solve a problem with background noise or distraction. Whether you are going to succeed in solving the mathematical problem is uncertain and undetermined because of the distracting neural noise. Yet if you concentrate and solve the problem nonetheless, I think we can say that you did it and are responsible for doing it even though it was undetermined whether you would succeed. The indeterministic noise would have been an obstacle to your solving the problem which you nevertheless overcame by your effort.

There are numerous other examples in the philosophical literature of this kind, where indeterminism functions as an obstacle to success without precluding responsibility. Consider an assassin who is trying to kill the prime minister, but might miss because of some undetermined events in his nervous system which might lead to a jerking or wavering of this arm. If he does hit his target, can he be held responsible? The answer (as J. L. Austin and Philippa Foot[16] successfully argued decades ago) is "yes," because he intentionally and voluntarily succeeded in doing what he was *trying* to do—kill the prime minister. Yet his killing the prime minister was undetermined. We might even say in a sense that he got lucky in killing the prime minister, when he could have failed. But it does not follow, if he succeeds, that killing the prime minister was not his action, not something he did; nor does it follow, as LP would require, that he was not responsible for killing the prime minister. Indeed, if anything is clear, it is that he both killed the prime minister and was responsible for doing so.

Or consider a husband who, while arguing with his wife, swings his arm down in anger on her favorite glass table top, intending to break it. Again we suppose that some indeterminism in the husband's efferent neural pathways makes the momentum of his arm indeterminate, so it is undetermined if the table will break right up to the moment when it is struck. Whether the husband breaks the table or not is undetermined. Yet it does not follow, if he succeeds, that breaking the table was not something he did; nor again does it follow, as LP would require, that he was not responsible for breaking it.[17] The inference sanctioned by LP from 'it was undetermined' to 'he was not responsible', is not valid. The above cases are counterexamples to it; and there are many more.

IV. Possible worlds and LP*

But one may grant this and still object that counterexamples to LP of these kinds do not amount to genuine exercises of free will involving SFAs, such as the businesswoman's, where there is conflict in the wills of the agents and they are supposed to choose freely and responsibly *whichever way* they choose. If the assassin and husband succeed in doing what they are trying to do (kill the prime minister, break the table) they will do it *voluntarily* (in accordance with their wills) and *intentionally* (knowingly and purposely). But if they *fail* because of the indeterminism, they will not fail voluntarily and intentionally, but "by mistake" or "accident," or merely "by chance." Thus, their "power" to do *otherwise* (if we should even call it a power) is not the usual power we associate with freedom of choice or action in self-formation, where the agents should be able to choose or act either way voluntarily or intentionally. The power to do otherwise of the assassin and the husband is more like Jane's "power" in (5) and (6) of section II, to choose to vacation in Colorado by a fluke or accident, after a long deliberation in which she had come to favor Hawaii.

As a consequence, while LP may fail for cases like those of the assassin, husband, and mathematical problem solver, another luck principle similar to LP might still be applicable to genuine exercises of free will involving SFAs, like the businesswoman's: if it is undetermined at t whether an agent *voluntarily* and *intentionally* does A at t or *voluntarily* and *intentionally* does otherwise, then the agent's doing one of these rather than the other at t would be a matter of *luck* or *chance,* and so could not be a free and responsible action. This principle—let us call it LP*—is fueled by the same intuitions that fuel LP. Indeed, it is a special case of LP, but one that is more difficult to deal with because it is not subject to counterexamples like those of the husband and the assassin; and it seems to be applicable to SFAs, like the businesswoman's, where failure is not merely a matter of mistake or accident.

To explore further the difficulties posed by LP*, let us look at the final and, I think, most powerful of the intuition pumps in support of LP-type principles mentioned in section II, namely, consideration (8). This was the argument of Strawson, Mele, Berofsky, Waller, Double, Bernstein, and Haji about two agents, or one agent in different possible worlds, with the same pasts.

Consider the version of this argument by Mele, which appeared in this JOURNAL and is a particularly revealing and challenging version of it. In the actual world, an agent John succumbs to the temptation to arrive late to a meeting, whereas his counterpart, John*, in a nearby possible world, whose physical and psychological history is the same as John's up to the moment of choice (as indeterminism requires), resists this temptation. Similarly, we can imagine a counterpart to the businesswoman, businesswoman*, in a nearby possible world who goes to her meeting instead of stopping to aid the assault victim, given the same past. But then, Mele argues, "if there is nothing about [these] agents' powers, capacities, states of mind, moral character and the like that explains this difference in outcome," since they are the same up to the moment of choice in the two possible worlds, "then the difference is just a matter of luck" (*op. cit.,* p. 583).[18] It would seem that John* got lucky in his attempt to overcome temptation, whereas John did not; and similarly, the businesswoman got lucky in her attempt to overcome temptation, while businesswoman* did not.

Let us first consider a general form of this argument that would support LP.

(a)   In the actual world, person P (for example, John, the businesswoman) does A at t.

On the assumption that the act is undetermined at t, we may imagine that:

(b)   In a nearby-possible world which is the same as the actual world up to t, P^* (P's counterpart with the same past) does otherwise (does B) at t.

(c) But then (since their pasts are the same), there is nothing about the agents' powers, capacities, states of mind, characters, dispositions, motives, and so on prior to t which explains the difference in choices in the two possible worlds.

(d) It is therefore a matter of luck or chance that P does A and P^* does B at t.

(e) P is therefore not responsible (praiseworthy or blameworthy, as the case may be) for A at t (and presumably P^* is also not responsible for B).

Call this the *luck argument*. The key assumption is the assumption of indeterminism, which leads to step (b). The remaining steps are meant to follow from (b), given (a).

Despite the fact that this argument looks like Mele's and has an initial plausibility, it is not his argument—and it is a good thing it is not. For the argument from (a)–(e) is invalid as it stands—for the same reasons that LP was invalid. Consider the husband and husband* (his counterpart in a nearby world who fails to break the wife's table). If the outcome is undetermined, husband and husband* also have "the same powers, capacities, states of mind, characters, dispositions, motives, and so on" up to the moment of breaking or not breaking the table, as the argument requires; and it is a matter of luck or chance that the table breaks in one world and not the other. But for all that, it does not follow, as (e) requires, that the husband is not responsible for breaking the table. The husband would have quite a task persuading his wife that he was not responsible for breaking the table on the grounds that it was a matter of luck or chance that it broke. ("Luck or chance did it, not me" is an implausible excuse.)

But, of course, as we noted, husband* is not also responsible for *failing* to break the table, since he does not fail to break it voluntarily or intentionally. He is responsible only for the attempt, when he fails. Similarly, assassin* would be responsible for the attempted murder of the prime minister, when he missed. What has to be explicitly added to the argument (a)–(e) to avoid counterexamples like these is the LP* requirement that *both* P and P^* *voluntarily* and *intentionally* do A and B respectively in their respective worlds. Specifically, we must add to premise (a) that P voluntarily and intentionally does A at t and to (b), that P^* voluntarily and intentionally does B at t, and then make the corresponding additions to (d) and (e). This will yield what we might call the LP* version of the luck argument rather than the LP version. And the stronger LP* version is clearly the one Mele intends, since John's choice in his example is supposed to be an SFA, like the businesswoman's choice in my example, where the agents can go either way voluntarily and intentionally. Moreover, this version of the argument—like LP* itself—is immune to counterexamples like those of the husband and the assassin.

V. Parallel processing

Nonetheless, despite immunity from these counterexamples, I think the LP* version of the luck argument, and LP* itself, also fail. But it is far less easy to show why. To do so, we have to take a closer look at SFAs and push the argument beyond where it has come thus far. Let it be granted that the businesswoman's case and other SFAs like John's are not like the examples of the husband and the assassin. The wills of the husband and assassin are already "set" on doing what they intend, whereas the wills of agents in SFAs, like the businesswoman and John, are not already settled or "formed" until they choose (hence the designation "self-forming actions").[19]

Thus, to get from examples like those of the husband and assassin to genuine SFAs, I think we must do two things. First, we must put the indeterminacy involved in the efferent neural pathways of the husband and assassin into the central neural processes of the businesswoman and other agents, like John, who are making efforts of will to overcome moral, prudential, and other temptations. This move has already been made in earlier sections. But to respond to LP* versions of the luck argument, like Mele's, I believe this move must also be combined with another—a kind of "doubling" of the example given earlier of solving the mathematical problem in the presence of background indeterministic noise.[20]

Imagine that the businesswoman is *trying* or making an effort to solve *two* cognitive problems at once, or to complete two competing (deliberative) tasks at once—to make a moral choice and to make a choice for her ambitions (corresponding to the two competing neural networks involved in the earlier description). With respect to each task, as with the mathematical problem, she is being thwarted in her attempt to do what she is trying to do by indeterminism. But in her case, the indeterminism does not have a mere external source; it is coming from her own will, from her desire to do the opposite. Recall that the two crossing neural networks involved are connected, so that the indeterminism which is making it uncertain that she will do the moral thing is coming from her desire to do the opposite, and vice versa. She may therefore fail to do what she is trying to do, just like the assassin, the husband, and the person trying to solve the mathematical problem. But I argue that, if she nevertheless *succeeds,* then she can be held responsible because, like them, she will have succeeded in doing *what she was trying to do.* And the interesting thing is that this will be true of her, *whichever choice is made,* because she was trying to make both choices and one is going to succeed.

Does it make sense to talk about agents trying to do two competing things at once in this way? Well, we know the brain is a parallel processor and that capacity, I believe, is essential for the exercise of free will. In cases of self-formation, agents are simultaneously trying to resolve plural and competing cognitive tasks. They are, as we say, of two minds. But they are not therefore two separate persons. They are not disassociated from either task.[21] The businesswoman who wants to go back and help the assault victim is the same ambitious woman who wants to go on to her meeting and close the sale. She is a complex creature, like most of us who are often torn inside; but hers is the kind of complexity needed for free will. And when she succeeds in doing one of the things she is trying to do, she will endorse that as *her* resolution of the conflict in her will, voluntarily and intentionally, as LP* requires. She will not disassociate from either outcome, as did Jane (in (5) of section II), who wondered what "happened to" her when she chose Colorado, or like the husband and assassin who did not also want to fail.[22]

But one may still object that the businesswoman makes one choice rather than the other *by chance,* since it was undetermined right up to the last moment which choice she would make. If this is so, we may have the picture of her first making an effort to overcome temptation (to go on to her meeting) and do the moral thing, and then at the last minute "chance takes over" and decides the issue for her. But this is the wrong picture. On the view just described, you cannot separate the indeterminism from the effort to overcome temptation in such a way that *first* the effort occurs *followed by* chance or luck (or vice versa). One must think of the effort and the indeterminism as fused; the effort *is* indeterminate and the indeterminism is a property of the effort, not something separate that occurs after or before the effort. The fact that the woman's effort of will has this property of being indeterminate does not make it any less her *effort.* The complex recurrent neural network that realizes the effort in the brain is circulating impulses in feedback loops and there is some indeterminacy in these circulating impulses. But the whole process is her effort of will and it persists right up to the moment when the choice is made. There is no point at which the effort stops and chance "takes over." She chooses *as a result of* the effort, even though she might have failed because of the indeterminism.

And just as expressions like 'She chose *by* chance' can mislead us in these contexts, so can expressions like 'She got lucky'. Ask yourself this question: Why does the inference 'He got lucky, *so he was not responsible*' fail when it does fail, as in the cases of the husband and the assassin? The first part of an answer goes back to the claim that 'luck', like 'chance', has question-begging implications in ordinary language which are not necessarily implications of "indeterminism" (which implies only the absence of deterministic causation). The core meaning of 'He got lucky', which *is* implied by indeterminism, I suggest, is that 'He succeeded *despite the probability or chance of failure';* and this core meaning does not imply lack of responsibility, if he succeeds.

If 'He got lucky' had further meanings in these contexts often associated with 'luck' and 'chance' in ordinary usage (for example, the outcome was not his doing, or occurred by *mere* chance, or he was not responsible for it), the inference would not fail for the husband and assassin, as it clearly does. But the point is that these further meanings of 'luck' and 'chance' do not follow *from the mere presence of indeterminism*. Second, the inference 'He got lucky, so he was not responsible' fails because *what* the assassin and husband succeeded in doing was what they were trying and wanting to do all along. Third, *when* they succeeded, their reaction was not "Oh dear, that was a mistake, an accident—something that *happened* to me, not something I *did*." Rather, they *endorsed* the outcomes as something they were trying and wanting to do all along, that is to say, knowingly and purposefully, not by mistake or accident.

But these conditions are satisfied in the businesswoman's case as well, *either way* she chooses. If she succeeds in choosing to return to help the victim (or in choosing to go on to her meeting) (i) she will have "succeeded despite the probability or chance of failure"; (ii) she will have succeeded in doing what she was trying and wanting to do all along (she wanted both outcomes very much, but for different reasons, and was trying to make those reasons prevail in both cases); and (iii) when she succeeded (in choosing to return to help) her reaction was not "Oh dear, that was a mistake, an accident—something that happened to me, not something I did." Rather, she endorsed the outcome as something she was trying and wanting to do all along; she recognized it as her resolution of the conflict in her will. And if she had chosen to go on to her meeting she would have endorsed that outcome, recognizing it as her resolution of the conflict in her will.

VI. The luck argument revisited

With this in mind, let us return to the LP* version of the argument from (a)–(e). I said that Mele clearly intends this stronger LP* version of the argument, since the force of his argument depends on the fact that John's choice in his example is a SFA, like the businesswoman's, instead of being like the actions of the husband and assassin. But if this is so, then John's situation will also be like the businesswoman's on the account just given of SFAs. Since both of them are simultaneously trying to do *both* of the things they may do (choose to help or go on, overcome the temptation to arrive late or not), they will do either with intent or on purpose, as a result of wanting and trying to do it—that is, intentionally and voluntarily. Thus, their "failing" to do one of the options will not be a mistake or accident, but a voluntary and intentional doing *of the other*.

Likewise, businesswoman* and John* are simultaneously trying to do both things in their respective worlds; and they will not "fail" to act on moral or weak-willed motives by mistake or accident, as the case may be, but by voluntarily and intentionally choosing to act on the opposing motives. The point is that in self-formation of these kinds (SFAs), failing is never *just* failing; it is always also a *succeeding* in doing something else we wanted and were trying to do. And we found that one can be responsible for succeeding in doing what one was trying to do, even in the presence of indeterminism. So even if we add the LP* requirement of more-than-one-way voluntariness and intentionality to the argument of (a)–(e), the argument remains invalid for cases like the businesswoman's and other SFAs, like John's.

But one might argue further, as Mele does, that John and John* (and businesswoman and businesswoman*) not only had the same capacities, motives, characters, and the like prior to choice, but they made exactly the same *efforts* as well. And this does seem to suggest that the success of one and failure of the other was a matter of mere luck or chance, so that John and the businesswoman were not responsible. But again the inference is too hasty. Note, first, that husband and husband* also made the same efforts (as well as having the same capacities, motives, and characters) up to the very moment of breaking of the table. Yet it does not follow that the husband is not responsible when he succeeds. And *both* the businesswoman and businesswoman*, and John and John*, are in the position of the husband in their respective worlds, since both will have succeeded in doing what they were trying to do.

But one may still want to object: if the businesswoman and businesswoman*, and John and John*, make exactly the same efforts, how can it *not* be a matter of chance that one succeeds and the other does not, in a way that makes them not responsible? To which I reply: But if they both succeeded in doing what they were trying to do (because they were simultaneously trying to do both things), and then having succeeded, they both *endorsed* the outcomes of their respective efforts (that is, their choices) as what they were trying to do, instead of disowning or disassociating from those choices, how then can we *not* hold them responsible? It just does not follow that, because they made exactly the same efforts, they chose *by* chance.

To say something was done "by chance" usually means (as in the assassin and husband cases when they fail), it was done "by mistake" or "accidentally," "inadvertently," "involuntarily," or "as an unintended fluke." But none of these things holds of the businesswoman and John either way they choose. Unlike husband*, businesswoman* and John do not fail to overcome temptation by mistake or accident, inadvertently or involuntarily. They consciously and willingly fail to overcome temptation *by* consciously and willingly choosing to act in selfish or weak-willed ways. So, just as it would have been a poor excuse for the husband to say to his wife when the table broke that "Luck or chance did it, not me," it would be a poor excuse for businesswoman* and John to say "Luck or chance did it, not me" when they failed to help the assault victim or failed to arrive on time.

Worth highlighting in this argument is the point that we cannot simply say the businesswoman and businesswoman* (or John and John*) made exactly the same *effort* (in the singular) in their respective possible worlds and one succeeded while the other failed. We must say they made exactly the same *efforts* (plural) in their respective worlds. Mentioning only one effort prejudices the case, for it suggests that the failure of that effort in one of the worlds was a *mere* mistake or accident, when the fact is that both of the agents (P and P*) made *both* efforts in *both* worlds. In one world, one of the efforts issued in a choice and in the other world, a different effort issued in a different choice; but neither was merely accidental or inadvertent in either world. I would go even further and say that we may also doubt that the efforts they were both making really were exactly the same. Where events are indeterminate, as are the efforts they were making, there is no such thing as exact sameness or difference of events in different possible worlds. Their efforts were not exactly the same, nor were they exactly different, because they were not exact. They were simply unique.[23]

One might try another line: perhaps we are begging the question in assuming that the outcomes of the efforts of the businesswoman and her counterpart were *choices* at all. If they were not choices to begin with, they could not have been voluntary choices. One might argue this on the grounds that (A) "If an event is undetermined, it must be something that merely happens and cannot be somebody's choice"; and (B) "If an event is undetermined, it must be something that merely happens, it cannot be something an agent does (it cannot be an action)." But to see how question-begging these assumptions are, one has only to note that (A) and (B) imply respectively (A') "If an event is a choice, it must be determined" ("All choices are determined") and (B') "If an event is an action, it must be determined" ("All actions are determined"). Are these supposed to be a priori or analytic truths? If so, then long-standing issues about freedom and determinism would be settled by fiat. If an event were not determined, it could not be a choice or action necessarily or by definition.[24]

This explains the businesswoman's suspicions when she exited the neuroscientists' offices. They told her that when she "chose" to go back to help the assault victim the day before, there was some indeterminism in her neural processes prior to choice. She accepted this as a correct empirical finding. But she was suspicious when the neuroscientists tried to get her to make the further inference from those findings which she did not really *choose* to help the assault victim yesterday. She refused to accept that conclusion, and rightly so. For in drawing it, they were going beyond their empirical findings and trying to foist on her the a priori assumption that if an event was undetermined, it could not have been her choice or could not have been something she did. She rightly saw that there was nothing in the empirical evidence that required her to say that. To choose is consciously and deliberately to form an intention to do something; and she did that, despite the indeterminism in her neural processes (as did businesswoman* when she chose to go on to her meeting).

VII. Final considerations: control and explanation

But it is one thing to say that she chose and another to say she chose *freely* and *responsibly*. This would require that she not only chose, but had voluntary *control* over her choice either way. We have not talked at length to this point about the matter of control (considerations (1) and (3) of section II) and must now do so. For this may be the reason why we may think the choices made by the businesswoman and businesswoman* (or John and John*) could not be responsible, if they were undetermined. We might deny that they had voluntary control over what they chose, where voluntary control means being able to bring about something in accordance with one's will or purposes (or, as we often say, the ability to bring something about "at will").

One thing does seem to be true about control which critics of indeterminist freedom have always maintained: indeterminism, wherever it appears, does seem to *diminish* rather than enhance agents' voluntary control (consideration (3) of section II). The assassin's voluntary control over whether or not the prime minister is killed (his ability to realize his purpose or what he is trying to do) is diminished by the undetermined impulses in his arm—and so also for the husband and his breaking the table. Moreover, this limitation is connected to another, which I think we must also grant—that indeterminism, wherever it occurs, functions as a *hindrance* or *obstacle* to our purposes that must be overcome by effort (consideration (3)).

But recall that in the businesswoman's case (and for SFAs generally, like John's), the indeterminism that is admittedly diminishing her ability to overcome selfish temptation, and *is* indeed a hindrance to her doing so, is coming from her own will—from her desire and effort to do the opposite—since she is simultaneously trying to realize two conflicting purposes at once. Similarly, her ability to overcome moral qualms is diminished by the fact that she also simultaneously wants and is trying to act on moral reasons. If we could look at each of the two competing neural networks involved separately, abstracting from the other, the situation would look analogous to the situations of the husband and the assassin. The agent would be trying to do something while being hindered by indeterminism coming from an external source. But, in fact, we cannot look at the two networks separately in this way because, in reality, they are connected and interacting. The indeterminism that is a hindrance to her fulfilling one is coming from its interactions with the other. The indeterminism, therefore, does not have an external source. It is internal to her will, and hence to her self, since she identifies with both networks and will identify with the choice reached by either of them as her choice.

The upshot is that, despite the businesswoman's diminished control over *each* option considered separately, due to a conflict in her will, she nonetheless has what I call *plural voluntary control* over the two options considered *as a set* (*ibid.*, 134–43). Having plural voluntary control over a set of options means being able to bring about *whichever* of the options you will or most want, *when* you will to do so, for the reasons you will to do so, without being coerced or compelled in doing so. And the businesswoman (or John) has this power, because whichever of the options she chooses (to help the victim or go on to her meeting) will be *endorsed* by her as what she wills or most wants to do at the moment when she chooses it (though not necessarily beforehand); she will choose it for the reasons she most wants to act on then and there (moral or selfish reasons, as the case may be); she need not have been coerced by anyone else into choosing one rather than the other; and she will not be choosing either compulsively, since neither choice is such that she could not have chosen it then and there, even if she most wanted to.[25]

One must add, of course, that such plural voluntary control is not the same as what may be called *antecedent determining control*—the ability to determine or guarantee which of a set of options will occur *before* it occurs (*ibid.*, 144). With respect to undetermined self-forming choices (SFAs), agents cannot determine or guarantee which choice outcome will occur *beforehand;* for that could only be done by predetermining the outcome. But it does not follow that, because one cannot determine which of a set of outcomes will occur before it occurs, one does not determine which of them occurs *when* it occurs. When the conditions of plural voluntary control are satisfied, agents exercise control over their present and future lives then and there by deciding.

But can we not at least say that, if indeterminism is involved, then *which* option is chosen is "arbitrary"? I grant that there is a sense in which this is true. An ultimate arbitrariness remains in all undetermined SFAs because there cannot, in principle, be sufficient or overriding *prior* reasons for making one set of competing reasons prevail over the other. But I argue that such arbitrariness relative to prior reasons tells us something important about free will. It tells us, as I have elsewhere expressed it, that every undetermined self-forming choice (SFA) "is the initiation of a 'value experiment' whose justification lies in the *future* and is not fully explained by the *past*. [Making such a choice], we say in effect, 'Let's try this. It is not required by my past, but is consistent with my past and is one branching pathway my life could now meaningfully take. I am willing to take responsibility for it one way or the other' " (*ibid.*, 145–46). To initiate and take responsibility for such value experiments whose justification lies in the future, is to "take chances' without prior guarantees of success. Genuine self-formation requires this sort of risk-taking and indeterminism is a part of it. If there are persons who need to be certain in advance just exactly what is the best or right thing to do in every circumstance (perhaps to be told so by some human or divine authority), then free will is not for them.

This point also throws light on why the luck argument fails, even in the stronger LP* version, despite its initial plausibility. Consider the move from step (c)—the agents *P* and *P** have the same powers, characters, motives, and the like, prior to *t* in the two possible worlds—to step (d), which says it was a matter of luck or chance that *P* did *A* and *P** did *B* at *t*. An important reason given for this move was that, if both agents have all the same prior powers, characters, motives, and the like, there can be no "explanation of the difference in choice" between the two agents in terms of their prior reasons or motives; and this is taken to imply that the difference in choices in the two worlds is a matter of luck or chance *in a way* that precludes responsibility.

But this move, like others discussed earlier, is too hasty. The absence of an explanation of the difference in choice in terms of prior reasons does not have the tight connection to issues of responsibility one might initially credit it with. For one thing, the absence of such an explanation does not imply (as I have been arguing throughout this paper) that businesswoman and businesswoman* (John and John*) (1) did not *choose* at all, nor does it imply that they did not both choose (2) *as a result of their efforts,* nor that they did not choose (3) *for reasons* (different reasons, of course) that (4) they most wanted to choose for *when* they chose, nor that they did not choose for those reasons (5) *knowingly* and (6) *on purpose* when they chose, and hence (7) *rationally,* (8) *voluntarily,* and (9) *intentionally.* None of these conditions is precluded by the absence of an explanation of the difference of choice in terms of prior reasons. Yet these are precisely the kinds of conditions we look for when deciding whether or not persons are responsible.

I suggest that the reason why these conditions are not excluded is that the explanation of the difference of choice in the two possible worlds which is missing is an explanation in terms of *sufficient* or *conclusive* reasons—one that would render an alternative choice, given the same prior reasons, irrational or inexplicable. And, of course, *that* sort of explanation is not possible for undetermined SFAs, when there is conflict in the will and the agent has good (but not decisive or conclusive) prior reasons for going either way. But neither is that sort of explanation required to say that an agent acts as the result of her effort for reasons she most wants to act on then and there. In sum, *you can choose responsibly for prior reasons that were not conclusive or decisive prior to your choosing for them.*

I said a moment ago that such arbitrariness relative to prior reasons tells us something important about free will—that every self-forming choice is the initiation of a value experiment whose justification lies in the future and cannot be fully explained by the past. It is worth adding in this regard that the term 'arbitrary' comes from the Latin *arbitrium,* which means 'judgment'—as in *liberum arbitrium voluntatis* ("free judgment of the will")—the medieval designation for free will. Imagine a writer in the middle of a novel. The novel's heroine faces a crisis and the writer has not yet developed her character in sufficient detail to say exactly how she will react. The author must make a "judgment" *(arbitrium)* about how she will react that is not determined by the heroine's already formed past, which does not give unique direction. In this sense, the author's judgment of how she will act is "arbitrary," but not entirely so. It has input from the hero-ine's fictional past and, in turn, gives input to her projected future.

In a similar manner, agents who exercise free will are both authors of, and characters in, their own stories at once. By virtue of "self-forming" judgments of the will *(arbitria voluntatis),* they are "arbiters" of their own lives, taking responsibility for "making themselves" out of past that, if they are truly free, does not limit their future pathways to one. If someone should charge them with not having a sufficient or conclusive prior reason for choosing as they did, they may reply as follows: "Perhaps so. But that does not mean I did not *choose*; and it does not mean I did not choose for *good* reasons, which I stand by and for which I take responsibility. If I lacked sufficient or conclusive prior reasons, that is because, like the heroine of the novel, I was not a fully formed person before I chose—and still am not, for that matter.[26] Like the author of the novel, I am in the process of writing a story and forming a person (who, in my case, is myself). It is a heavy burden, but an eminently human one."

Notes

This paper was prompted by a recent objection made in various forms against my view and other incompatibilist views of freedom and responsibility by Galen Strawson, Alfred Mele, Bernard Berofsky, Bruce Waller, Richard Double, Mark Bernstein, and Ishtiyaque Haji. (See footnote 10 for references.) The paper has benefitted from inter-changes with the above persons and with participants at a conference on my work on free will at the University of Arkansas in September, 1997: Gary Watson, Barry Loewer, Timothy O'Connor, Randolph Clarke, Christopher Hill, and Thomas Senor. It has also benefited from interchanges in conferences or in correspondence with John Martin Fischer, William Rowe, Nicholas Nathan, David Hodgson, Saul Smilansky, Kevin Magill, Peter van Inwagen, Derk Pereboom, Laura Ekstrom, Hugh McCann, and Ilya Prigogine. I am especially grateful to Mele and Strawson for pursuing me assiduously on these issues since the publication of my latest work, and for perceptive comments on the penultimate draft by Mele, Berofsky, and George Graham.

1. Ludwig Wittgenstein, *Culture and Value* (New York: Blackwell, 1980).

2. Daniel C. Dennett, *Elbow Room* (Cambridge, M.A: MIT Press, 1984), chap. 1 and 32–34, 64–65, 119–20, 169–70.

3. Robert Kane, *The Significance of Free Will* (New York: Oxford University Press, 1996), 10–14, 33–37.

4. For example, physicist A. H. Compton, *The Freedom of Man* (New Haven, CT: Yale University Press, 1935) and neurophysiologist John Eccles, *Facing Reality* (New York: Springer, 1970).

5. See, for example, Galen Strawson, who argues that, even if free will should be incompatible with determinism, indeterminism would be "no help" in enhancing either freedom or responsibility—"The unhelpfulness of indeterminism," *Philosophy and Phenomenological Research* 60.1 (2000), 149–155.

6. Arthur Schopenhauer, *Essay on the Freedom of the Will* (Indianapolis: Bobbs-Merrill, 1960), 47.

7. This dilemma for incompatibilist accounts of freedom is nicely described by Thomas Nagel, *The View from Nowhere* (New York: Oxford University Press, 1986), chap. 7.

8. Gottfried Wilhelm Leibniz, *Selections* (New York: Scribner's, 1951), 435.

9. Stephen M. Cahn makes a persuasive case for there being such a role—"Random choices," *Philosophy and Phenomenological Research* 37 (1977): 549–51.

10. Galen Strawson, "The impossibility of moral responsibility," *Philosophical Studies* 75 (1994): 5–24, and "The unhelpfulness of indeterminism," *op. cit.;* Alfred Mele, Review of my *The Significance of Free Will*, this JOURNAL, 95, 11 (November 1998): 581–84, and "Kane, luck, and the significance of free will," *Philosophical Explorations* (May 1999), 96–104; Bernard Berofsky, "Ultimate responsibility in a deterministic world," *Philosophy and Phenomenological Research* 60.1 (2000), 135–40; Bruce Waller, "Free will gone out of control," *Behaviorism* 16 (1988): 149–67; Richard Double, *The Non-reality of Free Will* (New York: Oxford University Press, 1991), p. 140; Mark Bernstein, "Kanean libertarianism," *Southwest Philosophy Review* 11 (1995): 151–57; Ishtiyaque Haji, "Indeterminism and Frankfurt-type examples," *Philosophical Explorations* 2.1 (1999), 42–58. Different, but related, concerns about indeterminism and agency are aired by Timothy O'Connor, "Indeterminism and free agency: three recent views," *Philosophy and Phenomenological Research,* 53 (1993): 499–526; and Randolph Clarke, "Free choice, effort and wanting more," *Philosophical Explorations* 2.1 (1999), 20–41.

11. I defend this point at length in *Free Will and Values* (Albany: SUNY Press, 1985), chap. 4 and chap. 5. It is also defended by Peter van Inwagen, "When is the will free?" in *Philosophical Perspectives,* vol. 3, ed. J. Tomberlain (Atascadero, CA: Ridgeview, 1989), 399–422. John Martin Fischer has described the view that van Inwagen and I defend as "restricted libertarianism," and has criticized it in "When the will is free," in Tomberlin, ed., *Philosophical Perspectives,* vol. 6, ed. J. Tomberlin (Atascadero, CA: Ridgeview, 1992), 423–51. Another critic is Hugh McCann, "On when the will is free," in G. Holmstrom-Hintikka and R. Tuomela, eds., *Contemporary Action Theory,* vol. 1, (Dordrecht: Kluwer, 1997), 219–32. Van Inwagen responds to Fischer in "When is the will not free?" *Philosophical Studies* 75 (1994): 95–114; and I respond in *The Significance of Free Will,* 32–43.

12. See *The Significance of Free Will*, 74–78. SFAs are also sometimes called "self-forming willings" or SFWs in that work (125ff.).

13. This, in broad outline, is the account developed in my *The Significance of Free Will*, chapters 8–10. In later sections below, I make important additions to it in response to criticisms.

14. See P. Huberman and G. Hogg, "Phase transitions in artificial intelligence systems," *Artificial Intelligence* 33 (1987): 155–72; C. Skarda and W. Freeman, "How brains make chaos in order to make sense of the world," *Behavior and Brain Sciences* 10 (1987): 161–95; A. Babloyantz and A. Destexhe, "Strange attractors in the human cortex," in *Temporal Disorder in Human Oscillatory Systems*, ed. L. Rensing (New York: Springer, 1985), 132–43.

15. Important recent defenses of the claim that indeterminism does not necessarily undermine control and responsibility include Clarke, "Indeterminism and control," *American Philosophical Quarterly* 32 (1995): 125–38; Carl Ginet, *On Action* (New York:

Cambridge University Press, 1990), chap. 6; Timothy O'Connor; and Laura Ekstrom, *Free Will: A Philosophical Study* (Boulder, CO: Westview, 2000).

16. J. L. Austin, "Ifs and cans," in his *Philosophical Papers* (New York: Oxford University Press, 1961), 153–80; Philippa Foot, "Free will as involving determinism," in *Free Will and Determinism*, ed. Bernard Berofsky (New York: Harper and Row, 1966), 95–108.

17. We must, of course, assume in both these examples that other (compatibilist) conditions for responsibility are in place—for example, that, despite his anger, the husband was not acting compulsively and would have controlled himself, if he had wished; that he knew what he was doing and was doing it intentionally to anger his wife, and so on (and similarly for the assassin). But the point is that nothing in the facts of either case precludes these assumptions from also being satisfied.

18. I have elsewhere denied that the pasts of the agents can be exactly the same, since, with indeterminist efforts, there is no exact sameness or difference (*The Significance of Free Will*, 171–74). Mele's argument is designed to work, however, whether this denial of exact sameness is assumed or not. So I do not make an issue of it here.

19. See *The Significance of Free Will*, 112–14.

20. This further "doubling" move is consistent with the theory put forward in *The Significance of Free Will*, and presupposes much of that theory, but is not made in that work. It is a further development especially provoked by Mele's argument discussed here as well as by criticisms of other persons since the book's publication, such as Strawson, Berofsky, Nathan, Watson, Clarke, O'Connor, Double, and Haji.

21. I account for this elsewhere in terms of the notion of a "self-network" (*The Significance of Free Will*, 137–42), a more comprehensive network of neural connections representing the general motivational system in terms of which agents define themselves as agents and practical reasoners. For further discussion of such a notion, see Owen Flanagan, *Consciousness Reconsidered* (Cambridge, MA: MIT, 1992), 207ff.

22. In response to my claim (*The Significance of Free Will*, 215) that "free willers [who engage in SFAs] are always trying to be better than they are by their own lights," by trying to overcome temptations of various sorts, Strawson asks: but "can't they also try to be worse than they are?"—"The unhelpfulness of indeterminism." He is right, of course; they can. I should have added what I am saying here, that free willers can and do *also* try to be as bad or worse than they are by resisting efforts to be better. Strange creatures indeed.

23. See *The Significance of Free Will*, pp. 171–74.

24. *Ibid.*, 183–86, for a fuller account of why indeterminism does not rule out action or choice.

25. *Ibid.*, 133–38, where a more detailed case is made for each of these claims.

26. Jan Bransen (in "Alternatives of oneself," *Philosophy and Phenomenological Research* 60.2 (2000), 381–400) has made an important distinction that is relevant here— between choosing "alternatives *for* oneself" and choosing "alternatives *of* oneself." Bransen notes that some choices in life are for different courses of action that will make a difference in what sort of person the chooser will become in future. In such cases, agents are not merely choosing alternatives for themselves but are choosing alternatives of themselves. Many SFAs, as I understand them, would be of this kind.

11

Toward A Credible Agent-Causal Account of Free Will

Randolph Clarke

Agent-causal accounts of free will, of the sort advanced in years past by Chisholm and Taylor,[1] are now widely regarded as discredited. Such accounts held that when an agent acts with free will, her action is not causally determined by any prior events. The agent herself was said to cause her action, and this causation by the agent was said not to consist in causation by an event or collection of events. An agent acting with this sort of freedom, it was claimed, acted with the ability to do otherwise. And what the agent did was not an accident or a matter of chance; the agent herself made it happen that she did what she did. She was an uncaused cause of her so acting.

Such accounts have been rejected chiefly for two reasons. First, they failed to provide an adequate account of the relations between an agent, her reasons for action, and her action, and hence they failed as accounts of rational free action.[2] Second, they did not provide an intelligible explication of what causation by an agent was supposed to be.[3]

It is, in my view, unfortunate that the notion of agent causation has been largely abandoned, and in this paper I hope to contribute to its rehabilitation. I will sketch an agent-causal account of free will that differs in important respects from those of Chisholm and Taylor; and I will argue that given this account, the first of the objections described above can be easily met, and that considerable progress can be made in meeting the second. If I am right, then the result is an important one, for a viable agent-causal account would provide an attractive alternative to compatibilist accounts of free will.

I. Rational free action

On Chisholm's and Taylor's accounts, when an agent acts with free will, her action (or some event that is a part of her action) is not caused by any events.[4] Indeed, Chisholm seems to believe that *any* action must be caused by an agent and not by any event.[5] The rationality problem arises directly from these requirements, for if an agent's action is not caused by her having certain reasons for action, then it is unclear how she can be said to have acted on those reasons and how her action can be said to be rational (and rationally explicable).

There are, I believe, two errors in Chisholm's and Taylor's requirements regarding the causes of actions. First, agent causation should be seen as required for acting with free will, but not for acting. An agent-causal account of free will might then be made consistent with the familiar analyses of action. And second, an agent-causal account should not deny that free actions are caused by prior events. Both of these mistakes can be avoided without sacrificing what is of value in an agent-causal account.

According to one of our most familiar pictures of deliberation and action, it is frequently the case when an agent acts that there is a variety of things that she can do, and she brings it about that she does one of these things in particular. The chief virtue of an agent-causal view, I believe, is that it gives a non-Orwellian account of how these two conditions can obtain.

Like any libertarian view, an agent-causal account makes room for the first of these conditions by requiring that determinism be false. Given indeterminism, it may often be the case when an agent acts that there are several different actions each of which it is naturally possible that she perform, where 'naturally possible' is explained as follows: at time t it is naturally possible that an event E occur (in our world) at time t′ just in case there is at least one possible world with the same laws of nature as ours and with a history exactly like ours up through time t in which E occurs at t′.[6]

Unlike most other libertarian accounts, an agent-causal account secures the second condition by taking it seriously and quite literally. An agent's bringing it about that she performs one in particular of the naturally possible actions is taken as a condition of production, and producing is taken to be causally bringing about. An agent's causing her performing a certain action is taken to be really that, and not really something quite different, such as the causation of her action by an event involving the agent. Finally, since agents or persons are held not to be themselves effects of prior causes, on agent-causal accounts agents constitute uncaused causes of their performing the particular actions they perform.

Agent-causal accounts thus secure an interesting condition of production, one that requires that, when an agent acts with free will, she is in a significant respect an originator of her action. This condition can be expressed as follows:

(CP) When an agent acts with free will, her action is causally brought about by something that (a) is not itself causally brought about by anything over which she has no control, and that (b) is related to her in such a way that, in virtue of its causing her action, she determines which action she performs.

When CP is fulfilled, an agent is a real point of origin of her action. She determines that she perform that action, and that determination by her is not determined by anything beyond her control.

Any account of free will that allows that all events (except perhaps the world's first event) are caused, that all causes are events, and that all causal chains go back in time, if not forever, then to the beginning of the universe will fail to secure CP, regardless of whether causal relations are deterministic or merely probabilistic. CP appears unsecured, too, if an uncaused event is the immediate cause of the agent's action. For then it is unclear how the agent could be related to that uncaused event in such a way that she controlled its occurrence, and by controlling its occurrence determined which action she would perform. CP *is* secured if the relation in question is taken to be identity. For then when an agent acts with free will, she herself causes her performing a certain action, and qua agent or person she is not the effect of any causes (although events involving her are).

Now, it is consistent with this much of the agent-causal account that earlier events, including the agent's having or coming to have certain reasons to act, cause her performing a certain action. For suppose that all events in our world (except perhaps a first event) are caused by earlier events, but that event causation is 'chancy' or probabilistic rather than deterministic.[7] Then, given the events up until now, there might be a certain chance, or single-case, objective probability (say, for example, .6) that a certain event E occur now, as well as a certain chance (.4) that E not occur now. Whatever happens now, past events cause it; but since they do not causally necessitate it, something else might have happened instead, in which case past events would have caused that something else. Suppose, further, that frequently when a human agent acts, it is naturally possible that she perform any one of several different actions each of which precludes her performing any of the others. Whichever of these actions she performs, earlier events probabilistically cause that action. It is consistent with these suppositions that often when a human agent acts, *she* causes her performing one rather than any of the other naturally possible actions. She brings it about that she performs that particular action. Yet, until her performance of that action, the chance that she would perform it remained somewhere between zero and one.

A libertarian view that affirms this account of human agency allows that an agent's behavior, besides being caused by her, is caused also by earlier events, among which are her having or coming to have certain beliefs, desires, preferences, aims, values, and so forth. This difference from the agent-causal views of Chisholm and Taylor stems from the recognition, here, that event causation may be probabilistic, and that probabilistic causation is not the threat to free will that causal necessitation is.[8] CP can thus be secured even if it is allowed that all events are caused by prior events.

The agent-causal account that I have sketched, then, is itself a kind of reconciliationism. It reconciles a traditionally libertarian claim—that freedom consists in being an undetermined determinant of one's action—with the apparently undeniable fact that human beings are part of the causal order, that all events involving human beings are causally brought about by earlier events. Such a view reconciles free will not with determinism but with the highly plausible thesis of universal event causation. There is a clear advantage to be gained from this sort of reconciliation, for it allows for our ability to predict and explain human behavior.

The account suggested here thus provides a reply to the following version of the rational-explicability objection. The agent exists prior to, as well as during and after, the performance of any one of her actions. Yet the action occurs at a certain time. The fact that the action is caused by the agent, then, cannot explain why the action occurs when it does rather than earlier or later. Hence, it is objected, on an agent-causal account, the timing of human actions cannot be explained.[9]

The reply is that, on the view sketched here, the timing of an action is explained as well as it is on a wholly event-causal account of human agency, given the assumption that event causation is nondeterministic. On the view I suggest, the occurrence of certain prior events will be a necessary condition of an agent's causing a certain event. Absent those prior events, the later event will not be naturally possible, and an agent can cause only what is naturally possible. The agent-causal view thus has the same resources as does a wholly event-causal view of human agency to explain why an agent performs a certain action at a certain time, rather than earlier or later. If there is an event, such as her acquiring new reasons, that explains why she acted then and not at some other time, then both sorts of views have available an explanation. If there is no such event, then neither sort of view has available an explanation. As I explain in more detail in Section III, although agent causation adds nothing to our ability to explain human behavior, neither does it subtract anything.

On the agent-causal account sketched here, when an agent acts with free will, the agent's beliefs and desires are among the causes of her behavior. But if this is so, how are event and agent causation related, and can agent-caused actions still be rational?

The best reply here, I believe, is to maintain that what an agent directly causes, when she acts with free will, is her acting on (or for) certain of her reasons rather than on others, and her acting for reasons ordered in a particular way by weight, importance, or significance as the reasons for which she performs that action. Her acting for that ordering of reasons is itself a complex event, one that consists, in part, of her behavior's being caused by those reasons.[10] What is agent-caused, then, is her performing that action for that ordering of reasons rather than, say, that action for a different ordering of reasons or another action for different reasons.[11]

In the simplest case, an agent has her reasons and she acts on them. Pam attends a lecture on Mapplethorpe, say, primarily because she is interested in his work and secondarily because she knows the speaker. She might also have some desire to accompany a second friend to an interesting movie that is showing at the same time. But she causes her acting on the first set of reasons, and on a particular ordering of them, instead. What she directly causes is her attending the lecture primarily because of her interest in Mapplethorpe's work and secondarily because of her friendship with the lecturer.

Now, if an agent's action is rational, then her acting *for* a particular ordering of reasons will be rational in light of the reasons the agent *has* to act. It will be rational in light of her overall constellation of motivational states. And there are a couple of questions on this point that are waiting to be addressed.

One question concerning the rationality of agent-caused actions is whether, when an agent acts with this sort of freedom, there could be at least one ordering of the reasons *for* which she acts such that her acting for that ordering would be rational in light of the reasons she *has* to act. The answer to this question is an easy 'yes'. If Pam has better reasons to attend the Mapplethorpe lecture than to go to the movie, then it is rational for her to act for those better reasons. It will be rationally explicable why she went to the lecture, and rationally explicable as well why she went to the lecture instead of going to the movies. Such explanations need refer to no more than the reasons for which she acted in going to the lecture.

It is important for a libertarian view that on a significant number of the occasions when an agent acts with free will, there is more than one action that she might rationally perform. Although our freedom of the will might consist partly in an ability to behave irrationally, free will is more desirable if it is the freedom to determine which of several genuine alternatives one will rationally pursue. A second rationality question, then, is whether the view sketched here allows for such alternative rationality.

It is often rationally indeterminate what we shall do and for what reasons we shall act. We are, for example, sometimes faced with choices among alternatives about which we are utterly indifferent. If I am given a choice of any one of several fine-looking apples, I may have no reason to pick any one of them rather than any other. In this kind of situation, my choice of any one of the apples will be as rational as would have been the choice of any other one. We also often face decisions where we have equally good reasons for making either of two or more choices. If I have until now taken as great an interest in surfing as in downhill skiing, I might as rationally choose to vacation at the beach as I might choose to go to the mountains.

There are other sorts of cases in which it is rationally indeterminate not only *for* which reasons an agent will act, but also how the reasons an agent *has* to act will be ordered. In making a decision, an agent will sometimes change the order in which she ranks considerations as reasons for action, and sometimes it may be as rational for her to change an ordering as it is for her to maintain it. Someone who smokes, for example, might have long judged that the health risks are less important to her than the pleasure she derives from smoking and the irritability and disruption that would result from quitting. If such a decision could be rational in the first place, then this agent might rationally continue to smoke. But it would surely not offend rationality if she one day reversed her ordering of reasons and decided to quit. Finally, an agent may face a decision that requires her to order considerations that she has not previously compared with each other; in some such cases there may be two or more new orderings each of which would be equally rational given her previous constellation of motivational states.

The important point to be made about all cases of rational indeterminacy is that the presence or absence of agent causation makes no difference to the rationality of the action. Whether such an action is agent-caused or not, there will be no contrastive rational explanation of it, one that would answer the question, 'Why did you choose this apple rather than that one?' or 'Why did you go to the beach rather than to the mountains?' This absence is due entirely to the structure of the situation and the agent's reasons. Such actions are nevertheless rationally explicable. I chose this apple because I wanted to eat an apple and it was as good as any other; I went to the beach because I like to surf. There is nothing rationally defective about an action of this sort; given the circumstances, it is as rational as can be.

II. Causation by an agent

I turn now to the objection concerning the intelligibility of the notion of agent causation. Chisholm has offered a definition of agent causation in terms of 'undertaking' or 'endeavoring.'[12] However, both of these terms suggest that agent causation is a kind of intentional action; and if that is so, it is unclear that it deserves the name 'causation' at all, since event causation, about which there are at least intelligible accounts, is not any kind of intentional action. Van Inwagen has proposed a different kind of analysis, one on which the agent causation of an action is held to consist wholly in the performance of an action a component event of which is uncaused by any event.[13] However, this approach fails to tell us in positive terms in what the causation by the agent consists, and indeed why the component event could not be entirely uncaused.

Certain features drawn from the views of Chisholm and Taylor, as well as from the view I have sketched here, suggest the beginnings of an account of agent causation. Agent causation is a relation, the first relatum of which is an agent or person and the second relatum of which is an event. Agents enter into such relations only as first relata, never as second relata. And an agent that is a relatum of such a relation is not identical to any event, property, fact, or state of affairs, nor to any collection of such things.[14] What is directly caused by an agent is her acting for a particular ordering or reasons.

What remains is to say just what this relation is. The prevailing tendency among agent causalists and their critics alike on this point has been to stress how different agent causation is from event causation and indeed how 'mysterious' the former is.[15] However, the proper line here, I believe, is to maintain that agent causation, if there is such a thing, is (or involves) *exactly* the same relation as event causation.[16] The only difference between the two kinds of causation concerns the types of entities related, not the relation. The question that needs to be addressed, then, is whether there is an intelligible account of the relation of causation that will serve in accounts of event causation as well as agent causation.

The most familiar accounts of event causation are reductionist, aiming to analyze causation in terms of such noncausal and non-nomological features as constant conjunction or counterfactual dependence, or in terms of the modalities of necessity and sufficiency. Certainly, if any of this type of account of event causation is correct, then agent causation cannot be the same relation as event causation. For agent causation plainly cannot be either the constant conjunction of an agent and an action type or the counterfactual dependence of an action on an agent, nor can it consist in an agent's being a necessary or sufficient condition for the performance of a particular action.[17] However, reductionist accounts are subject to grave difficulties,[18] and they are not the only sort of account around.

An attractive alternative is to take the causal relation to be among the basic constituents of the universe. Causation may be held to be a real relation between particulars, one that, although analyzable, is not reducible to noncausal and nonnomological properties and relations. There is a variety of such realist accounts of causation.[19] A common intuition underlying many is that reductionist accounts attempt to explain the more fundamental by the less fundamental. It is not, for example, because one event counterfactually depends on another that the second may be said to cause the first. Rather, according to a realist, such counterfactual dependence is to be explained in terms of causal relations and laws.[20]

One type of realist account of event causation can be sketched, in broad strokes, as follows. An event (particular) causes another just in case the relation of causation obtains between them. Two events can be so related only if they possess (or are constituted by) properties that are in turn related under a law of nature. Ultimately, then, causal relations are grounded in laws of nature, which consist of second-order relations among universals.

Such an account roughly resembles that favored by Tooley for event (or, as he would have it, state-of-affairs) causation.[21] Tooley maintains that the relations involved in this sort of account—causation, as well as the higher-order relations among universals—can be adequately specified, without reduction, by a set of postulates indicating the roles of these relations within the domain of properties and states of affairs.[22] If he is correct about this, then we have an analysis of the causal relation that can be employed in an account of agent causation. An agent causalist can say that it is the relation thus analyzed that obtains between a person and her action when she acts with free will; it is the very relation that, within the domain of properties and events or states of affairs, occupies the specified role.[23]

Moreover, an account that runs parallel, at a certain level of description, to that suggested for event causation would seem to be available for agent causation. An agent may be held to cause a particular action (more precisely: an event of acting on a certain ordering of reasons) just in case the relation of causation obtains between these two particulars. And an agent can be said to be so related to one of her actions only if these two particulars exemplify certain properties. Perhaps the only agents who cause things are those who have the property of being capable of reflective practical reasoning,[24] and perhaps such an agent directly causes only those events that constitute her acting for reasons. There might, in that case, be a law of nature to the effect that any individual who acts with such a capacity acts with free will.

Here is one way in which such a law might be construed. Suppose that it is necessarily true that if an action is performed with free will, then the agent causes her acting on the reasons on which she acts. (That there is such a necessary truth seems to be what, at bottom, agent causalists have always argued.) Suppose, further, that a necessary, but not logically sufficient, condition of acting with free will is that an agent act with a capacity for reflective, rational self-governance. Now suppose that it is a law in our world that if an agent possessing that capacity acts on reasons, then she acts with free will.[25] Here we have a contingent statement of natural necessity. Together with the supposed necessary truth, it implies the obtaining of the causal relation between agent and action.

Natural law, then, may subsume all free action without undermining the freedom with which human beings act. On this sort of account, the agent causation on which free will is held to depend is seen as thoroughly natural.

On the suggested account, then, agent causation is the obtaining of a relation between two particulars; the relation involved is the very same one that is involved in event causation. An agent's exercise of her causal power is simply the obtaining of this relation between her and an event. An agent need not *do* anything—if by that is meant perform some action—in order to cause something. Thus, agent causation is not fundamentally the performance of some special kind of action that then causes one's bodily movements. Nevertheless, the causal power that such an account attributes to agents is no more 'magical' than that which we attribute to events. For an event need not perform any action in order to cause another event, and event causation is not fundamentally the occurrence of some third event between cause and effect; it is fundamentally the obtaining of a relation between the two.

The upshot is that, on an agent-causal account, an agent's *control* over her behavior resides fundamentally in her *causing* what she does. Her control does not reside fundamentally in her performing some special sort of action. Since causing is bringing something about, producing it, or making it happen, causing seems to be the right sort of thing on which to base an agent's control over her behavior.

My suggestions concerning an account of agent causation are, of course, programmatic. It remains to be seen whether such an account can be fully worked out. Nevertheless, the alternative of a realist account of causation significantly weakens the charge that the notion of agent causation is mysterious or unintelligible. If a realist treatment of event causation is intelligible, then we fairly well understand, too, what is meant by the claim that agents cause their actions. And given a realist account of causation, what is expressed by the claim in question is, it seems to me, something that is true in some possible worlds. At this juncture, an objection that agent causation is metaphysically impossible would stand in need of some argument.[26]

III. Why believe it

Even if an agent-causal thesis is intelligible, however, and even if what it states is not something impossible, the question remains whether it is reasonable to believe that, in fact, human beings agent-cause at least some of their actions. I will first indicate what kind of argument is *not* available for such a view and then outline what seems to me the best argument that *can* be made.

First, if agent causation is as described here, then there is no observational evidence that could tell us whether our world is an indeterministic world with agent causation or an indeterministic world without it.[27] We do not introspectively observe agent causation, and even highly improbable behavior could occur in a world without agent causation.

A related point is that affirming agent causation would not improve our ability to predict and explain human behavior. Our beliefs about event causation play a crucial role in this kind of understanding of human agency. But those beliefs concern the conditions for the occurrence of some event, and beliefs about agent causation are about something quite different. Nevertheless, it should be evident that, since an agent-causal thesis does not require that there be any gaps in chains of event causes, agent causation does not undermine the predictive and explanatory significance of event causes.

Indeed, agent causation is consistent with its being the case that probabilistic laws of nature apply as thoroughly to human beings and their behavior as such laws apply to anything else. Thus, contrary to what Chisholm claims, agent causation is not a reason why "there can be no complete science of man."[28]

If prediction and explanation are paradigmatic of scientific understanding, it appears that agent causation neither contributes to nor detracts from such understanding. Its contribution, rather, would be to our understanding of ourselves as moral agents. We believe, most of us, that we are morally responsible for much of what we do. Agent causation, it may be argued, is a condition of the possibility of morally responsible agency.[29] Affirming something like the view sketched here, then, would give us an explication of how we can be what we seem, from the moral point of view, to be. Importantly, the explication provided would be one that is consistent with how we view ourselves from the scientific point of view.

The broader case for this view, as these last remarks suggest, constitutes a kind of transcendental argument, one that, in outline, runs as follows: (1) We are morally responsible agents; (2) If we are morally responsible agents, then we act with free will; (3) If we act with free will, then determinism is false; (4) If determinism is false and still we act with free will, then we agent-cause our actions; (5) If our acting with free will requires that we agent-cause our actions, then that freedom is as presented in the account sketched above.

I have not, of course, established these five propositions here. My aim has been only to argue for serious consideration of the account referred to in the last of them. The crucial steps of the argument are, of course, the rejection of compatibilism and of nonagent-causal libertarian views. What inclines many of us to follow those steps, I believe, is that we find unsatisfactory any view of free will that allows that everything that causally brings about an agent's action is itself causally brought about by something in the distant past. Certainly any freedom of the will that we enjoy on such a view, if not a complete fraud, is a pale imitation of the freedom that is characterized by an agent-causal account. If I am right that agent causation can be made intelligible and that agent-caused actions can be rational, then an agent-causal account certainly deserves close attention.[30]

Notes

1. Roderick M. Chisholm, "Freedom and action," in *Freedom and Determinism*, ed. Keith Lehrer (New York: Random House, 1966); "The agent as cause," in *Action Theory*, ed. Myles Brand and Douglas Walton (Dordrecht, The Netherlands: D. Reidel, 1976); and *Person and Object* (La Salle: Open Court, 1976), 53–88. Richard Taylor, *Action and Purpose* (Englewood Cliffs, NJ: Prentice Hall, 1966), 99–152; "Determinism and the theory of agency," in *Determinism and Freedom in the Age of Modern Science*, ed. Sydney Hook

(New York: Collier Books, 1979); and *Metaphysics* (Englewood Cliffs, NJ: Prentice Hall, 1983), 33–50.

2. The rationality objection is sometimes stated in terms of the intelligibility of the action or in terms of rational explicability. For versions of this objection, see C. D. Broad, *Ethics and the History of Philosophy* (London: Routledge & Kegan Paul, 1952), 215; Carl Ginet, *On Action* (Cambridge: Cambridge University Press, 1990), 13–14; and Irving Thalberg, "Agent causality and reasons for action," *Philosophia* 7 (1978): 555–566, esp. 564.

3. For examples of the intelligibility objection, see R. Kane, *Free Will and Values* (Albany: State University of New York Press, 1985), 72; and Gary Watson, "Free action and free will," *Mind* 96 (1987): 145–72, esp. 167.

4. See, for example, Chisholm's "Freedom and action," 17, and Taylor's *Action and Purpose*, 127.

5. Chisholm writes that "We must say that at least one of the events that is involved in any act is caused, not by any other event, but by the agent, by the man" ("Freedom and action," 29).

6. In this paper I focus on cases in which an agent acts with an ability to do otherwise. Certain features of the account I will sketch are more visibly displayed in light of such cases. However, I emphasize here that I do not believe that a libertarian need require, for free will, that an agent be able to do anything significantly different from what she actually does. If an agent has very good reason to perform an action of a certain type (A'ing), and if she has no reason not to, then, although it may be causally indeterminate *when* she A's, or exactly *how* she A's, it may not be naturally possible that she not A. So long as she is an undetermined determinant of her A'ing, it seems to me that it ought to be allowed that she acts with free will.

7. For a sample of discussions of nondeterministic causation, see G. E. M. Anscombe, "Causality and determination," in *The Collected Philosophical Papers of G. E. M. Anscombe,* vol. 2 (Oxford: Basil Blackwell, 1981); Ellery Eells, *Probabilistic Causality* (Cambridge: Cambridge University Press, 1991); David Lewis, "Causation," in *Philosophical Papers,* vol. 2 (Oxford: Oxford University Press, 1986), esp. 175–184; and Michael Tooley, *Causation: A Realist Approach* (Oxford: Clarendon Press, 1987), 289–296.

8. In fact, Chisholm, in one of his later discussions of free will, does draw a distinction that appears similar to this one. See Roderick M. Chisholm, "Comments and replies," *Philosophia* 7 (1978): 597–636, esp. 629. However, he and Taylor generally take causation to be causal necessitation, and they deny that free will is compatible with universal causation.

John Bishop, too, has argued that an agent-causal view need not rule out universal event causation. See his "Agent-causation," *Mind* 92 (1983): 61–79, esp. 76–79. However, there are two important differences between Bishop's approach and my own. First, his aim in "Agent-causation" is to advance an agent-causal account of *action,* and not just of acting with free will. (Hence, some of the problems with which he deals are not problems for me.) Second, Bishop suggests that agent causation is 'conceptually primitive', and he does not attempt to explicate it. (In section II below, I take some steps toward such an explication.)

In his later work, Bishop defends an event-causal theory of action. See *Natural Agency: An Essay on the Causal Theory of Action* (Cambridge: Cambridge University Press, 1989).

9. This version of the rational-explicability objection is expressed by C. D. Broad, *Ethics and the History of Philosophy,* 215, and by Carl Ginet, *On Action,* 13–14. Ginet notes that the objection can be stated as well in terms of explaining why one particular action rather than another is performed. The reply to this variation is analogous to that given to the variation concerning the timing of the action. Given the assumption that event causation is nondeterministic, the agent-causal view has the same resources as does a wholly event-causal account to provide the contrastive explanation. This point is covered in more detail in the remainder of Section I.

10. I say 'in part' because acting on or for certain reasons consists in more than the fact that one's action is caused by those reasons. The action must be nondeviantly caused by the reasons, and the reasons must constitute at least part of an explanation of the action. For a fuller account, see Robert Audi, "Acting for reasons," *Philosophical Review* 95 (1986): 511–546.

11. Even if agents can cause events, is it credible that an agent can affect whether her having certain reasons will have a certain effect, viz., her performing a certain action? I think so. After all, events can affect whether other events will have certain effects. Suppose that human agency is a wholly event-causal process. If it is cloudy, I acquire the belief that it is cloudy and might rain. If I believe that it is cloudy and might rain, then I might take my umbrella, but it is very likely that I will not. However, if I believe that it is cloudy and might rain, and then if my companion remarks that it is cloudy, then I will very likely take my umbrella. My companion's remark, or the absence of it, may causally affect whether the clouds and my belief will cause a certain action. The agent-causal case is disanalogous in that the agent, unlike my companion's remark, is not an event. But if agents, like events, can cause events, then it appears that agents can affect which effects certain events will have.

12. Roderick M. Chisholm, "The agent as cause;" and *Person and Object,* pp. 53–88.

13. Peter van Inwagen, "A definition of Chisholm's notion of immanent causation," *Philosophia* 7 (1978): 567–581.

14. Only a very minimal commitment as to the nature of a person is implied here. All that is implied is a denial of the bundle view, the view that a person is simply a collection of qualities or events. It is certainly *not* implied here that a person is a Cartesian ego, or a monad, or any sort of nonphysical thing. Nor is it implied that a person is a bare particular; on the contrary, on the view sketched here, an agent's causal powers depend on her attributes.

15. Taylor expresses this sort of view, as do Kane and Watson. See Richard Taylor, *Metaphysics,* 49; R. Kane, *Free Will and Values,* 72; and Gary Watson, "Free action and free will," 167.

16. Event causation may be probabilistic or deterministic, and a single world might contain both kinds. The causal relation itself need not differ in the two cases; the difference between them might reside in the fact that the underlying laws involve different higher-order relations. For an account of this sort, see Michael Tooley, *Causation: A Realist Approach.*

Perhaps it needs to be required that agent causation is deterministic. However, I am not sure that this is so. I see no problem in saying that, on the agent-causal account, the agent, together with her having certain reasons, jointly deterministically cause her acting on those reasons.

17. Certainly, if the agent had not existed, her action would not have occurred. However, it is not the agent's existing, nor her coming to exist, but rather the agent that is said to cause her action. Furthermore, no agent causalist wants to claim that an agent causes every event that would not have occurred had she not existed.

18. For criticism of reductionist accounts of causation, see Galen Strawson, "Realism and causation," *The Philosophical Quarterly* 37 (1987): 252–277; Michael Tooley, "Causation: reductionism versus realism," *Philosophy and Phenomenological Research* 50 (1990): 215–236; and the works cited in note 19 below.

19. John Bigelow and Robert Pargetter, "Metaphysics of causation," *Erkenntnis* 33 (1990): 89–119; Adrian Heathcote and D. M. Armstrong, "Causes and laws," *Nous* 25 (1991): 63–73; and Michael Tooley, *Causation: A Realist Approach*.

20. Bigelow and Pargetter write: "We take causation to be part of the basic furniture of nature, and as such it functions as an input into the explanation of modalities. It is widely agreed that the best account of modalities make appeal to the framework of possible worlds. There is less agreement on how possible worlds are to be construed. Most of the details on the nature of worlds are unimportant here. What is important is only the direction of explanation between causation and the nature of worlds. We support theories which use causation as part of an account of what there is in any given possible world. Thus causation enters into the explanation of modalities, and in particular, into the explanation of 'necessary and sufficient conditions,' and also of probabilities. Hence modal or probabilistic theories, even if they could be adjusted until they became extensionally correct, would nevertheless proceed in the wrong direction from an explanatory point of view." "Metaphysics of causation," 98.

21. Michael Tooley, *Causation: A Realist Approach*.

22. The terms defined in this manner themselves appear in the postulates, but they can be replaced by variables to give us a theory that employs only antecedently understood observational, quasilogical, and logical vocabulary. The theory succeeds in defining causation and the (two) relations involved in laws just in case there is a unique ordered triple of relations that satisfies the open formula of the theory.

The approach is one that is generally available for a realist treatment of theoretical terms. The technique employed is the Ramsey/Lewis method. For discussion of this method, see David Lewis, "How to define theoretical terms," in *Philosophical Papers,* vol. 1 (Oxford: Oxford University Press, 1983).

23. I owe this suggestion to David Lewis.

24. Several compatibilist accounts identify free will with a capacity to direct one's behavior by reflective practical reasoning. See, for example, T. M. Scanlon, "The significance of choice," in *The Tanner Lectures on Human Values,* vol. 8., ed. Sterling M. McMurrin (Salt Lake City: University of Utah Press, 1988), esp. 174; and Gary Watson, "Free action and free will," esp. 152–53. Acting with such a capacity is, I believe, a necessary condition of acting with free will, and an adequate libertarian account will need to affirm this. Whether having that capacity is lawfully associated with agent-causing one's actions is, of course, another matter.

25. This way of expressing the law seems to imply that intentionality enters into the law of nature that governs agent causation, and it might be objected that such an implication is incredible. I am not sure that it is. Many of us believe, anyway, that intentional states (or our having them) can enter into causal relations, and that it can be *because* a

certain state has a certain intentional content that state causes what it does. If the intentionality of mental states really is relevant to their causal roles, then we have one good reason to believe that intentionality somehow enters into the laws of nature that govern the causal relations of those states.

On the other hand, what if the intentional is anomalous? In that case, anyone who claims that the intentionality of mental states is causally relevant owes us an account of how that relevance is captured in the laws of nature. When we have that account, an agent causalist can use it for her own purposes.

26. It may be objected that, even if it is not impossible that a person should be a cause, nevertheless, on the view I have suggested, entities of two ontologically different sorts are said to be causes, and that (so the objection goes) is absurd. I do not think that it is. When it comes to accounts of 'ordinary' causation, some say the relata are events, some say aspects of events, some say states of affairs, and some say properties. Consider the hypothesis that, in fact, at least two of these sorts of entities are causes. I do not think that it asserts something that is impossible.

For an argument that entities of several ontologically different kinds are *indeed* relata of causation, see David H. Sanford, "Causal relata," in *Actions and Events: Perspectives on the Philosophy of Donald Davidson*, ed. Ernest LePore and Brian P. McLaughlin (Oxford: Basil Blackwell, 1985). I note that Sanford does *not* admit persons as causal relata.

27. Perhaps we could have evidence that our world was a deterministic world; but I take it that we don't.

28. Roderick M. Chisholm, "Freedom and action," 24.

29. There is a widespread conviction that it is just too much to believe that human beings have a causal power that is to be found nowhere else in nature. Here is one part of a reply to that conviction. If it is accepted that we are morally responsible for at least some of our actions, then it is already accepted that we are morally unique (at least among known natural agents). If it is, moreover, necessarily true that only an agent who agent-causes her actions is a morally responsible agent, then one cannot consistently believe that we are thus morally unique and at the same time reject the metaphysics of agent causation.

The second part of a reply is that, in fact, it is not necessary for an agent-causalist to maintain that only human agents are agent causes. It can be allowed that the laws governing agent causation are not as suggested above but also cover causation by agents who lack the reflective capacity that free agents have. In that case, agent causation is a necessary but not a sufficient condition for free will. A further necessary condition is that an agent act with a capacity rationally to reflect on the courses of action she might pursue and on the reasons for which she might pursue them, and to govern her behavior on the basis of such reflection.

30. I wish to thank audiences at Princeton University and North Carolina State University for comments on earlier versions of this paper. Many individuals provided helpful suggestions and criticisms; I am especially grateful to Gilbert Harman and David Lewis.

12

Agent-Causal Power

Timothy O'Connor

Our universe is populated, at bottom, by a vast number of partless particulars of a few basic kinds. Each of these particulars instantiates some of a small range of primitive qualities and stands in primitive relations with other particulars. We may conceive qualities as immanent universals that are numerically identical in their instances, along the lines championed by David Armstrong (1978), or as 'tropes' that are non-identical but exactly resembling in their instances, following C.B. Martin (1997). (Nothing of what follows hangs on which alternative one prefers.) In calling these qualities "primitive," we are contending that they are real existents whose being does not consist, even in part, in the existence or instantiation of other entities. The nature of these qualities is irreducibly dispositional: they are tendencies to interact with other qualities in producing some effect, or some range of possible effects. (Or, in certain cases—as we shall consider below—they may instead confer upon their possessor a tendency towards, or power to produce, some such effects.) It *may* be that the dispositional profile of a quality does not exhaust its nature, so that it has a further 'qualitative character,' or quiddity. Here again, we may be neutral on this question for present purposes.[1]

The formal character of a feature's dispositionality may be variable. For a couple centuries after Newton, it was usual to conceive dispositions deterministically: given the right circumstances, causes strictly necessitate their effects. But fundamental physics since the early twentieth century encourages the thought that dispositions may be probabilistic, such that there are objective probabilities less than one that a cause will produce its characteristic effect on a given occasion. On this view, deterministic propensities are simply a limiting case of probabilistic ones. What is more, it seems possible to conceive pure, unstructured tendencies, ones that are nondeterministic and yet have no particular probability of being manifested on a given occasion.

The qualities of composite particulars (if we do not here embrace eliminativism) are typically structural, consisting in the instantiation of qualities of and relations between the composite's fundamental parts.[2] Very often, the terms we use to refer to features of composites do not pick out such structural properties, since they are insensitive to minor variation in the composite's exact underlying state. (A water molecule's being in a structured arrangement of hydrogen and oxygen atoms persists through small-scale changes in its microphysical composition and state. Of course, there are also much more dramatic cases of underlying variation across instances consistent with applicability of the same macroscopic term, with functional terms providing obvious examples.) Here, we should say that the *concept* is satisfied in different cases in virtue of the instantiation of different structural qualities. Despite superficial ways of speaking, there is no distinctive causal power attached to the satisfaction of such a concept, as that would require the causal powers theorist to accept an objectionable form of double counting of causes, one for the macroscopic structural property (itself nothing over and above the instantiation of microscopic properties and relations) and one for the putative multiply-realized functional 'property.'

Such are some central elements of a causal powers metaphysic. There are many disputes of detail among its adherents—to the disputed matters already noted, we should add the nature of primitive external relations and the substantiality of space or spacetime.[3] Such disputes aside, the causal powers metaphysics stands opposed both to the neo-Humean vision that David Lewis (1983b, 1986c) popularized and the second-order Humean metaphysic of causal realism without causal powers defended in recent years by David Armstrong (1997) and Michael Tooley (1997).[4]

In what follows, I shall presuppose the ecumenical core of the causal powers metaphysics. The argument of this paper concerns what may appear at first to be a wholly unrelated matter, the metaphysics of free will. However, an adequate account of freedom requires, in my judgment, a notion of a distinctive variety of causal power, one which tradition dubs "agent-causal power." I will first develop this notion and clarify its relationship to other notions. I will then respond to a number of objections either to the possibility of a power so explicated or to its sufficiency for grounding an adequate account of human freedom.

1. The problem of freedom and agent-causal power

Central to the notion of metaphysical freedom of action, or free will, is the thought that what I do freely is something that is "up to me," as Aristotle says. A familiar, disputed line of reasoning, which turns upon the principle that where certain truths that are not up to an agent logically (and so unavoidably) entail some further truth, the latter truth is itself not up to the agent, concludes that nothing of what we do would be up to us were our actions to be embedded within a strictly deterministic universe.[5] But if determinism would threaten our freedom, so would the complete absence of any intelligible causation of our actions. So one might steer a middle course by supposing that the world is governed throughout by unfolding causal processes, just not deterministic ones. In particular, one might suppose that our free actions are caused by our own reasons-bearing states at the time of the action. An action's being "up to me," on this view, consists in the nondeterministic causal efficacy of certain of my reasons: I might have performed a different action in identical circumstances because there was a non-zero (and perhaps pronounced) chance that other reasons-bearing states had been efficacious in producing the action which they indicated.[6] However, according to many critics (myself among them), indeterminist event-causal approaches falter just here, in the fact that the free control they posit is secured by an *absence,* a removal of a condition (causal determination) suggested by the manifestly inadequate varieties of compatibilism. If there is no means by which I can take advantage of this looser connectivity in the flow of events, its presence can't confer a greater kind of control, one that *inter alia* grounds moral responsibility for the action and its consequences.[7] Given the causal indeterminist view, if I am faced with a choice between selfish and generous courses of action, each of which has some significant chance of being chosen, it would seem to be a matter of luck, good or bad, whichever way I choose, since I have no means directly to settle which of the indeterministic propensities gets manifested.

The familiar considerations just sketched lead certain philosophers to conclude that the kind of control necessary for freedom of action involves an ontologically primitive capacity of the agent directly to determine which of several alternative courses of action is realized. In these instances of *agent causation,* the cause of an event is not a state of, or event within, the agent; rather, it is the agent himself, an enduring substance.

I will not defend the claim that any actual agents have such a capacity. The philosophical claim is that agents must exercise such a capacity if they are to have metaphysical freedom, but it is an empirical claim whether human agents do exercise such a capacity (and thus do in fact act freely). Our concern is what such an agent-causal power would be, and, given the analysis, whether any agents *could* possibly have it, given fairly modest assumptions about the agents and their embeddedness within an environment.

We begin by considering what the notion of agent causation requires us to assume concerning the nature of the agent having such a power. It is commonly supposed that the notion requires a commitment to agents as partless and nonphysical entities. A radically distinct kind of power, the thought goes, requires a radically distinct kind of substance. And this seems further encouraged by my earlier contention that the causal powers metaphysics pushes one to regard typical 'high-level' features as structural properties wholly composed of microphysical properties arranged in a certain way.

But there is more to be said. While the tidiness of substance dualism has its appeal, it is in fact optional for the metaphysician who believes that human beings have ontologically fundamental powers (whether of freedom or consciousness or intentionality). For we may suppose that such powers are *emergent* in the following sense: (*i*) They are ontologically basic properties (token-distinct from any structural properties of the organism). (*ii*) As basic properties, they confer causal powers on the systems that have them, powers that non-redundantly contribute to the system's collective causal power, which is otherwise determined by the aggregations of, and relations between, the properties of the system's microphysical parts. Such non-redundant causal power necessarily means a difference even at the microphysical level of the system's unfolding behavior. (This is not a violation of the laws of particle physics but it is a supplement to them, since it involves the presence of a large-scale property that interacts with the properties of small-scale systems.) In respects (*i*) and (*ii*), emergent powers are no less basic ontologically than unit negative charge is taken to be by current physics. However, emergent and microphysical powers differ in that (*iii*) the appearance of emergent powers is caused (*not* 'realized') by the joint efficacy of the qualities and relations of some of the system's fundamental parts and it persists if and only if the overall system maintains the right kind of hierarchically-organized complexity, a kind which must be determined empirically but is insensitive to continuous small-scale dynamical changes at the microphysical level.[8]

One cannot give uncontroversial examples of emergent properties. Though there are ever so many macroscopic phenomena that seem to be governed by principles of organization highly insensitive to microphysical dynamics, it remains an open question whether such behavior is nonetheless wholly determined, in the final analysis, by ordinary particle dynamics of microphysical structures in and around the system in question.[9] Given the intractable difficulties of trying to compute values for the extremely large number of particles in any medium-sized system (as well as the compounding error of innumerable applications of approximation techniques used even in measuring small-scale systems), it may well forever be impossible in practice to attempt to directly test for the presence or absence of a truly (ontologically) emergent feature in a macroscopic system. Furthermore, it is difficult to try to spell out in any detail the impact of such a property using a realistic (even if hypothetical) example, since plausible candidates (e.g., phase state transitions or superconductivity in solid state physics, protein functionality in biology, animal consciousness) would likely involve the simultaneous emergence of multiple, interacting powers. Suffice it to say that if, for example, the multiple powers of a particular protein molecule were emergent, then the unfolding dynamics of that molecule *at a microscopic level* would diverge in specifiable ways from what an ideal particle physicist (lacking computational and precision limitations) would expect by extrapolating from a complete understanding of the dynamics of small-scale particle systems. The nature and degree of divergence would provide a basis for capturing the distinctive contribution of the emergent features of the molecule.

As sketchy as the foregoing has been, we must return to our main topic. I have suggested that we can make sense of the idea of ontologically emergent powers, ones that are at once causally dependent on microphysically-based structural states and yet ontologically primitive, and so apt to confer onto-logically primitive causal power. If this is correct, then the fact that agent causal power would be fundamental, or nonderivative, does not imply that the agent that deploys it be anything other than a mature human organism. It is simply an empirical question whether or not the dispositions of the ulti-mate particles of our universe include the disposition to causally generate and sustain agent-causal power within suitably organized conscious and intelli-gent agents.

One important feature of agent-causal power is that it is not directed to any particular effects. Instead, it confers upon an agent a power to cause a certain type of event within the agent: the coming to be of a state of intention to carry out some act, thereby resolving a state of uncertainty about which action to undertake. (For ease of exposition, I shall hereafter speak of "causing an intention," which is to be understood as shorthand for "causing an event which is the coming to be of a state of intention.") This power is multi-valent, capable of being exercised towards any of a plurality of options that are in view for the agent. We may call the causing of this intentional state a 'deci-sion' and suppose that in the usual case it is a triggering event, initiating the chain of events constituting a wider observable action.

Following agent causalists of tradition (such as Thomas Reid), I conceive agent-causal power as *inherently* goal-directed. It is the power of an agent to cause an intention in order to satisfy some desire or to achieve some aim. How should we understand this goal-directedness?

One way is a variation on a familiar view in action theory, the causal the-ory of action. The rough idea behind developed versions of the causal theory is that the agent's having a potential reason R actually motivated action A (and so contributes to its explanation) just in case R is a salient element in the set of causes that 'nondeviantly' produce A. (R might be, e.g., a belief–desire pair or a prior intention.) In line with this, one might be tempted to say that R actually motivated *an agent's causing of intention i* just in case R is among the set of causes that nondeviantly produce it.

However, it is not clear that anything *could* (in strict truth) produce a causally complex event of the form *an agent's causing of intention i*. On the causal powers theory, causation consists in the manifestation of a single disposition (limiting case) or the mutual manifestation of a plurality of properties that are, in C. B. Martin's term, 'reciprocal dispositional part-ners' (typical case). We sometimes speak of an external event's 'triggering' a disposition to act (as when the lighting of the fuse is said to trigger the dynamite's disposition to explode). And this way of speaking might tempt one to assert, in more explicit terms, that the lighting of the fuse directly caused the causally complex event, *the dynamite's emitting a large quantity of hot gas caused the rapid dislocation of matter in its immediate vicinity.* But neither of these statements can be taken at face value when it comes to the metaphysics of causation. The unstable chemical properties of the dynamite's active substance (nitroglycerin) would be involved in any number of effects relative to an appropriate wider circumstance. However, in each case, a variety of conditions C are exercising a *joint* disposition towards the particular effect, E. And nothing directly *produces their producing* of the effect, as this could only mean that the conditions C did not, after all, include all the factors involved in producing E. Granted, there is a perfectly good sense in which a prior event that produces one or more of C's elements may be said to *indirectly* cause C's causing E, in virtue of causing part of C itself to obtain. (So, the lighting of the fuse did lead more or less directly to the rapid burning process of the chemical substance, which event caused the production of the hot gas, which in turn caused the surrounding matter to be rapidly pressed outward.) But this indirect causing of a causal chain by virtue of causing the chain's first element cannot apply to instances of agent causation, for the simple reason that here the first element within the causal chain is not an event or condition, but a substance. It is not the event of the agent's existing at t that causes the coming to be of a state of intention—something that *could* have a cause—but the agent himself. The notion of *causing a substance,* qua substance, has no clear sense.[10]

Thus, we cannot coherently suppose that the obtaining of a reason in the agent may be said to be among the factors that causally *produce* the agent's causing an intention. But perhaps we can sensibly stop a little short of this supposition by supposing instead that the obtaining of the reason appropriately affects (in the typical case, by increasing) an *objective propensity of the agent* to cause the intention. On this latter suggestion, while nothing produces an instance of agent causation, the possible occurrence of this event has a continuously evolving, objective likelihood. Expressed differently, agent causal power is a structured propensity towards a class of effects (the formings of executive intentions), such that at any given time, for each causally possible, specific agent-causal event-type, there is a definite objective probability of its occurrence within the range (0, 1), and this probability varies continuously as the agent is impacted by internal and external influences. To emphasize: events that alter this propensity do *not* thereby tend toward the production of the agent's causing the coming to be of an intention (in the sense that they potentially contribute to the *causing* of this latter event). Even where the event promoted occurs, the effect of the influencing events is exhausted by their alteration of the relative likelihood of an outcome, which they accomplish by affecting the propensities of the agent-causal capacity itself. Where reasons confer probabilities in this manner, I will say that the reasons *causally structure* the agent-causal capacity.

It will perhaps be helpful to clarify what I have and have not just said. I am at this point taking it as provisionally given that we have a decent grasp on the very idea of agent causal power. I argued in the penultimate paragraph that we cannot coherently suppose reasons to constrain agent-causal power in one familiar way, that of tending to produce agent-causal events. I then tried to explicate another (albeit less familiar) way, that of structuring a propensity of an agent to produce an event *without thereby tending toward the production of* the agent's producing said event. However, I have in no way suggested that one could not coherently jettison the idea of agent causation in favor of an event-causal theory of action on which the having of reasons does indeed tend directly towards the production of one's executive intentions to act. This is the guiding idea of causal theories of action and, unlike some agent causationists such as Richard Taylor, I do not maintain that it is impossible to give a satisfactory theory of action along these lines. I would only insist that such a theory cannot capture the more ambitious notion of *freedom of action*. Here, I maintain, purely event-causal theories (whether deterministic or not) will inevitably fail. Thus, I am committed to supposing that there is more than one broad sort of way that the having of reasons might influence an intentional action. As with other propensities, the effect of events constituted by the having of reasons to act depends on surrounding circumstances. The agent-causal account I am advancing suggests that the presence of agent-causal power is one very important determinant on such effects. In the presence of such a power, the causal contribution of the having of reasons is exhausted by the alteration of the probability of a corresponding agent-causal event.

With this idea in hand, we can specify *one* way in which agent-causal events are inherently purposive. Necessarily, when an agent causes an intention i to occur at time t_1, he does so in the presence of a motivational state whose onset began at a time $t_0 < t_1$ and which had an appreciable influence on the probability between t_0 and t_1 of his causing of i. Let us say that when a reason R satisfies this description, the agent freely acted *on* R.[11]

The controverted metaphysics of agent-causation aside, this sufficient condition for acting on a reason is quite minimal. Some would contend that it is objectionably weak because it allows that I may act on a reason of which I am entirely unconscious. In such a case, it will be claimed, the reason is exerting a brutely causal influence, and not a rational influence.[12] In my view, this objection mistakenly seeks to assimilate all cases of reasons-guided activity into a single framework. I agree that *some* free actions manifest a heightened degree of conscious control and I try to capture what this might consist in immediately below. But we need to recognize that not even all free actions are created equal—freedom itself comes in degrees. If a reason inclines me to undertake an action but its content is unknown to me (if, say, I am aware merely that I have an inclination to undertake the action), the latter fact diminished my freedom, since I am thereby unable to subject my motivation to rational scrutiny. Nonetheless, if it remains open to me to undertake the action or not, I exhibit the goal-driven self-determination that is the core element of freedom of the will.[13]

Agents who act freely to any degree, then, directly produce the intentions that initiate and guide their actions, acting on an inclination that is the causal product of certain reasons they acquired (and subsequently retained) at some point prior to this causal activity. But sometimes, it would appear, there is more to be said about the way that reasons motivate freely undertaken actions. Often enough, not only am I conscious of certain reasons that favor the course of action I am choosing, I expressly choose the action for the purpose of achieving the goal to which those reasons point. This goal enters into the content of the intention I bring into being. In such cases, I cause the intention to A *for the sake of G,* where G is the goal of a prior desire or intention that, together with the belief that A-ing is likely to promote G, constitutes the consciously grasped reason *for* which I act. Now, since I freely and consciously bring the intention into being and thus give it just this purposive content, that purpose cannot but be one for which I am acting. What is more, a further explanatory connection between that reason and the choice is forged beyond the reason's influence on the choice's prior probability. This connection consists in the conjunction of the external relation of prior causal influence and the purely internal relation of sameness of content (the goal G). There may be several reasons that increase the likelihood that I would cause the intention to A. In the event that I do so, each of these reasons are ones *on* which I act. But if I am conscious of a particular reason, R, that promotes a goal G (and no other reason promotes that goal), and I cause the intention to A for the sake of G, then R plays a distinctive explanatory role, as shown by the fact that it alone can explain the goal-directed aspect of the intention's content. It alone is one *for* which I act.

It is commonly objected to nondeterministic accounts of human freedom that, despite what I've just said, undetermined actions cannot be explained by the agent's reasons since those reasons cannot account for why the agent performed action A rather than B, one of the alternatives that were also causally possible in the circumstances. This objection fails to appreciate that explanation need not always be contrastive. If there are truly indeterministic quantum mechanical systems capable of generating any of a plurality of outcomes, whatever results is not absolutely inexplicable. A perfectly good explanation may be given by citing the system and its relevant capacities that in fact produced the outcome, even if there is no explanation at all of why that outcome occurred rather than any of the others that might have. Similarly, if an agent is capable of causing any of a range of intentions that would result in different corresponding actions, the reason(s) that inclined the agent to do what he in fact does serve to explain it even though there may be no explanation of why he did that rather than any of the alternatives.

2. Arguments for the impossibility of agent-causal power

The possibility of agent causation has been widely doubted, especially in recent philosophy. Sometimes, the claim is that it is absolutely, or metaphysically, impossible insofar as it posits conditions that contradict certain necessary truths about certain ontological categories, such as that of event or substance. Other times, the form or impossibility is epistemic: agent causation, it is held, is incompatible with what we have excellent reason to believe are basic truths concerning the physics of our world; or with the relationship between the physics and any high-level processes to which basic physics gives rise; or with a general sort of ontological economy that obtains in our world (no superfluous explanatory features). I will now consider four reasons that some have put forward as grounds for doubting the coherence of agent causation, either absolutely, or with respect to some such general feature of our world.

FROM THE TIMING OF ACTIONS

C. D. Broad's oft-cited objection to the possibility of agent causation runs thus:

> I see no *prima facie* objection to there being events that are not completely determined. But, in so far as an event *is* determined, an essential factor in its total cause must be other *events*. How can an event possibly be determined to happen at a certain date if its total cause contained no factor to which the notion of date has any application? And how can the notion of date have any application to anything that is not an event? (1952: 215)

Broad's objection, or something like it, would have considerable force against an agent-causal view that maintained that nothing about the agent at the time of his action was explanatorily relevant to its performance. Such an "action" would indeed seem freakish, or inexplicable in any significant way. But no agent causationist imagines such a scenario. On the version of the view advanced here, the agent's capacity to cause action-triggering events is causally structured by the agent's internal state, involving the having of reasons and other factors, before and up to the time of the action. These events within the agent suffice to explanatorily ground the agent's causing the event to happen "at a certain date" without collapsing the view into one on which those events themselves produce the action.

Randy Clarke, an erstwhile defender of an agent-causal account of freedom, has recently claimed that a modified version of Broad's objection has some force.[14] Events, but not substances, are 'directly' in time in that their times are constituents of the events. By contrast, he maintains, "a substance is in time only in that events involving it…are directly in time." (This is supposed to be directly parallel to a reverse contention with respect to space, on which substances occupy space directly whereas events in their careers occupy a location only via its constituent object.) From this, he suggests, one can argue that the fact that effects are caused to occur at times "can be so only if their causes likewise occur at times—only, that is, if their causes are directly in time in the way in which events are but substances are not" (2003: 201).

The contention that drives this argument is obscure. It can easily be taken to suggest that events are ontologically more fundamental than objects, a contentious claim that any agent causationist will reject out of hand. But if this is not being claimed—as the reverse contention regarding occupation of space confirms—the point is unclear. What does it mean, exactly, to say that an object exists at a time "only in that" events it undergoes exist at that time? It cannot be the claim that the object's existing at that time metaphysically depends on the event's existing, as the object might have undergone another event at that time instead. If we weaken the claim to the plausible observation that, necessarily, an object exists at time t only if there is some event or other involving it that occurs at t, the dependence is no longer asymmetrical: for any event occurring at t that involves an object, O, necessarily, *that* event exists at t only if O exists at t. Since I can think of no other way of explicating the 'exists only in that' relation, I do not see here a promising basis for Broad's assertion that the cause of an event can only be another 'datable' entity.

FROM THE UNIFORMITY OF CAUSAL POWER

A second objection on which Clarke puts a great deal of weight begins with the following observation. If there is such a thing as agent causation, then there is a property or set of properties whose dispositional profile is precisely to confer on the agent a capacity to cause an intention to act. Notice how this contrasts with other causal powers in a very basic respect: the obtaining of properties that constitute 'event-causal' powers themselves tend towards certain effects (conditional on other circumstances). Hence,

> *Event-causal powers* are tendencies towards effects, i.e., the powers themselves are disposed to produce effects.
> *Agent-causal power* confers a capacity upon agents to produce effects, i.e., the power is not disposed to produce anything, it merely confers on its possessor a generic disposition to cause effects.

The uniformity objection to the thesis of agent causation is simply that it is doubtful that there can be any such property that fundamentally "works differently" (by conferring a power on its possessor to cause an effect) (2003: 192–3). If true, "causation would then be a radically disunified phenomenon" (2003: 208), and this is evidently a bad thing.

We may read this objection as making the claim that the ontological category of *property* has an abstract functional essence that includes the tendency in the presence of other properties towards the direct, joint production of certain effects. Is there reason to think that this is so? One reason to doubt it stems from the variety of property theories philosophers have advanced: transcendent vs. immanent universals vs. tropes; pure powers vs. Humean non-dispositional qualities vs. a 'dual-aspect' combination of the two. In the face of serious commitment to and elaboration of such diverse positions, one might think that the range of possibility is correspondingly broad. However, this sort of reason for rejecting the uniform dispositional essence thesis is not compelling. Nearly all philosophers holding one or another of the competing theories of properties just noted believes the truth of their favored theory to be necessary, with the other alleged entities judged to be impossibilities. And that seems the right thing to say, whatever one's view. In particular, if one rejects Humean qualities in favor of either the pure powers or dual aspect theory, then one should hold that, whatever the variation across possibility space when it comes to the specific kinds of properties there are, they all conform to the general features of one's property theory.[15]

Thus, one who maintains the uniformity thesis may allow that figuring out the right conception of properties is difficult while contending that, once we have embraced a general approach (here presumed to include irreducible dispositionality), we should presume an absolute unity of nature at a suitable level of abstraction. But at *what* level of abstraction should the thesis be applied? Consider that, in the advent of statistical laws in fundamental physics, many metaphysicians are now comfortable with the notion that there are nondeterministic dispositions varying in strength along a continuum, with deterministic potentialities merely being a limiting case. Consider further that, while properties typically work in tandem towards effects, a natural way of interpreting the phenomenon of radioactive particle decay is as an entirely self-contained process whose timing is radically undetermined by any sort of stimulus event. Finally, some adhere to the truth of (and still others to the possibility of) a view that all or many conscious mental properties are intrinsically intentional while this is true of no physical properties. None of these claims concerns free will, and yet all posit a kind of variability in the nature of dispositional properties that warrants classifying them into different basic types. Given these examples, it is hard to see why there may not be a further partition of types of the sort envisioned by the agent causationist.

Doubtless there is a unity across these divisions at *some* level of abstraction. But assuming the agent causationist's position is otherwise motivated, he may reasonably contend that it must be sufficiently abstract as to encompass the division his theory requires. Indeed, why may not the unity of *basic* dispositional properties simply consist in their making a net addition to the pool of causal powers?

FROM THE CONNECTION BETWEEN CAUSATION AND PROBABILITY-RAISING

A third consideration for doubting the possibility of agent causation (also given by Clarke 2003) takes as its point of departure that causation is somehow bound up with probability raising. As Clarke notes, it is difficult if not impossible to state a very precise thesis here. In most cases of indeterministic event causation, the obtaining of a causally relevant feature to some degree *raised* the probability of the effect in question—but not, or at least not obviously, in all cases. Given the fact that the obtaining of potential causes may screen off other factors that would otherwise potentially influence an outcome, we can readily imagine cases where something that actually contributed to an effect nonetheless rendered it either no more or even *less* likely than it would have been had that factor not obtained.[16] Still, he contends, there is "considerable plausibility" to the claim that a cause must be the sort of entity that can *antecedently affect the probability* of their effects. But an agent, as such, is not this sort of entity—clearly, only an event or enduring state could be. So the thesis of agent causation runs contrary to a plausible constraint on indeterministic causation by positing agents who are indeterministic causes of certain effects while necessarily not having a direct influence on the prior probability of those effects (203).

In reply, I suggest that Clarke's proposed constraint on admissible causes is at best a rough, first pass at capturing a conceptual connection between causal factors and probability transmission. And to the extent that there is a plausible intuition underlying it, my structured tendency account of agent causation conforms to it. On this account, agent causation is not something wholly disassociated from the evolving chain of probabilistic causes constituting the world's history. Agent causes act on the basis of prior factors that confer a positive objective probability on their occurrence. This should suffice to conform to any independently plausible, refined thesis that is intended to capture the vague intuition that probability transmission is a fundamental feature of causation. We may grant that, if one *already* believes on independent grounds that agent causation is impossible, then Clarke's more specific claim is a reasonable way to express the intuition. But in the present context, it seems to me a gratuitous strengthening of a general intuition in a way that arbitrarily precludes the possibility of agent causation.

FROM THE SUPERFLUITY/UNKNOWABILITY OF AGENT CAUSING THAT IS PROBABILISTICALLY CONSTRAINED

By constructing a picture on which agent causal power is causally structured by reasons and other factors, I have tried to integrate the view of human freedom it anchors into a view of the wider world as an evolving network of interacting powers. Critics of traditional, less constrained versions of the view have understandably complained that it depicts a godlike transcendence of natural forces. The present project suggests that the objectionable aspect is inessential, since it is possible to give freedom a human face.[17]

To other critics, however, that merely opens up other vulnerabilities. Eric Hiddleston charges that the view of agent causation as probabilistically structured renders it superfluous for explanatory purposes (2005b: 552–3). Any event that one might explain as caused by an agent whose power was probabilistically structured by reasons R1 and R2 might equally well and more economically be explained by the direct causal efficacy of R1 and R2, acting nondeterministically. Furthermore, the agent causal theorist practically invites such an alternative explanation when he allows that, in some cases, reasons do in fact bring about actions (though these would not be directly *free* actions).

An initial reply simply notes that the agent causationist will expect that cases where reasons directly bring about actions differ in detectable ways from those in which agent causal power is at work. Viewed from another direction, there is no reason to suppose that an agent whose agent-causal power was rendered inoperative with all else being left untouched would simply carry on exactly as before.

But Hiddleston, I believe, would wish to persist as follows: why would we have reason to posit agent causal power in the first place instead of a causal theory of action on which reasons are productive? It seems that nothing in the observable pattern of events could, even in principle, require us to ascribe certain events to agents as causes.[18]

In reply, I first question the premise that there are no distinctive features of agent-causal processes as against possible cases in which reasons nondeterministically produce actions. First, just given the way highly deliberate and unpressured choices seem to us to unfold, it seems doubtful that our reasons fix a probability for the precise timing of the action which they promote. At most, there is an interval of time in which a possible choice is likely to occur, with the likelihood being subject to fluctuation as the agent deliberates. It seems, on some occasions, that I am capable of putting off decisions or continuing to search for reasons pro and con various courses of action, and that there are not fixed probabilities of my ceasing to dither at particular moments. (This is consistent with assuming that there is a high conditional probability for the agent's causing intention i at t_1 on i's occurring at t_1.) One might construct a model analogous to the way physicists model particle decay, on which a sample of a radioactive substance of a given mass has an associated probability distribution that measures the likelihood for each moment over an interval of its having lost half its mass by that time. But any such model generally applied to the case of freely making a choice would seem contrived.

Second, the agent causationist can plausibly suppose that while there is a probability of an agent's causing an intention to A, there is no particular probability of that intention's having a further goal-directed content in the sense I spoke of as acting *for*, and not just *on*, a reason. That is, there may be a probability of 0.6 that an agent will, within a specified interval of time, cause an intention to A, but no probabilities to its having the precise content of simply *A*, *A-for-the-sake-of-G1*, or *A-for-the-sake-of-G2*.

I put forward these two suggestions with some diffidence, as they are grounded in vague intuitions concerning how actions seem to us to unfold. A more firmly-grounded response to the 'no evidence' objection is that, even if there weren't these differences from possible cases of indeterministic causation by reasons, we have a general explanatory reason to accept that agents are sometimes causes. The thesis that agents are sometimes causes, in my view, best reflects the phenomenology of many of our actions and it is required by our (related) native belief that most human adults are free and morally responsible agents.

In general respects, the explanatory appeal to agent causation is similar to the appeal to causal realism. The skeptical Humean insists that all we need are the observable patterns among events, (allegedly) conceived nondispositionally. According to the realist, we must go deeper, explaining the patterns themselves in terms of the structured propensities of the world's basic features. Humean complaints that primitive causation is an 'occult' metaphysical relation are just so much throwing dust in the air and complaining that one cannot see. We have an intuitive grasp—albeit one that is highly general, needing elucidation—on the idea of causal power and it is fundamental to our naïve conception of the world around us. Now, Hiddleston himself is no Humean. As it happens, however, he endorses Nancy Cartwright's (1989) idiosyncratic claim to provide a purely *empirical*, neutral case for the existence of event-causal dispositions, a case that turns on the nature of successful scientific practice in isolating causal influences. (And so he thinks there is a principled asymmetry concerning the possibility of evidence for event and agent-causal dispositions.) Here, I can only join hands with many others in confessing not to understand exactly how Cartwright's argument is supposed to go—how it is that the convinced Humean cannot give an alternate interpretation (however perverse to my realist eyes on non-empirical grounds) of what is observed and the empirical inferences and theorizing based upon it.

Many philosophers (including Hiddleston) dispute the claim that our experience of acting in any way supports the thesis that human agents are sometimes (literally) causes. Randy Clarke writes:

> I do not find it a credible claim that ordinary human agents have any experience, or any belief arising directly from experience, the content of

which is correctly characterized in terms of agent causation...Ordinary human agents, it seems plain, lack the concept of substance causation. A representation of free action as substance-caused (or as consisting on the substance causation of some event internal to the action) is a sophisticated philosophical construction...(2003: 206–7)

Now, something in the neighborhood of Clarke's remarks is surely correct. It takes philosophical reflection to attain a clear grasp on the idea of agents *qua* substance as causes, as distinct from either events internal to the agent as causes or the bogus Humean surrogate of patterns of (actual or counterfactual) regularity among events internal to the agent. But, for all that, it may be (and I contend *is*) the case that (a) the content of the experience-in-acting of ordinary human agents involves a fairly inchoate sense of themselves as bringing about their actions and that (b) the reflective account that best captures this inchoate content is the agent-causal account. I observe that this position on the ordinary *experience* of agency is supported by Daniel Wegner, a prominent cognitive psychologist who goes on to argue that our experience of agency is deeply illusory.[19]

FROM THE INSUFFICIENCY (FOR FREEDOM) OF AGENT CAUSING THAT IS PROBABILISTICALLY CONSTRAINED

Recall that an apparent difficulty facing an alternative, causal indeterminist account of human freedom—an account that eschews agent causation in favor of a nondeterministic causation of choices by one's reasons—is that it appears to be a matter of luck which of the undetermined possibilities is realized in a particular case. Given the presence of desires and intentions of varying strength, making certain outcomes more likely than others, the agent possesses no further power to determine which outcome in fact is brought about. The determination is a product of the propensities of the agent's states, and the agent doesn't seem to directly control which propensity will 'fire.' If we imagine two identical agents in identical circumstances, with one agent nondeterministically choosing alternative A and the other choosing B, it seems a matter of luck from the standpoint of the agents themselves which alternative occurs in which person.

Supposing there is a power of agent causation has the virtue that it seems to avoid this 'problem of luck' facing other indeterministic accounts.[20] Agent causation is precisely the power to directly determine which of several causal possibilities is realized on a given occasion. However, Derk Pereboom has recently argued that this is so only if agent causation does not conform to pre-given indeterministic tendencies.[21] He writes:

...to answer the luck objection, the causal power exercised by the agent must be of a different sort from that of the events that shape the agent-causal power, and on the occasion of a free decision, the exercise of these causal powers must be token-distinct from the exercise of the causal powers of the events. Given this requirement, we would expect the decisions of the agent-cause to diverge, in the long run, from the frequency of choices that would be extremely likely on the basis of the events alone. If we nevertheless found conformity, we would have very good reason to believe that the agent-causal power was not of a different sort from the causal powers of the events after all, and that on the occasion of particular decisions, the exercise of these causal powers was not token-distinct. Or else, this conformity would be a wild coincidence... (2005: 246)

Though Pereboom expresses the matter in epistemological terms, I take it that he intends to be making a linked pair of metaphysical claims, as follows. If agent-causal power is to truly enable the agent directly to determine which causally-possible choice obtains, and so overcome the luck objection plaguing other accounts of freedom, then it must be a different sort of power from event-causal powers such as the propensities of one's reasons, such that its exercise is token-distinct from the exercise of any of these event-causal powers. And the latter condition can be met only if the outcomes of agent-causal events are not strictly governed by the propensities of any relevant set of obtaining event-causal powers.

The agent causationist readily endorses the first of these conditionals, on a straightforward reading of "different sort of power" and "token-distinct exercise." After all, the view posits a fundamental, irreducible power of agents to form intentions. But the second conditional directly rejects the viability of any account on which agent causal power is probabilistically structured by reasons. Why does Pereboom assert it? His thought seems to be that if the event of one's having certain reasons along with other prior events ensure that one's choices will fit a certain pattern—more accurately, make the pattern-fitting likely, given a sufficiently large number of cases—then one's supposed agent-causal power in choosing is at best a shadowy accompaniment to the event-causal power. In truth, it is no power at all, as it adds nothing to the mix of factors already in play. With no authority to act on its own, its presence makes no discernible difference to what occurs in the aggregate. If it would be a matter of luck, beyond my direct control, which of my indeterministic propensities happens to be realized on any given occasion, were the causal indeterminist account correct, then adding the ability to 'directly determine' the outcome wouldn't help if I am ineluctably constrained by those very propensities.

It is easy to feel the pull of this thought, but it should be resisted. First, we insist upon the importance of the distinction between (the persisting state or event of one's having) reasons *structuring* one's agent-causal power in the sense of conferring objective tendencies towards particular actions and reasons *activating* that power by producing one's causing a specific intention. On the view I have described, nothing other than the agent himself activates the agent causal power in this way. To say that I have an objective probability of 0.8 to cause the intention to join my students at the local pub ensures nothing about what I will in fact do. I can resist this rather strong inclination just as well as act upon it. The probability simply measures relative likelihood and serves to predict a distribution of outcomes were I to be similarly inclined in similar circumstances many times over (which of course I never am in actual practice). The reason that the alternative, causal indeterminist view is subject to the luck objection is *not* that it posits objective probabilities to possible outcomes but that it fails to posit a kind of single-case form of control by means of which the agent can determine what happens in each case. After all, were the causal indeterminist picture modified so that agents choices are caused but not determined by appropriate internal states whose propensities, while nondeterministic, lacked definite measure, the problem of luck or control would remain. Again, that problem concerns not prior influence but the ability to settle what occurs on the occasion of a causally undetermined outcome. The agent causationist's solution is to posit a basic capacity of just that sort, while allowing that the capacity is not situated within an indifferent agent, but one with evolving preferences and beliefs. Surely having preferences does not undermine control!

* * *

Causation is a primitive, yet fairly simple concept. Reflective theorizing, both philosophical and scientific, has yielded a variety of forms in which it can be coherently conceived. Absent convincing reason to think one of these imagined forms is defective in some unobvious way, we ought to deem it possible. It has been the aim of the present essay to specify a coherent way we might think about the idea of agent-causal power, an idea that has guided some who theorize about freedom of the will and that is even deemed intuitively attractive by some who resist it. It may be metaphysically impossible that there be such a thing, but I have yet to encounter a convincing argument for it.

Notes

1. For discussion, see especially Molnar 2003, Heil and Martin 1999, and Hawthorne 2001.

2. David Armstrong has been the key contemporary figure in developing the idea of structural properties as part of a 'sparse' ontology. Nonetheless, he waffles a bit in his understanding of their reducibility. He speaks of them as something subtly 'extra'—distinct from the underlying instances of properties and relations but strongly supervening

upon them (Armstrong 1997: 37).But this is hard to square with his adamant contention that they are an "ontological free lunch." (See the discussion on 34–45.)

3. On the nature of fundamental external relations, see Molnar 2003, (chap.10), Ellis 2001, and the skeptical discussion in Armstrong's contribution to Armstrong, Martin, and Place 1996.

4. I characterize the Armstrong-Tooley view as a gratuitously complicated kind of Humeanism because, despite their intentions, second-order relational structure to the world (their N (F, G) necessitation relation) cannot *explain* first-order facts (instances of G regularly following instances of F) since the second-order relations presuppose the supposed explananda. Were God to construct a Tooley-Armstrong world, determining the distribution of first-order F and G facts must precede decisions about N (F, G) facts.

5. Peter van Inwagen has heavily influenced discussion of this argument over the last thirty years by his careful formulation of the argument. See van Inwagen 1983 and O'Connor 2000 for a friendly amendment.

6. The most prominent advocate of this view of freedom has been Robert Kane. Kane has developed his view in a number of writings culminating in *The Significance of Free Will*.

7. A few preceding sentences are borrowed from O'Connor and Churchill 2004.

8. Concepts of emergence have a long history—one need only consider Aristotle's notion of irreducible substantial forms. Their coherence is also a matter of controversy. For an attempt to sort out the different ideas that have carried this label, see O'Connor and Wong 2002. And for a detailed exposition and defense of the notion I rely on in the text, see O'Connor and Wong 2005.

9. For numerous examples of such phenomena, see Laughlin, Pines, Schmalian, Stojkovic, and Wolynes 2000.

10. See O'Connor 2000, 52–55, for further discussion.

11. I first developed the distinction in the text between *acting on* and *acting for* a reason in O'Connor 2005.

12. Nikolaj Nottelmann raised this objection to me in discussion

13. For further discussion of the idea of degrees of freedom, see O'Connor 2005.

14. 2003: 201–2. Clarke does not claim that this argument is individually decisive. Instead, he presents several considerations, including some that I present below, that he believes to tell against the possibility of agent causation and that cumulatively make the impossibility of agent causation more likely than not. I will argue to the contrary that none of the main considerations he adduces has significant force.

15. A complication here is that one version of the causal powers theory maintains that there are two fundamental kinds of properties and relations: those whose nature is dispositional and certain 'framework' relations such as spatio-temporal relations. (See Ellis 2001.) Suppose this is correct. Even so, one may argue for the abstract functional uniformity of all properties falling on the powers side of this division.

16. Clarke cites (203) putative illustrations in Dowe 2000: 33–40, Salmon 1984: 192–202, and Ehring 1997: 36. For a deft and thorough development of a theory of indeterministic event causal powers, see Hiddleston 2005a.

17. Another recent effort along these lines is O'Connor 2005. Randolph Clarke 2003 is similarly an attempt to give a recognizably human version of the agent causal account of freedom. John Churchill and I give reasons for rejecting Clarke's approach in our 2004.

18. Clarke (2003: 206) endorses the undetectability claim while denying that it gives reason to reject the possibility of agent causation.

19. See Wegner 2002, (chap. 1). I criticize Wegner's case for the illusory character of what he terms "conscious willing" in my 2005: 220–26.

20. In addition to causal indeterminist and agent causal theories of freedom, there is noncausal indeterminism, on which control is an intrinsic, noncausal feature of free choices or actions. For versions of this view, see Goetz 1988, Ginet 1990, McCann 1998, and Pink 2004.

21. Others have recently argued that agent causation does not necessarily avoid the problem of luck (or, as it sometimes put, the "problem of control"). See Haji 2004, Widerker 2005, and Mele 2006. I will not here address their ways of pressing the issue, though I find their arguments even less compelling than the one by Pereboom that I discuss in the text. Pereboom (2005: 243–44) also rejects the arguments of Mele and Haji.

References

Armstrong, D. 1978. *A Theory of Universals. Vol.2 of Universals and Scientific Realism.* Cambridge: Cambridge University Press.

Armstrong, D. 1997. *A World of States of Affairs.* Cambridge, UK: Cambridge University Press.

Armstrong, D., U.T. Place, and C.B. Martin. 1996. *Dispositions: A Debate.* London: Routledge Press.

Broad, C.D. 1952. "Determinism, indeterminism, and libertarianism," in *Ethics and the History of Philosophy: Selected Essays,* by C. D. Broad, 195–217. New York: Humanities Press.

Cartwright, N. 1989. *Nature's Capacities and Their Measurement.* Oxford: Oxford University Press.

Clarke, R. 2003. *Libertarian Accounts of Free Will.* New York: Oxford University Press.

Dowe, P. 2000. *Physical Causation.* Cambridge: Cambridge University Press.

Ehring, D. 1997. *Causation and Persistence.* New York: Oxford University Press.

Ellis, B. 2001. *Scientific Essentialism.* Cambridge: Cambridge University Press.

Ginet, C. 1990. *On Action.* Cambridge: Cambridge University Press.

Goetz, S. 1988. "A noncausal theory of agency," *Philosophy and Phenomenological Research* **49**: 303–16.

Haji, I. 2004. "Active control, agent-causation, and free action," *Philosophical Explorations* **7**(2): 131–48.

Hawthorne, J. 2001. "Causal structuralism," *Philosophical Perspectives* **15**: 361–78.

Heil, J, and C.B. Martin. 1999. "The ontological turn," *Midwest Studies in Philosophy* **23**: 34–60.

Hiddleston, E. 2005a. "Causal powers," *The British Journal for the Philosophy of Science* **56**(1): 27–59.

Hiddleston, E. 2005b. "Critical notice: Timothy O'Connor, *Persons and causes,*" *Noûs* **39**(3): 541–56.

Kane, R. 1996. *The Significance of Free Will.* New York: Oxford University Press.

Laughlin, R. B., D. Pines, J. Schmalian, B. Stojkovic, and P. Wolynes. 2000. "The middle way," *Proceedings of the National Academy of Sciences* **97** (January 4): 32–37.

Lewis, D. 1983. *Philosophical Papers*, Vol.1. New York: Oxford University Press.

Lowe, E. J. 2002. *A Survey of Metaphysics*. Oxford: Oxford University Press.

Martin, C. B. 1997. "On the need for properties: the road to pythagoreanism and back," *Synthese* **112**: 193–231.

McCann, H. 1998. *The Works of Agency*. Ithaca, NY: Cornell University Press.

Mele, A. 2006. *Free Will and Luck*. New York: Oxford University Press.

Molnar, G. 2003. *Powers: A Study in Metaphysics*, ed. S. Mumford. Oxford: Oxford University Press.

O'Connor, T. 2000. *Persons and Causes: The Metaphysics of Free Will*. New York: Oxford University Press.

O'Connor, T. 2005. "Freedom with a human face," *Midwest studies in philosophy* **29**: 207–27.

O'Connor, T, and J. Churchill. 2004. "Reasons explanation and agent control: in search of an integrated account," *Philosophical Topics* **32**: 241–54.

O'Connor, T, and H. Y. Wong. 2002. "Emergent properties," *Stanford online encyclopedia of philosophy*. http://plato.stanford.edu/entries/properties-emergent/.

O'Connor, T, and H. Y. Wong. 2005. "The metaphysics of emergence," *Noûs* **39**: 659–79.

Pereboom, D. 2005. "Defending hard incompatibilism," *Midwest Studies in Philosophy* **29**: 228–47.

Pink, T. 2004. *Free Will: A Very Short Introduction*. Oxford: Oxford University Press.

Salmon, W. 1984. *Scientific Explanation and the Causal Structure of the World*. Princeton, NJ: Princeton University Press.

Tooley, M. 1987. *Causation: A Realist Approach*. Oxford: Clarendon Press.

Van Inwagen, P. 1983. *An Essay on Free Will*. Oxford: Clarendon Press.

Wegner, D. 2002. *The Illusion of Conscious Will*. Cambridge, MA: MIT Press.

Widerker, D. 2005. "Agent-causation and control," *Faith and Philosophy* **22** 1: 87–98.

PART 5

Suggested Further Readings

V. Libertarian Alternatives—Soft and Hard

A critical overview and analysis of various libertarian views is presented in:

Clarke, Randolph. 2003. *Libertarian Accounts of Free Will*. Oxford: Oxford University Press.

Other "soft" libertarian accounts include:

Balaguer, Mark. 2004. "A coherent, naturalistic, and plausible formulation of libertarian free will," *Noûs* 38: 379–406.

Ekstrom, Laura Waddell. 2000. "Indeterminist free action," in Laura Ekstrom, *Agency and Responsibility: Essays on the Metaphysics of Freedom*. Boulder, Co.: Westview Press.

McCall, Storrs & E.J. Lowe. 2005. "Indeterminist free will," *Philosophy and Phenomenological Research*, 70.3: 681–90.

Sorabji, Richard. 1980. *Necessity, Cause and Blame*. London: Duckworth.

Wiggins, David. 2003. "Towards a reasonable libertarianism," in G. Watson, ed., *Free Will*. Oxford: Oxford University Press.

Critical discussions relating to soft libertarian views can be found in:

Clarke, Randolph. 1995. "Indeterminism and control," *American Philosophical Quarterly* 32: 125–38.

Dennett, Daniel. 2003. *Freedom Evolves*. London: Allen Lane, Chapter 4.

Russell, Paul. 1984. "Sorabji and the dilemma of determinism," *Analysis* 44: 166–72.

Watson, Gary. 1999. "Soft libertarianism and hard compatibilism," *Journal of Ethics* 3/4: 351–65. (Reprinted in Gary Watson, *Agency and Answerability*, New York: Oxford University Press, 2004.)

On "hard" libertarianism:

Clarke, Randolph. 2005. "Agent causation and the problem of luck," *Pacific Philosophical Quarterly* 86/3: 408–21.

O'Connor, Timothy. 2000. *Persons and Causes: The Metaphysics of Free Will*. Oxford: Oxford University Press.

See also:

Ginet, Carl. 1997. "Freedom, responsibility and agency," *The Journal of Ethics* **1**.1: 374–80. (Reprinted in R. Kane, ed., *Free Will*. Oxford: Blackwell, 2002.)

Pink, Thomas. 2011. "Freedom and action without causation," in R. Kane, ed., *The Oxford Handbook of Free Will*. 2nd ed. New York: Oxford University Press, Chapter 17.

Steward, Helen. 2012. *A Metaphysics of Freedom*. Oxford: Oxford University Press.

Compatibilism: Hierarchical Theories and Manipulation Problems

13

Freedom of the Will and the
Concept of a Person

Harry G. Frankfurt

What philosophers lately come to accept as analysis of the concept of a person is not actually analysis of *that* concept at all. Strawson, whose usage represents the current standard, identifies the concept of a person as "the concept of a type of entity such that *both* predicates ascribing states of consciousness *and* predicates ascribing corporeal characteristics...are equally applicable to a single individual of that single type." [1] But there are many entities besides persons that have both mental and physical properties. As it happens—though it seems extraordinary that this should be so—there is no common English word for the type of entity Strawson has in mind, a type that includes not only human beings but animals of various lesser species as well. Still, this hardly justifies the misappropriation of a valuable philosophical term.

Whether the members of some animal species are persons is surely not to be settled merely by determining whether it is correct to apply to them, in addition to predicates ascribing corporeal characteristics, predicates that ascribe states of consciousness. It does violence to our language to endorse the application of the term 'person' to those numerous creatures which do have both psychological and material properties but which are manifestly not persons in any normal sense of the word. This misuse of language is doubtless innocent of any theoretical error. But although the offense is "merelyverbal," it does significant harm. For it gratuitously diminishes our philosophical vocabulary, and it increases the likelihood that we will overlook the important area of inquiry with which the term 'person' is most naturally associated. It might have been expected that no problem would be of more central and persistent concern to philosophers than that of understanding what we ourselves essentially are. Yet this problem is so generally neglected that it has been possible to make off with its very name almost without being noticed and, evidently, without evoking any widespread feeling of loss.

There is a sense in which the word 'person' is merely the singular form of 'people' and in which both terms connote no more than membership in a certain biological species. In those senses of the word which are of greater philosophical interest, however, the criteria for being a person do not serve primarily to distinguish the members of our own species from the members of other species. Rather, they are designed to capture those attributes which are the subject of our most humane concern with ourselves and the source of what we regard as most important and most problematical in our lives. Now these attributes would be of equal significance to us even if they were not in fact peculiar and common to the members of our own species. What interests us most in the human condition would not interest us less if it were also a feature of the condition of other creatures as well.

Our concept of ourselves as persons is not to be understood, therefore, as a concept of attributes that are necessarily species-specific. It is conceptually possible that members of novel or even of familiar nonhuman species should be persons; and it is also conceptually possible that some members of the human species are not persons. We do in fact assume, on the other hand, that no member of another species is a person. Accordingly, there is a presumption that what is essential to persons is a set of characteristics that we generally suppose—whether rightly or wrongly—to be uniquely human.

It is my view that one essential difference between persons and other creatures is to be found in the structure of a person's will. Human beings are not alone in having desires and motives, or in making choices. They share these things with the members of certain other species, some of whom even appear to engage in deliberation and to make decisions based upon prior thought. It seems to be peculiarly characteristic of humans, however, that they are able to form what I shall call "second-order desires" or "desires of the second order."

Besides wanting and choosing and being moved *to do* this or that, men may also want to have (or not to have) certain desires and motives. They are capable of wanting to be different, in their preferences and purposes, from what they are. Many animals appear to have the capacity for what I shall call "first-order desires" or "desires of the first order," which are simply desires to do or not to do one thing or another. No animal other than man, however, appears to have the capacity for reflective self-evaluation that is manifested in the formation of second-order desires.[2]

I.

The concept designated by the verb 'to want' is extraordinarily elusive. A statement of the form "*A* wants to *X*"—taken by itself, apart from a context that serves to amplify or to specify its meaning—conveys remarkably little information. Such a statement may be consistent, for example, with each of the following statements: (a) the prospect of doing *X* elicits no sensation or introspectible emotional response in *A*; (b) *A* is unaware that he wants to *X*;(c) *A* believes that he does not want to *X*; (d) *A* wants to refrain from *X*-ing; (e) *A* wants to *Y* and believes that it is impossible for him both to *Y* and to *X*; (f) *A* does not "really" want to *X*; (g) *A* would rather die than *X*; and so on. It is therefore hardly sufficient to formulate the distinction between first-order and second-order desires, as I have done, by suggesting merely that someone has a first-order desire when he wants to do or not to do such-and-such, and that he has a second-order desire when he wants to have or not to have a certain desire of the first order.

As I shall understand them, statements of the form "*A* wants to *X*" cover a rather broad range of possibilities.[3] They may be true even when statements like (a) through (g) are true: when *A* is unaware of any feelings concerning *X*-ing, when he is unaware that he wants to *X*, when he deceives himself about what he wants and believes falsely that he does not want to *X*, when he also has other desires that conflict with his desire to *X*, or when he is ambivalent. The desires in question may be conscious or unconscious, they need not be univocal, and *A* may be mistaken about them. There is a further source of uncertainty with regard to statements that identify someone's desires, however, and here it is important for my purposes to be less permissive.

Consider first those statements of the form "*A* wants to *X*" which identify first-order desires—that is, statements in which the term 'to *X*' refers to an action. A statement of this kind does not, by itself, indicate the relative strength of *A*'s desire to *X*. It does not make it clear whether this desire is at all likely to play a decisive role in what *A* actually does or tries to do. For it may correctly be said that *A* wants to *X* even when his desire to *X* is only one among his desires and when it is far from being paramount among them. Thus, it may be true that *A* wants to *X* when he strongly prefers to do something else instead; and it may be true that he wants to *X* despite the fact that, when he acts, it is not the desire to *X* that motivates him to do what he does. On the other hand, someone who states that *A* wants to *X* may mean to convey that it is this desire that is motivating or moving *A* to do what he is actually doing or that *A* will in fact be moved by this desire (unless he changes his mind) when he acts.

It is only when it is used in the second of these ways that, given the special usage of 'will' that I propose to adopt, the statement identifies *A*'s will. To identify an agent's will is either to identify the desire (or desires) by which he is motivated in some action he performs or to identify the desire (or desires) by which he will or would be motivated when or if he acts. An agent's will, then, is identical with one or more of his first-order desires. But the notion of the will, as I am employing it, is not coextensive with the notion of first-order desires. It is not the notion of something that merely inclines an agent in some degree to act in a certain way. Rather, it is the notion of an *effective* desire— one that moves (or will or would move) a person all the way to action. Thus the notion of the will is not coextensive with the notion of what an agent intends to do. For even though someone may have a settled intention to do X, he may nonetheless do something else instead of doing X because, despite his intention, his desire to do X proves to be weaker or less effective than some conflicting desire.

Now consider those statements of the form "A wants to X" which identify second-order desires—that is, statements in which the term 'to X' refers to a desire of the first order. There are also two kinds of situation in which it may be true that A wants to want to X. In the first place, it might be true of A that he wants to have a desire to X despite the fact that he has a univocal desire, altogether free of conflict and ambivalence, to refrain from X-ing. Someone might want to have a certain desire, in other words, but univocally want that desire to be unsatisfied.

Suppose that a physician engaged in psychotherapy with narcotics addicts believes that his ability to help his patients would be enhanced if he understood better what it is like for them to desire the drug to which they are addicted. Suppose that he is led in this way to want to have a desire for the drug. If it is a genuine desire that he wants, then what he wants is not merely to feel the sensations that addicts characteristically feel when they are gripped by their desires for the drug. What the physician wants, insofar as he wants to have a desire, is to be inclined or moved to some extent to take the drug.

It is entirely possible, however, that, although he wants to be moved by a desire to take the drug, he does not want this desire to be effective. He may not want it to move him all the way to action. He need not be interested in finding out what it is like to take the drug. And insofar as he now wants only to *want* to take it, and not to *take* it, there is nothing in what he now wants that would be satisfied by the drug itself. He may now have, in fact, an altogether univocal desire *not* to take the drug; and he may prudently arrange to make it impossible for him to satisfy the desire he would have if his desire to want the drug should in time be satisfied.

It would thus be incorrect to infer, from the fact that the physician now wants to desire to take the drug, that he already does desire to take it. His second-order desire to be moved to take the drug does not entail that he has a first-order desire to take it. If the drug were now to be administered to him, this might satisfy no desire that is implicit in his desire to want to take it. While he wants to want to take the drug, he may have *no* desire to take it; it may be that *all* he wants is to taste the desire for it. That is, his desire to have a certain desire that he does not have may not be a desire that his will should be at all different than it is.

Someone who wants only in this truncated way to want to X stands at the margin of preciosity, and the fact that he wants to want to X is not pertinent to the identification of his will. There is, however, a second kind of situation that may be described by 'A wants to want to X'; and when the statement is used to describe a situation of this second kind, then it does pertain to what *A* wants his will to be. In such cases the statement means that *A* wants the desire to *X* to be the desire that moves him effectively to act. It is not merely that he wants the desire to *X* to be among the desires by which, to one degree or another, he is moved or inclined to act. He wants this desire to be effective—that is, to provide the motive in what he actually does. Now when the statement that *A* wants to want to *X* is used in this way, it does entail that *A* already has a desire to *X*. It could not be true both that *A* wants the desire to *X* to move him into action and that he does not want to *X*. It is only if he does want to *X* that he can coherently want the desire to *X* not merely to be one of his desires but, more decisively, to be his will.[4]

Suppose a man wants to be motivated in what he does by the desire to concentrate on his work. It is necessarily true, if this supposition is correct, that he already wants to concentrate on his work. This desire is now among his desires. But the question of whether or not his second-order desire is fulfilled does not turn merely on whether the desire he wants is one of his desires. It turns on whether this desire is, as he wants it to be, his effective desire or will. If, when the chips are down, it is his desire to concentrate on his work that moves him to do what he does, then what he wants at that time is indeed (in the relevant sense) what he wants to want. If it is some other desire that actually moves him when he acts, on the other hand, then what he wants at that time is not (in the relevant sense) what he wants to want. This will be so despite the fact that the desire to concentrate on his work continues to be among his desires.

II.

Someone has a desire of the second order either when he wants simply to have a certain desire or when he wants a certain desire to be his will. In situations of the latter kind, I shall call his second-order desires "second-order volitions" or "volitions of the second order." Now it is having second-order volitions, and not having second-order desires generally, that I regard as essential to being a person. It is logically possible, however unlikely, that there should be an agent with second-order desires but with no volitions of the second order. Such a creature, in my view, would not be a person. I shall use the term 'wanton' to refer to agents who have first-order desires but who are not persons because, whether or not they have desires of the second order, they have no second-order volitions.[5]

The essential characteristic of a wanton is that he does not care about his will. His desires move him to do certain things, without its being true of him either that he wants to be moved by those desires or that he prefers to be moved by other desires. The class of wantons includes all nonhuman animals that have desires and all very young children. Perhaps it also includes some adult human beings as well. In any case, adult humans may be more or less wanton; they may act wantonly, in response to first-order desires concerning which they have no volitions of the second order, more or less frequently.

The fact that a wanton has no second-order volitions does not mean that each of his first-order desires is translated heedlessly and at once into action. He may have no opportunity to act in accordance with some of his desires. Moreover, the translation of his desires into action may be delayed or precluded either by conflicting desires of the first order or by the intervention of deliberation. For a wanton may possess and employ rational faculties of a high order. Nothing in the concept of a wanton implies that he cannot reason or that he cannot deliberate concerning how to do what he wants to do. What distinguishes the rational wanton from other rational agents is that he is not concerned with the desirability of his desires themselves. He ignores the question of what his will is to be. Not only does he pursue whatever course of action he is most strongly inclined to pursue, but he does not care which of his inclinations is the strongest.

Thus a rational creature, who reflects upon the suitability to his desires of one course of action or another, may nonetheless be a wanton. In maintaining that the essence of being a person lies not in reason but in will, I am far from suggesting that a creature without reason may be a person. For it is only in virtue of his rational capacities that a person is capable of becoming critically aware of his own will and of forming volitions of the second order. The structure of a person's will presupposes, accordingly, that he is a rational being.

The distinction between a person and a wanton may be illustrated by the difference between two narcotics addicts. Let us suppose that the physiological condition accounting for the addiction is the same in both men, and that both succumb inevitably to their periodic desires for the drug to which they are addicted. One of the addicts hates his addiction and always struggles desperately, although to no avail, against its thrust. He tries everything that he thinks might enable him to overcome his desires for the drug. But these desires are too powerful for him to withstand, and invariably, in the end, they conquer him. He is an unwilling addict, helplessly violated by his own desires.

The unwilling addict has conflicting first-order desires: he wants to take the drug, and he also wants to refrain from taking it. In addition to these first-order desires, however, he has a volition of the second order. He is not a neutral with regard to the conflict between his desire to take the drug and his desire to refrain from taking it. It is the latter desire, and not the former, that he wants to constitute his will; it is the latter desire, rather than the former, that he wants to be effective and to provide the purpose that he will seek to realize in what he actually does.

The other addict is a wanton. His actions reflect the economy of his first-order desires, without his being concerned whether the desires that move him to act are desires by which he wants to be moved to act. If he encounters problems in obtaining the drug or in administering it to himself, his responses to his urges to take it may involve deliberation. But it never occurs to him to consider whether he wants the relations among his desires to result in his having the will he has. The wanton addict may be an animal, and thus incapable of being concerned about his will. In any event he is, in respect of his wanton lack of concern, no different from an animal.

The second of these addicts may suffer a first-order conflict similar to the first-order conflict suffered by the first. Whether he is human or not, the wanton may (perhaps due to conditioning) both want to take the drug and want to refrain from taking it. Unlike the unwilling addict, however, he does not prefer that one of his conflicting desires should be paramount over the other; he does not prefer that one first-order desire rather than the other should constitute his will. It would be misleading to say that he is neutral as to the conflict between his desires, since this would suggest that he regards them as equally acceptable. Since he has no identity apart from his first-order desires, it is true neither that he prefers one to the other nor that he prefers not to take sides.

It makes a difference to the unwilling addict, who is a person, which of his conflicting first-order desires wins out. Both desires are his, to be sure; and whether he finally takes the drug or finally succeeds in refraining from taking it, he acts to satisfy what is in a literal sense his own desire. In either case he does something he himself wants to do, and he does it not because of some external influence whose aim happens to coincide with his own but because of his desire to do it. The unwilling addict identifies himself, however, through the formation of a second-order volition, with one rather than with the other of his conflicting first-order desires. He makes one of them more truly his own and, in so doing, he withdraws himself from the other. It is in virtue of this identification and withdrawal, accomplished through the formation of a second-order volition, that the unwilling addict may meaningfully make the analytically puzzling statements that the force moving him to take the drug is a force other than his own, and that it is not of his own free will but rather against his will that this force moves him to take it.

The wanton addict cannot or does not care which of his conflicting first-order desires wins out. His lack of concern is not due to his inability to find a convincing basis for preference. It is due either to his lack of the capacity for reflection or to his mindless indifference to the enterprise of evaluating his own desires and motives.[6] There is only one issue in the struggle to which his first-order conflict may lead: whether the one or the other of his conflicting desires is the stronger. Since he is moved by both desires, he will not be altogether satisfied by what he does no matter which of them is effective. But it makes no difference to *him* whether his craving or his aversion gets the upper hand. He has no stake in the conflict between them and so, unlike the unwilling addict, he can neither win nor lose the struggle in which he is engaged. When a *person* acts, the desire by which he is moved is either the will he wants or a will he wants to be without. When a *wanton* acts, it is neither.

III.

There is a very close relationship between the capacity for forming second-order volitions and another capacity that is essential to persons—one that has often been considered a distinguishing mark of the human condition. It is only because a person has volitions of the second order that he is capable both of enjoying and of lacking freedom of the will. The concept of a person is not only, then, the concept of a type of entity that has both first-order desires and volitions of the second order. It can also be construed as the concept of a type of entity for whom the freedom of its will may be a problem. This concept excludes all wantons, both infrahuman and human, since they fail to satisfy an essential condition for the enjoyment of freedom of the will. And it excludes those suprahuman beings, if any, whose wills are necessarily free.

Just what kind of freedom is the freedom of the will? This question calls for an identification of the special area of human experience to which the concept of freedom of the will, as distinct from the concepts of other sorts of freedom, is particularly germane. In dealing with it, my aim will be primarily to locate the problem with which a person is most immediately concerned when he is concerned with the freedom of his will.

According to one familiar philosophical tradition, being free is fundamentally a matter of doing what one wants to do. Now the notion of an agent who does what he wants to do is by no means an altogether clear one: both the doing and the wanting, and the appropriate relation between them as well, require elucidation. But although its focus needs to be sharpened and its formulation refined, I believe that this notion does capture at least part of what is implicit in the idea of an agent who *acts* freely. It misses entirely, however, the peculiar content of the quite different idea of an agent whose *will* is free.

We do not suppose that animals enjoy freedom of the will, although we recognize that an animal may be free to run in whatever direction it wants. Thus, having the freedom to do what one wants to do is not a sufficient condition of having a free will. It is not a necessary condition either. For to deprive someone of his freedom of action is not necessarily to undermine the freedom of his will. When an agent is aware that there are certain things he is not free to do, this doubtless affects his desires and limits the range of choices he can make. But suppose that someone, without being aware of it, has in fact lost or been deprived of his freedom of action. Even though he is no longer free to do what he wants to do, his will may remain as free as it was before. Despite the fact that he is not free to translate his desires into actions or to act according to the determinations of his will, he may still form those desires and make those determinations as freely as if his freedom of action had not been impaired.

When we ask whether a person's will is free we are not asking whether he is in a position to translate his first-order desires into actions. That is the question of whether he is free to do as he pleases. The question of the freedom of his will does not concern the relation between what he does and what he wants to do. Rather, it concerns his desires themselves. But what question about them is it?

It seems to me both natural and useful to construe the question of whether a person's will is free in close analogy to the question of whether an agent enjoys freedom of action. Now freedom of action is (roughly, at least) the freedom to do what one wants to do. Analogously, then, the statement that a person enjoys freedom of the will means (also roughly) that he is free to want what he wants to want. More precisely, it means that he is free to will what he wants to will, or to have the will he wants. Just as the question about the freedom of an agent's action has to do with whether it is the action he wants to perform, so the question about the freedom of his will has to do with whether it is the will he wants to have.

It is in securing the conformity of his will to his second-order volitions, then, that a person exercises freedom of the will. And it is in the discrepancy between his will and his second-order volitions, or in his awareness that their coincidence is not his own doing but only a happy chance, that a person who does not have this freedom feels its lack. The unwilling addict's will is not free. This is shown by the fact that it is not the will he wants. It is also true, though in a different way, that the will of the wanton addict is not free. The wanton addict neither has the will he wants nor has a will that differs from the will he wants. Since he has no volitions of the second order, the freedom of his will cannot be a problem for him. He lacks it, so to speak, by default.

People are generally far more complicated than my sketchy account of the structure of a person's will may suggest. There is as much opportunity for ambivalence, conflict, and self-deception with regard to desires of the second order, for example, as there is with regard to first-order desires. If there is an unresolved conflict among someone's second-order desires, then he is in danger of having no second-order volition; for unless this conflict is resolved, he has no preference concerning which of his first-order desires is to be his will. This condition, if it is so severe that it prevents him from identifying himself in a sufficiently decisive way with *any* of his conflicting first-order desires, destroys him as a person. For it either tends to paralyze his will and to keep him from acting at all, or it tends to remove him from his will so that his will operates without his participation. In both cases he becomes, like the unwilling addict though in a different way, a helpless bystander to the forces that move him.

Another complexity is that a person may have, especially if his second-order desires are in conflict, desires and volitions of a higher order than the second. There is no theoretical limit to the length of the series of desires of higher and higher orders; nothing except common sense and, perhaps, a saving fatigue prevents an individual from obsessively refusing to identify himself with any of his desires until he forms a desire of the next higher order. The tendency to generate such a series of acts of forming desires, which would be a case of humanization run wild, also leads toward the destruction of a person.

It is possible, however, to terminate such a series of acts without cutting it off arbitrarily. When a person identifies himself *decisively* with one of his first-order desires, this commitment "resounds" throughout the potentially endless array of higher orders. Consider a person who, without reservation or conflict, wants to be motivated by the desire to concentrate on his work. The fact that his second-order volition to be moved by this desire is a decisive one means that there is no room for questions concerning the pertinence of desires or volitions of higher orders. Suppose the person is asked whether he wants to want to want to concentrate on his work. He can properly insist that this question concerning a third-order desire does not arise. It would be a mistake to claim that, because he has not considered whether he wants the second-order volition he has formed, he is indifferent to the question of whether it is with this volition or with some other that he wants his will to accord. The decisiveness of the commitment he has made means that he has decided that no further question about his second-order volition, at any higher order, remains to be asked. It is relatively unimportant whether we explain this by saying that this commitment implicitly generates an endless series of confirming desires of higher orders, or by saying that the commitment is tantamount to a dissolution of the pointedness of all questions concerning higher orders of desire.

Examples such as the one concerning the unwilling addict may suggest that volitions of the second order, or of higher orders, must be formed deliberately and that a person characteristically struggles to ensure that they are satisfied. But the conformity of a person's will to his higher-order volitions may be far more thoughtless and spontaneous than this. Some people are naturally moved by kindness when they want to be kind, and by nastiness when they want to be nasty, without any explicit forethought and without any need for energetic self-control. Others are moved by nastiness when they want to be kind and by kindness when they intend to be nasty, equally without forethought and without active resistance to these violations of their higher-order desires. The enjoyment of freedom comes easily to some. Others must struggle to achieve it.

IV.

My theory concerning the freedom of the will accounts easily for our disinclination to allow that this freedom is enjoyed by the members of any species inferior to our own. It also satisfies another condition that must be met by any such theory, by making it apparent why the freedom of the will should be regarded as desirable. The enjoyment of a free will means the satisfaction of certain desires—desires of the second or of higher orders—whereas its absence means their frustration. The satisfactions at stake are those which accrue to a person of whom it may be said that his will is his own. The corresponding frustrations are those suffered by a person of whom it may be said that he is estranged from himself, or that he finds himself a helpless or a passive bystander to the forces that move him.

A person who is free to do what he wants to do may yet not be in a position to have the will he wants. Suppose, however, that he enjoys both freedom of action and freedom of the will. Then he is not only free to do what he wants to do; he is also free to want what he wants to want. It seems to me that he has, in that case, all the freedom it is possible to desire or to conceive. There are other good things in life, and he may not possess some of them. But there is nothing in the way of freedom that he lacks.

It is far from clear that certain other theories of the freedom of the will meet these elementary but essential conditions: that it be understandable why we desire this freedom and why we refuse to ascribe it to animals. Consider, for example, Roderick Chisholm's quaint version of the doctrine that human freedom entails an absence of causal determination.[7] Whenever a person performs a free action, according to Chisholm, it's a miracle. The motion of a person's hand, when the person moves it, is the outcome of a series of physical causes; but some event in this series, "and presumably one of those that took place within the brain, was caused by the agent and not by any other events" (18). A free agent has, therefore, "a prerogative which some would attribute only to God: each of us, when we act, is a prime mover unmoved" (23).

This account fails to provide any basis for doubting that animals of subhuman species enjoy the freedom it defines. Chisholm says nothing that makes it seem less likely that a rabbit performs a miracle when it moves its leg than that a man does so when he moves his hand. But why, in any case, should anyone *care* whether he can interrupt the natural order of causes in the way Chisholm describes? Chisholm offers no reason for believing that there is a discernible difference between the experience of a man who miraculously initiates a series of causes when he moves his hand and a man who moves his hand without any such breach of the normal causal sequence. There appears to be no concrete basis for preferring to be involved in the one state of affairs rather than in the other.[8]

It is generally supposed that, in addition to satisfying the two conditions I have mentioned, a satisfactory theory of the freedom of the will necessarily provides an analysis of one of the conditions of moral responsibility. The most common recent approach to the problem of understanding the freedom of the will has been, indeed, to inquire what is entailed by the assumption that someone is morally responsible for what he has done. In my view, however, the relation between moral responsibility and the freedom of the will has been very widely misunderstood. It is not true that a person is morally responsible for what he has done only if his will was free when he did it. He may be morally responsible for having done it even though his will was not free at all.

A person's will is free only if he is free to have the will he wants. This means that, with regard to any of his first-order desires, he is free either to make that desire his will or to make some other first-order desire his will instead. Whatever his will, then, the will of the person whose will is free could have been otherwise; he could have done otherwise than to constitute his will as he did. It is a vexed question just how 'he could have done otherwise' is to be understood in contexts such as this one. But although this question is important to the theory of freedom, it has no bearing on the theory of moral responsibility. For the assumption that a person is morally responsible for what he has done does not entail that the person was in a position to have whatever will he wanted.

This assumption *does* entail that the person did what he did freely, or that he did it of his own free will. It is a mistake, however, to believe that someone acts freely only when he is free to do whatever he wants or that he acts of his own free will only if his will is free. Suppose that a person has done what he wanted to do, that he did it because he wanted to do it, and that the will by which he was moved when he did it was his will because it was the will he wanted. Then he did it freely and of his own free will. Even supposing that he could have done otherwise, he would not have done otherwise; and even supposing that he could have had a different will, he would not have wanted his will to differ from what it was. Moreover, since the will that moved him when he acted was his will because he wanted it to be, he cannot claim that his will was forced upon him or that he was a passive bystander to its constitution. Under these conditions, it is quite irrelevant to the evaluation of his moral responsibility to inquire whether the alternatives that he opted against were actually available to him.[9]

In illustration, consider a third kind of addict. Suppose that his addiction has the same physiological basis and the same irresistible thrust as the addictions of the unwilling and wanton addicts, but that he is altogether delighted with his condition. He is a willing addict, who would not have things any other way. If the grip of his addiction should somehow weaken, he would do whatever he could to reinstate it; if his desire for the drug should begin to fade, he would take steps to renew its intensity.

The willing addict's will is not free, for his desire to take the drug will be effective regardless of whether or not he wants this desire to constitute his will. But when he takes the drug, he takes it freely and of his own free will. I am inclined to understand his situation as involving the over determination of his first-order desire to take the drug. This desire is his effective desire because he is physiologically addicted. But it is his effective desire also because he wants it to be. His will is outside his control, but, by his second-order desire that his desire for the drug should be effective, he has made this will his own. Given that it is therefore not only because of his addiction that his desire for the drug is effective, he may be morally responsible for taking the drug.

My conception of the freedom of the will appears to be neutral with regard to the problem of determinism. It seems conceivable that it should be causally determined that a person is free to want what he wants to want. If this is conceivable, then it might be causally determined that a person enjoys a free will. There is no more than an innocuous appearance of paradox in the proposition that it is determined, ineluctably and by forces beyond their control, that certain people have free wills and that others do not. There is no incoherence in the proposition that some agency other than a person's own is responsible (even *morally* responsible) for the fact that he enjoys or fails to enjoy freedom of the will. It is possible that a person should be morally responsible for what he does of his own free will and that some other person should also be morally responsible for his having done it.[10]

On the other hand, it seems conceivable that it should come about by chance that a person is free to have the will he wants. If this is conceivable, then it might be a matter of chance that certain people enjoy freedom of the will and that certain others do not. Perhaps it is also conceivable, as a number of philosophers believe, for states of affairs to come about in a way other than by chance or as the outcome of a sequence of natural causes. If it is indeed conceivable for the relevant states of affairs to come about in some third way, then it is also possible that a person should in that third way come to enjoy the freedom of the will.

Notes

1. P. F. Strawson, *Individuals* (London: Methuen, 1959), 101–102. Ayer's usage of 'person' is similar: "it is characteristic of persons in this sense that besides having various physical properties…they are also credited with various forms of consciousness." A. J. Ayer, *The Concept of a Person* (New York: St. Martin's Press, 1963), 82. What concerns Strawson and Ayer is the problem of understanding the relation between mind and body, rather than the quite different problem of understanding what it is to be a creature that not only has a mind and a body but is also a person.

2. For the sake of simplicity, I shall deal only with what someone wants or desires, neglecting related phenomena such as choices and decisions. I propose to use the verbs 'to want' and 'to desire' interchangeably, although they are by no means perfect synonyms. My motive in forsaking the established nuances of these words arises from the fact that the verb 'to want', which suits my purposes better so far as its meaning is concerned, does not lend itself so readily to the formation of nouns as does the verb 'to desire'. It is perhaps acceptable, albeit graceless, to speak in the plural of someone's "wants." But to speak in the singular of someone's "want" would be an abomination.

3. What I say in this paragraph applies not only to cases in which 'to X' refers to a possible action or inaction. It also applies to cases in which 'to X' refers to a first-order desire and in which the statement that 'A wants to X' is therefore a shortened version of a statement—'A wants to want to X'—that identifies a desire of the second order.

4. It is not so clear that the entailment relation described here holds in certain kinds of cases, which I think may fairly be regarded as nonstandard, where the essential difference between the standard and the nonstandard cases lies in the kind of description by which the first-order desire in question is identified. Thus, suppose that *A* admires *B* so fulsomely that, even though he does not know what *B* wants to do, he wants to be effectively moved by whatever desire effectively moves *B*; without knowing what *B*'s will is, in other words, *A* wants his own will to be the same. It certainly does not follow that *A* already has, among his desires, a desire like the one that constitutes *B*'s will. I shall not pursue here the questions of whether there are genuine counterexamples to the claim made in the text or of how, if there are, that claim should be altered.

5. Creatures with second-order desires but no second-order volitions differ significantly from brute animals, and, for some purposes, it would be desirable to regard them as persons. My usage, which withholds the designation 'person' from them, is thus somewhat arbitrary. I adopt it largely because it facilitates the formulation of some of the points I wish to make. Hereafter, whenever I consider statements of the form "*A* wants to want to *X*," I shall have in mind statements identifying second-order volitions and not statements identifying second-order desires that are not second-order volitions.

6. In speaking of the evaluation of his own desires and motives as being characteristic of a person, I do not mean to suggest that a person's second-order volitions necessarily manifest a *moral* stance on his part toward his first-order desires. It may not be from the point of view of morality that the person evaluates his first-order desires. Moreover, a person may be capricious and irresponsible in forming his second-order volitions and give no serious consideration to what is at stake. Second-order volitions express evaluations only in the sense that they are preferences. There is no essential restriction on the kind of basis, if any, upon which they are formed.

7. "Freedom and action," in *Freedom and Determinism*, ed. K. Lehrer (New York: Random House, 1966), 11–44.

8. I am not suggesting that the alleged difference between these two states of affairs is unverifiable. On the contrary, physiologists might well be able to show that Chisholm's conditions for a free action are not satisfied, by establishing that there is no relevant brain event for which a sufficient physical cause cannot be found.

9. For another discussion of the considerations that cast doubt on the principle that a person is morally responsible for what he has done only if he could have done otherwise, see my "Alternate possibilities and moral responsibility," this JOURNAL 66, 23 (December 4, 1969): 829–39.

10. There is a difference between being *fully* responsible and being *solely* responsible. Suppose that the willing addict has been made an addict by the deliberate and calculated work of another. Then it may be that both the addict and this other person are fully responsible for the addict's taking the drug, while neither of them is solely responsible for it. That there is a distinction between full moral responsibility and sole moral responsibility is apparent in the following example. A certain light can be turned on or off by flicking either of two switches, and each of these switches is simultaneously flicked to the "on" position by a different person, neither of whom is aware of the other. Neither person is solely responsible for the light's going on, nor do they share the responsibility in the sense that each is partially responsible; rather, each of them is fully responsible.

14

Puppeteers, Hypnotists, and Neurosurgeons
Richard Double

Perhaps the best-known recent compatibilist account of free will is the reason-sensitive view (Levin's word) endorsed by Harry Frankfurt (Frankfurt, 1971), Gary Watson (Watson, 1975), Michael Levin (Levin, 1979), Keith Lehrer (Lehrer, 1980), Daniel Dennett (Dennett, 1984), and others. Although specifics vary, these accounts share the belief that determined human decisions can be free provided we enjoy a certain relation between our decisions and our reflections about our decisions. Reason-sensitive ("R-S") accounts face counter-examples involving hypothesized external agents who cause us to have our reflective attitudes, thereby purportedly satisfying reason-sensitivity while leaving us unfree. In this paper I show how such criticisms of R-S accounts depend upon two premises which I argue can be neutralized.

I. The objection to R-S accounts

I extract from Frankfurt's work a "generic" R-S account that I believe captures the view also defended by the others:

> *Original R-S account:* S's decision *d* is free if and only if S is able to bring *d* into accord with S's reflective judgments about the desirability of *d*.

Critics have proposed thought-experiments to make explicit what they take to be the implicit inadequacy of R-S accounts. An obvious challenge is to imagine that some external agent unbeknownst to us gives us our second-order volitions, thereby, satisfying reason-sensitivity yet leaving us unfree. Michael Slote uses the example of hypnotism:

> Robert, who is genuinely undecided between two conflicting first-order desires X and Y, is visited by a hypnotist who decides to "solve" his problem by putting him in a trance and inducing in him a second-order

volition in favor of X; as a result of having this second-order volition, Robert then acts to satisfy X, never suspecting that his decisiveness has been induced by the hypnotist. The example...seems adequate...to point up the conceptual insufficiency of "rationality" conditions of free action. For we would all surely deny that Robert acts of his own free will...(Slote 1980, 137)

In a similar vein Watson criticizes Dennett's R-S view:

If someone offers a certain analysis of freedom, which turns out to be fully compatible with being totally under the control of the Nefarious Neurosurgeon, that is a serious difficulty for the analysis. (Watson 1986, 519)

Robert Kane poses the problem in terms of a "covert non-constraining controller" who makes a controlled agent "a means and not an end in himself because he does not ultimately determine his own purposes or ends" (Kane 1985, 34). With slight amendments one might add Peter van Inwagen's case of Martian remote control of volition-determination devices in our brains (van Inwagen 1983, 109) and Richard Taylor's "ingenious physiologist" who induces volitions in us by pushing buttons (Taylor 1974, 50).

The objection raised by these purported counter-examples is this:

(a) All reason-sensitive versions of free will are compatible with the presence of an undetected puppeteer (hypnotist, neurosurgeon) who determines the nature of our second-order volitions.

(b) The presence of such a puppeteer would result in our *not* having free will.

(c) Therefore, no reason-sensitive version of free will is sufficient for distinguishing free from unfree decisions.

Although this argument is valid (or at least could be reworded to be valid),[1] I shall provide reasons for rejecting each premise. As a mnemonic, I shall call the denial that all R-S accounts are compatible with puppeteers "the Metaphilosophical reply" and the denial of the second premise "the Irrelevancy reply." Interestingly, support for both replies comes from (different places in) Dennett's work.

II. The metaphilosophical reply

Dialectically speaking, if one thought both that reason-sensitivity makes our decisions free and that the addition of external controllers would result in our losing our freedom, the simplest tactic would be to disallow puppeteers by adding an additional condition to one's R-S account that does just that. The beginnings of this metaphilosophical reply can be gleaned from Dennett's reminder that although

> a superhuman intelligence could...control...us...but this superhuman, after all, is just another one of those imaginary agents we needn't worry about. Perhaps there could be such agents, for all we know, inhabiting other planets. It would be as reasonable for us to dread them as it is unreasonable for us to conjure them into existence on the premise of determinism...The environment, not being an agent, does not control us. Dennett, 1984, 61)

I take Dennett's argument to be:

(i) One is controlled only if an agent controls you.

(ii) In actual cases of determinism there is no agent controlling our decisions.

(iii) Therefore, in actual cases of determinism we are not controlled by nature (or anything).

(iv) Therefore, the possibility of controlling agents does not count against the compatibility of determinism and free decisions in cases where there are no controlling agents.

Given this argument it is easy to formulate an amended account that contradicts the premise that all R-S versions of free will are compatible with the existence of puppeteers:

> *Metaphilosophically Amended Account*: S's decision *d* is free to the extent that: (1) S is able to bring *d* into accord with S's reflective judgments about the desirability of *d* (2) There is no other agent who causes S to have those reflective judgments about *d*.

We might lend some support to this amended account by appeal to some considerations associated with the Putnam-Kripke view of language. We could say that in the normal case the original R-S account is adequate to fix the reference of "free decisions" due to a commonsense characteristic of free decisions, *viz.*, the fact that our second-order volitions control our first-order ones. The original account fails for the puppeteer counter-examples, however, since it ignores the equally important but easily overlooked "microstructural" nature of free decisions, namely, that free decisions require a normal etiology that excludes being brought about by external agents. The right microstructure is needed, we might say, in the case of "free decision" no less than it is needed in "water," "gold," and "lemon," not because free will is a natural kind, but because the right microstructure is *part* of the complex of properties that constitute free will. On this view, there is nothing paradoxical about an otherwise free reason-sensitive decision being made unfree if it traces to a puppeteer provided that is how the concept of free will is. One might interpret

Dennett's remarks this way: if there is no puppeteer, then we should not worry about our freedom (although we may not be able to assuage our philosophical worries that the concept of freedom "should" be nicely principled).

It may be objected that the Metaphilosophical reply, at most, saves R-S accounts from the puppeteer objection only if puppeteers provide a stronger threat to the freedom of reason-sensitive actions than simple determinism *per se*. But, if the puppeteer is portrayed as a non-intervener (like Bouwsma's evil genius), then the puppeteer poses the same problem for R-S accounts that determinism does, and, hence, if determinism *per se* is destructive of our freedom, then so is the puppeteer. So, to finish our reply to the puppeteer objection, we must show why determinism does not undermine our freedom on the R-S accounts. To do this, we must face the determinism objection head on.

III. The irrelevancy reply

In discussing van Inwagen's example of Martian remote control of our mental states, George Schlesinger suggests that the incompatibilist at least consider the reply that "it would make no essential difference whether our acts were determined by extraterrestrials or by nature" (Schlesinger 1985, 226). Another source of the Irrelevancy reply is found in Dennett's earlier *Brainstorms*. There Dennett asks whether a neurosurgeon could implant just one belief into our heads. Dennett answers

> ... One cannot directly and simply cause or implant a belief, for a belief is essentially something that has been *endorsed* (by commission or omission) by the agent on the basis of its conformity with the rest of his beliefs ... A parallel point can be made about desires and intentions. Whatever might be induced in me is either fixed and obsessive, in which case I am not responsible for where it leads me, or else, in 'MacIntyre's phrase, "can be influenced or inhibited by the adducing of some logically relevant consideration," in which case I am responsible for *maintaining* it. (Dennett 1978, 252—3)

The dilemma Dennett poses for intentional states seems directly applicable to the artificial implantation of second-order volitions by a puppeteer or as the result of simple determinism: if my second-order volitions are themselves not amenable to rational consideration and revision, then they are not themselves reason-sensitive and my first-order volitions are, therefore, unfree. Yet, if my second-order volitions are amenable to rational self-evaluation, then I have endorsed them, they "are mine" irrespective of their etiology, and my resultant first-order volitions are free. Either way, the truth of determinism is irrelevant to the viability of the R-S account.

It is worth noting that this way of developing the Irrelevancy reply builds more into the R-S account than appeared in our original version. Whereas the original R-S account required only that S be able to bring S's decisions into account with the second-order volitions, we now require that S's second-order volitions themselves be subject to rational consideration.[2] ("Subject to" is important, since that qualification avoids both the charge that this requirement generates an infinite regress of reason-sensitivity and the charge that we are free only if we actually reflect upon our second-order volitions.) We express this additional condition to a first approximation:

Initial Irrelevancy Amended Account: S's decision *d* is free to the extent that (1) S is able to bring *d* into accord with S's reflective judgments about the desirability of *d* (2) S's reflective judgments about the desirability of *d* are subject to rational evaluation and revision owing to that evaluation.

One might object that the Irrelevancy reply is near-sighted because it overlooks the question of the causal origin of subjects' rational or obsessive stances towards implanted second-order volitions. "Don't you see," it might be objected, "that one's 'reason-sensitive' evaluation of one's second-order volitions are still the product of determinism. This shows that even allowing the distinction between reasonable and obsessive stances towards higher-order volitions, we cannot reach a point where the reason-sensitivity at stake is truly the subject's. Your volitions (of whatever order), irrespective of their reason-sensitivity, are not really *yours* if they can be traced back deterministically. You cannot control your decisions if they come to you from an outside source."

This objection takes us to the heart of the issue. The advocate of the Metaphysical reply must allow that our rational reflections about our second-order volitions, our reflections about *these* reflections and so on would be determined. But the aim of R-S accounts is not to reach some point where our reason-sensitivity stands outside of determinism. The advocate of the Irrelevancy reply maintains that if the ultimate result of determinism is reason-sensitive decisions, then the fact that the mental states involved are determined is simply irrelevant to the reasonability, and, thus, freedom of the decisions.

I think the real challenge to those who adopt the Irrelevancy reply is to build a picture of free will that is sufficiently rich so that in the process of understanding why free will is desirable we will see that even if we add determinism or puppeteers to the picture, freedom is no longer threatened. The seminal R-S accounts of Frankfurt and Watson did not fully explicate the intricacy needed to capture the free will concept and left critics with lingering doubts that a richer account could avoid. To make our Irrelevancy amended account fully explicit, we need to imagine what characteristics our decisions would need to have so that they remain *ours* irrespective of determinism. Given my skepticism about the feasibility of reductive analyses (See Stich, 1983, 77), I believe that the most we should hope for is a specification of conditions that generally capture our intuitions regarding clear cases. To do so I appeal to the social psychology literature concerning cognitive failure (Nisbett and Ross 1980) to arrive at five conditions (elaborated elsewhere—Double 1987) which I call *autonomy variables.*

First, if we are to critically evaluate our decisions, we need accurate representations of the beliefs, desires, fears, and the other mental states that are relevant to our decisions. I call this variable *self-knowledge.* A second variable, *reasonability,* marks the attitude of one who wishes to subject one's mental states to scrutiny for truth, consistency, and normative suitability. Reasonability is what Lindley (1986, 47) calls "active theoretical rationality," the disposition for critical self-assessment. *Intelligence* is a covering term for the intellectual skills we use in self-assessment; it includes abilities like memory, learning, as well as deductive, inductive, and statistical inference. Intelligence is to reason-ability as strength is to Superman's good intentions. *Efficacy* is the power to bring one's will and those psychological states that bear on one's will into accord with one's accurate (self-knowledgeable), reasonable, and intelligent efforts. Finally, *unity* is the presupposition that there is one single agent to whom the other four variables apply.

I would be pleased if I could specify the exact degree to which I believe that each variable must be satisfied for decisions to satisfy my account, but I cannot. For one thing, our metaphilosophical position counts against it. For another, a rationality view of free will must face the fact that not all decisions need to meet the same criteria of ratiocination. I can freely and mindlessly decide to pick up one pencil rather than another to begin my work; yet if I am similarly mindless in my choice of a career, my decision is not free.

So, I think there are grey areas between the clearly free and clearly unfree decisions, and that our account should reflect this:

Irrelevancy Amended Autonomy Variable Account: S's decision *d* is free to the extent that S is able to bring *d* into accord with S's reflective judgments about the desirability of *d*, that is,

(1) S knows that nature of the beliefs, desires, and other mental states that bring about *d*; if they were caused by the purposive intervention of an external agent, S knows this also. (self-knowledge)

(2) S goes through critical and nondogmatic consideration of *d* and the mental states that bring about *d* in cases where such consideration is appropriate. (reasonability)

(3) S's reasoning concerning *d* and those other states meet normative standards of intellectual skill. (intelligence)

(4) S possesses the power, at each step in the reflective and decision-making processes, to bring about subsequent mental states according to the normative standards of (2) and (3). (efficacy)[3]

(5) There is a single agent to whom variables (1)–(4) apply. (unity)

The force of this expanded account rests on the following intuition. If you knew that your decisions satisfied the autonomy variable account, then you should regard yourself free whether determinism or a puppeteer resides at the front of the causal sequence that ends in your decisions. You have everything you should want by way of rational control. The incompatibilist will point out that you lack contra-causal freedom whereby your decisions might have come out differently given your identical states at the moment of the decisions; there are familiar arguments, though, that this would not be an increase in your power, but would undermine the rationality of your decisions (Double, 1988). Since we have argued through the metaphilosophical reply that puppeteers are no more of a problem for R-S accounts than mere determinism, our answer to the counter-examples of Slote, Watson, Kane, van Inwagen, and Taylor is clear: if the autonomy variable account is satisfied, we have all we need with respect to free will.

Let me make one final attempt to address incompatibilist worries, specifically Kane's worry that determinism, like external controllers, would be demeaning to human dignity:

> ...the controlled agent is not free in the dignity-grounding sense. It is the controller and not the controlled agent who is ultimately responsible for the outcome...The controlled agent is a means and not an end in himself because he does not ultimately determine his own purposes or ends. He has a "kind of freedom," but not the true freedom of being an end in himself, which confers dignity on human beings. (Kane, 1985, 34)

I begin my reply with a thought-experiment of my own. Imagine that on Earth and on its molecule-for-molecule replica Twin Earth there are two persons who are likewise qualitatively identical (including the states of their Cartesian minds, if they have them), call them "Jim" and "Twin Jim."[4] Imagine also that (i) all of Jim's and Twin Jim's decisions are qualitatively identical, as are their entire psychological histories, and (ii) some of Jim's decisions satisfy the libertarian notion of freedom (that is, there are other causally possible Earths where Jim's decisions are different given the conditions that hold on Earth), while all of Twin Jim's decisions are determined. Now, if the dignity objection to determinism is sound, it seems that Jim, but not Twin Jim, is sometimes worthy of dignity. But how can that be? They have done all the same things for the same reasons—they are qualitatively indistinguishable physically, intellectually, emotionally, and so on. If Jim and Twin Jim differ with respect to freedom or dignity, then these characteristics are "doubly supervenient." That is, freedom and dignity would have to supervene not on the actual states of Jim and Twin Jim, which are, afterall, qualitatively identical, but on the modal status of the actual states of the two. Although this is not incoherent,

I think it is problematic enough to set us searching for a deterministic interpretation of dignity.

We need to get clear about what we are supposed to risk losing if determinism is true. Although Kane does not define the notion of "dignity-grounding," it seems that Kane is relying on the intuition that dignity is something we lose if we are unmasked as "big foolish clocks." This makes dignity something that is essentially *relational* in that one possesses or lacks dignity not in virtue of the intrinsic nature of oneself and one's decisions, but in virtue of one's causal background. Against this intuition, I would suggest a view of human dignity wherein those qualities that confer dignity are intrinsically valuable and, hence, not subject to diminution by relational properties. Consider some of the wide range of properties whose criteria are neutral with respect to the determinism/indeterminism distinction. *Pace* some libertarian thinkers (Popper, 1965), it seems that one's line of reasoning is logically valid or not owing to its adherence to valid rules of logic, irrespective of whether the reasoning was determined or not.[5] Or consider a moral property such as compassion: are one's actions and feelings less compassionate if they turn out to be determined? Or take a nonmoral virtue such as the diligence to stay with a difficult task until completion. In all these cases, which I think represent the sort of intrinsic qualities that give humans dignity, I think the determinism question is logically irrelevant: the criteria of logical soundness, compassion, and diligence are neutral with respect to whether the actions and character traits involved are determined or not. But since these sorts of things seem to be constitutive of human dignity, I think human dignity has nothing to fear from determinism *per se*.

Whether the universe is constructed such that one's decision is the only one possible or such that one's decision might have been different is not an intrinsic characteristic of the decision itself. Thus, if one's ability to make decisions can possess intrinsic value, something I also take to support human dignity, then that ability can be intrinsically valuable whether or not determinism is true. Thus, I do not think that determinism is demeaning to human dignity, and reject the dignity objection to the Irrelevancy reply.

IV. Conclusion

The objection to R-S accounts that was raised by the possibility of external agents requires the acceptance of two premises, *viz.*, that all R-S accounts allow for puppeteers and that puppeteers necessarily make us unfree. The Metaphilosophical reply shows that to the extent that puppeteers are more problematic than determinism *per se*, puppeteers may be explicitly excluded since they violate our paradigm of free will. The Metaphilosophical reply also suggests that we should not expect our mature R-S account to supply logically necessary and sufficient conditions for free will, but rather give us answers that agree with our intuitions regarding paradigms of free and unfree decisions. The Irrelevancy reply completed our reply to incompatibilists who continue to object that determinism *per se* destroys the R-S program. It may be debated whether my autonomy variable account is a satisfactory way to spell out the Irrelevancy reply, but I think that this type of approach suggests the way to vindicating the R-S view from an important type of objection.

Notes

I am grateful to Robert Kane, George Schlesinger, and the editor for valuable help with earlier drafts of this paper.

1. I take the following reformulation to be formally valid:

> For all R-S accounts, it is possible that both the R-S account is satisfied for S and there is an undetected external agent who determines the nature of S's second-order volitions.
> All cases of such additional agency would result in S's being unfree.
> Therefore, for all R-S accounts, it is possible that the R-S account is satisfied for S and S is unfree.
> Therefore, for all R-S accounts, it is not the case that the satisfaction of the R-S account for S necessarily implies that S is free.

2. The requirement that one's second-order volitions be subject to rational evaluation enables our Irrelevancy amended account to withstand Watson's sound objection that Frankfurt's original R-S version was defective because it allowed our second-order volitions to be capricious. See Watson, 1975, 108–9.

3. What I call *efficacy* is provided a rigorous treatment as *control* in Lehrer 1980.

4. For a similar example designed to show that ancestral determination does not, *ipso facto*, defeat compatibilist analyses of our ability to do otherwise, see Lehrer 1976, 264–6.

5. We might add that since doing logic is to engage in a normative activity in the sense of drawing *correct* inferences, we have at least one clear precedent of determined persons possessing a normative property.

References

Dennett, D. 1978. *Brainstorms*. Cambridge, MA: MIT Press.

Dennett, D. 1984. *Elbow Room*. Cambridge, MA: MIT Press.

Double, R. 1987. "Autonomy variables as a supplement to rationality accounts of free will." Draft.

Double, R. 1988. "Libertarianism and rationality," *Southern Journal of Philosophy* 26/3: 431–439.

Fischer, J. 1986. *Moral Responsibility*. Ithaca, NY: Cornell University Press.

Frankfurt, H. 1971. "Freedom of the will and the concept of a person," *Journal of Philosophy*, 5–20, reprinted in Watson, 1982, 81–95 (page numbers are to Watson volume).

Kane, R. 1985. *Free Will and Values*. Albany: SUNY Press.

Lehrer, K. 1976. "'Can' in theory and practice: a possible worlds analysis," in Brand, M. and Walton, D., eds., *Action Theory*. Dordrecht-Holland: Reidel, 241–270.

Lehrer, K. 1980. "Preferences, conditionals and freedom," in van Inwagen, P., ed., *Time and Cause*. Dordrecht-Holland: Reidel, 187–201.

Levin, M. 1979. *Metaphysics and the Mind-Body Problem*. Oxford: Oxford University Press.

Lindley, R. 1986. *Autonomy*. Atlantic Heights, N.J.: Humanities Press.

Nisbett, R. and Ross. L. 1980. *Human Inference: Strategies and Shortcomings of Social Judgment*. Englewood Cliffs, NJ: Prentice-Hall.

Popper, K. 1965. "Of clocks and clouds," Arthur Holly Compton Memorial Lecture (St. Louis, Washington University).

Schlesinger, G. 1985. "Review of van Inwagen (1983)," in *Canadian Philosophical Reviews*, 224–226.

Slote, M. 1980. "Understanding free will," in Fischer 1986, 124–139.

Stich, S. 1983. *From Folk Psychology to Cognitive Science: The Case Against Belief*. Cambridge, MA: MIT Press.

Taylor, R. 1974. *Metaphysics (second edition)*. Englewood Cliffs, N.J.: Prentice-Hall.

van Inwagen, P. 1983. *An Essay on Free Will*. Oxford: Oxford University Press.

Watson, G. 1975. "Free agency," in Watson 1982, 96–110.

Watson, G. 1982. *Free Will*. Oxford: Oxford University Press.

Watson, G. 1986. "Review of Dennett 1984," in *Journal of Philosophy*, 517–522.

PART 6

Suggested Further Readings

VI. Compatibilism: Hierarchical Theories and Manipulation Problems

Essays discussing Frankfurt's views on freedom can be found in:

Buss, Sarah & Lee Overton, eds. 2002. *The Contours of Agency*. Cambridge, MA: MIT Press.

See also:

Bratman, Michael. 2003. "A desire of one's own," *Journal of Philosophy* **100**: 221–42.

Double, Richard. 1991. *The Non-Reality of Free Will*. New York: Oxford University Press.

Dworkin, Gerald. 1970. "Acting freely," *Nous* **4**: 367–83.

Frankfurt, Harry. 1987. "Identification and wholeheartedness," in *Responsibility, Character, and the Emotions: New Essays on Moral Psychology*, ed. F. D. Schoeman. Cambridge: Cambridge University Press, 34–56.

Kennett, Jeanette. 2003. *Agency and Responsibility*. New York: Oxford University Press.

Locke, Don. 1975. "Three concepts of free action I." *Proceedings of the Aristotelian Society* Supplemental Vol. **II**: 95–112.

Slote, Michael. 1980. "Understanding free will," *Journal of Philosophy* **77**: 136–51.

Taylor, Charles. 1976. "Responsibility for self," in *Identities of Persons*, A.O. Rorty, ed. Berkeley, CA: University of California Press.

Vellman, David. 1992. "What happens when someone acts?" *Mind* **101**: 461–81. (Reprinted in J. Fischer and M. Ravizza, eds., *Perspectives on Moral Responsibility*. Ithaca: Cornell University Press, 1993.)

Watson, Gary. 1975. "Free agency," *Journal of Philosophy* **72**: 205–20.

Wolf, Susan. 2005. "Freedom within reason," in *Personal Autonomy*, J.S. Taylor, ed. New York: Cambridge University Press.

Compatibilism: Reason-Based Alternatives

15

Sanity and the Metaphysics of Responsibility

Susan Wolf

Philosophers who study the problems of free will and responsibility have an easier time than most in meeting challenges about the relevance of their work to ordinary, practical concerns. Indeed, philosophers who study these problems are rarely faced with such challenges at all, since questions concerning the conditions of responsibility come up so obviously and so frequently in everyday life. Under scrutiny, however, one might question whether the connections between philosophical and nonphilosophical concerns in this area are real.

In everyday contexts, when lawyers, judges, parents, and others are concerned with issues of responsibility, they know, or think they know, what in general the conditions of responsibility are. Their questions are questions of application: Does this or that particular person meet this or that particular condition? Is this person mature enough, or informed enough, or sane enough to be responsible? Was he or she acting under posthypnotic suggestion or under the influence of a mind-impairing drug? It is assumed, in these contexts, that normal, fully developed adult human beings are responsible beings. The questions have to do with whether a given individual falls within the normal range.

By contrast, philosophers tend to be uncertain about the general conditions of responsibility, and they care less about dividing the responsible from the nonresponsible agents than about determining whether, and if so why, any of us are ever responsible for anything at all.

In the classroom, we might argue that the philosophical concerns grow out of the nonphilosophical ones, that they take off where the nonphilosophical questions stop. In this way, we might convince our students that even if they are not plagued by the philosophical worries, they ought to be. If they worry about whether a person is mature enough, informed enough, and sane enough to be responsible, then they should worry about whether that person is metaphysically free enough, too.

The argument I make here, however, goes in the opposite direction. My aim is not to convince people who are interested in the apparently nonphilosophical conditions of responsibility that they should go on to worry about the philosophical conditions as well, but rather to urge those who already worry about the philosophical problems not to leave the more mundane, prephilosophical problems behind. In particular, I suggest that the mundane recognition that *sanity* is a condition of responsibility has more to do with the murky and apparently metaphysical problems which surround the issue of responsibility than at first meets the eye. Once the significance of the condition of sanity is fully appreciated, at least some of the apparently insuperable metaphysical aspects of the problem of responsibility will dissolve.

My strategy is to examine a recent trend in philosophical discussions of responsibility, a trend that tries, but I think ultimately fails, to give an acceptable analysis of the conditions of responsibility. It fails due to what at first appear to be deep and irresolvable metaphysical problems. It is here that I suggest that the condition of sanity comes to the rescue. What at first appears to be an impossible requirement for responsibility—the requirement that the responsible agent have created her- or himself—turns out to be the vastly more mundane and noncontroversial requirement that the responsible agent must, in a fairly standard sense, be sane.

Frankfurt, Watson, and Taylor

The trend I have in mind is exemplified by the writings of Harry Frankfurt, Gary Watson, and Charles Taylor. I will briefly discuss each of their separate proposals, and then offer a composite view that, while lacking the subtlety of any of the separate accounts, will highlight some important insights and some important blind spots they share.

In his seminal article "Freedom of the Will and the Concept of a Person,"[1] Harry Frankfurt notes a distinction between freedom of action and freedom of the will. A person has freedom of action, he points out, if she (or he) has the freedom to do whatever she wills to do—the freedom to walk or sit, to vote liberal or conservative, to publish a book or open a store, in accordance with her strongest desires. Even a person who has freedom of action may fail to be responsible for her actions, however, if the wants or desires she has the freedom to convert into action are themselves not subject to her control. Thus, the person who acts under posthypnotic suggestion, the victim of brainwashing, and the kleptomaniac might all possess freedom of action. In the standard contexts in which these examples are raised, it is assumed that none of the individuals is locked up or bound. Rather, these individuals are understood to act on what, at one level at least, must be called *their own desires*. Their exemption from responsibility stems from the fact that their own desires (or at least the ones governing their actions) are not up to them. These cases may be described in Frankfurt's terms as cases of people who possess freedom of action, but who fail to be responsible agents because they lack freedom of the will.

Philosophical problems about the conditions of responsibility naturally focus on an analysis of this latter kind of freedom: What *is* freedom of the will, and under what conditions can we reasonably be thought to possess it? Frankfurt's proposal is to understand freedom of the will by analogy to freedom of action. As freedom of action is the freedom to do whatever one wills to do, freedom of the will is the freedom to will whatever one wants to will. To make this point clearer, Frankfurt introduces a distinction between First-order and second-order desires. First-order desires are desires to do or to have various things; second-order desires are desires about what desires to have or what desires to make effective in action. In order for an agent to have both freedom of action and freedom of the will, that agent must be capable of governing his or her actions by first-order desires *and* capable of governing his or her First-order desires by second-order desires.

Gary Watson's view of free agency[2]—free and responsible agency, that is—is similar to Frankfurt's in holding that an agent is responsible for an action only if the desires expressed by that action are of a particular kind. While Frankfurt identifies the right kind of desires as desires that are supported by second-order desires, however, Watson draws a distinction between "mere" desires, so to speak, and desires that are *values*. According to Watson, the difference between free action and unfree action cannot be analyzed by reference to the logical form of the desires from which these various actions arise, but rather must relate to a difference in the quality of their source. Whereas some of my desires are just appetites or conditioned responses I find myself "stuck with," others are expressions of judgments on my part that the objects I desire are good. Insofar as my actions can be governed by the latter type of desire—governed, that is, by my values or valuational system—they are actions that I perform freely and for which I am responsible.

Frankfurt's and Watson's accounts may be understood as alternate developments of the intuition that in order to be responsible for one's actions, one must be responsible for the self that performs these actions. Charles Taylor, in an article entitled "Responsibility for Self,"[3] is concerned with the same intuition. Although Taylor does not describe his view in terms of different levels or types of desire, his view is related, for he claims that our freedom and responsibility depends on our ability to reflect on, criticize, and revise our selves. Like Frankfurt and Watson, Taylor seems to believe that if the characters from which our actions flowed were simply and permanently *given* to us, implanted by heredity, environment, or God, then we would be mere vehicles through which the causal forces of the world traveled, no more responsible than dumb animals or young children or machines. But like the others, he points out that, for most of us, our characters and desires are not so brutely implanted—or, at any rate, if they are, they are subject to revision by our own reflecting, valuing, or second-order desiring selves. We human beings—and as far as we know, only we human beings—have the ability to step back from ourselves and decide whether we are the selves we want to be. Because of this, these philosophers think, we are responsible for our selves and for the actions that we produce.

Although there are subtle and interesting differences among the accounts of Frankfurt, Watson, and Taylor, my concern is with features of their views that are common to them all. All share the idea that responsible agency involves something more than intentional agency. All agree that if we are responsible agents, it is not just because our actions are within the control of our wills, but because, in addition, our wills are not just psychological stales *in* us, but expressions of characters that come *from* us, or that at any rate are acknowledged and affirmed *by* us. For Frankfurt, this means that our wills must be ruled by our second-order desires; for Watson, that our wills must be governable by our system of values; for Taylor, that our wills must issue from selves that are subject to self-assessment and redefinition in terms of a vocabulary of worth. In one way or another, all these philosophers seem to be saying that the key to responsibility lies in the fact that responsible agents are those for whom it is not just the case that their actions are within the control of their wills, but also the case that their wills are within the control of their *selves* in some deeper sense. Because, at one level, the differences among Frankfurt, Watson, and Taylor may be understood as differences in the analysis or interpretation of what it is for an action to be under the control of this deeper self, we may speak of their separate positions as variations of one basic view about responsibility: the *deep-self view.*

The deep-self view

Much more must be said about the notion of a deep self before a fully satisfactory account of this view can be given. Providing a careful, detailed analysis of that notion poses an interesting, important, and difficult task in its own right. The degree of understanding achieved by abstraction from the views of Frankfurt, Watson, and Taylor, however, should be sufficient to allow us to recognize some important virtues as well as some important drawbacks of the deep-self view.

One virtue is that this view explains a good portion of our pretheoretical intuitions about responsibility. It explains why kleptomaniacs, victims of brainwashing, and people acting under posthypnotic suggestion may not be responsible for their actions, although most of us typically are. In the cases of people in these special categories, the connection between the agents' deep selves and their wills is dramatically served—their wills are governed not by their deep selves, but by forces external to and independent from them. A different intuition is that we adult human beings can be responsible for our actions in a way that dumb animals, infants, and machines cannot. Here the explanation is not in terms of a split between these beings' deep selves and their wills; rather, the point is that these beings *lack* deep selves altogether. Kleptomaniacs and victims of hypnosis exemplify individuals whose selves are *alienated* from their actions; lower animals and machines, on the other hand, do not have the sorts of selves from which actions *can* be alienated, and so they do not have the sort of selves from which, in the happier cases, actions can responsibly flow.

At a more theoretical level, the deep-self view has another virtue: It responds to at least one way in which the fear of determinism presents itself.

A naive reaction to the idea that everything we do is completely determined by a causal chain that extends backward beyond the times of our births involves thinking that in that case we would have no control over our behavior whatsoever. If everything is determined, it is thought, then what happens happens, whether we want it to or not. A common, and proper, response to this concern points out that determinism does not deny the causal efficacy an agent's desires might have on his or her behavior. On the contrary, determinism in its more plausible forms tends to affirm this connection, merely adding that as one's behavior is determined by one's desires, so one's desires are determined by something else.[4]

Those who were initially worried that determinism implied fatalism, however, are apt to find their fears merely transformed rather than erased. If our desires are governed by something else, they might say, they are not *really* ours after all—or, at any rate, they are ours in only a superficial sense.

The deep-self view offers an answer to this transformed fear of determinism, for it allows us to distinguish cases in which desires are determined by forces foreign to oneself from desires which are determined *by* one's self— by one's "real," or second-order desiring, or valuing, or deep self, that is. Admittedly, there are cases, like that of the kleptomaniac or the victim of hypnosis, in which the agent acts on desires that "belong to" him or her in only a superficial sense. But the proponent of the deep-self view will point out that even if determinism is true, ordinary adult human action can be distinguished from this. Determinism implies that the desires which govern our actions are in turn governed by something else, but that something else will, in the fortunate cases, be our own deeper selves.

This account of responsibility thus offers a response to our fear of determinism; but it is a response with which many will remain unsatisfied. Even if my actions are governed by my desires and my desires are governed by my own deeper self, there remains the question: Who, or what, is responsible for this deeper self? The response above seems only to have pushed the problem further back.

Admittedly, some versions of the deep-self view, including Frankfurt's and Taylor's, seem to anticipate this question by providing a place for the ideal that an agent's deep self may be governed by a still deeper self. Thus, for Frankfurt, second-order desires may themselves be governed by third-order desires, third-order desires by fourth-order desires, and so on. Also, Taylor points out that, as we can reflect on and evaluate our prereflective selves, so we can reflect on and evaluate the selves who are doing the first reflecting and evaluating, and so on. However, this capacity to recursively create endless levels of depth ultimately misses the criticism's point.

First of all, even if there is no *logical* limit to the number of levels of reflection or depth a person may have, there is certainly a psychological limit—it is virtually impossible imaginatively to conceive a fourth-, much less an eighth-order, desire. More important, no matter how many levels of self we posit, there will still, in any individual case, be a last level—a deepest self about whom the question "What governs it?" will arise, as problematic as ever. If determinism is true, it implies that even if my actions are governed by my desires, and my desires are governed by my deepest self, my deepest self will still be governed by something that must, logically, be external to myself altogether. Though I can step back from the values my parents and teachers have given me and ask whether these are the values I really want, the "I" that steps back will itself be a product of the parents and teachers I am questioning.

The problem seems even worse when one sees that one fares no better if determinism is false. For if my deepest self is not determined by something external to myself, it will still not be determined by *me*. Whether I am a product of carefully controlled forces or a result of random mutations, whether there is a complete explanation of my origin or no explanation at all, *I* am not, in any case, responsible for my existence; I am not in control of my deepest self.

Thus, though the claim that an agent is responsible for only those actions that are within the control of his or her deep self correctly identifies a necessary condition for responsibility—a condition that separates the hypnotized and the brainwashed, the immature and the lower animals from ourselves, for example—it fails to provide a sufficient condition of responsibility that puts all fears of determinism to rest. For one of the fears invoked by the thought of determinism seems to be connected to its implication that we are but intermediate links in a causal chain, rather than ultimate, self-initiating sources of movement and change. From the point of view of one who has this fear, the deep-self view seems merely to add loops to the chain, complicating the picture but not really improving it. From the point of view of one who has this fear, responsibility seems to require being a prime mover unmoved, whose deepest self is itself neither random *nor* externally determined, but is rather determined *by* itself—who is, in other words, self-created.

At this point, however, proponents of the deep-self view may wonder whether this fear is legitimate. For although people evidently can be brought to the point where they feel that responsible agency requires them to be ultimate sources of power, to the point where it seems that nothing short of self-creation will do, a return to the internal standpoint of the agent whose responsibility is in question makes it hard to see what good this metaphysical status is supposed to provide or what evil its absence is supposed to impose.

From the external standpoint, which discussions of determinism and indeterminism encourage us to take up, it may appear that a special metaphysical status is required to distinguish us significantly from other members of the natural world. But proponents of the deep-self view will suggest this is an illusion that a return to the internal standpoint should dispel. The possession of a deep self that is effective in governing one's actions is a sufficient distinction, they will say. For while other members of the natural world are not in control of the selves that they are, we, processors of effective deep selves, are in control. We can reflect on what sons of beings we are, and on what sorts of marks we make on the world. We can change what we don't like about ourselves, and keep what we do. Admittedly, we do not create ourselves from nothing. But as long as we can revise ourselves, they will suggest, it is hard to find reason to complain. Harry Frankfurt writes that a person who is free to do what he wants to do and also free to want what he wants to want has "all the freedom it is possible to desire or to conceive."[5] This suggests a rhetorical question: If you are free to control your actions by your desires, and free to control your desires by your deeper desires, and free to control those desires by still deeper desires, what further kind of freedom can you want?

The condition of sanity

Unfortunately, there is a further kind of freedom we can want, which it is reasonable to think necessary for responsible agency. The deep-self view fails to be convincing when it is offered as a complete account of the conditions of responsibility. To see why, it will be helpful to consider another example of an agent whose responsibility is in question.

JoJo is the favorite son of Jo the First, an evil and sadistic dictator of a small, undeveloped country. Because of his father's special feelings for the boy, JoJo is given a special education and is allowed to accompany his father and observe his daily routine. In light of this treatment, it is not surprising that little JoJo takes his father as a role model and develops values very much like Dad's. As an adult, he does many of the same sorts of things his father did, including sending people to prison or to death or to torture chambers on the basis of whim. He is not *coerced* to do these things, he acts according to his own desires. Moreover, these are desires he wholly *wants* to have. When he steps back and asks, "Do I really want to be this sort of person?" his answer is resoundingly "Yes," for this way of life expresses a crazy sort of power that forms part of his deepest ideal.

In light of JoJo's heritage and upbringing—both of which he was power-less to control—it is dubious at best that he should be regarded as responsible for what he does. It is unclear whether anyone with a childhood such as his could have developed into anything but the twisted and perverse sort of person that he has become. However, note that JoJo is someone whose actions are controlled by his desires and whose desires are the desires he wants to have: That is, his actions are governed by desires that are governed by and expressive of his deepest self.

The Frankfurt–Watson–Taylor strategy that allowed us to differentiate our normal selves from the victims of hypnosis and brainwashing will not allow us to differentiate ourselves from the son of Jo the First. In the case of these earlier victims, we were able to say that although the actions of these individuals were, at one level, in control of the individuals themselves, these individuals themselves, qua agents, were not the selves they more deeply wanted to be. In this respect, these people were unlike our happily more integrated selves. However, we cannot say of JoJo that his self, qua agent, is not the self he wants it to be. It *is* the self he wants it to be. From the inside, he feels as integrated, free, and responsible as we do.

Our judgment that JoJo is not a responsible agent is one that we can make only from the outside—from reflecting on the fact, it seems, that his deepest self is not up to him. Looked at from the outside, however, our situation seems no different from his—for in the last analysis, it is not up to any of us to have the deepest selves we do. Once more, the problem seems metaphysical—and not just metaphysical, but insuperable. For, as I mentioned before, the problem is independent of the truth of determinism. Whether we are determined or undetermined, we cannot have created our deepest selves. Literal self-creation is not just empirically, but logically impossible.

If JoJo is not responsible because his deepest self is not up to him, then we are not responsible either. Indeed, in that case responsibility would be impossible for anyone to achieve. But I believe the appearance that literal self-creation is required for freedom and responsibility is itself mistaken.

The deep-self view was right in pointing out that freedom and responsibility requires us to have certain distinctive types of control over our behavior and our selves. Specifically, our actions need to he under the control of our selves, and our (superficial) selves need to be under the control of our deep selves. Having seen that these types of control are not enough to guarantee us the status of responsible agents, we are tempted to go on to suppose that we must have yet another kind of control to assure us that even our deepest selves are somehow up to us. But not all the things necessary for freedom and responsibility must be types of power and control. We may need simply to *be* a certain way, even though it is not within our power to determine whether we are that way or not.

Indeed, it becomes obvious that at least one condition of responsibility is of this form as soon as we remember what, in everyday contexts, we have known all along—namely, that in order to be responsible, an agent must be sane. It is not ordinarily in our power to determine whether we are or are not sane. Most of us, it would seem, are lucky, but some of us are not. Moreover, being sane does not necessarily mean that one has any type of power or control an insane person lacks. Some insane people, like JoJo and some actual political leaders who resemble him, may have complete control of their actions, and even complete control of their acting selves. The desire to be sane is thus not a desire for another form of control; it is rather a desire that one's self be connected to the world in a certain way—we could even say it is a desire that one's self be *controlled by* the world in certain ways and not in others.

This becomes clear if we attend to the criteria for sanity that have historically been dominant in legal questions about responsibility. According to the M'Naughten Rule, a person is sane if (1) he knows what he is doing and (2) he knows that what he is doing is, as the case may be, right or wrong. Insofar as one's desire to be sane involves a desire to know what one is doing—or more generally, a desire to live in the real world—it is a desire to be controlled (to have, in this case, one's *beliefs* controlled) by perceptions and sound reasoning that produce an accurate conception of the world, rather than by blind or distorted forms of response. The same goes for the second constituent of sanity—only, in this case, one's hope is that one's *values* be controlled by processes that afford an accurate conception of the world.[6] Putting these two conditions together, we may understand sanity, then, as the minimally sufficient ability cognitively and normatively to recognize and appreciate the world for what it is.

There are problems with this definition of sanity, at least some of which will become obvious in what follows, that make it ultimately unacceptable either as a gloss on or an improvement of the meaning of the term in many of the contexts in which it is used. The definition offered does seem to bring out the interest sanity has for us in connection with issues of responsibility, however, and some pedagogical as well as stylistic purposes will be served if we use sanity hereafter in this admittedly specialized sense.

The sane deep-self view

So far I have argued that the conditions of responsible agency offered by the deep-self view are necessary but not sufficient. Moreover, the gap left open by the deep-self view seems to be one that can be filled only by a metaphysical, and, as it happens, metaphysically impossible addition. I now wish to argue, however, that the condition of sanity, as characterized above, is sufficient to fill the gap. In other words, the deep-self view, supplemented by the condition of sanity, provides a satisfying conception of responsibility. The conception of responsibility I am proposing, then, agrees with the deep-self view in requiring that a responsible agent be able to govern her (or his) actions by her desires and to govern her desires by her deep self. In addition, my conception insists that the agent's deep self be sane, and claims that this is *all* that is needed for responsible agency. By contrast to the plain deep-self view, let us call this new proposal the *sane deep-self view*.

It is worth noting, to begin with, that this new proposal deals with the case of JoJo and related cases of deprived childhood victims in ways that better match our pretheoretical intuitions. Unlike the plain deep-self view, the sane deep-self view offers a way of explaining why JoJo is not responsible for his actions without throwing our own responsibility into doubt. For, although like us, JoJo's actions flow from desires that flow from his deep self, unlike us, JoJo's deep self is itself insane. Sanity, remember, involves the ability to know the difference between right and wrong, and a person who, even on reflection, cannot see that having someone tortured because he failed to salute you is wrong plainly lacks the requisite ability.

Less obviously, but quite analogously, this new proposal explains why we give less than full responsibility to persons who, though acting badly, act in ways that are strongly encouraged by their societies—the slaveowners of the 1850s, the Nazis of the 1930s, and many male chauvinists of our fathers' generation, for example. These are people, we imagine, who falsely believe that the ways in which they are acting are morally acceptable, and so, we may assume, their behavior is expressive of or at least in accordance with these agents' deep selves. But their false beliefs in the moral permissibility of their actions and the false values from which these beliefs derived may have been inevitable, given the social circumstances in which they developed. If we think that the agents could not help but lie mistaken about their values, we do not blame them for the actions those values inspired.[7]

It would unduly distort ordinary linguistic practice to call the slaveowner, the Nazi, or the male chauvinist even partially or locally insane. Nonetheless, the reason for withholding blame from them is at bottom the same as the reason for withholding it from JoJo. Like JoJo, they are, at the deepest level, unable cognitively and normatively to recognize and appreciate the world for what it is. In our sense of the term, their deepest selves are not fully *sane*.

The sane deep-self view thus offers an account of why victims of deprived childhoods as well as victims of misguided societies may not be responsible for their actions, without implying that we are not responsible for ours. The actions of these others are governed by mistaken conceptions of value that the agents in question cannot help but have. Since, as far as we know, our values are not, like theirs, unavoidably mistaken, the fact that these others are not responsible for their actions need not force us to conclude that we are not responsible for ours.

But it may not yet be clear why sanity, in this special sense, should make such a difference—why, in particular, the question of whether someone's values are unavoidably *mistaken* should have any bearing on their status as responsible agents. The fact that the sane deep-self view implies judgments that match our intuitions about the difference in status between characters like JoJo and ourselves provides little support for it if it cannot also defend these intuitions. So we must consider an objection that comes from the point of view we considered earlier which rejects the intuition that a relevant difference can be found.

Earlier, it seemed that the reason JoJo was not responsible for his actions was that although his actions were governed by his deep self, his deep self was not up to him. But this had nothing to do with his deep self's being mistaken or not mistaken, evil or good, insane or sane. If JoJo's values are unavoidably mistaken, our values, even if not mistaken, appear to be just as unavoidable. When it comes to freedom and responsibility, isn't it the unavoidability, rather than the mistakenness, that matters?

Before answering this question, it is useful to point out a way in which it is ambiguous: The concepts of avoidability and mistakenness are not unequivocally distinct. One may, to be sure, construe the notion of avoidability in a purely metaphysical way. Whether an event or state of affairs is unavoidable under this construal depends, as it were, on the tightness of the causal connections that bear on the event's or state of affairs' coming about. In this sense, our deep selves do seem as unavoidable for us as JoJo's and the others' are for them. For presumably we are just as influenced by our parents, our cultures, and our schooling as they are influenced by theirs. In another sense, however, our characters are not similarly unavoidable.

In particular, in the cases of JoJo and the others, there are certain features of their characters that they cannot avoid *even though these features are seriously mistaken, misguided, or bad*. This is so because, in our special sense of the term, these characters are less than fully sane. Since these characters lack the ability to know right from wrong, they are unable to revise their characters on the basis of right and wrong, and so their deep selves lack the resources and the reasons that might have served as a basis for self-correction. Since the deep selves *we* unavoidably have, however, are sane deep selves—deep selves, that is, that unavoidably *contain* the ability to know right from wrong—we unavoidably do have the resources and reasons on which to base self-correction. What this means is that though in one sense we are no more in control of our deepest selves than JoJo et al., it does not follow in our case, as it does in theirs, that we would be the way we are, even if it is a bad or wrong way to be. However, if this does not follow, it seems to me, our absence of control at the deepest level should not upset us.

Consider what the absence of control at the deepest level amounts to for us: Whereas JoJo is unable to control the fact that, at the deepest level, he is not fully sane, we are not responsible for the fact that, at the deepest level, we are. It is not up to us to *have* minimally sufficient abilities cognitively and normatively to recognize and appreciate the world for what it is. Also, presumably, it is not up to us to have lots of other properties, at least to begin with—a fondness for purple, perhaps, or an antipathy for beets. As the proponents of the plain deep-self view have been at pains to point out, however, we do, if we are lucky, have the ability to revise our selves in terms of the values that are held by or constitutive of our deep selves. If we are lucky enough both to have this ability and to have our deep selves be sane, it follows that although there is much in our characters that we did not choose to have, there is nothing irrational or objectionable in our characters that we are compelled to keep.

Being sane, we are able to understand and evaluate our characters in a reasonable way, to notice what there is reason to hold on to, what there is reason to eliminate, and what, from a rational and reasonable standpoint, we may retain or get rid of as we please. Being able as well to govern our superficial selves by our deep selves, then, we are able to change the things we find there is reason to change. This being so, it seems that although we may not be *metaphysically* responsible for ourselves—for, after all, we did not create ourselves from nothing—we are *morally* responsible for ourselves, for we are able to understand and appreciate right and wrong, and to change our characters and our actions accordingly.

Self-creation, self-revision, and self-correction

At the beginning of this chapter, I claimed that recalling that sanity was a condition of responsibility would dissolve at least some of the appearance that responsibility was metaphysically impossible. To see how this is so, and to get a fuller sense of the sane deep-self view, it may be helpful to put that view into perspective by comparing it to the other views we have discussed along the way.

As Frankfurt, Watson, and Taylor showed us, in order to be free and responsible we need not only to be able to control our actions in accordance with our desires, we need to be able to control our desires in accordance with our deepest selves. We need, in other words, to be able to *revise* ourselves—to get rid of some desires and traits, and perhaps replace them with others on the basis of our deeper desires or values or reflections. However, consideration of the fact that the selves who are doing the revising might themselves be either brute products of external forces or arbitrary outputs of random generation made us wonder whether the capacity for self-revision was enough to assure us of responsibility—and the example of JoJo added force to the suspicion that it was not. Still, if the ability to revise ourselves is not enough, the ability to create ourselves does not seem necessary either. Indeed, when you think of it, it is unclear why anyone should want self-creation. Why should anyone be disappointed at having to accept the idea that one has to get one's start somewhere? It is an idea that most of us have lived with quite contentedly all along. What we do have reason to want, then, is something more than the ability to revise ourselves, but less than the ability to create ourselves. Implicit in the sane deep-self view is the idea that what is needed is the ability to *correct* (or improve) ourselves.

Recognizing that in order to be responsible for our actions, we have to be responsible for our selves, the sane deep-self view analyzes what is necessary in order to be responsible for our selves as (1) the ability to evaluate ourselves sensibly and accurately, and (2) the ability to transform ourselves insofar as our evaluation tells us to do so. We may understand the exercise of these abilities as a process where by we *take* responsibility for the selves that we are but did not ultimately create. The condition of sanity is intrinsically connected to the first ability; the condition that we be able to control our superficial selves by our deep selves is intrinsically connected to the second.

The difference between the plain deep-self view and the sane deep-self view, then, is the difference between the requirement of the capacity for self-revision and the requirement of the capacity for self-correction. Anyone with the first capacity can *try* to take responsibility for himself or herself. However, only someone with a sane deep self—a deep self that can see and appreciate the world for what it is—can self-evaluate sensibly and accurately. Therefore, although insane selves can try to take responsibility for themselves, only sane selves will properly be accorded responsibility.

Two objections considered

At least two problems with the sane deep-self view are so glaring as to have certainly struck many readers. In closing, I shall briefly address them. First, some will be wondering how, in light of my specialized use of the term "sanity," I can be so sure that "we" are any saner than the nonresponsible individuals I have discussed. What justifies my confidence that, unlike the slaveowners, Nazis, and male chauvinists, not to mention JoJo himself, we are able to understand and appreciate the world for what it is? The answer to this is that nothing justifies this except widespread intersubjective agreement and the considerable success we have in getting around in the world and satisfying our needs. These are not sufficient grounds for the smug assumption that we are in a position to see the truth about *all* aspects of ethical and social life. Indeed, it seems more reasonable to expect that time will reveal blind spots in our cognitive and normative outlook, just as it has revealed errors in the outlooks of those who have lived before. But our judgments of responsibility can only be made from here, on the basis of the understandings and values that we can develop by exercising the abilities we do possess as well and as fully as possible.

If some have been worried that my view implicitly expresses an over-confidence in the assumption that we are sane and therefore right about the world, others will be worried that my view too closely connects sanity with being right about the world, and fear that my view implies that anyone who acts wrongly or has false beliefs about the world is therefore insane and so not responsible for his or her actions. This seems to me to be a more serious worry, which I am sure I cannot answer to everyone's satisfaction.

First, it must be admitted that the sane deep-self view embraces a conception of sanity that is explicitly normative. But this seems to me a strength of that view, rather than a defect. Sanity *is* a normative concept, in its ordinary as well as in its specialized sense, and severely deviant behavior, such as that of a serial murderer or a sadistic dictator, does constitute evidence of a psychological defect in the agent. The suggestion that the most horrendous, stomach-turning crimes could be committed only by an insane person—an inverse of Catch-22, as it were—must be regarded as a serious possibility, despite the practical problems that would accompany general acceptance of that conclusion.

But, it will be objected, there is no justification, in the sane deep-self view, for regarding only horrendous and stomach-turning crimes as evidence of insanity in its specialized sense. If sanity is the ability cognitively and normatively to understand and appreciate the world for what it is, then *any* wrong action or false belief will count as evidence of the absence of that ability. This point may also be granted, but we must be careful about what conclusion to draw. To be sure, when someone acts in a way that is not in accordance with acceptable standards of rationality and reasonableness, it is always appropriate to look for an explanation of why he or she acted that way. The hypothesis that the person was unable to understand and appreciate that an action fell outside acceptable bounds will always be a possible explanation. Bad performance on a math test always suggests the possibility that the testee is stupid. Typically, however, other explanations will be possible, too—for example, that the agent was too lazy to consider whether his or her action was acceptable, or too greedy to care, or, in the case of the math testee, that he or she was too occupied with other interests to attend class or study. Other facts about the agent's history will help us decide among these hypotheses.

This brings out the need to emphasize that sanity, in the specialized sense, is defined as the *ability* cognitively and normatively to understand and appreciate the world for what it is. According to our commonsense understandings, having this ability is one thing and exercising it is another—at least some wrong-acting, responsible agents presumably fall within the gap. The notion of "ability" is notoriously problematic, however, and there is a long history of controversy about whether the truth of determinism would show our ordinary ways of thinking to be simply confused on this matter. At this point, then, metaphysical concerns may voice themselves again—but at least they will have been pushed into a narrower, and perhaps a more manageable, corner.

The sane deep-self view does not, then, solve all the philosophical problems connected to the topics of free will and responsibility. If anything, it highlights some of the practical and empirical problems, rather than solves them. It may, however, resolve some of the philosophical, and particularly, some of the metaphysical problems, and reveal how intimate are the connections between the remaining philosophical problems and the practical ones.

Notes

1. Harry Frankfurt, "Freedom of the will and the concept of a person," *Journal of Philosophy* 68 (1971): 5–20.

2. Gary Watson, "Free agency," *Journal of Philosophy* 72 (1975): 205–20.

3. Charles Taylor, "Responsibility for self," in *The Identities of Persons*, ed. A. E. Roily (Berkeley: University of California Press, 1976), 281–99.

4. See, e.g., David Hume, *A Treatise of Human Nature* (Oxford: Oxford University Press, 1967), 399–406, and R. E. Hobart, "Free will as involving determination and inconceivable without it," *Mind* 43 (1934).

5. Frankfurt, 16.

6. Strictly speaking, perception and sound reasoning may not be enough in ensure the ability to achieve an accurate conception of what one is doing and especially to achieve a reasonable normative assessment of one's situation. Sensitivity and exposure to certain realms of experience may also be necessary for these goals. For the purpose of this essay, I understand "sanity" to include whatever it takes to enable one to develop an adequate conception of one's world. In other contexts, however, this would be an implausibly broad construction of the term.

7. Admittedly, it is open to question whether these individuals were in fact unable in help having mistaken values, and indeed, whether recognizing the errors of their society would even have required exceptional independence strength of mind. This is presumably an empirical question, the answer to which is extraordinarily hard to determine. My point here is simply that *if* we believe they are unable to recognize that their values are mistaken, we do not hold them responsible for the actions that flow from these values, and *if* we believe their ability to recognize their normative errors is impaired, we hold them less than fully responsible for the relevant actions.

16

My Compatibilism

John Martin Fischer

I. Introduction

Thinking about it in one way, compatibilism seems very plausible. For now, take "compatibilism" to be the doctrine that both some central notion of freedom and also genuine, robust moral responsibility are compatible with the doctrine of causal determinism (which, among other things, entails that every bit of human behavior is causally necessitated by events in the past together with the natural laws). Of course, compatibilism, as thus understood, does not in itself take any stand on whether causal determinism is true.

Compatibilism can seem plausible because it appears so obvious to us that we (most of us) are at least sometimes free and morally responsible, and yet we also realize that causal determinism could turn out to be true. That is, for all we know, it is true that all events (including human behavior) are the results of chains of necessitating causes that can be traced indefinitely into the past. Put slightly differently, I could certainly imagine waking up some morning to the newspaper headline, "Causal Determinism Is True!" (Most likely this would not be in the *National Inquirer* or even *People*—but perhaps the New York Times...) I could imagine reading the article and subsequently (presumably over some time) becoming convinced that causal determinism is true—that the generalizations that describe the relationships between complexes of past events and laws of nature, on the one hand, and subsequent events, on the other, are universal generalizations with 100% probabilities associated with them. And I feel confident that this would not, nor should it, change my view of myself and others as (sometimes) free and robustly morally responsible agents—deeply different from other animals. The mere fact that these generalizations or conditionals have 100% probabilities associated with them, rather than 99.9% (say), would not and should not have any effect on my views about the existence of freedom and moral responsibility. My basic views of myself and others as free and responsible are and should be resilient with respect to such a discovery about the arcane and "close" facts pertaining to the generalizations of physics. (This of course is not to say that these basic views are resilient to *any* empirical discovery—just to this sort of discovery.)

So, when I deliberate I often take it that I am free in the sense that I have more than one option that is genuinely open to me. Since causal determinism (in the sense sketched above) might, for all we know be true, compatibilism seems extremely attractive. Similarly, it is very natural to distinguish those agents who are compelled to behave as they do from those who act freely; we make this distinction, and mark the two classes of individuals, in common sense and also the law. But since causal determinism might, for all we know, be true, compatibilism is extremely attractive. If casual determinism turned out to be true, and incompatibilism were also true, then it would seem that all behavior would be put into one class—the distinctions we naturally and intuitively draw in common sense and law would be in jeopardy of disappearing.

And yet there are deep problems with compatibilism. Perhaps these are what have led some philosophers to condemn it in such vigorous terms: "wretched subterfuge," (Kant), "quagmire of evasion," (James), and "the most flabbergasting instance of the fallacy of changing the subject to be encountered anywhere in the complete history of sophistry...[a ploy that] was intended to take in the vulgar, but which has beguiled the learned in our time" (Wallace Matson).

In this short essay I will start by highlighting the attractions of compatibilism and sketching and motivating an appealing version of traditional compatibilism. I shall then present a basic challenge to such a compatibilism. Given this challenge, I suggest an alternative version of compatibilism, which I call "semicompatibilism," and I develop some of the advantages of such an approach. My goal will be to present the beginning of a defense of semicompatibilism (highlighting the main attractions), rather than a detailed elaboration or full defense of the doctrine.

II. The lure of compatibilism

As I pointed out above, often it seems to me that I have more than one path open to me. The paths into the future branch out from the present, and they represent different ways I could proceed into the future. When I deliberate now about whether to go to the lecture or to the movies tonight, I now think I genuinely can go to the lecture, and I genuinely can go to the movies (but perhaps I cannot do both). And I often have this view about the future—the view of the future as a "garden of forking paths" (in Borges' wonderful phrase). But I also can be brought to recognize that, for all I know, causal determinism is true; its truth would not necessarily manifest itself to me phenomenologically. Thus, compatibilism is extremely attractive: it allows me to keep both the view that I (sometimes at least) have more than one path genuinely open to me and also that causal determinism may be true. (I can keep both of these views in the same mental compartment, so to speak; they need not be compartmentalized into different mental slots or thought to apply to different realms or perspectives.)

It is incredibly natural—almost inevitable phenomenologically—to think that I could either go to the movies or to the lecture tonight, that I could either continue working on this essay or take a coffee break, and so forth. It would be jarring to discover that, despite the appearance of the availability of these options, only one path into the future is genuinely available to me. A compatibilist need not come to the one-path conclusion, in the event that theoretical physicists conclusively establish that the conditionals discussed above have associated with them 100% probabilities, rather than (say) 99.9% probabilities. A compatibilist can embrace the resiliency of this fundamental view of ourselves as agents who (help to) *select* the path the world takes into the future, among various paths it genuinely *could* take. A compatibilist can capture the intuitive idea that a tiny difference (between 100% and 99.9%) should not make such a huge difference (between our having more than one genuinely available pathway into the future and this pervasive phenomenological fact being just a big delusion). How could such a small change—of the sort envisaged in the probabilities associated with the arcane conditionals of theoretical physics—make such a big difference?

Similarly, it is natural and extraordinarily "basic" for human beings to think of ourselves as (sometimes at least) morally accountable for our choices and behavior. Typically, we think of ourselves as morally responsible precisely in virtue of exercising a distinctive kind of freedom or control; this freedom is traditionally thought to involve exactly the sort of "selection" from among genuinely available alternative possibilities alluded to above. When an agent is morally responsible for his behavior, we typically suppose that he could have (at least at some relevant time) done otherwise.

The assumption that we human beings—most of us, at least—are morally responsible agents (at least sometimes) is extremely important and pervasive. In fact, it is hard to imagine human life without it. (At the very least, such life would be very different from the way we currently understand our lives—less richly textured and, arguably, not better or more attractive.) A compatibilist need not give up this assumption, even if he were to wake up to the headline, "Causal Determinism Is True!" (and he were convinced of its truth). Nor need the compatibilist give up any of his basic metaphysical views—apparently *a priori* metaphysical truths that support his views about free will—simply because the theoretical physicists have established that the relevant probabilities are 100% rather than 99%. Wouldn't it be bizarre to give up a principle such as that the past is fixed and out of our control or that logical truths are fixed and out of our control, simply because one has been convinced that the probabilities in question are 100% rather than 99%. A compatibilist need not "flipflop" in this weird and unappealing way.

In ordinary life, and in our moral principles and legal system, we distinguish individuals who behave freely from those who do not. Sam is a "normal" adult human being, who grew up in favorable circumstances (roughly those described in the American TV series, *Leave It To Beaver*). He has no unusual neurophysiological or psychological anomalies or disorders, and he is not in a context in which he is manipulated, brainwashed, coerced, or otherwise "compelled" to do what he does. More specifically, no factors that uncontroversially function to undermine, distort, or thwart the normal human faculty of practical reasoning or execution of the outputs of such reasoning are present. He deliberates in the "normal way" about whether to deliberately withhold pertinent information on his income tax forms, and, although he knows it is morally wrong, he decides to withhold the information and cheat on his taxes anyway.

According to our common-sense way of looking at the world and even our more theoretical moral and legal perspectives, Sam freely chooses to cheat on his income taxes and freely cheats. It is plausible that, given the assumptions I have sketched, he was free just prior to his decision and action *not* to so decide and behave. Insofar as Sam selected his own path, he acted freely and can be held both morally and legally accountable for cheating on his taxes.

On the other hand, we tend to exempt certain agents from *any* moral responsibility in virtue of their lacking even the *capacity* to control their choices and actions; we take it that such individuals are so impaired in their cognitive and/or executive capacities that they cannot *freely* select their path into the future (even if various paths present themselves as genuinely available). Such agents may have significant brain damage or neurological or psychological disorders in virtue of which they are not even capable of exercising the distinctive human capacity of control in any morally significant context. Other agents may have the basic features that underwrite this capacity, but they nevertheless are locally rather than globally exempt from moral responsibility.

On the common-sense view, even as structured and refined by moral and legal analysis, agents who are brainwashed (without their consent), involuntarily subjected to hypnosis or subliminal advertising or other forms of behavioral conditioning, or even direct stimulation of the brain, are not morally responsible for the relevant behavior. But they may be morally responsible for choices and actions that are not the result of these "stock" examples of freedom-undermining and thus responsibility-undermining factors.

Of course, there are difficult cases of significant coercion, or pressure that falls short of genuine compulsion, or subliminal suggestion that is influential but not determinative, about which reasonable persons may disagree. Further, there is considerable controversy over the role and significance of early childhood experiences, deprivations, poverty, physical and psychological abuse, and so forth. But even though there are "hard cases", common sense—and moral and legal theory—has it that there are clear cases of freedom and responsibility, on the one hand, and clear cases of the lack of it, on the other.

A compatibilist can maintain this distinction, even if it turns out that the physicists convince us that the probabilities associated with the relevant conditionals—the conditionals linking the past and laws with the present in physics—are 100%, rather than 99.9%. And this is a significant and attractive feature of compatibilism. Incompatibilism would seem to lead to a collapse of the important distinction between agents such as Sam and thoroughly manipulated or brainwashed or coerced agents. A compatibilist need not deny what seems so obvious, even if the conditionals have attached to them probabilities of 100%: there is an important difference between agents such as Sam, who act freely and can be held morally responsible, and individuals who are completely or partially exempt from moral responsibility in virtue of *special* hindrances and disabilities that impair their functioning. Again, a compatibilist's view of human beings as (sometimes) both free and morally responsible agents is *resilient* to the particular empirical discovery that causal determinism is true. Wouldn't it be bizarre if our basic view of ourselves as free and morally responsible, and our distinction between responsible agents and those who are insane or literally unable to control their behavior, would hang on whether the probabilities of the conditionals are 99.9% or 100%? Again, how can such a tiny change make such a monumental difference?

III. A compatibilist account of freedom

One might distinguish between the forward-looking aspects of agency, including practical reasoning, planning, and deliberation, and the backward-looking aspects of agency, including accountability and moral (and legal) responsibility. I have noted that it is extremely natural and plausible—almost inevitable—to think of ourselves as (sometimes at least) having more than one path branching into the future. This same assumption appears to frame both our deliberation and (retrospectively) our attributions of responsibility. I shall here take it that the possibilities in question are the *same* in both forward-looking and backward-looking aspects of agency: when we deliberate, we naturally presuppose that we have different paths into the future, and when we assign responsibility, we suppose (typically) that the relevant agent had available to him a different path.

In both forward-looking and backward-looking contexts, it is appealing to suppose that the relevant sort of possibility or freedom is analyzed as a certain sort of choice-dependence. That is, when I'm deliberating, it is plausible to suppose that I genuinely can do whatever it is that I would do, if I were so to act: I can go to the movies later insofar as I would go to the movies, if I were to choose to go to the movies, and I can go to the lecture insofar as I would go to the lecture, if I were to choose to go to the lecture, and so forth. On this view, I can do, in the relevant sense of "can", whatever is a (suitable) function of my "will" or choices: the scope of my deliberation about the future is the set of paths along which my behavior is a function of my choices. I do not deliberate about whether to jump to the moon, because (in part at least) I would not successfully jump to the moon, even if I were to choose to jump to the moon.

Similarly, given the assumption of the unity of forward-looking and backward-looking features of agency, the alternative possibilities pertinent to the attribution of responsibility are understood in terms of choice-dependence. That is, on this approach an agent is morally responsible for a certain action only if he could have done otherwise, and he could have done otherwise just in case he would have done otherwise, if he had chosen to do otherwise.

This compatibilist analysis of freedom (or the distinctive sort of possibility relevant to deliberation and responsibility) is called the "conditional analysis" because it suggests that our freedom can be understood in terms of certain conditional statements ("if-then" statements). More specifically, the conditional analysis commends to us the view that an agent S's freedom to do X can be understood in terms of the truth of a statement such as, "If S were to choose (will, decide, and so forth) to do X, S would do X." The subjunctive conditional specifies the relevant notion of "dependence." The analysis seems to capture important elements of our intuitive picture of what is within the legitimate scope of our deliberation and planning for the future. It also helps to sort out at least some cases in which agents are not morally responsible for their behavior—and to distinguish these from cases in which agents are responsible. If someone is kidnapped and chained, he is presumably not morally responsible for not helping someone in distress insofar as he would still be in chains (and thus would not succeed in helping), even if he were to choose (decide, will) to help.

But despite its considerable attractions, the conditional analysis, as presented thus far, has fatal problems—problems that should be seen to be fatal even by the compatibilist. First, note that it may be that some upshot is choice-dependent in the way specified by the conditional analysis, and yet there may be some factor that (uncontroversially) impairs or hinders the relevant agent's capacity for choice (in the circumstances in question). This factor could render the agent powerless (in the sense presumably relevant to moral responsibility), even though the upshot is choice-dependent.

So consider the following example due to Keith Lehrer.[1] As a boy, Thomas had a terrible and traumatic experience with a snake. He thus has a pathological aversion to snakes that renders him psychologically incapable of bringing himself to choose to touch a snake (much less pick one up), even as an adult. A snake is in a basket right in from of Thomas. Whereas it is true that *if* Thomas were to choose to pick up the snake, he would do so, it is nevertheless true that Thomas cannot choose to pick up the snake. Intuitively, Thomas cannot pick up the snake—and yet the conditional analysis would have it that he can (in the relevant sense). This is a problem that even a compatibilist should see as significant; the problem clearly does not come from causal determination *per se*. The general form of the problem is that the relevant subjunctive conditional can be true consistently with the actual operation of some factor that intuitively (and apart from any contentious views about the compatibility of causal determinism and freedom) makes it the case that the agent is psychologically incapable of choosing (the act in question) and thus unable to perform the act. Factors that would seem to render an agent psychologically incapable of choice (and which could be seen to do so even by a compatibilist) might include past trauma, subliminal advertising, aversive conditioning, hypnosis, and even direct electric stimulation of the brain.

To make the point starkly, an individual could have his brain directly manipulated (without his consent) so as to choose Y. This would presumably render it true that he cannot do X, even though it might well be the case that *if* he had chosen to do X, he would have done X. (Of course, if the individual were to choose X, then he would not have been subject to the actual manipulation to which he has been subjected—manipulation that issues in his choosing Y.) Think of a demonic (or even well-intentioned) neuroscientist (or even a team including very nice neurophilosophers and neuroscientists!) who can manipulate parts of the brain by using (say) a laser; metaphorically, the laser beam can be thought of as a line that comes from some external source— some source physically external to the individual who is being manipulated and out of his control—at the "end" of which is the individual's choice to do Y. The neuroscientist knows the systematic workings of the brain so that she knows what sort of laser-induced manipulation is bound to produce a choice to do Y. Under such circumstances, it would seem ludicrous to suppose that the individual is free to do X; and yet it may well be true that *if* he were to choose X, the neuroscientist would not have intervened and the individual would successfully do X. The upshot is choice-dependent, but the individual is clearly powerless (in the relevant sense).

Some compatibilists about freedom and causal determinism have given up on the conditional analysis in light of such difficulties. Others have sought to give a more refined conditional analysis. So we might distinguish between the generally discredited "simple" conditional analysis, and what might be called the "refined" conditional analysis. Different philosophers have suggested different ways of refining the simple analysis, but the basic idea is somehow to rule out the factors that uncontroversially (that is, without making any assumptions that are contentious within the context of an evaluation of the compatibility of causal determinism and freedom) render an agent unable to choose (and thus unable to act). Along these lines, one might try something like this: An agent S can do X just in case (i) if S were to choose to do X, S would do X, and (ii) the agent is not subject to clandestine hypnosis, subliminal advertising, psychological compulsion resulting from past traumatic experiences, direct stimulation of the brain, neurological damage due to a fall or accident, and so forth...

An obvious problem with the refined analysis is the "and so forth..." It would seem that an indefinitely large number of other conditions (apparently heterogeneous in nature) could in principle be thought to issue in the relevant sort of incapacity. Additionally, there should be a certain discomfort in countenancing as part of the analysis a list of disparate items with no explanation of what ties them together as a class; from a philosophical point of view, condition (ii) posits an unseemly miscellany. How could one evaluate a proposed addition to the list in a principled way?

Perhaps the compatibilist could simply admit these problems and revise condition (ii) in the following way: (ii') the agent is not subject to *any* factor that would uncontroversially (that is, without making any assumptions that are contentious within the context of an evaluation of the compatibility of causal determinism and freedom) render an agent unable to choose the act in question (and thus unable to act). Despite the obvious problems of incompleteness in this analysis, it might capture something useful; it might capture much of what a compatibilist means by the relevant notion of freedom.

Unfortunately, the proposed revision renders the analysis completely useless in seeking to resolve the controversial issue of whether causal determinism is compatible with freedom (in the relevant sense). This is because all actual choices will be the result of a causally deterministic sequence, if causal determinism is true. Since causal determination obviously is *not* a factor that uncontroversially renders an agent unable to choose (and thus unable to act), the revised analysis will have results congenial to compatibilism. But it would be dialectically unfair to the incompatibilist to suppose that the revised analysis can be seen uncontroversially to be acceptable; that is, it would clearly beg the question against the incompatibilist to contend that the refined conditional analysis can be seen to be a plausible analysis of the sort of freedom that is under consideration.

To see this more clearly, recall again the metaphor of the line from the neuroscientist to the individual's choice. When the neuroscientist uses clandestine and unconsented-to manipulation by a laser beam, it is plausible that the individual could not have chosen otherwise. Note that, under the circumstances, the only way the individual would have chosen otherwise (would have chosen X instead of Y) would have been if the neuroscientist had not employed the laser beam as she actually did; that is, it was a necessary condition of the individual's choosing otherwise that the line not have been present, as it were. But the incompatibilist will ask how exactly causal determination of the choice to do *Y* is any different from the neuroscientist's employment of her laser beam to manipulatively induce a choice to do *Y*. The laser beam is not experienced as coercive—it is by hypothesis not experienced at all. The laser is a "subtle" and phenomenologically inaccessible influence that starts entirely "outside" the agent (physically external to the agent and not within his control) and issues (via a process over which the agent has no control) in a choice to do *Y*. But if causal determinism is true, then there is *some* causally deterministic sequence that starts entirely "outside" the agent (physically external to the agent and not within his control) and issues (via a deterministic process) in a choice to do *Y*. The incompatibilist will legitimately ask what exactly the difference between the laser beam and the causally deterministic sequence is? Metaphorically, they are both lines that start outside the agent and end with the same choice, and both lines must be "erased" to get a different choice.

Now a compatibilist might grant this, but insist on a crucial point—that not all causal sequences are "created equal." More specifically, the compatibilist wishes to insist that not all causally deterministic sequences undermine freedom; a straightforward and "upfront" commitment of the compatibilist is to the idea that we can distinguish among causally deterministic sequences, and, more specifically, that we can distinguish those that involve "compulsion" (or some freedom- and responsibility-undermining factor) from those that do not. Returning to the pictorial metaphor: it may well be that an individual cannot choose or do otherwise when being manipulated by the neuroscientist's laser beam—in this case the individual cannot erase the line from the neuroscientist to his choice. On the other hand, according to the compatibilist, there is no reason to suppose that I am not free either to go to the lecture or go to the movies later. Even if I do in fact go to the movies, there is no reason—no reason stemming merely from the truth of causal determinism—to suppose that my behavior is causally determined in a *special way*—a way uncontroversially recognized to rule out freedom and responsibility. Thus, even if I do in fact go to the movies later, the compatibilist might say that there is no reason (stemming merely from the truth of causal determinism) to think that I will not be free (at the relevant time) to go to the lecture instead—and thus no reason to suppose that I will not be free (at the relevant time) to erase the line that does in fact connect the past to my choice to go to the movies.

IV. The Consequence argument

Yes, it is a basic commitment of the compatibilist—to which I promise we will return below—that not all causally deterministic sequences undermine freedom equally. But there is nevertheless an argument that presents a significant challenge to this commitment and also to the commonsense idea that we can be confident in distinguishing cases of freedom and responsibility from cases where some freedom- and responsibility-undermining factor operates. This argument is a "skeptical argument," rather like the skeptical argument from the possibility of illusion to the conclusion that we don't know what we ordinarily take ourselves to know about the external world. The skeptical argument in epistemology employs basic ingredients of common sense to challenge other parts of common sense; that is, it employs ordinary ideas about the possibility of illusion and the concept of knowledge (putatively) to generate the intuitively jarring result that we don't know what we take ourselves to know about the external world. Similarly, the skeptical argument about our freedom employs ordinary ideas about the fixity of the past and the fixity of the natural laws (putatively) to generate the intuitively jarring result that we are not ever free, if causal determinism turns out to be true (something we can't rule out *a priori*). If this skeptical argument is sound, it calls into question *any* compatibilist analysis of freedom (that is, freedom of the sort under consideration—involving the capacity for selection among open alternatives). If the argument is sound, then not only both the simple and refined conditional analysis, but *any* compatibilist analysis (of the relevant sort of freedom) must be rejected. It is thus an extremely powerful and disturbing argument. I think that any honest and serious discussion of compatibilism must address this argument, to which I turn now.

The skeptical argument has been around in one form or another for a very long time. Actually, a structurally similar argument was originally presented thousands of years ago; then, the worry was fatalism (more specifically, the idea that the truth values of statements about the future must be fixed and thus we lack freedom). Then in the Middle Ages the worry stemmed from the doctrine of God's essential omniscience. In the Modern era, our attention has focused primarily (although by no means exclusively) on the threat posed by science—more specifically, the possibility that causal determinism is true. At this point, we simply do not know whether causal determinism is true or not. If it turns out to be true, then all our behavior could in principle be deduced from a complete description of the past and laws of nature. Alternatively, if causal determinism is true, then true propositions about the past and propositions that express the laws of nature entail all our current and future choices and actions.

Here's the argument (very informally). Suppose that causal determinism is indeed true. Given the definition of causal determinism, it follows that my current choice to continue typing (and not take an admittedly much-needed coffee break) is entailed by true propositions about the past and laws of nature. Thus, if I were free (just prior to my actual choice) to choose (and subsequently do) otherwise, then I must have been free so to behave that the past would have been different or the natural laws would have been different.

But intuitively the past is "fixed" and out of my control and so are the natural laws. I cannot now do anything that is such that, if I were to do it, the past would have been different (say, John F. Kennedy never would have been assassinated) or the natural laws would be different (say, some things would travel faster than the speed of light [if I've got the natural law in question correct!]). It appears to follow that, despite the natural and almost ineluctable sense I have that I am (sometimes, at least) free to choose and do otherwise, I am never free to choose and do otherwise, if causal determinism obtains.

Although the compatibilist wishes to say that not all causally deterministic sequences equally threaten freedom, the Consequence Argument—so-called by Peter van Inwagen because under causal determinism all our behavior is the consequence of the past plus the laws of nature—appears to imply that causal determinism *per se* rules out the relevant sort of freedom.[2] If the Consequence Argument is sound—and it relies on intuitively plausible ingredients, such as the fixity of the past and natural laws—then the common-sense distinction between cases of "compulsion" and ordinary cases in which moral responsibility is present would vanish, if causal determinism were true; and since we do not know that causal determinism is false, our basic views about ourselves (as free and morally responsible agents) would be called into question.

Recall that it would be uncontroversial that I would not be morally responsible if I were subjected to clandestine (and unconsented to) manipulation by a neuroscientist's laser beam. As I said above, in such a context, in order for a different choice to have occurred, the laser beam must not have connected the neurosurgeon with my actual choice. Similarly, if causal determinism were true, then the Consequence Argument brings out the fact that—even in the most "ordinary" circumstances (that is, in the absence of anything that would uncontroversially constitute compulsion)—in order for a different choice to have occurred, the past or the natural laws would have had to have been different: the "line" connecting the past to my choice (via the laws) would have had to have been broken (or erased). The line posited by causal determination appears to be equivalent to the laser beam.

Another way to look at the ingredients that go into the Consequence Argument is to consider the intuitive idea that (as Carl Ginet puts the point) my freedom now is the freedom to add to the given past, holding fixed the laws of nature.[3] In terms of our metaphor, my freedom (on this view) is the freedom to draw a line that *extends* the line that connects the actual past with the present (holding fixed the natural laws). The future may well be a garden of forking paths, but the forking paths all branch off a single line (presumably). The Consequence Argument throws into relief an intuitively jarring implication of compatibilism: the compatibilist cannot embrace the almost undeniable picture of our freedom as the freedom to add to the past, given the laws. If the past is a set of dots, then for our freedom truly to be understandable, we must be able to connect the dots—in more ways than one. Some have said that responsibility involves "making a connection" with values of a certain sort, or "tracking values" in a certain way; but there is even a more fundamental way in which our freedom involves making a connection: we must be able to connect our current actions with our past (holding the natural laws fixed).

In my opinion, the Consequence Argument is a powerful and highly plausible argument. On the other hand, it certainly falls short of being indisputably sound. Some compatibilists—Multiple-Pasts Compatibilists—are willing to say that we can sometimes so act that the past would have been different from what it actually was; alternatively, these compatibilists say that our freedom need not be construed as the freedom to extend the given past, holding the natural laws fixed. On such a view, I might have access to a possibility with a different past associated with it (a possible world with a different past from the actual past) insofar as there are no special "obstacles" in the actual course of events (or the actual world) that "block" such access. Other compatibilists—Local-Miracle Compatibilists—are willing to say that we can sometimes so act that a natural law that actually obtains would not have obtained; some such compatibilists are also willing to countenance small changes in the past as well as the laws. On this sort of view, I might have access to a possibility (or possible world) with slightly different natural laws from those that obtain actually, as long as these alternative scenarios do not involve widespread and big changes in the laws. This view is defended in a classic paper by David Lewis (1981)[4].

So there is room for compatibilism about causal determinism and the sort of freedom that involves genuine access to alternative possibilities, even in light of the Consequence Argument; excellent philosophers have opted for some response to the Consequence Argument (such as Local-Miracle or Multiple-Pasts Compatibilism). As I said above, the Consequence Argument is not indisputably sound, and thus there is no knockdown argument available that the responses are inadequate.

I do in fact find the Consequence Argument highly plausible, and I am inclined to accept its soundness. I thus think it is important to argue that there is an attractive kind of compatibilism that is indeed consistent with accepting the Consequence Argument as sound. The doctrine of semicompatibilism is the claim that causal determinism is compatible with moral responsibility, quite apart from whether causal determinism rules out the sort of freedom that involves access to alternative possibilities. Note that semicompatibilism in itself does not take a stand on whether the Consequence Argument is sound; it is consistent with acceptance or rejection of the Consequence Argument. My main goal is to defend semicompatibilism, although I am also inclined to accept the soundness of the Consequence Argument. The total package of views I am inclined to accept includes more than semicompatibilism, but semicompatibilism is the principle doctrine I seek to defend here.

V. Semicompatiblism and the Frankfurt-examples

Let's say you are driving your car and it is functioning normally. You want to go to the coffee house, so you guide the car to the right (into the parking lot for the coffee house). Your choice to go to the coffee house is based on your own reasons in the normal way, and the car's steering apparatus functions normally. Here you have a certain distinctive kind of control of the car's movements—you have "guidance control" of the car's going to the right. This is more than mere causation or even causal determination; you might have causally determined the car's going to the right by sneezing (and thus jerking the steering wheel to the right) or having an epileptic seizure (and thus slumping over the wheel and causing it to turn to the right) without having exercised this specific and distinctive sort of *control*. Supposing that there are no "special" factors at work—that is, no special psychological impairments, brain lesions, neurological disorders, causal determination, and so forth— and imagining (as above) that the car's steering apparatus is not broken, you had it in your power (just prior to your actual decision to turn to the right) to continue going straight ahead, or to turn the car to the left, and so forth. That is, although you exercise guidance control in turning the car to the right, you presumably (and apart from special assumptions) possessed freedom to choose and do otherwise: you had "regulative control" over the car's movements. In the normal case, we assume that agents have both guidance and regulative control—a signature sort of control of the car's movements, as well as a characteristic kind of control *over* the car's movements.

Whereas these two sorts of control are typically presumed to go together, they can be prized apart. Suppose that everything is as above, but that the steering apparatus of your car is broken in such a way that, if you had tried to guide the car in any direction other than the one in which you actually guide it, it would have gone to the right anyway—in just the trajectory it actually traveled. The defect in the steering apparatus plays no role in the actual sequence of events, but it would have played a role in the alternative scenario (or range of such scenarios). Given this sort of preemptive overdetermination, although you exhibit guidance control of the car's going to the right, you do *not* have regulative control over the car's movements: it would have gone in precisely the same way, no matter what you were to choose or try.

Of course, in this context you *do* possess *some* regulative control: you could have chosen otherwise, and you could have tried to guide the car in some other direction. This is reminiscent of John Locke's famous example in his *Essay Concerning Human Understanding*. Here a man is transported into a room while he is asleep. When the man awakens, he considers leaving, but he decides to stay in the room for his own reasons. Locke says he voluntarily chooses to stay in the room and voluntarily stays in the room. Unbeknownst to the man, the door to the room is locked, and thus he could not have left the room. According to Locke, the man voluntarily stays in the room, although he does not have the power to leave the room. He exhibits a certain sort of control of his staying in the room (what I would call guidance control), even though he cannot do otherwise than stay in the room (and thus he lacks regulative control over staying in the room). But note that, as in the second car example above, the man could have chosen to leave the room, and he could have tried to do so.

Can structurally similar examples be given in which there is guidance control but *no* regulative control? This is where the "Frankfurt-examples" come in. The contemporary philosopher, Harry Frankfurt, has sought to provide just such an example. One could say that he seeks to put the locked door inside the mind (in terms of Locke's example). In Locke's example, some factor (the locked door) plays no role in the individual's deliberations or choice, and yet its presence renders it true that the individual could not have done otherwise (could not have left the room). Frankfurt posits some factor that plays an analogous role in the context of the agent's mind: it plays no role in the agent's actual deliberations or choice, and yet its presence (allegedly) renders it true that the individual could not have chosen otherwise (or done otherwise). If Frankfurt's examples work, then one could in principle entirely prize apart guidance control from regulative control.

Here is my favorite version of a Frankfurt-type case. Jones has left his political decision until the last moment, just as some diners leave their decision about what to order at a restaurant to the moment when the waiter turns to them. In any case, Jones goes into the voting booth, deliberates in the "normal" way, and chooses to vote for the Democrat. On the basis of this choice, Jones votes for the Democrat. Unbeknownst to Jones, he has a chip in his brain that allows a very nice and highly progressive neurosurgeon (Black) to monitor his brain. The neurosurgeon wants Jones to vote for the Democrat, and if she sees that Jones is about to do so, she does not intervene in any way—she merely monitors the brain. If, on the other hand, the neurosurgeon sees that Jones is about to choose to vote for the Republican, she swings into action with her nifty electronic probe and stimulates Jones' brain in such a way as to ensure that he chooses to vote for the Democrat (and goes ahead and votes for the Democrat). Given the set-up, it seems that Jones freely chooses to vote for the Democrat and freely votes for the Democrat, although he could not have chosen or done otherwise: it seems that Jones exhibits guidance control of his vote, but he lacks regulative control over his choice and also his vote. The neurosurgeon's chip and electronic device has brought Locke's locked door into the mind. Just as the locked door plays no role in Locke's man's choice or behavior but nevertheless renders it true that he could not have done otherwise, the Black's set-up plays no role in Jones' actual choice or behavior, but it apparently renders it true that he could not have chosen or done otherwise.

How exactly does the neurosurgeon's device reliably know how Jones is about to vote? Frankfurt himself is vague about this point, but let us imagine that Jones's brain registers a certain neurological pattern if Jones is about to choose to vote for the Democrat, and a different pattern if Jones is about to choose to vote Republican. The chip can subtly convey this information to the neurosurgeon, which she can then use to good effect. Of course, the mere possibility of exhibiting a certain neurological pattern is not sufficiently robust to ground ascriptions of moral responsibility, on the picture that requires access to alternative possibilities. That is, if moral responsibility requires the sort of control that involves selection from among various paths that are genuinely open to an agent, the mere possibility of involuntarily exhibiting a certain neurological pattern would not seem to count as the relevant sort of "selection." Put slightly differently, just as it is not enough to secure moral responsibility that a different choice could have *randomly* occurred, it does not seem to be enough to secure moral responsibility that a different neurological pattern could have been exhibited *involuntarily*. Such an exiguous possibility is a mere "flicker of freedom" and not sufficiently robust to ground moral responsibility, given the picture that requires regulative control for moral responsibility. How could something as important as moral responsibility come from something so thin—and something entirely involuntary?

It is tempting then to suppose that one could have a genuine kind of control—guidance control—that can be entirely prized apart from regulative control and that is all the freedom required for moral responsibility. So even if the Consequence Argument were valid and thus all casually deterministic sequences were equally potent in ruling out the sort of control that requires access to alternative possibilities (regulative control), it would *not* follow that all causally deterministic sequences equally threaten guidance control and moral responsibility. That is, if moral responsibility does not require the sort of control that involves access to alternative possibilities, then this opens the possibility of defending a kind of compatibilism, even granting the soundness of the Consequence Argument.

But various philosophers have resisted the temptation to suppose that one can expunge all vestiges of regulative control while at the same time preserving guidance control. They have pointed out that the appearance that Frankfurt-type cases can help to separate guidance from (all) regulative control may be misleading. Perhaps the most illuminating way to put their argument is in terms of a dilemma. The first horn assumes that indeterminism is true in the Frankfurt-examples; in particular, it assumes that the relationship between the "prior sign" (read by the progressive neurosurgeon, Black) and the choice is causally indeterministic. It follows that right up until the time Jones begins to choose, he can begin to choose otherwise; after all, the prior sign (together with other factors) falls short of causally determining the actual choice. Thus, there emerges a robust alternative possibility—the possibility of beginning to choose otherwise. This is no mere flicker of freedom; although it may be blocked or thwarted before it is completed or comes to fruition, it is nevertheless a voluntary episode—the initiation of choice.

The second horn of the dilemma assumes that causal determinism is true in the examples. Given the assumption of causal determination, it would appear to be straightforwardly question-begging to say that Jones is obviously morally responsible for his choice and behavior (despite lacking genuine access to alternative possibilities). After all, this (the compatibility of causal determination and moral responsibility) is precisely what is at issue!

The dilemma is powerful, but I am not convinced that it presents an insuperable objection to the employment of the Frankfurt-examples as part of a general strategy of defending compatibilism; as a matter of fact, I reject it. First, there have been various attempts at providing explicitly indeterministic versions of the Frankfurt-cases, and I think some of them are promising. I don't think it is obvious that one could not construct a Frankfurt-example (under the explicit assumption of causal indeterminism) in which there are *no* robust alternative possibilities. Recall that it is not enough for the proponent of the regulative control requirement to identify just any sort of alternative possibility; rather, he needs to find an alternative possibility that is sufficiently *robust* to ground attributions of moral responsibility, given the regulative control picture. If the ground of moral responsibility is a certain sort of *selection* from genuinely available paths into the future, then paths with mere accidental or arbitrary events would seem to be irrelevant. This is the idea of the irrelevance of exiguous alternatives. In my view, to seek to get responsibility out of mere flickers of freedom is akin to alchemy. Here I am in agreement with the libertarian, Robert Kane, who insists on the "dual-voluntariness" constraint on moral responsibility.[5]

On the second horn of the dilemma, causal determinism is assumed. I agree that it would be dialectically rash to conclude precipitously from mere inspection of the example presented above that Jones is morally responsible for his choice and voting behavior. Rather, my approach would be rather more circumspect. First, I would note that the distinctive contribution of the Frankfurt-examples is to suggest that if Jones is not morally responsible for his choice and behavior, this is *not* because he lacks genuine access to (robust) alternative possibilities. After all, in the example, Black's set-up is sufficient for Jones's choosing and acting as he actually does, but intuitively it is *irrelevant* to Jones's moral responsibility. That is, we can identify a factor— Black's elaborate set-up—that is (perhaps in conjunction with other features of the example) sufficient for Jones's actual kind of choice and behavior, but it plays no actual role in Jones's deliberations or actions; Black's set-up could have been subtracted from the situation and the actual sequence would have flowed in exactly the way it actually did. When something is in this way irrelevant to what happens in the actual sequence issuing in an agent's choice and behavior, it would seem to be irrelevant to his moral responsibility.

So the distinctive element added by the Frankfurt-type examples, under the assumption of causal determinisim, is this: if the relevant agent is not morally responsible, it is not because of his lack of regulative control. Alternatively, we could say that they show that it is not the lack of genuine access to alternative possibilities (regulative control) in itself (and apart from pointing to other factors) that rules out moral responsibility. Now we can ask whether there is some other factor—some factor that plays a role in the actual sequence—that rules out moral responsibility, if causal determinism obtains. We will turn to a more thorough and careful consideration of such "actual-sequence factors" below. For now, I simply wish to note that there is nothing question-begging or dialectically inappropriate about how I have invoked the Frankfurt-examples thus far (on the second horn), and their distinctive role is to call into question the relevance or importance of regulative control in grounding moral responsibility (in the way presented described above).

Taking stock, in Section IV I presented the Consequence Argument. I did not officially endorse its conclusion, although I am inclined to believe that the argument is valid and further that its premises are based on extremely plausible ingredients. I suggested that it would be prudent to seek a defense of compatibilism that does not presuppose that the Consequence Argument is unsound. Here I have presented the rudimentary first steps toward the elaboration of just such a compatibilism. I have invoked the Frankfurt-examples (the prototypes of which are in John Locke) to support the contention that moral responsibility does not require regulative control (or the sort of freedom that involves genuine access to alternative possibilities), but only guidance control. (In the following section, I shall give a sketch of an account of guidance control.) Further, I have suggested that (thus far at least) there is no reason to suppose that causal determinism is inconsistent with guidance control. Better: I have contended that even if causal determinism threatens regulative control, it does not thereby threaten guidance control. In a more comprehensive defense of the sort of compatibilism I find attractive, one would explore whether there are other reasons (apart from regulative control) in virtue of which causal determinism is incompatible with moral responsibility (and offer reasons why it isn't).

VI. An account of guidance control

An insight from the Frankfurt-cases helps to shape the account of guidance control: moral responsibility is a matter of the history of an action (or behavior)—of how the actual sequence unfolds—rather than the genuine metaphysical availability of alternative possibilities. On this view, alternative scenarios or non-actual possible worlds might be relevant to moral responsibility in virtue of helping to specify or analyze modal properties of the actual sequence, but not in virtue of indicating or providing an analysis of genuine access to alternative possibilities.

Note that, in a Frankfurt-type case, the actual sequence proceeds "in the normal way" or via the "normal" process of practical reasoning. In contrast, in the alternative scenario (which never actually gets triggered and thus never becomes part of the actual sequence of events in our world), there is (say) direct electronic stimulation of the brain—intuitively, a different way or a different kind of mechanism. (By "mechanism" I simply mean, roughly speaking, "way"—I do not mean to reify anything.) I assume that we have intuitions at least about clear cases of "same mechanism," and "different mechanism." The actually operating mechanism (in a Frankfurt-type case)—ordinary human practical reasoning, unimpaired by direct stimulation by neurosurgeons, and so forth—is in a salient sense responsive to reasons. That is, holding fixed that mechanism, the agent would presumably choose and act differently in a range of scenarios in which he is presented with good reasons to do so.

The above discussion suggests the rudiments of an account of guidance control of action. On this account, we hold fixed the kind of mechanism that actually issues in the choice and action, and we see whether the agent responds suitably to reasons (some of which are moral reasons). My account presupposes that the agent can recognize reasons, and, in particular, recognize certain reasons as moral reasons. The account distinguishes between reasons-recognition (the ability to recognize the reasons that exist) and reasons-reactivity (choice in accordance with reasons that are recognized as good and sufficient), and it makes different demands on reasons-recognition and reasons-reactivity. The sort of reasons-responsiveness linked to moral responsibility, on my view, is "moderate reasons-responsiveness."

A bit more carefully, we can build up to the conditions for moderate reasons-responsiveness by starting with "weak reasons-responsiveness":

> An agent is *weakly reasons-responsive* when a certain kind K of mechanism, which involves the agent's rational consideration of reasons relevant to the situation, issues in action, and in *at least some alternative circumstances* in which there are sufficient reasons for her to do otherwise than she actually does, she would be receptive to these reasons and would have chosen and done otherwise by the efficacy of the same mechanism that actually results in the action.[6]

Now moderate reasons-responsiveness is the same as weak reasons-responsiveness, except for the following changes:

> a) In the alternative situation in which there is sufficient reason to do otherwise and the agent does otherwise, the agent performs the action for that (sufficient) reason.

b) The agent must show regularity in recognizing reasons—the agent must be receptive to a pattern of reasons. (This condition rules out situations in which an agent is weakly reasons-responsive but recognizes only random elements in a pattern of reasons.)

c) The agent must be receptive to a range of reasons that includes moral reasons.[7]

But one could exhibit the right sort of reasons-responsiveness as a result (say) of clandestine, unconsented-to electronic stimulation of the brain (or hypnosis, brainwashing, and so forth). So moderate reasons-responsiveness of the actual-sequence mechanism is necessary but not sufficient for moral responsibility. I contend that there are two elements of guidance control: reasons-sensitivity of the appropriate sort and mechanism ownership. That is, the mechanism that issues in the behavior must (in an appropriate sense) be the *agent's own* mechanism. (When one is secretly manipulated through clandestine mind control as in *The Manchurian Candidate*, one's practical reasoning is not *one's own*.)

I argue for a subjective approach to mechanism ownership. On this approach, one's mechanism becomes one's own in virtue of one's having certain beliefs about one's own agency and its effects in the world, that is, in virtue of *seeing oneself in a certain way*. (Of course, it is *not* simply a matter of saying certain things—one actually has to have the relevant constellation of beliefs.) On my view, an individual becomes morally responsible in part at least by taking responsibility; he makes his mechanism his own by taking responsibility for acting from that kind of mechanism. In a sense, then, one acquires control by *taking control*.

More carefully, the conditions for taking responsibility for the mechanism on which one acts are as follows:

a) The individual must see himself as an agent; he must see that his choices and actions are efficacious in the world. This condition includes the claim that the individual sees that if he were to choose and act differently, different upshots would occur in the world.

b) The individual must accept that he is a fair target of the reactive attitudes as a result of how he exercises this agency in certain contexts.

c) The individual's view of himself specified in the first two conditions must be based, in an appropriate way, on the evidence.[8]

I ended my 1981 paper, "Responsibility and Control," by saying that we must "decode the information in the actual sequence" leading to behavior for which the agent can legitimately be held morally responsible and ascertain whether it is compatible with causal determination. The account of guidance control—with the two chief ingredients, moderate reasons-responsiveness and mechanism-ownership—are the secrets revealed by close scrutiny of the actual sequence, and I have argued that they are entirely compatible with causal determination. (Note that they are also entirely compatible with causal indeterminism; thus, on my approach, moral responsibility does *not* hang on a thread.)

Further, I have shown how we can build a *comprehensive* account of guidance control from an account of guidance control of *actions*.[9] That is, we can develop an account of guidance control of omissions, consequence-particulars, consequence-universals, and perhaps even emotions and character traits by invoking certain basic ingredients contained in the account of guidance control of actions. I argue that it is a point in favor of my account of moral responsibility that it can give a comprehensive account that builds on simple, basic ingredients. Additionally, I contend that this comprehensive account systematizes our intuitive judgments about a wide range of examples involving moral responsibility. It thus helps us to achieve a philosophical homeostasis, or, in John Rawls's famous term, a reflective equilibrium.

VII. Conclusion: the lure of semicompatibilism

John Perry has told me that I need a new name for the position, and I agree that "semicompatibilism" is not very exciting. (My only consolation is that the other names for positions in the free will debates are equally uninspiring; could you imagine going to the barricades for "hard incompatibilism"?) What is important, however, is not what's in the name, but what's in the doctrine. In this essay I have focused mainly on trying to explain the appeal of this form of compatibilism. That is, I have attempted to provide a *general* motivation for compatibilism, and also an explanation of the appeal of *this specific form* of compatibilism (as opposed to traditional compatibilism). The idea here has not been to develop detailed elaborations of the ideas or sustained defenses of the positions; rather, I have simply presented in sketchy form the attractions of the overall view (and some of the difficulties faced by its competitors).

One of the main virtues of compatibilism is that our deepest and most basic views about our agency—our freedom and moral responsibility—are not held hostage to views in physics. A semicompatibilist would not have to revise these beliefs in light of a future discovery of the truth of causal determinism. Nor need he be prepared to revise his basic metaphysical views—such as that the past is fixed or the laws of nature are fixed or that powerlessness can be transmitted via the Principle of Transfer of Powerlessness—in light of such a discovery. A libertarian, it seems, must claim that he knows from his armchair (or philosophical Barca-Lounger) that causal determinism is false; but how could we know in advance such an empirical thesis? These are significant virtues of semicompatibilism: a proponent of this doctrine need not purport to know *apriori* some (presumably) empirical thesis in physics, or be prepared to give up his basic views about our agency, or engage in unattractive "metaphysical flipflopping" (giving up some or one's basic metaphysical principles in light of some empirical truth in physics).

Semicompatibilism combines the best features of compatibilism and incompatibilism. It can accommodate the most compelling insights of the incompatibilist (as crystallized in the Consequence Argument) and also the basic appeal of compatibilism—that not all causally deterministic sequences equally rule out the sort of control that grounds moral responsibility. Thus, semicompatibilism allows us to track common sense (suitably conceptualized in moral and legal theory) in making distinctions between those factors that operate in such a way as to undermine responsibility and those that do not. And a semicompatibilist need not give up the idea that sometimes individuals robustly deserve punishment for their behavior, whereas on other occasions they robustly deserve moral commendation and reward. That is, a semicompatibilist need not etiolate or reconfigure the widespread and natural idea that individuals *morally deserve* to be treated harshly in certain circumstances, and kindly in others. We need not in any way damp down our revulsion at heinous deeds, or our admiration for human goodness and even heroism. Thus, even if the name is unexciting, the idea is beautiful.[10]

Notes

1. Lehrer discusses such cases in various places, including Keith Lehrer, "'Can' in theory and practice: a possible-worlds analysis," in *Action Theory*, ed. Myles Brand and Kendall Walton (Dordrecht, The Netherlands: Reidel, 1976), 241–70.

2. Peter Van Inwagen, *An Essay on Free Will* (Oxford: Clarendon Press, 1983).

3. Carl Ginet, *On Action* (Cambridge, U.K.: Cambridge University Press, 1990), 102–103.

4. Lewis, David, "Are we free to break the laws?" *Theoria* 47 (1981): 112–21.

5. Robert Kane, *The Significance of Free Will* (New York: Oxford University Press, 1996), 109–15.

6. John Martin Fischer, *The Metaphysics of Free Will* (Oxford: Blackwell, 1994), 164.

7. John Martin Fischer and Mark Ravizza, *Responsibility and Control: A Theory of Moral Responsibility* (New York: Oxford University Press, 1998), 69–82. In presenting the view in a clear and condensed way, I am very grateful to Derk Pereboom, *Living Without Free Will* (New York: Cambridge University Press), 108–109.

8. Fischer and Ravizza 1998, 210–14.

9. Fischer and Ravizza 1998.

10. This essay is (in part) based on my contribution to John Martin Fischer, Robert Kane, Derk Pereboom, and Manuel Vargas, *Four Views on Free Will* (Oxford: Blackwell,

2007), 44–84. I have attempted to present, defend, and elaborate semicompatibilism in Fischer 1994; Fischer and Ravizza 1998; and John Martin Fischer, *My Way: Essays on Moral Responsibility* (New York: Oxford University Press, 2006). For further reflections on various features of my account of guidance control (and thus the freedom-relevant component of moral responsibility), see John Martin Fischer, "The free will revolution," part of a book symposium on John Martin Fischer and Mark Ravizza, *Responsibility and Control: A Theory of Moral Responsibility, Philosophical Explorations* 8 (2005), 145–56; "The free will revolution (continued)," (part of a special issue on the work [pertaining to moral responsibility] of John Martin Fischer), *Journal of Ethics* 10 (2006), 315–45; "*My Way* and life's highway," *Journal of Ethics* 12 (2008), 167–89.

There are certain features of my account of guidance control that a disconcerting cohort of (otherwise!) thoughtful philosophers have found rather less than irresistible, especially the subjective element and the contention that "reactivity is all of a piece". In the trio of articles referred to in the paragraph above, I argue (among other things) that (if need be) I could adjust my account so as to do without these contentious features while still maintaining all of my major claims: that moral responsibility does not require regulative control, that causal determination is compatible with moral responsibility, that moral responsibility is an essentially historical notion, and so forth.

I am grateful to Derk Pereboom for helpful comments on a previous version of this paper.

PART 7

Suggested Further Readings

VII. Compatibilism: Reason-Based Alternatives

Bok, Hilary. 2001. *Freedom and responsibility*. Princeton, NJ: Princeton University Press.

Dennett, Daniel. 1984. *Elbow room*. Cambridge, MA: MIT Press.

Fischer, John M., and Mark Ravizza. 1998. *Responsibility and Control*. Cambridge: Cambridge University Press.

Russell, Paul. 2002. "Pessimists, pollyannas and the new compatibilism," in *The Oxford handbook of free will*, ed. Robert Kane. New York: Oxford University Press.

Scanlon, T. M. 1988. "The significance of choice," *The Tanner Lectures on Human Values*. Brasenose College, Oxford University.

Scanlon, T. M. 1998. *What We Owe to Each Other*. Cambridge, MA: Harvard University Press.

Wallace, R. Jay. 1994. *Responsibility and the Moral Sentiments*. Cambridge, MA: Harvard University Press.

Wolf, Susan. 1990. *Freedom Within Reason*. Oxford: Oxford University Press.

Autonomy and History

17

Autonomy and Personal History[1]

John Christman

I. Introduction

Virtually any appraisal of a person's welfare, integrity, or moral status, as well as the moral and political theories built on such appraisals, will rely crucially on the presumption that her preferences and values are in some important sense her own. In particular, the nature and value of political freedom is intimately connected with the presupposition that actions one is left free to do flow from desires and values that are truly an expression of the 'self-government' of the agent. However, we all know that no person is self-made in the sense of being a fully formed and intact 'will' blossoming out of nowhere. Our values and preferences are explained by essential reference to a variety of influences that have come to bear on our development throughout our personal histories. What is needed, then, is to establish an account of self-determination or autonomy that would help determine just when and if the values and preferences we find ourselves with deserve the centrality that moral and political theories place on them.

I intend here to defend a theory of individual autonomy. I will do this in three stages: I will first argue for the necessity of an account of autonomy as an essential aspect of human freedom; second, I will spell out one influential approach to the concept of autonomy and show how powerful criticisms can be waged against it; I will then develop a new account which avoids these difficulties and which is defensible in its own right. The new theory is unique in that I focus on the manner in which the agent *came to have* a set of desires rather than her attitude towards the desires at any one time. The key element of autonomy is, in my view, the agent's acceptance or rejection of the process of desire formation or the factors that give rise to that formation, rather than the agent's identification with the desire itself. I will argue that this theory succeeds where others have failed in capturing the essence of self-government, which for many expresses a basic component of the value structure of a free and just society.

II. Terminology: autonomy and freedom

Although some use the term 'autonomy' as simply interchangeable with 'freedom' in certain contexts, I take these to refer to separate, though complementary, properties of a person's life and action.[2] 'Freedom' has been taken to refer essentially to the absence of various types of restraints (internal or external, positive or negative)[3] that might stand between an agent's desires and the performance of her actions. But even if one utilizes a rich concept of restraint, this characterization of freedom leaves something crucial out of account. For example, subliminal advertising might induce a person to *prefer* something they otherwise would not, and hence actions based on that preference will not be done freely. However, it would be incorrect to say that the person was unfree because she was restrained from doing *that* act, for she did it. And it is not that she had 'no choice,' for we can imagine that she faced no restraints in performing some alternative action. What renders her unfree, however, is that she would not *prefer* any other action. The preference that guides her action has itself been tainted by manipulation.[4]

These observations lead to the question of the scope of the property of autonomy. Gerald Dworkin argues, for example, that freedom refers to individual acts that a person is or is not free to do, while "the question of autonomy [is] one that can only be assessed over extended portions of a person's lie. It is a dimension of assessment that evaluates a whole way of living one's life."[5] However, I think Dworkin is wrong here about whether autonomy is, at its most basic level of application, simply a property of whole persons, or persons' whole lives. Consider the fact that people will, in some aspects of their lives, make decisions autonomously, while in others they are moved by external, heteronomous, factors affecting decision-making. A person with an uncontrollable phobia, for example, may display all of the level-headedness and freedom of thought characteristic of autonomy in aspects of her life not affected by the phobia. Construing autonomy as an all-or-nothing property of a person's whole life (or a whole person) obscures the need for an account of the autonomous formation of single (or 'localized') desires. Autonomy at the more 'global' level should simply amount to perhaps an aggregation of this property. The property of being autonomous *tout court*, then, is parasitic on the property of autonomy for isolated preferences and values.[6] What all this suggests is that autonomy—at the level of preference—is an additional component of an account of free action: additional, that is, to the standard triadic account restraints.[7] Moreover, as I will argue, what is prima in an analysis of autonomy is a special property of preference or belief[8] *formation* and not merely a characteristic of a person's entire life.

III. The received model and its problems

I will begin the task of constructing a theory of autonomy with an examination of a model first put forward by Gerald Dworkin. His approach to the question of when a person is autonomous utilizes the notions of higher and lower order desires, the so called 'split-level' view of the self. Lower order desires (LODs) have as their object actual actions of the agent: a desire to *do* X or Y; higher order desires (HODS), however, have as their object other, lower order desires: a desire to desire to do X or Y. At this meta-level of evaluation, a person will 'identify' with some set of wants, goals and preferences. Dworkin's 'full formula for autonomy,' then, can be spelled out this way:

> A person is autonomous if he identifies with his desk, goals, and values, and such identification is not influenced in ways which make the process of identification in some way alien to the individual. spelling out the conditions of procedural independence involves distinguishing those ways of influencing people's reflective and...critical faculties which subvert them from those which promote and improve them.[9]

The two components of the model focus on, respectively, the special relation a person has with those desires that are 'authentic'—identification—and the necessity that this identification is not itself manipulated or constrained.[10]

I will now focus on the central defects of the Dworkin account, ones which I think are avoided in the replacement theory I suggest in the next section. These difficulties surround the condition of identification, the question of preference formation, and what I call the 'incompleteness' problem.

Identification takes place when an agent reflects critically on a desire and, at the higher level, approves of having the desire. But there are two possible readings of the identification condition: either one sees identification as simple *acknowledgment* of what desires I find myself with at a time, or one builds into the notion an *evaluation* of the having of that desire. The former view would amount to simply a judgment about what desires I have at a time, rather than an evaluation of those desires. This is what, in a different context, Galen Strawson has called 'integration.' An agent identifies with a desire, adapting Strawson's view, when from his own point of view, its "being involved in the determination of the action (citable in true rational explanations of it) *just* is his being so involved."[11]

But on this view, one can *acknowledge* that a desire is truly one's own no matter *how* one came to have the desire. Even the desires that are the result of obviously heteronomous processes can be viewed as being a (regrettable) part of oneself, maybe something one cannot change and for a time something one is simply 'stuck with.' In this way I can just as readily 'identify' with those *non*-autonomous aspects of myself as the more 'authentic' parts. So here identification can appear to *conflict* with (an intuitive sense of) autonomy.

On the second reading of the identification condition, I not only acknowledge having a desire, I approve of my having it. But to be autonomous in this way, I would have to be in some sense *perfect* (in my own eyes), since it would be conceptually impossible to have an autonomous desire of which I do not approve. Moreover, the account needs to defend the view that there is something special about the higher order desires we find ourselves with, by virtue of which we approve of our other desires. Mere higher order disapproval amounts to nothing more than a conflict of wants, one at one level and one at another.[12]

Recognizing that there are problems with the condition of authenticity (identification), Dworkin has revised his theory recently and dropped this requirement altogether.[13] His new position is that, irrespective of whether the agent identifies with the desires in question, what is necessary for autonomy is "some ability both to alter one's preferences and to make them effective in one's actions" (17). So identification per se is no longer necessary. This step, which I think is in the right direction, still faces problems. It is true that for many of the preferences that I care most deeply about, I lack, in some way, the ability to reject or alter them. This is because they are too much entrenched into my personality by processes of self-development that I participated in and approved of. But, for example, I would not say that my desire to study philosophical questions, which for me has this character, is not autonomous.[14] My autonomy in that area would only be questionable if the process by which those desires were developed proceeded against my will, as it were.

I turn now to the most serious difficulty. The thrust of the objection is this: we can imagine a person who lives a completely subservient life and who also identifies with the first order desires that comprise such a life. Socialization and fierce conditioning throughout the person's life lead her to adopt, let us say, the life of complete subservience as her true calling. Thus, on the hierarchical analysis, she passes the test of autonomy since her HODs are consistent with her LODs. She approves of the LODs, and identifies with them. However, she is (ex hypothesi) a manipulated individual whose choice of lifestyle and values are not her own in a real sense. Her values, even at the second level, are the blind product of her upbringing and conditioning.

Moreover, as Irvine Thalberg has armed. the condition of Procedural Independence included in the Dworkin model merely introduces an infinite regress. Since the acts of identification must themselves be autonomous, another act of identification taking place at a higher level is required by the theory. And since this act must also be carried out in a way that reflects Procedural Independence, then a fourth level must be postulated, and so on. Hence the regress.[15]

One might be tempted to dodge this charge by dropping the requirement of independence, saying that as long as second order approval has taken place, the person is autonomous. This effectively implies that a person can have autonomous first order desires despite having non-autonomous higher order desires. This introduces what could be labelled the 'ab initio' problem, in that it involves the claim that desires can be autonomous without foundations. But this renders this response implausible on its face, for certainly a person cannot be autonomous at a lower level of desire when those very desires are the result of manipulation further up the hierarchy of preferences. In this way, an account of autonomy should not reduce that characteristic to simply 'radical choice.'

So either the acts of critical reflection which convey authenticity onto the person's desires are autonomous, or they are not autonomous. If they are, then the account of autonomy simply goes back one step and the same question arises at this level. If they are not, then this gives rise to the ab initio problem; i.e., a desire cannot be autonomous if it was evaluated by a desire that was not itself autonomous. Now if it is required that the acts of critical reflection that convey autonomy are themselves autonomous, then either they are autonomous in the *same way* that LODs are autonomous, which gives rise to the regress problem, or they are autonomous in a different way, in which case we are owed an account of this new way. This last possibility raises what we could call the 'incompleteness problem.'

It is important to see how general the regress/ab initio/incompleteness problems are. *Any* account of rational action that presupposes that the desires that move an agent are 'accepted' by her will invite an infinite regress of desires in the explanation of this acceptance. For either a desire descended to the agent without her awareness or approval (which seems a troublesome basis for the rationality of action), the agent was able to judge whether or not this desire was acceptable. If the latter is the case (as must be on hierarchical 'approval' models), then the judgment about the desire will have to be based on (other) desires of the agent. Then the question arises about these new desires and their being approved or not by the agent, from which flows the infinite regress of desires.[16] (Notice that none of these arguments depends on the truth or falsity of determinism.)

As a final attempt to save the model, let us consider a recent attempt by Harry Frankfurt to respond to the infinite regress problem (as it applies to his own model of the person, one which mirrors Dworkin's account of autonomy). Frankfurt's rejoinder pursues the line of the second disjunct above, namely that higher order approval of an act of identification with a desire is not necessary for that identification to indicate the freedom (for our purposes, autonomy) of the agent. The higher order approval which characterizes this identification, however, must be *decisive* for this to suffice for the person's autonomy. An act of identification is 'decisive,' Frankfurt explains, "if and only if it is made without reservation . . . . [that is], it is made in the belief that no further accurate inquiry would require [the person] to change his mind."[17]

Frankfurt goes on to explain and defend this view, but it nevertheless does not look promising as a solution. If by 'decisive approval' Frankfurt means that a person endorses a desire according to the agents own lights and given the information she has and her preferences at the time, then the possibility exists that a thoroughly manipulated individual could be declared autonomous. Imagine someone who has been secretly hypnotized to want strawberries, where the hypnotist includes a directive to ignore any information concerning the hypnosis itself. Such a person would 'decisively' endorse the desire for strawberries and no new information she might gather would dissuade her of her preference. But such a person is surely not autonomous relative to this desire for strawberries. On the other hand, if Frankfurt accepted the judgment that this person is *lacking* autonomy despite the decisive identification with the desire, this would imply that identification is insufficient for autonomy. We would then be left wondering what the missing condition is (that the hypnosis victim lacks). This is another example of the incompleteness problem.[18]

On these models of autonomy, the determination of autonomy can take place simply by *structural* analysis. That is, a person's desires can be determined to be autonomous or not by taking a 'time slice' of the person and asking what her attitude would be about the desires she has at the time (or whether they are integrated).[19] If she identifies with them (or if they cohere), then they pass the test; if not, then she is not autonomous. We have seen, however, that identification in such a context is ambiguous and does not give convincing results concerning a judgment of a person's autonomy. The problem here, I think, is just this 'time slice' approach. What is suggested by the criticisms we have discussed, I would argue, is that what is crucial in the determination of the autonomy of a desire is the manner in which the desire was *formed*— the conditions and factors that were relevant during the (perhaps lengthy) process of coming to have the value or desire. And these conditions may have little to do with how the agent evaluates the desire itself (qua desire).

IV. A new model

To motivate the contours of the new model, we should imagine a person who seems (intuitively and pre-theoretically) an obvious case of someone lacking autonomy. Say a friend or family member has spent two intensive weeks on the grounds of a religious cult and now mindlessly mouths the credo of the sect, showing few signs of her former self. Say that our pre-theoretic reaction to this is to judge that she is not autonomous in expressing these new attitudes. If we were taken to justify our judgment, what sorts of claims would we need to make? Generally, we would have to speculate about the conditions under which her 'character change' has taken place and about what makes them inconsistent with her autonomy. We would have to speculate further that she did not submit to the regimen of 'programming' with the full knowledge of its nature and effects; i.e., it was not part of a strategy of self-change that might have included a decision to pursue a new lifestyle. This suggests that the central focus for autonomy must make particular reference to the processes of preference formation, in particular what makes them 'manipulative' in a way crucially different from 'normal' processes of self-development.

I wish, then, to shift the focus of the inquiry about autonomy to the conditions of the formation of the desire. This will eliminate the need for the condition of identification (as such) altogether. For it will not be crucial to determine what the agent's evaluation of the *desire* is at a particular time. What matters is what the agent thinks about the *process* of coming to have the desire, and whether she resists that process when (or if) given the chance. The conditions of autonomy must, then, set out the conditions that determine the agent's 'participation' in this process of preference formation. We must ask if the person would have or did resist the adoption of a value or desire and for what reasons. In addition, it is relevant whether any factors are present during these (perhaps hypothetical) evaluations which effectively undercut a person's ability to make these judgments about her past. The conditions of the new model of autonomy, then, must attempt to capture this requirement: that the agent was in a position to resist the development of a desire and she did not. This suggests the following conditions:

(i) A person P is autonomous relative to some desire D if it is the case that P did not resist the development of D when attending to this process of development, or P *would not have* resisted that development had P attended to the process;

(ii) The lack of resistance to the development of D did not take place (or would not have) under the influence of factors that inhibit self-reflection;

and

(iii) The self-reflection involved in condition (i) is (minimally) rational and involves no self-deception.

These conditions will be explained and defended. The motivating idea behind the theory is that autonomy is achieved when an agent is in a position to be aware of the changes and development of her character and of why these changes come about. This self-awareness enables the agent to foster or resist such changes. And while doing so the agent cannot be self-deceived or irrational (in a minimal sense). This implies that she must be free from the influence of factors that disrupt these cognitive capacities.

Of course much needs to be explained in these conditions. First, as the second clause of (i) indicates, the test may need to be hypothetical; some individuals may not resist the development of a desire when this occurs, but they *would have* done so under conditions that make this possible. A person 'attends to' the development of a desire when she is in a position to focus on the processes and conditions that led to the adoption of that desire. That is, a relevantly full description of the steps of reasoning or the causal processes that led her to have this desire is available for her possible consideration. This reflectiveness assumes that an agent can become aware of the beliefs and desires that move her to act. Call this the 'transparency' of her motivating reasons. What I mean by this is the ability of an agent to bring to conscious awareness a belief or desire—either in the form of a mental representation or a proposition—concentrate on its meaning.[20] I will say more of this below.

More must be said, then, about what these 'processes' are like and how an agent can make judgments about them. The processes that give rise to a change in desire (or the development of a new desire) are various and can be described at any number of levels. In any case, the process will involve events which are spatio-temporally contiguous with the person which result in a new or altered preference. On the one hand, the process can involve a change in a belief—the agent comes upon new information—where the person can in principle examine the reasons for the new belief and its relation to other things already desired. I may find out that a certain store has a sale going on for an item I want to buy. This creates in me a new desire to go to that store. In these cases, the process—a reasoning process—must be one the agent is guided by without irrationality or self-deception.[21] Preference changes must be the result of deliberations (perhaps hypothetical ones the agent would have if she turned her attention to the question) that do not involve inconsistencies and, by implication, mistakes in logical inference. If they do, then the resulting desire cannot be said to be a true outgrowth of the person as she is—the assortment of her beliefs, desires, and values at a time; for then the desire would have merely a *mistaken* or *inaccurate* connection with these prior beliefs and desires.

In the other kinds of desire formation processes no alteration in the set of beliefs of the agent takes place. The explanations of such preference changes will be purely causal. The reason I have a desire for food right now, for example, is that I haven't eaten since this morning (plus a variety of physical facts about me). No epistemic element is relevant to the explanation of this new desire. In these cases it is hard to be specific about the level of description of these processes that the agent must consider, for theories vary as to the exact causal explanation of these transitions. But I don't think these issues need resolution for our purposes. All that must be hue is that the agent would not resist—that is, take action to counteract—the process, were she to understand it. The level of description, then, can be any one which the agent is capable of considering and which is not patently inconsistent with some verifiably true description at another (deeper) level. For the most part, though, causal processes that do not involve epistemic steps in the development of a desire will not be ones that the agent could resist even if made aware of them. No amount of detailed information about my gastro-intestinal mechanisms will make it possible for me to stop being hungry right now. Hence, this is not an autonomous desire since I would prefer to go on working longer without this nagging urge to eat.

To sum up, the processes that issue in a change in desire for an agent either involve changes in beliefs or they do not. If they do, then the autonomous agent is one whose process of reasoning is internally consistent (in a weak sense). That is, the reasoning process that results in the new preference does not contain manifest contradictions. If the process is purely causal, in the sense that it includes no strictly epistemic steps, then it must not be one that the agent could not resist if she turned her attention to it, if she is to be autonomous in regard to it. But in both kinds of cases, the reflection that is required by autonomy must involve certain cognitive faculties that are characteristic of a person with a settled and accurate conception of herself.

In all these cases of judgment and reflection, certain conditions of normal cognitive functioning are necessary for autonomy to be established. I will now elaborate on the two conditions necessary for adequate self-reflection.

1. RATIONALITY

Many disputes concerning the nature and scope of autonomy turn crucially on the question of whether (and in what sense) an agent must be rational to be autonomous. The question is complicated by the variety of requirements for rationality that are presented and defended. Some views are 'internalist,' like the claim that individuals are rational if they have consistent beliefs and desires,[22] or that the rational agent will choose the best means to maximize expected satisfaction (given an overriding desire to maximize happiness). Other requirements can be considered 'externalist'[23] and are thus more stringent: for example, the requirement that the beliefs upon which an agent's conditional desires rest are based on an (objectively speaking) adequate degree of evidence.

While I cannot argue for it in detail here, I would defend the claim that only minimal 'internal' conditions for rationality (like consistency of beliefs and desires) would be plausible as conditions for autonomy. For to demand more—for example, that one's beliefs (upon which conditional desires rest) be confirmed by objectively relevant evidence—would make the property of autonomy divergent from the idea of *self*-government that provides its intuitive base. Requiring an 'externalist' rationality condition for autonomy implies that people will not be considered autonomous (and therefore not free) even if they are acting on well-formed, considered, and consistent reasons for action.[24] Isaiah Berlin puts the point more forcefully: "once I take this view [that autonomy requires 'externalist' rationality], I am in a position to ignore the actual wishes of men or societies, to bully, oppress, torture them in the name...of their 'real' selves, in the secure knowledge that whatever is the true goal of man (happiness, the performance of duty...) must be identical with his freedom— the free choice of his 'true,' albeit often submerged and inarticulate, self."[25]

The demand that autonomous agents have internally consistent beliefs and transitive desires is in some ways too stringent itself: few of us have examined all our beliefs and preferences and tested them for this standard. And if we did, few if any of us would pass. What this requirement must capture, though, is the necessity that the autonomous person is not being guided by *manifestly inconsistent* desires or beliefs. Those preferences or beliefs that are in obvious conflict, ones which the agent could bring easily to consciousness and recognize as incompatible, are what one would label 'manifestly inconsistent.' This idea will be picked up below in the requirement that the agent cannot be self-deceived to be autonomous.

What this requirement for consistency entails, however, is that the autonomous agent does not act on the basis of mistaken inferences or violation of logical laws. If I believe that 'p' and I believe that 'if p then q,' but I desire something X which is based on the belief that 'not-q,' then the desire for X is not autonomous. These conditions should not be seen as less stringent than, for example, the axioms of standard decision theory, wherein the agent is rational if she chooses the action that will maximize her expected utility. As long as a highest order desire to maximize utility can be attributed to the agent, then the consistency I describe will be achieved only when the agent conforms to this set of requirements.

Nor do I mean to imply here that autonomy only demands the consistency of desires and beliefs about 'means' and says nothing about the ends that an agent may have. The final ends and purposes that an agent has must also be consistent with the rest of the judgments, values, and beliefs to which she has committed herself. And a good deal of conflict at this level can occur within an agent.[26]

What I am ruling out here are conditions that go beyond internal consistency and make the property of being autonomous an open-ended and vague characteristic. If I can always become more autonomous by gathering more evidence, then we would want to know the conditions for when I become 'autonomous enough' to justify the various normative propositions about me that are connected to the question of my autonomy. I reject the externalist rationality condition since I want to develop and defend this threshold of normal autonomy. Moreover, I think that the property of autonomy must not collapse into the property of 'reasonable person' where the idea of being self-governing is indistinguishable from the idea of being, simply, smart.

This requirement of minimal rationality is also better able to capture what is 'heteronomous' about so-called 'compulsive' desires. What is problematic about compulsive desires is not merely that they are compulsive— uncontrollable at the moment of effectiveness—but rather that they often are in manifest conflict with the agent's other desires. To see that compulsiveness alone does not defeat autonomy, consider a sprinter gearing up for the starting gun in a race. At the moment just after the firing of the gun, the desire to run is in every way compulsive and uncontrollable. But we would not call such an agent lacking in autonomy, for this compulsion is part of a consistent strategy undertaken under conditions that meet our historical test set out above (let us imagine). What *would* render the judgment that such a person is not autonomous would be the additional fact that at the moment just after the gun fires, she has another desire *not* to run (say she hears someone yell for her to stop). In that case the irresistible desire to run is not autonomous because of this inconsistency. So only if there is a manifest conflict in the set of desires moving an agent is there a problem with compulsive desires.

In rejecting the externalist rationality requirement, it may seem that I am ignoring the ways that autonomy can be lost as a result of others deliberately manipulating or cutting off a person's access to true information (in ways that still leave the person with a consistent belief set).[27] It is also true that one's desire set is partly related to beliefs one has about what is available, possible, or valuable. Although I do not give the question full treatment here, I think that my general account of autonomy can be applied to belief formation more or less without alteration. One is autonomous if one comes to have one's desires *and* beliefs in a manner which one accepts. If one desires a state of affairs by virtue of a belief which is not only false but is the result of distorted information given to one by some conniving manipulator, one is not autonomous just in case one views such conditions of belief formation as unacceptable (subject to the other conditions I discuss). All that I would reject in this vein is the view that one lacks autonomy *simply* because one's beliefs are false.

2. SELF-AWARENESS

The second cognitive requirement for autonomy is that the (perhaps hypothetical) judgments of the processes of preference formation cannot involve self-deception. I base this claim on the admittedly rough idea that a person is choosing or judging 'for herself' only when she is in tune with the settled aspects of herself that apply to the judgment at hand. This means that the motivating desires and beliefs she has at a time must be 'transparent' to her. They must be relatively easily brought to consciousness and subject to reflection. Hence, self-deception, or exposure to factors which make self-awareness impossible, will be inconsistent with autonomy, since it will rule out the possibility of effective *self*-government. If the 'self' doing the 'governing' is dissociated, fragmented, or insufficiently transparent to itself, then the process of self-determination sought for in a concept of autonomy is absent or incomplete.

According to a penetrating analysis of self-deception by M. R. Haight, self-deception involves, among other things, the strategic refusal on the part of the agent to bring clearly to consciousness a proposition that the agent, for other reasons she accepts, knows to be true. The agent engages in an active process of suppression of facts that are inconsistent with propositions that the agent wants very much to hold onto (a person's belief, for example, that she does not have cancer in the face of a competent doctor's diagnosis).[28] The requirement of self-awareness, then, will resemble minimal rationality rather closely, in that for both conditions the agent is not autonomous if there are beliefs, plausibly attributable to the agent, which are manifestly inconsistent. In the case of self-deception, this inconsistency is 'buried' by the agent's tactics of not focusing her awareness on the suppressed belief. If she faced the evidence for the suppressed proposition squarely, she would realize that there is a direct contradiction between it (along with the suppressed proposition itself) and the 'cover story' she is telling herself.

This condition is also intended to rule out those individuals plagued with severe neuroses, (most cases of) weakness of the will, and simple anomie. When these conditions involve a fragmentation of the self, when the cognitive mechanisms whereby we are normally able to make transparent the desires and beliefs that motivate us are defective, then we are not autonomous. Delusion, paranoia, and other psychopathologies will be inconsistent with autonomy because of the suffering agent's inability to make consistent and reflective judgments about her own set of desires by which she is moved to action. Those individuals, for example, whose suppression of beliefs and desires freeze them to inaction when they are conscious of other reasons they have to act, are not autonomous on the present account. I take this to be a description, albeit a superficial one, of many instances of anomie and weakness of will.[29]

So the test for autonomy is met when the agent would not resist the processes that result in her desire and her lack of resistance is not the product of (minimal) irrationality or self-deception.

V. Avoiding the regress

It should be pointed out that although the condition of 'not resisting the formation of a desire' is a way of avoiding the ambiguities of 'identification,' resisting may in some ways simply be the converse of identifying. The crucial difference, though, is that 'identification' is a relation between the judging person and her *desire*, while 'not resisting' is a relation between the person and the *process* of coming to have the desire. And while it may be the case that a person does not resist a process of desire formation *because* she wants to have the desire in question, what matters for autonomy is that she is not moved by desires whose genesis is outside of her control. I have argued that it is not that I approve of the desire that is crucial but that I was given, by the conditions present, the chance to approve of the *manner* by which I developed the desire.

Now it must be stressed here how this model is able to avoid the regress problem that I suggested faced all other views of autonomy that included conditions of self-appraisal. It seems at first glance as if it may not, for whether or not a person chooses to resist or foster the development of a desire is of course a *choice*, and choices are the result of desires (and beliefs). So the regress threatens again since the question arises whether this desire (the one motivating the choice) is an autonomous one or not. But the claim that all accounts of autonomy that include a condition of self-appraisal are subject to the regress depends on the premise that the only account of the authenticity of the acts of appraisal that comprise autonomy must refer to other preferences of the agent.[30] But as the model put forth here makes clear, this is not the only possibility. For on this view, the regress is cut off at the first level. If the act of appraisal of the processes by which a desire developed in an agent is carried out with sufficient self-awareness and minimal rationality then that act of appraisal (and non-resistance) is sufficient for the autonomy of the desire. The threat of regress is avoided since we do not postulate another level of desire in order to evaluate whether a person resists the development of a desire in question.

Condition (ii) is intended, then, to rule out the possibility of a person's failing to resist the development of a desire, it being the case that this failure was *itself* manipulated. Imagine the new cult member we discussed above. One reason we are inclined to say she is lacking in autonomy is that, although she may well (retrospectively) *not* disapprove of the development of her desires, we are inclined to presume that this second order acceptance is also the result of her conditioning. For a person to be autonomous, it must be hue that during the processes where she might have resisted these developing desires, she wasn't also under the influence of manipulating factors that inhibit the person's ability to reflect on her desires and those processes that helped form them. These will be factors whose presence undermines an agent's rationality and self-awareness, by virtue of which she could critically appraise the development of desires and values she finds herself with.

The essential aspect of such influences, then, will be whether or not they crucially affect a person's *reflective capabilities*—those cognitive capacities we discussed above: minimal rationality and self-awareness (non-self-deception). These capacities enable the agent to appraise and revise certain aspects of herself and the factors which affect her desires and beliefs. Such things as hypnosis, some drugs, certain educational techniques, and the like, have the effect of rendering the agent less able to evaluate, from her own point of view, the processes by which she has come to develop a certain desire or value. Her vision is clouded, as it were. We could call these sorts of factors 'reflection-constraining factors' (RCFs) because of their tendency to reduce the agent's ability to reflect on her own desires.

These factors will be those which vitiate the normal cognitive processes of an agent that involve reflection and evaluation of the agent's own states (what some have called 'meta-cognition'). They disturb the capacities of rationality and self-awareness that are necessary for autonomy. The latter capacity is impaired when the desire(s) that are in fact motivating the agent to act cannot be brought clearly into conscious focus, perhaps because of induced self-denial or merely an inability to concentrate. An example might be the relentless harangue of a cult leader who invokes such fear and anxiety in his listeners that they are unable to step back and reflect on the changes they themselves are going through. The desires they adopt are the result of reducing dissonance (caused by the fear of crossing the guru) more than for reasons they would otherwise accept. This level of anxiety makes the subjects unable to calmly reflect on the process of preference change (or on the desires themselves), and hence self-awareness is made impossible. Similarly, there are crucial differences in pedagogical techniques concerning the ability of students to reflect and critically appraise the educational methods and principles to which they are being subjected. The surer we (observers) are that the student was prevented from so reflecting, the less we can attribute autonomy to her vis-à-vis the resulting desires and values, even if their development is not resisted.

Though it often cannot be known directly whether a person is in a position to reflect clearly, certain indicators of the presence of RCFs and/or the failure of the capacities necessary for autonomy can be listed: failure on the part of the agent to bring (otherwise) salient aspects of a representation or a motivating desire to consciousness;[31] failures of concentration that inhibit the ability to recognize (otherwise) salient relations between aspects of objects or their mental representations; failures in the judgment of (normal) causal and inferential connections between objects or propositions. These indicators are symptoms of the general failure of self-awareness and rationality that autonomy demands.

One question that may arise here, though, is this: if we can stipulate the nature of these factors which inhibit the capacity of a person to reflect on her desire and its genesis, then why not make this simply the sole condition for autonomy? That is, why not quire only that if the person is not under the influence described, then she is autonomous; and if so, then she is not? The reason for resisting this suggestion is simply that people often will subject themselves, in ways and under conditions that manifest autonomy, to factors and influences that severely undercut their reflective capacities. This is done, however, to accomplish things (or states of mind) that cannot otherwise be achieved. People submit to hypnosis to quit smoking, for example, where part of the therapy might be that the agent is less able to re-evaluate the hypnosis itself when it has taken effect (to prevent backsliding, say). Such hypnosis is then a reflection-constraining factor in our sense, but it would be a mistake to call the person's lack of a desire to smoke non-autonomous because of it. Many would report being *more* free as a result, free from the constraining addiction. The utilization of 'self-manipulating' methods of preference change need not vitiate that judgment. What must *not* be true, however, is that the person's judgment and evaluations of her states are *all* the product of these influences. At some point, the person had to have undertaken the exposure to these factors while not under the influence of such factors for her autonomy to be preserved.

So while the descriptions of the various processes by which we come to have a desire are in some sense 'objective' (for example, cognitive scientists might be able to tell us how they operate), the judgment concerning the acceptance or resistance of those processes is *subjective*. How I came to have the desires and values I have is in large part not up to me, but whether I continue to act on them and fail to revise them—make them autonomous—*is* up to me.[32]

It will be instructive to return once again to the example of the 'brainwashed' friend that helped motivate intuitions concerning autonomy. What the present model does is give substance to the pre-theoretic judgment that a critique of the process of value change is needed to support the intuition that the person is not autonomous after the change. The key factor that separates normal autonomy-supporting processes from heteronomous ones is whether the agent was inhibited in her ability to reflect on her own mental states and the forces that affect them. If she were made aware (before the fact) of the ways that the cult members induce change (controlling sleep and eating, denying people contact with friends and relatives, exploiting emotional vulnerabilities of individuals and playing on their fears, etc.), would she resist submitting to these techniques and their effects? And if, after the change, she does not take issue with these processes, is there evidence that the practices destroyed her ability to reflect? Or, further, did her acceptance of these techniques rest on inconsistent beliefs, faulty reasoning or self-deception? If the answer to any of these questions is yes, then we have grounds to consider her non-autonomous. What makes these processes incompatible with autonomy (not to mention pernicious) is not simply that the agent changes her values, or that she is exposed to continuous argumentation, but that she is physically and psychologically being prevented from reflecting on herself and her environment.

It should be emphasized how the model I have defended diverges from the original Dworkin approach. First, the theory developed here focuses crucially on the *formation* of preferences which, I argued, was the true locus of the property of autonomy. Second, the condition of identification as such is no longer required. Third, the description of the illegitimate factors that must be absent for autonomy to be established is spelled out to avoid both the problem of an infinite regress and the 'incompleteness' problem the Dworkin model faced.[33]

VI. Conclusion

The central idea of the new account can be stated in one (rather baroque) sentence: an agent is autonomous vis-à-vis some desire if the influences and conditions that gave rise to the desire were factors that the agent approved of or did not resist, or would not have resisted had she attended to them, and that this judgment was or would have been made in a minimally rational, non-self-deceived manner. One implication of this theory is that people could turn out to be autonomous despite having desires for subservient, demeaning, or even evil things and lifestyles. I don't take this to be a defect of the model. It only reveals that the conception of autonomy we are discussing is "content neutral."[34] There are good theoretical reasons for a content neutral conception, since for any desire (no matter how evil, self-sacrificing, or slavish it might be) we can imagine cases where an agent would have *good reason* to have such a desire. Hence, we can also imagine that the person is autonomously guided by those good reasons in formulating that desire, and so by that token we can imagine it as autonomously formed. So since we can imagine *any* preference as being autonomously formed, given a fantastic enough situation, then it cannot be the content of the preference *itself* that determines its autonomy. It is always the *origin* of desires that matters in judgments about autonomy.

Also, it should be noted here how the account I have developed relates to the guiding assumptions of traditional liberal political theory, in particular its 'atomism.' Some radical critics of liberalism press the claim that since our characters are completely molded by our social and political background, then autonomy in the liberal atomistic sense is a dangerous illusion. It is illusory because it presupposes that we can stand outside of our histories and judge ourselves, and it is dangerous in that it is held up as an ideal which, since it is impossible to attain, merely serves to prop up the (unacceptable) status quo. I have great sympathy for the latter claim, especially when liberal theories do in fact rest on false or illusory presuppositions about human independence. (The examples I would give of this are some versions of microeconomics or political contractarianism which simply assume away the problem of the nature and genesis of preferences.) But the first claim—that people cannot be defined independent of their cultural surroundings and hence that they cannot judge themselves—demands a full-blown social psychological theory to support it. In my own case, for example, the social and political milieu of which I am and have been a part is that of the United States. But given the values and policies dominant here now and in the recent past, this is a culture from which I could hardly before profoundly alienated and of which I could scarcely be more critical. What part of it, then, is so deeply intertwined with my character that I am unable to judge that aspect of myself? We are owed a fairly robust answer to such questions before much of this radical critique of autonomy gets off the ground. Until then, it is still an essential part of any normative political theory to have an account of the authenticity of desires and values of the individuals which are the subjects of those theories.

On the other hand, the 'historical' approach to the notion of autonomy that I defend here is in line with these departures from liberalism. My contention that the formation of desires is what is crucial to their authenticity is similar to the claim that since one's social and cultural history is the determining factor in one's perspective on the world, one can only judge oneself in light of that history and its effect on one's development as a person. However, my view remains 'atomist' in that the fulcrum of the determination of autonomy remains the point of view of the agent herself. I rejected attempts to give a thoroughly externalist or objective account of individual autonomy for the reasons I have described. After all, what I am giving an account of is the property of *individual* autonomy (not 'ideal' autonomy or the autonomy realized in 'true consciousness' or the like). Now I do not pursue the question of whether the circumstances of a modern, patriarchal, capitalist state are such that the conditions for autonomy I describe are systematically denied to large classes of people. But what this model would demand in the name of autonomy are governmental policies whose effect is to leave intact or promote individuals' abilities to reflect on the manner they develop as persons and on the conditions that shape that development.

Notes

1. A version of this paper was read at the Eastern Division meeting of the American Philosophical Association in New York, December 1987. I would like to thank Joel Marks for his comments there. I am especially grateful to Eleonore Stump for a number of conversations and comments on this topic, and to Richmond Campbell, Robert Young and the late Irving Thalberg for their written comments on earlier drafts of the paper. I am also grateful to the editors of the *Canadian Journal of Philosophy* for their helpful comments.

2. For a survey of the various conceptions of autonomy in the recent philosophical literature, cf. John Christman, "Constructing the inner citadel: recent work on autonomy," *Ethics* **99** (1988): 109–24.

3. This is, of course, the sense of 'freedom' relevant to moral and political debates. For a discussion of the various conceptions of freedom in this sense, see W.D. Parent, "Some recent work on the concept of liberty," *American Philosophical Quarterly* 11 (1974): 149–67. The notion of internal and external restraints is explained in Joel Feinberg, *Social Philosophy* (Englewood Cliffs, NJ: Prentice Hall 1973), chap. 1. There Feinberg uses the

terms 'compulsion' and 'constraint' interchangeably, and in doing so, I think he confuses the very issue I discuss.

4. Even if 'internal restraints' are included among the kinds of things that diminish freedom, things like hypnosis or subliminal messages do not, internally or externally, *stop* a person from doing something. Quite the opposite: they *force* a person to (prefer to) do something.

5. *The Theory and Practice of Autonomy* (Cambridge: Cambridge University Press, 1988), 16.

6. Cf. Wright Neely: "freedom is not just a matter of doing as one desires, but requires, in addition, that we should have something to say about what we desire" ("Freedom and desire," *Philosophical Review* **83** [1974] 37). This brings the account of autonomy into line with the debate in the philosophy of the social sciences over the problem of 'endogeneity of preferences.' Cf., for example, Jon Elster, *Sour Grapes* (Cambridge: Cambridge University Press, 1983). Also, for an account of autonomy that resists the reduction to reference only to preferences, see Robert Young, "Autonomy and the inner self," reprinted in John Christman, ed., *The Inner Citadel: Essays on Individual Autonomy* (New York: Oxford University Press, 1989), 77–90.

7. This does not preclude any of a variety of claims about the contingent relation between autonomy and freedom, i.e., that freedom is contingently necessary for the further *development* of a person's autonomy: cf. Robert Young, *Personal Autonomy: Beyond Negative and Positive Liberty* (New York: St. Martin's Press 1986), chap. 2. Similarly, this will not rule out (in fact it complements) the use of the term 'autonomy' to refer to a right to these conditions, or the right to be treated with *respect* for one's capacity to act under such conditions.

8. I say 'belief' here, but for the most part my discussion concerns autonomous *preferences*. Whether or not this model can be applied to belief formation is left open (though see my discussion of this in section IV [1] below). Also, the terms 'desire' and 'preference' are used broadly to mean 'motive,' 'value,' or any 'positively valenced' attitude a person might have vis-à-vis a state of affairs.

9. Dworkin, "The concept of autonomy," in *Science and Ethics*, ed. R. Haller, (Amsterdam: Rodopi, 1981), 212. Dworkin has since published an updated version of this essay where he reverses certain aspects of his view: cf. *The Theory and Practice of Autonomy*, ch. 1. His revisions are treated below.

10. Harry Frankfurt puts forth a similar account in his well known work concerning freedom of the will. Although Frankfurt introduces the notion of 'volitions' to capture those desires that an agent actually wants to issue in action (to be one's will), the components of the theory are essentially the same. And, as we will see, the problems are also the same. Cf. "Freedom of the will and the concept of a person," reprinted in *The Inner Citadel*, ed. John Christman (New York: Oxford University Press, 1989), 63–76.

11. Galen Strawson, *Freedom and Belief* (Oxford: Oxford University Press 1986), 245

12. This is a problem that Gary Watson and others have raised about models such as this: some of the desires we identify with we do so not simply because we desire them but because we view them as desirable, objectively. This suggests at least that the requirement of identification is ambiguous. Cf. Watson, "Free agency," in *The Inner Citadel*, 109–22. Cf. also Irving Thalberg, "Hierarchical analyses of unfree action," in *The Inner Citadel*, 123–36; and Marilyn Friedman, "Autonomy and the split-level self." For another

(albeit unsuccessful, I think) response to the charge that the condition of identification is implausibly vague, cf. Young, *Personal Autonomy*, 43–47.

13. Cf. *The Theory and Practice of Autonomy*, chap. 1. The problems Dworkin adduces with the condition of identification, however, differ from those discussed here.

14. Dworkin comments on disabilities such as these and says that they are compatible with autonomy (ibid., 17). But if that is true, it is not clear what the requirements for the ability in question really are.

15. For a discussion of this charge, cf. Thalberg, 129–35, and Friedman, 22–23. For development of the reply given in the text, cf. John Christman, "Autonomy: a defense of the split-level self," *Southern Journal of Philosophy* **25** (1987) 281–93.

16. Strawson argues along these lines in chap. 2. He concludes, however, that this shows that free action is conceptually impossible. If my arguments below are successful it will be clear that this is not so.

17. "Identification and wholeheartedness," in *Responsibility, Character, and the Emotions*, ed. F. Schoeman, 27–45, at 37 (Cambridge, UK: Cambridge University Press, 1987) 27–45, at 37.

18. Another reading of 'decisive,' however, might be this: in light of an 'objective' analysis of all relevant information having to do with the agent's desire, the agent need go no further in investigating and evaluating her desire. That is, no matter what the agent *herself* knows or wants, there are objectively good reasons for her to identify with the desire in question. This amounts to adding an 'external' rationality condition as a requirement of autonomy. But this move effectively separates the property of autonomy from the actual decisions and judgments of real people; hence, this component of freedom would fail to capture the idea of *self*-government that is the motivating concept behind autonomy. I develop this point in section IV (1) below. Dworkin also discusses these criticisms and responds to them in *The Theory and Practice of Autonomy*, 18–20. However, his response does not, in my view, succeed in galvanizing his theory against the incompleteness problem.

19. Integration views are ones where, for example, "autonomy is achieved in virtue of a…process of integration within a person's hierarchy of motivations, intermediate standards and values, and highest principles" (Friedman, 34). Only when this complete integration takes place—with no level commanding special status in the conferring of autonomy—can we say that a person is autonomous. The major defect in integration views of autonomy, however, is this: a person can be manipulated and conditioned to such an extent that she gains a coherent and integrated set of desires as a result, but one which is totally the result of external manipulation. And it will not do to spread the integration conditions over a person's entire life, saying that a person is autonomous (over her whole life) only if each desire she has conforms to an overall coherent life plan, or in relation to her entire character. Again, a person might have been so severely conditioned to want to do what her brainwashers say she must that she will continue to develop her life along *those very directives* if not otherwise interfered with. An entire life can be 'coherently' manipulated just as a single set of desires can.

20. Herbert Fingarette, in *Self-Deception* (London: Routledge and Kegan Paul, 1969) describes the act of 'spelling out' to oneself one's beliefs. This is similar to what I have in mind here. For a critical discussion of Fingarette, cf. M. R. Haight, *A Study of Self-Deception* (Atlantic Highlands, NJ: Humanities Press 1980), chap. 7. This notion of transparency might be resisted by those influenced by Freud who are convinced that much of

our motivational structure is not immediately transparent to us (without therapy, dream interpretation or the like). I do not wish to dispute this. I only claim here that *insofar as* a person's motives are subject to reflective consideration by the agent under normal conditions, she is autonomous. If therapy is necessary to make this possible, then therapy is necessary to make autonomy possible.

21. Jon Elster, in *Sour Grapes*, provides a topology of changes in belief and desire that is informative here. Some of the changes he labels 'autonomous' and others not.

22. 'Consistent beliefs and desires' is ambiguous in several ways. By 'consistency of beliefs' I mean that the set of beliefs could all be true a single possible world (though as I explain in the text, the consistency requirement I adopt is that there can be no manifest inconsistencies in the belief set). In the case of consistency of preference, it is common to require that they be transitive, complete, and continuous. These are very stringent requirements, though, because most people have not compiled a complete ranking of all the available objects of preference. Hence, by 'consistency of desires' I will mean simple transitivity of those desires plus consistency of the beliefs upon which they rest (if any).

23. The distinction I am describing closely parallels Richard Brandt's distinction between 'subjective' and 'objective' rationality. Cf. Brandt, *A Theory of the Good and the Right* (Oxford: Oxford University Press 1979) 72ff.

24. For consideration of this question, cf. Young, *Personal Autonomy*, chap. 2; Richard Lindley, *Autonomy* (New York: Macmillan, 1986), and Lawrence Haworth, *Autonomy: An Essay in Philosophial Psychology and Ethics* (New Haven, CT: Yale University Press 1986) Part I.

25. "Two concepts of liberty," in *Four Essays on Liberty* (Oxford: Oxford University Press 1969) 133

26. For example, Lawrence Haworth (*Autonomy*, ch. 2) argues that 'full rationality' is a necessary condition for what he calls 'normal autonomy.' Full rationality involves critically analyzing one's ends (as well as beliefs about means) in accordance with one's other beliefs, higher principles and values, future preferences one expects to have, and present preferences one has about the future. Wholesale avoidance of manifest inconsistency of the sort I defend would ensure that this kind of condition is also met.

27. Cf. Elster, *Sour Grapes,* for a discussion of this. I am grateful to Richmond Campbell for calling my attention to the need for this qualification.

28. Cf. Haight, *A Study* of *Self-Deception,* ch. 6

29. For a more detailed analysis of these conditions and their relation to autonomy, cf. Robert Young, "Autonomy and the inner self," *The Inner Citadel*, 81–89.

30. David Zimmerman notices the necessity of this premise and also denies it (though for reasons different from mine). Cf. "Hierarchical motivation and freedom of the will," *Pacific Philosophical Quarterly* **62** (1981) 354–68.

31. For a discussion of this phenomenon within a general theory of self-deception, cf. Robert Audi, "Self deception and rationality," in M. Martin, ed., *Self-Deception and Self-Understanding* (Lawrence, KS: University Press of Kansas, 1985) 169–94.

32. A full defense of my approach to autonomy would involve an exhaustive account and criticism of alternative 'non-subjective' views which this is intended to replace. I cannot give such an exhaustive argument here, though the simple answer to the non-subjectivist could be put as follows: imagine any process which you stipulate as resulting in the subversion of autonomy, and I can imagine a person who (given a

fantastic enough hypothetical situation) would want her choices to be formed that way, and this desire is itself an autonomous one. What follows is that, since for that person, the choice generation procedure is an expression of 'self-government' of the crucial sort, she should not be labeled non-autonomous because she chooses unconventional means for getting what she wants.

33. It may illuminate this suggestion to contrast it with a similar view put forth by Robert Young in "Autonomy and socialization," (*Mind* **89** (1980): 565–76). Young argues that we display autonomy if, after "the processes of our socialization are brought to the level of consciousness...the possibility is there for us either to get free of desires we'd prefer not to have or to identify with previously unrecognized motivations" (573–74). In other words, if our identification with our desires survives bringing to consciousness an awareness of the processes that brought about that desire, the person is autonomous vis-à-vis that desire. This account has much in common with my view, though I avoid the notion of identification and I add conditions to respond to the 'regress' and 'incompleteness' problems. Young's view would still run afoul of the kinds of counterexamples we have discussed if the conditioning has been so fierce as to manipulate identification with the desires even *after* the person gains knowledge of the source of the preference.

34. Cf. Gerald Dworkin's updated view (*The Theory and Practice of Autonomy,* chap. 2) where he also defends a 'content neutral' conception.

18

Responsibility & Globally Manipulated Agents[1]

Michael McKenna

Recently there has been a heightened level of discussion amongst compatibilists and incompatibilist regarding the status of globally manipulated agents. These agents are manipulated not merely by way of causing them to acquire some singular characteristic, such as a particular desire or a new belief. This sort of isolated manipulation is known as *local manipulation*. By contrast, *globally manipulated* agents are covertly "tinkered with" by massive causal influence, influence that results in installing or altering a large swath of their psychological characteristics.

Incompatibilists have exploited variations upon global manipulation cases in an effort to create conditions in which an agent is covertly brought to satisfy and then act from some proposed Compatibilist-friendly Agential Structure (CAS). CAS is meant to provide sufficient conditions for moral responsibility and the freedom required for it. Working with one concrete example or another, incompatibilists proceed to argue as follows:

1) It is intuitively clear that agents so manipulated into satisfying CAS do not act of their own free will and are not morally responsible for what they do.
2) Determinism is in no relevant manner any different than is this sort of manipulation—it is just a different way to bring about the very same result (the satisfaction of CAS).
3) Therefore, CAS is inescapably incomplete; free will and moral responsibility are incompatible with determinism.

Call this the Manipulation Argument (MA). With the conclusion to MA in hand, the incompatibilist further advances her thesis by arguing that some deeper feature of agency is required for free will and moral responsibility, something that is lacking in any version of CAS. This feature will render free will and moral responsibility immune from these troubling manipulation cases. The answer: Morally responsible agents must be the ultimate undetermined originators of their actions; nothing but the agents themselves can settle for them how they shall act and what sorts of persons they shall be.

For instance, Robert Kane develops a version of MA based upon the socially engineered inhabitants of Skinner's Walden Two. His target is Harry Frankfurt's (1971) compatibilist proposal. "All citizens," Kane writes, "can have and do whatever they want or chose; and they can will to do what they want—that is, their first-order desires always conform to their second-order desires" (1996, 65). This is just what is required by Frankfurt's specification of CAS. But, Kane objects, these citizens "lack free will in a deeper sense" (65). And this is because, according to Kane, their wills and purposes are not their own but are instead covertly created by the social engineers who are manipulating them. (See also Pereboom's formulation of MA (2001, 110–7).)

1. Frankfurt's defiant stand

Since it was Frankfurt whom Kane was targeting, it is instructive to consider how Frankfurt would respond to him. In considering a different global manipulation case, Frankfurt writes:

> What we need most essentially to look at is, rather, certain aspects of the psychic structure that is coincident with the person's behavior ....
>
> A manipulator may succeed, through his interventions, in providing a person not merely with particular feelings and thoughts but with a new character. That person is then morally responsible for the choices and the conduct to which having this character leads. We are inevitably fashioned and sustained, after all, by circumstances over which we have no control. The causes to which we are subject may also change us radically, without thereby bringing it about that we are not morally responsible agents. It is irrelevant whether those causes are operating by virtue of the natural forces that shape our environment or whether they operate through the deliberate manipulative designs of other human agents. (2002, 27–8)

How would Frankfurt handle Kane's case of Walden Two? He would deny the first premise of MA and argue that if the people in Walden Two are appropriately manipulated so as to satisfy everything that he demands for CAS, then they do act of their own free will and are morally responsible for their conduct.

Frankfurt's treatment of these sorts of manipulation cases has been received by many with dismay, and he has been accused of biting a gigantic bullet, a mortar shell. Intuition, it is thought, speaks so strongly against Frankfurt's response that either the compatibilists should concede defeat, or instead they should find some other way to resist MA. Rather than accept the counterintuitive result, compatibilists should seek some relevant difference between these globally manipulated agents and merely causally determined agents, thereby resisting the second premise in MA.

In this paper, I offer a modest defense of Frankfurt against several of his compatibilist critics. These critics hold that agents in global manipulation cases like Kane's Walden Two do not act of their own free will and are not morally responsible for what they do. I will not attempt to prove decisively on compatibilist grounds that in these manipulation cases, the agents do act of their own free will and are morally responsible. I will only try to show that the presumption that they clearly are not is overstated. There are ways to accommodate our intuitive uneasiness about these cases in a manner consistent with Frankfurt's assessment of them. I begin with a sketch of the alternative proposal offered by some of Frankfurt's compatibilist critics.

2. Historical considerations and a more cautious compatibilist approach

In roughly the last decade a greater number of compatibilists have found reason to adopt an historical thesis. Although the prospect of an historical compatibilist position had been in the making for some time, three especially compelling historical compatibilist theses have recently emerged, one by John Martin Fischer and Mark Ravizza (1998), another by Ishtiyaque Haji (1998), and yet another by Alfred Mele (1995).[2] Each merits serious attention. For the purposes of this paper, however, the differences between their intriguing views are irrelevant. What does matter is that they defend something like the proposition that the concepts of free will and moral responsibility are historical. Drawing upon the distinction between internalism and externalism, each has argued for some variation upon the claim that an agent's status as free and morally responsible at a time is dependent upon considerations external to the state of the agent at that time—considerations that are compatible with determinism. Just like on certain externalist views, meaning isn't all in the head, neither is free will or moral responsibility. The causal history of how an agent came to be in the relevant internal state at that time also has a bearing on her putative status as a free and morally responsible agent.

To develop their historical theses, these compatibilists distinguish between *current time-slice* or *nonhistorical* properties on the one hand, and *historical* properties on the other (Fischer and Ravizza 1998, 171–3; Haji 1998, 108–9; and Mele 1995, 146–7). The current time-slice or nonhistorical properties are qualities an item has at a time that do not depend upon truths about any earlier time. Being spherical, for example, is a current time-slice or nonhistorical property. Whether an object at a particular time is spherical in no way depends upon any fact about it at any other time. On the other hand, a piece of paper's being a genuine dollar bill, or a burn's being a sunburn requires a particular history.

For instance, in accounting for the historical dimension of autonomy, a near cousin of moral responsibility, Mele requires that an agent not have acquired important elements of her springs of action in a manner that bypassed her ability to evaluate them critically (1995, 131–43). What are these elements?[3] Mele works from the psychologically credible assumption that agents sometimes act from practically unsheddable values and principles. A value or principle is unsheddable for a person at a time if, at that time, under normal psychological conditions, it is not up to her whether or not she holds it (1995, 153–4). For example, it is now not up to me that I value my wife's welfare. I could not simply "will" that her flourishing does not matter to me. It is, for me, a practically fixed feature of my current psychological make up that I love her as I do and therefore value her welfare. A noteworthy feature of unsheddable values and principles as I understand them, one that will figure in subsequent consideration of Mele's view, is that they should not be thought of as functioning the way that a compulsive disorder or a hypnotic suggestion would. For example, persons who act from unsheddable values are not coerced into so acting. And it is consistent with the possession of an unsheddable value that one *not* act upon it, that she acts contrary to what she judges best in light of that value. Thus, the possession of an unsheddable value is not like an "actional straightjacket," not in the way that a compulsive desire is thought to be.

Mele argues that if unsheddable values or principles were installed in a person by means of a process that bypassed her ability to critically assess them, and if she did not participate in the sustaining or preserving them, then when she acts upon them, she does not act of her own free will and is not morally responsible for what she does. This is because she had no opportunity to decide for herself whether or not to take on or preserve these values or principles. Normally developing human persons typically do acquire their values and principles in a manner in which they have the opportunity to reflect upon them, forsake some and embrace others (a process that is compatible with determinism). Over time, some values or principles might solidify into features of a person's character so that in normal psychological circumstances, it is not practically possible to eschew them. Still, when acting from them, there is no reason to think that these agents do not act of their own free wills, or that they are not morally responsible for what they do.

According to the historical compatibilists Fischer and Ravizza, Haji, and Mele, at least one necessary condition of the Compatibilist-friendly Agential Structure (CAS) is an historical one. An agent might come to achieve all of the other necessary conditions for CAS but the historical condition(s), and she would as a result of this failure *not* act of her own free will or be morally responsible for her conduct. These externalist and historical accounts of free will and moral responsibility can be contrasted with Frankfurt's internalist and nonhistorical account. Frankfurt writes:

> …to the extent that a person identifies with the springs of his actions, he takes responsibility for those actions and acquires moral responsibility for them; moreover, the questions of how the actions and his identifications

with their springs are caused are irrelevant to the questions of whether he performs them freely or is morally responsible for performing them (1975, as appearing in Frankfurt, 1988, 54).

So, according to Frankfurt, it matters not a bit how a person came to have the psychic structure that she does have at a moment in time. So long as she satisfies at the proximal time of her action all that on Frankfurt's account is required for CAS, then when she acts from this structure, she does so of her own free will and is morally responsible for what she does.

3. More global manipulation cases used in the service of historical compatibilism

All three of the historical compatibilist positions I have mentioned take it that global manipulation cases like that of Kane's Walden Two provide powerful intuitive support for the historical component of their respective theses. Beginning with the assumption that clearly these sorts of manipulated agents are not free or morally responsible, they reason in roughly the following way: What is wrong in Walden Two is that the process of manipulation whereby persons are brought to satisfy everything that Frankfurt demands for CAS is a process that in some way distorts or impairs the proper historical development of a human person, a development that allows a person to come to be a well functioning morally responsible agent. To press their historical theses, each offers global manipulation cases that are presumed to add intuitive support to the judgment we are supposed to reach about a case like that of Walden Two—that the agents in these manipulation scenarios are not free or morally responsible.

Fischer and Ravizza draw upon the examples discussed by Don Locke. These examples are modifications of ones due to John Wisdom and Richard Taylor (Fischer and Ravizza 1998, 196; and Locke 1975, 104–6). In Wisdom's, the Devil fixes all of a man's desires. In Taylor's, neurologists manipulate desires through manipulating brain states. Locke amends these cases so as to satisfy fully Frankfurt's account of CAS. (The details of Locke's amendments are irrelevant to the point at issue.) Haji works from examples such as his case Psychogen:

> In Psychogen, Jenny (in the absence of her consent or knowledge) is modeled, via transformation psychosurgery, into a psychological twin of Jim the adept financial manager. When, just after awakening from her surgery, Jenny makes a brilliant investment decision and acts on it, we don't think that she is morally praiseworthy for her action. In a sense, we can say that her action is not "truly her own" as it issues from an evaluative

scheme that is not "truly her own"; her engineered-in scheme is unauthentic. Psychogen, then, strongly suggests that moral appraisability presupposes action generated on the basis of an authentic evaluative scheme. (1998, 108)

By appealing to historical considerations unique to each of their respective theories, Fischer and Ravizza, and Haji show why it is that in these cases, like in Kane's Walden Two, the globally manipulated agents featured in them are not free or responsible.

Fischer and Ravizza's case, and also Haji's, would work perfectly well for treatment in the remainder of this paper. But I find the best one, certainly the most entertaining, to be Mele's case involving Ann and Beth (1995, 145). Here is a recent recounting of the case by Mele:

> Ann is a free agent and an exceptionally industrious philosopher. She puts in twelve solid hours a day, seven days a week, and she enjoys almost every minute of it. Beth, an equally talented colleague, values many things above philosophy for reasons that she has refined and endorsed on the basis of careful critical reflection over many years. Beth identifies with and enjoys her own way of life, and she is confident that it has a breadth, depth, and richness that long days in the office would destroy. Their dean wants Beth to be like Ann. Normal modes of persuasion having failed, he decides to circumvent Beth's agency. Without the knowledge of either philosopher, he hires a team of psychologists to determine what makes Ann tick and a team of new-wave brainwashers to make Beth like Ann. The psychologists decide that Ann's peculiar hierarchy of values accounts for her productivity, and the brainwashers instill the same hierarchy in Beth while eradicating all competing values—via new-wave brainwashing, of course. Beth is now, in the relevant respect, a "psychological twin" of Ann. She is an industrious philosopher who thoroughly enjoys and highly values her philosophical work. Largely as a result of Beth's new hierarchy of values, whatever upshot Ann's critical reflection about her own values and priorities would have, the same is true of critical reflection by Beth. Her critical reflection, like Ann's, fully supports her new style of life.
>
> Naturally, Beth is surprised by the change in her. What, she wonders, accounts for her remarkable zest for philosophy? Why is her philosophical work now so much more enjoyable? Why are her social activities now so much less satisfying and rewarding than her work? Beth's hypothesis is that she simply has grown tired of her previous mode of life, that her life had become stale without her recognizing it, and that she finally has come fully to appreciate the value of philosophical work. When she carefully reflects on her values, Beth finds that they fully support a life

dedicated to philosophical work, and she wholeheartedly embraces such a life and the collection of values that supports it. (2006)

Poor Beth. It is clear that something is very wrong in the way that the dean handled Beth. The question, however, is what is wrong about it, and how ought we to understand Beth and her conduct now that she is this "revised" person?

Consider how Mele treats the case of Beth, and note that he takes it as *evidence in support of an historical conclusion* that we should judge that Beth is not autonomous (free and responsible):

> Ann, by hypothesis, freely does her philosophical work; but what about Beth? In important respects, she is a clone of Ann—and by design, not accident. Her own considered values were erased and replaced in the brainwashing process. Beth did not consent to the process. Nor was she even aware of it; she had no opportunity to resist. By instilling new values in Beth and eliminating old ones, the brainwashers gave her life a new direction, one that clashes with the considered principles and values she had before she was manipulated. Beth's autonomy was violated. And it is difficult not to see her now, in light of all this, as heteronomous—and unfree—to a significant extent in an important sphere of her life. If that perception is correct, then given the psychological similarities between the two agents, the difference in their current status regarding freedom would seem to lie in how they *came* to have certain of their psychological features, hence in something *external* to their present psychological constitutions. That is, the crucial difference is *historical*; free agency is in some way history-bound. (2006)

It is especially important to note that Mele is not drawing the conclusion that Beth is not autonomous—not free and responsible—on the basis of other considerations meant to establish an historical conclusion, considerations then brought to bear on the case of Beth. Rather, *because* we think that Beth is not free and responsible we are *thereby* supposed to draw historical conclusions about the nature of free and responsible agency. Well, must we?

4. A detour: historical manipulation cases

Before considering whether a compatibilist must respond to a case like that of Mele's Beth by drawing historical conclusions, it is worth considering other sorts of global manipulation cases. For it might be thought that the historical compatibilist takes herself to be immune to *any* global manipulation case. In my estimation, it is important for all compatibilists to grant that there is no way to foreclose the possibility that the causes figuring in the creation of a determined morally responsible agent could be artificially fabricated, that is, could be produced by a process of global manipulation. Should the compatibilists rest their thesis on a denial of this proposition, *surely they will fail*. Why? It is at least metaphysically possible to bring about relevantly similar causal processes to those arising from a determining world (see McKenna 2004, 216–7). For example, couldn't an incompatibilist like Kane simply revise the example he works from and fashion an instance of MA that includes the addition of any compatibilist-friendly historical requirements, whether it is Fischer and Ravizza's, Haji's, or Mele's? If so, wouldn't the historical compatibilists then *have* to grant that sometimes an agent when appropriately manipulated is no different than a determined agent? Hence, they too would be willing to grant the second premise of MA, just like Frankfurt was willing to do in the face of a nonhistorical example like Walden Two. In these historical cases, just like Frankfurt responded to the nonhistorical case, the historical compatibilists would have to deny premise one of MA and argue that agents so manipulated into satisfying their preferred historical versions of CAS *do* act of their own free will and *are* morally responsible for that they do. In fact, this is just how both Fischer and Mele have handled this sort of consideration.

In a published exchange between Fischer and members of an audience, following Fischer's reply to a criticism put to him by Kane, Carl Ginet presented Fischer with an example that speaks directly to this dialectical situation. Ginet said:

> I would like to lay on John a wild example, maybe the ultimate manipulation scenario. In your treatment of [Kane's] Walden Two case you say, "Well I have hope that we can find some relevant difference that will strike us all, some account of the difference." I was thinking about your response to that kind of example and I thought, well, here is the example we really need: Suppose there are some super-human intelligences somewhere in the galaxy and they come to understand the laws of nature thoroughly. Suppose that determinism is true. At least they understand enough about the laws of nature that when they look at what happened on our planet they can understand exactly why everything happens. They can explain it causally. So one of them decides to run a sort of super Truman Show. What they do is they take an actual human life and observe it from the beginning. Then they say, we are going to reproduce that life in all its details. And they do. They know in advance how to do it. They are super human intelligences and can hold in their minds all of the details. They can create an embryo, etc., the same environment of the actual normal person. It could have been you, or me. Now here, I take it that there are no relevant differences to the history of the person or their surroundings. I myself have a clear intuition that in this Super Truman Show the person is not morally responsible for any of their actions. ([my braces] 2000, 414–5)

Perhaps one might think that Fischer would resist Ginet by arguing that there is some relevant difference between a person merely determined to live that life and one who is manipulated via a Truman Show type scenario into living out that history. Thus, in this case as well, Fischer would be denying premise two of a suitably amended instance of MA. But this is not the strategy Fischer adopts. Here is how he responds to Ginet's Super Truman Show example:

> Yes, that is where we disagree. I think that it shows why you are naturally inclined toward incompatibilism and I am naturally inclined toward compatibilism. My intuition is that the world you describe might be the actual world, if there is a God and God has certain kinds of knowledge and set it up to work in a certain way. My own intuition is that it might have been the case that God set up the world and knew in advance its entire history, maybe middle knowledge or some other mechanism. But as long as what we do issues from reasons-responsive mechanisms [Fischer's demand for CAS], it does not eliminate our responsibility. (2000, 415)

Clearly, Fischer grants that *some* instances of global manipulation are freedom and responsibility conferring.

Interestingly, Mele has very recently fashioned an argument that builds from a case that is strikingly like Ginet's Super Truman Show example. Here is his example:

> Diana creates a zygote Z in Mary. She combines Z's atoms as she does because she wants a certain event E to occur thirty years later. From her knowledge of the state of the universe just prior to her creating Z and the laws of nature of her deterministic universe, she deduces that a zygote with precisely Z's constitution located in Mary will develop into an ideally self-controlled agent who, in thirty years, will judge, on the basis of rational deliberation, that it is best to A and will A on the basis of that judgment, thereby bringing about E. If this agent, Ernie, has any unsheddable values at the time, they play no role in motivating his A-ing. Thirty years later, Ernie is a mentally healthy person who regularly exercises his powers of self-control and has no relevant compelled or coercively produced attitudes. Furthermore, his beliefs are conducive to informed deliberation about all matters that concern him, and he is a reliable deliberator. So he satisfies a version of my proposed compatibilist sufficient conditions for having freely A-ed. (2006)

Using this example to support the first premise, Mele sketches the following argument for incompatibilism, *The Zygote Argument*:

1. Because of the way his zygote was produced in his deterministic universe, Ernie is not a free agent and is not morally responsible for anything.

2. Concerning free action and moral responsibility, there is no significant difference between the way Ernie's zygote comes to exist and the way any normal human zygote comes to exist in a deterministic universe.

3. So determinism precludes free action and moral responsibility. (2006)

Notice that premises one and two of Mele's Zygote Argument are very similar to the premises of MA.[4]

Mele proceeds to argue that premise two of the Zygote Argument is true. He agrees that there is no way for the compatibilist to foreclose the metaphysical possibility that the causes figuring in the creation of a determined morally responsible agent could be artificially fabricated. As regards premise one of the argument, Mele writes:

> If it is assumed that premise 2 is true, what should compatibilists say about premise 1? They should say that it is false. Compatibilists believe that there are free, morally responsible agents in some deterministic worlds and that the zygotes of many of them, at least, come to be in the normal way. Given their compatibilism and the assumption that premise 2 is true, Ernie should strike them as free and morally responsible (in light of his properties as an agent). (2006)

So Mele, like Fischer, agrees that ultimately, when pressed with the right sort of case, the compatibilist—even the historical compatibilist—must accept the possibility that a properly globally manipulated agent might turn out to be one who acts of her own free will and is morally responsible for what she does.[5]

It should not be taken as a weakness of Fischer's or Mele's position that it cannot stave off *any* manipulation case. It is merely a mark of the subtlety of each position that each has the resources to handle different sorts of manipulation cases differently.[6] Once the requisite historical considerations are factored into the examples, perhaps there is no longer great intuitive weight speaking against the judgment that the agents featured in them are free and responsible. On the other hand, it is noteworthy that, ultimately, even the finest efforts to advance compatibilism along historical lines require that sometimes a proper response to a carefully crafted instance of MA involves accepting that the agent featured in it is free and responsible. This should give the compatibilist some reason to look very carefully at the nonhistorical cases like Fischer and Ravizza's Devil/Neurologist, Haji's Psychogen, or Mele's Ann and Beth. For, recall, our intuitions about the nonhistorical cases are alleged by the historical compatibilists to help establish the historical thesis. It is not that the historical thesis is demonstrated on other grounds and so helps us to draw intuitive judgments about them. This invites the question, is there any other way to explain our intuitive resistance to judging globally manipulated agents free and morally responsible in the nonhistorical cases? If so, then the cases might not speak so forcefully for the historical thesis after all.[7]

5. Suzie Instant: the case of a free and responsible globally manipulated agent?

Mele claims that it is difficult not to see Beth as unfree in a significant sphere of her life. Let me see if I can make it less difficult. Let us restrict our attention to the sphere of Beth's life that issues from her unsheddable values. To begin, I remind the reader of a consideration that is easy to lose sight of in this sort of dialectic. As pointed out above, these constituents in the mental economy of a well-functioning agent should not be thought of like irresistible desires or compulsive disorders. They are not actional straightjackets. A person might have a value that is unsheddable for her, maybe even one that counts for her as a deep value (one that helps guide her in settling upon how to live her life), and it might be that in relevant circumstances, she acts contrary to its prescriptions. This could be because she acts from weakness of will, or because she has other competing values that conflict with it (due to some unexpected contingency), or for any other of a number of considerations. But the key point here is that if an agent possesses a certain sort of control over her conduct that she can exercise strongly or weakly, or even just unexpectedly (maybe out of curiosity to see how her life might go if she placed less emphasis on a certain value), then she might be able to control her own conduct in such a way that she does not act upon values—even deep values—that for her are unsheddable.

I want to get to the case of Ann and Beth indirectly. So set it aside just for the moment. Consider instead a different case completely unrelated to the Ann and Beth case. Consider instead the case of Suzie, who is created by a god at an instant and who is placed in a determined world. Suzie is created to be a psychologically healthy woman indistinguishable from any other normally functioning thirty-year-old person whom any of us might encounter. To get this result, she is given a huge set of beliefs according to which she has lived a normal human life for thirty years. For instance, she believes (falsely) that she had a twelfth birthday and that her daddy bought her a pony. Furthermore, Suzie has some range of values and principles that are unsheddable. In Suzie's case, she has a set of false beliefs about how she came to acquire her now unsheddable values. She thinks that she acquired them through a process of sustained effort over the years leading up to what she thinks is her thirtieth. She takes pride in this fact and believes that she is responsible for this process and that she engaged in it freely. (On this point, clearly she is mistaken.) Also, assume that she is a richly self-controlled person who is able to resist the inclination to act with weakness of will (a nonhistorical requirement

Mele specifies for CAS, 1995), that she satisfies something like Frankfurt's hierarchical account of freely willed conduct (Frankfurt 1971). Furthermore, she is reasons-responsive in the manner that Fischer and Ravizza (1998) and also Haji (1998) require (*sans* any historical component). In short, Suzie satisfies the juiciest nonhistorical demands of the Compatibilist-friendly Agential Structure. Add to all of this the fact that she has a robust and relatively consistent range of beliefs about her history (which for her are false), like those that any psychologically healthy person would have.

Now suppose that Suzie is presented with the option to do one of two things, A or B. One option, B, involves a violation of a value that is unsheddable for her. The other option, A, involves acting from one of her unsheddable values. Suzie A's, acting as her unsheddable value counsels. Supposing that compatibilism is true, it is not clear to me that Suzie did not act freely or responsibly. I can't see how a causal history that zeroed in on this Suzie all in an instance—let us just call her Suzie Instant—renders Suzie Instant unfree in a way that she would not be if instead some causal history or other unfolded over the course of thirty years. Note that, as I have been careful to point out, when Suzie A'ed from her unsheddable value, she was *not* compelled to do so. Her doing so was *nothing like* acting upon an irresistible desire. It would be natural to say that she A'ed freely—in at least some non-question begging, restricted sense of freely, say freely*.

To press the point, suppose that every now and then this same god who created Suzie Instant visits another possible world and there creates another thirty-year-old Suzie, Suzie Normal, in the normal zygote manner. Other times she creates a (seemingly) thirty-year-old Suzie, Suzie Instant, at an instant. Now suppose that Suzie Normal at the age of thirty arrives at the precise point where she comes to be a nonhistorical duplicate of Suzie Instant. Suzie Normal faces the exact same choice between options A and B as Suzie Instant faces. Just like Suzie Instant, Suzie Normal opts to do A. If we agreed with Mele's results of the Zygote Argument, it seems that compatibilists should be prepared to say that Suzie Normal A'ed of her own free will and is morally responsible for doing so. The crunch is now upon us: How is it that Suzie Instant is rendered not free and morally responsible when she A's at the relevant time merely by virtue of the fact that the causal history giving rise to her action came compressed in a momentary package where Suzie Normal's history chugged along over the course of thirty years? A difference here seems arbitrary.[8]

6. If Suzie Instant is free and responsible, why not Mele's Beth?

Suppose that it is arbitrary to claim that Suzie Instant is not free and responsible but Suzie Normal is. Here we have a case and some attendant intuitions speaking on behalf of a nonhistorical conclusion as regards the case of Suzie

Instant. But of course, intuitions about varying cases can compete. So it is time for Suzie Instant, Suzie Normal, Ann, and Beth to meet. Let's start with Suzie Instant and Ann, and let us stick with a case in which each A as opposed to B in such a way that their respective acts of A'ing issue from their respective unsheddable values. Recall, unlike Beth, Ann acquired her wonderful professorial values under her own steam, with the sort of history that Mele finds to be freedom and responsibility conferring. Suppose that by mere cosmic accident, not even by the intentional design of the god who brought Suzie Instant into existence, Suzie Instant is a nonhistorical qualitative duplicate of Ann. She is so right down to her (false) beliefs about her history. If Ann recalls the hours of labor she spent knocking out her last article, Suzie Instant (falsely) recalls the hours of labor that she thinks she spent. Her psychic life, her memory of how she came to be is just as Ann's is. I submit that if Ann and Suzie Instant behaved in the same ways in the same circumstances, Suzie Instant's conduct should be regarded as free and responsible if Ann's is. If this result seems dubious, just start one step away from this. Make the cosmic accident that this god created Suzie Normal to be a qualitative duplicate of Ann, living out the very same life and history as Ann right up to the moment when Ann A's instead of B's. If we agree with the results of Mele's Zygote Argument, we should be prepared to treat the case of Suzie Normal no differently than we treat the case of Ann. But now, as I have argued above, we should treat the case of Suzie Instant no differently than we treat the case of Suzie Normal. Hence, we should treat Suzie Instant's case no differently than we treat Ann's.

But now, *if* we have established that we should treat the case of Suzie Instant no differently than we treat the case of Ann (and I do not mean to suggest that we have established this point), what are we to make of our intuitions about poor Beth? Should we use the leverage established with the Suzie Instant case to push a similar treatment in the case of Beth? *If* so, we could force the conclusion that when Beth A's, she should be regarded as free and responsible, just like Ann and Suzie Instant. Or should we use our resistance to treating Beth as A'ing freely and responsibly as leverage to draw historical conclusions? Then we could instead force the conclusion that Suzie Instant is not free and morally responsible in her A'ing, despite the seemingly arbitrary differences between Suzie Instant and Suzie Normal.

I fear that this could quickly degenerate into a stalemate with no resources for settling the matter beyond the tug of competing intuitions elicited by competing examples. I would like to offer further considerations on behalf of the nonhistorical compatibilist like Frankfurt that might help pull the case of Beth into the nonhistorical camp, allowing it to be claimed, without alarming counterintuitive results, that Beth A's freely and is morally responsible for doing so.

How are we to do this? To begin, if the case of Beth or any like case is to do the work that the historical theorists want it to do, we have always to hold firmly in our minds when thinking about the case that the agent in question, Beth in this case, satisfies the very richest of compatibilist-friendly nonhistorical properties. In these terms, she is *just as* morally competent of an individual as any other who comes to be so through a "proper" history. This is one reason that I take it to be especially important to emphasize that acting upon unsheddable values is not like a case of compulsion or acting from an irresistible desire. Thinking in these terms, ask yourself how indeed *you* would think of and respond to Beth or to Suzie Instant were you to have a certain moral transaction with one of them.[9] Imagine the case even as one in which you were informed of Beth or Suzie Instant's bizarre causal history. Would it be realistic not to make relevant moral demands of them, not to be prepared to respond with appropriate morally reactive attitudes in response to certain sorts of actions? A quick reaction might suggest that it would be realistic. But fill out the case just a bit, imagine a moral transgression, a direct harm done to one of your children; or a morally laudatory act, a sincere offer to render aid to another clearly in need. Would the fact that Beth or Suzie Instant came about in such a weird manner truly give you sufficient reason to conclude that they are not morally responsible (blameworthy or praiseworthy) *for what they did*, and should not be treated accordingly? Intuitions waiver here. It can seem quite credible to claim that the right way to think of either and to respond to either would be to see either as a "real" person, that is, a fully competent moral agent. Of course, these considerations hardly tip the scale in favor of the nonhistorical compatibilist. But there is more to say.

One consideration that seems to be overlooked in these discussions is that there are more moral judgments to go around than those that have to do just with the relevant action figuring in the manipulation case at issue. The relevant action in the case of Ann, Beth, and Suzie Instant is A'ing in accord with some unsheddable value. Of course, there are intuitively jarring features in the case of Beth (less so for the case of Suzie Instant). But these can be accommodated by calling attention to *further* judgments of freedom and responsibility beyond those that concern the act of A'ing. One clear difference between Ann on the one hand, and both Beth and Suzie Instant on the other, is that Ann is morally responsible for coming to have the unsheddable values that she has, as well as, presumably, other features of her character. She acquired these characteristics of her own free will. Beth and Suzie Instant did not. The nonhistorical compatibilist who wishes to push a Frankfurt-style hard-line reply in the cases of Beth and Suzie Instant can argue that Ann, Beth, and Suzie Instant are all equally free and equally morally responsible *with respect to their acts of A'ing*. But Ann is free and morally responsible for more than what Beth and Suzie Instant are free and morally responsible for. What explains away the counterintuitive appearance of the judgment that Beth is free and morally responsible for A'ing is a failure to give sufficient attention to this fact.

But there is yet more to be said to distinguish the cases. Beth, unlike either Ann or Suzie Instant, was dorked with in a highly objectionable way. (Some might be inclined to a more evocative four letter word than "dork.") She was coerced into possessing unsheddable values that were in conflict with other values that, presumably, she did acquire of her own free will—her pre-dorked-with values. She was robbed of these other values, ones she invested her self in. In this way, Beth *was done wrong*. Something about her own self was taken from her.[10] (And, as Jimmy Hendrix might put it, "That ain't too cool.") Perhaps part of our reluctance to treat Beth as freely and responsibly A'ing is that we wrongly think that in making such a judgment, we are not recognizing the quite clear violations of Beth's rights as a person. But we can recognize that Beth freely and responsibly A'ed and *still* draw appropriate moral judgments about the moral wrongs done to Beth and how she deserves to be treated in light of that history. What, we might ask, could count as a proper moral response to Beth for her having suffered from someone else deciding for her what kind of person she should be? This question can be given a rich answer even if, now that she is this different (sort of) person, we are warranted in thinking that she is a person who acts freely and responsibly for what she now does.[11]

I hope that I have said enough to show that the nonhistorical compatibilist is not without resources to handle relevant global manipulation cases via a Frankfurt-style hard-line reply, despite the fact that other compatibilists take these cases as strong evidence for an historical conclusion. First of all, some cases, such as the one involving Suzie Instant and Suzie Normal, invite a nonhistorical conclusion, not an historical one. These help place pressure on examples like Mele's example of poor Beth, gently inviting the thought that perhaps, as peculiar as it might seem, Beth does act freely and is morally responsible when she A's. Naturally, such a thought is not conclusive. The historical theorists will want to push in the other direction, *from* the case of Beth, *to* the case of Suzie Instant.

But the nonhistorical compatibilist has more to say beyond calling attention to competing intuitions about cases. She can attempt to draw further differences in our judgments about Ann, Beth, and Suzie Instant beyond those regarding questions about their freedom and responsibility with respect to their acts of A'ing. Focusing upon these further considerations might help lessen the counterintuitive appearance of the claim that agents like Beth and Suzie Instant are just as free and responsible for their acts of A'ing as someone like Ann is.

8. Conclusion

Many philosophers have recently denounced Harry Frankfurt's tough stand on certain manipulation cases, arguing contrary to Frankfurt that the agents featured in them do not act of their own free will and are not morally responsible for what they do. Many of Frankfurt's compatibilist critics have instead culti-vated historical theses, and they have used these sorts of manipulation cases as evidence in support of their historical compatibilist accounts. In this paper I have argued that Frankfurt has a reasonable basis for his treatment of these cases. There are cases of global manipulation, such as that of Suzie Instant, in which it is not at all clear why the agent would not be regarded as free and responsible. Furthermore, in the cases in which it *seems* clear that the agents featured in them are not free and responsible, as in Mele's case of Beth, there are relevant moral judgments one can identify that help to ameliorate the intuitive uneasiness of judging such agents as free and responsible for their "manipulated" actions. Sometimes these further judgments concern the dis-tinct point that an agent like Beth or Suzie Instant is not morally responsible for coming to be who she is (where another agent like Ann is). Sometimes these further judgments concern the distinct judgment that an agent like Beth was done wrong in being psychically violated. The crucial point is that there is a way to lessen the force of the indictment against Frankfurt.

Notes

1. I am grateful to John Martin Fischer, Ishtiyaque Haji, Alfred Mele, Kristen Mickelson, Cyrus Panjvani, Derk Pereboom, Matt Talbert, and Manuel Vargas for com-ments on an earlier draft of the original paper, which appeared in *Philosophical Topics* 32 (2004): 169–92. The current, abridged piece is reprinted with kind permission from the editors and University of Arkansas Press.

2. So as not to mislead, Mele himself wishes to remain agnostic about the truth of compatibilism. Without endorsing it, he means only to work out a credible version of it.

3. For ease of presentation, in the remainder of this paper I will set aside Mele's dis-cussion of autonomy and shall present his treatment as it applies directly to free will and moral responsibility (though this will involve a slight albeit harmless misrepresentation of his position).

4. Recently, Berofsky has constructed a different sort of example that generates results much like the example Mele uses (Berofsky, 2005). Berofsky imagines an omni-scient global controller who has control over early environment and wants to get an agent to act in a certain way later in life. To achieve this result without impairing the agent's ability to evolve historically in normal and psychologically healthy ways, the control-ler must over later times manipulate future environmental conditions so as to allow the agent to evolve properly, and thereby have the right sort of history. Yet still, the agent is manipulated in the sense that the agent eventually comes to the actional juncture at which she does just what the manipulator arranged for her to do.

5. Here is one minor qualification about Mele's use of the zygote example: Mele takes care to insure that when Ernie A's and thereby brings about E, he does not act from any unsheddable values in A'ing. But if, in creating Z in Mary, Dianna created a causal path-way whereby at earlier stages in his life, Ernie came to accept certain values through a process of critical reflection; and if those values later in his life became unsheddable for

Ernie; and if these unsheddable values in turn figured in Ernie's A'ing; then the compatibilist should be just as prepared to accept that Ernie A'ed of his own free will and was morally responsible for doing so. In written correspondence, Mele agrees with this point.

6. For a further development of this compatibilist strategy see Haji and Cuypers (2004).

7. After completing this paper, I learned that Manuel Vargas also adopts a strategy similar to the one I have developed here. See his "On the Importance of History for Responsible Agency" (2004).

8. For an impressive treatment of agents like Suzie Instant, see David Zimmerman's excellent paper, "Born Yesterday: Personal Autonomy for Agents Without a Past" (1999).

9. Ish Haji has offered a friendly warning about the point developed in this paragraph. He rightly points out that there is a distinction between what he calls "overt blame" and the status of being blameworthy—the latter being a status a person can satisfy even if further variables make it so that it would not be morally justified for one (or anyone) to overtly blame the person. (A similar point could be made for praise.) One might resist the point made in this paragraph by agreeing that in such a bizarre situation it could be regarded as reasonable or even morally justified to overtly blame Beth or Suzie Instant, but this would not by itself prove that Beth or Suzie Instant *is* blameworthy. Agreed. But the point I wish to make here is a gentle one. I do not mean to claim that an inclination to think it proper to overtly blame Beth or Suzie Instant would be decisive grounds to conclude that either is blameworthy. I mean only that the former is suggestive that the latter might not be as far fetched as some see to think it is. For, while it is true that the conditions for overt blame (even justified overt blame) can come apart form the conditions for blameworthiness, the default presumption is that it is only justified to overly blame those who are blameworthy.

10. Nomy Arpaly makes a similar point about these sorts of cases (2003, 128).

11. It is worth asking, how would Beth regard herself from her own point of view? Given that she now is this "new person," how would she think of her own agency in terms of her freedom or responsibility, and how would she wish others to treat her?

References

Arpaly, Nomy. 2003. *Unprincipled Virtue: An Inquiry into Moral Agency*. New York: Oxford University Press.

Berofsky, Bernard. 2005. "Global Control and Freedom," *Philosophical Studies* 131.2: 419–445.

Buss, Sarah, and Lee Overton. eds. 2002. *Contours of Agency: Essays on Themes from Harry Frankfurt*. Cambridge, MA: MIT Press.

Fischer, John Martin. 2000. "Excerpts from John Martin Fischer's discussion with members of the audience," *Journal of Ethics* 4: 408–17.

Fischer, John Martin, and Mark Ravizza. 1998. *Responsibility and Control: An Essay on Moral Responsibility*. Cambridge: Cambridge University Press.

Frankfurt, Harry. 1971. "Freedom of the will and the concept of a person," *Journal of Philosophy* 68: 5–20.

Frankfurt, Harry. 1975. "Three concepts of free action," *Proceedings of the Aristotelian Society*. Reprinted in Frankfurt 1988, 47–57.

Frankfurt, Harry. 1988. *The Importance of What We Care About*. Cambridge: Cambridge University Press.

Frankfurt, Harry. 2002. "Reply to John Martin Fischer," in Buss and Overton, eds., 2002.

Haji, Ishtiyaque. 1998. *Moral Appraisability*. New York: Oxford University Press.

Haji, Ishtiyaque and Stefaan Cuypers. 2004. "Responsibility and the problem of manipulation reconsidered," *International Journal of Philosophical Studies* **12**: 439–64.

Kane, Robert. 1996. *The Significance of Free Will*. Oxford: Oxford University Press.

Locke, Don. 1975. "Three concepts of free action: I," *Proceedings of the Aristotelian Society*, suppl. **49** 95–112.

McKenna, Michael. 1998. "The limits of evil and the role of moral address: a defense of Strawsonian compatibilism," *Journal of Ethics* 2: 123–42.

McKenna, Michael. 2004. "The relationship between autonomous and morally responsible agency," in *Personal Autonomy*. ed., J. S. Taylor, 2004, 205–34.

Mele, Alfred. 1995. *Autonomous Agents*. New York: Oxford University Press.

Mele, Alfred. 2006. *Free Will and Luck*. New York: Oxford University Press.

Pereboom, Derk. 2001. *Living Without Free Will*. Cambridge: Cambridge University Press.

Schoeman, Ferdinand, ed. 1987. *Responsibility, Character, and the Emotions: New Essays in Moral Psychology*. Cambridge: Cambridge University Press.

Taylor, James Stacey, ed. 2004. *Personal Autonomy*. New York: Cambridge University Press.

Vargas, Manuel. 2004. "On the importance of history for responsible agency," *Philosophical Studies* 127.3: 351–382.

Wallace, R. Jay. 1994. *Responsibility and the Moral Sentiments*. Cambridge, MA: Harvard University Press.

Wolf, Susan. 1987. "Sanity and the metaphysics of responsibility," in *Responsibility, Character, and the Emotions: New Essays in Moral Psychology*, ed. Ferdinand Schoeman, New York: Cambridge University Press, 1987.

Zimmerman, David. 1999. "Born yesterday: personal autonomy for agents without a past," *Midwest Studies in Philosophy* 23: 236–66.

PART 8

Suggested Further Readings

VIII. Autonomy and History

Cuypers, Stefaan. 2006. "The trouble with externalist compatibilist autonomy," *Philosophical Studies* 129:171–96.

Fischer, J. M. 2004. "Responsibility and manipulation," *The Journal of Ethics* 8: 145–77.

Haji, Ishtiyaque. 2008. "Authentic springs of action and obligation," *The Journal of Ethics* 12:239–61.

Haji, Ishtiyaque and Stefaan E. Cuypers. 2004. "Moral responsibility and the problem of manipulation reconsidered," *International Journal of Philosophical Studies* 12.4: 439–64.

McKenna, Michael. 2008. "A hard-line reply to Pereboom's four-case manipulation argument," *Philosophy and Phenomenological Research* 76: 142–59.

Mele, Alfred. 1995. *Autonomous Agents*. New York: Oxford University Press.

Mele, Alfred. 2008. "Manipulation, compatibilism, and moral responsibility," *The Journal of Ethics* 12:263–86.

Pereboom, Derk. 2008. "A hard-line reply to the multiple-case manipulation argument," *Philosophy and Phenomenological Research* 77/1: 160–70.

Russell, Paul. 2010. "Selective hard compatibilism," in Joseph Campbell, Michael O'Rourke and Harry Silverstein, eds., *Action, Ethics and Responsibility: Topics in Contemporary Philosophy*, Vol. 7. Cambridge, MA: MIT Press.

Shabo, Seth. 2010. "Uncompromising source incompatibilism," *Philosophy and Phenomenological Research* 80.2: 350–83.

Todd, Patrick. 2011. "A new approach to manipulation arguments," *Philosophical Studies* 152.1:127–33.

Zimmerman, David. 1999. "Born yesterday: personal autonomy for agents without a past," *Midwest Studies in Philosophy* 23: 236–66.

PART NINE

Skepticism, Illusionism, and Revisionism

19

The Impossibility of Ultimate Moral Responsibility

Galen Strawson

1.

There is an argument, which I will call the Basic Argument, which appears to prove that we cannot be truly or ultimately morally responsible for our actions. According to the Basic Argument, it makes no difference whether determinism is true or false. We cannot be truly or ultimately morally responsible for our actions in either case.

The Basic Argument has various expressions in the literature of free will, and its central idea can be quickly conveyed. (1) Nothing can be *causa sui*—nothing can be the cause of itself. (2) In order to be truly morally responsible for one's actions one would have to be *causa sui*, at least in certain crucial mental respects. (3) Therefore nothing can be truly morally responsible.

In this paper I want to reconsider the Basic Argument, in the hope that anyone who thinks that we can be truly or ultimately morally responsible for our actions will be prepared to say exactly what is wrong with it. I think that the point that it has to make is obvious, and that it has been underrated in recent discussion of free will—perhaps because it admits of no answer. I suspect that it is obvious in such a way that insisting on it too much is likely to make it seem less obvious than it is, given the innate contra-suggestibility of human beings in general and philosophers in particular. But I am not worried about making it seem less obvious than it is so long as it gets adequate attention. As far as its validity is concerned, it can look after itself.

A more cumbersome statement of the Basic Argument goes as follows.[1]

(1) Interested in free action, we are particularly interested in actions that are performed for a reason (as opposed to 'reflex' actions or mindlessly habitual actions).

(2) When one acts for a reason, what one does is a function of how one is, mentally speaking. (It is also a function of one's height, one's strength, one's place and time, and so on. But the mental factors are crucial when moral responsibility is in question.)

363

(3) So if one is to be truly responsible for how one acts, one must be truly responsible for how one is, mentally speaking—at least in certain respects.

(4) But to be truly responsible for how one is, mentally speaking, in certain respects, one must have brought it about that one is the way one is, mentally speaking, in certain respects. And it is not merely that one must have caused oneself to be the way one is, mentally speaking. One must have consciously and explicitly chosen to be the way one is, mentally speaking, in certain respects, and one must have succeeded in bringing it about that one is that way.

(5) But one cannot really be said to choose, in a conscious, reasoned, fashion, to be the way one is mentally speaking, in any respect at all, unless one already exists, mentally speaking, already equipped with some principles of choice, 'P1'—preferences, values, pro-attitudes, ideals—in the light of which one chooses how to be.

(6) But then to be truly responsible, on account of having chosen to be the way one is, mentally speaking, in certain respects, one must be truly responsible for one's having the principles of choice P1 in the light of which one chose how to be.

(7) But for this to be so one must have chosen P1, in a reasoned, conscious, intentional fashion.

(8) But for this, that is, (7), to be so one must already have had some principles of choice P2, in the light of which one chose P1.

(9) And so on. Here we are setting out on a regress that we cannot stop. True self-determination is impossible because it requires the actual completion of an infinite series of choices of principles of choice.[2]

(10) So true moral responsibility is impossible because it requires true self-determination, as noted in (3).

This may seem contrived, but essentially the same argument can be given in a more natural form. (1) It is undeniable that one is the way one is, initially, as a result of heredity and early experience, and it is undeniable that these are things for which one cannot be held to be in any way responsible (morally or otherwise). (2) One cannot at any later stage of life hope to accede to true moral responsibility for the way one is by trying to change the way one already is as a result of heredity and previous experience. For (3) both the particular way in which one is moved to try to change oneself, and the degree of one's success in one's attempt at change, will be determined by how one already is as a result of heredity and previous experience. And (4) any further changes that one can bring about only after one has brought about certain initial changes will in turn be determined, via the initial changes, by heredity and previous experience. (5) This may not be the whole story, for it may be that some changes in the way one is are traceable not to heredity and experience but to the influence of indeterministic or random factors. But it is absurd to suppose that indeterministic or random factors, for which one is *ex hypothesi* in no way responsible, can in themselves contribute in any way to one's being truly morally responsible for how one is.

The claim, then, is not that people cannot change the way they are. They can, in certain respects (which tend to be exaggerated by North Americans and underestimated, perhaps, by Europeans). The claim is only that people cannot be supposed to change themselves in such a way as to be or become truly or ultimately morally responsible for the way they are, and hence for their actions.

2.

I have encountered two main reactions to the Basic Argument. On the one hand it convinces almost all the students with whom I have discussed the topic of free will and moral responsibility.[3] On the other hand it often tends to be dismissed, in contemporary discussion of free will and moral responsibility, as wrong, or irrelevant, or fatuous, or too rapid, or an expression of metaphysical megalomania. I think that the Basic Argument is certainly valid in showing that we cannot be morally responsible in the way that many suppose. And I think that it is the natural light, not fear, that has convinced the students I have taught that this is so. That is why it seems worthwhile to restate the argument in a slightly different—simpler and looser—version, and to ask again what is wrong with it.

Some may say that there is nothing wrong with it, but that it is not very interesting, and not very central to the free will debate. I doubt whether any non-philosopher or beginner in philosophy would agree with this view. If one wants to think about free will and moral responsibility, consideration of some version of the Basic Argument is an overwhelmingly natural place to start. It certainly has to be considered at some point in a full discussion of free will and moral responsibility, even if the point it has to make is obvious. Belief in the kind of absolute moral responsibility that it shows to be impossible has for a long time been central to the Western religious, moral, and cultural tradition, even if it is now slightly on the wane (a disputable view). It is a matter of historical fact that concern about moral responsibility has been the main motor—indeed the *ratio essendi*—of discussion of the issue of free will. The only way in which one might hope to show (1) that the Basic Argument is not central to the free will debate would be to show (2) that the issue of moral responsibility is not central to the free will debate. There are, obviously, ways of taking the word 'free' in which (2) can be maintained. But (2) is clearly false nonetheless.[4]

In saying that the notion of moral responsibility criticized by the Basic Argument is central to the Western tradition, I am not suggesting that it is some artificial and local Judaeo–Christian–Kantian construct that is found nowhere else in the history of the peoples of the world, although even if it were that would hardly diminish its interest and importance for us. It is natural to suppose that Aristotle also subscribed to it,[5] and it is significant that anthropologists have suggested that most human societies can be classified either as 'guilt cultures' or as 'shame cultures.' It is true that neither of these two fundamental moral emotions necessarily presupposes a conception of oneself as truly morally responsible for what one has done. But the fact that both are widespread does at least suggest that a conception of moral responsibility similar to our own is a natural part of the human moral-conceptual repertoire.

In fact the notion of moral responsibility connects more tightly with the notion of guilt than with the notion of shame. In many cultures shame can attach to one because of what some member of one's family—or government—has done, and not because of anything one has done oneself; and in such cases the feeling of shame need not (although it may) involve some obscure, irrational feeling that one is somehow responsible for the behaviour of one's family or government. The case of guilt is less clear. There is no doubt that people can feel guilty (or can believe that they feel guilty) about things for which they are not responsible, let alone morally responsible. But it is much less obvious that they can do this without any sense or belief that they are in fact responsible.

3.

Such complications are typical of moral psychology, and they show that it is important to try to be precise about what sort of responsibility is under discussion. What sort of 'true' moral responsibility is being said to be both impossible and widely believed in?

An old story is very helpful in clarifying this question. This is the story of heaven and hell. As I understand it, true moral responsibility is responsibility of such a kind that, if we have it, then it *makes sense*, at least, to suppose that it could be just to punish some of us with (eternal) torment in hell and reward others with (eternal) bliss in heaven. The stress on the words 'makes sense' is important, for one certainly does not have to believe in any version of the story of heaven and hell in order to understand the notion of true moral responsibility that it is being used to illustrate. Nor does one have to believe in any version of the story of heaven and hell in order to believe in the existence of true moral responsibility. On the contrary: many atheists have believed in the existence of true moral responsibility. The story of heaven and hell is useful simply because it illustrates, in a peculiarly vivid way, the *kind* of absolute or ultimate accountability or responsibility that many have supposed themselves to have, and that many do still suppose themselves to have. It very clearly expresses its scope and force.

But one does not have to refer to religious faith in order to describe the sorts of everyday situation that are perhaps primarily influential in giving rise to our belief in true responsibility. Suppose you set off for a shop on the evening of a national holiday, intending to buy a cake with your last ten pound note. On the steps of the shop someone is shaking an Oxfam tin. You stop, and it seems completely clear to you that it is entirely up to you what you do next. That is, it seems to you that you are truly, radically free to choose, in such a way that you will be ultimately morally responsible for whatever you do choose. Even if you believe that determinism is true, and that you will in five minutes time be able to look back and say that what you did was determined, this does not seem to undermine your sense of the absoluteness and inescapability of your freedom, and of your moral responsibility for your choice. The same seems to be true even if you accept the validity of the Basic Argument stated in §1, which concludes that one cannot be in any way ultimately responsible for the way one is and decides. In both cases, it remains true that as one stands there, one's freedom and true moral responsibility seem obvious and absolute to one.

Large and small, morally significant or morally neutral, such situations of choice occur regularly in human life. I think they lie at the heart of the experience of freedom and moral responsibility. They are the fundamental source of our inability to give up belief in true or ultimate moral responsibility. There are further questions to be asked about why human beings experience these situations of choice as they do. It is an interesting question whether any cognitively sophisticated, rational, self-conscious agent must experience situations of choice in this way.[6] But they are the experiential rock on which the belief in true moral responsibility is founded.

4.

I will restate the Basic Argument. First, though, I will give some examples of people who have accepted that some sort of true or ultimate responsibility for the way one is is a necessary condition of true or ultimate moral responsibility for the way one acts, and who, certain that they are ultimately morally responsible for the way they act, have believed the condition to be fulfilled.[7]

E. H. Carr held that "normal adult human beings are morally responsible for their own personality." Jean-Paul Sartre talked of "the choice that each man makes of his personality," and held that "man is responsible for what he is." In a later interview he judged that his earlier assertions about freedom were incautious; but he still held that "in the end one is always responsible for what is made of one" in some absolute sense. Kant described the position very clearly when he claimed that "man *himself* must make or have made himself into whatever, in a moral sense, whether good or evil, he is to become. Either condition must be an effect of his free choice; for otherwise he could not be held responsible for it and could therefore be *morally* neither good nor evil." Since he was committed to belief in radical moral responsibility, Kant held that such self-creation does indeed take place, and wrote accordingly of "man's character, which he himself creates," and of "knowledge of oneself as a person who... is his own originator." John Patten, a former British Minister for Education and a Catholic apparently preoccupied by the idea of sin, claimed that "it is... self-evident that as we grow up each individual chooses whether to be good or bad." It seems clear enough that he saw such choice as sufficient to give us true moral responsibility of the heaven-and-hell variety.[8]

The rest of us are not usually so reflective, but it seems that we do tend, in some vague and unexamined fashion, to think of ourselves as responsible for—answerable for—how we are. The point is quite a delicate one, for we do not ordinarily suppose that we have gone through some sort of active process of self-determination at some particular past time. Nevertheless it seems accurate to say that we do unreflectively experience ourselves, in many respects, rather as we might experience ourselves if we did believe that we had engaged in some such activity of self-determination.

Sometimes a part of one's character—a desire or tendency—may strike one as foreign or alien. But it can do this only against a background of character traits that are not experienced as foreign, but are rather 'identified' with (it is a necessary truth that it is only relative to such a background that a character trait can stand out as alien). Some feel tormented by impulses that they experience as alien, but in many a sense of general identification with their character predominates, and this identification seems to carry within itself an implicit sense that one is, generally, somehow in control of and answerable for how one is (even, perhaps, for aspects of one's character that one does not like). Here, then, I suggest that we find, semi-dormant in common thought, an implicit recognition of the idea that true or ultimate moral responsibility for what one does somehow involves responsibility for how one is. Ordinary thought is ready to move this way under pressure.

There is, however, another powerful tendency in ordinary thought to think that one can be ultimately morally responsible even if one's character is ultimately wholly non-self-determined—simply because one is fully self-consciously aware of oneself as an agent facing choices. I will return to this point later on.

5.

Let me now restate the Basic Argument in very loose—as it were conversational—terms. New forms of words allow for new forms of objection, but they may be helpful nonetheless.

(1) You do what you do, in any situation in which you find yourself, because of the way you are.

So

(2) To be truly morally responsible for what you do you must be truly responsible for the way you are—at least in certain crucial mental respects.

Or:

(1) What you intentionally do, given the circumstances in which you (believe you) find yourself, flows necessarily from how you are.

Hence

(2) You have to get to have some responsibility for how you are in order to get to have some responsibility for what you intentionally do, given the circumstances in which you (believe you) find yourself.

Comment: once again the qualification about 'certain mental respects' is one I will take for granted. Obviously one is not responsible for one's sex, one's basic body pattern, one's height, and so on. But if one were not responsible for anything about oneself, how could one be responsible for what one did, given the truth of (1)? This is the fundamental question, and it seems clear that if one is going to be responsible for any aspect of oneself, it had better be some aspect of one's mental nature.

I take it that (1) is incontrovertible, and that it is (2) that must be resisted. For if (1) and (2) are conceded the case seems lost, because the full argument runs as follows.

(1) You do what you do because of the way you are.

So

(2) To be truly morally responsible for what you do you must be truly responsible for the way are—at least in certain crucial mental respects.

But

(3) You cannot be truly responsible for the way you are, so you cannot be truly responsible for what you do.

Why can't you be truly responsible for the way you are? Because

(4) To be truly responsible for the way you are, you must have intentionally brought it about that you are the way you are, and this is impossible.

Why is it impossible? Well, suppose it is not. Suppose that

(5) You have somehow intentionally brought it about that you are the way you now are, and that you have brought this about in such a way that you can now be said to be truly responsible for being the way you are now.

For this to be true

(6) You must already have had a certain nature N in the light of which you intentionally brought it about that you are as you now are.

But then

(7) For it to be true you and you alone are truly responsible for how you now are, you must be truly responsible for having had the nature N in the light of which you intentionally brought it about that you are the way you now are.

So

You must have intentionally brought it about that you had that nature N, in which case you must have existed already with a prior nature in the light of which you intentionally brought it about that you had the nature N in the light of which you intentionally brought it about that you are the way you now are...

Here one is setting off on the regress. Nothing can be *causa sui* in the required way. Even if such causal 'aseity' is allowed to belong unintelligibly to God, it cannot plausibly be supposed to be possessed by ordinary finite human beings. "The *causa sui* is the best self-contradiction that has been conceived so far," as Nietzsche remarked in 1886:

it is a sort of rape and perversion of logic. But the extravagant pride of man has managed to entangle itself profoundly and frightfully with just this nonsense. The desire for 'freedom of the will' in the superlative meta-physical sense, which still holds sway, unfortunately, in the minds of the half-educated; the desire to bear the entire and ultimate responsibility for one's actions oneself, and to absolve God, the world, ancestors, chance, and society involves nothing less than to be precisely this *causa sui* and, with more than Baron Münchhausen's audacity, to pull oneself up into existence by the hair, out of the swamps of nothingness... (*Beyond Good and Evil*, §21)

The rephrased argument is essentially exactly the same as before, although the first two steps are now more simply stated. It may seem pointless to repeat it, but the questions remain. Can the Basic Argument simply be dismissed? Is it really of no importance in the discussion of free will and moral responsibility? (No and No.) Shouldn't any serious defence of free will and moral responsibility thoroughly acknowledge the respect in which the Basic Argument is valid before going on to try to give its own positive account of the nature of free will and moral responsibility? Doesn't the argument go to the heart of things if the heart of the free will debate is a concern about whether we can be truly or ultimately morally responsible in the absolute way that we ordinarily suppose? (Yes and Yes)

We are what we are, and we cannot be thought to have made ourselves *in such a way* that we can be held to be free in our actions *in such a way* that we can be held to be morally responsible for our actions *in such a way* that any punishment or reward for our actions is ultimately just or fair. Punishments and rewards may seem deeply appropriate or intrinsically 'fitting' to us in spite of this argument, and many of the various institutions of punishment and reward in human society appear to be practically indispensable in both their legal and non-legal forms. But if one takes the notion of justice that is central to our intellectual and cultural tradition seriously, then the evident consequence of the Basic Argument is that there is a fundamental sense in which no punishment or reward is ever ultimately just. It is exactly as just to punish or reward people for their actions as it is to punish or reward them for the (natural) colour of their hair or the (natural) shape of their faces. The point seems obvious, and yet it contradicts a fundamental part of our natural self-conception, and there are elements in human thought that move very deeply against it. When it comes to questions of responsibility, we tend to feel that we are somehow responsible for the way we are. Even more importantly, perhaps, we tend to feel that our explicit self-conscious awareness of ourselves as agents who are able to deliberate about what to do, in situations of choice, suffices to constitute us as morally responsible free agents in the strongest sense, whatever the conclusion of the Basic Argument.

6.

I have suggested that it is step (2) of the restated Basic Argument that must be rejected, and of course it can be rejected, because the phrases 'truly responsible' and 'truly morally responsible' can be defined in many ways. I will briefly consider three sorts of response to the Basic Argument, and I will concentrate on their more simple expressions, in the belief that truth in philosophy, especially in areas of philosophy like the present one, is almost never very complicated.

(i) The first response is *compatibilist*. Compatibilists believe that one can be a free and morally responsible agent even if determinism is true.

Roughly, they claim, with many variations of detail, that one may correctly be said to be truly responsible for what one does, when one acts, just so long as one is not caused to act by any of a certain set of constraints (kleptomaniac impulses, obsessional neuroses, desires that are experienced as alien, post-hypnotic commands, threats, instances of *force majeure*, and so on). Clearly, this sort of compatibilist responsibility does not require that one should be truly responsible for how one is in any way at all, and so step (2) of the Basic Argument comes out as false. One can have compatibilist responsibility even if the way one is is totally determined by factors entirely outside one's control.

It is for this reason, however, that compatibilist responsibility famously fails to amount to any sort of true *moral* responsibility, given the natural, strong understanding of the notion of true moral responsibility (characterized above by reference to the story of heaven and hell). One does what one does entirely because of the way one is, and one is in no way ultimately responsible for the way one is. So how can one be justly punished for anything one does? Compatibilists have given increasingly refined accounts of the circumstances in which punishment may be said to be appropriate or intrinsically fitting. But they can do nothing against this basic objection.

Many compatibilists have never supposed otherwise. They are happy to admit the point. They observe that the notions of true moral responsibility and justice that are employed in the objection cannot possibly have application to anything real, and suggest that the objection is therefore not worth considering. In response, proponents of the Basic Argument agree that the notions of true moral responsibility and justice in question cannot have application to anything real; but they make no apologies for considering them. They consider them because they are central to ordinary thought about moral responsibility and justice. So far as most people are concerned, they are the subject, if the subject is moral responsibility and justice.

(ii) The second response is *libertarian*. Incompatibilists believe that freedom and moral responsibility are incompatible with determinism, and some of them are libertarians, who believe that that we are free and morally responsible agents, and that determinism is therefore false. In an ingenious statement of the incompatibilist-libertarian case, Robert Kane argues that agents in an undetermined world can have free will, for they can "have the power to make choices for which they have ultimate responsibility." That is, they can "have the power to make choices which can only and finally be explained in terms of their own wills (i.e., character, motives, and efforts of will)."[9] Roughly, Kane sees this power as grounded in the possible occurrence, in agents, of efforts of will that have two main features: first, they are partly indeterministic in their nature, and hence indeterminate in their outcome; second, they occur in cases in which agents are trying to make a difficult choice between the options that their characters dispose them to consider. (The paradigm cases will be cases in which they face a conflict between moral duty and non-moral desire.)

But the old objection to libertarianism recurs. How can this indeterminism help with moral responsibility? Granted that the truth of determinism rules out true moral responsibility, how can the falsity of determinism help? How can the occurrence of partly random or indeterministic events contribute in any way to one's being truly morally responsible either for one's actions or for one's character? If my efforts of will shape my character in an admirable way, and in so doing are partly indeterministic in nature, while also being shaped (as Kane grants) by my already existing character, why am I not merely lucky?

The general objection applies equally whether determinism is true or false, and can be restated as follows. We are born with a great many genetically determined predispositions for which we are not responsible. We are subject to many early influences for which we are not responsible. These decisively shape our characters, our motives, the general bent and strength of our capacity to make efforts of will. We may later engage in conscious and intentional shaping procedures—call them S-procedures—designed to affect and change our characters, motivational structure, and wills. Suppose we do. The question is then why we engage in the particular S-procedures that we do engage in, and why we engage in them in the particular way that we do. The general answer is that we engage in the particular S-procedures that we do engage in, given the circumstances in which we find ourselves, because of certain features of the way we already are. (Indeterministic factors may also play a part in what happens, but these will not help to make us responsible for what we do.) And these features of the way we already are—call them character features, or C-features—are either wholly the products of genetic or environmental influences, deterministic or random, for which we are not responsible, or are at least partly the result of earlier S-procedures, which are in turn either wholly the product of C-features for which we are not responsible, or are at least partly the product of still earlier S-procedures, which are turn either the products of C-features for which we are not responsible, or the product of such C-features together with still earlier S-procedures—and so on. In the end, we reach the first S-procedure, and this will have been engaged in, and engaged in the particular way in which it was engaged in, as a result of genetic or environmental factors, deterministic or random, for which we were not responsible.

Moving away from the possible role of indeterministic factors in character or personality formation, we can consider their possible role in particular instances of deliberation and decision. Here too it seems clear that indeterministic factors cannot, in influencing what happens, contribute to true moral responsibility in any way. In the end, whatever we do, we do it either as a result of random influences for which we are not responsible, or as a result of non-random influences for which we are not responsible, or as a result of influences for which we are proximally responsible but not ultimately responsible. The point seems obvious. Nothing can be ultimately *causa sui* in any respect at all. Even if God can be, we can't be.

Kane says little about moral responsibility in his paper, but his position seems to be that true moral responsibility is possible if indeterminism is true. It is possible because in cases of "moral, prudential and practical struggle we ... are truly 'making ourselves' in such a way that we are ultimately responsible for the outcome." This 'making of ourselves' means that "we can be ultimately responsible for our present motives and character by virtue of past choices which helped to form them and for which we were ultimately responsible" (op. cit: 252). It is for this reason that we can be ultimately responsible and morally responsible not only in cases of struggle in which we are 'making ourselves,' but also for choices and actions which do not involve struggle, flowing unopposed from our character and motives.

In claiming that we can be ultimately responsible for our present motives and character, Kane appears to *accept* step (2) of the Basic Argument. He appears to accept that we have to 'make ourselves,' and so be ultimately responsible for ourselves, in order to be morally responsible for what we do.[10] The problem with this suggestion is the old one. In Kane's view, a person's 'ultimate responsibility' for the outcome of an effort of will depends essentially on the partly indeterministic nature of the outcome. This is because it is only the element of indeterminism that prevents prior character and motives from fully explaining the outcome of the effort of will (op. cit.: 236). But how can this indeterminism help with moral responsibility? How can the fact that my effort of will is indeterministic in such a way that its outcome is indeterminate make me truly responsible for it, or even help to make me truly responsible for it? How can it help in any way at all with moral responsibility? How can it make punishment—or reward—ultimately just?

There is a further, familiar problem with the view that moral responsibility depends on indeterminism. If one accepts the view, one will have to grant that it is impossible to know whether any human being is ever morally responsible. For moral responsibility now depends on the falsity of determinism, and determinism is unfalsifiable. There is no more reason to think that determinism is false than that it is true, in spite of the impression sometimes given by scientists and popularizers of science.

(iii) The third response begins by accepting that one cannot be held to be ultimately responsible for one's character or personality or motivational structure. It accepts that this is so whether determinism is true or false. It then directly challenges step (2) of the Basic Argument. It appeals to a certain picture of the self in order to argue that one can be truly free and morally responsible in spite of the fact that one cannot be held to be ultimately responsible for one's character or personality or motivational structure.

This picture has some support in the 'phenomenology' of human choice—we sometimes experience our choices and decisions as if the picture were an accurate one. But it is easy to show that it cannot be accurate in such a way that we can be said to be truly or ultimately morally responsible for our choices or actions.

It can be set out as follows. One is free and truly morally responsible because one's self is, in a crucial sense, independent of one's character or personality or motivational structure—one's CPM, for short. Suppose one is in a situation which one experiences as a difficult choice between A, doing one's duty, and B, following one's non-moral desires. Given one's CPM, one responds in a certain way. One's desires and beliefs develop and interact and constitute reasons for both A and B. One's CPM makes one tend towards A or B. So far the problem is the same as ever: whatever one does, one will do what one does because of the way one's CPM is, and since one neither is nor can be ultimately responsible for the way one's CPM is, one cannot be ultimately responsible for what one does.

Enter one's self, S. S is imagined to be in some way independent of one's CPM. S (i.e., one) considers the deliverances of one's CPM and decides in the light of them, but it—S—incorporates a power of decision that is independent of one's CPM in such a way that one can after all count as truly and ultimately morally responsible in one's decisions and actions, even though one is not ultimately responsible for one's CPM. Step (2) of the Basic Argument is false because of the existence of S.[11]

The trouble with the picture is obvious. S (i.e., one) decides on the basis of the deliverances of one's CPM. But whatever S decides, it decides as it does because of the way it is (or else because partly or wholly because of the occurrence in the decision process of indeterministic factors for which it—i.e. one—cannot be responsible, and which cannot plausibly be thought to contribute to one's true moral responsibility). And this returns us to where we started. To be a source of true or ultimate responsibility, S must be responsible for being the way it is. But this is impossible, for the reasons given in the Basic Argument.

The story of S and CPM adds another layer to the description of the human decision process, but it cannot change the fact that human beings cannot be ultimately self-determining in such a way as to be ultimately morally responsible for how they are, and thus for how they decide and act. The story is crudely presented, but it should suffice to make clear that no move of this sort can solve the problem.

"Character is destiny," as Novalis is often reported as saying.[12] The remark is inaccurate, because external circumstances are part of destiny, but the point is well taken when it comes to the question of moral responsibility. Nothing can be *causa sui*, and in order to be truly morally responsible for one's actions one would have to be *causa sui*, at least in certain crucial mental respects. One cannot institute oneself in such a way that one can take over true or assume moral responsibility for how one is in such a way that one can indeed be truly morally responsible for what one does. This fact is not changed by the fact that we may be unable not to think of ourselves as truly morally responsible in ordinary circumstances. Nor is it changed by the fact that it may be a very good thing that we have this inability—so that we might wish to take steps to preserve it, if it looked to be in danger of fading. As already remarked, many human beings are unable to resist the idea that it is their capacity for fully explicit self-conscious deliberation, in a situation of choice, that suffices to constitute them as truly morally responsible agents in the strongest possible sense. The Basic Argument shows that this is a mistake. However self-consciously aware we are, as we deliberate and reason, every act and operation of our mind happens as it does as a result of features for which we are ultimately in no way responsible. But the conviction that self-conscious awareness of one's situation can be a sufficient foundation of strong free will is very powerful. It runs deeper than rational argument, and it survives untouched, in the everyday conduct of life, even after the validity of the Basic Argument has been admitted.

7.

There is nothing new in the somewhat incantatory argument of this paper. It restates certain points that may be in need of restatement. "Everything has been said before," said André Gide, echoing La Bruyère, "but since nobody listens we have to keep going back and beginning all over again." This is an exaggeration, but it may not be a gross exaggeration, so far as general observations about the human condition are concerned.

The present claim, in any case, is simply this: time would be saved, and a great deal of readily available clarity would be introduced into the discussion of the nature of moral responsibility, if the simple point that is established by the Basic Argument were more generally acknowledged and clearly stated. Nietzsche thought that thoroughgoing acknowledgement of the point was long overdue, and his belief that there might be moral advantages in such an acknowledgement may deserve further consideration.[13]

Notes

1. From Galen Strawson, *Real Materialism and Other Essays* (Oxford: Clarendon Press, 2008). First published 1994 in *Philosophical Studies*.

2. That is, the infinite series must have a beginning and an end, which is impossible.

3. Two have rejected it in fifteen years. Both had religious commitments, and argued, on general and radical sceptical grounds, that we can know almost nothing, and cannot therefore know that true moral responsibility is not possible in some way that we do not understand.

4. It is notable that both Robert Kane (1989) and Alfred Mele (1995), in two of the best recent incompatibilist discussions of free will and autonomy, have relatively little to say about moral responsibility.

5. Cf. *Nichomachean Ethics* III. 5.

6. Cf. MacKay (1960) and the discussion of the 'Genuine Incompatibilist Determinist' in Strawson 1986: 281–6.

7. I suspect that they have started out from their subjective certainty that they have ultimate moral responsibility. They have then been led by reflection to the realization that they cannot really have such moral responsibility if they are not in some crucial way responsible for being the way they are. They have accordingly concluded that they are indeed responsible for being the way they are.

8. Carr in *What Is History?*, 89; Sartre in *Being and Nothingness, Existentialism and Humanism*, 29, and in the *New Left Review* 1969 (quoted in Wiggins 1975); Kant in *Religion within the Limits of Reason Alone*, 40, *The Critique of Practical Reason*, 101 (Ak. V. 98), and in *Opus Postumum*, 213; Patten in *The Spectator*, January 1992.

These quotations raise many questions which I will not consider. It is often hard, for example, to be sure what Sartre is saying. But the occurrence of the quoted phrases is significant on any plausible interpretation of his views. As for Kant, it may be thought to be odd that he says what he does, in so far as he grounds the possibility of our freedom in our possession of an unknowable, non-temporal noumenal nature. It is, however, plausible to suppose that he thinks that radical or ultimate self-determination must take place even in the noumenal realm, in some unintelligibly non-temporal manner, if there is to be true moral responsibility.

9. Kane 1989: 254. I have omitted some italics.

10. He cites van Inwagen 1989 in support of this view.

11. Cf. C. A. Campbell 1957.

12. e.g., by George Eliot in *The Mill on the Floss*, bk. 6, chap. 6. Novalis wrote "Oft fühl ich jetzt…[und] je tiefer einsehe, dass Schicksal und Gemüt Namen eines Begriffes sind"—"I often feel, and ever more deeply realize, that fate and character are the same concept." He was echoing Heracleitus, Fragment 119 DK.

13. Cf. R. Schacht 1983: 304–9. The idea that there might be moral advantages in the clear headed admission that true or ultimate moral responsibility is impossible has been developed in another way by Saul Smilansky (1994).

References

Aristotle., c. 330 BCE /1953. *Nichomachean Ethics*. Trans. J. A. K. Thomson. London: Allen and Unwin.

Campbell, C.A. 1957. "Has the self 'free will'?" In *On Selfhood and Godhood*, by C. A. Campbell. London: Allen and Unwin.

Carr, E. H. 1961. *What is History?* London: Macmillan.

Eliot, G. 1860/1960. *The Mill on the Floss*. Harmondsworth, UK: Penguin.

Kane, R. 1989. "Two kinds of incompatibilism," *Philosophy and Phenomenological Research* 50: 219–54.

Kant, I. 1785/1956. *Critique of Practical Reason*, trans. L. W. Beck. Indianapolis: Bobbs-Merrill.

Kant, I. 1793/1960. *Religion Within the Limits of Reason Alone*, trans. T. M. Greene and H. H. Hudson. New York: Harper and Row.

Kant, I. 1993. *Opus Postumum*, trans. E. Förster and M. Rosen. Cambridge: Cambridge University Press.

MacKay, D. M. 1960. "On the logical indeterminacy of free choice," *Mind* 69: 31–40.

Mele, A. 1995. *Autonomous Agents: From Self-Control to Autonomy*. New York: Oxford University Press.

Nietzsche, F. 1886/1966. *Beyond Good and Evil*, trans. Walter Kaufmann. New York: Random House.

Novalis. 1802. *Heinrich von Ofterdingen*, ed. Friedrich Schlegel. Berlin: n.p.

Sartre, J.-P. 1943/1969. *Being and Nothingness*, trans. Hazel E. Barnes. London: Methuen.

Sartre, J.-P. 1946/1989. *Existentialism and Humanism*, trans. Philip Mairet. London: Methuen.

Schacht, R. 1983. *Nietzsche*. London: Routledge and Kegan Paul.

Smilansky, S. 1994. "The ethical advantages of hard determinism," *Philosophy and Phenomenological Research* 54.2: 355–63.

Strawson, G. 1986. *Freedom and Belief*. Oxford: Clarendon Press.

van Inwagen, P. 1989. "When is the will free?" *Philosophical Perspectives* 3: 399–422.

Wiggins, D. 1975. "Towards a reasonable libertarianism," in *Essays on Freedom of Action*, ed. T. Honderich. London: Routledge.

20

Free Will: From Nature to Illusion

Saul Smilansky

We have to believe in free will to get along.
—C.P. SNOW

Sir Peter Strawson's "Freedom and Resentment" (1982, first published in 1962) was a landmark in the philosophical understanding of the free will problem. It has been widely influential and subjected to penetrating criticism (e.g., Galen Strawson 1986 Ch.5, Watson 1987, Klein 1990 Ch.6, Russell 1995 Ch.5). Most commentators have seen it as a large step forward over previous positions, but as ultimately unsuccessful. This is where the discussion within this philosophical direction has apparently stopped, which is obviously unsatisfactory. I shall attempt to defend a novel position, which purports to provide, in outline, the next step forward. The position presented is based on the descriptively central and normatively crucial role of illusion in the issue of free will. Illusion, I claim, is the vital but neglected *key* to the free will problem. It is not claimed that we need to induce illusory beliefs concerning free will, or can live with beliefs we fully realise are illusory—both of these positions would be highly implausible. Rather, my claim is that illusory beliefs are in place, and that the role they play is largely positive. The proposed position, which may be called 'Illusionism,' can be defended independently from its derivation from Strawson's 'reactive naturalism,' but it is helpful to present the progression in this way. Since the role of illusion emerges only at a late stage of the train of arguments pertaining to free will, we will get to the final destination by 'free-riding' most of the way on Strawson's train, and then continue a bit further by ourselves, into the uncharted and dangerous Land of Illusion.

This paper consists of six parts. Part 1 sets out reactive naturalism. Part 2 explains why it has been thought to improve on previous positions on free will. Part 3 shows why reactive naturalism is inadequate. Part 4 elaborates on the problems whose solution requires illusion. Part 5 presents Illusionism and motivates it philosophically. Part 6 reviews the road from reactive naturalism to Illusionism.

379

I.

Strawson's 'Humean Naturalism.' Naturalism, in the sense I am concerned with here, is a sort of 'Humean' response to scepticism about our common free-will-related practices and reactions. It will be called here 'reactive-naturalism' and 'naturalism' interchangeably. This sort of naturalism considers scepticism as idle in view of the natural inclinations of humanity, given which there is no need for countering the sceptic or, indeed, for offering any justification at all of our basic beliefs and attitudes (Strawson 1987, 38–41). Like the compatibilist, the naturalist claims that morality and human life are not dramatically affected by the absence of libertarian free will. However, he rests his case not on an analysis of the philosophical implications of this absence but on its insignificance in 'real life.'

Considering the predominance of human reactive attitudes and their centrality in human life, indeed, in being human, any intellectual considerations, such as the truth of determinism, cannot seriously be posed as a threat. And, even if we can imagine having a choice whether to engage in inter-personal relations, founded as they are on reactive attitudes, rational choice would be based on the expected gains and losses to human life, and the outcome would be clear (Strawson 1982, 70). Strawson claims that the nature of morality is largely analogical, in that our demands for other persons' good will towards third parties (or demands from ourselves) resemble those we make for good will towards ourselves. This analogy is sustained by the various excusing conditions, in the particular irrelevance of considerations of the truth of determinism to them, and in the ridiculous nature of suggestions that the truth of determinism might abolish this part of life, the moral sphere being intimately connected with the sphere of inter-personal relations (74).

II.

THE ATTRACTIONS OF REACTIVE-NATURALISM

II.1. *Preliminaries.* Reactive naturalism is a strange position to hold on the free will problem, since it is not really about whether we do or do not *have* free will or moral responsibility in an independent sense, in the way that traditional positions (libertarianism, compatibilism and hard determinism) clearly are. Rather, reactive naturalism focuses on our emotional lives and asks whether, in the light of our emotional make-up, common views are liable to be affected. That such a position can be a contender at all must be due then to a serious state of affairs; this is indeed the case. This state is, broadly:

(A) There is no libertarian free will.
(B) Compatibilism is insufficient as a basis for moral responsibility and related matters.
(C) We need to maintain common free-will-related attitudes and practices, so that compatibilist distinctions in terms of control and its absence should largely continue to be followed.
(D) Other alternatives, such as utilitarian, are inadequate.

In considering the free will problem, the first[1] question is whether libertarian free will really exists, i.e., the libertarian Coherence/Existence Question. The second question is whether—if it does not—we are in trouble. It can be called the Compatibility Question, namely, are moral responsibility and related notions compatible with determinism (or with the absence of libertarian free will irrespective of determinism)? Compatibilism and hard determinism are the opponents on the Compatibility Question. Reactive naturalism, like the Illusionism I am offering, is best understood as an answer to the third-level question of the consequences of pessimistic answers to the first two questions—namely, that there is no libertarian free will, and that compatibilism is insufficient and hence we are in trouble. It can be called the Consequences Question.

It is the despair from the possibility of grounding our ethical and personal free-will-related beliefs, practices and reactions on libertarianism, compatibilism or any other traditional alternative, which brought naturalism to the scene.

II.2. *Why Not Libertarian Free Will?* First a few words on (A), i.e., the claim that there is no libertarian free will. I shall assume, with Strawson, that libertarian free will is incoherent (Strawson 1980, 265). In a nutshell, the conditions required by an ethically satisfying sense of libertarian free will, which would give us anything beyond sophisticated formulations of compatibilism, are self-contradictory, and hence cannot be met. This is so irrespective of determinism or causality. Attributing moral worth to a person for her decision or action requires that it follow from what she is, morally. The decision or action cannot be produced by a random occurrence and count morally. We might think that two different decisions or actions can follow from a person, but which one does, say, a decision to steal or not to steal, again cannot be random but needs to follow from what she is, morally. But what a person is, morally, cannot ultimately be under her control. We might think that such control is possible if she creates herself, but then it is the early self that creates a later self, leading to vicious infinite regress. The libertarian project was worthwhile attempting: it was supposed to allow a deep moral connection between a given act and the person, and yet not fall into being merely an unfolding of the arbitrarily given, whether determined or random. But it is not possible to find any way in which this can be done.

Libertarians may well not be satisfied with my cursory treatment, but this should be accepted for the sake of the current discussion, for we need to journey far. We may then say that my argument, like that of Strawson, is primarily addressed to those who are not assured of the belief in the existence of libertarian free will.

II.3. *Why Not Compatibilism?* I will now say something on (B), i.e., on why I think that compatibilism, its partial validity not-withstanding, is grimly insufficient. Not only is compatibilism a widely prevalent view in philosophy, and hence I need to combat the complacency it encourages if I am to motivate the need for illusion, but this need will emerge from the situation that makes compatibilism inadequate. (The case made here is my own, and it is not claimed that Strawson would view matters in exactly the same way.)

We can make sense of the notion of autonomy or self-determination on the compatibilist level but, if there is no libertarian free will, no one can be ultimately in control, ultimately responsible, for this self and its determinations. *Everything* that takes place on the compatibilist level, irrespective of the local distinctions in respect of control, becomes on the ultimate hard determinist level 'what was merely *there*,' ultimately deriving from causes beyond the control of the participants. If people lack libertarian free will, their identity and actions flow from circumstances beyond their control. To a certain extent, people can change their character, but that which changes or does not change remains itself a result of something, and there is always a situation in which the self-creating person could not have created herself, but was just what she was, as it were, 'given,' Being the sort of person one is, and having the desires and beliefs one has, are ultimately something which one cannot control, which cannot be one's fault, it is one's luck. And one's life, and everything one does, is an unfolding of this. Let us call this the 'ultimate perspective' and contrast it with the 'compatibilist perspective,' which takes the person as a 'given' and enquires about her various desires, choices and actions.

Consider the following quotation from a compatibilist:

> The incoherence of the libertarian conception of moral responsibility arises from the fact that it requires not only authorship of the action, but also, in a sense, authorship of one's self, or of one's character. As was shown, this requirement is unintelligible because it leads to an infinite regress. The way out of this regress is *simply to drop* the second-order authorship requirement, which is what has been done here (Vuoso 1987; my emphasis).

The difficulty is that there is an *ethical basis* for the libertarian requirement and, even if it cannot be fulfilled, the idea of 'simply dropping it' masks how *problematic* the result may be in terms of fairness and justice. The fact remains that if there is no libertarian free will a person being punished *may suffer justly* in compatibilist terms for what is ultimately her luck, for what follows from being what she is—ultimately beyond her control, a state which she had no real opportunity to alter, hence neither her responsibility nor her fault. With all the importance of compatibilist distinctions, a morally serious compatibilist cannot escape the conclusion that if this person suffers—however justly in compatibilist terms—she is, from an important perspective, a victim. For it was *given* that being who she was she would (compatibilistically freely) choose as she did, and suffer the consequences.

A similar criticism applies to other moral and non-moral ways of perceiving and treating people. The compatibilist cannot maintain the libertarian-based view of moral worth or of the grounds for respect, and what she has to offer is a much shallower sort of meaning and justification. Desert, be it of praise or punishment, can make sense only on a shallow compatibilist level, where the underlying causes of the good or bad motives are not queried. Ultimately people are not deserving, they are simply the way they have been made, and hence equal in value, i.e., equally lacking in desert-based value. Compatibilism, in sum, is morally, even humanly, shallow, for it depends on our remaining on the level of people as more or less 'givens,' i.e., on blindness as to what we learn when we push our inquiries further, into the causes of this 'given,' beyond the limited internal compatibilist perspective. The picture of moral reality and of personal aspects of worth that we can aspire to as compatibilists is often tragic and inherently shallow. It is those two charges, of a shallowness, and of a complacent compliance with the injustice of not acknowledging lack of fairness and desert, and in particular ultimate-level victimisation, which form the backbone of my case against compatibilism.

II.4. *Why Not Hard Determinism?* If there is no libertarian free will and if compatibilism is insufficient, should we not then opt for hard determinism, which denies the reality of free will and moral responsibility in any sense? I will now briefly defend (C) above, namely the need to retain some of the 'form of life' based on the value put on distinctions made in terms of compatibilist free will. I share with most free will philosophers the belief in the at least partial validity of compatibilism. In broad outline, the basis for this position combines the reality of distinctions in terms of local free choice even in a world without libertarian free will, such as a deterministic world, and the possibility to motivate ethically the making use of these distinctions. (Again, Strawson would not share this view in its particulars, but since this is not a work of historical interpretation this need not concern us. He *would* certainly share the thought that hard determinism should not guide our practice.)

The kleptomaniac and the alcoholic differ from the common thief and common drinker in the deficiency of their capacity for local reflective control over their actions (see e.g., Glover 1970, 136; cf. Fischer 1994 for a recent sophisticated compatibilist formulation). Here everyone should agree. But the point is that such differences are *morally significant*: in some ways the compatibilistically free may also be victims, as viewing things from the ultimate perspective has helped us to see, and yet the importance of the commonplace compatibilist level distinctions will often be great. Consider, for instance, the notion of a valid Will and Testament made by a person wishing to arrange the distribution of her property after her death. The idea of a valid will requires that it be made of one's 'free will.' There are likely to be border-line difficulties but, in general, we are able to identify what it *is about* the agent and the situation when signing a document which makes the signatory's action free in a sense we care about (even without libertarian free will), and what limitations of free will (such as coercion and insanity) invalidate the will. And it is fairly obvious *why* we want to make use of these factors in our ethical judgements, reactions and social practices. We want our last wishes to be respected, as well as defence if our will is tampered with, and an ethically decent social order will follow the compatibilist distinctions.

More generally, we want to be members of a Community of Responsibility where our choices will determine the moral attitude we receive, with the accompanying possibility of being morally excused when our actions are not within our reflective control, e.g., when they result from a brain tumor. The exceptions and excuses commonly presented by compatibilism should, in general, continue to carry weight. For if people are to be respected, their nature as purposive agents capable and desirous of choice needs to be catered for. We have to enable people to live as responsible beings in the Community of Responsibility, with their lives based largely on their choices, to note and give them *credit* for their good actions, and to take account of situations in which they *lacked* the abilities, capacities and opportunities to choose freely, and are therefore not responsible in the compatibilist sense. Even without libertarian free will, it is reasonable to desire that compatibilist distinctions concerning control affect the way one is treated, and to see this as a condition for civilised existence.

Such a community is possible on the basis of compatibilist-level distinctions. Except in extreme situations, we have no reason to accept at face value the words and deeds of a woman who admits that she continuously takes advantage of people and treats them shabbily but claims, as an excuse, that 'this is in her nature.' Admittedly, it may be more difficult for her to control herself or to change than it is for others but this can be only a mitigating element, and would not lead us to accept her presentation of things as simply an acceptable excuse. We shall see her self-justification as, at best, bad faith but more probably as an attempt at self-serving manipulation. One is not normally in a *passive* relationship with such features of one's behaviour, and is an agent who deliberates, decides and acts out one's decisions, not a spectator of forces carrying one along. This element of 'up-to-usness' is why the compatibilist perspective is available, why we are allowed to hold this woman accountable and why we are permitted to attempt to influence her within a responsibility-based moral structure. Such a Community of Responsibility allows people to live lives of integrity based upon their choices, and is also a basis for a fair division of burdens. As Will Kymlicka points out: "It is unjust if people are disadvantaged by inequalities of their circumstances, but it is equally unjust for me to demand that someone else pay for the costs of my choices" (Kymlicka, quoted in Cohen 1989, 933). Hence, with all the moral importance of the absence of libertarian free will, we need not and must not escape from living according to the basic ethical paradigm of control and responsibility.[2]

We see, then, that we are in serious trouble, for (A) libertarian free will does not exist, (B) compatibilism is greatly insufficient, but (C) the basic free-will-related practices and reactions should be maintained.[3] Naturalism attempts to offer, as we have seen, a defence of our common attitudes and practices in this predicament.

III.

Why Not Reactive-Naturalism? Reactive-naturalism offers a highly significant contribution to the debate. When examined closely, however, it is much weaker than it seems at first, and if the basic attitude it favours is to be sustained it is necessary to interpret it along the lines of Illusionism.

III.1. *Revisionist Naturalism.* Naturalism can be seen to split into two versions: a tough-minded, revisionist naturalism, and a softer, passive account. Revisionist naturalism seeks to change the perception that there is a theoretical need to justify common attitudes and practices, holding that there is no need for general grounding and that the reactions themselves provide all the (self-) grounding required. Strawson sometimes expresses views akin to revisionist naturalism (e.g., 1987, 32–3). In greater detail, Jonathan Bennett might be interpreted as working towards such a position in his attempt to apply Strawson's work to the issue of punishment (1980; cf. Wallace 1994). Bennett suggests that we see the reactive attitudes as the limiting addition (constituting 'justice') to the regular consequentialist considerations regarding punishment, and this explains why we should not 'punish' the innocent, for example—we cannot resent them, and to 'punish' the innocent would be harmful to our reactive lives (48–9).

There is likely to be much affinity between the structure of our reactive lives and the basic ethical intuitions requiring the existence of free will. This depends, however, on the reality of distinctions in control, which influence our knowledge when a reaction is *appropriate*. Our reactive attitudes are not independent and self-validating. The concerns of the basic ethical intuition and reactive attitudes may differ and, in any case, the needs of our reactive lives cannot be the main consideration. Justice, for instance, involves matters other than safeguarding the reactive attitudes. If we doubt whether free action exists in a significant sense, this must be crucial to the view we take of the justification of blame and punishment, for example. Even with Strawson's paradigmatic attitude, resentment, a belief *transcending and underlying* the attitude itself seems necessary. As Joel Feinberg says: "It is clear, I think, that resentment without an ostensible desert basis is not resentment" (Feinberg 1970, 71).

Similarly, the wish to preserve the reactive attitudes could hardly be widely accepted as a basis for morality. Revisionist naturalism can be confronted with the same type of criticism that naturalism itself levelled at consequentialism in the free will context—that, like the consequentialist 'effects of blame,' safe-guarding the reactive attitudes is just not the *kind* of reason bound up with free-will-related moral life, and will not be recognised by most people as appropriate. Dependency on grounds is inherent in the notions under consideration, such as resentment, blame and punishment. The reactive attitudes follow the existence of such grounds (e.g., gratitude has to be deserved), and cannot in themselves replace it.

III.2. *Non-Revisionist Naturalism.* Perhaps a non-revisionist, passive naturalism is sufficient? Perhaps all the naturalist requires is that *in practice* common attitudes and behaviour remain constant, whatever the theoretical case may be. However, even on its own naturalistic terms, naturalism is inadequate. Even someone such as Paul Russell, who follows Hume and Strawson in discounting the need for general justification of our moral attitudes as such, thinks that Strawson is too optimistic as to the stability of specific attitudes and practices (Russell 1992). But why are reactive attitudes insufficient?

III.3. *Justice.* One problem that has real practical substance concerns justice. It is not required that people think of some alternative moral position, unrelated to the reactive attitudes. It is enough that some segments of the population should become *cynical* or *doubtful*, about the moral difference between the guilty and innocent (in traditional terms) in the light of the causal role of crimogenic environments, in order for any confidence as to the assurance provided by reactive attitudes to be shaken. In such a case we might face a threat to the basis of moral life in the requirement for considering free will as a condition for punishment. Societies with very different conceptions of justice existed, and even if they cannot be reinstated, significant doubts as to the justness of our own institutions, resulting in an uncaring cynicism, cannot be ruled out.

A sense of 'justice' has often been closely connected with feelings of revenge, concern with the existence of free will being non-existent or meagre: it has often been thought that 'just' revenge could be taken on the tribesmen or countrymen of the guilty person, without undue concern for their lack of responsibility. Today such attitudes are still expressed in societies organised largely on the basis of kinship, resulting in blood-feuds. Many terrorist actions, such as blowing up civilian airlines or buses in the name of 'just' revenge, show the same disregard for the value of considering free will. Such beliefs, emotions and practices were long considered natural, and the danger has not been eradicated. Consider also the prevalence for hundreds of years in Christian Europe of the sentiment that Jews, as such, should suffer, because of the alleged role of some Jews in the Roman crucifixion of Jesus. Other religious beliefs, such as the common conception of Original Sin under certain interpretations, might also betray the lack of concern with 'up-to-usness.' Here we are faced with situations where even the *minimal* content of free will—agency—is not considered necessary in order for punishment to be just.[4]

Let us call the ethical demand for considering the existence of free will in justifying, e.g., blame and punishment, the 'Core Conception' of justice. I believe that current acceptance of the Core Conception, in some societies, has a good claim to represent moral progress, perhaps the best claim there is: think about enlightened attitudes towards the 'punishment' of the innocent or collective 'punishment,' for example. This progress is more fragile than we are wont to think. Moreover, such threats need not even arise from within the free will issue. There are various intellectual and social currents which might harm the value put upon free will. The call for 'efficiency' in the fight against crime might suffice here. The point is that even a mild weakening of free will beliefs might reduce their power to make us *resist* such external influences.

III.4. *Respect.* We can highlight many of these points by considering the issue of (self-)respect. Just as with the issue of justice, I think consideration of this topic shows Strawson's position to be too optimistic. This becomes apparent if we substitute 'respect' for 'resentment' and consider the matter of 'Freedom and Respect,' respect being an attitude much more dependent on complex cognitive beliefs than resentment. Resentment may linger when we cease to see the issue of (dis)respect as pertaining to a person, in light of the issue of free will. We can hardly continue to respect ourselves in the same way if we really internalise the belief that all action and achievement is ultimately down to luck and not ultimately attributable to us. And there is every reason to believe that many educated people can internalise this thought to a degree that will *suffice* to cause serious harm to their self-respect. Similarly with the appreciation of and respect for others.

Moreover, the non-revisionist naturalist position, to the extent that it is deemed convincing, is itself harmful to our self-respect. If attitudes of respect are thought unjustifiable on the deepest level because of the lack of an ultimate basis for them in free will, then to say that it is 'unavoidable' that we hold such attitudes means that we are caught in a humiliating state. To continue with the same attitudes and practices involving libertarian desert and worth when we know that there is no libertarian free will is hardly conducive to self-respect, even if no real choice is involved.

In sum, the issue of (self-)respect illuminates the danger of the ultimate hard determinist insight, and shows the weakness of a position such as Strawson's. Firstly, we realise that what we seek is a deep basis for being worthy of respect, and this Strawson cannot give us. The quest for respect is a quest for true appreciation and value, and cannot be satisfied in the way that the need for some of the more 'emotional' reactive attitudes perhaps can. Secondly, we see that Strawson relies too heavily on our natural proneness to the reactive attitudes as a means of upholding these values, since many people may come to doubt the basis for their self-respect. Finally, even where they are effective, Strawson's pragmatic assurances are only comforting at the price of a further reduction in our self-respect, due to their very nature, and because of our very need for what might be taken to be mere palliatives.[5]

III.5. *Why Not Reactive-Naturalism? Conclusion.* Reactive-naturalism originally appeared as a strong position for, unlike other compatibilist stances, it in a way encompassed the common libertarian assumptions, while neutralising them, so that they seemed to result, in practice, in compatibilist conclusions. But as we saw, this crucially depends on assuming that the reactive attitudes guarantee the status quo, with the cognitive status of the assumptions and resulting actions following the reactive attitudes. And this is unconvincing.

Free will and moral responsibility are the stuff of our beliefs and convictions and not mere secretions of our natural reactions. Instinctive nature is not in complete mastery in matters of free will, and our personal and ethical convictions can be led up grim paths if the absence of libertarian free will is internalised, as it may be, in part. Our ethical common-sense is not 'built-in,' and even those reactive attitudes that are more or less unavoidable cannot guarantee it. Reactive naturalism is a useful antidote to extreme cognitivism concerning free will, but in it the pendulum has swung too far the other way. Despite the role of the reactive attitudes, the free will problem can be important in practice, perhaps mainly in less subjective and moral areas, because we can have limited threats to the central values involved, threats that are perhaps largely unavoidable in the modern world, and should not be avoided by abandoning the Core Conception values, even if they could be.

IV.

Elaborating 'The Problem.' In order to see how illusion is crucial, we must deepen our understanding of the difficulties which (would) prevail without it. There are fatal weaknesses in naturalism as a solution; but why is there an urgent problem in the first place? We have already seen some difficulties. In what follows I will give a number of further illustrations.

IV.1. *The Question of Innocence.* The danger concerning respect for moral innocence was mentioned above. Even in a world with-out libertarian free will, the idea that only those who deserve to be punished in light of their free actions may be punished is a condition for any civilised moral order (cf. Hart 1970). 'Punishment' of those who did not perform the act for which they are 'punished,' or did so act but lacked control over their action in any sense, is the paradigm of injustice. Yet while the justification for these values does not require libertarian free will, in practice they might be at risk were the lack of libertarian free will internalised. Consider Anscombe's passionate remark that "If someone really thinks, *in advance,* that it is open to question whether such an action as procuring the judicial execution of the innocent should be quite excluded from consideration—I do not want to argue with him; he shows a corrupt mind" (Anscombe 1981, 40). Surely, if a moral system that seeks to pre-serve and guard vigilantly the common conception of innocence is to function well, such a sentiment should be prevalent, almost instinctive. But if this is to be so, the worst thing one could do would be to point out that, ultimately, none of this makes sense—because the 'guilty' are, ultimately, no more guilty than others. In a world imbued with a deterministic outlook the ethical-emotional weight of the Dreyfus affair, for example, is scarcely comprehensible.

IV.2. *The Ultimate Conclusion as a Practical Threat to the Taking of Responsibility.* We cannot tell people that they must behave in a certain way, that it is morally crucial that they do so, but then, if they do not, turn and say that this is (in every case) excusable, given whatever hereditary and environ-mental influences have operated in their formation. Psychologically, the attri-bution of responsibility to people so that they may be said to justly deserve gain or loss for their actions requires (even *after* the act) the absence of the notion that the act is an unavoidable outcome of the way things were, is ulti-mately beyond anyone's control. Morality has a crucial interest in confront-ing what can be called the *Present Danger of the Future Retrospective Excuse,* and in restricting the influence of the ultimate hard determinist level. To put it bluntly: people as a rule ought not to be fully aware of the ultimate inevita-bility of what they have done, for this will affect the way in which they hold themselves responsible. The knowledge that such an escape from responsibil-ity, based on retrospective ultimate judgement, will be available in the *future* is likely to affect the *present* view, and hence cannot be fully admitted even in its *retrospective* form. We often want a person to blame himself, feel guilty, and even see that he deserves to be punished. Such a person is not likely to do all this if he internalises the ultimate perspective, according to which in the actual world nothing else could in fact have occurred, he could not strictly have done anything else except what he did do.

IV.3. *Failure.* It might also be interesting to reflect upon *failure.* The threat of failure is central to the widespread motivation to study, work, and in general make an effort, i.e., in motivating achievement. The sense of achievement and the self-respect it generates are in everybody's interest; unfortunately these ideas make no sense without the notion of failure. Hence we need the idea of failure in order to be given the opportunity to succeed. By now, however, it will be obvious that the ultimate perspective poses a great threat here. If the boy at fifteen is to make something of himself, it cannot be the case that, were he to fail, at sixty he would have an easy way of dismissing his plight as all along beyond his control, for hard determinist reasons. Moreover, such an easy erasure of failure cannot but affect the fate of the sense of achievement: it cannot be that failure is thought not to be in the end up to one, while attainment miraculously remains so. A cultural climate of guaranteed excuse is not conducive to effort and for encouraging success, nor is it a firm foundation for (self-)respect.

IV.4. *A Sense of Value*. From the ultimate hard determinist perspective, all people—whatever their efforts and sacrifices—are morally equal: i.e., there cannot be any means of generating 'real' moral value. As we have seen, there is a sense in which our notion of moral self-respect, which is intimately connected with our view of our choices, actions and achievements, withers when we accept the ultimate perspective. From the latter any sense of moral achievement disappears, as even the actions of the 'moral hero' are simply an unfolding of what he happens to be *no matter how devoted he has been, how much effort he has put in, how many tears he has shed, how many sacrifices he has willingly suffered*. True *appreciation*, deeply *attributing* matters to someone in a sense that will make him worthy, is impossible if we regard him and his efforts as merely determined products. All that the compatibilist can offer us in terms of value, although important in itself, is meagre protection from the cold wind that attacks us when we come close to reaching the luck-imbued ultimate level. There is an obvious practical danger here to our moral motivation, which can be named the *Danger of Worthlessness*. But the concern is not only to get people to function adequately as moral agents, but with the very meaning we can find in our lives.

IV.5. *Remorse and Integrity*. If a person takes the ultimate hard determinist perspective, it is not only others who seem to disappear as moral agents—but in some way the person herself is reduced. In retrospect her life, her decisions, that which is most truly her own, appear to be accidental phenomena of which she is the mere *vehicle*, and to feel moral remorse for any of it, by way of truly *owning up* to it, seems in some deep sense to be misguided. Feelings of remorse are inherently tied to the person's self-perception as a morally responsible agent (see Taylor 1985, 107).

It sharpens our focus not to dwell upon those happy to escape accountability, but rather upon those who have good will. Here we confront what can be termed the *Danger of Retrospective Dissociation*, the difficulty of feeling truly responsible after action. One can surrender the right to make use of the 'ultimate level excuse' for normative reasons, and yet perhaps not be able to hold oneself truly responsible (e.g., to engage in remorse), if one has no grain of belief in something like libertarian free will. One can, after all, accept responsibility for matters that were not up to one in any sense, such as for the actions of others, for normative reasons. But here we are dealing with a different matter: not with the acceptance of responsibility in the sense of 'willingness to pay,' but rather with feeling *compunction*. Compunction seems conceptually problematic and psychologically dubious when it concerns actions that, it is understood, ultimately one could not in fact help doing. But such genuine feelings of responsibility (and not mere acceptance of it) are crucial for being responsible selves! We see here the *intimacy* of the connection between moral and personal integrity and beliefs about free will; hence the danger of realising the truth also looms large.

Here the common person's incompatibilist intuitions, for all of their vagueness and crudeness, have captured something that has escaped philosophical compatibilists. Once this larger view of the need to have workable beliefs and sustaining self-images is taken we can no longer contemplate with equanimity the decline of libertarian-based beliefs. When we appreciate that it is not merely 'external' or 'theoretical' conclusions which may emerge, but that internalised beliefs regarding the free will problem could enter into our retrospective beliefs about *ourselves,* we see that the difficulties caused by the absence of ultimate-level grounding are likely to be great, generating acute psychological discomfort for many people and threatening morality—if, that is, we do not have illusion at our disposal.

IV.6. *The 'Problem': Some Concluding Reflections.* The difficulties we have seen can be divided into two types. Firstly, reactions and practices which are at least partially valid (have compatibilist grounding) will not be sufficiently adhered to if the absence of libertarian free will is realised. The compatibilist categories are not erased by the absence of libertarian free will, but *over-reaction* to this absence may in practice occur. Secondly, the absence of libertarian free will is *in itself* grimly significant, hence its realisation is potentially problematic irrespective of the danger to the compatibilistically-valid reactions and practices. Even if people continue to respect the compatibilist categories, they may come to see that the lack of libertarian free will is, say, corrosive of their self-respect. As we shall see shortly, illusion assists us with these two problems.

Belief can be fairly stable concerning libertarian free will but, if this current stability-point is broken, it is not the partially valid compatibilist categories that will be upheld. Rather, the risk is that belief will collapse to its next 'natural' stability-point, to the denial of meaning to free will and moral responsibility: as it were, *"If all is determined, everything is permitted."* And even when this is not the case, the poverty of the best that the compatibilist has to offer in terms of worth and desert is disheartening, and this grim situation can be realised to some extent.

In theory, alternatives to the concern with free will also present themselves: for example, a purely aesthetic view of life that does not treat achievements as reflecting on a person's value, except for a merely quasi-aesthetic ranking. Such abandonment of value and of self is at best a marginal possibility, at least within the framework of anything resembling Western forms of thought. Note that this extends beyond those with deep moral concerns. A true understanding of what is at stake concerning non-moral self-respect, for example, would lead one to the same conclusion. *There is no real substitute for the framework of achievement, desert and value based on free action.* And within that framework, a deep view not diverted by illusion will find itself face-to-face with darkness.

V.

ILLUSION AS A 'SOLUTION'

V.1. *What Is Illusionism?* Illusionism is the position that illusion often has a *large and positive* role to play in the issue of free will. In arguing for the importance of illusion I claim that we can see why it is useful, that it is a reality, and that by and large it ought to continue. As I noted above, it is not claimed that we need to induce illusory beliefs concerning free will, or can live with beliefs we fully realise are illusory. Rather, my claim is that illusory beliefs are in place, and that the role they play is largely positive. Humanity is fortunately deceived on the free will issue, and this seems to be a condition of civilised morality and personal value.

The importance of illusion flows from the basic structure of the free will problem that we have seen. It flows in two ways: first, indirectly, from the fundamental dualism on the Compatibility Question—the partial and varying validity of *both* compatibilism and hard determinism. The partial validity of compatibilism does not reduce the need for illusion so much as it complicates it and adds to it, because of the need to guard the compatibilist concerns and distinctions, and the contrast and dissonance with the ultimate hard determinist perspective. Secondly, illusion flows directly and more deeply—from the meaning of the very absence of the sort of grounding that libertarian free will was thought to provide. We cannot live adequately with the dissonance of the two valid sides of the fundamental dualism, nor with a complete awareness of the deep significance of the absence of libertarian free will. We have to face the fact that there are basic beliefs that morally ought not to be abandoned, although they might destroy each other, or are even partly based on incoherent conceptions. At least for most people, these beliefs are potentially in need of motivated mediation and defence by illusion, ranging from wishful thinking to self-deception.

The sense of 'illusion' that I am using combines the falsity of the belief with some motivated role in forming and maintaining that belief, as in standard cases of wishful thinking or self-deception. However, it suffices that the beliefs are false and that this conclusion would be resisted were a challenge to arise; it is not necessary for us to determine the current level of illusion concerning free will.

V.2. *Why Is There a Need for Illusion?* Our previous results supply the resources for an answer. Let us concentrate, for the sake of simplicity, on the concerns of a strictly 'practical' point of view: if the basic ethical concern for free will, the Core Conception, is taken seriously, while the absence of libertarian free will is to some extent realised, and illusion does not prevail, then the ultimate level conclusion might tend to dominate in practice. It might very well pose a danger—especially because of the human tendency to over-simplify—to the 'common form of life' and to the strict observance of the corresponding moral order. Many people would find it hard to think that the partial compatibilist truth *matters,* as in fact it ethically does, if they realised the sense in which both the compatibilistically free and the unfree were merely performing according to their mould. And this might lead them to succumb to 'pragmatic' consequentialist temptations, or an unprincipled nihilism. The ultimate hard determinist perspective does not leave sufficient moral and psychological 'space' for compatibilistically-defensible reactive attitudes and moral order. The fragile compatibilist-level plants need to be defended from the chill of the ultimate perspective in the hothouse of illusion. *Only if we do not see people from the ultimate perspective can we live in a way which compatibilism affirms*—blaming, selectively excusing, respecting, being grateful, and the like.

Within these parameters, there is a *prima facie* case for a large measure of motivated obscurity regarding the objections to libertarian free will: if libertarian assumptions *carry on their back* the compatibilist distinctions, which would not be adhered to sufficiently without them, an illusion which defends these libertarian assumptions seems to be just what we need.[6] The partial validity of the compatibilist distinctions is unlikely to overcome the practical salience of the ultimate perspective in such a situation, unless illusion intervenes. Determinists are not likely to cherish and maintain adequately the respect due to people in the light of their free actions, nor a free will-based moral order in general. The ethical importance of the paradigm of free will and responsibility as a basis for desert should be taken very seriously, but the ultimate perspective threatens to *present* it as a farce, a mere game without foundation. Likewise with the crucial idea of a personal sense of value and appreciation that can be gained through our free actions: this is unlikely to be adequately maintained by individuals in their self-estimates, nor warmly and consistently projected by society. A broad loss of moral and personal confidence can be expected. The idea of action-based desert, true internal acceptance of responsibility, respect for effort and achievement, deep ethical appreciation, excusing the innocent—all these and more are threatened by the 'levelling' or homogenising view arising from the ultimate perspective. Illusion is crucial in pragmatically safeguarding the compatibilistically-defensible elements of the 'common form of life' *Illusion is, by and large, a condition for the actual creation and maintenance of adequate moral and personal reality.*

V.3. *How Does Illusion Function?* When illusion plays a role, things can, in practice, work out. Two schematic answers can be made. Significant realisation of the absence of libertarian free will and concern about ultimate level injustice, for example, can remain more or less limited to part of the population, say, those more concerned with policy-making (an 'elitist solution'). This maintains the widespread 'intuition' that, for instance, 'punishing' the innocent is an abomination whereas criminals deserve 'to pay,' while permitting the amelioration of treatment, resulting from the recognition, by some, that ultimately things are not morally that simple. Complex patterns of self-and-other deception emerge here. But, in addition to all the general practical and moral difficulties with elitist solutions, which we cannot consider here, elitism can in any case be only a partial solution concerning free will. For, in the light of the reasons that we have already seen, people without illusions would have great difficulty in functioning.

The major solution will be one where, since two beliefs are vaguely but simultaneously held, yet commonly not set side by side (often, I claim, due to the presence of a motivated element), their contrary nature is not fully noticed. When acting in the light of compatibilist insights we suspend the insights of the ultimate hard determinist perspective (which we in any case are likely to be only dimly aware of). We *keep ourselves* on the level of compatibilist distinctions about local control, and do not ask ourselves about the deeper question of the 'givenness' of our choosing self; resisting threats to our vague, tacit libertarian assumptions. As Bernard Williams put it: "To the extent that the institution of blame works coherently, it does so because it attempts less than morality would like it to do... [it] takes the agent together with his character, and does not raise questions about his freedom to have chosen some other character" (1985, 194). The result is not philosophically neat, but that, after all, is its merit: the original reality was that we face practical dangers if we try to make our (incoherent or contradictory) conceptions *too clear,* but that we ought not to give any of them up entirely. Illusion, in short, allows us to have 'workable beliefs.'

We can *expect* people to be able to function adequately when they are compatibilistically free. There is ample basis in compatibilist local control for doing so, and enlisting such functioning is a condition of civilisation. When we remain on the compatibilist level, distinctions and excuses emerge which allow for normal human interaction, for our reactive lives, for the accumulation of moral credit and discredit and for moral discernment. However, awareness of the ultimate inevitability of any level of functioning endangers *good* functioning, and *darkens* our fundamental ways of appreciating ourselves as well as others; hence illusion is required. Illusion not only functions in motivated resistance to threats to our beliefs; but it also offers a positive view *underlying* our attitudes and practices. The affirmation of the responsible self is furthered by the vague tacit belief that one was and is able to do otherwise in the libertarian sense, and can have no general escape from the burden of responsibility. It is not that we find out the truth and then say "Let's keep quiet about this," but that illusion is intimately *entangled* with our free-will-related beliefs, reactions and practices. However, some awareness of deterministic elements can be useful, mitigating resentment of others or self-recriminations. Illusion allows us the advantages of the libertarian picture together with the mitigating element, without full awareness either of the incoherence of the libertarian picture or of the contrariness of the compatibilist and ultimate perspectives.

The interaction between illusion and reality is subtle: illusion is often the handmaiden of reality and, indeed, its constant support. Matters such as the acceptance of personal responsibility, adherence to the values and practices of a Community of Responsibility, and the sense of pride at having done 'all that one could,' are of immense value and find some grounding on the compatibilist level. They can be a non-illusory reality. However, they often depend upon lack of awareness of the ultimate perspective: illusion does not turn everything into falsehood but, on the contrary, is often the condition for the *emergence* of a valid and morally necessary reality.

Moreover, even those elements of our self-understanding that are solely illusory (and not compatibilistically-grounded reality merely assisted by illusion) may nevertheless be very important in themselves. Illusion not only helps to sustain independent reality, but is also *in itself* a sort of 'reality,' simply by virtue of its existence. The falseness of beliefs does not negate the fact that they exist for the believer. This is the way in which the libertarian beliefs exist. In addition to supporting the compatibilist non-illusory basis, illusion also *creates* a mental reality, such as a particular sense of worth, appreciation and moral depth associated with belief in libertarian free will, which would not exist without it. The effects of this illusory 'reality' are sometimes positive. In a number of ways, then, illusion serves a crucial *creative* function, which is a basis for social morality and personal self-appreciation, in support of the compatibilist forms and beyond them.

The idea of illusion as morally necessary is repugnant and demeaning. As David Wiggins aptly put it:

> If a dilemma exists here it should first be acknowledged and felt as such. Only barbarism and reaction can benefit by concealment. If the unreformed notion of responsibility, the notion which is our notion, is a sort

of metaphysical joke must we not at the very least create some safe time
or place in everyday life to laugh at it? (Wiggins 1973, 55).

Nevertheless, I do not see any resources left to combat the ethical necessity of
illusion in the free will case.

VI.

From Naturalism to Illusionism. Revisionist naturalism sought to neutralise
problems such as we saw by saying that we need not care, that there is no
need to justify our attitudes and practices. Non-revisionist naturalism was
more modest, merely insisting that in practice not much can change, and that
for this reason there is little room for concern. Both stances were found to
be unconvincing. We can understand the 'conservative' instinct of naturalism but see that illusion is required. The insights of naturalism can be better
defended in combination with an illusionistic element. We end up with the
broad conclusion that our priority should be to live with the assumption of
libertarian free will although there is no basis for this other than our very
need to live with this assumption; but as we cannot accept this way of seeing
things, and confront dangers to our beliefs, illusion must play a central role
in our lives.

Reactive naturalism is important for Illusionism. Firstly, the failure of
naturalism's 'don't-worry' attitude leads to Illusionism. Naturalism has been
seen by many as the last hope of compatibilism, and its weaknesses lead to
recognition of the *role* and the *need* for illusion. Those who came to naturalism out of despair of previous alternatives now need to take a further step
towards Illusionism. It can be said that naturalism and Illusionism are the
last competitors. It is not by chance that they are located at the stage of the
third question, the Consequences Question, unlike the more traditional positions. The progression to the third question reflects our acknowledgement
that the answer to the Compatibility Question (are moral responsibility and
the associated notions compatible with the absence of libertarian free will?),
for all its importance, is not conclusive, and, moreover, that the deep meaning
and practical significance of the free will issue is not fully encapsulated in the
absence of libertarian free will and the answer to the Compatibility Question.
The move to the third question (which asks about the consequences following
from our previous results), and the insufficiency of naturalism on that question, serve to firmly identify illusion as the deep factor in the free will issue.

Finally, even more crucially, naturalism indicates the basis for illusion's
practical *actualisation.* Naturalism's partial success, and not only its limitation, is instructive here. We are 'naturally' tacit libertarians, and 'naturally'
resist threats to free-will-related beliefs, attitudes and practices: even when

the defence of not seeing threats to libertarian free will in the first place is breached, the damage can be contained. The naturalistic foundation not only paves the way for illusion, but sets it at the heart of the human condition. Illusion is not some external, pragmatic, temporary way of coping with philosophical conclusions, but the very way humanity lives.[7]

Notes

1. The free will problem can be structured in various ways, but the way presented here seems most useful: if there were libertarian free will, much of the point in asking the Compatibility Question would disappear, and so on. Nevertheless, one may begin by asking if compatibilism is insufficient and then move on to see whether libertarian free will could help. In any case, reactive naturalism emerges at the end of such traditional explorations and, I claim, Illusionism follows from the weaknesses of reactive naturalism.

2. We need to combine the insights of compatibilism and hard determinism into a joint position, for neither on its own is adequate; see Smilansky (1993) and Smilansky (2000, Part I).

3. Further views, such as utilitarianism, can be thought to be relevant. I cannot consider the general merits of utilitarianism here, but it seems to me to be fundamentally alien to the deep concerns of the free will issue. It is radically at odds with moral phenomenology: the seriousness of moral appraisal depends on our not viewing judgements merely as manipulative ways of influencing people, which can in principle be applied to the blameless if it is socially useful to do so. People would not be willing to be blamed, would not accept blame as appropriate, were it not assumed that they deserve blame on account of their freely taken actions. Utilitarianism is also opposed to our deepest moral intuitions (the inherent concern with control in general and the abhorrence for the 'punishment' of the innocent example in practice). Even if one accepts utilitarianism the role of illusion with respect to free will can be demonstrated, but this paper can be taken to address those whose basic ethical views are not (only) utilitarian. I cannot consider other positions here.

4. Natural human inclinations have not always been sufficient to safeguard our core conception. For more historical examples, from the ancient Greeks, medieval societies, and anthropology, see Sayre (1932, 977 and 981); Adkins (1960, 57, 68, 167); Hibbert (1963, 201f.); Von Furer-Haimendorf (1967, 216); Pollock and Maitland (1968 vol.2, 470f.).

5. I consider the issue of free will and self-respect in greater detail in Smilansky (1997) and Smilansky (2000, section 6.4).

6. There are many complex ways in which illusion may be functional concerning free will, which we cannot consider here (see Smilansky 2000, section 8.4). We have focused on the main way, helping maintain false libertarian beliefs.

7. I am very grateful to Giora Hon, Hugh LaFollette, Iddo Landau, Jimmy Lenman, Andrew Moore, Paul Russell, Peter Strawson, Ralph Walker, and Jo Wolff, for helpful comments on drafts of this paper. Earlier versions were presented to the philosophy departments at Cardiff, Glasgow, the University of Kent at Canterbury, and Reading, and I have benefited from comments made by the participants.

References

Adkins, Arthur W. H. 1960. *Merit and Responsibility*. Oxford: Clarendon Press.

Anscombe, G. E. M. 1981. "Modern moral philosophy," *Collected Philosophical Papers*. Vol. 3. Oxford: Blackwell.

Bennett, Jonathan. 1980. "Towards a theory of punishment," *Philosophic Exchange* 3: 43–54.

Feinberg, Joel. 1970. "Justice and personal desert," *Doing and Deserving*, by Joel Feinberg. Princeton, NJ: Princeton University Press.

Fischer, John Martin. 1994. *The Metaphysics of Free Will*. Oxford: Blackwell.

Furer-Haimendorf, Christoph von. 1967. *Morals and Merit: A Study of Values and Social Controls in South Asian Societies*. London: Weidenfeld and Nicolson.

Glover, Jonathan. 1970. *Responsibility*. London: Routledge and Kegan Paul.

Hart, H. L. A. 1970. *Punishment and Responsibility*. Oxford: Clarendon Press.

Hibbert, Christopher. 1963. *The Roots of Evil*. London: Weidenfeld and Nicolson.

Klein, Martha. 1990. *Determinism, Blameworthiness and Deprivation*. Oxford: Oxford University Press.

Kymlicka, Will. 1989. Quoted in G.A. Cohen, "On the currency of egalitarian justice," *Ethics*. 99: 906–44.

Pollock, Frederick, and Frederic William Maitland. 1968. *The History of English Law*. 2d. ed. Vol. 2. Cambridge: Cambridge University Press.

Russell, Paul. 1992. "Strawson's way of naturalizing responsibility," *Ethics* 102: 287–302.

Russell, Paul. 1995. *Freedom and Moral Sentiment*. New York: Oxford University Press.

Sayre, Francis Bowes. 1932. "Mens rea," *Harvard Law Review*, 45: 974–1026.

Snow, C. P. 1983. In *Snow: An Oral Biography*, by John C. Halperin. Brighton, UK. Harvester.

Smilansky, Saul. 1993. "Does the free will debate rest on a mistake?", *Philosophical Papers*, 22: 173–88.

Smilansky, Saul. 1997. "Can a determinist respect herself?" In *Freedom and Moral Responsibility: General and Jewish Perspectives*, ed. C. H. Manekin and M.Kellner, 85–98. College Park: University of Maryland Press.

Smilansky, Saul. 2000. *Free Will and Illusion*. Oxford: Oxford University Press.

Strawson, Galen. 1986. *Freedom and Belief*. Oxford: Oxford University Press.

Strawson, P. F. 1980. "P. F. Strawson replies," in *Philosophical Subjects*, ed. Zak Van Straaten. Oxford: Clarendon Press.

Strawson, P. F. 1982. "Freedom and resentment," in *Free Will*, ed. Gary Watson. Oxford: Oxford University Press.

Strawson, P. F. 1987. *Skepticism and Naturalism*. London: Methuen.

Taylor, Gabriele. 1985. *Pride, Shame, and Guilt*. Oxford: Clarendon Press.

Vuoso, George. 1987. "Background, responsibility and excuse," *Yale Law Journal*, 96: 1661–1686.

Wallace, R. Jay. 1994. *Responsibility and the Moral Sentiments*. Cambridge, MA: Harvard University Press.

Watson, Gary. 1987. "Responsibility and the limits of evil: variations on a Strawsonian theme," in *Responsibility, Character and the Emotions*, ed. Ferdinand Schoeman. Cambridge: Cambridge University Press, 256–286.

Wiggins, David. 1973. "Towards a reasonable libertarianism," in *Essays on Actions and Events*, ed. Ted Honderich. London: Routledge and Kegan Paul.

Williams, Bernard. 1985. Ethics and the Limits of Philosophy. London: Fontana.

21

How to Solve the Problem of Free Will

Manuel Vargas

1. Take-backs

Let me start off by acknowledging that the title of this essay is both presumptuous and completely misleading.

First, I don't think there is anything that has sole claim to being *the* problem of free will. There are a number of distinct philosophical puzzles that have gone under the label "the problem of free will." For example, there is the question of what sort of power or variety of control we need in order to be properly held morally responsible. There is also the question of what sort of freedom we must have for us to have true beliefs about our powers when we deliberate about what to do. There is also the question of whether and how it makes sense to say that we cause things, or initiate new chains of events, as opposed to our just transmitting the effects of prior causes. You *could* think that the answer to all these things—and others I haven't mentioned—comes to the same thing. However, I am inclined to think that they do not, and that anyway, we ought not start off by supposing that they do.

Second, I'm not really going to try to *solve* any of the problems of free will. Instead, I am going to show *how* we can solve it. The idea is to give you a general recipe or formula for constructing a solution to it. Elsewhere, I have tried to bake that cake given by the recipe, but my aspiration here is much more limited. I just want to convince you that this recipe looks good enough to be worth trying out on your own time.

Third, I'm aware that all of this sounds *really* presumptuous. Lots of thoughtful folks have thought really hard about the various problems of free will. Many of them have offered purported solutions to the problem of free will. However, it isn't as though any of those accounts has widespread support. So, you might wonder, what makes this account so special?

In reply: well, yeah, this looks bad. Nevertheless, I think we've been very close to an adequate solution to at least one version of the free will problem for some time now, and all we have needed is a distinction or two and a bit more clarity about some methodological issues. My contribution to these matters is to put a few pieces in place that allow us to see our way through to a solution, the larger pieces of which have been developed by many others.

So now that I've taken back nearly everything promised in the title, I should say what I'm actually going to do. First, I'll say a bit about conventional solutions to one version of the free will problem. My focus will be on what is dissatisfying about them. Then, I'll consider whether we should just accept that we don't have free will. I'll argue that we shouldn't, because there is a possibility—and a plausible one at that—that we have overlooked. I'll then discuss the shape of this possibility and how it provides us with the outlines of a satisfactory resolution to the free will problem.

2. The problem with which we are concerned

The version of the problem of free will I am interested in trying to solve is the problem of explaining what free will is and whether we have it, where by "free will" I mean a feature, power, or ability of responsible agents that is especially distinctive of them being morally responsible.

I say "especially distinctive" rather than "required" because there are many features of agents—beliefs, desires, intentions, emotions, social connections, consciousness, and so on—the absence of which may preclude moral responsibility in some or another circumstance, but that are nevertheless not distinctive of specifically responsible agency. However, for my purposes, free will is the kind of thing that shows up in distinctively (morally) responsible agents. In particular, something about free will should help explain why agents with it can be properly held responsible.

There are some things I could say to motivate such presumptions, but I'm content to leave them as undefended premises in what follows.

In focusing on a responsibility-centric conception of free will, it behooves me to clarify that the variety of responsibility that is at stake here is *moral* responsibility. I am interested in a notion of responsibility connected to the licensing of moral praise and blame—blameworthiness, you might say. This is distinct from, for example, causal and legal responsibility. I might be worthy of moral blame for snickering loudly at your choice of trousers or your manner of speaking, but it would not follow that under the law there is anything for which I am thereby responsible. Causal and moral responsibility come apart as well: a bad alternator might be causally responsible for my car not starting, but there is no moral fault to be found with the alternator.

One complexity about moral responsibility is that it admits of both direct and indirect cases. When I surreptitiously put beef stock in food for vegetarian friends, I am directly responsible for serving them non-vegetarian food. But there are outcomes of my choices for which I can be responsible that are less certain but morally salient possible outcomes of what I do that I foresee, or could foresee. So, if I plan to pursue a high-speed road race immediately following an extended tequila-shooting contest with my drinking team, it seems plausible to think that I will be responsible for a wide range of disastrous results that will follow in the wake of my undertaking that two-stage adventure. When I pass out at the wheel, moments before my car goes shooting off a cliff into the Pacific Ocean, I will not be absolved from responsibility when my teammates point out that I was unconscious at the time I went off the cliff. If still sufficiently articulate, they might belligerently proclaim that consciousness is widely regarded as a requirement for responsibility, and I was manifestly unconscious when my car left the road. But we would do well to ignore them. After all, my responsibility here is very real, if indirect.

So, in the following, I am interested in a distinctive agential power, a power that directly and indirectly supports moral responsibility.

3. The standard solutions and what's wrong with them

There are a number of purported solutions to "the" problem of free will, but two in particular have garnered the lion's share of adherents: *libertarianism* and *compatibilism*.

Libertarianism is ordinarily characterized as the conjunction of two different commitments. The first is *incompatibilism*, or the view that free will is incompatible with determinism.[1] The second is a commitment to the *existence* of free will. So, a libertarian thinks that if determinism were true, we wouldn't have free will. But we do have free will, insists the libertarian, which commits him or her to the view that we are not determined.

Although historically significant, and not without conceptual utility, I think the focus on determinism is more than a little misleading. There aren't many physicists or philosophers who think that determinism is true as a description of low-level physical particles. (Oddly, social scientists remain great enthusiasts of determinism.[2]) So it should strike you as a bit strange to worry about whether free will is incompatible with determinism.

Instead, it seems to me, the real concern should be whether we possess forms of agency sufficient to sustain practices of moralized praising and blaming, given a scientifically informed, independently plausible picture of the world. After all, even if determinism is true, there might be any number of other things that could threaten our having free will—whether it is neuroscience, discoveries about how the psychology of our agency functions, and so on. Determinism is only one threat, and perhaps the least scientifically credible threat, at that.

Still, determinism has a kind of pride of place in these discussions. One reason is that it remains useful as a way of characterizing an influential class of views. Even if many of us remain suspicious about determinism as a characterization of the universe as a whole, it remains possible that we might learn that determinism, or something very close to it, obtains in the parts of the universe in which our agency functions. What the libertarian insists is that were we to learn that our actions were determined in this way, that would be sufficient to show that we are not free and responsible.

Compatibilism is the other view with a plausible claim on a plurality of adherents, at least amongst those who have joined these debates. By compatibilism, I mean the view that free will is compatible with determinism. In recent years, there has been some dispute about the scope of this and related terms, for example, whether it is possible that one can be a compatibilist about moral responsibility without being a compatibilist about free will. Although there is a good deal to say about these matters, I will bracket them. For present purposes, I will use "compatibilism" and "incompatibilism" to refer to the view that *both* free will and moral responsibility are, respectively, compatible and incompatible with determinism.

I claimed that in this section I would say why the standard solutions to "the" problem of free will don't work. Nothing I will say here is immune to reply by even an average defender of the views I criticize. Still, my hope is to make some remarks that will resonate with those who have cast their eyes at least once on the standard approaches, and walked away not entirely convinced.

Libertarianism does a fine job of capturing many threads of ordinary, commonsense thinking about the nature of our agency in the world. There is a growing body of experimental research that shows that when people reflect on questions of free will in the abstract, many of us tend to have broadly incompatibilist reactions (Nichols and Knobe 2007; Roskies and Nichols 2008; Sarkissian et al. 2010). And, overwhelmingly, people seem to think that even if the rest of the world is deterministic, at least human choice-making is not (Nichols and Knobe 2007). So even if not everyone is pre-philosophically (or perhaps more accurately, at the first stages of doing philosophy) a libertarian when thinking about matters in the abstract, a good many people seem to be.

Libertarianism has a second virtue. It piggy-backs on the considerable (if imperfect) virtues of classic arguments for incompatibilism. I won't rehearse them here, but there is a body of powerful arguments for incompatibilism. They can be resisted in various ways, with various degrees of dialectical sophistication. However, incompatibilism gets some claim to being intuitive from the fact that familiar arguments for incompatibilism do seem to codify a very natural way of thinking about free will. What it takes to resist these arguments is oftentimes a very subtle interpretation of powers, laws of nature, abilities, and so on. The nuances of these views, and the complex arguments it takes to make such views credible to even other philosophers, seem to me to be prima facie considerations against their credibility as descriptions of ordinary convictions.

Finally, I think the intuitiveness of libertarianism is perhaps connected to a diverse set of other influences. The legacy of dualism, various religious traditions, and a tendency to read off one's metaphysics from confusions about phenomenology and the explanatory frameworks for human action have all given libertarianism a foothold in our imagination of human agency.

Despite its considerable intuitive appeal, libertarianism has several shortcomings. I will mention two: doubts about its plausibility and worries about the moral cost it carries.

First: once you see what it takes to make good on the commitments of libertarian pictures of agency—the postulation of a special and radically different metaphysics for humans (e.g., agent causal libertarianism), the existence of indeterministic mechanisms in very specific places in human deliberation and not others (event causal libertarianism), or the postulation of uncaused events in the production of human action (uncaused event libertarianism)—it is easy to feel uneasy. The accounts can feel like armchair neuroscience, or they seem to invoke an entirely *ad hoc* metaphysics, postulated solely to preserve a picture that we have no independent motivation for believing in, beyond the fact that we seem greatly invested in perpetuating practices of moralized praising and blaming. And that, I think, is a real problem. If we were to sit back and ask our selves what we have good reason to believe about our agency, solely on the evidence, it is hard to imagine that we'd come up with libertarianism.

Now this isn't really an argument against libertarianism. For all I've said, libertarians might be right. Our agency might indeed have whatever properties are described by your favorite libertarian theory. Still, I've never seen good evidence for thinking that we are, in fact, agents of the sort libertarians describe. At best, we get hints that, for example, some brain processes are not deterministic. But this feels a bit like trying to prove the existence of fairies by noting that there are some small creatures with translucent wings. In neither case is consistency with the known facts an argument for the actuality of the additional posit. And there is almost always an additional posit; no libertarian thinks that raw indeterminism is sufficient for free will. The indeterminism has to happen in particular ways at particular times, and this is precisely what there is virtually no evidence for. So, it seems, libertarianism is an undermotivated attempt to preserve a pre-scientific picture of humans as radically distinct and separate from the physical, material world.

There is a second reason to worry about libertarianism. The worry is this: given the fact that libertarianism has little or no evidence in its favor, beyond our hope that it is true, adherence to libertarianism seems to undermine our grounds for holding one another responsible. That is, it makes the justification for our blaming and punishing hinge on the hope or aspiration that we are libertarian agents, a hope or aspiration for which *there is no positive evidence and considerable disagreement about whether anyone possesses the requisite power* (Pereboom 2001, 161, 198–99; Pereboom 2006, 562–64; Vargas 2009).

A concrete example may make this point clearer. Consider *Fiery*. Fiery is a skeptical subject of a significant moral blame, and likely, punishment. Perhaps she faces the death penalty, if that is permissible, and if not, then some very significant censure where that variety or some large quantum of that censure (whether blame or punishment) depends on the presumption of her being a libertarian agent. Now, let us imagine that Fiery demands to know *why* such treatment is justified.

Her libertarian persecutor must acknowledge that we have no evidence to support the hope that underwrites our treatment of her—that is, the hope that Fiery is, indeed, a libertarian agent. But Fiery will surely protest: the mere *possibility* that she deserves some extra quantum of blame or punishment beyond that required for, say, rehabilitation, does not, by itself, make such treatment justified. After all, Fiery insists, there is also a chance that she—and everyone else—might not be libertarian agents. Indeed, this strikes her (especially now!) as considerably more plausible than her prosecutor's insistence that libertarianism is true.

Fiery is surely right about this much: if she is indeed not responsible, it would be grossly unjust to hold her accountable to any degree beyond the degree of blame and punishment warranted by non-libertarian considerations. On the presumption that one should avoid gross injustice when one can do so, and that it is wrong to blame when there is no evidence that the target is responsible, the only defensible course of action is to abandon holding Fiery (and everyone else) responsible in whatever degree the presumption of libertarian agency entails. So, it seems to me, we had better have a justification for blame that runs deeper than the wish or hope that we are libertarian agents.

So: libertarianism's purported solution to this version of the free will problem is not much of a solution.

Let us turn to consider the other purported solution to the problem of free will: compatibilism. Like libertarianism, compatibilism has some claim of capturing our pre-philosophical convictions. For example, there is a body of research that shows that when it comes down to brass tacks, when we think about concrete, particular cases in which there is a clear victim, we seem quick to blame and condemn regardless of whether or not we are told the world is deterministic (Nahmias et al. 2006; Nichols and Knobe 2007; Woolfolk et al. 2006).

So, it seems, compatibilism has some claim on us too. The dialectic here is complicated, and more complicated than I can adequately address in this essay. Here's the upshot, though: for all of compatibilism's virtues, it will always seem like a cheat to a good many of us. Many of us persist in having incompatibilist convictions. Although there are clearly cases in which a strong majority of folks give compatibilist reactions to various prompts, incompatibilist reactions never completely disappear, remaining at roughly a quarter to a third of responses among the populations where these things have been studied.

We could argue about which set of cases is more revealing—perhaps there is an error in our thinking caused by emotion-triggering cases with personalized victims, or perhaps it is only when emotions are engaged that we see the true moral significance of an act—but I think there is no easy path to the resolution of this dispute. Instead, I think we should just accept that (for good or bad reasons) as a matter of ordinary convictions, we have a mixed picture of the requirements for moral responsibility. If that is right, though, then any philosophical account of moral responsibility that is going to satisfy those convictions will need to sometimes invoke libertarian convictions.

Some compatibilists have insisted that one of the appealing features of compatibilism is that it does not make our moral responsibility "hang on a thread" (Fischer 2006, 6). And, one might think, that such considerations might give us some reason for jettisoning lingering libertarian convictions. But we must be careful here. It might be appealing if our theory of free will ensured that we are responsible, but this doesn't (by itself) seem like a good reason to think that a thoroughgoing compatibilist theory is *true*. After all, I find it appealing to think that there is an afterlife awaiting me, perhaps with an endless supply of the finest mezcals, bourbons, and Belgian beer (plus, video games!...and my spouse and kids...and friends and extended family (that I like) and video games, quite plausibly). But as widespread a view about the afterlife as this might be (allowing for substitution about the precise details), we might wonder if the fact of its being appealing and its possibility of playing an organizing role in my life should yet constitute a reason for thinking that such an afterlife exists.

So, I think conventional compatibilist theories are in an odd position. They are plausible only to the extent to which they ignore the very convictions that gave us a problem that needs solving. The way they solve the problem is by denying we ever had the problematic commitments in the first place. And, independent appeals to how nice it would be to insulate our moral practices from threat does not seem to constitute a very compelling reason to think the view is true.

To sum up: the problem with standard solutions is that they don't seem to do a very good job of solving that problem. Libertarians offer us accounts that would be nice to believe, but they don't give us very good reasons for believing in them. Compatibilists offer us solutions, but solutions that seem to work only by insisting there was no real problem to be solved in the first place.

Given that conventional solutions seem unfortunately aspirational or disingenuously evasive, we might conclude that the only solution is to acknowledge that we do not have free will. Indeed, one might think, far too many philosophers have been callow about this, scared of embracing the tough but radical conclusion. So, we might think, at least *we* shall be tough enough to stare the problem in its face and deal with it honestly and with integrity.[3]

Perhaps there is a matter of disposition here: some philosophers are drawn to more radical conclusions and others regard such conclusions as proof of an argument gone wrong. My own view is that we can be dissatisfied with conventional libertarian and compatibilists accounts, and still think that the no free will view is woefully undermotivated. Let me explain.

4. What's wrong with the nay-sayers

We can make some progress by starting with a distinction between *diagnostic* and *prescriptive* theorizing.

When we face a philosophical puzzle, we can try to provide a diagnosis of what is going on. In providing that diagnosis, we offer a description of the state of our thinking, and ideally, an explanation of how we came to have the problem that exercises us. So, a diagnostic account of free will is one that endeavors to describe the contours of our thinking that have given rise to the problem of free will.

However, we might pursue a different project. We could endeavor to provide an account of how, all things considered, we ought to think about some subject matter. This may or may not overlap with how we currently think about things. Sometimes how we ought to think about things just is how we think about them. Other times, what we conclude is that we ought to think about things somewhat differently than we do. So, for example, at one point in time a popular view was that water was one of the four basic indivisible substances of the universe. When the chemical theory of water gained acceptance, presumably these people did not conclude that water did not exist. Rather, they concluded that the nature of water was different than they had imagined it to be.

Don't let the example from the history of science mislead. Moral, social, and legal categories have all changed over time as a result of various pressures—some empirical, some conceptual, some normative. Few of our received notions have remained unmolested by the expansion of human learning and the accretions of diverse cultural practices.

It is the possibility of a gap between what we think and what we ought to think that offers us a way out of the familiar debates about free will. Here's my suggestion: we can resolve a number of problems familiar to us under the rubric of "free will" if we permit ourselves to take seriously the possibility that free will might not be the sort of thing we supposed it to be. Moreover, once we have seen how such an account might go, and we reflect on our pre-philosophical convictions as we find them, what we might conclude is that we have no good reason to hold on to various presuppositions about free will, presuppositions that have precisely led to our conception of free will *as a problem*.

In suggesting this possibility, I don't mean to downplay the fact that such an account would leave us with some hard work. For example, we would need some story of how we can go about characterizing free will without just appealing to our received convictions or the intuitions we find ourselves having. (My answer: think about the role of the concept, the work it does, and what notions and practices it regulates.) And, we would need some reason to think that the proposed prescriptive account is an account of free will and not some other things. (Roughly, the test is to ask whether it is capable of doing the bulk of the conceptual and social practice-coordinating roles we associate with free will). But if we can provide reasonable enough answers to these things, we move tantalizingly close to a resolution to exhausting and exhausted-seeming debates about free will.[4]

In general, there are at least two classes of cases where jettisoning significant convictions widely associated with some notion have been appealing: (1) in the case of scientific discoveries (e.g., the advent of the chemical theory of water displacing, say, broadly Empedoclean and Aristotelian pictures of water) and (2) in the case of ideas whose function or role in our life has to do with social regulation, and where background presumptions and/or motivating social pressures have shifted sometimes in response to empirical data and/or to new forms of social organization. Examples include, perhaps, marriage, social class position (e.g., as reflecting stratifications reflective of God's favor), race (as a biological essence vs. a social kind), and so on. In each of these cases, we came to fundamentally re-conceive the matter. Indeed, the whole of morality might have plausibly been subject to such transformation in conviction.

Recall the state of ethics among the European intelligentsia at the end of the 19th century. God's obituary was being written, and more than a few thoughtful people, including Nietzsche and Dostoevsky, wondered whether God's non-existence would entail that "everything is permitted." Here's one reason people might have thought that: if you thought that the nature, content, and significance of morality is essentially settled by God's will, and if you thought God doesn't exist, then moral claims will likely look to you to be false, nonsense, or at least not binding.

There are different ways to read the subsequent history of ethical theorizing. On one reading, we are still working out the fact that without God, there is no hope for an adequate foundation for morality. A different, and perhaps more common view (at least in the overwhelmingly atheist-inclined world of Anglophone philosophy) is the thought that the proper lesson from the death of God was not that morality doesn't exist, but that the foundation of morality was rather different than many people supposed. Rather than God's existence and His commands being essential to morality, it turns out that something else (say, what we would universally will under full information in ideal conditions, or what would produce the greatest welfare, or what we would agree to if concerned to create a system of cooperation, or...) is the core of morality.

This basic pattern of concept change should seem, with a bit of reflection, somewhat familiar: we have a cherished way of thinking about something, a way that helps make sense of our lives and orders important practices; it becomes threatened by some new consideration or an overturning of some old presumption; people rush to declare that the old notion is now bankrupt and to be rejected; but then others rush in to advocate a transformation or rehabilitation of the old view, which now rejects the troublesome element or presupposition that was previously thought to be essential to the notion. Sometimes the rehabilitation sticks and sometimes it doesn't. Whether it does is a function of any number of factors, but at least in the case of ideas that play some role in social regulation, one prominent factor is surely whether or not the proposed transformation still permits a similar kind of social regulation as the pre-revised notion.

So now, finally, we get to the heart of the matter: can we go in for a revised notion of free will, one that does without the (to some, apparently essential) incompatibilist elements? That is, is our notion of free will the kind of thing that is enough of a social regulation-like idea to admit to this sort of transformation? I think so.

Recall an idea I mentioned at the beginning, that there are various notions of free will that philosophers have bandied about. I'm not sure that all the notions out there that have some claim on being labeled "free will" are sufficiently social regulation-ish to make this idea plausible in all of those cases. However, if we focus on the notion of control that is required to license moral praise and blame, then the answer is very plausibly *yes*. This idea, that we are concerned with something intimately tied to social practices, gives those of us with *this* interest—i.e., free will understood in terms of a condition on moral responsibility—some reason to think we should be *revisionists* rather than eliminativists or nihilists about free will. That is to say: we can think that a philosophically adequate account of free will will conflict with aspects of our ordinary commitments.[5] Crucially, the revisionist holds that such conflicts are permissible (and indeed, predictable) whenever we reject a particularly troublesome aspects of our ordinary views—say, libertarian commitments— because we've found some other way to secure what is at stake.

Of course, there are some who will insist that, manifestly, free will should *not* be understood in this way. Perhaps you are among them, thinking that free will is a kind of property of our agency that we have or don't, and that it can be analyzed independently of moral or social concerns. If this is nothing more than noting that you are interested in a different notion of free will than the one with which I am concerned, that's fine. Perhaps I want to think about chocolate and you want to think about sauerkraut. But suppose you intend this as an objection to the same notion I'm interested in, and that this notion is to be understood in terms of some metaphysical property, the status of which is independent of anything in the realm of morality or social regulation. On your view, the permissibility of the moral concerns *presumes* or *depends* on whether or not we have this metaphysical property. Call this *the metaphysical reading*.

Here, there are two things to say. First, we can repeat the dialectic: we might *think* some independent metaphysical nature is the core of a responsibility-centric notion of free will, but we could be in error about this, and an otherwise plausible account of free will that dispenses with this presumption is partly an argument against the presumption of the metaphysical reading. Second, even if we grant that the metaphysical reading is an essential part of something we in fact care about, it remains open to us to object that this is merely another one of a long line of mysterious properties according to which we regulate our social and moral lives, but that turns out to be otiose to the concerns for which we've postulated the property. In this, the metaphysical conception of free will might be like blood purity, succubi, immaterial souls, and the divine right of kings: you *could* believe in such things, but we don't *need* to believe in such things if, for example, we wish to regulate our social lives in ways that are both mutually justifiable and that permit us to flourish.

So, *if* (and at this stage of the argument that's all it is) there is a notion of responsible agency and a justifiable system of praising and blaming that can adequately function without an incompatibilist metaphysics, then it looks like this is all we need to be revisionists, instead of eliminativists or nihilists about this notion of free will. And (once again) *if* we locate such a notion, then we might find ourselves in the fortunate position of not missing those libertarian elements of our self-conception, anyway.

On the approach I am suggesting, in the face of libertarianism's implausibility, the main question before us is whether we still have reason to go on roughly as before. If we do not have reason to go on roughly as before, then eliminativism becomes more plausible. If however we can locate some reasons to continue as before, then revisionism is surely the more credible option.

5. How to solve the problem

Suppose you decided to take seriously the thought that free will might be different than we sometimes tend to think, but that it should be the sort of thing intimately tied to the business of moralized praising and blaming. How might you go about trying to construct an account of what that might be?

There are at least two options available to you. I call them *repurposing revisionism* and *systematic revisionism*. The first option is the easiest: take any traditional compatibilist theory you like, declare that it is only prescriptive and not diagnostic, and *voilà!*, you have a revisionist theory. The virtue of this approach is that you have some already existing theories at your disposal. The downside is that those theories tend to have been constructed in a context where the concern for intuitiveness played an important role in the construction of the theory. Most compatibilist theories have not started with the question of what could justify our practices of praising and blaming (and the typical web of connected judgments and attitudes), but have instead begun from trying to capture our intuitive judgments and ordinary patterns of the ways we in fact praise and blame. So, you might worry that these accounts will contain elements in them that were developed out of a concern for commitments or intuitions that the revisionist can reject.

Systematic revisionism constitutes a more demanding but also more appealing alternative. On this approach, the strategy is to begin with a picture of what we want a theory of moral responsibility to *do*. On the model I favor, the goal of the theory is to identify features of agency that can play an appropriate role in explaining the justification of our practices of praising and blaming and that helps explain how familiar judgments and attitudes about freedom and responsibility make sense in a framework that minimizes *ad hoc* metaphysical commitments.

The last two ideas can be expressed in terms of commitments to *normative adequacy* and to *naturalistic plausibility* (or perhaps less dogmatically, *scientific plausibility*). Roughly, the idea is that we want our theory of free will to be beholden to three things: (1) some conceptual role (in this case: a distinctive agential feature whose presence and operation licenses moralized praising and blaming); (2) explanatory and justifying tasks connected to the particular conceptual role identified by the account (in this case: an account of why this power would be the sort of thing that licenses praise and blame); and (3) a picture of the capacity or power that constitutes free will that does not put us at odds with our epistemically best pictures of the world (in this case: no libertarianism, and the aspiration to not run afoul of our scientific understanding of how agency operates). So, proposed departures from our ordinary ways of thinking won't be unprincipled if they are responsive to these concerns.

There are several advantages for any account developed along these lines. First, it would have the following advantage over conventional compatibilist accounts: it need not deny the existence and deep-rootedness of incompatibilist commitments among ordinary folks. Second, it needn't be committed to armchair neuroscience, old-fashioned speculative metaphysics, or other troublesome endeavors that arise when philosophers attempt to sketch pictures that commit us to very particular and otherwise unmotivated views about how future science will unfold. Third, it would provide us with a principled explanation for why the identified powers matter, how it is that these things—despite their running afoul of some of received convictions—are the sorts of things that properly underpin attributions of freedom and responsibility.

Of course, these advantages are conditional on actually generating a revisionist account that satisfies the afore-mentioned constraints on revisionist theory-building. So, more needs to be said.

6. Outlines of a solution

Now is the part of the story in which I downplay the demand for an account that would provide the antecedent of the extravagant conditional claims in the previous section. I do this for good reason: it is far beyond the scope of the present discussion to present a worked-out account of how a systematically revisionist, prescriptively compatibilist account of free will might go, for such an account necessarily involves thorny details far beyond the scope of a single chapter (Vargas, 2013). Moreover, as I emphasized at the outset, the aim of this particular essay is less to convince you to embrace my particular account than it is to make plausible a general approach that might intrigue those who remain unhappy with the more familiar options.

Although in what remains of this essay I say a bit about my preferred approach, I do not mean to suggest that there are not other revisionist accounts that could be given. Indeed, revisionism constitutes a class of theories, of which there are many possible instances. So, what follows should not be taken to be the definitive statement of what any revisionist account should look like. On the contrary, it would be best if we were in a position where we could select among multiple competing revisionist accounts, weighing contrasting advantages and disadvantages of theories, liberated from the shackles of our otiose or problematic intuitions.

Of course, I'd be delighted if the brief sketch that follows were sufficient to convince you to follow up on the details, but I'll be happy enough if I make plausible the thought that we are tantalizingly close to a solution to the problem of free will.

Let's start with the question of what, if anything, could justify praise and blame—apart from our being libertarian agents. This is a reasonable place to start precisely because we have yoked our picture of free will to the role it plays in moral responsibility. Given this framework, here's an appealing answer: praise and blame would be justified if they played some role in attaining some other end whose value is substantial and clear. Here's one such end:

enhancing our agency, in particular, our capacity to recognize and respond to moral considerations. To the extent to which our practices of moral responsibility, including praise and blame, play some appropriate role in supporting and enhancing the ongoing success of such agency (both in terms of responsiveness to moral considerations and in terms of the scope of context of actions in which such agency operates sufficiently well), we have a plausible justification for praising and blaming.

I'm glossing over a number of important details here. For example, on the picture I favor, the relationship between praising and blaming practices and the modest teleology that structures those practices is two-tiered: the ground level practices are not themselves goal-structured in their content or how they are ordinarily regarded—the teleology is only in the justification of those non-consequentialist elements. Moreover, the standards of praise and blame have their own internal logic, one that roughly tracks a concern for quality of will.

Here's what all of this has to do with free will: free will is the capacity we have to recognize and respond to moral considerations. This is a picture on which the possession of free will partly explains *why* we can be morally responsible. Without our having free will, responsibility practices lose their point, for there would be no agency of the relevant sort to enhance. It is also a picture that explains why free will is distinctively valuable. It is in virtue of having free will that we are the sorts of morally significant creatures that we are.

Of course, free will in the absence of a suite of standard agential capacities (for example, the ability to foresee consequences of action, to reason instrumentally, to settle on plans that get filled in over time, and so on) will be uninteresting. So there are some background presumptions about other agential capacities, but assuming their presence, then free will possesses a kind of explanatory power in understanding the normatively structured social practices that fill our daily lives.

Important to my account is the idea that the capacities to recognize and respond to moral considerations are multiply realizable. Indeed, their nature and structure are not stable across contexts. Bracketing some complexities, the picture is one on which the metaphysical realizers of free will vary: what constitutes a sufficient degree of responsiveness to moral considerations is not the same in all cases. This variation is partly a function of the justifying teleology of the responsibility system and the variable psychological constraints we operate under. Given that circumstances plausibly structure the capacities we have, a practicable system of normatively ideal standards for considerations-responsiveness will vary across contexts.

This picture also entails that our having free will is not an all-or-nothing affair, and that it is the kind of thing that we might grow to have in some contexts while simultaneously lacking it in other contexts. One byproduct of this picture is an original way of rewriting talk of alternative capacities. It is one on which the relevant notion of alternative possibilities is not to be extracted from the brute features of the metaphysics of agents, but instead from a complex relation consisting of the metaphysics of the agent and the agent's position in a web of normatively structured interests and practices.

What this means is that our having free will is not an intrinsic feature about us, but a partly relational notion. In turn, this means that we can ask questions about the circumstances of action, and whether our local moral ecology is conducive to our being responsible agents. The questions of whether, and how, and to what extent we build such circumstances are difficult questions that I have not attempted to answer. If I am right, the deepest problem that threatens our having free will is not a matter of high metaphysics, but rather the contexts in which we exercise our agency and the political challenges of structuring our environments to better support responsible agency.

My hope is that the preceding sketch is sufficiently provocative to make plausible the idea that we have considerable resources available to us, if we wish to walk down a revisionist path. If I am right, we have free will, and it is compatible with what we know about our agency and the world. It is not the notion of free will we started off looking for, but it is a notion that leads us away from responsibility nihilism.

7. Is revisionism just another cheat?

Among the many memorable condemnations of compatibilism, one of the best is Kant's remark that it is a "wretched subterfuge." Given that the account I have suggested is prescriptively compatibilist (although *not* diagnostically compatibilist), we might wonder whether it amounts to yet another wretched subterfuge.

In reply: even if my version of revisionism is wretched, it is most certainly not a subterfuge. My account begins with the idea that an adequate theory of free will costs us something. It costs us a piece of our self-conception, that part of our self-conception that sees us distinguished from the ordinary causal order of the universe, possessed of a unique ability to screen off the past and initiate new chains of causation disconnected from prior facts. What free will skeptics would like you to think is that this concession means that we lack free will and moral responsibility, just as some 19th-century atheists would have had you believe that the death of God entailed that everything is permitted.

Of course, it might turn out that we lack free will for some other reason, apart from our being part of the natural causal order. And, it might turn out that morality is bunk not because God doesn't exist but because there is no way to, say, draw a distinction between moral norms and merely local cultural conventions. Nevertheless, the mere fact that things are not as they first seem is not proof that they do not exist. It might only be proof that some more thinking is required before we understand what we are talking about.

Notes

1. Definitions of determinism are plentiful. For our purposes, we can assume that determinism is the view that (post-Big Bang) everything has a cause, and that causes are not probabilistic in any interesting way (i.e., the probability of a given cause bringing about an effect is always either 1 or 0). So, a post-Big Bang world that had uncaused events would not be deterministic. Nor would a world in which there were sometimes causes that had, say, only a 75% probability of bringing about some effect.

2. Chris Franklin has persuasively argued that much of the grip that determinism has exercised over the imaginations of scientists has arisen out of a concern to expunge uncertainty from their models and out of a confused (if historically influential) model of science (Franklin, in progress).

3. As Nietzsche once noted: "It is certainly not the least charm of a theory that it is refutable; it is precisely thereby that it attracts the more subtle minds. It seems that the hundred-times-refuted theory of the 'free will' owes its persistence to this charm alone; someone is always appearing who feels himself strong enough to refute it" (Nietzsche 1966, 18).

4. Notice that if we accept the possibility of some notion's nature being other than we ordinarily conceive it to be, this does not preclude nihilism-warranting discoveries. If nothing or too many diverse things play the relevant realizer in the world, this would be reason for taking seriously the nihilist's recommendation. On this approach, eliminativism is not eliminated, but its likelihood is reduced.

5. More precisely: a theory is revisionist whenever its prescription *conflicts* with the diagnosis. Cases in which a theory merely refines some commitment or the theory stakes a claim or injunction on some subject about which we have no antecedent commitments is not revisionist in the sense with which I am concerned.

References

Fischer, John Martin. 2006. *My Way: Essays on Moral Responsibility*. New York: Oxford University Press.

Franklin, Christopher. In progress. "The scientific plausibility of libertarianism."

Nahmias, Eddy, Stephen Morris, Thomas Nadelhoffer, and Jason Turner. 2006. "Is incompatibilism intuitive?" *Philosophy and Phenomenological Research* 73.1: 28–53.

Nichols, Shaun, and Joshua Knobe. 2007. "Moral responsibility and determinism: the cognitive science of folk intuitions," *Noûs* 41.4: 663–85.

Nietzsche, Friedrich Wilhelm. 1966. *Beyond Good and Evil*, trans. Walter Kaufmann. New York: Vintage Books.

Pereboom, Derk. 2001. *Living Without Free Will*. Cambridge: Cambridge University Press.

Pereboom, Derk. 2006. "Kant on transcendental freedom," *Philosophy and Phenomeno-logical Research* **73**.3: 537–67.

Roskies, Adina, and Shaun Nichols. 2008. "Bringing responsibility down to earth," *Journal of Philosophy* **105**.7: 371–88.

Sarkissian, Hagop, Amita Chatterjee, Felipe de Brigard, Joshua Knobe, Shaun Nichols, and Smita Sirker. 2010. "Is belief in free will a cultural universal?" *Mind and Language* **25**.3: 346–58.

Vargas, Manuel. 2009. "Revisionism about free will: a statement & defense." *Philosophical Studies* **144**.1: 45–62.

Vargas, Manuel. 2013. *Building Better Beings: A Theory of Moral Responsibility*. Oxford: Oxford University Press.

Woolfolk, Robert L., John Doris, and John Darley. 2006. "Identification, situational constraint, and social cognition: studies in the attribution of moral responsibility," *Cognition* **100**: 283–401.Part 9

Suggested Further Readings

IX. Scepticism, Illusionism, and Revisionism

Bernstein, Mark H. 2005. "Can we ever be really, truly, ultimately, free?" *Midwest Studies in Philosophy* 29.1: 1–12.

Clarke, Randolph. 2005. "On an argument for the impossibility of moral responsibility," *Midwest Studies in Philosophy* 29.1: 13–24.

Harris, Sam. 2012. *Free Will*. New York: Free Press.

Honderich, Ted. 2002. *How Free are You?* 2nd edition. Oxford: Oxford University Press.

Honderich, Ted, 2011. "Effects, determinism, neither compatibilism nor incompatibilism, consciousness," in Robert Kane, ed., *The Oxford Handbook of Free Will*, 2nd ed. New York: Oxford University Press.

Smilansky, Saul. 2000. *Free Will and Illusion*. New York: Oxford University Press.

Smilansky, Saul, 2011. "Free will, fundamental dualism, and the centrality of illusion," in Robert Kane, ed., *The Oxford Handbook of Free Will*, 2nd ed. New York: Oxford University Press.

Strawson, Galen. 1986. *Freedom and Belief*. Oxford: Clarendon Press.

Strawson, Galen, 2002. "The bounds of freedom," in R. Kane. ed., *The Oxford Handbook of Free Will*. New York: Oxford University Press.

Sommers, Tamler. 2012. *Relative Justice: Cultural Diversity, Free Will and Moral Responsibility*. Princeton: Princeton University Press.

Vargas, Manuel. 2011. "Revisionist accounts of free will," in Robert Kane, ed., *The Oxford Handbook of Free Will*, 2nd ed. New York: Oxford University Press.

Vargas, Manuel. 2013. *Building Better Beings: A Theory of Moral Responsibility*. Oxford: Oxford University Press.

PART TEN

Optimism, Pessimism, and Their Modes

22

Optimistic Skepticism about Free Will

Derk Pereboom

Introduction

One of the main concerns at stake in the historical free will debate is whether the sort of free will required for moral responsibility is compatible with the causal determination of our actions by factors beyond our control. Since Hume, the concern has prominently been extended to whether this sort of free will is compatible with indeterminacy in action. The position for which I argue is that free will, characterized in this way, is incompatible with this type of causal determination, and with the kind of indeterminacy of action that Hume had in mind. It is important to recognize that the term "moral responsibility" is used in a variety ways, and that the type of free will or control required for moral responsibility in several of these senses is uncontroversially compatible with the causal determination of action by factors beyond our control. But there is one particular sense of moral responsibility that has been at issue in the historical debate. It is this: for an agent to be morally responsible for an action is for it to belong to her in such a way that she would deserve blame if she understood that it was morally wrong, and she would deserve credit or perhaps praise if she understood that it was morally exemplary. The desert at issue here is basic in the sense that the agent, to be morally responsible, would deserve the blame or credit just because she has performed the action, given sensitivity to its moral status, and not by virtue of consequentialist or contractualist considerations. Moral responsibility in this sense is presupposed by our retributive reactive attitudes, and it is thus the variety of moral responsibility that P. F. Strawson famously brings to the fore in his essay "Freedom and Resentment" (1962).

There are other senses of moral responsibility that have not been a focus of the free will debate. For example, an agent could be considered morally responsible if it is legitimate to expect her to respond to such questions as: "Why did you decide to do that? Do you think it was the right thing to do?" and to evaluate critically what her actions indicate about her moral character.

Engaging in such interactions might well be reasonable in light of the way in which they contribute to our own and others' moral improvement (Arthur Kuflik, in conversation; for a related conceptions see Scanlon 1998 and Bok 1998). However, incompatibilists would not think that being morally responsible in this "answerability" sense is even *prima facie* incompatible with determinism. The type of moral responsibility that incompatibilists do claim not to be compatible with determinism is instead the sense characterized by basic desert and the reactive attitudes that presuppose it. From this point on, unless otherwise indicated, I will use the term "moral responsibility" to refer to this particular type.

Spinoza (1677/1985: 440–44, 483–84, 496–97) maintained that due to very general facts about the nature of the universe we human beings lack the sort of free will required for moral responsibility. About this I think he is right. More specifically, he argues that it is because of the truth of causal determinism that we lack this sort of free will; he is thus a *hard determinist*. By contrast, I am agnostic about the truth of causal determinism. I contend, like Spinoza, that we would not be morally responsible if determinism were true, but also that we would lack moral responsibility if indeterminism were true and the causes of our actions were exclusively states or events—this is the notion of indeterminacy of action that Hume arguably had in mind (1737/1978). For such indeterministic causal histories of actions would be as threatening to this sort of free will as deterministic histories are. However, it might be that if we were undetermined agent causes—if we as substances had the power to cause decisions without being causally determined to cause them—we would then have this type of free will. But although our being undetermined agent causes has not been ruled out as a coherent possibility, it is not credible given our best physical theories. Thus I do not claim that our having the sort of free will required for moral responsibility is impossible. Rather, I don't take a stand on whether it is possible or not. Nevertheless, since the only account on which we might in fact have this kind of free will is not credible given our best physical theories, we must take seriously the prospect that we are in fact not free in the sense required for moral responsibility. I call the resulting skeptical position *hard incompatibilism*. At the same time, I defend the optimistic view that conceiving of life without this type of free will would not be devastating to morality or to our sense of meaning in life, and in certain respects it may even be beneficial (for contrasting pessimistic views, see Smilansky 2000, and Russell 2000).

Furthermore, I reject an incompatibilism for which the availability of alternative possibilities is crucial to explaining moral responsibility, and accept instead an incompatibilism that ascribes the more significant role to an action's causal history. I argue that an agent's moral responsibility for an action would be explained primarily by the action's having a causal history in which she is the source of her action in a specific way. I thus opt for *source* as opposed to *leeway* incompatibilism. Agent-causal libertarianism is commonly conceived as an incompatibilist position in which an agent can be the source of her action in the way required for moral responsibility, and as a result proponents of this view are typically source incompatibilists. However, one might also be a source incompatibilist and seriously doubt that we have the sort of free will required for moral responsibility, and this is the position I advocate (Pereboom 2001).

A manipulation argument against compatibilism

Defending hard incompatibilism requires facing up to compatibilism. I believe that the strongest argument against the compatibilist begins with the intuition that if someone is causally determined to act by other agents, for example, by scientists who manipulate her brain, then she is not morally responsible for that action (Taylor 1974, cf. Ginet 1990; Kane 1996; Mele 2006). The argument continues by showing that there are no differences between cases like this and otherwise similar ordinary deterministic examples that can justify the claim that while an agent is not morally responsible when she is manipulated, she can nevertheless be responsible in the ordinary deterministic examples. The non-responsibility intuition remains strong even if when manipulated the agent satisfies the conditions on moral responsibility advocated by the prominent compatibilist theories. My multiple-case argument first of all develops examples of actions that involve such manipulation and in which these compatibilist conditions on moral responsibility are satisfied (1995, 2001). These cases, taken separately, indicate that it is possible for an agent not to be morally responsible even if the compatibilist conditions are satisfied, and that as a result these conditions are inadequate. But the argument has more force by virtue of setting out three such cases, each progressively more like a fourth, which the compatibilist might envision to be realistic, in which the action is causally determined in a natural way. An additional challenge for the compatibilist is to point out a relevant and principled difference between any two adjacent cases that would show why the agent might be morally responsible in the later example but not in the earlier one. I argue that this can't be done. I contend that the agent's non-responsibility generalizes from at least one of the manipulation examples to the ordinary case.

In the set-up, in each of the four cases Professor Plum decides to kill Ms. White for the sake of some personal advantage, and succeeds in doing so. The cases are designed so that his act of murder conforms to the prominent compatibilist conditions. This action meets certain conditions advocated by Hume: the action is not out of character, since for Plum it is generally true that selfish reasons typically weigh heavily—too heavily when considered from the moral point of view; while in addition the desire that motivates him to act is nevertheless not irresistible for him, and in this sense he is not constrained to act (Hume 1739/1978). The action fits the condition proposed by Harry Frankfurt (1971): Plum's effective desire (i.e., his will) to murder White conforms appropriately to his second-order desires for which effective desires he will have. That is, he wills to murder her, and he wants to will to do so, and he wills this act of murder because he wants to will to do so. The action also satisfies the reasons-responsiveness condition advocated by John Fischer and Mark Ravizza (1998): Plum's desires can be modified by, and some of them arise from, his rational consideration of the reasons he has, and if he knew that the bad consequences for himself that would result from killing White would be much more severe than they are actually likely to be, he would have refrained from killing her for that reason. Also, this action meets the condition advanced by Jay Wallace (1994): Plum has the general ability to grasp, apply, and regulate his actions by moral reasons. For instance, when egoistic reasons that count against acting morally are weak, he will typically regulate his behavior by moral reasons instead. This ability also provides him with the capacity to revise and develop his moral character over time, a condition that Alfred Mele emphasizes (1995). Now, supposing that causal determinism is true, is it plausible that Professor Plum is morally responsible for his action?

Each of the four cases I will now describe features different ways in which Plum's murder of White might be causally determined by factors beyond his control. In a first type of counterexample (Case 1) to these prominent compatibilist conditions, neuroscientists manipulate Plum in a way that directly affects him at the neural level, but so that his mental states and actions feature the psychological regularities and counterfactual dependencies that are compatible with ordinary agency (Pereboom, 2001: 121; McKenna 2008):

> Case 1: A team of neuroscientists is able to manipulate Professor Plum's mental state at any moment through the use of radio-like technology. In this case, they do so by pressing a button just before he begins to reason about his situation. This causes Plum's reasoning process to be egoistic, which the neuroscientists know will deterministically result in his decision to kill White. Plum does not think and act contrary to character since his reasoning processes are not infrequently egoistic. His effective first-order desire to kill White conforms to his second-order desires. The process of deliberation from which his action results is reasons-responsive; in particular, this type of process would have resulted in his refraining from killing White in some situations in which the reasons were different. Still, his reasoning is not in general exclusively egoistic, since he often regulates his behavior by moral reasons, especially when the egoistic reasons are relatively weak. He is also not constrained, in the sense that he does not act because of an irresistible desire—the neuroscientists do not induce a desire of this kind.

In Case 1, Plum's action satisfies all the compatibilist conditions we just examined. But intuitively, he is not morally responsible for the murder, because his action is causally determined by what the neuroscientists do, which is beyond his control. Consequently, it would seem that these compatibilist conditions are not sufficient for moral responsibility—even if all are taken together.

This example might be filled out in response to those who have asked whether Plum in Case 1 (or in a previous version of this example) meets certain minimal conditions of agency because he is too disconnected from reality, or because he himself lacks ordinary agential control (Fischer 2004: 156; Mele 2005: 78; Baker 2006: 320; Demetriou 2010). This concern highlights the fact that in this example two desiderata must be secured at the same time: the manipulation must preserve satisfaction of intuitive conditions of agency, and it must render it plausible that Plum is not morally responsible. It turns out that these two desiderata can be met simultaneously. Agency is regularly preserved in the face of certain involuntary momentary external influences. Finding out that the home team lost makes one irritable and more egoistic, and news of winning a prize more generous, but the conditions of agency remain intact. Still we commonly suppose that such influences are typically compatible with moral responsibility. However, we can imagine an egoism-enhancing momentary influence that preserves agency but plausibly does undermine moral responsibility. Suppose that by way of neural intervention the manipulators enhance Plum's disposition to reason self-interestedly at the requisite time, so that they know that it is causally ensured that he will decide to kill Ms. White (see also Shabo 2010: 376). Like finding out that the home team has lost, this intervention would not undermine Plum's agency, but intuitively it does render him non-responsible for his action.

Next consider a scenario more like the ordinary situation than Case 1:

Case 2: Plum is like an ordinary human being, except that neuroscientists have programmed him at the beginning of his life so that his reasoning is frequently but not always egoistic (as in Case 1), with the consequence that in the particular circumstances in which he now finds himself, he is causally determined to engage in the egoistic reasons-responsive process of deliberation and to have the set of first- and second-order desires that result in his decision to kill White. Plum has the general ability to regulate his behavior by moral reasons, but in his circumstances, due to the egoistic character of his reasoning, he is causally determined to make his decision. The neural realization of his reasoning process and of the resulting decision is exactly the same as it is in Case 1 (although the external causes are different). At the same time, he does not act because of an irresistible desire.

Again, although Plum satisfies the compatibilist conditions, intuitively he is not morally responsible. So Case 2 also shows that the prominent compatibilist conditions, either individually or in conjunction, are not sufficient for moral responsibility. Moreover, it would seem unprincipled to claim that here, by contrast with Case 1, Plum is morally responsible because the length of time between the programming and the action is now great enough. Whether the programming occurs a few seconds before or forty years prior to the action seems irrelevant to the question of his moral responsibility. Causal determination by factors beyond his control plausibly explains Plum's not being morally responsible in the first case, and I think we are forced to say that he is not morally responsible in the second case for the same reason.

Imagine next a scenario more similar yet to the ordinary situation:

> Case 3: Plum is an ordinary human being, except that he was causally determined by the rigorous training practices of his household and community in such a way that his reasoning processes are often but not exclusively rationally egoistic (as in Cases 1 and 2). This training took place when he was too young to have the ability to prevent or alter the practices that determined this aspect of his character. This training, together with his particular current circumstances, causally determines him to engage in the egoistic reasons-responsive process of deliberation and to have the first and second-order desires that result in his decision to kill White. Plum has the general ability to regulate his behavior by moral reasons, but in his circumstances, due to the egoistic nature of his reasoning processing, he is causally determined make his decision. The neural realization of his reasoning process and of his decision is the same as it is in Cases 1 and 2. Here again his action is not due to an irresistible desire.

For the compatibilist to argue successfully that Plum is morally responsible in Case 3, he must adduce a feature of these circumstances that would explain why he is morally responsible here but not in Case 2. It seems there is no such feature. In all of these examples, Plum meets the prominent compatibilist conditions for morally responsible action, so a divergence in judgment about moral responsibility between these examples won't be supported by a difference in whether these conditions are satisfied. Causal determination by factors beyond Plum's control most plausibly explains the absence of moral responsibility in Case 2, and we should conclude that he is not morally responsible in Case 3 for the same reason.

Therefore it appears that Plum's exemption from responsibility in Cases 1 and 2 generalizes to the nearer-to-normal Case 3. Does it generalize to the ordinary deterministic case?

> Case 4: Physicalist determinism is true—everything in the universe is physical, and everything that happens is causally determined by virtue

of the past states of the universe in conjunction with the laws of nature. Plum is an ordinary human being, raised in normal circumstances, and again his reasoning processes are frequently but not exclusively egoistic (as in Cases 1–3). His decision to kill White results from his reasons-responsive process of deliberation, and he has the specified first and second-order desires. The neural realization of his reasoning process and decision is just as it is in Cases 1–3. Again, he has the general ability to grasp, apply, and regulate his behavior by moral reasons, and it is not due to an irresistible desire that he kills White.

Given that we are constrained to deny moral responsibility in Case 3, could Plum be responsible in this ordinary deterministic situation? It appears that there are no differences between Case 3 and Case 4 that might justify the claim that Plum is not responsible in Case 3 but is in Case 4. In each of these cases Plum satisfies the prominent compatibilist conditions on moral responsibility. In each the neural realization of his reasoning process and decision is the same, although the causes differ. One distinguishing feature of Case 4 is that the causal determination of Plum's crime is not brought about by other agents (Lycan 1997). But the claim that this is a relevant difference is implausible. Imagine a further case that is exactly the same as Case 1 or Case 2, except that Plum's states are induced by a spontaneously generated machine—a machine with no intelligent designer. Here also Plum would lack morally responsibility.

The best explanation for why the agent isn't responsible in these four cases is that he is causally determined by factors beyond his control in each. Because there are no differences between Cases 1 and 2, 2 and 3, and 3 and 4 that can explain in a principled way why he would not be responsible in the first of each pair but would be in the second, we are driven to the conclusion that he is not responsible in Case 4. The salient common factor in these cases that can plausibly explain why the agent is not responsible is that he is causally determined by factors beyond his control to act as he does. This is the best explanation for his non-responsibility in each of the cases. (See Todd 2011 for a important way to strengthen this argument[1]; for objections, see Fischer 2004, 2006; Mele 2005, 2006; Baker 2006; McKenna 2003, 2008; Demetriou 2010; Nelkin 2011; for further replies see Pereboom 2005, 2008a, 2008b. Thanks to all of these philosophers for motivating the revisions to the argument featured in this presentation).

Source incompatibilism

Why opt for a source as opposed to a leeway position? I argue that an example of the kind devised by Frankfurt supplies an effective challenge to the leeway position (Frankfurt 1969). In such examples an agent considers performing some action, but an intervener is concerned that she will not come through. So if the agent were to show some sign that she will not or might not perform the action, the intervener would arrange matters so that she would perform it anyway. Consider one of Fischer's examples: Jones will decide to kill Smith only if Jones blushes beforehand. Jones's failure to blush (by a certain time) can then function as the prior sign that would trigger the intervention that would cause her to kill Smith. Suppose that Jones acts without intervention. We might well have the intuition that she is morally responsible for killing Smith, although she could not have done otherwise than to kill Smith, and despite the fact that she could not even have formed an alternative intention. Jones could have failed to blush, but Fischer contends that such a "flicker of freedom" is of no use to the libertarian, since it is not *robust* enough to play a part in grounding her moral responsibility (Fischer 1994, 131–59).

Here is a proposal for what is required for an alternative possibility to be robust:

> *Robustness*: For agent to have a robust alternative to her immoral action A, that is, an alternative relevant per se to explaining why she is blameworthy for A, it must be that
> (a) she instead could have voluntarily acted or refrained from acting as a result of which she would be blameless, and
> (b) that for at least one such exempting acting or refraining, she is cognitively sensitive to its being available to her, with the result that she believes to some significant degree that had she voluntarily so acted or refrained she would be, or would likely be, blameless. (Pereboom 2012)[2]

The core intuition that underlies the proposal to ground moral responsibility in the accessibility of alternative possibilities is of the following sort: to be blameworthy for an action, the agent must have been able to do something that would have precluded her from being blameworthy for what she does, at least to the degree she's blameworthy; she must have been able to do something that would have resulted in her being "off the hook" (Pereboom 2001: 1). Thus for an alternative possibility to be robust, it must first of all satisfy this condition: she could have willed something other than what she actually willed such that by willing it she would thereby have been precluded from the moral responsibility she actually has for the action (cf. Otsuka 1998). But in addition, the epistemic element of Robustness—that she must have been cognitively sensitive to the fact that by willing otherwise she would have been precluded from the responsibility she actually has—is motivated by the following sort of consideration. Suppose that the only way Joe could have avoided deciding to take an illegal deduction on his tax form—a choice he does in fact make—is by voluntarily taking a sip from his coffee cup, for unbeknownst to him, the coffee was laced with a drug that induces compliance with the tax code. In this situation, he could have behaved voluntarily in such a manner that would have precluded the choice for which he was in fact blameworthy, as a result of which he would have been morally non-responsible for it. But whether he could have voluntarily taken the sip from the coffee cup, not being cognitively sensitive to the fact that as a result of doing so he would have been blameless, is intuitively irrelevant to explaining whether he is morally responsible for his choice.

The most significant objection that has been raised against the earlier kinds of Frankfurt-style arguments, such as the one where blushing signals the act at issue, was initially suggested by Robert Kane and then systematically developed by David Widerker and Carl Ginet (Kane 1985: 51; 1996, 142–44, 191–92; Widerker 1995: 247–61; 2006; Ginet 1996). The general form of the Kane/Widerker/Ginet objection is this: in Frankfurt-style cases generally, the actual situation will feature a sign that occurs prior to the action at issue that signals the fact that intervention is not required. If in the proposed case this prior sign causally determined the action, or if it were associated with some factor that did, the intervener's predictive ability could be explained. However, then the incompatibilist would not and could not be expected to have the intuition that the agent is morally responsible. But if the relationship between the prior sign and the action were not causally deterministic in such ways, then it will be the case that the agent could have done otherwise despite the occurrence of the prior sign. Either way, an alternative-possibilities condition on moral responsibility emerges unscathed.

I have proposed a type of Frankfurt-style case that avoids this objection (Pereboom 2000; 2001: 18–19; 2003, 2009a, 2012; see also Hunt 2000, 2005 for a similar example; see Fischer 2010 for an argument that the earlier cases are effective). Its distinguishing features are these: the cue for intervention must be a necessary condition for the agent's availing herself of any robust alternative possibility (without the intervener's device in place), while this cue is not itself a robust alternative possibility, and the absence of this cue at any specific time is not a sufficient condition for the agent's performing the action. Here is the most recent version of this example (Pereboom 2012):

> *Tax Cut*: Jones can vote for or against a modest tax cut for those in his high-income group by pushing either the 'yes' or the 'no' button in the voting booth. Once he has entered the voting booth, he has exactly two minutes to vote, and a downward-to-zero ticking timer is prominently displayed. If he does not vote, he will have to pay a fine, substantial enough so that in his situation he is committed with certainty to voting (either for or against), and this is underlain by the fact that the prospect of the fine, together with background conditions, causally determines him to vote. Jones has concluded that voting for the tax cut is barely on balance

morally wrong, since he believes it would not stimulate the economy appreciably, while adding wealth to the already wealthy without helping the less well off, despite how it has been advertised. He is receptive and reactive to these general sorts of moral reasons: he would vote against a substantially larger tax cut for his income group on account of reasons of this sort, and has actually done so in the past. He spends some time in the voting booth rehearsing the relevant moral and self-interested reasons. But what would be required for him to decide to vote against the tax cut is for him to vividly imagine that his boss would find out, whereupon due to her political leanings she would punish him by not promoting him to a better position. In this situation it is causally necessary for his not deciding to vote for the tax cut, and to vote against it instead, that he vividly imagine her finding out and not being promoted, which can occur to him involuntarily or else voluntarily by his libertarian free will. Jones is sensitive to the fact that imagining this punishment scenario will put him in a motivational position to vote against. But so imagining is not causally sufficient for his deciding to vote against the tax cut, for even then he could still, by his libertarian free will, either decide to vote for or against (without the intervener's device in place). However, a neuroscientist has, unbeknownst to him, implanted a device in his brain, which, were it to sense his vividly imagining the punishment scenario, would stimulate his brain so as to causally determine the decision to vote for the tax cut. Jones's imagination is not exercised in this way, and he decides to vote in favor while the device remains idle.[3]

In this situation, Jones could be morally responsible—blameworthy, in particular—for choosing to vote in favor of the tax cut by the deadline despite the fact that for this he has no robust alternative possibility.

This case does feature an alternative possibility that is accessible to the agent—Jones's vividly imagining the punishment scenario. However, relative to his responsibility for deciding to vote in favor of the tax cut by the deadline, this alternative is not robust. First of all, absent the intervener's device, it is not the case that by vividly imagining the scenario Jones would have avoided responsibility for deciding to vote in favor by the deadline. In these ordinary circumstances, this exercise of the imagination is compatible with his nevertheless being strongly inclined to vote for the tax cut, and indeed with actually deciding to vote in favor. Still, one might object, due to the intervener's device, by vividly imagining the punishment scenario at some time during this interval Jones would have voluntarily done something whereby he would have avoided the blameworthiness he actually incurs. Had he exercised his imagination in this way, the device would have been activated, and he would not then have been blameworthy for deciding to vote in favor by the deadline. But Jones is not cognitively sensitive to the fact doing so would preclude him from responsibility for making the decision he does by the deadline. Moreover, he has no reason whatsoever to believe that the intervention would then take place and that as a result he would be precluded from this responsibility for his choice. Nevertheless, it remains intuitive that Jones is actually morally responsible for deciding to vote in favor of the tax cut by the deadline.

For proponents of the leeway position, the accessibility of alternative possibilities is crucial to explaining why an agent would be morally responsible. The *Tax Cut* argument provides reason to reject the leeway view, and to affirm instead that moral responsibility would be explained primarily by the agent's being the action's source in the appropriate way. According to source incompatibilism, which I endorse, moral responsibility requires that the agent be the source of her action in a way incompatible with her being causally determined to act by factors beyond her control. It might well be that alternative possibilities—not necessarily of the robust sort—are entailed by her being the source of her action in this way (Pereboom 2001: 37, 2003: 197). But these alternative possibilities would not have the primary role in explaining an agent's moral responsibility. Rather, they would be a consequence of the factor that did: the agent's being the source of her action in the right way.

Against libertarianism

Defending hard incompatibilism also requires confronting libertarianism. Two contending versions of libertarianism are the event-causal and agent-causal types.[4] In event-causal libertarianism, actions are caused solely by *events*—such as *Joe's currently desiring to receive a substantial tax refund*, or *Anne's currently believing that she can help someone in trouble*. It is often assumed that all causation in the physical world is fundamentally by events, and not by things such as atoms, organisms, and agents, which we call *substances*. Although we might say, for example, that a missile—a substance—destroyed an airplane, when speaking more accurately, the idea is that we should say instead that *the missile's hitting the airplane at noon yesterday*—an event—caused the destruction. If we are more precise about what it is in the physical world that causes effects, it turns out to be events, not substances. In solidarity with this position, event-causal libertarians contend that actions are caused solely by events, and indeterminacy in the production of actions by appropriate events is a highly significant requirement for moral responsibility (Kane 1996; Ekstrom 2000; Balaguer 2009, Franklin 2011b).

According to agent-causal libertarianism, free will of the sort required for moral responsibility is accounted for by the existence of agents who possess a causal power to make choices without being determined to do so (Taylor 1966, 1974; Chisholm 1976; O'Connor 2000; Clarke 2003). In this view, it is crucial that the kind of causation involved in an agent's making a free choice is not reducible to causation among events involving the agent, but is rather irreducibly an instance of a substance causing a choice not by way of events. The agent, fundamentally as a substance, has the causal power to make choices without being determined to do so.

Critics of libertarianism have contended that if actions are undetermined, agents will lack the control in action required for moral responsibility. The classical presentation of this objection is found in Hume's *Treatise of Human Nature*, and it has become known as the "luck" objection (Hume 1739/1978: 411–2; cf. Mele 2006). There are several distinct versions of this objection (Franklin 2011b). I believe that event-causal libertarianism is undermined by one in particular, but that agent-causal libertarianism might well evade it (cf. O'Connor 2000, Clarke 2003). The strongest challenge to the agent-causal position is rather one based on our best physical theories. Our choices produce physical events in the brain and in the rest of the body, and these events are, according to these theories, governed by physical laws. A libertarian view must make it credible that our choices could be free in the sense it advocates given the evidence we have about these physical laws. The concern is that agent-causal libertarianism does not meet this standard.

The version of the luck objection that in my view reveals the deepest problem for event-causal libertarianism is what I call the *disappearing agent* (DA) objection (2001, 2004, 2007):

> *DA objection*: Consider a decision made in a context in which moral reasons favor one action, prudential reasons favor a distinct and incompatible action, and the net strength of these sets of reasons are in close competition. On an event-causal libertarian picture, the relevant causal conditions antecedent to the decision—agent-involving events—would leave it open whether the decision will occur, and the agent has no further causal role in determining whether it does. With the causal role of the antecedent events already given, whether the decision occurs is not settled by any causal factor involving the agent. In fact, given the causal role of all causally relevant antecedent events, *nothing settles* whether the decision occurs. Thus, plausibly, on the event-causal libertarian picture, agents lack the control required for moral responsibility.

The objection is not that agents will have no causal role in producing decisions, but that causal role that available to agents will be insufficient for the control moral responsibility demands. For on the event-causal libertarian view, the agent will "disappear" at the exact point at which moral responsibility for her decision requires her to exercise control.

To illustrate, consider Kane's example of a businesswoman—let's call her Anne—who has the option of deciding to stop to help an assault victim, whereupon she would be late for an important meeting at work, or not deciding to stop, which would allow her to make it to the meeting on time. For simplicity, suppose the relevant antecedent conditions are, against stopping, *Anne's desiring at t not to annoy her boss*, and *Anne's believing at t that if she is late for the meeting her boss will give her a difficult time*; and for stopping, *Anne's desiring at t to help people in trouble*, and *Anne's belief that she can be effective in helping the assault victim*. Suppose the motivational force of each of these pairs of conditions is for her about the same. On an event-causal libertarian theory, with the causal role of these antecedent conditions already given, both Anne's deciding to stop and her not deciding to stop are significantly probable outcomes. Suppose she in fact decides to stop. There is nothing else about Anne that can settle whether the decision to stop occurs, since in this view her role in producing a decision is exhausted by antecedent states or events in which she is involved. If at this point nothing about Anne can settle whether the decision occurs, then, plausibly, she lacks the control required for moral responsibility for it. So it seems that on an event-causal libertarian view there is no provision that allows the agent to have control over whether the decision occurs or not (in the crucial sorts of cases), and for this reason she lacks the control required for moral responsibility for it.

Libertarians agree that an action's resulting from a deterministic sequence of causes that traces back to factors beyond the agent's control would rule out her moral responsibility for it. The deeper point of the luck objection is that if this sort of causal determination rules out moral responsibility, then it is no remedy simply to provide slack in the causal net by making the causal history of actions indeterministic. Such a move would yield one requirement for moral responsibility—the absence of causal determinism for decision and action—but it would not supply another—sufficiently enhanced control (Clarke 1996, 2003). In particular, it would not provide the capacity for an agent to be the source of her decisions and actions that, according to many incompatibilists, is unavailable in a deterministic framework.

The agent-causal libertarian's solution is to specify a way in which the agent could have this enhanced control, which involves the power to settle which of the antecedently possible decisions actually occurs. The suggested remedy is to reintroduce the agent as a cause, this time not merely as involved in events, but rather fundamentally as a substance. The agent-causal libertarian claims that we possess a special causal power—a power for an agent, fundamentally as a substance, to cause a decision without being causally determined to cause it (Chisholm 1966, O'Connor 2000, Clarke 2003, Griffiths 2010).

I argue that the agent-causal position has not been shown to be incoherent (Pereboom 2004). However, can agent-causal libertarianism be reconciled with what we would expect given our best physical theories? Consider first the supposition that all the events in the physical world are governed by deterministic laws. In this agent-causal picture, when an agent makes a free decision, she causes the decision without being causally determined to do so. On the path to action that results from this undetermined decision, changes in the physical world, for instance in her brain or some other part of her body, are produced. But it would seem that we would at this point encounter divergences from these laws. For the changes in the physical world that result from the undetermined decision would themselves not be causally determined, and they would thus not be governed by deterministic laws. One might object that it is possible that the physical changes that result from every free decision just happen to dovetail with what could in principle be predicted on the basis of the deterministic laws, so nothing actually occurs that diverges from these laws. But this proposal would seem to involve coincidences too wild to be credible. For this reason, agent-causal libertarianism is not plausibly reconcilable with the physical world's being governed by deterministic laws.

On some interpretations of quantum mechanics, however, the physical world is not in fact deterministic, but is rather governed by probabilistic statistical laws. But wild coincidences would also arise on this suggestion. Consider the class of possible actions each of which has a physical component whose antecedent probability of occurring is approximately 0.32. It would not violate the statistical laws in the sense of being logically incompatible with them if, for a large number of instances, the physical components in this class were not actually realized close to 32% of the time. Rather, the force of the statistical law is that for a large number of instances it is correct to *expect* physical components in this class to be realized close to 32% of the time. Are free choices on the agent-causal libertarian model compatible with what the statistical law would have us to expect about them? If they were, then for a large enough number of instances the possible actions in our class would almost certainly be freely chosen near to 32% of the time. But if the occurrence of these physical components were settled by the choices of agent-causes, then their actually being chosen close to 32% of the time would amount to a wild coincidence. The proposal that agent-caused free choices do not diverge from what the statistical laws predict for the physical components of our actions would be so sharply opposed to what we would expect as to make it incredible (for objections to this argument, see O'Connor 2003, 2008; Clarke 2003: 181, n. 31, 2011; for replies see Pereboom 2005).

At this point, the libertarian agent-causalist might propose that there are indeed divergences from the probabilities that we would expect absent agent-causes, and that these divergences are located at the interface between the agent-cause and that part of the physical world that it directly affects—an interface very likely to be found in the brain. But the issue for this proposal is that we have no evidence that such divergences occur. This difficulty yields a strong reason to reject this approach.

Thus the various kinds of libertarianism face significant problems. Because compatibilism is vulnerable to the argument from manipulation cases, the position that remains is hard incompatibilism, which denies that we have the sort of free will required for moral responsibility. The concern for this stance is not that there is considerable empirical evidence that it is false, or that there is a powerful argument that it is somehow incoherent, and false for that reason. Rather, the crucial questions it faces are practical: What would life be like if we believed it was true? Is this a sort of life that we can cope with?[5]

Hard incompatibilism and wrongdoing

Accepting hard incompatibilism requires giving up our ordinary view of ourselves as blameworthy for immoral actions and praiseworthy for those that are morally exemplary. At this point one might object that giving up our belief in moral responsibility would have harmful consequences, perhaps so harmful that thinking and acting as if this skeptical view is true is not a feasible option. So even if the claim that we are morally responsible turns out to be false, there might yet be weighty practical reasons to believe that we are, or at least to treat people as if they were morally responsible.

For instance, one might think that if we gave up the belief that people are blameworthy and praiseworthy, we could no longer legitimately judge any actions as wrong or even bad, or as right or good. But this thought seems mistaken. Even if we came to believe that some perpetrator of genocide was not blameworthy due to a degenerative brain disease, we would still hold that his actions were morally wrong, or at least that it was bad that he acted as he did. So, in general, denying blameworthiness would not appear to threaten judgments of wrongness or badness, and, likewise, denying praiseworthiness would not seem to undercut assessments of rightness or goodness (for a contrary view, see Haji (1998, 2002).

Perhaps treating wrongdoers as blameworthy is often required for effective moral education and improvement. If we resolved never to treat people as blameworthy, we might be left with insufficient leverage to reform immoral behavior (Nichols 2007; for a response see Pereboom 2009b). But this proposal would have us treat people as blameworthy—by, for example, expressing anger toward them just because of what they have done—when they do not deserve it, which would seem morally wrong. If people are not morally responsible for immoral behavior, treating them as if they were seems unfair. However, it is possible to achieve moral reform by methods not threatened by this sort of unfairness, and in ordinary situations such practices could arguably be as successful as those that presuppose moral responsibility. Instead of treating people as if they deserved blame, the free will skeptic can turn to moral admonition and encouragement, which presuppose only that the offender has done wrong. These methods can effectively communicate a sense of right and wrong, and they might well issue in salutary reform.

But does hard incompatibilism have resources adequate for contending with criminal behavior? Here it would appear to be at a disadvantage, and if so, practical considerations might generate good reasons to treat criminals as if they were morally responsible. First, if this skeptical view is true, a retributivist justification for criminal punishment is unavailable, for it asserts that a criminal deserves pain or deprivation just for committing the crime, while hard incompatibilism rejects this basic-desert claim. And retributivism is among the most naturally compelling ways to justify criminal punishment.

By contrast, a theory that justifies criminal punishment on the ground that punishment educates criminals morally is not threatened by hard incompatibilism specifically. So one might suggest that the free will skeptic should endorse a view of this kind. However, we lack strong empirical evidence that punishing criminals results in moral education, and without such evidence, it would be wrong to punish them to achieve this aim. It is generally wrong to harm a person for the sake of realizing some good without strong evidence that the harm will produce the good. In addition, even if we had impressive evidence that punishment is effective in morally educating criminals, we should prefer non-punitive ways of achieving this aim, whether or not criminals are morally responsible.

According to deterrence theories, punishing criminals is justified for the reason that it deters future crime. The two most-discussed deterrence theories, the utilitarian view and the version that grounds the right to punish on the right to self-defense and defense of others, are not imperiled by hard incompatibilism *per se*. But they are questionable on other grounds. The utilitarian theory, which claims that punishment is justified when and because it maximizes utility, faces well-known objections. It would require punishing the innocent when doing so would maximize utility; in certain situations it would prescribe punishment that is unduly severe; and it would authorize harming people merely as means to the safety of others. The kind of deterrence theory that grounds the right to punish in the right of individuals to defend themselves and others against immediate threats (Farrell 1985: 38–60) is also objectionable. For when a criminal is sentenced to punishment he most often does not pose an immediate threat to anyone, since he is then in the custody of the law, and this fact about his circumstances distinguishes him from those who can legitimately be harmed on the basis the right of self-defense and defense of others.

There is, however, an intuitively legitimate theory of crime prevention that is neither undercut by the skeptical view, nor threatened by other sorts of considerations. This theory draws an analogy between the treatment of criminals and the treatment of carriers of dangerous diseases. Ferdinand Schoeman (1979) argues that if we have the right to quarantine carriers of serious communicable diseases to protect people, then for the same reason we also have the right to isolate the criminally dangerous. Notice that quarantining a person can be justified when she is not morally responsible for being dangerous to others. If a child is infected with a deadly contagious virus that was transmitted to her before she was born, quarantine can still be legitimate. Now imagine that a serial killer poses a grave danger to a community. Even if he is not morally responsible for his crimes (say because no one is ever morally responsible), it would be as legitimate to isolate him as it is to quarantine a non-responsible carrier of a serious communicable disease.

It would be morally wrong to treat carriers of communicable diseases more severely than is required to protect people from the resulting threat. Similarly, it would be wrong to treat criminals more harshly than is required to protect society against the danger posed by them. Moreover, just as moderately dangerous diseases may allow for only measures less intrusive than quarantine, so moderately serious criminal tendencies might only justify responses less intrusive than detention. Furthermore, I suspect that a theory modeled on quarantine would not justify measures of the sort whose legitimacy is most in doubt, such as the death penalty or confinement in the worst prisons we have. It would also demand a degree of concern for the rehabilitation and well-being of the criminal that would alter much of current practice. Just as society must seek to cure the diseased it quarantines, so it would be required to try to rehabilitate the criminals it detains. In addition, if a criminal cannot be rehabilitated, and if protection of society demands his indefinite confinement, there would be no justification for making his life more miserable than is needed to guard against the danger he poses.

Meaning in life

If hard incompatibilism is true and we came to recognize this, could we legitimately retain a sense of achievement for successes that make our lives fulfilled, happy, or worthwhile (Honderich 1988)? It might be argued that on the supposition of this skeptical view there would be no genuine achievements, for an agent cannot have an achievement for which she is not also praiseworthy. However, achievement is not as closely tied to praiseworthiness as this objection would have it. If an agent hopes to achieve success in a project she undertakes, and if she accomplishes what she hoped for, intuitively this outcome would be an achievement of hers even if she is not praiseworthy for it—although the sense in which it is her achievement might be diminished. For instance, if a teacher hopes that her efforts will result in well-educated children, and they do, there remains a clear sense in which she has achieved what she hoped for, even if it turns out she is not praiseworthy for what she has accomplished.

One might be concerned that accepting hard incompatibilism would instill an attitude of resignation to whatever the future holds in store and would undercut our motivation for achievement. But this is not clearly correct. Even if what we understand about our behavioral dispositions and our environment provides evidence our futures turning out in a particular way, it can often be reasonable to hope that they will turn out differently. For this to be so, it may sometimes be important for us to lack complete knowledge of our dispositions and environmental conditions. Suppose that someone reasonably believes that he has a disposition that would be an impediment to realizing something he hopes to achieve. But because he does not know whether this disposition will in fact have this effect, it remains open for him—that is, not ruled out by anything he knows or believes—that another disposition he has will allow him to transcend the impediment. For example, imagine that someone aspires to become a successful politician, but he is concerned that his fear of public speaking will keep this from happening. He does not know for sure whether this fear will in fact frustrate his ambition, since it is open for him that he will overcome this problem, perhaps due to a disposition for resolute self-discipline in transcending obstacles of this sort. Thus he might reasonably hope that he will overcome his fear and succeed in his ambition.

At the same time, one might concur with Saul Smilansky that although determinism allows for a limited foundation of the sense of self-worth that derives from achievement and virtue, the free will skeptic's perspective can nevertheless be "extremely damaging to our view of ourselves, to our sense of achievement, worth, and self-respect," especially when it comes to achievement in the formation of one's own moral character. In response to this concern, Smilansky argues that it would be best for us to foster the illusion that we have free will (Smilansky 1997, 2000). I agree with Smilansky that there is a kind of self-respect that presupposes that we have the sort of free will required for moral responsibility, and that this self-respect would be undermined if hard incompatibilism were true. I question, however, whether Smilanksy is right about how damaging it would be for us to relinquish this sort of self-respect, and whether an appeal to illusion is required as a remedy.

Note first that our sense of self-worth—our sense that we have value and that are lives are worth living—is to a non-trivial extent due to features we possess not produced by our will, let alone by free will. People place great value on natural beauty, native athletic ability, and intelligence, none of which result from our voluntary efforts. We also value efforts that are voluntary in the sense that they are willed by us—in productive work and altruistic behavior, and in the formation of moral character. But how much does it matter to us that these voluntary efforts are also *freely* willed? Perhaps Smilansky overestimates how much we care.

Consider how someone comes to have a good moral character. Not implausibly, this character was formed to some significant degree by upbringing, and the belief that this is so is widespread. Parents typically regard themselves as having failed in raising their children if they turn out with immoral dispositions, and parents often take great care to bring their children up to prevent such a result. Accordingly, people often come to believe that they have the good moral character they do largely because they were raised with love and skill. But those who come to believe this about themselves seldom experience dismay because of it. People tend not to become dispirited upon coming to believe that their good moral character is not their own doing, and that they do not deserve significant praise or respect for it. By contrast, they often come to feel more fortunate and thankful. Suppose, however, that there are some who would be overcome with dismay. Would it be justified or even desirable for them to foster the illusion that they nonetheless deserve praise and respect for producing their moral character? I suspect that most people would eventually be able to accept the truth without incurring significant loss. All of this, I believe, would also hold for those who come to believe that they do not deserve praise and respect for producing their moral character because they are not, in general, morally responsible in the basic desert sense.

Emotions, reactive attitudes, and personal relationships

P. F. Strawson (1962) contends that the justification for judgments of blameworthiness and praiseworthiness has its foundation in the reactive attitudes—emotional reactions to how people voluntarily behave—attitudes such as moral resentment, guilt, gratitude, forgiveness, and love. Because moral responsibility has this type of foundation, the truth or falsity of determinism is irrelevant to whether we are justified in regarding agents as morally responsible. This is because these reactive attitudes are required for the kinds of interpersonal relationships that make our lives meaningful, and so even if we were able to give up the reactive attitudes, we would never have sufficient practical reason to do so. Strawson believes that it is in fact psychologically impossible for us to relinquish our reactive attitudes altogether, but in a limited range of cases we can adopt what he calls the "objective attitude," which he conceives as a cold and calculating stance:

> To adopt the objective attitude to another human being is to see him, perhaps, as an object of social policy; as a subject for what, in a wide range of sense, might be called treatment; as something certainly to be taken account, perhaps precautionary account, of; to be managed or handled or cured or trained; perhaps simply to be avoided...The objective attitude may be emotionally toned in many ways: it may include repulsion or fear, it may include pity or love, though not all kinds of love. But it cannot include the range of reactive feelings and attitudes which belong to involvement or participation with others in interpersonal human relationships; it cannot include resentment, gratitude, forgiveness, anger, or the sort of love which two adults can sometimes be said to feel reciprocally, for each other. (Strawson 1962)

Strawson suggests that if determinism did threaten our reactive attitudes, and we were able to give them up, we would face the prospect of adopting this objective attitude toward everyone, and as a result our interpersonal relationships would be damaged. But because we have extremely good practical reasons for maintaining these relationships, we would never have sufficient practical reason to adopt the objective attitude in most cases. As a result we would not have sufficient reason to relinquish our reactive attitudes, and thus to stop regarding people as morally responsible.

I think it's plausible that if we persistently maintained an objective attitude toward others, as Strawson describes it, our interpersonal relationships would be seriously threatened.[6] However, I deny that we would have good reason to adopt this stance if we came to accept the skeptical view about free will. Some of the reactive attitudes would then in fact be challenged, because some of them, such as moral resentment and indignation, would have the false presupposition that the person who is the object of the attitude is morally responsible in the basic desert sense. But the reactive attitudes we would want to retain either would not be threatened in this way, or else have analogues or aspects that would not have false presuppositions. The attitudes that would survive do not amount to the objective attitude, and they would be sufficient to sustain good interpersonal relationships.

It is plausible that to a certain degree moral resentment and indignation are beyond our power to affect. Even supposing that a free will skeptic is thoroughly committed to morality and rationality, and that she is admirably in control of her emotions, she might well be unable to eliminate these attitudes. So we might continue to expect people to be morally resentful or indignant in certain circumstances. But at the same time we have the ability to prevent, temper, and sometimes to dispel these attitudes, and given the skeptical conviction, we might do so for the sake of morality and rationality. Modifications of this sort might well be good for interpersonal relationships.

One might reply that in relationships moral resentment and indignation are crucial to effective communication of wrongdoing, and if we dispelled or modified these attitudes, relationships would be damaged. However, when someone is wronged in a relationship, she typically has further attitudes not threatened by the skeptical view whose expression can have the communicative role at issue. These attitudes include being alarmed or distressed about what another has done, and moral concern, sadness, or sorrow for him (Pereboom 2009b; for a contrary view, see Nichols 2007). Moral resentment is thus not clearly required for effective communication in interpersonal relationships.

Forgiveness might seem to presuppose that the person being forgiven is blameworthy, and if this is so, this attitude would also be threatened by hard incompatibilism.[7] But certain key features of forgiveness would not be endangered, and they are sufficient to sustain the role forgiveness has in relationships. Suppose a friend repeatedly mistreats you, and in consequence you decide to end your relationship with him. However, he then apologizes to you, indicating his recognition that his actions were wrong, a wish that he had not mistreated you, and a commitment to refrain from the immoral behavior. Because of this you decide not to end the friendship. In this case, the aspect of forgiveness that is consistent with the skeptical position is a willingness to cease to regard past immoral behavior as a reason to weaken or end a relationship. A feature often associated with forgiveness that would be undercut is the disposition to disregard the friend's blameworthiness. But since the skeptic denies blameworthiness (in the sense that involves basic desert), she no longer needs a willingness to disregard blameworthiness for good interpersonal relationships.

One might object that accepting hard incompatibilism would jeopardize the self-directed attitudes of guilt and repentance, and that this would be especially bad for relationships. Without guilt and repentance, we would not only be incapable of restoring relationships damaged due to wrongdoing, but, in addition, it would become more difficult to restore the moral integrity of those who have done wrong. For without the attitudes of guilt and repentance, we would no longer have the psychological mechanisms that can play these roles. Note first, however, that it would be because guilt essentially involved a belief that one is blameworthy that this attitude would be challenged by the skeptical view. It is for this reason that repentance would also seem to be (indirectly) threatened, for a sense of guilt would seem required to motivate repentance. Imagine, however, that in your relationship with another person you have acted immorally, but because you endorse skepticism about free will, you do not believe that you are blameworthy in the basic-desert sense. Instead, you acknowledge that you were the agent of wrongdoing, you feel genuine sorrow because of what you have done to another person, and you deeply regret having acted as you did. Moreover, because you are committed to doing what is right and to your own moral improvement, you resolve not to act in this way in the future, and you communicate this to the other person. None of these measures threatened are threatened by hard incompatibilism (see Pereboom 2009b for further discussion).

Gratitude would seem to presuppose that the agent to whom one is grateful is morally responsible for a beneficial act, whereupon the skeptical view would jeopardize gratitude. But as in the case of forgiveness, certain core aspects of this attitude would remain unaffected, and these aspects can provide what is required for good interpersonal relationships. Gratitude involves, first of all, being thankful toward someone who has acted beneficially. True, being thankful toward someone often involves the belief that she is praiseworthy for some action in the basic desert sense. Still, one can be thankful to a young child for some kindness without believing that she is morally responsible for it. This aspect of gratitude could be retained even without the presupposition of praiseworthiness. Usually gratitude also involves joy in response to a person for what she has done. But no feature of hard incompatibilism poses a threat to the legitimacy of this sort of joy and of expressing it. Expressing joy can bring about the same sense of harmony and goodwill typically produced by a sense of gratitude unmodified by free will skepticism, and thus on this point the skeptical view is not at a disadvantage.

Is the kind of love that mature adults have for each other in good relationships endangered by a hard incompatibilist conviction, as Strawson's line of argument suggests? Consider first whether for loving someone it is significant that the person who is loved possesses and exercises free will in the sense required for moral responsibility. Parents love their children rarely, if ever, for the reason that they possess this sort of free will, or decide to do what is right by free will, or deserve to be loved due to freely-willed action. When adults love each other, it is also very seldom, if at all, for these sorts of reasons. In addition to moral character and action, factors such as intelligence, appearance, style, and resemblance to certain others in one's personal history all might play a part. Plausibly, morally admirable qualities are particularly important in occasioning, enriching, and maintaining love. But even if there is an aspect of love that we see as a deserved response to morally admirable qualities, it is unlikely that love would be diminished at all if we came to believe that these qualities are not brought about or sustained by freely willed decisions. Such admirable qualities are loveable whether or not we think of agents as deserving praise for having them.

One might contend that we want to be freely loved by others—to be loved by them by their own free will. However, the love that parents have for their children is typically independent of the parents' will altogether, and we don't regard love of this sort as deficient. Kane acknowledges this fact about parents' love, and he recognizes that romantic love is similar in this respect. But he argues that there is a kind of love we very much want that would be ruled out if love were always causally determined by factors beyond our control (Kane 1996: 88). The plausibility of Kane's idea might be enhanced by reflecting on how you would react if you found out that someone you love was causally determined to love you by a benevolent manipulator.

Setting aside *free* will for a moment, we might ask: when does the will play any role at all in engendering love? When a relationship is disintegrating, people will sometimes decide to try to restore the love they once had for one another. When a student finds himself in conflict with a roommate from the outset, he might choose to do what he can to improve the relationship. When a marriage is arranged, the partners may decide to take steps to promote love for each other. In these kinds of circumstances, we want others to make decisions that would produce or maintain love. However, this is not to say that we would want such choices to be freely willed in the sense required for moral responsibility. It is not clear that appreciable value would be added by such a decision's being free in this sense. Moreover, although in some circumstances we might want others to make such relationship-enhancing decisions, we would typically prefer love that did not require choices of this sort. This is so not only for intimate romantic relationships—where it is undeniable—but also for friendships and for relationships between parents and children.

But imagine that Kane's view was vindicated, and we did desire a kind of love that is freely willed in the sense required for basic-desert moral responsibility. We would then desire a kind of love that would be impossible if hard incompatibilism were true. Still, the sorts of love not undercut by this skeptical position would be sufficient for good interpersonal relationships. If we can aspire to the kind of love parents typically have for their children, or the type romantic lovers share, or the sort had by friends who are devoted to each other, and whose friendship was deepened through their interactions, then the prospect of fulfillment through interpersonal relationships remains intact (see Pereboom 2009b for further discussion).

Thus a hard incompatibilist conviction does not pose a threat to good interpersonal relationships. It might well undermine certain attitudes that typically have a role in such relationships. Moral resentment and indignation would likely be irrational for the free-will skeptic, since these attitudes would have presuppositions she believes to be false. But these attitudes are either not required for good relationships, or they have analogues that could play their typical beneficial role. Moreover, love—the attitude most essential to good interpersonal relationships—does not appear to be placed at risk by such a view at all. Love of another involves, fundamentally, wishing for the other's good, taking on her aims, and a desire to be together with her, and none of this is undercut by hard incompatibilism.

The good in hard incompatibilism

The skeptical view also holds out the prospect of substantial benefits for human life. Of all the attitudes associated with the belief that we are morally responsible, anger seems most closely connected with it. Discussions about moral responsibility typically focus not on how we regard morally exemplary agents, but rather on our attitudes toward wrongdoers. Examples designed to elicit a strong intuition that an agent is morally responsible usually feature action that is especially malevolent, and the intuition typically involves sympathetic anger. It might be, then, that our attachment to the belief that we are morally responsible derives to a significant degree from the role anger has in our emotional lives. Perhaps we sense that giving up the assumption of responsibility is threatening because the rationality of anger would be unjustified as a result.

The type of anger at issue is the sort directed toward a person who is believed to have behaved immorally, and it comprises both moral resentment and indignation. Let us call this attitude *moral anger*. Not all anger is moral anger. One kind of non-moral anger is directed toward someone because his abilities are lacking in some way or he has performed poorly in some situation. At times we are angry with machines for malfunctioning. Sometimes our anger has no object. But most human anger is moral anger.

Such anger has a significant part in our moral psychology. It motivates us to resist abuse, discrimination, and oppression. But expression of moral anger often has harmful effects for those toward whom it is directed, and also for those expressing the anger. Frequently its expression is intended to cause little else than emotional or physical pain. As a result, moral anger has a tendency to damage relationships, hinder the functioning of organizations, and unsettle societies. In extreme cases, it can motivate people to torture and kill.

The realization that expression of moral anger can be damaging generates a strong requirement that it be morally justified when it occurs. The demand to morally justify behavior that is harmful is generally very strong, and expression of moral anger is often harmful. This demand is made more urgent by our degree of attachment to this emotion, which is fueled by the satisfaction we frequently have in expressing it. Often we justify expression of such anger by contending that wrongdoers are morally responsible in the basic-desert involving sense for what they have done. If we became convinced that we do not have the sort of free will required for moral responsibility, we would regard such justifications as illegitimate. About the view that we lack this sort of free will Spinoza says: "this doctrine contributes to the social life insofar as it teaches us to hate no one, to disesteem no one, to mock no one, to be angry at no one…" (1677/1985: 490). Given the concerns to which expression of moral anger gives rise, our coming to believe that we lack this sort of free will may on balance be a good thing.

Notes

1. Todd argues that proponents of manipulation arguments have assumed too heavy a burden: they do not need make it plausible that manipulated agents are not morally responsible, only that their responsibility is mitigated, for compatibilists will have as difficult a time explaining mitigation as they would explaining non-responsibility.

2. Thanks to Dana Nelkin, James Hobbs, Jonathan Vance, and Kevin Timpe for comments that led to a revision of a previous version of this criterion (in Pereboom 2000, 2001).

3. As I argue in Pereboom (2012), this example can be embellished to answer one of Carl Ginet's (2002) objections to *Tax Evasion*, in particular to the (2000, 2001) version of this example. Ginet contends that at the precise time Joe makes the decision to take the illegal tax deduction, he might have been activating the necessary condition for refraining instead, and that this alternative possibility is robust: "for had J taken it, he would at t1 have been refraining from a willing—to do B [decide to take the illegal deduction] right then—such that by so refraining he would have avoided responsibility for doing

B right then and would have been aware that he was avoiding responsibility for doing B right then (that being such an obvious implication of his not doing B right then, of which he of course would have been aware)." David Palmer (2011) and Christopher Franklin (2011a) also develop this kind of objection. Here, in essence, is my response. Imagine first an agent, Adam, who is causally determined to perform some immoral action during the time interval t0-t3, but the specific time during this interval he decides is up to him. Suppose he actually decides at t1. The incompatibilist has to agree that Adam is not blameworthy for making the decision at t1, but at best only responsible in some neutral sense for deciding then and not at some other time during the interval. And crucially, the reason the leeway incompatibilist must give for his not being blameworthy for deciding at t1 is that he has no (robust) alternative to making his decision by t3. According to the leeway incompatibilist it has to be the unavailability of some alternative possibility that explains why Adam is not blameworthy for his decision. In this case, causal determination is what excludes Adam's blameworthiness, and the leeway incompatibilist maintains that in general, causal determination rules out blameworthiness because it precludes alternative possibilities. The only plausible candidate is the unavailability of an alternative to making the decision by t3, and thus on the leeway incompatibilist view, this unavailability would have to be sufficient for Adam's not being blameworthy at t1.

We can draw the following consequence for Jones's situation in *Tax Cut*. Suppose that Jones decides to vote for the tax cut at t1, a minute before the deadline t3. The leeway incompatibilist will not be able to defend the claim that Jones's deciding at t1 to vote in favor of the tax cut with the intervener's device in place is as blameworthy, and for the same reasons, as would be his deciding to vote in favor by t3 without the device in place. For with the device in place, the leeway incompatibilist cannot explain Jones's blameworthiness for making his decision at t1, but only his responsibility in a neutral sense for making the decision at t1 rather than at some other available instant. Although, as in Adam's situation, Jones does have an alternative to deciding at t1—for example, continuing to deliberate at t1—this will be insufficient to explain Jones's blameworthiness for making his decision at t1. For Jones has no robust alternative to making his decision by t3, and as in Adam's situation, for the leeway incompatibilist this will be sufficient for Jones's not being blameworthy for making his decision at t1. But it's nonetheless our strong intuition that Jones is blameworthy for deciding to vote in favor at t1, for which the leeway incompatibilist now has no explanation.

4. A third type is non-causal libertarianism, advocated by Ginet (1990), Hugh McCann (1998), and Stewart Goetz (2008). An often-cited objection to this type of libertarianism is that control in action is fundamentally a causal matter, and in particular such theories cannot secure the type of control in action required for moral responsibility (O'Connor 2000, Clarke 2003). But this position remains intriguing, especially given the sorts of concerns that arise for the other types of libertarianism.

5. In responding to these questions, I have been inspired by others who have done excellent work in answering them, including Spinoza (1677/1985), Galen Strawson (1986), Ted Honderich (1988), Bruce Waller (1990), and Saul Smilansky (2000).

6. For a contrary view, see Sommers 2007; Shabo (2011) defends Strawson against Sommers.

7. See Nelkin (2008, 2011) for reasons to think that forgiveness does not have this presupposition.

References

Baker, Lynne R. 2006. "Moral responsibility without libertarianism," *Noûs* **40:** 307–330.

Balaguer, Mark. 2009. *Free Will as an Open Scientific Problem*. Cambridge, MA: MIT Press.

Bok, Hilary. 1998. *Freedom and Responsibility*. Princeton, NJ: Princeton University Press.

Chisholm, Roderick. 1976. *Person and Object*. La Salle, IL: Open Court.

Clarke, Randolph. 1996. "Agent causation and event causation in the production of free action," *Philosophical Topics* **24:** 19–48.

Clarke, Randolph. 2003. *Libertarian Theories of Free Will*. New York: Oxford University Press.

Clarke, Randolph. 2011. "Are we free to obey the laws?" *American Philosophical Quarterly* **47.4:** 389–401.

Demetriou, Kristin. 2010. "The soft-line solution to Pereboom's four-case argument," *Australasian Journal of Philosophy* **88:** 595–617.

Ekstrom, Laura W. 2000. *Free Will: A Philosophical Study*. Boulder, CO: Westview.

Farrell, Daniel M. 1985. "The justification of general deterrence," *Philosophical Review* **104:** 367–394.

Fischer, John Martin. 1994. *The Metaphysics of Free Will*. Oxford: Blackwell.

Fischer, John Martin. 2004. "Responsibility and manipulation," *Journal of Ethics* **8:** 145–177. Reprinted in Fischer (2006).

Fischer, John Martin. 2006. *My Way*. New York: Oxford University Press.

Fischer, John Martin. 2010. "The Frankfurt cases: the moral of the stories," *Philosophical Review* **119:** 315–336.

Fischer, John Martin, and Mark Ravizza. 1998. *Responsibility and Control: A Theory of Moral Responsibility*. New York: Cambridge University Press.

Fischer, John Martin, Robert Kane, Derk Pereboom, and Manuel Vargas. 2007. *Four Views on Free Will*. Oxford: Blackwell.

Frankfurt, Harry G. 1969. "Alternate possibilities and moral responsibility," *Journal of Philosophy* **66:** 829–839.

Frankfurt, Harry G. 1971. "Freedom of the will and the concept of a person," *Journal of Philosophy* **68:** 5–20.

Franklin, Christopher. 2011a. "Neo-Frankfurtians and buffer cases: the new challenge to the principle of alternative possibilities," *Philosophical Studies* **152:** 189–207.

Franklin, Christopher. 2011b. "Farewell to the luck (and mind) argument," *Philosophical Studies*, **156.2:** 199–230.

Ginet, Carl. 1990. *On Action*. Cambridge: Cambridge University Press.

Ginet, Carl. 1996. "In defense of the principle of alternative possibilities: why I don't find Frankfurt's arguments convincing," *Philosophical Perspectives* **10:** 403–417.

Ginet, Carl. 2002. "Review of *Living Without Free Will*," *Journal of Ethics* **6:** 305–309.

Goetz, Stewart. 2008. *Freedom, Teleology, and Evil*. London: Continuum.

Griffiths, Meghan. 2010. "Why agent-caused actions are not lucky," *American Philosophical Quarterly* **47:** 43–56.

Haji, Ishtiyaque. 1998. *Moral Accountability*. New York: Oxford University Press.

Haji, Ishtiyaque. 2002. *Deontic Morality and Control*. Cambridge: Cambridge University Press.

Honderich, Ted. 1988. *A Theory of Determinism*. Oxford: Oxford University Press.

Hume, David. 1739/1978. *A Treatise of Human Nature*. Oxford: Oxford University Press.

Hunt, David. 2000. "Moral responsibility and unavoidable action," *Philosophical Studies* **97**: 195–227.

Hunt, David. 2005 "Moral responsibility and buffered alternatives," *Midwest Studies in Philosophy* **29**: 126–145.

Kane, Robert. 1985. *Free Will and Values*. Albany: State University of New York Press.

Kane, Robert. 1996. *The Significance of Free Will*. New York: Oxford University Press.

Lycan, William G. 1997. *Consciousness*. Cambridge, MA: MIT Press.

McCann, Hugh. 1998. *The Works of Agency*. Ithaca, NY: Cornell University Press.

McKenna, Michael. 2003. "Robustness, control, and the demand for morally significant alternatives," in *Freedom, Responsibility, and Agency: Essays on the Importance of Alternative Possibilities,* ed. Michael McKenna and David Widerker. Aldershot, UK: Ashgate, 210–216.

McKenna, Michael. 2008. "A hard-line reply to Pereboom's four-case argument," *Philosophy and Phenomenological Research* **77**: 142–159.

Mele, Alfred. 1995. *Autonomous Agents*. New York: Oxford University Press.

Mele, Alfred. 2005. "A critique of Pereboom's 'four-case' argument for incompatibilism," *Analysis* **65**: 75–80.

Mele, Alfred. 2006. *Free Will and Luck*. New York: Oxford University Press.

Moya, Carlos. 2011. "On the very idea of a robust alternative," *Critica, Revista Hispanoamericana de Filosofia* **43.128**: 2–26.

Nelkin, Dana. 2008. "Responsibility and rational abilities: defending an asymmetrical view," *Pacific Philosophical Quarterly* **89**: 497–515.

Nelkin, Dana. 2011. *Making Sense of Freedom and Responsibility*. Oxford: Oxford University Press.

Nichols, Shaun. 2007. "After incompatibilism: a naturalistic defense of the reactive attitudes," *Philosophical Perspectives* **21**: 405–428.

O'Connor, Timothy. 2000. *Persons and Causes*. New York: Oxford University Press.

O'Connor, Timothy. 2003. "Review of *Living without Free Will*," *Philosophical Quarterly* **53**: 308–310.

O'Connor, Timothy. 2008. "Agent-causal power," in *Dispositions and Causes,* ed. Toby Handfield. Oxford: Clarendon Press, 189–214.

Otsuka, Michael. 1998. "Incompatibilism and the avoidability of blame," *Ethics* **108**: 685–701.

Palmer, David. 2011. "Pereboom on the Frankfurt cases," *Philosophical Studies* **153.2**: 261–272.

Pereboom, Derk. 1995. "Determinism *al dente*," *Noûs* **29**: 21–45.

Pereboom, Derk. 2000. "Alternative possibilities and causal histories," *Philosophical Perspectives* **14**: 119–137.

Pereboom, Derk. 2001. *Living Without Free Will*. Cambridge: Cambridge University Press.

Pereboom, Derk. 2003. "Source incompatibilism and alternative possibilities," in *Freedom, Responsibility, and Agency: Essays on the Importance of Alternative*

Possibilities, ed. Michael McKenna and David Widerker. Aldershot, UK: Ashgate, 185–199.

Pereboom, Derk. 2004. "Is our conception of agent causation incoherent?" *Philosophical Topics* **32:** 275–286.

Pereboom, Derk. 2005. " Defending hard incompatibilism," *Midwest Studies in Philosophy* **29,** 228–47.

Pereboom, Derk. 2007. "Hard incompatibilism," and "Response to Kane, Fischer, and Vargas," in *Four Views on Free Will,* ed. Robert Kane, John Martin Fischer, Derk Pereboom, and Manuel Vargas. Oxford: Blackwell, 85–125, 191–203.

Pereboom, Derk. 2008a. "A hard-line reply to the multiple-case manipulation argument," *Philosophy and Phenomenological Research* **77,** 2008: 160–70.

Pereboom, Derk. 2008b. "Defending hard incompatibilism again," in *Essays on Free Will and Moral Responsibility,* ed. Nick Trakakis and Daniel Cohen. Newcastle, UK: Cambridge Scholars Press, 1–33.

Pereboom, Derk. 2009a. "Further thoughts about a Frankfurt-style argument," *Philosophical Explorations* **12** (2010): 109–118.

Pereboom, Derk. 2009b. "Free will, love and anger," *Ideas y Valores* **141:** 5–25.

Pereboom, Derk. 2012. "Frankfurt examples, derivative responsibility, and the timing objection," *Philosophical Issues* **22.1:** 298–315.

Russell, Paul. 2000. "Compatibilist-fatalism," in *Moral Responsibility and Ontology,* ed. Ton van den Beld. Dordrecht, The Netherlands: Kluwer, 199–218.

Scanlon, Thomas. 1998. *What We Owe to Each Other.* Cambridge, MA: Harvard University Press.

Schoeman, Ferdinand D. 1979. "On incapacitating the dangerous," *American Philosophical Quarterly* **16:** 27–35.

Shabo, Seth. 2010. "Uncompromising source incompatibilism," *Philosophy and Phenomenological Research* **80:** 349–383.

Shabo, Seth. 2012. "Incompatibilism and personal relationships: another look at Strawson's objective attitude," *Australasian Journal of Philosophy* **90.1:** 131–147.

Smilansky, Saul. 1997. "Can a determinist help herself?" in *Freedom and Moral Responsibility: General and Jewish Perspectives,* ed. C. H. Manekin and M. Kellner. College Park: University of Maryland Press, 85–98.

Smilansky, Saul. 2000. *Free Will and Illusion.* Oxford: Oxford University Press.

Sommers, Tamler. 2007. "The objective attitude," *Philosophical Quarterly* **57,** 321–41.

Spinoza, Baruch. 1677/1985. *The Collected Works of Spinoza.* Vol.1, *Ethics,* ed. and trans. Edwin Curley. Princeton, NJ: Princeton University Press.

Strawson, Galen. 1986. *Freedom and Belief.* Oxford: Oxford University Press.

Strawson, Peter F. 1962. "Freedom and resentment," *Proceedings of the British Academy* **48:** 1–25.

Taylor, Richard. 1966. *Action and Purpose.* Englewood Cliffs, NJ: Prentice Hall.

Taylor, Richard. 1974. *Metaphysics,* 4th ed. Englewood Cliffs, NJ: Prentice Hall.

Todd, Patrick. 2011. "A new approach to manipulation arguments," *Philosophical Studies* **152:** 127–133.

Wallace, R. Jay. 1994. *Responsibility and the Moral Sentiments.* Cambridge, MA: Harvard University Press.

Waller, Bruce. 1990. *Freedom Without Responsibility*. Philadelphia: Temple University Press.

Widerker, David. 1995. "Libertarianism and Frankfurt's attack on the principle of alternative possibilities," *Philosophical Review* **104**: 247–261.

Widerker, David. 2006. "Libertarianism and the philosophical significance of Frankfurt scenarios," *Journal of Philosophy* **103**: 163–187.

23

Compatibilist-Fatalism: Finitude, Pessimism, and the Limits of Free Will

Paul Russell

> To escape pessimism is, as we all know, no easy task.
> —WILLIAM JAMES ("THE DILEMMA OF DETERMINISM")

Compatibilists argue, famously, that it is a simple incompatibilist confusion to suppose that determinism implies fatalism. Incompatibilists argue, on the contrary, that determinism implies fatalism, and thus cannot be consistent with the necessary conditions of moral responsibility. Despite their differences, however, both parties are agreed on one important matter: the refutation of fatalism is essential to the success of the compatibilist strategy. In this paper I argue that compatibilism requires a richer conception of fatalistic concern; one that recognizes the *legitimacy* of (pessimistic) concerns about the origination of character and conduct. On this basis I argue that any plausible compatibilist position must concede that determinism has fatalistic implications of some significant and relevant kind, and thus must allow that agents may be legitimately held responsible in circumstances where they are subject to fate. The position generated by these compatibilist concessions to incompatibilism will be called "compatibilist-fatalism."

I.

Compatibilist-fatalism has two key components:

(1) It claims that the truth of determinism is compatible with conditions of responsibility. I will call this the 'responsibility-compatibilist claim.' (Its contrary will be called the 'responsibility-incompatibilist claim.')

(2) It claims that determinism implies conditions of universal fatalism. I will call this the 'fatalism claim.'

There is near unanimous agreement in both compatibilist and incompatibilist camps that it is incoherent to combine these two claims, since an agent cannot be both responsible and subject to fate. Compatibilists and incompatibilists have, nevertheless, very different reasons for taking this view. Indeed, their superficial agreement conceals fundamental differences about the nature and significance of *fatalism* itself.

With remarkable consistency compatibilists have been very clear about why they believe that the fatalistic claim should be rejected. It is, they maintain, a product of simple confusion—a confusion that gives illegitimate support to incompatibilism. The compatibilist argument against the fatalism claim—let us call it the 'refutation argument'—is very familiar. In an influential statement of classical compatibilism R.E. Hobart gives the following brief account of the refutation argument:

> Fatalism says that my morrow is determined no matter how I struggle. This is of course a superstition. Determinism says that my morrow is determined through my struggle... The stream of causation runs through my deliberations and decisions, and if it did not run as it does run, the event would be different.[1]

According to this view, then, determinism is the thesis that everything that occurs, including our deliberations and decisions, are causally *necessitated* by antecedent conditions. Fatalism, by contrast, is the doctrine that our deliberations and decisions are causally *ineffective* and make no difference to the course of events. In circumstances of fatalism what happens does not depend on how the agent deliberates. The relevant outcome will occur no matter what the agent decides. Clearly, however, determinism does not imply fatalism. While there are some circumstances in which deliberation is futile (i.e. 'local fatalism'), deliberation is nevertheless generally effective in a deterministic world.[2]

Let us call those who accept the responsibility-compatibilist claim but reject the fatalist claim 'orthodox-compatibilists.' Orthodox-compatibilist understanding of the relationship between responsibility and fate seems clear enough—indeed, one of its attractions is its simplicity. In circumstances where a person is subject to fate, her deliberations and decisions cannot change the course of events. Whatever occurs in these circumstances does not depend on the agent's deliberations. Accordingly, if it were true that determinism implied universal fatalism then it would follow that no one would be responsible—since no one would be able to influence or alter what occurs.[3] However, as the refutation argument makes plain, none of these consequences follows from the truth of determinism. Responsibility-incompatibilism, therefore, has no legitimate foundation in the fatalism claim that incompatibilists mistakenly try to draw from the thesis of determinism.

Incompatibilists defend the fatalism claim and reject the (orthodox) compatibilist's refutation-argument.[4] The incompatibilist reply to the refutation argument turns, crucially, on an alternative interpretation of *fate*. The incompatibilist maintains that compatibilist accounts of 'fate,' interpreted in terms of the causal ineffectiveness of an agent's deliberations and actions, is wholly inadequate, and that in consequence it evades not only real difficulties of a fatalistic character, but also related difficulties about the conditions of moral responsibility. Incompatibilist concern about fate is not—as on the refutation argument—directed to the issue of the causal influence *of the agent* but rather at the issue concerning the causal influence *on the agent*. An agent is said to be subject to 'fate,' on this account, if her character and conduct does not (ultimately) originate with the person concerned. The incompatibilist maintains that determinism implies universal fatalism in the sense that—however complex the mechanisms at work may be—the causal chains eventually reach outside the agent and, hence, no person is *the real originator or ultimate source* of her conduct and character. When an agent is not the (ultimate) source of her actions then, the incompatibilist argues, the person is subject to fate.

Compatibilists and incompatibilists, evidently, conceive of 'fate' in quite different terms. For the compatibilist a person is subject to fate only if their circumstances are such that they are unable to causally *contribute* to the course of events in some relevant respect. Let us call this account of fate, as developed in the refutation argument, the concept of 'contributory-fate.' Incompatibilists do not (or need not) deny that contributory-fate is one mode of fatalistic concern nor need they suppose that determinism implies that contributory-fatalism holds universally.[5] What the incompatibilist maintains is that there is another mode of fatalistic concern that arises from a backward-looking perspective (and is, as I will explain, intimately linked with problems of responsibility). The question that concerns us from this perspective is whether or not the agent is the ultimate source or true originator of her character and conduct. An agent is subject to 'fate,' in this sense, if her circumstances are such that her character and conduct have origins and sources that (ultimately) extend beyond her control.[6] Let us call this alternative, incompatibilist conception of fate 'origination-fate.' The essence of the incompatibilist position is that determinism implies that origination-fate is the universal condition and thus renders responsibility impossible.[7]

Issues of responsibility and fatalism are intimately and inextricably woven-together on the standard incompatibilist account. Incompatibilists object to the compatibilist's refutation argument on the ground that it constitutes a superficial response on this issue (i.e., fate) and argue that it reflects a one-sided, forward-looking pragmatic perspective that fails to capture—or even acknowledge—difficulties arising from the backward-looking perspective (i.e., matters of origination as opposed to contribution). According to the incompatibilist, the very same shortcomings can be found in compatibilist views on responsibility and for reasons that are rooted in and run parallel to the failings of the refutation argument.[8] Incompatibilists grant that it is possible to advance a 'superficial' conception of responsibility that is essentially pragmatic and forward-looking in nature, and this can be reconciled with determinism. What cannot be reconciled with determinism, however, is deep responsibility.[9] Deep responsibility is concerned not with the causal efficacy of the attitudes and practices of blaming and punishing, but rather with whether these attitudes and practices are deserved or merited. To understand (deep) responsibility in these terms involves a change of perspective from forward-looking to backward-looking considerations. Only from this perspective can we understand the retributive aspects of responsibility which the compatibilist's (superficial) forward-looking account cannot capture.

It is at this point that incompatibilists draw on their defense of the fatalism claim and use it to support their responsibility-incompatibilist conclusion. Attributions of desert, claims the incompatibilist, rest with an agent's capacity for *self-determination*, and this requires the metaphysics of indeterminism. The incompatibilist maintains, in other words, that it will not suffice to establish a person's responsibility to show, simply, that her deliberations and conduct are causally effective in the world. On the contrary, what is required is to show that the choices and actions originate with the agent—and that is why we hold the agent accountable. Clearly, then, since determinism implies universal origination-fatalism, it makes responsibility impossible. It is in this manner that the responsibility-incompatibilist claim and fatalism claim are inextricably bound together on the standard incompatibilist account.[10]

II.

The success of any compatibilist strategy depends on showing that 'origination,' understood in terms of indeterministic metaphysics, is not a necessary condition of moral responsibility and that a suitably 'deep' account of responsibility can be provided within the restrictions imposed by compatibilist commitments. It is not possible in this context to provide any full-scale defense of the case for responsibility-compatibilism. For our purposes, however, this is not necessary. All that is necessary is to describe the general structural features of the case for responsibility-compatibilism in order to assess its significance for the *distinct* prospects of compatibilist-fatalism (as contrasted with orthodox-compatibilism). Suffice it to say, that if there is nothing of a convincing nature to be said in support of the responsibility-compatibilist claim then both orthodox-compatibilism *and* compatibilist-fatalism collapse—since this claim is common to both.

There are two independent but merging strands in contemporary compatibilist thinking that promise a 'deeper' and more 'robust' compatibilist account of moral responsibility. Both these strands can be described under the general heading of 'naturalized responsibility.' The first strand is closely associated, in the contemporary context, with P. F. Strawson's highly influential paper "Freedom and Resentment."[11] The view advanced is that circumstances of responsibility must be understood in terms of the natural workings of moral sentiment. Human beings, it is argued, are inescapably subject to moral emotions under certain conditions, and no general 'theoretical' considerations concerning the truth of determinism can discredit—much less dislodge—our human commitment to these emotional responses. To suppose otherwise is to 'over-intellectualize' these matters. The most notable strength of this strand of naturalized responsibility is that it distances itself from the cruder utilitarian, forward-looking features of classical compatibilism, without making any concessions to the metaphysics of libertarianism. The Strawsonian strategy, therefore, plugs a significant 'gap' in the compatibilist position and provides a substantial basis for accounting for backward-looking, desert-based considerations consistent with compatibilist commitments. To this extent, compatibilists are better placed to provide their account of responsibility with the kind of 'depth' which it plainly requires.

Although the Strawsonian strand of naturalized responsibility (plausibly) addresses a number of traditional incompatibilist objectives, it has its own significant vulnerabilities. The most important of these is, perhaps, that taken by itself it fails to explain on what basis individuals are or are not appropriate objects of moral sentiment.[12] More specifically, without some account of the relevant *capacities* required of moral agents, the theory remains entirely open to the incompatibilist counter-argument that what is required is some mode of contra-causal freedom. The second strand of contemporary naturalized responsibility, however, appears to plug this gap in the position very neatly. What is required is an account of moral capacity that can account for freedom of the *will* as well as freedom of action. Various models of 'hierarchical' or 'real self' theories provide this.[13] Moral freedom, it is argued, is not simply a matter of being able to act according to your own will, unimpeded by external constraints. It also involves a capacity to reflect on the structure of your own will and form preferences about which desires move you to action. On the basis of a higher-order capacity of this kind agents are able to 'identify' with or 'repudiate' their own will—something that is essential to being capable of moral conduct and an appropriate object of moral sentiment. It is a general capacity of this nature that distinguishes fully responsible human adults from animals and children who (in some degree) do not enjoy such a capacity and thus are not (fully) responsible. The crucial point remains, however, that this sort of higher-capacity involves no contra-causal or libertarian metaphysical commitments.

Although it would be entirely premature to declare this two-pronged defense of the responsibility-compatibilist claim a success (as clearly the matters raised continue to be strenuously debated), it is nevertheless fair to say that this general approach provides substantial support for the position taken.[14] Let us say, therefore, that the responsibility-compatibilist claim has substantial (although not conclusive) support. The issue that concerns us is what the implications of this are for the compatibilist position in respect of the matter of fatalism. The view that is most widely accepted on this issue is plain. If responsibility-compatibilism is accepted, then the fatalism claim must be rejected, as both cannot be accepted.

Let us call the assumption that responsibility and fate *exclude* each other the 'exclusion thesis.' Both orthodox-compatibilists and incompatibilists accept the exclusion thesis although, as I have explained, they accept it for very different reasons. The exclusion thesis, however, provides a very quick way of dealing with the issue of fatalism once the responsibility-compatibilist claim is established. The exclusion thesis eliminates the possibility that conditions of universal fatalism could persist in conditions when agents are still morally responsible. Hence, if agents are responsible, conditions of universal fatalism cannot hold. In short, if we accept the responsibility-compatibilist claim, and the exclusion thesis, then we *must* reject the fatalism claim. If this is correct, then compatibilist-fatalism is an untenable position.

If a case can be made for compatibilist-fatalism it must be able to show that there is some basis for accepting the fatalism claim without compromising the responsibility-compatibilist claim (thereby showing the exclusion thesis to be false). Another way of expressing this is to say that there must be issues of fatalism that survive the (assumed) success of responsibility-compatibilism. On the face of it, however, this is odd, as incompatibilist concern about the fatalistic implications of determinism (i.e., in respect of origination-fate) are generally motivated by worries about responsibility-incompatibilism. The puzzle is, that if determinism has no responsibility-incompatibilist implications then the issue of origination-fatalism seems to be empty.[15]

III.

In order to explain the distinctive commitments of compatibilist-fatalism it will be useful to employ the terminology of 'optimism' and 'pessimism.'[16] These labels are illuminating for understanding the free will debate because they indicate that the various parties involved have certain concerns or interests that motivate the positions that they take. In other words, these labels make plain that the issues at stake are not merely theoretical (conceptual) puzzles that require clarification but, rather, they are matters that are in some sense emotionally charged. The language of 'pessimism,' in particular, is indicative of the fact that incompatibilists find some implications of determinism troubling or disturbing.[17] For the incompatibilist determinism suggests a picture of human beings that is (somehow) disillusioning and, thus, the incompatibilist wants this thesis to be false. Compatibilists, by contrast, do not share these concerns and believe, indeed, that they are misguided and a product of (philosophical) confusion. Since compatibilists find nothing 'troubling' or 'disturbing' about the thesis of determinism—and nothing about it motivates a desire that it be false—they may be characterized as 'optimists.'

Any position that accepts the fatalism claim seems to be committed to pessimistic motivations of some kind. In the case of incompatibilism these pessimistic motivations, as we have noted, are closely tied to concerns about the conditions of responsibility. These concerns are not endorsed by compatibilist-fatalists since they accept the (contrary) responsibility-compatibilist claim. The obvious question arises, therefore, given their commitment to the fatalism claim, what are the pessimistic motivations of the compatibilist-fatalist? Clearly compatibilist-fatalists hold that determinism implies universal origination-fatalism and there is something 'troubling' or 'disturbing' about this which lies beyond the scope of issues of responsibility. However, the source of this pessimism remains obscure.

What is essential to compatibilist-fatalism is the view that while origination-fatalism does not undermine or discredit our (natural) commitment to moral responsibility, it nevertheless does not leave our conception of ourselves as *real* agents in the world undiminished. A well-known passage of Spinoza's *Ethics* identifies this source of pessimistic concern and describes it in the following terms:

> Most of those who have written about the emotions and human conduct seem to be dealing not with natural phenomena that follow the common laws of Nature but with phenomena outside Nature. They appear to go so far as to conceive man in Nature as a kingdom within a kingdom. They believe that he disturbs rather than follows Nature's order, and has absolute power over his actions, and is determined by no other source than himself.[18]

Spinoza's observations appear in a context in which he is seeking to explain the source of deep *resistance* to any naturalized, deterministic conception of human life. Although much of this resistance is motivated by incompatibilist concerns about the threat to the fabric of moral responsibility, Spinoza's remarks bypass them. Instead, his remarks are addressed directly at the issue of agency. The specific dimension of pessimistic concern is captured through the metaphor of 'sovereignty.' In conceiving of human beings as 'a kingdom within a kingdom' we conceive of ourselves as subject, not to the alien laws that govern all nature, but rather to laws that pertain uniquely to human (rational) life. Our sense of 'sovereignty,' therefore, is tied to our belief that we are distinct from nature, not (a reducible) part of it. Through our capacity for sovereignty, so conceived, we are not only independent of nature, but also *above* it. We are above it—qua sovereign—because we govern nature without being governed by it (i.e., we are not subject to its laws).[19] From this perspective we take ourselves to be something more than (sophisticated and complex) causal intermediaries. We conceive of ourselves as starting points that intervene in the order of things. Finally, the metaphor of sovereignty brings with it a conception of beings who are worthy of a particular kind of dignity—the dignity due to beings who are sovereign over both themselves and nature.

Clearly, from this perspective, we want much more than simply to be morally accountable to each other. What is at stake here is our conception of ourselves as (actively) *ordering nature* rather than being (passively) *ordered by nature*. This distinction depends on a capacity for spontaneous self-determination and thus cannot be sustained in conditions of universal origination-fatalism. Any optimism secured on the basis of responsibility-compatibilism, therefore, must be significantly tempered by a pessimism rooted in these reflections. Although we may concede that universal origination-fatalism poses no threat to the fabric of responsibility, it nevertheless has troubling implications for aspects of our self-conception that lie outside this sphere (something that is obscured by incompatibilist arguments that focus exclusively on issues of responsibility). Only those who are unmoved by the issue of 'sovereignty,' and place no value on it, can draw any other conclusion.

What reply can orthodox-compatibilists offer to this line of reasoning? The first point to note is that it will not do to fall back on the refutation argument. The pessimistic concerns of the compatibilist-fatalist are not motivated by any simple confusion between determinism and contributory-fatalism. On the contrary, compatibilist-fatalists (along with incompatibilists) object to the refutation argument on the ground that it fails to draw the relevant distinction between origination and contributory fate and is, consequently, blind to the very different concerns that arise from the former. Furthermore, the entire line of reasoning that develops from the refutation argument proceeds from the same one-sided, forward-looking perspective that generated serious shortcomings in the efforts of classical compatibilists to address incompatibilist concerns about responsibility. Since compatibilism has overcome its blindness to backward-looking claims in respect of responsibility, so too it must face the issues raised by origination-fatalism in a more direct manner.

The orthodox-compatibilist may argue that it is possible to address these concerns about origination without accepting the fatalism claim. It may be argued, for example, that the resources of naturalized responsibility provide an effective basis from which to discredit the specific concerns that the compatibilist-fatalist has raised. What is supposed to be troubling about determinism is that it makes genuine origination or (true) self-determination impossible. If there is any foundation to the pessimistic concerns that support the fatalism claim, this seems to be it. Against this, however, it can be argued that hierarchical or real self theories of freedom provide a substantial account of self-determination and self-control without any appeal to indeterministic metaphysics. All that is required is a suitably complex description of the higher-order capacities of human beings to reflect on their own character and motivation and restructure their own wills on this basis. It is simply incorrect, on this account, to suppose that any agent in a deterministic framework is incapable of altering or amending his character and the structure of his own will. Agents with the relevant capacities of the sort described (i.e., two-level freedom) are not passive in these respects. Indeed, with capacities of these (natural) kinds we can, to a large extent, conceive of ourselves as 'self-made-selves.'[20] Whatever residue of pessimistic concern survives responsibility-compatibilism, therefore, is effectively discredited by these considerations.

Does this orthodox-compatibilist counter-argument—let us call it the *revised* refutation argument'—serve to discredit the distinct pessimistic concerns that motivate the compatibilist fatalist? The revised refutation argument is obviously an improvement on the original argument. It does not, for example, suggest that the defender of the fatalism claim makes the crude mistake of supposing that determinism implies universal *contributory*-fatalism. More importantly, this revised effort to refute the fatalism claim does not deny the general legitimacy of concerns that arise from a backward-looking perspective about the issue of origination of character and conduct. What is argued is that determinism provides no basis for pessimistic concerns of this kind and to this extent the concerns are unreasonable. The resources of higher-order capacities are more than adequate to account for talk of self-determination and self-control (i.e., some form of 'sovereignty') and they do so without relying on the obscure metaphysics of libertarianism to fill this particular gap.

The strength of the revised argument is that it shows that compatibilists can provide a more sophisticated account of self-determination and freedom of will, which is a clear improvement on the more limited (classical) compatibilist accounts of freedom understood in terms of unimpeded action. Nevertheless, it is not evident that the case against the fatalism claim can be secured by means of the revised refutation argument. The (higher-order) moral capacities described may well serve as the relevant basis on which to distinguish individuals who are appropriate objects of moral sentiment from those who are not. (Indeed, for reasons that have been explained, the case for responsibility-compatibilism depends on this.) However, capacities of these kinds are not capable of addressing the specific difficulties that are suggested by reflection on the implications of (universal) origination-fatalism.

First, the compatibilist-fatalist may grant that human beings have capacities of self-determinism of the sort described without in any way conceding that these capacities are of such a nature as to allow agents to reinvent themselves as they please. Any account of these capacities, so construed, is self-evidently an exaggeration. Clearly there are many other forces of an external nature that condition character and the conduct that flows from it. Accordingly, the scope and extent of the human capacity for self-determination of this sort is much more limited and restricted than orthodox-compatibilist talk of 'self-made-selves' suggests.[21] Second, and more importantly, even if these powers of self-control were as extensive as defenders of the revised refutation argument imply, they entirely fail to address the more basic concern that sustains the fatalism claim. The specific concern is that ultimately nothing that the agent is or does originates with the agent—the causal source can always be traced to factors lying outside the agent. Granted a deterministic framework, when and how an agent actually *exercises* such capacities of rational self-criticism and redirection will depend, ultimately, on factors that lie beyond the agent.[22] This brings us back full circle to the specific implication of determinism that compatibilist-fatalists find disturbing: determinism implies that no agent is the ultimate source of her own character and conduct.[23]

This basic concern is, of course, very familiar in literature critical of compatibilist efforts to account for self-determination. It is, however, particularly important to note that while libertarian efforts to explain what ultimate agency consists in may be judged hopelessly obscure, the aspiration itself is motivated by a general worry that is clear enough: namely, that compatibilist accounts of self-determination are essentially superficial since such agents are, inescapably, conditioned by factors that they have no control over. Clearly, then, the revised refutation argument, fails to discredit this fundamental concern. It may be argued, furthermore, that this conclusion is especially disturbing if the compatibilist is right and our natural commitment to responsibility persists in face of these (fatalistic) conditions.[24]

IV.

In face of this reply to the revised refutation argument, orthodox-compatibilists may suggest another way of discrediting the pessimistic concerns that seem to sustain the fatalism claim. What is not clear, they may argue, is what sort of 'origination' or 'self-determination' is required to avoid these fatalistic anxieties. More specifically, the desire to be a (pure) self-determinator, so conceived, is simply incoherent and, thus, no real sense can be made of the pessimistic concerns that lie behind the fatalism claim.[25] Moreover, insofar as any sense can be made of this desire for (pure) self-determination it appears, on examination, less than desirable. So the orthodox-compatibilist reply is this: the objective of 'overcoming' origination-fate in the terms suggested is neither coherent nor obviously attractive in itself. To this the orthodox-compatibilist may also add that it is important to note that the problem of fate, conceived in terms of worries about origination (rather than contribution), is not limited to the metaphysics of determinism. On the contrary, the metaphysics of indeterminism generates its own 'fatalistic' worries in this regard. That is, even if there are real 'breaks in the causal chain,' and 'spontaneous willings' occur, it is not evident that this serves to secure 'genuine agency.' This is because (pure) 'spontaneity' seems to undermine genuine agency no less than the chains of causal necessity. The underlying point is, of course, that the ideal of 'genuine agency' is simply a confused illusion that cannot stand up to critical scrutiny. Given this, the pessimistic concerns that are supposed to sustain the fatalism claim can be dismissed as wholly unreasonable.

This rejoinder seeks to discredit the pessimistic motivations of the compatibilist-fatalist by arguing that there is no plausible *alternative* metaphysics that could overcome these difficulties (i.e., regarding ultimate self-determination or origination). This is not a convincing way to discredit these concerns about origination-fatalism. The obvious point is that while it may be granted that there is no alternative metaphysics that serves to insulate us from these pessimistic concerns about the ultimate origination of character and conduct, this does not show that these concerns are somehow bogus or without foundation. Consider, for example, the analogous debate concerning the doctrine of the immortality of the soul. Many philosophers—especially religiously minded philosophers—have argued that we have reason to want to be immortal, to exist for all eternity. Accordingly, faced with arguments for human mortality (i.e., naturalistic conceptions of human beings) these philosophers maintain that mortalism has pessimistic implications. Against pessimism of this nature, defenders of mortalism may argue (in parallel reasoning with orthodox-compatibilists) that the desire for immortality is neither coherent in itself nor an obviously attractive ideal—to the extent that we can conceive of it being realized.

Clearly, however, those who find mortalism a source of pessimism (i.e., troubling; difficult, disillusioning, and so on) may readily grant the truth of the mortalist's claims concerning the doctrine of immortality. Nevertheless, it simply does not follow that if one grants that the desire for immortality involves an ideal or aspiration that is doubtfully coherent and (on reflection) doubtfully attractive, then there is no basis for being troubled by reflections on human mortality.[26] On the contrary, reflection on this specific aspect of the human condition provides a reasonable basis for being troubled *whatever view we take*. There is no guarantee that some trouble-free optimistic alternative must be 'available' to us. Indeed, in the case of human mortality/immortality the truth seems otherwise. What is troubling about human mortality is that it confronts us with the limits of human existence—our inevitable and inescapable *finitude* as beings in the world. Clearly, then, while we may not want to be immortal, and we may agree there is no coherent account of what we would want if we sought immortality, we may still have some reasonable basis for finding the limits of human existence and individual finitude matters that unsettle and disturb us in important respects (so long as we are tolerably reflective on the matter). This feature of the human condition is something that we cannot contemplate with optimistic calm and serenity.[27]

Parallel reasoning is available to the compatibilist-fatalist. Against this position it is argued that concerns about the fatalistic implications of determinism rely upon an ideal of (pure) self-determination that is neither coherent nor, on reflection, attractive. From this the orthodox-compatibilist concludes that there is no basis for the pessimistic anxieties that are supposed to sustain the fatalism claim. To this, however, the compatibilist-fatalist may reply that, however incoherent and unattractive the ideal of pure (uncondi-tioned) agency may be, what is troubling about origination-fatalism is that it confronts us with *the limits of human agency*—the inescapable fact that the ultimate source of our character and conduct lies beyond us.[28] Our finitude and place in the order of nature has implications for our conception of our-selves as genuine agents. We may not want to be (God-like) self-creators, and we may agree that there is no available coherent interpretation of this ideal, and yet consistently maintain that reflections on these limits concerning the origination of human agency are disturbing and troubling in ways that are analogous to reflections about human mortality. To insist on (easy) optimism in face of such thoughts about the human condition is a form of 'superficial-ity' to which (orthodox) compatibilists are much too prone.

V.

There is one final reply to the compatibilist-fatalist that may now be pre-sented. The fatalism claim receives whatever support it has on the basis of the pessimistic concerns that it generates from reflections about origination. The orthodox-compatibilist may simply insist that none of these concerns move him, or *trouble* him, in the least. It may be argued, moreover, that it is the compatibilist-fatalist who is guilty of 'over-intellectualizing' this whole issue by appealing to 'theoretical' considerations regarding origination in order to *compel* a particular affective response (i.e., pessimism)—but this cannot be done.

This reply, however, is one that the orthodox-compatibilist should be reluctant to employ. The orthodox-compatibilist has tried to *discredit* the fatalism claim by showing that, in some way or other, it depends on confu-sion and/or illusion. In reply it has been shown that these attempts to refute the fatalism claim are themselves confused or manifest a shallow apprecia-tion of fatalistic concern. The compatibilist-fatalist may grant, at this stage, that their concerns may not be shared by everyone and that it is impossible to argue someone into the relevant attitude (i.e., pessimism) once all relevant considerations have been made clear. Nevertheless, if it is impossible to com-pel pessimistic attitudes in face of such considerations, it is no less impossible to compel optimism. As there seems to be no identifiable confusion lying behind either the optimistic or pessimistic attitude in these circumstances, a stalemate results. This situation, however, leaves orthodox-compatibilists unable to discredit the pessimism that sustains the fatalism claim. All that can be said in reply is that the orthodox-compatibilist does not share it, which is clearly a different matter. It suffices, therefore, that the pessimism that moti-vates the commitment to the fatalism claim has not been discredited, and the orthodox-compatibilist is mistaken to suppose that it can be.

The compatibilist-fatalist may also argue that the best explanation for the fact that orthodox-compatibilists are unable to share this pessimism is that they have not sufficiently exercised their reflective imagination. To rem-edy this, they may suggest that appropriate reflection on especially striking cases will help to make clear why pessimistic concerns about origination are called for.[29] As I have explained, however, it would be a mistake to represent the pessimistic concerns that sustain commitment to the fatalism claim as simply the end-result of a process of pure reasoning, as clearly such con-cerns also require some relevant *sensibility*. (Consider, again, the analogy with pessimistic reflections on death.) This is why the cultivation of artis-tic imagination is of such obvious significance in this context; since many great works of literature and drama are devoted to the central message of compatibilist-fatalism: that responsibility and fate come fused together in human life.[30]

Another possibility is to show that the orthodox-compatibilist's inability to share this mode of pessimism is rooted in confusion about the *quality* of the pessimism involved. Pessimism varies in its quality as well as its source. The quality of pessimism generated by contributory-fatalism may be charac-terized as one of *despair*, produced by a sense of impotence. To conceive of ourselves as 'puppets' or 'dolls,' for example, would certainly be awful and justify despair.[31] The pessimism associated with origination-fatalism, how-ever, is not of this character.

Origination-fatalism, I have argued, focuses on our awareness of human finitude and its relevance to agency. This basic concern is well captured by John Macquarrie in the context of a discussion of existentialist philosophy.

> Man is thrown into existence, each one is thrown into his own particular existential situation. From the human point of view, it is rather like the throw of a dice .... As we see it from the purely human point of view, we all start out as different people with different endowments in different situations, and there is as little assignable reason for the differences as there is for the dice turning up one number rather than another.[32]

As these remarks suggest, the pessimism of compatibilist-fatalism is not so much a sense of despair rooted in impotence but rather one of being *dis-concerted*, rooted in awareness of *finitude and contingency*.[33] Closely associ-ated with the sense of finitude and contingency is, I suggest, a sense of the absurdity of human life.[34] In this context it takes the form of an (uncomfort-able) awareness of the gap between our aspiration to 'sovereignty' and being 'self-made-selves,' and the recognition, as conveyed by the fatalism claim, that this is an illusion. It is evident, therefore, that the pessimism involved in endorsing the fatalism claim, so interpreted, is of a very different kind from the pessimism associated with contributory-fatalism (i.e., as featured in the refutation argument). Much of the orthodox-compatibilist resistance to the pessimism of compatibilist-fatalism is based, I suggest, in a confusion between these two very different modes of fatalistic concern and the distinct sensibilities associated with them.

It should now be clear what the optimistic and pessimistic commitments of compatibilist-fatalism come to. In respect of the issue of responsibility, the compatibilist-fatalist maintains that the resources of naturalized responsibility are rich enough to provide firm support for the responsibility-compatibilist claim. (This is an issue that I have left open, except for the proviso that a strong enough case can be made for this claim to give it considerable credibility.) In respect of the fatalism claim, compatibilist-fatalists hold that the refutation argument is blind to pessimistic concerns about *origination*. Moreover, even the more substantial revised version of the refutation argument (employing the resources of naturalized responsibility) cannot discredit or dislodge the source of pessimism that sustains commitment to the fatalism claim. So interpreted, compatibilist-fatalism involves *mixed* optimistic and pessimistic elements, and to this extent it addresses both compatibilist and incompatibilist concerns.

VI.

My objective in this paper has not been to defend compatibilist-fatalism but to consider its merits in relation to orthodox (non-fatalistic) compatibilism. Both forms of compatibilism accept the responsibility-compatibilist claim: that is, the claim that determinism does not discredit the attitudes and practices associated with moral responsibility. Where they diverge is on the matter of fatalism. Compatibilist-fatalists accept a claim that is generally associated with incompatibilism, namely, that determinism has fatalistic implications. The discussion in this paper, therefore, has been primarily concerned to provide an interpretation and defense of the fatalism claim from the perspective of those who are already (i.e., independently) committed to the responsibility-compatibilist claim. For reasons that have been explained, this is an unusual and controversial position for any compatibilist to adopt.[35]

I have described a number of different approaches that the orthodox-compatibilist may take in order to discredit the specific pessimistic motivations associated with the fatalism claim. All of them, I argue, are unsuccessful. It follows from this that any plausible compatibilism must take the form of—or accept the legitimacy of—compatibilist-fatalism.[36] An obvious corollary of this is that a plausible compatibilism must reject the exclusion thesis.[37] A particular merit of compatibilistfatalism is that it recognizes the (deep) source of incompatibilist intuitions as rooted in backward-looking concerns about the origination of character and conduct and, related to this, it avoids the one-sided superficiality of the (classical) refutation argument. When these points are properly established, I maintain, the compatibilist is better placed to provide a more nuanced and appropriate response to the (pessimistic) concerns of the incompatibilist

A plausible compatibilism, I conclude, must embrace a richer conception of fatalistic concern and allow for the possibility that agents may be legitimately held responsible in circumstances where they are subject to fate. The significance of this should be clear. Hitherto all forms of compatibilism have been orthodox in character: they reject the fatalism claim and are homogeneously 'optimistic.' The central thesis of this paper is that compatibilism can (or must) take the form of compatibilist-fatalism and, thereby, accept that determinism has fatalistic implications without compromising its commitment to naturalized responsibility.

Notes

I am grateful to Ton van den Beld, Richard Double, Richard Gale, Walter Glannon, David Gauthier, Saul Smilansky, Jay Wallace, and Allen Wood for helpful comments and suggestions on earlier drafts of this paper. For further helpful comments and discussion I would like to thank audiences at Simon Fraser, Washington (Seattle), British Columbia, Edinboro (Pennsylvania), Virginia and, especially, the Utrecht conference on "Moral Responsibility and Ontology" (1998).

1. R.E. Hobart, "Free will as involving determination and inconceivable without it," reprinted in *Free Will and Determinism*, ed. Bernard Berofsky (New York: Harpers & Row, 1966), 82.

2. Daniel Dennett is the most prominent contemporary defender of the (classical) refutation argument. As an example of 'local fatalism' he describes circumstances where a person has thrown himself off the Golden Gate Bridge and then asks if this is really such a good idea. For this person, Dennett observes, "deliberation has indeed become impotent." See Dennett, *Elbow Room: The Varieties of Free Will Worth Wanting* (Oxford: Clarendon Press, 1984), 104. The point is, however, that these circumstances are 'abnormal' in a deterministic world and deliberation is generally effective, not futile (106).

3. The sort of fatalistic circumstances that the refutation argument is concerned with (i.e., situations that concern the 'causal impotence' or 'futility' of deliberation—*Elbow Room*, 15, 104, 106) may nevertheless vary in significant ways. Compare, for instance, Dennett's 'bogeymen' examples such as being controlled by 'the Peremptory Puppeteer' and 'the Hideous Hypnotist' (*Elbow Room*, 8–9). As Dennett points out, the phenomenology of agency/fatalism is very different in these cases.

4. There are exceptions to this generalization. See, e.g., Isaiah Berlin, *Four Essays on Liberty* (Oxford: Oxford University Press, 1969), xiii. Although Berlin accepts the refutation argument and its associated understanding of fatalism, he nevertheless argues for the responsibility-incompatibilist claim on independent grounds.

5. Some incompatibilists, of course, object to deterministic metaphysics on the ground that it implies 'mechanism,' and this is incompatible with the sort of purposive explanations that are essential to responsible agency. This distinct and more radical line of incompatibilist reasoning (which Dennett labels as worries about 'sphexishness,' *Elbow Room*, 10–14) is not essential to their position. On this see Watson's introduction to *Free Will*, ed. Gary Watson (Oxford University Press, 1982), 11–14.

6. For a discussion and interpretation of the relevance of the origination/contribution distinction for the free will debate see Robert Nozick, *Philosophical Explanations* (Oxford: Oxford University Press, 1981), 313. Nozick interprets fatalism as denying that our actions have any 'contributory value,' and the problem of causal determinism as the suggestion that our actions would be left without 'originatory value.'

7. For an influential and illuminating discussion that articulates these incompatibilist intuitions see Thomas Nagel, "Moral luck," reprinted in Watson, ed., (1982), esp. 183 on 'genuine agency' and 'shrinking' responsibility. Another similarly important and interesting discussion of these matters is presented in Gary Watson, "Responsibility and the limits of evil: variations on a Strawsonian theme," reprinted in *Perspective on Moral Responsibility*, ed. J. M. Fischer and M. Ravizza (Ithaca, NY Cornell University Press, 1993), esp. 143–44 on 'origination' and the 'historical dimension' of responsibility. Both Nagel and Watson (consistent with usual incompatibilist concerns) emphasize the relevance of worries about 'origination' for issues of responsibility.

8. It is no coincidence, for example, that Dennett's account of responsibility is wholly pragmatic and forward-looking in character (*Elbow Room*, 156–65). On this see Gary Watson's review of *Elbow Room* in the *Journal of Philosophy* 83 (1986): 517–22.

9. Susan Wolf, *Freedom within Reason* (New York: Oxford University Press, 1990), 40–45.

10. See, in particular, Nagel's remarks on "the contributions of fate" and their tendency "to erode most of the moral assessments we find it natural to make" ("Moral luck," esp. 176, 180, 182). I note in passing that not all incompatibilists would accept that their position should be interpreted in terms of concerns about "origination." Some, for example, may articulate their incompatibilism in terms of the issue of 'alternate possibilities' or 'freedom to do otherwise." Incompatibilist concerns of this nature, however, depend on a particular ('categorical') interpretation of these requirements which on analysis, it may be argued, reflect (deeper) concerns about origination. It suffices, in any case, that concerns about origination constitute a standard incompatibilist perspective on the free will issue. For the purpose of concise presentation, therefore, I will not elaborate on these complexities.

11. P. F. Strawson, "Freedom and resentment," reprinted in *Free Will*, ed. Gary Watson, 59–80. Strawson's paper is also reprinted in *Perspectives on Moral Responsibility*, ed. Fischer and Ravizza, see also the editors' introduction for a helpful discussion of various responses and criticisms of Strawson (4–25).

12. I develop this line of criticism of Strawson in "Strawson's way of naturalizing responsibility," *Ethics* 102 (1992): 287–302 (see esp. 296–97, 300–301). See also Watson's related discussion of Strawson's difficulties in accounting for 'exempting conditions,' "Responsibility and the limits of evil," esp. 125–26.

13. Dennett's *Elbow Room* is an important contribution to this aspect of contemporary compatibilist thinking. Other influential accounts of this kind include Harry

Frankfurt, "Freedom of the will and the concept of a person," and Gary Watson, "Free agency," both reprinted in *Free Agency*, ed. Gary Watson. Closely related to the second strand of naturalized responsibility is the issue of 'reflexivity' and 'reason-responsiveness.' Dennett, among others, devotes considerable attention to this matter. See esp. *Elbow Room*, chap.2.

14. There is considerable variation in the specific ways that these two strands of naturalized responsibility are developed and articulated. Compare, for example, the Humean way of developing and blending these themes as presented in Paul Russell, *Freedom and Moral Sentiment: Hume's Way of Naturalizing Responsibility* (New York: Oxford University Press, 1995), with the essentially Kantian account presented in R. Jay Wallace, *Responsibility and the Moral Sentiments* (Cambridge, MA.: Harvard University Press, 1994). It is also important to note that not all contemporary compatibilists accept both of the two strands described above (see, e.g., note 8 above on Dennett).

15. Some incompatibilists may argue that their pessimism about the fatalistic implications of determinism are not entirely based on worries about responsibility, although this is their primary concern. Insofar as incompatibilists have fatalistic concerns independent of the issue of responsibility they share common cause with compatibilist-fatalists—as I will explain.

16. This terminology is a prominent feature of Strawson's discussion in "Freedom and resentment," where it is used to describe the positions of the major parties in the free will dispute: incompatibilists being 'pessimists,' compatibilists being 'optimists."

17. In *Elbow Room*, Dennett interprets his own defense of compatibilism as a vindication of 'optimism' over 'pessimism' (*Elbow Room*, 18–19, 169). His discussion makes clear that from an orthodox-compatibilist perspective incompatibilist claims are not innocuous as they generate negative emotions such as 'fear,' 'anxiety,' 'dread,' and so on. Dennett's general conclusion is that all such incompatibilist 'pessimism' can be effectively discredited and shown to be motivated by various kinds of (philosophical) confusion and/or illusion. This includes, notably, pessimism about fate.

18. Spinoza, *Ethics* (Indianapolis: Hackett, 1992), 102 (Part 3, preface); translation by Samuel Shirley.

19. The metaphor of being 'governed by nature' may be taken to suggest that Nature (somehow) 'controls' us for its own ends and purposes. This would involve confusion and should be avoided. For this reason it is important to distinguish worries about origination-fatalism from worries about supernatural-fate. In the case of supernatural-fate it is argued, not only that the ultimate source of character and conduct does not lie with the agent (and thus has an external source) but, moreover, the external source is some supernatural agent or cosmic being who 'manipulates' or 'directs' our (human) lives according to some (alien) design or plan. Worries about loss of 'sovereignty,' however, need not presuppose any such 'bogeyman' to be at work. In general, there is no reason to suppose that a mistake of this kind is required to motivate pessimistic concerns about origination-fatalism. (One of the unsatisfactory aspects of Dennett's efforts to defuse worries about fatalism is that he tends to assimilate worries about origination with worries about supernatural-fate: see *Elbow Room*, 7–17, and chap.3.)

20. The expression is Dennett's (*Elbow Room*, chap.4, esp. 100) and it is indicative of the extent of his 'optimism' on such matters. See also the papers by Frankfurt and Watson cited in note 13 above.

21. Dennett notes himself (*Elbow Room*, 85, 156) that "a completely self-made self, one hundred per cent responsible for its own character, [is] an impossibility." The question arises, however, what percentage is required for a 'self' to be 'self-made'—will any percentage do? It should also be noted that Dennett does not claim that we avoid worries about fatalism to the extent that we are 'self-made-selves.' On the contrary, since he accepts the (classical) refutation argument, and its narrow conception of fate as contributory-fate, all that is required to avoid worries about 'fate,' he claims, is for deliberation and action to be causally effective.

22. There are variations on this general problem in compatibilist literature. Wallace, for example, suggests that "powers of reflective self-control" constitute the relevant moral capacities required for responsible agency. (See the discussion concerning moral capacities above.) These powers, he says, involve the possession of the ability to grasp and apply moral reasons, and to regulate behavior on this basis. (*Responsibility and the Moral Sentiments*, 157) However, as Wallace concedes, agents may possess these powers and yet have no ability to determine the way that they are exercised in particular circumstances (180–94, 201–14). This is, however, precisely what is required for 'sovereignty.' Hence, even if Wallace's defense of responsibility-compatibilism is accepted, the concerns about origination-fatalism remain unanswered.

23. For a brief account of this matter see Russell, *Freedom & Moral Sentiment*, 128–30.

24. In respect of this, consider Watson's illuminating and suggestive reflections on the significance of the case of Robert Harris. ["Responsibility and the limits of evil," 137–46]. Harris was a notably brutal Californian killer (i.e., when viewed as a 'victimizer') and also the product of an exceptionally brutal childhood (i.e., when viewed as a 'victim'). Watson interprets the significance of the 'historical' considerations relating to Harris's childhood and moral development in terms of their tendency to influence our reactive attitudes (i.e., to produce 'ambivalence': 137–38). There is, however, another way of looking at this case, more in keeping with compatibilist-fatalism. Reflection on such circumstances press the thought upon us that who we are, and what we are responsible for to other human beings, depends ultimately on factors that we have no control over. These reflections are even more troubling when, as Watson puts it, we "turn our gaze inward" and recognize "that one's moral self is such a fragile thing" (139). In contrast with this view, orthodox-compatibilism suggests that historical considerations of this kind are untroubling so long as they do not discredit or dislodge our (natural) commitment to reactive attitudes.

25. It is, in particular, a notorious stumbling block of libertarian metaphysics that it is unable to make clear what is required for 'genuine agency' beyond simple indeterminism. The difficulties facing the libertarian are well described in the closing passages of Nagel's "Moral luck"; Nagel's *The View from Nowhere* (New York: Oxford University Press, 1986), chap.7; and also Galen Strawson, *Freedom and Belief* (Oxford: Clarendon Press, 1986), chap.2.

26. The many difficulties associated with making sense of the thesis of immortality are well known. An interesting discussion of the desirability of immortality is presented in Bernard Williams, "The Makropulos case," in *Problems of the Self* (Cambridge: Cambridge University Press, 1973).

27. "We cannot look squarely at either death or the sun." LaRochfoucauld, *Maxims*, No.26.

28. The only way to evade these pessimistic reflections about origination-fatalism is to provide some (coherent) account of 'genuine agency' that is premised on indeterministic metaphysics. For recent libertarian efforts along these lines see the various papers in *Agents, Causes & Events: Essays on Indeterminism and Free Will*, ed. Timothy O'Connor (Oxford: Oxford University Press, 1995).

29. Consider, for example, Watson's discussion of Robert Harris, as cited in note 24 above.

30. The compatibilist-fatalist, as explained, interprets the specific way that responsibility and fate "come fused together in human life" in terms of (rejecting) the exclusion thesis and distinguishing between origination and contributory fatalism.

31. Dennett associates the pessimism generated by the 'bugbear' of fatalism with the condition of 'puppets' or 'dolls'—something that really is a "terrible condition" (*Elbow Room*, chap.1).

32. John Macquarrie, *Existentialism* (Harmondsworth, UK: Penguin, 1973), 191.

33. This sense of the contingency of human existence, and its relevance to our view of ourselves as (responsible) agents who are nevertheless 'thrown' into our own particular circumstances, is something that many moral theories (most notably Kantianism) strongly resist. On this see Bernard Williams, "Moral luck: a postscript," reprinted in *Making Sense of Humanity* (Cambridge, UK: Cambridge University Press, 1995), 246.

34. My comments here draw on Thomas Nagel's influential discussion of our sense of the absurd as it relates to human life: "The absurd," reprinted in *Mortal Questions* (Cambridge: Cambridge University Press, 1979).

35. Despite this, some may be tempted to question the freshness of compatibilist-fatalism on the ground that each of its two component claims are (very) familiar. It should be clear, however, that the particular interest of this position does not rest with its two component claims considered in isolation from each other but rather with the effort to combine two claims that have traditionally been treated by both the major parties in the free will dispute as incompatible—a thesis which compatibilist-fatalism rejects. I am unaware of any compatibilist thinker who has defended the 'mixed' optimist/pessimist position of compatibilist-fatalism as described. See, however, Saul Smilansky, "Does the free will problem rest on a mistake," *Philosophical Papers* 22 (1993): 173–88. Smilansky pursues themes that are very relevant to the position taken in this paper.

36. The qualifying clause in this sentence (i.e., 'or accept the legitimacy of') provides scope for the weaker position that allows that some compatibilists, after due reflection, may remain untroubled by any considerations regarding origination. (See section V above.) On the assumption that there is no confusion about the source and quality of the pessimism at issue nor any failure of due reflection in such cases, but only a divergence of sensibility, then orthodox-compatibilism may be judged no less—and no more—legitimate than compatibilist-fatalism. As I have indicated, however, it may be argued that a failure to be troubled by considerations regarding origination is best explained in terms of a lack of appropriate reflection, and that a suitable sensibility can be cultivated on the basis of such reflection.

37. Incompatibilists, of course, remain committed to the exclusion thesis insofar as it is essential to their defense of the responsibility-incompatibilist claim.

PART 10

Suggested Further Readings

X. Optimism, Pessimism, and their Modes

For a classic statement of (behaviouristic) optimism associated with "hard determinism" see:

Skinner, B.F. 1977. *Walden 2*. Upper Saddle River, NJ: Pearson. (Selections reprinted in R. Kane, ed., *Free Will*. Oxford: Blackwell, 2002.)

See also:

Cuypers, Stefaan. Forthcoming (online November 2011). "Moral shallowness, metaphysical megalomania and compatibilist-fatalism," *Ethical Theory and Moral Practice*.

Pereboom, Derk. 2001. *Living Without Free Will*. Cambridge: Cambridge University Press.

Sommers, Tamler. 2007. "The objective attitude," *Philosophical Quarterly* 57: 321–41.

Waller, Bruce. 2011. *Against Moral Responsibility*. Cambridge, MA: MIT Press.

PART ELEVEN

The Phenomenology of Agency
and Experimental Philosophy

24

Do We Have Free Will?

Benjamin Libet

I have taken an experimental approach to this question. Freely voluntary acts are preceded by a specific electrical change in the brain (the 'readiness potential,' RP) that begins 550 ms. before the act. Human subjects became aware of intention to act 350–400 ms *after* RP starts, but 200 ms. before the motor act. The volitional process is therefore *initiated* unconsciously. But the conscious function could still control the outcome; it can veto the act. Free will is therefore not excluded. These findings put constraints on views of how free will may operate; it would not initiate a voluntary act but it could *control* performance of the act. The findings also affect views of guilt and responsibility.

But the deeper question still remains: Are freely voluntary acts subject to macro-deterministic laws or can they appear without such constraints, non-determined by natural laws and 'truly free'? I shall present an experimentalist view about these fundamental philosophical opposites.

The question of free will goes to the root of our views about human nature and how we relate to the universe and to natural laws. Are we completely defined by the deterministic nature of physical laws? Theologically imposed fateful destiny ironically produces a similar end-effect. In either case, we would be essentially sophisticated automatons, with our conscious feelings and intentions tacked on as epiphenomena with no causal power. Or, do we have some independence in making choices and actions, not completely determined by the known physical laws?

I have taken an experimental approach to at least some aspects of the question. The operational definition of free will in these experiments was in accord with common views. First, there should be no external control or cues to affect the occurrence or emergence of the voluntary act under study; i.e., it should be endogenous. Secondly, the subject should feel that he/she wanted to do it, on her/his own initiative, and feel he could control what is being done, when to do it or not to do it. Many actions lack this second attribute. For example, when the primary motor area of the cerebral cortex is stimulated, muscle contractions can be produced in certain sites in the body. However, the subject (a neurosurgical patient) reports that these actions were imposed by the stimulator, i.e., that he did not will these acts. And there are numerous clinical disorders in which a similar discrepancy between actions and will occurs. These include the involuntary actions in cerebral palsy, Parkinsonism, Huntington's chorea, Tourette's syndrome and even obsessive compulsions to act. A striking example is the 'alien hand syndrome.' Patients with a lesion in a fronto-medial portion of premotor area may find that the hand and arm on the affected side performs curious purposeful actions, such as undoing a buttoned shirt when the subject is trying to button it up; all this occurs without or even against the subject's intention and will. (Cf. Spence and Frith 1999, 23.)

Timing of brain processes and conscious will

Performance of 'self-paced' voluntary acts had, surprisingly, been found to be preceded by a slow electrical change recordable on the scalp at the vertex (Kornhuber & Deecke, 1965). The onset of this electrical indication of certain brain activities preceded the actual movement by up to 1 sec or more. It was termed the 'Bereitschaft-potential' or 'readiness potential' (RP). To obtain the RP required averaging the recordings in many self-paced acts. Subjects were therefore asked to perform their acts within time intervals of 30 sec. to make the total study manageable. In our experiments, however, we removed this constraint on freedom of action; subjects performed a simple flick or flexion of the wrist at any time they felt the urge or wish to do so. These voluntary acts were to be performed capriciously, free of any external limitations or restrictions (Libet *et al*. 1982). RPs in these acts began with onsets averaging 550 msec. before activation of the involved muscle (fig. 1).

The brain was evidently beginning the volitional process in this voluntary act well before the activation of the muscle that produced the movement. My question then became: *when* does the *conscious* wish or intention (to perform the act) appear? In the traditional view of conscious will and free will, one would expect conscious will to appear before, or at the onset, of the RP, and thus command the brain to perform the intended act. But an appearance of conscious will 550 msec. or more before the act seemed intuitively unlikely. It was clearly important to establish the time of the conscious will relative to the onset of the brain process (RP); if conscious will were to *follow* the onset of RP, that would have a fundamental impact on how we could view free will.

To establish this temporal relation required a method for measuring the time of appearance of the conscious will in each such act. Initially, that seemed to me an impossible goal. But after some time it occurred to me to try having the subject report a 'clock-time' at which he/she was *first aware* of the

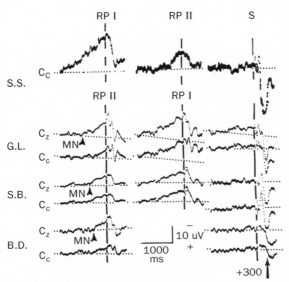

FIGURE 1 Readiness potentials (RP) preceding self-initiated voluntary acts. Each horizontal row is the computer-averaged potential for 40 trials, recorded by a DC system with an active electrode on the scalp, either at the midline-vertex (C_z) or on the left side (contralateral to the performing right hand) approximately over the motor/premotor cortical area that controls the hand (C_c).

When every self-initiated quick flexion of the right hand (fingers or wrist) in the series of 40 trials was (reported as having been) subjectively experienced to originate spontaneously and with no pre-planning by the subject, RPs labelled type II were found in association. (Arrowheads labelled MN indicate onset of the 'main negative' phase of the vertex recorded type II RPs in this figure; see Libet et al. 1982. Onsets were also measured for 90% of the total area of RP). When an awareness of a general intention or preplanning to act some time within the next second or so was reported to have occurred before some of the 40 acts in the series, type I RPs were recorded (Libet et al., 1982). In the last column, labelled S, a near-threshold skin stimulus was applied in each of the 40 trials at a randomized time unknown to the subject, with no motor act performed; the subject was asked to recall and report the time when he became aware of each stimulus in the same way he reported the time of awareness of wanting to move in the case of self-initiated motor acts.

The solid vertical line through each column represents 0 time, at which the electromyogram (EMG) of the activated muscle begins in the case of RP series, or at which the stimulus was actually delivered in the case of S series. The dashed horizontal line represents the DC baseline drift.

For subject S.S., the first RP (type I) was recorded before the instruction 'to let the urge come on its own, spontaneously' was introduced; the second RP (type II) was obtained after giving this instruction in the same session as the first. For subjects G.L., S.B. and B.D., this instruction was given at the start of all sessions. Nevertheless, each of these subjects reported some experiences of loose preplanning in some of the 40-trial series; those series exhibited type I RPs rather than type II. Note that the slow negative shift in scalp potential that precedes EMGs of self-initiated acts (RP) does not precede the skin stimulus in S series. However, evoked potentials following the stimulus are seen regularly to exhibit a large positive component with a peak close to +300 ms. (arrow indicates this time); this P300 event-related potential had been shown by others to be associated with decisions about uncertain events (in this case, the time of the randomly delivered stimulus), and it also indicates that the subject is attending well to the experimental conditions.

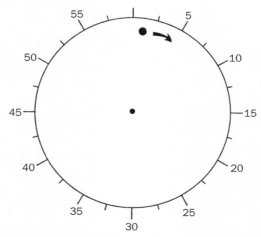

FIGURE 2 Oscilloscope 'clock.' Spot of light revolves around periphery of screen, once in 2.56 sec. (instead of 60 sec. for a sweep-second hand of a regular clock). Each marked off 'second' (in the total of 60 markings) represents 43 msec. of actual time here. The subject holds his gaze to the centre of the screen. For each performed quick flexion of the wrist, at any freely chosen time, the subject was asked to note the position of the clock spot when he/she first became aware of the wish or intention to act. This associated clock time is reported by the subject later, after the trial is completed.

wish or urge to act (fig. 2) (Libet *et al.* 1983a). The clock had to be much faster than the usual clock, in order to accommodate time differences in the hundreds of msec. For our clock, the spot of light of a cathode ray oscilloscope was made to revolve around the face of the scope like the sweep-second hand of an ordinary clock, but at a speed approximately 25 times as fast. Each of the marked off 'seconds' around the periphery was thus equivalent to about 40 msec. When we tried out this method we were actually surprised to find that each subject reported times for *first awareness of wish to act* (W) with a reliability of 20 msec., for each group of 40 such trials. A test for the accuracy of such reports was also encouraging. In this, the subject remained relaxed and did *not* perform any voluntary act. Instead, a weak electrical stimulus was delivered to the skin of the same hand. The stimulus was applied at random times in the different trials. The experimental observers knew the actual time for each stimulus. The subject did not know this actual time but was asked to report the clock-time at which he felt each such stimulus. Subjects accomplished this with an error of only −50 msec.

THE EXPERIMENT

In the actual experiment, then, each RP was obtained from an averaged electrical recording in 40 trials. In each of these trials the subject performed the sudden flick of the wrist whenever he/she freely wanted to do so. After each of these trials, the subject reported W, the clock-time associated with the first awareness of the wish to move (Libet *et al.* 1983a).

BRAIN INITIATES VOLUNTARY ACT UNCONSCIOUSLY

The results of many such groups of trials are diagrammed in fig. 3. For groups in which all the voluntary acts were freely spontaneous, with no reports of rough pre-planning of when to act, the onset of RP averaged –550 msec. (before the muscle was activated). The W times for first awareness of wish to act averaged about –200 msec., for all groups. This value was the same even when subjects reported having pre-planned roughly when to act! If we correct W for the –50 msec. error in the subjects' reports of timings of the skin stimuli, we have an average corrected W of about –150 msec. Clearly, the brain process (RP) to prepare for this voluntary act began about 400 msec. before the appearance of the conscious will to act (W). This relationship was true for every group of 40 trials and in every one of the nine subjects studied. It should also be noted that the actual difference in times is probably greater than the 400 msec; the actual initiating process in the brain probably starts before our recorded RP, in an unknown area that then activates the supplementary motor area in the cerebral cortex. The supplementary motor area is located in the midline near the vertex and is thought to be the source of our recorded RP.

Self-initiated act: sequence

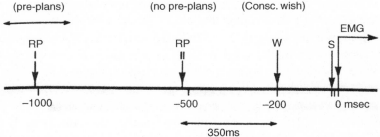

FIGURE 3 Diagram of sequence of events, cerebral and subjective, that precede a fully self-initiated voluntary act. Relative to 0 time, detected in the electromyogram (EMG) of the suddenly activated muscle, the readiness potential (RP)(an indicator of related cerebral neuronal activities) begins first, at about –1050 ms. when some pre-planning is reported (RP I) or about –550 ms. with spontaneous acts lacking immediate pre planning (RP II). Subjective awareness of the wish to move (W) appears at about –200 ms., some 350 ms. after onset even of RP II; however, W does appear well before the act (EMG). Subjective timings reported for awareness of the randomly delivered S (skin) stimulus average about –50 ms. relative to actual delivery time. (From Libet 1989.)

Any role for conscious will?

The initiation of the freely voluntary act appears to begin in the brain unconsciously, well before the person consciously knows he wants to act! Is there, then, any role for conscious will in the performance of a voluntary act? (see Libet 1985). To answer this it must be recognized that conscious will (W) does appear about 150 msec. before the muscle is activated, even though it follows onset of the RP. An interval of 150 msec. would allow enough time in which the conscious function might affect the final outcome of the volitional process. (Actually, only 100 msec. is available for any such effect. The final 50 msec. before the muscle is activated is the time for the primary motor cortex to activate the spinal motor nerve cells. During this time the act goes to completion with no possibility of stopping it by the rest of the cerebral cortex.)

Potentially available to the conscious function is the possibility of stopping or vetoing the final progress of the volitional process, so that no actual muscle action ensues. *Conscious-will could thus affect the outcome* of the volitional process even though the latter was initiated by unconscious cerebral processes. Conscious-will might block or veto the process, so that no act occurs.

The existence of a veto possibility is not in doubt. The subjects in our experiments at times reported that a conscious wish or urge to act appeared but that they suppressed or vetoed that. In the absence of the muscle's electrical signal when being activated, there was no trigger to initiate the computer's recording of any RP that may have preceded the veto; thus, there were no *recorded* RPs with a vetoed intention to act. We were, however, able to show that subjects could veto an act planned for performance at a pre-arranged time. They were able to exert the veto within the interval of 100 to 200 msec. before the pre-set time to act (Libet *et al.*, 1983b). A large RP preceded the veto, signifying that the subject was indeed *preparing* to act, even though the action was aborted by the subject. All of us, not just experimental subjects, have experienced our vetoing a spontaneous urge to perform some act. This often occurs when the urge to act involves some socially unacceptable consequence, like an urge to shout some obscenity at the professor. (Incidentally, in the disorder called Tourette's syndrome, subjects do spontaneously shout obscenities. These acts should not be regarded as freely voluntary. No RP appears before such an act. A quick reaction to an unwarned stimulus also lacks a preceding RP, and it is not a freely voluntary act.)

Another hypothetical function for conscious will could be to serve as a 'trigger' that is required to enable the volitional process to proceed to final action. However, there is no evidence for this, such as there is for a veto function, and the 'trigger' possibility also seems unlikely on other grounds. For example, voluntary acts that become somewhat 'automatic' can be performed with no reportable conscious wish to do so; the RP is rather minimal in amplitude and duration before such automatic acts. Automatic acts clearly go to completion without any conscious trigger available.

DOES THE CONSCIOUS VETO HAVE A PRECEDING UNCONSCIOUS ORIGIN?

One should, at this point, consider the possibility that the conscious veto itself may have its origin in preceding unconscious processes, just as is the case for the development and appearance of the conscious will. If the veto itself were to be initiated and developed unconsciously, the choice to veto would then become an unconscious choice of which we *become* conscious, rather than a consciously causal event. Our own previous evidence had shown that the brain 'produces' an awareness of something only after about a 0.5 sec. period of appropriate neuronal activations (see reviews by Libet 1993; 1996).

Some have proposed that even an unconscious initiation of a veto choice would nevertheless be a genuine choice made by the individual and could still be viewed as a free will process (e.g., Velmans 1991). I find such a proposed view of free will to be unacceptable. In such a view, the individual would not consciously control his actions; he would only become aware of an unconsciously initiated choice. He would have no direct conscious control over the nature of any preceding unconscious processes. But, a free will process implies one could be held consciously responsible for one's choice to act or not to act. We do not hold people responsible for actions performed unconsciously, without the possibility of conscious control. For example, actions by a person during a psychomotor epileptic seizure, or by one with Tourette's syndrome, etc., are not regarded as actions of free will. Why then should an act unconsciously developed by a normal individual, a process over which he also has no conscious control, be regarded as an act of free will?

I propose, instead, that the conscious veto may *not* require or be the direct result of preceding unconscious processes. The conscious veto is a *control* function, different from simply becoming aware of the wish to act. There is no logical imperative in any mind–brain theory, even identity theory, that requires specific neural activity to precede and determine the nature of a conscious control function. And, there is no experimental evidence against the possibility that the control process may appear without development by prior unconscious processes.

Admittedly, to be conscious of the decision to veto does mean one is aware of the event. How may one reconcile this with my proposal? Perhaps we should re-visit the concept of awareness, its relation to the content of awareness, and the cerebral processes that develop both awareness and its contents. Our own previous studies have indicated that *awareness* is a unique phenomenon in itself, distinguished from the contents of which one may become aware. For example, awareness of a sensory stimulus can require similar durations of stimulus trains for somatosensory cortex and for medial lemniscus. But the *content* of those awarenesses in these two cases is different, in the subjective timings of sensations (Libet *et al.*, 1979). The content of an unconscious mental process (e.g. correct detection of a signal in the brain *without any awareness* of the signal) may be the same as the content *with awareness* of the signal. But to become aware of that same content required that stimulus duration be increased by about 400 msec. (see Libet *et al.*, 1991).

In an endogenous, freely voluntary act, awareness of the intention to act is delayed for about 400 msec. after brain processes initiate the process unconsciously (Libet *et al.*, 1983a; Libet, 1985). Awareness developed here may be thought of as applying to the whole volitional process; that would include the content of the conscious urge to act and the content of factors that may affect a conscious veto. One need not think of awareness of an event as restricted to one detailed item of content in the whole event.

The possibility is not excluded that factors, on which the decision to veto (control) is *based*, do develop by unconscious processes that precede the veto. However, the *conscious decision to veto* could still be made without direct specification for that decision by the preceding unconscious processes. That is, one could consciously accept or reject the programme offered up by the whole array of preceding brain processes. The *awareness* of the decision to veto could be thought to require preceding unconscious processes, but the *content* of that awareness (the actual decision to veto) is a separate feature that need not have the same requirement.

What significance do our findings have for voluntary acts in general?

Can we assume that voluntary acts other than the simple one studied by us also have the same temporal relations between unconscious brain processes and the appearance of the conscious wish/will to act? It is common in scientific researches to be limited technically to studying a process in a simple system; and then to find that the fundamental behaviour discovered with the simple system does indeed represent a phenomenon that appears or governs in other related and more complicated systems. For example, the charge on a single electron was measured by Milliken in one isolated system, but it is valid for electrons in all systems. It should also be noted that RPs have been found by other investigators to precede other more complex volitional acts, such as beginning to speak or to write; they did not, however, study the time of appearance of the conscious wish to begin such acts. We may, therefore, allow ourselves to consider what general implications may follow from our experimental findings, while recognizing that an extrapolation to encompass voluntary acts in general has been adopted.

We should also distinguish between *deliberations* about what choice of action to adopt (including pre-planning of when to act on such a choice) and the final intention actually 'to act now.' One may, after all, deliberate all day about a choice but never act; there is *no voluntary act* in that case. In our experimental studies we found that in some trials subjects engaged in some conscious pre-planning of roughly when to act (in the next second or so). But even in those cases, the subjects reported times of the conscious wish to actually act to be about −200 msec.; this value was very close to the values reported for fully spontaneous voluntary acts with no pre-planning. The onset of the unconscious brain process (RP) for preparing to act was well before the final conscious intention 'to act now' in all cases. These findings indicated that the sequence of the volitional processes 'to act now' may apply to all volitional acts, regardless of their spontaneity or prior history of conscious deliberations.

Ethical implications of how free will operates

The role of conscious free will would be, then, not to initiate a voluntary act, but rather to *control* whether the act takes place. We may view the unconscious initiatives for voluntary actions as 'bubbling up' in the brain. The conscious-will then selects which of these initiatives may go forward to an action or which ones to veto and abort, with no act appearing.

This kind of role for free will is actually in accord with religious and ethical strictures. These commonly advocate that you 'control yourself.' Most of the Ten Commandments are 'do not' orders.

How do our findings relate to the questions of when one may be regarded as guilty or sinful, in various religious and philosophical systems. If one experiences a conscious wish or urge to perform a socially unacceptable act, should that be regarded as a sinful event even if the urge has been vetoed and no act has occurred? Some religious systems answer 'yes.' President Jimmy Carter admitted to having had urges to perform a lustful act. Although he did not act, he apparently still felt sinful for having experienced a lustful urge.[1] But any such urges would be initiated and developed in the brain unconsciously, according to our findings. The mere appearance of an intention to act could not be controlled consciously; only its final consummation in a motor act could be consciously controlled. Therefore, a religious system that castigates an individual for simply having a mental intention or impulse to do something unacceptable, even when this is not acted out, would create a physiologically insurmountable moral and psychological difficulty.

Indeed, insistence on regarding an unacceptable urge to act as sinful, even when no act ensues, would make virtually all individuals sinners. In that sense such a view could provide a physiological basis for 'original sin'! Of course, the concept of 'original sin' can be based on other views of what is regarded as sinful.

Ethical systems deal with moral codes or conventions that govern how one behaves toward or interacts with other individuals; they are presumably dealing with actions, not simply with urges or intentions. Only a motor act by one person can directly impinge on the welfare of another. Since it is the performance of an act that can be consciously controlled, it should be legitimate to hold individuals guilty of and responsible for their acts.

Determinism and free will

There remains a deeper question about free will that the foregoing considerations have not addressed. What we have achieved experimentally is some knowledge of how free will may operate. But we have not answered the question of whether our consciously willed acts are fully determined by natural laws that govern the activities of nerve cells in the brain, or whether acts and the conscious decisions to perform them can proceed to some degree independently of natural determinism. The first of these options would make free will illusory. The conscious feeling of exerting one's will would then be regarded as an epiphenomenon, simply a by-product of the brain's activities but with no causal powers of its own.

First, it may be pointed out that free choices or acts are *not predictable*, even if they should be completely determined. The 'uncertainty principle' of Heisenberg precludes our having a complete knowledge of the underlying molecular activities. Quantum mechanics forces us to deal with probabilities rather than with certainties of events. And, in chaos theory, a random event may shift the behaviour of a whole system, in a way that was not predictable. However, even if events are not predictable in practice, they might nevertheless be in accord with natural laws and therefore determined.

Let us re-phrase our basic question as follows: *Must* we accept determinism? Is non-determinism a viable option? We should recognize that both of these alternative views (natural law determinism vs. non-determinism) are unproven theories, i.e., unproven in relation to the existence of free will. Determinism has, on the whole, worked well for the physical observable world. That has led many scientists and philosophers to regard any deviation from determinism as absurd and witless, and unworthy of consideration. But there has been no evidence, or even a proposed experimental test design, that definitively or convincingly demonstrates the validity of natural law determinism as the mediator or instrument of free will.

There is an unexplained gap between the category of physical phenomena and the category of subjective phenomena. As far back as Leibniz it was pointed out that if one looked into the brain with a full knowledge of its physical makeup and nerve cell activities, one would see nothing that describes subjective experience. The whole foundation of our own experimental studies of the physiology of conscious experience (beginning in the late 1950s) was that externally observable and manipulable brain processes and the related reportable subjective introspective experiences must be studied simultaneously, as independent categories, to understand their relationship. The assumption that a deterministic nature of the physically observable world (to the extent that may be true) can account for subjective conscious functions and events is a speculative *belief,* not a scientifically proven proposition.

Non-determinism, the view that conscious-will may, at times, exert effects not in accord with known physical laws, is of course also a non-proven speculative belief. The view that conscious will can affect brain function in violation of known physical laws, takes two forms. In one it is held that the violations are not detectable, because the actions of the mind may be at a level below that of the uncertainty allowed by quantum mechanics. (Whether this last proviso can in fact be tenable is a matter yet to be resolved). This view would thus allow for a non-deterministic free will without a perceptible violation of physical laws. In a second view it may be held that violations of known physical laws are large enough to be detectable, at least in principle. But, it can be argued, detectability in actual practice may be impossible. That difficulty for detection would be especially true if the conscious will is able to exert its influence by minimal actions at relatively few nerve elements; these actions could serve as triggers for amplified nerve cell patterns of activity in the brain. In any case, we do not have a scientific answer to the question of which theory (determinism or non-determinism) may describe the nature of free will.

However, we must recognize that the almost universal experience that we can act with a free, independent choice provides a kind of *prima facie* evidence that conscious mental processes can causatively control some brain processes (Libet 1994). As an experimental scientist, this creates more difficulty for a determinist than for a non-determinist option. The phenomenal fact is that most of us feel that we do have free will, at least for some of our actions and within certain limits that may be imposed by our brain's status and by our environment. The intuitive feelings about the phenomenon of free will form a fundamental basis for views of our human nature, and great care should be taken not to believe allegedly scientific conclusions about them which actually depend upon hidden *ad hoc* assumptions. A theory that simply interprets the phenomenon of free will as illusory and denies the validity of this phenomenal fact is less attractive than a theory that accepts or accommodates the phenomenal fact.

In an issue so fundamentally important to our view of who we are, a claim for illusory nature should be based on fairly direct evidence. Such evidence is not available; nor do determinists propose even a potential experimental design to test the theory. Actually, I myself proposed an experimental design that could test whether conscious will could influence nerve cell activities in the brain, doing so via a putative 'conscious mental field' that could act without any neuronal connections as the mediators (Libet 1994). This difficult though feasible experiment has, unfortunately, still to be carried out. If it should turn out to confirm the prediction of that field theory, there would be a radical transformation in our views of mind–brain interaction.

My conclusion about free will, one genuinely free in the non-determined sense, is then that its existence is at least as good, if not a better, scientific option than is its denial by determinist theory. Given the speculative nature of both determinist and non-determinist theories, why not adopt the view that we do have free will (until some real contradictory evidence may appear, if it ever does). Such a view would at least allow us to proceed in a way that accepts and accommodates our own deep feeling that we do have free will. We would not need to view ourselves as machines that act in a manner completely controlled by the known physical laws. Such a permissive option has also been advocated by the neurobiologist Roger Sperry (see Doty 1998).[2]

I close, then, with a quotation from the great novelist Isaac Bashevis Singer that relates to the foregoing views. Singer stated his strong belief in our having free will. In an interview (Singer 1968), he volunteered that 'The greatest gift which humanity has received is free choice. It is true that we are limited in our use of free choice. But the little free choice we have is such a great gift and is potentially worth so much that for this itself life is worthwhile living.'

Notes

1. President Carter was drawing on a Christian tradition deriving from the following two verses in the 'Sermon on the Mount': "[Jesus said], 'Ye have heard that it was said by them of old time, Thou shalt not commit adultery: But I say unto you, That whosoever looketh on a woman to lust after her hath committed adultery with her already in his heart'" (*Matthew*, 5.27–28).

2. The belief by many people that one's fate is determined by some mystical reality or by divine intervention produces a difficult paradox for those who also believe we have free will and are to be held responsible for our actions. Such a paradox can arise in the Judeo-Christian view that (a) God is omnipotent, knows in advance what you are going to do and controls your fate, while (b) also strongly advocating that we can freely determine our actions and are accountable and responsible for our behaviour. This difficulty has led to some theological attempts to resolve the paradox. For example, the Kabbalists proposed that God voluntarily gave up his power to know what man was going to do, in order to allow man to choose freely and responsibly, and to possess free will.

References

Doty, R.W. 1998. "Five mysteries of the mind, and their consequences," in *Views of the Brain: A Tribute to Roger W. Sperry,* ed. A. Puente. Washington, DC: American Psych. Association.

Kornhuber, H., and L. Deecke. 1965. "Hirnpotentialanderungen bei willkurbewegun-gen und passive bewegungen des menschen: bereitschaftspotential und reafferente potentiale," *Pfluegers Arch Gesamte Physiol Menschen Tiere* **284**: 1–17.

Libet, B. 1985. "Unconscious cerebral initiative and the role of conscious will in voluntary action," *Behavioral and Brain Sciences* **8**: 529–66.

Libet, B. 1989. "Conscious subjective experience vs. unconscious mental functions: a theory of the cerebral processes involved," in *Models of Brain Function*, ed. R.M.J. Cotterill. New York: Cambridge University Press, 68–79.

Libet, B. 1993. "The neural time factor in conscious and unconscious mental events," in Ciba Foundation Symposium, no.174, *Experimental and Theoretical Studies of Consciousness*. Chichester, UK: Wiley.

Libet, B. 1994. "A testable field theory of mind-brain interaction," *JCS* **1.1**: 119–26.

Libet, B. 1996. "Neural time factors in conscious and unconscious mental function," in *Toward a Science of Consciousness*, eds. S.R. Hameroff, A. Kaszniak, and A. Scott, Cambridge, MA: MIT Press, 156–171.

Libet, B., C.A. Gleason, E.W. Wright, and D.K. Pearl. 1983a. "Time of conscious intention to act in relation to onset of cerebral activity (readiness potential): the unconscious initiation of a freely voluntary act," *Brain* **106**: 623–642.

Libet, B., E.W. Wright, and C.A. Gleason. 1983b. "Preparation or intention-to-act, in relation to pre-event potentials recorded at the vertex," *Electroenceph. & Clin. Neurophysiology* **56**: 367–372.

Libet, B., D.K. Pearl, D.E. Morledge, C.A. Gleason, Y. Hosobuchi, and N.M. Barbaro. 1991. "Control of the transition from sensory detection to sensory awareness in man by the duration of a thalamic stimulus: the cerebral time-on factor," *Brain* **114**: 1731–1757.

Libet, B., E.W. Wright, Jr., B. Feinstein, and D.K. Pearl. 1979. "Subjective referral of the timing for a conscious sensory experience: a functional role for the somatosensory specific projection system in man," *Brain* **102**: 191–222.

Libet, B., E.W. Wright, and C.A. Gleason. 1982. "Readiness potentials preceding unrestricted spontaneous pre-planned voluntary acts," *Electroenceph. & Clin. Neurophysiology* **54**: 322–325.

Singer, I.B. 1968. Interview by H. Flender, in *Writers at Work* (1981), ed. G. Plimpton. New York: Penguin.

Spence, S.A. and C.D., Frith. 1999. "Towards a functional anatomy of volition," *Journal of Consciousness Studies* **6** (8–9): 11–29.

Velmans, M. 1991. "Is human information processing conscious?" *Behavioral and Brain Sciences* **3**: 651–669.

25

The Phenomenology of Free Will

Eddy Nahmias, Stephen Morris, Thomas Nadelhoffer
and Jason Turner

Introduction

Theories of free will are more plausible when they capture our intuitions and
experiences than when they explain them away. Thus, philosophers generally
want their theories of free will to aptly describe the experiences we have when
we make choices and feel free and responsible for our actions. If a theory
misdescribes our experiences, it may be explaining the wrong phenomenon,
and if it suggests that our experiences are illusory, it takes on the burden of
explaining this illusion with an error theory.

Compatibilists conceive of free will in a way that is compatible with causal
determinism; libertarians have a more robust conception of free will that
requires, at a minimum, indeterminism. While the two camps agree that we
have free will, their differing conceptions of it are often manifested in disagreements about the phenomenology of free will. In practice, however, they tend
to agree that this phenomenology can be discovered by introspecting on their
own experiences and describing what they find. If claims about the phenomenology of free will were uncontroversial, this practice would not be worri-
some. But they are controversial, as evidenced by the philosophers' conflicting
accounts of it. Furthermore, introspective reports about the relevant experiences are likely influenced by the theoretical commitments of the philosopher
doing the introspection. Introspection does not simply present 'pure' content
to be analysed; rather, by the time philosophers develop theories of free will,
they introspect through the lens of their theoretical commitments.

While we believe that it is crucial to 'trust the subject' in order to study
the nature of conscious experience, we worry that philosophers with theoretical axes to grind may be the wrong subjects to trust. Rather, since the phenomenology of free will plays an important role in the theoretical debates,
we see a need to collect systematic data about the relevant experiences of
ordinary people. It's not that such 'folk phenomenology' reveals theory-free

descriptions of the experience of free will: ordinary people's phenomenological descriptions will also be influenced by their theories and conceptual
schemes. Rather, 'folk phenomenology' comprises the set of claims philosophers' theories should accord with if they want to gain any support from phenomenological considerations.

We first discuss three disputes in which libertarians and compatibilists offer
conflicting phenomenological descriptions and explain why it matters whose
description is more accurate. We then discuss psychological research that might
shed light on these debates. Though this research is limited, it offers some useful
data and methodologies. We supplement this research with some pilot studies
of our own, not in order to resolve these questions about the phenomenology of
free will but rather to motivate further research in this area. (We did not want to
encourage a move away from the armchair without getting out of our own.)

We conclude that further empirical research on the phenomenology of
free will must be carried out, and that such research, though difficult, is possible. We also suggest that libertarians have the burden of finding empirical
evidence supporting the accuracy of their phenomenological descriptions,
since, on the one hand, the research we discuss in fact favours compatibilist descriptions, and on the other hand, libertarian theories demand more
from the phenomenology. Libertarian phenomenological claims are generally more robust than their compatibilist counterparts, so stronger empirical support is required to substantiate them. More importantly, libertarian
phenomenological descriptions set more demanding veridicality conditions,
since their theories require more demanding metaphysical conditions than
compatibilist theories do. This raises the question: Why should we believe we
need libertarian free will unless we feel like we have it? Why shouldn't we be
satisfied with the less demanding compatibilist conception of free will if it is
in fact consistent with our experiences?

Motivating the project

We will lump people's experiences of deliberating, making decisions, and feeling free and responsible for their actions together under the umbrella term 'the
phenomenology of free will.'[1] One might think that exploring this phenomenology would have a rich history. Yet despite the intrinsic value of understanding the phenomenology of these philosophically controversial topics, there are
surprisingly few sustained research programs that investigate them.

Taking a cue from recent empirical work on 'folk intuitions,'[2] we think
the best way to understand the phenomenology of free will—if there is one—is
to find out what ordinary people's experiences are like. If this is not possible,
philosophers' competing introspective descriptions will remain in yet another
free-will stalemate. If we can understand this phenomenology, however, then

this will at least situate the burden of proof: if libertarian descriptions of our experiences are right, then compatibilists must explain why it shouldn't matter if those experiences are illusory, and if compatibilist descriptions are right, then libertarians must explain why we need to satisfy conditions for free will more demanding than what is suggested by our experiences. It is thus worth trying to attain a more systematic understanding of the phenomenology of free will. And, as the articles in this collection suggest, we have reason to think such an understanding is attainable. Cognitive scientists and philosophers are increasingly interested in studying first-person experiences, recognizing both the need to 'trust the subject' and to develop more reliable methods for gathering data about such experiences so as to warrant this trust.[3]

Most philosophers seem to believe that there is no need to do such research on folk phenomenology because the relevant data can be procured by introspecting on their own experiences.[4] Perhaps they assume that most people experience free will in roughly the same way and, if people reflect properly on these experiences, they will offer similar descriptions. So, philosophers, reflective by training, can offer phenomenological descriptions adequate, if not superior, to those offered by the folk. Regardless of the rationale, we find the tendency of philosophers to project their own phenomenology and intuitions onto the folk—a practice we call the 'universality assumption'—problematic. As we'll see, this assumption crops up when philosophers make phenomenological claims, but it is challenged by the conflicts among these claims. Perhaps different philosophers' experiences are fundamentally different in a way that leads them to adopt diverse theoretical views, or perhaps their theoretical commitments have influenced their experiences or the way they describe them.

Either way, there is a problematic connection between philosophers' theoretical claims and their phenomenological claims. As David Velleman suggests, "the experience of freedom serves, in some philosophical theories, as a datum from which conceptual consequences are derived. The conceptual problem of freedom thus becomes intertwined with the phenomenological problem" (1989, 32). If possible, then, we need to find out whose descriptions of the experience of free will more accurately reflect pre-philosophical phenomenology. If we find that none does, we need to consider the consequences—for instance, that philosophers should no longer present phenomenology as support for their theory of free will.

In what ways do philosophers disagree about the experiences associated with free will? We identify three debates between libertarians and compatibilists driven, in part, by differing phenomenological descriptions:

(1) Categorical vs. conditional analyses of 'could have done otherwise.'
(2) Free actions as caused by the agent or as caused by the agents' mental states.
(3) 'Close-call decisions' vs. 'confident decisions' as paradigms of free action.

As we elucidate these disputes, notice how difficult it is to distinguish philosophers' conceptual claims from their *phenomenological* claims. Notice also the underlined passages illustrating the 'universality assumption' that we suggest leads philosophers to downplay the systematic 'folk phenomenology' we're calling for.

1. THE ABILITY TO DO OTHERWISE

Libertarians say an action is free only if, *given all conditions as they are at and up until the moment of choice*, the agent is able to act or choose in more than one way. Traditional compatibilists disagree, suggesting instead that the ability to do otherwise can be analysed as a conditional ability or in terms of general capacities to respond appropriately in the relevant circumstances.[5]

Unsurprisingly, they also disagree about how to describe the experience of choice. For instance, the libertarian C. A. Campbell writes: "Everyone must make the introspective experiment for himself: but I may perhaps venture to report…that I cannot help believing that *it lies with me here and now, quite absolutely, which of two genuinely open possibilities I adopt*" (1951, 463).[6] Keith Lehrer says that such an experience "accurately describes what I find by introspecting, and I cannot believe that others do not find the same" (1960, 150). And John Searle asks his readers to "reflect very carefully on the character of the experiences you have as you engage in normal, everyday human actions" and tells them, "You will sense the possibility of alternative courses of action built into these experiences…that we could be doing something else right here and now, that is, *all other conditions remaining the same*. This, I submit, is the source of our own unshakable conviction of our own free will" (1984, 95). None of these philosophers concludes from these experiences that we in fact *have* an unconditional ability to do otherwise, but they do suggest that if we *don't* have such an ability, free will is an illusion. Our *experience* would be illusory.[7] If so, the burden of proof is on the compatibilist: if free will is compatible with determinism, then why does it *feel* like it isn't?

Some compatibilists have shouldered this burden, accepting the libertarian description of the feeling of free will but explaining why it does not accurately capture the sort of freedom necessary for moral responsibility.[8] Other compatibilists, however, reject the libertarian description altogether. For instance, Adolf Grunbaum writes: "Let us carefully examine the content of the feeling that on a certain occasion we could have acted other than the way we did…. This feeling simply discloses that we were able to act in accord with our strongest desire at that time, and that *we could indeed have acted otherwise if a different motive had prevailed at the time*" (in Lehrer, 1960, 149). J.S. Mill agrees: "When we think of ourselves hypothetically as having acted otherwise than we did, *we always suppose a difference in the antecedents*: we picture ourselves having known something we did not know...or as having desired something...more or less than we did' (in Boyle *et al.*, 1976, 49).

Libertarians and compatibilists hence offer competing phenomenological descriptions to support their competing conceptual analyses of the ability to do otherwise. The question is whether or not we experience our choices as sufficiently caused by conditions at the moment of choice, such that a different choice would require some difference in those conditions (internal or external). If people experience their choices as following a causal sequence involving desires, beliefs, and reasons via a deliberative process, this would put pressure on the libertarian claim that people feel they could choose one way or the other *all things* (including desires, beliefs, and reasons) being equal. Conversely, the libertarian position would get support if, when people make choices, they feel as though they, as agents, add some 'causal oomph' to make otherwise undetermined events go one way or the other. This idea leads to a second dispute.

2. THE AGENT AS CAUSE?

Libertarians often suggest that we experience ourselves as active causes somewhere in the process of decision-making, whereas compatibilists often describe the deliberative process more passively, with our decisions 'flowing from' our desires and beliefs. The libertarian view is most explicit in theories of *agent causation* which hold that free actions are caused in a unique way, not by other events but by the agent herself.[9] Timothy O'Connor writes of agent causation that it "is appealing because it captures the way we experience our own activity. It does not seem to me (at least ordinarily) that I am caused to act by the reasons which favor doing so; it seems to be the case, rather, that *I produce my own decisions in view of* those reasons, and could have, in an unconditional sense, decided differently" (1995, 196). Horgan *et al.* (2003), though not endorsing the metaphysics of agent causation, agree that "your phenomenology presents your own behavior to you as having *yourself as its source*, rather than (say) presenting your own behavior to you as having your own occurrent mental events as its source" (225).

Compatibilists, however, are less apt to describe an agent's mental states as causes distinct from the agent herself. They analyse free actions (roughly and with caveats) as actions appropriately caused by the agent's beliefs and desires. W. T. Stace, for instance, claims, "Acts freely done are those whose immediate causes are psychological states in the agent" (1952, 257), and Joseph Priestly suggests that "all that a man can possibly be *conscious of* ... [is] that nothing hinders his choosing or taking whichsoever of the fruits *appears to him more desirable*" (in Boyle *et al.* 1976, 28). David Hume argued, contra the agent causationist Thomas Reid, that "our idea of power is not copied from any sentiment or consciousness of power within ourselves."[10] Similarly,

Daniel Dennett suggests that "we have to wait to see how we are going to decide something, and when we do decide, it bubbles up to consciousness from we know not where. We do not witness it being *made*; we witness its *arrival*" (1984, 78). He argues that we do not experience, but rather *construct*, a self as source of our decisions, "building a psychological theory of 'decision'...by inserting decisions where theory demands them, not where we have first-hand experience of them" (80).

Such compatibilists suggest that it is the theoretical demands of libertarian conceptions of free will that motivate, and perhaps influence, phenomenological claims about the experience of a 'self as source.' The burden of proof, they suggest, is on the libertarian to show that we actually have a 'thick' experience of ourselves as agent-causes that goes beyond our experience of our mental states causing our decisions and actions. Another way this phenomenological dispute plays out in the free will debate is in the different types of choices libertarians and compatibilists point to as paradigmatic of free will.

3. CLOSE CALLS VS. CONFIDENT DECISIONS

Since libertarians argue that free will requires the ability to do otherwise in the precise circumstances of choice, they point to those choices where we feel, given our reasons and desires, we could choose either way. Hence, the paradigmatic experiences of free will involve 'close-call' decisions, where we feel we have nearly equal motivation and/or reasons for alternative actions. Compatibilists, on the other hand, emphasize our ability to deliberate effectively to reach a decision about what we really want to do (or feel we should do). Hence, the paradigmatic experiences of free will involve 'confident' decisions, where we feel that, at least *after* deliberation, our reasons for choosing one alternative clearly outweigh the others.[11]

Some libertarians argue that free will is *only* possible when one's reasons and motivations remain closely balanced—otherwise the agent would have sufficient reasons or desires to causally determine his action. Peter van Inwagen suggests that a person exercises free will rarely, only when he faces choices "in which it is not obvious to the agent, even after reflection, and when all the facts are in, how he ought to choose" (1989, 234). Robert Kane requires such close calls for "self-forming actions" in which "there is a tension and uncertainty in our minds about what to do.... The uncertainty and tension we feel at such soul-searching moments of self-formation is reflected in the indeterminacy of our neural processes themselves" (2002, 228).[12]

On the contrary, some compatibilists suggest that we are most in control of our actions when we overcome uncertainty and tension by ruling out all but the one alternative we feel confident we should act on. Daniel Dennett, for instance, presents Martin Luther's claim, "Here I stand; I can do no other," as a paradigmatic instance of free action (1984, 133). Similarly, Harry Frankfurt suggests an agent is free when she acts on "a desire with which [she] is *satisfied*," where the feeling of satisfaction is "a state constituted just by the absence of any tendency or inclination to alter its condition" (1991, 104). And Susan Wolf suggests that, given the ability to choose on the basis of good reasons, the ability to choose otherwise is "a very strange ability to want, if it is an ability at all" (1990, 56).[13]

It should be no surprise that libertarians focus on the experience of close calls, since their view rests on the ability of agents to choose one way or another given the exact same conditions, an ability that only seems attractive when we experience closely balanced desires for either alternative. And it should also be no surprise that compatibilists focus on the experience of confident choices, since their view rests on the ability of agents to arrive at and act on decisions about what they really want, so the less conflict the better. What we would like to know is whether ordinary people associate acting of their own free will with the experience of confident decisions or close-call decisions.

Although there are undoubtedly other disagreements about the phenomenology of free will, we believe the three disputes described above represent the most significant conflicts between libertarians and compatibilists. Since the philosophers cannot agree on the phenomenology of free will, we suggest systematic psychological research on the relevant experiences of non-philosophers. If such research vindicates the libertarians' description, they can back up their claim that compatibilists offer a "wretched subterfuge" for what we want out of free will. If, instead, it vindicates the compatibilists' description, they can back up their claim that we don't want out of free will what the libertarians say we need (and could not have if determinism were true). The 'losing' side would then need to mount an argument either against the research itself, against the folk's (or rival philosophers') ability to get in touch with the relevant experiences, or against the relevance of phenomenology to the theoretical debate.

Of course, we may find that neither side's phenomenological descriptions are vindicated, because both are, in a sense, accurate. Perhaps people experience some choices in the libertarian way and others in the compatibilist way. Or perhaps some people experience deliberation and choice the way libertarians say, and other people experience it the way compatibilists say. This possibility would show the universality assumption to be mistaken.[14] But we should try to find out whether this is the case. And until such research has been conducted, philosophers should not talk about the phenomenology as if it is univocal and hence *prima facie* support for their theory.[15]

Even if systematic investigation of people's phenomenology in fact vindicates one of the conflicting descriptions offered by philosophers, this alone may not vindicate one of the conflicting *theories* of free will. The other side can still attack the alleged connection between the phenomenological facts and the conceptual conclusions or argue that phenomenology is entirely irrelevant. But as it stands (as illustrated by philosophers' claims about our shared experiences of free will), phenomenology plays a significant role in the debate. Our point is that such use of phenomenology is premature until we get some evidence from a larger sample size of people who are less subject to the theoretical influences of the philosophical debate.[16]

Psychological research on the phenomenology of free will

We've seen that philosophers have used their own phenomenology to support their analyses of free will. But their phenomenological descriptions conflict. Despite these conflicts, philosophers tend to assume that their own introspection sufficiently describes the experiences of ordinary people, so from their perspective, there has been no need for intersubjective studies on the 'folk phenomenology' of free will. There is thus a gap between introspection from the armchair and systematic research.

Unfortunately, we have been able to find little research that fills this gap. There are few studies on the *experiences* involved in choice, deliberation, voluntary action, etc. Admittedly, many research paradigms require subjects to deliberate and make choices, including work in cognitive dissonance, attribution theory, and game theory. These areas of research, however, fall within the behaviourist and cognitive psychology traditions, and they typically focus on the *objective* conditions for decision-making with no real systematic probe of subjects' experiences.[17]

When we look for psychological research on subjects' experiences, we find much less to work with. This is likely because the traditions that focused on such data—namely, introspectionism and phenomenology—fell to behaviourism. Surprisingly, even within those traditions, there seems to be little research devoted specifically to the experiences involved in deliberation and decision-making.[18] Some introspectionists worked on volition, but they said little about the experiences of deliberating and choosing that precede voluntary action. Exceptions include Narziss Ach (1905) and Michotte and Prum (1910), who carried out introspective studies on the phenomenology of action; these studies are discussed in Haggard and Johnson's contribution to this collection (2003), where they also point out the dearth of such research: "No studies of action phenomenology, to our knowledge, have achieved the harmonious combination of rigour of experimental control, depth of introspective report, and power of quantitative psychophysics" (77).

Here we discuss an American introspectionist who followed up on these studies: Honoria Wells' *Phenomenology of Acts of Choice,* which was published in 1927 during the dying years of introspectionism and has not been discussed since. Like most introspectionists, Wells used a small number of subjects (six including herself), all trained in the methods of introspection and educated in the relevant theoretical debates. The subjects learned the tastes of eight liquids and then were presented, over hundreds of trials, with two liquids at a time. They chose one to drink and immediately offered "a full report of all the processes which had been introspectable... from the moment when the two alternatives were presented to the...choice" (4–5).[19]

Relevant to our interests, subjects tended to report a negative affect experienced with 'close-call decisions'. In such cases, "the normal trend of conative activity in the act of choice is impeded.... Displeasure, and other affectively toned contents such as dismay, discomfort, confusion, surprise, etc. make their appearance" (77). Subjects report feeling less *control* over their choices when faced with similarly valenced alternatives: "Until the resolve to let things go, consciousness was very troubled; a great feeling of impotence" (77). Subjects were more apt to experience control over their choice when they were able to reach a confident conclusion about what they wanted than when they chose in a close-call situation.

Furthermore, subjects' reports generally have a passive tone. They usually describe thoughts and desires 'coming into' consciousness and their choices following automatically, even in the close-call cases Wells describes as 'effortful choices.' Here are two representative reports (the nonsense words label the liquids): "*Ziv* seemed to be attracting me rather than my determining it. I seemed to be passive. *Ziv* seemed to draw me. Chose *Ziv* and drank with pleasure" (80); "*Meb-Vab* present in a sort of jumble. Clear knowledge both very unpleasant. Nearly equally so.... Oscillation. Distinct feeling of strain...I accepted rather than chose *Mep*" (85).

Such results challenge the libertarian description of the phenomenology of free will. They suggest that when subjects were not theorizing about how deliberation and decision-making occur, they described the process in relatively passive terms: subjects were aware of the need to choose, of various desires and thoughts coming to mind, and of these desires and thoughts leading to a decision. A problem with introspectionist methodology, however, is that it *does* lend itself to theorizing (the diverse training methods of subjects is often cited as one of the causes of introspectionism's demise). While many of the reports offered by Wells' subjects used ordinary language and sound natural, when they introduced the theoretical language in which they were trained, they sounded unnatural and, well...theoretical: "I could distinguish a sort of mental movement towards *Tauk*. Still more hesitation, a distinct reference to 'self.' I designated *Laip* with a strong consciousness of action" (138). Subjects did not use the term 'consciousness of action' or refer to 'the self' in early trials.[20] Rather, they had reported "something in the choice they were missing," and were told to "observe this point very attentively in subsequent experiments." Indeed, they soon began to mention the theoretical terms they knew from the literature: "Having once caught the experience of

Self-activity, [subjects] were able to identify it in subsequent though weaker experience.... And this is in no sense an unscientific method of observing phenomena. In microscopic work, for example, an inexperienced begin-ner...misses[objects],although they are plainly there for the [experienced] observer who is looking for them" (144).

In this way, introspectionists justified the need for training: just as the biologist must be trained to notice and label objects under a microscope, the introspector must be trained to notice and label certain conscious phe-nomena. But while the objects under the microscope *are* there whether the observer can pick them out or not, it is not clear whether mental states that one must *learn* to notice are actually there waiting to be discovered. People can learn, laden with a theory, to experience things in a new way, perhaps a different way from observers trained under different theories and, more importantly, a different way from untrained folk.

On the other hand, perhaps Wells' subjects developed an ability to describe an experience of 'self-as-source,' as suggested by the libertarian, which untrained folk also experience but cannot easily access or describe. This runs us into a fundamental difficulty of this project. Our goal is to understand the phenomenology of free will in a way that informs the theoret-ical debate without tainting the phenomenology itself. But one might argue that, without training, the phenomenology of free will is either too difficult to apprehend or to describe or both. So, even if there *is* a folk phenomenology of free will, we may be unable to get systematic descriptions of it from folk who have yet to be trained in some relevant way.

Again, however, a major motivation behind our proposed methodology is that we are sceptical of well-trained philosophers' introspective descriptions of the phenomenology. We believe that reports gathered from laypersons will be minimally tainted by *philosophical* theory. For this purpose, it would be helpful for psychologists, perhaps guided by the questions raised in the phil-osophical debate, to reconsider the basic introspectionist project of gather-ing first-person reports, even offering some guidance about how to attend to conscious phenomena, while avoiding the introspectionists' tendency to train subjects in the theoretical debates. If the data from subjects' reports can be triangulated with behavioural and neuropsychological data, all the better.[21] Below, we describe our own attempt to use the 'talk aloud' method to gather concurrent reports from minimally trained subjects about their thoughts and feelings during deliberation and choice.

First, we will briefly describe two more areas of research on the experience of freedom. Five decades after Wells' study, decades during which behaviourism reigned in America, the cognitive psychologist Ivan Steiner proposed "that we ought somehow to legitimatise and dignify research in which all dependent vari-ables are abstracted from subjects' responses to inquiries concerning their feel-ings of control and choice. Perhaps that sounds outrageously phenomenological, but…until someone discovers a better way of gaining access to those experiences, we ought to listen to what subjects have to say" (in Perlmuter and Monty 1979, 20–21). This research on 'perceived freedom' sheds some light on our questions, though unfortunately Steiner's call to arms did not generate a sustained research effort on people's experiences of feeling free and making choices.

Perceived freedom studies present subjects with descriptions of agents making decisions and then ask subjects to judge the agents' level of freedom (or responsibility) in making the decision. Some studies show that subjects attribute higher freedom to agents when they act on a choice that accords with their clear preferences or their character traits than when they choose between two nearly equally attractive alternatives or act in other situations of uncertainty. Furthermore, attributions of responsibility track these judgments of freedom of choice.[22] These results suggest that, at least when judging others, people see confident choices, based on the agent's preferences or character traits, as more indicative of free will and responsibility than close-call choices. Steiner reports: "people experience choice when they seem in one way or another to control the decision-making process: They select an alternative they greatly desire; they confidently select among available options" (25). Unfortunately, these experiments don't tell us much about people's *own* experiences, including experiences of the ability to do otherwise or of the 'self as source.' It is difficult to know whether subjects are imagining their own experiences as if they were in the place of the agents they read about or engaging their theories about how to describe such agents.

Malcolm Westcott attempted a more extensive study of people's own experiences of freedom. His *Psychology of Human Freedom* (1988) offers a useful history of the neglect of such research: "Much as the phenomena of human freedom cry out for study from a human science viewpoint, there has not been much response" (118). He then describes several surveys and interviews he conducted on these topics. Unfortunately, though, Westcott's work includes issues that go well beyond the scope of the philosophical debates about free will. His interviews involve questions like, "Under what conditions do you feel free?" Unsurprisingly, the results tap into a range of experiences of freedom that go beyond deliberation and decision-making.

Nonetheless, some of his results are relevant to the question of close calls vs. confident decisions. Westcott developed seven generic descriptions of situations and surveyed subjects on how free (or unfree) they felt when they experienced such situations. The descriptions that drew the strongest ratings for freedom were 'self-direction' (taking steps towards a long-term goal), 'absence of responsibility,' and 'exercise of a skilled behavior,' which roughly fit the description of confident decisions. On the other hand, being 'faced with two important, apparently equal choices and deciding between them' drew the lowest rating among Westcott's categories, suggesting people do not experience close-call decisions as paradigmatic of freedom.

Westcott also tabulated subjects' descriptions of feeling *lack* of freedom into categories including, in order of frequency, 'prevention from without,' 'diffuse unpleasant affect,' and 'conflict and indecision.' These results also lend support to compatibilist descriptions, which emphasize freedom from external constraint and confident decisions. Though his results are of only limited relevance to our questions, Westcott's methodologies of surveying people about their experiences and interviewing them in a controlled way are interesting, and we have adopted these general strategies in the studies we describe below.

Pilot studies on the phenomenology of free will

So far we've seen that philosophers offer conflicting claims about the phenomenology of free will but make no real attempt to test their claims on a sample size larger than one. And psychologists tend to study the objective conditions and behaviours involved in decision-making rather than the first-person experiences of the subjects. We have found just a few attempts to break this trend. Unfortunately, we lack the resources to *remedy* this gap between philosophers' claims and psychological research, but we hope to motivate further efforts to close it. We offer preliminary studies as a good-faith effort to go beyond armchair speculation, while being well aware of their limitations. Notwithstanding, we hope our efforts will encourage philosophers, when they make empirical claims—including claims about our experiences—to present their problems and distinctions in such a way that they can be empirically tested.

Our initial study used specific questions with fixed responses drawn right from the philosophical debate. Here subjects are offering reports of remembered experiences and may be inclined to offer their theories rather than their phenomenology, problems we've already discussed. But it is important to note that when *philosophers* report their own experiences, they are likely to be reporting memories tainted by their own well-developed theories rather than their concurrent phenomenology. So, we thought it would be helpful to see what the folk say in response to alternatives suggested by the descriptions philosophers have offered.

The survey draws from competing libertarian and compatibilist accounts of our experience of the ability to choose otherwise, as described above:

> Imagine you've made a tough decision between two alternatives. You've chosen one of them and you think to yourself, 'I could have chosen otherwise' (it may help if you can remember a particular example of such a decision you've recently made).

Which of these statements best describes what you have in mind when you think, 'I could have chosen otherwise'?

A. 'I could have chosen to do otherwise even if everything at the moment of choice had been exactly the same.'
B. 'I could have chosen to do otherwise only if something had been different (for instance, different considerations had come to mind as I deliberated or I had experienced different desires at the time).'
C. Neither of the above describes what I mean.

We gave this survey to 96 undergraduates taking introductory philosophy classes (none had yet studied the free will problem): 62% offered the 'compatibilist response' (B); 35% offered the 'libertarian response' (A); and 3% answered 'neither.'[23]

Obviously this study indicates no clear consensus on how to describe the experience of being able to choose otherwise, at least when subjects are given these two alternatives.[24] However, the fact that significantly more subjects picked the 'compatibilist description' over the 'libertarian description' is somewhat surprising, especially given how passive the compatibilist description is. Libertarians might respond that the subjects assumed the 'something' that had to be different was some factor which they could control, everything else remaining the same—e.g., control over whether a desire or reason came to mind or over their relative strengths in their deliberative process. Compatibilists, in turn, might wonder whether people actually feel they have control over whether specific desires or reasons come to mind or over their influence on one's decisions.

Ultimately the goal is to get a sense of where precisely in the process of deliberation people feel they exercise control, how much control they feel they have, and how it seems to them to exercise it. What we need to do is catch people in the act of deliberating and deciding—or better, to get them to catch themselves in the act and tell us what it seems like to them. To attempt this, we adapted the talk-aloud method developed by Anders Ericsson and Herbert Simon (1993).[25] As a response to the behaviourists' almost complete neglect of subjects' verbal reports, but wary of errors made by introspectionists, Ericsson and Simon tested whether asking subjects to say out loud, but not explain, all the thoughts they are aware of while performing a cognitive task would disrupt 'the course or structure of the thought processes.' Numerous experiments suggest the talk-aloud method is in fact a valid instrument to probe subjects' cognitive processes. Usually the method is used for problem-solving tasks, though a few studies have been done on decision-making.[26] However, because these studies do not report the type of data we are interested in, we tried one of our own.

We devised descriptions of three apartments among which subjects were asked to deliberate and choose as if they were really going to live in one the next year. Following the basic talk-aloud protocol, we asked subjects to verbalize any thoughts (and feelings) they have as they performed practice tasks and the experimental task. Among our (twelve) subjects the general trend was simply to mention the features of the apartments they liked and disliked. As they read the descriptions and while they deliberated, they simply said aloud things like, "Hardwood floors—I like that," "Five miles from campus—that's too far," "I'm choosing apartment C because it has a washer/dryer," etc. It is difficult to discern whether subjects were reporting their thoughts or explaining their decisions or both. But, given the history of talk-aloud studies as well as our subjects' post-experimental responses that their reports were accurate accounts of what they were aware of, it may be that for *this* sort of decision at least, the process looks similar to what we found in Wells' introspectionist study: subjects are aware of their reactions to the information presented to them and in most cases decide based on being most attracted to one of the alternatives. The subjects described the process in passive terms and did not mention anything suggestive of a self that determines the outcome of an otherwise undetermined choice.

It may be that the experiences we're interested in are too 'thin' to be noticed easily or are too difficult to describe fully. Or perhaps they are so normal that we typically don't notice them (unless they are disrupted). Subjects usually had a pretty easy time picking one of the apartments—maybe the experience of making a decision becomes more salient in close-call situations. Perhaps to get interesting results using the talk-aloud method, the decision has to be moral or prudential.[27] Or we may just have to train our subjects a little more to get them to pay attention to what they normally take for granted, though we would then face the problem of inducing subjects to report experiences they might otherwise not have had.

Ultimately, we need a better way of finding out where to begin such studies. Here, the best idea may be to trust subjects to be the experts on their own experiences and use a qualitative research technique used primarily in the social sciences: the phenomenological interview. This technique involves extensive interviews with subjects about particular experiences, treating the subjects as co-investigators of the phenomena. The interviews begin with open-ended questions (e.g., "Tell me about your experience of time" [Pollio *et al.* 1997, 104]). From there, the interviewer lets the subject do most of the talking, directing the discussion with various "what?" and "how?" questions, but few demands for "why?" explanations. The transcripts of numerous subjects are then coded by several experimenters to quantify the data. We attempted such interviews with a few subjects, but have not yet coded any results.[28]

We recognize that some psychologists are likely to be wary of this methodology, given the difficulty of obtaining reliable quantitative data and the various research paradigms, such as attribution theory, suggesting that we are *not* experts about the way our minds work (though claims about our limited understanding of our mental *processes* need not challenge our ability to report how things seem to us, for instance, as we deliberate and act). Nonetheless, we need reports from subjects who are minimally tainted by philosophical theory while delving into the details of first-personal experiences neglected by most mainstream psychological practices. Refining the phenomenological interview to serve these practices may be a valuable *first* step in developing more quantitative studies.

Conclusions

While the research we have conducted does provide some insight into what folk experiences of free will are like, it does not provide conclusive answers to many of the questions we began with. The relevant research does not yet exist. No one has systematically explored the experiences philosophers claim are central to the phenomenology of free will—namely, whether we experience ourselves as being able to choose otherwise *all things being equal*, whether we experience our *selves* as causal agents in the process of choosing, and whether the paradigmatic experiences of free will involve close calls or confident decisions. One reason for the dearth of studies on these questions is surely the difficulty of carrying out such research. The questions are not precisely formulated. The connections between people's conceptual/theoretical views and their phenomenology are not well understood. And the methods for studying phenomenology in a scientific way are in their adolescence, since they were largely neglected until cognitive scientists and philosophers became more interested in the scientific study of consciousness.

The philosophical debate about the phenomenology of free will thus faces a dilemma: either it is impossible (or prohibitively difficult) to get the data needed to vindicate one side's phenomenological descriptions of free will over the other's, or it *is* possible. If it is impossible, then, at a minimum, philosophers should stop suggesting that their theories of free will best fit our experiences of free will. More significantly, philosophers would have to get a better handle on what *is* motivating their conflicting analyses of free will. If the foundational disputes in the debate (e.g., about how to understand the ability to do otherwise) ultimately come down to a conflict of intuitions or different ways of experiencing the world, then it is unclear what *could* resolve the disputes. And if phenomenology is entirely irrelevant to the conceptual analysis of free will, it would be helpful to understand why that is so.

However, it is unlikely that phenomenology is entirely irrelevant to the philosophical debates about free will, as demonstrated by philosophers' practice of introspecting on and describing their own experiences. So, if it *is* possible to uncover the relevant data about the phenomenology, then even though we are admittedly some distance from realizing that goal, we should strive for it. In this endeavour, philosophers can play a crucial role in setting more precise questions for researchers to answer. Success in answering such questions would allow us not only to understand an essential aspect of human psychology, but perhaps also to advance one of the most deadlocked debates in the history of philosophy.

Based on the preliminary evidence we have presented in this paper, libertarians should be especially concerned to find phenomenological data to support their theories. The research we have discussed above supports the compatibilist description of the phenomenology more than the libertarian description, though not, of course, decisively. First, in Wells' study, Westcott's surveys, and perceived freedom experiments, individuals' perception of freedom was stronger in confident decisions than in close calls. Second, we found that a majority of subjects associate 'could have done otherwise' with hypothetical rather than categorical ("all things being equal") descriptions. Finally, our talk-aloud studies found no evidence of agents experiencing themselves as the causal source of their choices, and Wells' subjects usually used similarly passive language to describe their deliberations and decision-making, at least until they were prompted to use the theoretical concepts. Hence, libertarians should consider finding ways to probe the relevant phenomenology to find evidence that we in fact have the rich experiences they suggest we all share— e.g., of an unconditional ability to do otherwise and of the 'self as source' of action—evidence we did not find.[29] Of course, since libertarians' descriptions of the phenomenology are more substantial, it will be more difficult to do the research necessary to substantiate them.

Furthermore, libertarian theories of free will are more metaphysically demanding than compatibilist theories, requiring at a minimum indeterminism (in a specific place) and sometimes agent-causal powers. If these demands turn out *not* to be required by our experiences, then we may reasonably ask why we should accept a theory that makes such demands rather than accepting a compatibilist theory that more accurately accords with our experiences. In any case, to determine whether libertarians or compatibilists are in fact misdescribing the phenomenology to fit the theory, we first need to study the phenomenology itself.[30]

Notes

1. We are using 'phenomenology' throughout to mean roughly the way experiences seem from the first-person point of view. The plural 'phenomeno*logies* of free will' may be more accurate, since there may not be homogenous experiences associated with what either the folk or philosophers mean by 'free will'. The list of relevant experiences may include voluntariness, efforts of will (or self-control), authorship, intention formation,

etc. (see Horgan *et al.*, 2003). We focus our discussion below on three issues central to the philosophical debates about free will.

2. See, for example, Knobe (2003), Mele (2003), Nadelhoffer (2005; 2004), Nahmias *et al.* (2005), Nichols (2004), Stich & Doris (2003), and Weinberg *et al.* (2001).

3. See also Jack & Shallice (2001), Nahmias (2002a), and Vermersch (1999).

4. Others may simply neglect the phenomenology, perhaps believing it is irrelevant to theoretical debates. As Horgan *et al.* note, "there has been a widespread, and very unfortunate, tendency to ignore the phenomenology of doing altogether—and to theorize about human agency without acknowledging its phenomenology at all" (2003, 332).

5. Compatibilists who, following Harry Frankfurt, reject the necessity of the ability to do otherwise nonetheless accept that agents must have general capacities to choose otherwise if conditions were different in relevant respects (e.g., to be responsive to reasons).

6. For these quotations, we've italicized the portion that illustrates the relevant claims about the phenomenology and underlined the portion that illustrates the 'universality assumption.'

7. Some psychologists writing about free will, notably Daniel Wegner (2002), offer evidence that our experience of consciously willing our actions does not accurately represent the mechanisms responsible for causing our actions, and hence our experiences are illusory. They usually assume something like the libertarian description of the phenomenology as their starting point. See Nahmias (2002b).

8. Hard determinists (incompatibilists who believe we do not have free will) tend to agree with the libertarian description of the phenomenology, but they argue, contra the compatibilist, that it does capture the sort of freedom necessary for moral responsibility, a type of freedom we do not have.

9. Other 'event-causal' libertarians eschew the problematic metaphysics of agent causation and require only that indeterministic events occur in specific places as an agent comes to act (see Ginet, 1990 and Kane, 2002). However, they generally agree about the phenomenology; Ginet writes of the "actish phenomenal quality": "My impression at each moment is that *I* at that moment, and nothing prior to that moment, determine which of several open alternatives is the next sort of bodily exertion I voluntarily make" (1990, 90).

10. *Enquiry* (section VII).

11. See Nahmias (2006) for further discussion of this debate.

12. See also Campbell (1951) and O'Connor (2000).

13. Compare Descartes' *Meditation IV*, 58.

14. It would also suggest an interesting explanation for the interminable nature of the free will debate: some philosophers' phenomenology leads them to develop libertarian views and others to develop compatibilist views, and when they whittle the arguments down to the disputed premises, they end up just banging their (fundamentally different) heads against each other.

15. Of course, neither side must claim that we *never* experience free will in the way the other side describes. Rather, they may be picking out particular experiences as the paradigmatic instances of free will. Here, it looks like we may also need to explore what ordinary folk's *intuitions* about free will and responsibility are (see Nahmias *et al.*, 2005).

16. One might worry that ordinary people's experiences are subject to other problematic influences, such as the theoretical views imported from their religious or scientific beliefs. While this poses a problem (which may, however, be testable), our goal is at least

to gain a better understanding of the experiences as reported by the folk the philosophers *say* they speak for.

17. In attribution research, for instance, subjects are sometimes asked to explain why they make decisions but not to describe the experience of making decisions. Libet (1985) and Wegner (2002) also neglect systematic exploration of the phenomenology of conscious will.

18. See Pfander (1977) for one example from the phenomenology tradition.

19. Wells also took physiological measurements during the experiments, such as galvanometric responses. Her attempt to correlate verbal reports with objective measures is an oft-overlooked method used by many introspectionists, one which we should replicate today (with fMRI scans, etc.).

20. These terms come from the work of Ach and Michotte & Prum which Wells was defending against theories advanced by Robert Wheeler.

21. See, for instance, Jack & Shallice (2001), Nahmias (2002a), and articles in this collection.

22. See Trope (1978), Kruglanski & Cohen (1973; 1974), and Upshaw (1979).

23. Responses were counterbalanced for order.

24. We ran a related survey to test J.L. Austin's famous claim about missing a short putt, "It is not that I should have holed it if conditions had been different: that might of course be so, but I am talking about conditions as they precisely were, and asserting that I could have holed it" (1970, 218). We asked subjects to imagine missing a short putt and thinking to themselves, "I could have made that putt"; then to pick among these descriptions of that sentence: A) I could have made that putt under the exact same conditions; B) I could have made that putt under very similar conditions; C) I could have made that putt only if something had been different; D) I make putts like that sometimes and I miss them sometimes; E) None of the above. Results did not support Austin's claims: Of 33 subjects, 43% answered C and 24% answered D, while only 24% answered A (9% picked B or E).

25. See also Ericsson's contribution to this volume (2003).

26. See Williamson & Ranyard (2000) and Svenson & Karlsson (1986).

27. We'd like to adopt a study from game theory which offers subjects $50 and the choice to keep as much as they want or give as much as they want to the Red Cross, obtaining talk aloud reports about their deliberations.

28. See Karlsson (1988) for such an approach to studying these experiences.

29. See Nichols (2004) for data that offers some support for the libertarian description.

30. For helpful comments, we thank Al Mele, Shaun Nichols, George Graham and participants of 'The Phenomenology of Agency' workshop (University of Arizona, 2003), as well as the editors of this collection and three anonymous referees.

References

Ach, N. 1905. *Über die Willenstätigkeit und das Denken*. Göttingen: Vandenhoeck & Ruprecht.

Austin, J. L. 1970. "Ifs and cans," in *Philosophical Papers,* ed. J. O. Urmson and G. J. Warnock. London: Oxford University Press, 205–231.

Boyle, J. M., Jr., G. Grisez, and O. Tollefson. 1976. *Free Choice: A Self-Referential Argument.* Notre Dame, IN: University of Notre Dame Press.

Campbell, C. A. 1951. "Is 'freewill' a pseudo-problem?" *Mind* **60.240:** 441–465.

Dennett, D. C. 1984. *Elbow Room: The Varieties of Free Will Worth Wanting.* Cambridge, MA: MIT Press.

Ericsson, A. 2003. "Valid and non-reactive verbalization of thought during performance of tasks: towards a solution to the central problems of introspection as a source of scientific data," *Journal of Consciousness Studies* **10.**9–10: 1–18.

Ericsson, A., and H. Simon. 1993. *Protocol Analysis.* Cambridge, MA: MIT Press.

Frankfurt, H. 1991. *Necessity, Volition, and Love.* New York: Cambridge University Press.

Ginet, C. 1990. *On Action.* Cambridge: Cambridge University Press.

Haggard, P., and H. Johnson. 2003. "Experiences of voluntary action," *Journal of Consciousness Studies* **10.**9–10: 72–84.

Horgan, T., J. Tienson, and G. Graham. 2003. "The phenomenology of first-person agency," in *Physicalism and Mental Causation,* ed. S. Walter and H. Heckman. Exeter, UK: Imprint Academic, 232–341.

Jack, A. I., and T. Shallice. 2001. "Introspective physicalism as an approach to the science of consciousness," *Cognition* **79.**1–2: 161–196.

Kane, R. 2002. "Free will: new directions for an ancient problem," in *Free Will,* ed. R. Kane. Malden, MA: Blackwell, 222–248.

Karlsson, G. 1988. "A phenomenological psychological study of decision and choice," *Acta Psychologica* **68:** 7–25.

Knobe, J. 2003. "Intentional action and side-effects in ordinary language," *Analysis* **63:** 190–193.

Kruglanski, A., and M. Cohen. 1973. "Attributing freedom and personal causation," *Journal of Personality and Social Psychology* **26.2:** 245–250.

Kruglanski, A., and M. Cohen. 1974. "Attributing freedom in the decision context: effects of the choice alternatives, degree of commitment, and predecision uncertainty," *Journal of Personality and Social Psychology* **30.1:** 178–187.

Lehrer, K. 1960. "Can we know that we have free will by introspection?" *Journal of Philosophy* **57.5:** 145–57.

Libet, Benjamin. 1985. "Unconscious cerebral initiative and the role of conscious will in voluntary action," *Behavioral and Brain Sciences* **8:** 529–566.

Mele, A. R. 2003. "Intentional actions: controversies, data, and core hypotheses," *Philosophical Psychology* **16:** 325–340.

Michotte, A., and E. Prum. 1910. "Le choix volontaire et ses antécédents immédiats," *Arch de Psychol* **38–39:** 8–205.

Nadelhoffer, T. 2004. "The Butler problem revisited," *Analysis* **64.3:** 277–284.

Nadelhoffer, T. 2005. "Skill, luck, and folk ascriptions of intentional action," *Philosophical Psychology* **18.3:** 341–352.

Nahmias, E. 2002a. "Verbal reports on the contents of consciousness: reconsidering introspectionist methodology," *Psyche* **8.**21: 1–23.

Nahmias, E. 2002b. "When consciousness matters: a critical review of Daniel Wegner's *The Illusion of Conscious Will,*" *Philosophical Psychology* **15.4:** 527–541.

Nahmias, E. 2006. "Close calls and the confident agent: free will, deliberation, and the ability to do otherwise," *Philosophical Studies* **131.3:** 627–667.

Nahmias, E., S. Morris, T. Nadelhoffer, and J. Turner. 2005. "Surveying freedom: folk intuitions about free will and moral responsibility," *Philosophical Psychology* **18.5:** 561–584.

Nichols, S. 2004. "The folk psychology of free will," *Mind and Language* **19.5:** 473–502.

O'Connor, T. 1995. "Agent causation," in *Agents, Causes, and Events*, ed. T. O'Connor. New York: Oxford University Press, 173–200.

O'Connor, T. 2000. *Persons and Causes: The Metaphysics of Free Will.* New York: Oxford University Press.

Perlmuter, L., and R. Monty, eds. 1979. *Choice and Perceived Control.* Hillsdale, NJ: Lawrence Erlbaum.

Pfänder, Alexander. 1967. *The Phenomenology of Willing and Motivation*, trans. H. Spiegelberg. Evanston, IL: Northwestern University Press.

Pollio, H., T. Henley, and C. Thompson. 1997. *The Phenomenology of Everyday Life.* Cambridge: Cambridge University Press.

Searle, J. 1984. *Minds, Brains, and Science.* Cambridge, MA: Harvard University Press.

Stace, W. T. 1952. *Religion and the Modern Mind.* New York: J.B. Lippincott.

Stich, S., and J. Doris. 2003. "As a matter of fact: empirical perspectives on ethics," in *The Oxford Handbook of Contemporary Analytic Philosophy*, ed. F. Jackson and M. Smith. Oxford: Oxford University Press.

Svenson, O., and G. Karlsson. 1986. "Attractiveness of decision-making alternatives characterized by numerical and non-numerical information," *Scandinavian Journal of Psychology* **27:** 74–84.

Trope, Y. 1978. "Extrinsic rewards, congruence between dispositions and behaviors, and perceived freedom," *Journal of Personality and Social Psychology* **36.6:** 588–597.

van Inwagen, P. 1989. "When is the will free?" *Philosophical Perspectives* **3:** 399–422.

Velleman, D. 1989. "Epistemic freedom," in *The Possibility of Practical Reason*. New York: Oxford University Press, 2000.

Vermersch, P. 1999. "Introspection as practice," *Journal of Consciousness Studies* **6.2–3:** 17–42.

Upshaw, H. 1979. "Attitude toward the reasons for one's actions: a determinant of perceived freedom," *Personality and Social Psychology Bulletin* **5.2:** 182–185.

Wegner, D. 2002. *The Illusion of Conscious Will.* Cambridge, MA: MIT Press.

Weinberg, J., S. Nichols, and S. Stich. 2001. "Normativity and epistemic intuitions," *Philosophical Topics* **29.1–2:** 429–460.

Wells, H. M. 1927. "The phenomenology of acts of choice: an analysis of volitional consciousness," *British Journal of Psychology, Monograph Supplements* **4.11.**

Westcott, M. 1988. *The Psychology of Human Freedom: A Human Science Perspective and Critique.* New York: Springer-Verlag.

Williamson, J., and R. Ranyard. 2000. "A conversation-based process tracing method for use with naturalistic decisions: an evaluation study," *British Journal of Psychology* **91:** 203–221.

Wolf, S. 1990. *Freedom Within Reason.* New York: Oxford University Press.

26

Moral Responsibility and Determinism: The Cognitive Science of Folk Intuitions

Shaun Nichols and Joshua Knobe

1. Introduction

The dispute between compatibilists and incompatibilists must be one of the most persistent and heated deadlocks in Western philosophy. Incompatibilists maintain that people are not fully morally responsible if determinism is true, i.e., if every event is an inevitable consequence of the prior conditions and the natural laws. By contrast, compatibilists maintain that even if determinism is true our moral responsibility is not undermined in the slightest, for determinism and moral responsibility are perfectly consistent.[1]

The debate between these two positions has invoked many different resources, including quantum mechanics, social psychology, and basic metaphysics. But recent discussions have relied heavily on arguments that draw on people's intuitions about particular cases. Some philosophers have claimed that people have incompatibilist intuitions (e.g., Kane 1999, 218; Strawson 1986, 30; Vargas 2006); others have challenged this claim and suggested that people's intuitions actually fit with compatibilism (Nahmias et al. 2005). But although philosophers have constructed increasingly sophisticated arguments about the implications of people's intuitions, there has been remarkably little discussion about *why* people have the intuitions they do. That is to say, relatively little has been said about the specific psychological processes that generate or sustain people's intuitions. And yet, it seems clear that questions about the sources of people's intuitions could have a major impact on debates about the compatibility of responsibility and determinism. There is an obvious sense in which it is important to figure out whether people's intuitions are being produced by a process that is generally reliable or whether they are being distorted by a process that generally leads people astray.

Our aim here is to present and defend a hypothesis about the processes that generate people's intuitions concerning moral responsibility. Our hypothesis is that people have an incompatibilist theory of moral responsibility that is elicited in some contexts but that they also have psychological mechanisms that can lead them to arrive at compatibilist judgments in other contexts.[2] To support this hypothesis, we report new experimental data. These data show that people's responses to questions about moral responsibility can vary dramatically depending on the way in which the question is formulated. When asked questions that call for a more abstract, theoretical sort of cognition, people give overwhelmingly incompatibilist answers. But when asked questions that trigger emotions, their answers become far more compatibilist.

2. Affect, blame, and the attribution of responsibility

In their attempts to get a handle on folk concepts and folk theories, naturalistic philosophers have proceeded by looking at people's intuitions about particular cases (e.g., Knobe 2003a, 2003b; Nahmias et al. 2005; Nichols 2004a; Weinberg et al. 2001; Woolfolk et al. 2006). The basic technique is simple. The philosopher constructs a hypothetical scenario and then asks people whether, for instance, the agent in the scenario is morally responsible. By varying the details of the case and checking to see how people's intuitions are affected, one can gradually get a sense for the contours of the folk theory. This method is a good one, but it must be practiced with care. One cannot simply assume that all of the relevant intuitions are generated by the same underlying folk theory. It is always possible that different intuitions will turn out to have been generated by different psychological processes.

Here we will focus especially on the role of *affect* in generating intuitions about moral responsibility. Our hypothesis is that, when people are confronted with a story about an agent who performs a morally bad behavior, this can trigger an immediate emotional response, and this emotional response can play a crucial role in their intuitions about whether the agent was morally responsible. In fact, people may sometimes declare such an agent to be morally responsible despite the fact that they embrace a theory of responsibility on which the agent is not responsible.

Consider, for example, Watson's (1987) interesting discussion of the crimes of Robert Harris. Watson provides long quotations from a newspaper article about how Harris savagely murdered innocent people, showing no remorse for what he had done. Then he describes, in equally chilling detail, the horrible abuse Harris had to endure as he was growing up. After reading all of these vivid details, it would be almost impossible for a reader to respond by calmly working out the implications of his or her theory of moral responsibility. Any normal reader will have a rich array of reactions, including not only abstract theorizing but also feelings of horror and disgust. A reader's intuitions about such a case might be swayed by her emotions, leaving her with a conclusion that contravened her more abstract, theoretical beliefs about the nature of moral responsibility.

Still, it might be thought that this sort of effect would be unlikely to influence people's reactions to ordinary philosophical examples. Most philosophical examples are purely hypothetical and thinly described (often only a few sentences in length). To a first glance at least, it might seem that emotional reactions are unlikely to have any impact on people's intuitions about examples like these. But a growing body of experimental evidence indicates that this commonsense view is mistaken. This evidence suggests that affect plays an important role even in people's intuitions about thinly described, purely hypothetical cases (Blair 1995; Greene et al. 2001; Nichols 2002; Haidt et al. 1993).

It may seem puzzling that affect should play such a powerful role, and a number of different models of the role of emotion in evaluative thought have been proposed. We will discuss some of these models in further detail in sections 5, 6, and 7. In the meantime, we want to point to one factor that appears to influence people's affective reactions. A recent study by Smart and Loewenstein (2005) shows that when a transgressor is made more 'determinate' for subjects, subjects experience greater negative affect and are more punitive towards that agent as a result. In the study, subjects play a game in which they can privately cooperate or defect. Each subject is assigned an identifying number, but none of the subjects knows anyone else's number. The experimenter puts the numbers of the defectors into an envelope. The cooperators are subsequently allowed to decide whether to penalize a defector. The cooperator is informed that he will pick a number out of the envelope to determine which defector will be penalized (or not). The manipulation was unbelievably subtle. In the *indeterminate* condition, subjects decide how much to penalize *before* they draw the number; in the *determinate* condition, subjects decide how much to penalize *after* they draw the number. Despite this tiny difference, Smart and Loewenstein found a significant effect—subjects in the determinate condition gave worse penalties than subjects in the indeterminate condition. Furthermore, subjects filled out a self-report questionnaire on how much anger, blame, and sympathy they felt, and subjects in the determinate condition felt more anger and blame than subjects in the indeterminate condition. Finally, using mediational statistical analysis, Smart and Loewenstein found that determinateness impacts punitiveness by virtue of provoking stronger emotions.

As we shall see, previous studies of people's moral responsibility intuitions all featured determinate agents and therefore were designed in a way that would tend to trigger affective reactions. Our own study provides an opportunity to see how people's intuitions are altered when the stimuli are designed in a way that keeps affective reactions to a minimum.

3. Intuitions about free will and responsibility

Incompatibilist philosophers have traditionally claimed both that ordinary people believe that human decisions are not governed by deterministic laws and that ordinary people believe that determinism is incompatible with moral responsibility (e.g., Kane 1999; Strawson 1986). These claims have been based, not on systematic empirical research, but rather on anecdote and informal observation. For example, Kane writes, "In my experience, most ordinary persons start out as natural incompatibilists" (1999, 217). (As will be clear below, we think Kane is actually getting at something deep about our intuitions here.) In recent years, philosophers have sought to put claims like this one to the test using experimental methods. The results have sometimes been surprising.

First, consider the claim that ordinary people believe that human decisions are not governed by deterministic laws. In a set of experiments exploring the lay understanding of choice, both children and adults tended to treat moral choices as indeterminist (Nichols 2004a). Participants were presented with cases of moral choice events (e.g., a girl steals a candy bar) and physical events (e.g., a pot of water comes to a boil), and they were asked whether, if everything in the world was the same right up until the event occurred, the event *had to* occur. Both children and adults were more likely to say that the physical event had to occur than that the moral choice event had to occur. This result seems to vindicate the traditional claim that ordinary people in our culture believe that at least some human decisions are not determined.

Experimental study has not been so kind to the traditional claim that ordinary people are incompatibilists about responsibility. Woolfolk, Doris and Darley (2006) gave participants a story about an agent who is captured by kidnappers and given a powerful 'compliance drug.' The drug makes it impossible for him to disobey orders. The kidnappers order him to perform an immoral action, and he cannot help but obey. Subjects in the 'low identification condition' were told that the agent did not want to perform the immoral action and was only performing it because he had been given the compliance drug. Subjects in the 'high identification condition' were told that the agent wanted to perform the immoral action all along and felt no reluctance about performing it. The results showed a clear effect of identification: subjects in the high identification condition gave higher ratings of responsibility for the agent than subjects in the low identification condition. This result fits beautifully with the compatibilist view that responsibility depends on identification (e.g., Frankfurt 1988). However, subjects in both conditions showed an overall tendency to give low ratings of responsibility for the agent. So these results don't pose a direct threat to the view that people are incompatibilists about responsibility.

The final set of studies we'll review poses a greater problem for the view that people are intuitive incompatibilists. Nahmias, Morris, Nadelhoffer and Turner (2005) find that participants will hold an agent morally responsible even when they are told to assume that the agent is in a deterministic universe. For instance, they presented participants with the following scenario:

> Imagine that in the next century we discover all the laws of nature, and we build a supercomputer which can deduce from these laws of nature and from the current state of everything in the world exactly what will be happening in the world at any future time. It can look at everything about the way the world is and predict everything about how it will be with 100% accuracy. Suppose that such a supercomputer existed, and it looks at the state of the universe at a certain time on March 25th, 2150 A.D., twenty years before Jeremy Hall is born. The computer then deduces from this information and the laws of nature that Jeremy will definitely rob Fidelity Bank at 6:00 PM on January 26th, 2195. As always, the supercomputer's prediction is correct; Jeremy robs Fidelity Bank at 6:00 PM on January 26th, 2195.

Participants were subsequently asked whether Jeremy is morally blameworthy for robbing the bank. The results were striking: 83% of subjects said that Jeremy was morally blameworthy for robbing the bank. In two additional experiments with different scenarios, similar effects emerged, suggesting that lay people regard moral responsibility as compatible with determinism. These findings are fascinating, and we will try to build on them in our own experiments.

Of course, it is possible to challenge the experiments on methodological grounds. For instance, the scenarios use technical vocabulary (e.g., "laws of nature," "current state"), and one might wonder whether the subjects really understood the scenarios. Further, one might complain that determinism is not made sufficiently salient in the scenarios. The story of the supercomputer focuses on the predictability of events in the universe, and many philosophers have taken the predictability of the universe to be less threatening to free will than causal inevitability. Although one might use these methodological worries to dismiss the results, we are not inclined to do so. For we think that Nahmias and colleagues have tapped into something of genuine interest.[3] They report three quite different scenarios that produce much the same effect. In each of their experiments, most people (60–85%) say that the agent is morally responsible even under the assumption that determinism is true. Moreover, the results coincide with independent psychological work on the assignment of punishment. Viney and colleagues found that college students who were identified as determinists were no less punitive than indeterminists (Viney et al. 1982) and no less likely to offer retributivist justifications for punishments (Viney et al. 1988).[4] So, we will assume that Nahmias et al. are right that when faced with an agent intentionally doing a bad action in a deterministic setting, people tend to hold the agent morally responsible.

But if people so consistently give compatibilist responses on experimental questionnaires, why have some philosophers concluded that ordinary people are incompatibilists?[5] Have these philosophers simply been failing to listen to their own undergraduate students? We suspect that something more complex is going on. On our view, most people (at least in our culture) really do hold incompatibilist theories of moral responsibility, and these theories can easily be brought out in the kinds of philosophical discussions that arise, e.g., in university seminars. It's just that, in addition to these theories of moral responsibility, people also have immediate affective reactions to stories about immoral behaviors. What we see in the results of the experiments by Nahmias and colleagues is, in part, the effect of these affective reactions. To uncover people's underlying theories, we need to offer them questions that call for more abstract, theoretical cognition.

4. Experimental evidence: first phase

We conducted a series of experiments to explore whether participants will be more likely to report incompatibilist intuitions if the emotional and motivational factors are minimized. In each experiment, one condition, the *concrete* condition, was designed to elicit greater affective response; the other condition, the *abstract* condition, was designed to trigger abstract, theoretical cognition. We predicted that people would be more likely to respond as compatibilists in the concrete condition.

Before we present the details of the experiments, we should note that there are many ways to characterize determinism. The most precise characterizations involve technical language about, for example, the laws of nature. However, we think it's a mistake to use technical terminology for these sorts of experiments, and we therefore tried to present the issue in more accessible language.[6] Of course, any attempt to translate complex philosophical issues into simpler terms will raise difficult questions. It is certainly possible that the specific description of determinism used in our study biased people's intuitions in one direction or another. Perhaps the overall rate of incompatibilist responses would have been somewhat higher or lower if we had used a subtly different formulation.

One should keep in mind, however, that our main focus here is on the *difference* between people's responses in the concrete condition and their responses in the abstract condition. Even though we use exactly the same description of determinism in these two conditions, we predict that people will give compatibilist responses in the concrete condition and incompatibilist responses in the abstract condition. Such an effect could not be dismissed as an artifact of our description of determinism. If a difference actually does emerge, we will therefore have good evidence for the view that affect is playing some role in people's compatibilist intuitions.

All of our studies were conducted on undergraduates at the University of Utah,[7] and all of the studies began with the same setup. Participants were given the following description of a determinist universe and an indeterminist universe:

> Imagine a universe (Universe A) in which everything that happens is completely caused by whatever happened before it. This is true from the very beginning of the universe, so what happened in the beginning of the universe caused what happened next, and so on right up until the present. For example one day John decided to have French Fries at lunch. Like everything else, this decision was completely caused by what happened before it. So, if everything in this universe was exactly the same up until John made his decision, then it *had to happen* that John would decide to have French Fries.
>
> Now imagine a universe (Universe B) in which *almost* everything that happens is completely caused by whatever happened before it. The one exception is human decision making. For example, one day Mary decided to have French Fries at lunch. Since a person's decision in this universe is not completely caused by what happened before it, even if everything in the universe was exactly the same up until Mary made her decision, it *did **not** have to happen* that Mary would decide to have French Fries. She could have decided to have something different.
>
> The key difference, then, is that in Universe A every decision is completely caused by what happened before the decision—given the past, each decision *has to happen* the way that it does. By contrast, in Universe B, decisions are not completely caused by the past, and each human decision *does **not** have to happen* the way that it does.
>
> 1. Which of these universes do you think is most like ours? (circle one)
>
> **Universe A   Universe B**
>
> Please briefly explain your answer:

The purpose of this initial question was simply to see whether subjects believe that our own universe is deterministic or indeterministic. Across conditions, nearly all participants (over 90%) judged that the indeterministic universe is most similar to our own.

After answering the initial question, subjects received a question designed to test intuitions about compatibilism and incompatibilism. Subjects were randomly assigned either to the *concrete* condition or to the *abstract* condition. We ran several different versions, but we will focus on the most important ones. In one of our concrete conditions, subjects were given the following question:

In Universe A, a man named Bill has become attracted to his secretary, and he decides that the only way to be with her is to kill his wife and 3 children. He knows that it is impossible to escape from his house in the event of a fire. Before he leaves on a business trip, he sets up a device in his basement that burns down the house and kills his family.

Is Bill fully morally responsible for killing his wife and children?

YES   NO

In this condition, most subjects (72%) gave the compatibilist response that the agent was fully morally responsible. This is comparable to results obtained in experiments by Nahmias and colleagues. But now consider one of our abstract conditions:

In Universe A, is it possible for a person to be fully morally responsible for their actions?

YES   NO

In this condition, most subjects (86%) gave the *incompatibilist* response!

In short, most people give the compatibilist response to the concrete case, but the vast majority give the *incompatibilist* response to the abstract case. What on earth could explain this dramatic difference? Let's first consider a deflationary possibility. Perhaps the concrete condition is so long and complex that subjects lose track of the fact that the agent is in a determinist universe. This is a perfectly sensible explanation. To see whether this accounts for the difference, we ran another concrete condition in which the scenario was short and simple. Subjects were given all the same initial descriptions and then given the following question:

In Universe A, Bill stabs his wife and children to death so that he can be with his secretary. Is it possible that Bill is fully morally responsible for killing his family?

YES   NO

Even in this simple scenario, 50% of subjects gave the compatibilist response, which is still significantly different from the very low number of compatibilist responses in the abstract condition.[8]

As we noted above, there are many ways of describing determinism, and the overall rate of incompatibilist responses might have been higher or lower if we had used a somewhat different description. Still, one cannot plausibly dismiss the high rate of incompatibilist responses in the abstract condition as a product of some subtle bias in our description of determinism. After all, the concrete condition used precisely the same description, and yet subjects in that condition were significantly more likely to give compatibilist responses.[9]

These initial experiments replicated the finding (originally due to Nahmias et al.) that people have compatibilist intuitions when presented with vignettes that trigger affective responses. But they also yielded a new and surprising result. When subjects were presented with an abstract vignette, they had predominantly *incompatibilist* intuitions. This pattern of results suggests that affect is playing a key role in generating people's compatibilist intuitions.

5. Psychological models

Thus far, we have been providing evidence for the claim that different folk intuitions about responsibility are produced by different kinds of psychological processes. But if it is indeed the case that one sort of process leads to compatibilist intuitions and another leads to incompatibilist intuitions, which sort of process should we regard as the best guide to the true relationship between moral responsibility and determinism?

Before we can address this question, we need to know a little bit more about the specific psychological processes that might underlie different types of folk intuitions. We therefore consider a series of possible models. We begin by looking at three extremely simple models and then go on to consider ways that elements of these simple models might be joined together to form more complex models.

THE PERFORMANCE ERROR MODEL

Perhaps the most obvious way of explaining the data reported here would be to suggest that strong affective reactions can bias and distort people's judgments. On this view, people ordinarily make responsibility judgments by relying on a tacit theory, but when they are faced with a truly egregious violation of moral norms (as in our concrete cases), they experience a strong affective reaction which makes them unable to apply the theory correctly. In short, this hypothesis posits an *affective performance error*. That is, it draws a distinction between people's underlying representations of the criteria for moral responsibility and the performance systems that enable them to apply those criteria to particular cases. It then suggests that people's affective reactions are interfering with the normal operation of the performance systems.

The performance error model draws support from the vast literature in social psychology on the interaction between affect and theoretical cognition. This literature has unearthed numerous ways in which people's affective reactions can interfere with their ability to reason correctly. Under the influence of affective or motivational biases, people are less likely to recall certain kinds of relevant information, less likely to believe unwanted evidence, and less likely to use critical resources to attack conclusions that are motivationally neutral (see Kunda 1990 for a review). Given that we find these biases in so many other aspects of cognition, it is only natural to conclude that they can be found in moral responsibility judgments as well.

More pointedly, there is evidence that affect sometimes biases attributions of responsibility. Lerner and colleagues found that when subjects' negative emotions are aroused, they hold agents more responsible and more deserving of punishment, *even when the negative emotions are aroused by an unrelated event* (Lerner et al. 1998). In their study, subjects in the *anger* condition watched a video clip of a bully beating up a teenager, while subjects in the *emotion-neutral* condition watched a video clip of abstract figures (Lerner et al. 1998, 566). All subjects were then presented with what they were told was a different experiment designed to examine how people assess responsibility for negligent behaviors. Subjects in the anger condition (i.e., those who had been seen the bully video) gave higher responsibility ratings than subjects in the emotion-neutral condition. So, although the subjects' emotions were induced by the film, these emotions impacted their responsibility judgments in unrelated scenarios. The most natural way to interpret this result is that the emotion served to bias the reasoning people used in making their assessments of responsibility.

Proponents of the performance error model might suggest that a similar phenomenon is at work in the experiments we have reported here. They would concede that people give compatibilist responses under certain circumstances, but they would deny that there is any real sense in which people can be said to hold a compatibilist view of moral responsibility. Instead, they would claim that the compatibilist responses we find in our concrete conditions are to be understood in terms of performance errors brought about by affective reactions. In the abstract condition, people's underlying theory is revealed for what it is—incompatibilist.

AFFECTIVE COMPETENCE MODEL

There is, however, another possible way of understanding the role of affect in the assessment of moral responsibility. Instead of supposing that affect serves only to bias or distort our theoretical judgments, one might suggest that people's affective reactions actually lie at the core of the process by which they ordinarily assign responsibility. Perhaps people normally make responsibility judgments by experiencing an affective reaction which, in combination with certain other processes, enables an assessment of moral responsibility. Of course, it can hardly be denied that some people also have elaborate theories of moral responsibility and that they use these theories in certain activities (e.g., in writing philosophy papers), but the proponents of this second view would deny that people's cold cognitive theories of responsibility play any real role in the process by means of which they normally make responsibility judgments. This process, they would claim, is governed primarily by affect.

This 'affective competence' view gains some support from recent studies of people with deficits in emotional processing due to psychological illnesses. When these people are given questions that require moral judgments, they sometimes offer bizarre patterns of responses (Blair 1995; Blair et al. 1997; Hauser et al. 2007). In other words, when we strip away the capacity for affective reactions, it seems that we are not left with a person who can apply the fundamental criteria of morality in an especially impartial or unbiased fashion. Instead, we seem to be left with someone who has trouble understanding what morality is all about. Results from studies like these have led some researchers to conclude that affect must be playing an important role in the fundamental competence underlying people's moral judgments (Blair 1995; Haidt 2001; Nichols 2004b; Prinz 2007).

Proponents of this view might suggest that the only way to really get a handle on people's capacity for moral judgment is to look at their responses in cases that provoke affective reactions. When we examine these cases, people seem to show a marked tendency to offer compatibilist responses, and it might therefore be suggested that the subjects in our studies should be regarded as compatibilists. Of course, we have also provided data indicating that these subjects provide incompatibilist answers when given theoretical questions, but it might be felt that studying people's theoretical beliefs tells us little or nothing about how they really go about making moral judgments. (Think of what would happen if we tried to study the human capacity for language by asking people theoretical questions about the principles of syntax!) Thus, affective competency theorists might maintain that the best way to describe our findings would be to say that people's fundamental moral competence is a compatibilist one but that some people happen to subscribe to a theory that contradicts this fundamental competence.

CONCRETE COMPETENCE MODEL

Finally, we need to consider the possibility that people's responses are not being influenced by affect in any way. Perhaps people's responses in the concrete conditions are actually generated by a purely cognitive process. Even if we assume that the process at work here can only be applied to concrete cases, we should not necessarily conclude that it makes essential use of affect. It might turn out that we have an entirely cognitive, affect-free process that, for whatever reason, can be applied to concrete questions but not to abstract ones.

One particularly appealing version of this hypothesis would be that people's intuitions in the concrete conditions are generated by an innate 'moral responsibility module.'[10] This module could take as input information about an agent and his or her behavior and then produce as output an intuition as to whether or not that agent is morally responsible. Presumably, the module would not use the same kinds of processes that are used in conscious reasoning. Instead, it would use a process that is swift, automatic, and entirely unconscious.

Here, the key idea is that only limited communication is possible between the module and the rest of the mind. The module takes as input certain very specific kinds of information about the agent (the fact that the agent is a human being, the fact that he knows what he is doing, etc.), but the vast majority of the person's beliefs would be entirely inaccessible to processes taking place inside of the module. Thus, the module would not be able to make use of the person's theory about the relationship between determinism and moral responsibility. It might not even be able to make use of the person's belief that the agent is in a deterministic universe. Because these beliefs would be inaccessible inside of the module, the conclusions of the module could differ dramatically from the conclusions that the person would reach after a process of conscious consideration.

HYBRID MODELS

Thus far, we have been considering three simple models of responsibility attribution. It would be possible, however, to construct more complex models by joining together elements of the three simple ones we have already presented. So, for example, it might turn out that moral responsibility judgments are subserved by a module but that the workings of this module are sometimes plagued with affective performance errors, or that the fundamental competence underlying responsibility judgments makes essential use of affect but that this affect somehow serves as input to a module, and many other possible hybrids might be suggested here.

Since we are unable to consider all of the possible hybrid models, we will focus on one that we find especially plausible. On the hybrid model we will be discussing, affect plays two distinct roles in the assignment of moral responsibility. Specifically, affect serves *both* as part of the fundamental competence underlying responsibility judgments *and* as a factor that can sometimes lead to performance errors. To get a sense for what we mean here, imagine that you are trying to determine whether certain poems should be regarded as 'moving', and now suppose you discover that one of the poems was actually written by your best friend. Here, it seems that the basic competence underlying your judgment would involve one sort of affect (your feelings about the poems) but the performance systems enabling your judgment could be derailed by another sort of affect (your feelings about the friend). The hybrid model in question would suggest that a similar sort of process takes place in judgments of moral responsibility. The competence underlying these judgments does make use of affect, but affect can also be implicated in processes that ultimately lead to performance errors.

Proponents of this model might suggest that affect does play an important role in the competence underlying moral responsibility judgments but that the effect obtained in the experiments reported here should still be treated as a performance error.[11] In other words, even if we suppose that affect has an important role to play in moral responsibility judgments, we can still conclude that the basic competence underlying these judgments is an incompatibilist one and that the responses we find in our concrete conditions are the result of a failure to apply that competence correctly.

6. Experimental evidence: second phase

Now that we have described some of the psychological models that might explain our results, we can explore a bit more deeply whether experimental evidence counts against any of the models. One key question is whether or not the compatibilist responses in our experiments are really the product of affect. We compared concrete conditions with abstract conditions, and we suggested that the concrete descriptions triggered greater affective response, which in turn pushed subjects toward compatibilist responses. However, it's possible that what really mattered was concreteness itself, not any affect associated with concreteness. That is, it's possible that the compatibilist responses were not influenced by affect but were elicited simply because the scenario involved a particular act by a particular individual. Indeed, this is exactly the sort of explanation one would expect from the responsibility module account. Fortunately, there is a direct way to test this proposal.

To explore whether concreteness alone can explain the compatibilist responses, we ran another experiment in which the affective salience varied across the two questions, but concreteness was held constant. Again, all subjects were given the initial descriptions of the two universes, A and B, and all subjects were asked which universe they thought was most similar to ours. Subjects were randomly assigned either to the *high affect* or *low affect* condition. In the *high affect* condition, subjects were asked the following:

> As he has done many times in the past, Bill stalks and rapes a stranger. Is it possible that Bill is fully morally responsible for raping the stranger?

In the *low affect* condition, subjects were asked:

> As he has done many times in the past, Mark arranges to cheat on his taxes. Is it possible that Mark is fully morally responsible for cheating on his taxes?

In addition, in each condition, for half of the subjects, the question stipulated that the agent was in Universe A; for the other half the agent was in Universe B. Thus, each subject was randomly assigned to one of the cells in Table 1.

What did we find? Even when we used these exclusively concrete scenarios, there was a clear difference between the high affect and low affect cases. Among subjects who were asked about agents in a *determinist* universe, people were much more likely to give the incompatibilist answer in the low affect case than in the high affect case. Indeed, most people said that it is *not* possible that the tax cheat is fully morally responsible, and a clear majority said that it *is* possible that the rapist is fully morally responsible. By contrast, for subjects who were asked about an agent in an indeterminist universe, most people said that it is possible for the agent to be fully morally responsible, regardless of whether he was a tax cheat or a rapist.[12] See Table 2.

These results help to clarify the role that affect plays in people's responsibility attributions Even when we control for concreteness, we still find that affect impacts people's intuitions about responsibility under determinism. The overall pattern of results therefore suggests that affect is playing an important role in the process that generates people's compatibilist intuitions.

We now have good evidence that affect plays a role in compatibilist judgments. But there remains the difficult question of whether what we see in these responses is the result of an affective competence or an affective performance error. Let's consider whether one of these models provides a better explanation of the experiment we just reported.

We think that the affective performance error model provides quite a plausible explanation of our results. What we see in the tax cheat case is that, when affect is minimized, people give dramatically different answers

TABLE 1
Experimental Design.

	Agent in indeterminist universe	Agent in determinist universe
High affect case		
Low affect case		

TABLE 2
Experimental Results.

	Agent in indeterminist universe	Agent in determinist universe
High affect case	95%	64%
Low affect case	89%	23%

depending on whether the agent is in a determinist or indeterminist universe. On the performance error hypothesis, these responses reveal the genuine competence with responsibility attribution, for in the low affect cases, the affective bias is minimized. When high affect is introduced, as in the serial rapist case, the normal competence with responsibility attribution is skewed by the emotions; that explains why there is such a large difference between the high and low affect cases in the determinist conditions.

Now let's turn to the affective competence account. It's much less clear that the affective competence theorist has a good explanation of the results. In particular, it seems difficult to see how the affective competence account can explain why responses to the low-affect case drop precipitously in the determinist condition, since this doesn't hold for the high affect case. Perhaps the affective competence theorist could say that low affect cases like the tax cheat case fail to trigger our competence with responsibility attribution, and so we should not treat those responses as reflecting our normal competence. But obviously it would take significant work to show that such everyday cases of apparent responsibility attribution don't really count as cases in which we exercise our competence at responsibility attribution. Thus, at first glance, the performance error account provides a better explanation of these results than the affective competence account.

Of course even if it is true that our results are best explained by the performance error account, this doesn't mean that affect is irrelevant to the normal competence. As noted in the previous section, one option that strikes us as quite plausible is a hybrid account on which (i) our normal competence with responsibility attribution does depend on affective systems, but (ii) affect also generates a bias leading to compatibilist responses in our experiments.

Although our experiment provides some reason to favor the performance error account of the compatibilist responses we found, it seems clear that deciding between the affective performance error and the affective competence models of compatibilist responses is not the sort of issue that will be resolved by a single crucial experiment. What we really need here is a deeper understanding of the role that affect plays in moral cognition more generally. (Presumably, if we had a deeper understanding of this more general issue, we would be able to do a better job of figuring out how empirical studies could address the specific question about the role of affect in judgments of moral responsibility.) But our inability to resolve all of the relevant questions immediately is no cause for pessimism. On the contrary, we see every reason to be optimistic about the prospects for research in this area. Recent years have seen a surge of interest in the ways in which affect can influence moral cognition—with new empirical studies and theoretical developments coming in all the time—and it seems likely that the next few years will yield important new insights into the question at hand.

7. Philosophical implications

Our findings help to explain why the debate between compatibilists and incompatibilists is so stubbornly persistent. It seems that certain psychological processes tend to generate compatibilist intuitions, while others tend to generate incompatibilist intuitions. Thus, each of the two major views appeals to an element of our psychological makeup.

But the experimental results do not serve merely to give us insight into the causal origins of certain philosophical positions; they also help us to evaluate some of the arguments that have been put forward in support of those positions. After all, many of these arguments rely on explicit appeals to intuition. If we find that different intuitions are produced by different psychological mechanisms, we might conclude that some of these intuitions should be given more weight than others. What we need to know now is which intuitions to take seriously and which to dismiss as products of mechanisms that are only leading us astray.

Clearly, the answer will depend partly on which, if any, of the three models described above turns out to be the right one, and since we don't yet have the data we need to decide between these competing models, we will not be able to offer a definite conclusion here. Our approach will therefore be to consider each of the models in turn and ask what implications it would have (if it turned out to be correct) for broader philosophical questions about the role of intuitions in the debate over moral responsibility.

PERFORMANCE ERROR MODEL

If compatibilist intuitions are explained by the performance error model, then we shouldn't assign much weight to these intuitions. For on that model, as we have described it, compatibilist intuitions are a product of the distorting effects of emotion and motivation. If we could eliminate the performance errors, the compatibilist intuitions should disappear.

Note that the performance error model does not claim that people's compatibilist intuitions are actually *incorrect*. What it says is simply that the process that generates these intuitions involves a certain kind of error. It is certainly possible that, even though the process involves this error, it ends up yielding a correct conclusion. Still, we feel that the performance error model has important philosophical implications. At the very least, it suggests that the fact that people sometimes have compatibilist intuitions does not itself give us reason to suppose that compatibilism is correct.

The philosophical implications of the performance error model have a special significance because the experimental evidence gathered thus far seems to suggest that the basic idea behind this model is actually true. But the jury is still out. Further research might show that one of the other models is in fact more accurate, and we therefore consider their philosophical implications as well.

AFFECTIVE COMPETENCE MODEL

On the affective competence model, people's responses in the concrete conditions of our original experiment are genuine expressions of their underlying competence. The suggestion is that the compatibilist responses people give in these conditions are not clouded by any kind of performance error. Rather, these responses reflect a successful implementation of the system we normally use for making responsibility judgments, and that system should therefore be regarded as a compatibilist one.

In many ways, this affective competence model is reminiscent of the view that P. F. Strawson (1962) puts forward in his classic paper 'Freedom and Resentment.' On that view, it would be a mistake to go about trying to understand the concept of moral responsibility by seeking to associate it with some sort of metaphysical theory. Rather, the best place to start is with an examination of the 'reactive attitudes' (blame, remorse, gratitude, etc.) and the role they play in our ordinary practice of responsibility attribution.

Yet, despite the obvious affinities between the affective competence model and Strawson's theory, it is important to keep in mind certain respects in which the affective competence model is making substantially weaker claims. Most importantly, the model isn't specifically claiming that people proceed *correctly* in the concrete conditions. All it says is that people's responses in these conditions reflect a successful implementation of their own underlying system for making responsibility judgments. This claim then leaves it entirely open whether the criteria used in that underlying system are themselves correct or incorrect.

For an analogous case, consider the ways in which people ordinarily make probability judgments. It can be shown that people's probability judgments often involve incorrect inferences, and one might therefore be tempted to assume that people are not correctly applying their own underlying criteria for probabilistic inference. But many psychologists reject this view. They suggest that people actually are correctly applying their underlying criteria and that the mistaken probabilistic inferences only arise because people's underlying criteria are themselves faulty (see, e.g., Tversky and Kahneman 1981; 1983).

Clearly, a similar approach could be applied in the case of responsibility judgments. Even if people's compatibilist intuitions reflect a successful implementation of their underlying system for making responsibility judgments, one could still argue that this underlying system is itself flawed. Hence, the affective competence model would vindicate the idea that people's core views about responsibility are compatibilist, but it would be a mistake to regard the model as an outright vindication of those intuitions.

CONCRETE COMPETENCE MODEL

The implications of the concrete competence model depend in a crucial way on the precise details of the competence involved. Since it is not possible to say anything very general about all of the models in this basic category, we will focus specifically on the implications of the claim that people's responsibility attributions are subserved by an encapsulated module.

As a number of authors have noted, modularity involves a kind of trade-off. The key advantages of modules are that they usually operate automatically, unconsciously, and extremely quickly. But these advantages come at a price. The reason why modules are able to operate so quickly is that they simply ignore certain sources of potentially relevant information. Even when we know that the lines in the Müller-Lyer illusion are the same length, we still have the visual illusion. Perhaps in the assignment of moral responsibility, we are dealing with a similar sort of phenomenon—a 'moral illusion.' It might be that people have a complex and sophisticated theory about the relationship between determinism and moral responsibility but that the relevant module just isn't able to access this theory. It continues to spit out judgments that the agent is blameworthy even when these judgments go against a consciously held theory elsewhere in the mind.

Of course, defenders of compatibilism might point out that this argument can also be applied in the opposite direction. They might suggest that the module itself contains a complex and sophisticated theory to which the rest of the mind has no access. The conclusion would be that, unless we use the module to assess the relationship between determinism and moral responsibility, we will arrive at an impoverished and inadequate understanding. This type of argument definitely seems plausible in certain domains (e.g., in the domain of grammatical theory). It is unclear at this point whether something analogous holds true for the domain of responsibility attribution.[13]

REFLECTIVE EQUILIBRIUM

Our concern in this section has been with philosophical questions about whether knowledge of particular mental processes is likely to give us valuable insight into complex moral issues. Clearly, these philosophical questions should be carefully distinguished from the purely psychological question as to whether people *think* that particular mental processes give them insight into these issues. Even if people think that a given process is affording them valuable moral insight, it might turn out that this process is actually entirely unreliable and they would be better off approaching these issues in a radically different way.

Still, we thought it would be interesting to know how people themselves resolve the tension between their rival intuitions, and we therefore ran one final experiment. All subjects were given a brief description of the results from our earlier studies and then asked to adjudicate the conflict between the compatibilist and incompatibilist intuitions. Given that people's intuitions in the concrete conditions contradict their intuitions in the abstract conditions, would they choose to hold on to the concrete judgment that Bill is morally responsible or the abstract judgment that no one can be responsible in a deterministic universe?[14] The results showed no clear majority on either side. Approximately half of the subjects chose to hold onto the judgment that the particular agent was morally responsible, while the other half chose to hold onto the judgment that no one can be responsible in a deterministic universe.[15] Apparently, there is no more consensus about these issues among the folk than there is among philosophers.

9. Conclusion

As we noted at the outset, participants in the debate over moral responsibility have appealed to an enormous variety of arguments. Theories from metaphysics, moral philosophy, philosophy of mind and even quantum mechanics have all been shown to be relevant in one way or another, and researchers are continually finding new ways in which seemingly unrelated considerations can be brought to bear on the issue. The present paper has not been concerned with the full scope of this debate. Instead, we have confined ourselves to just one type of evidence—evidence derived from people's intuitions.

Philosophers who have discussed lay intuitions in this area tend to say either that folk intuitions conform to compatibilism or that they conform to incompatibilism. Our actual findings were considerably more complex and perhaps more interesting. It appears that people have *both* compatibilist *and* incompatibilist intuitions. Moreover, it appears that these different kinds of intuitions are generated by different kinds of psychological processes. To assess the importance of this finding for the debate over moral responsibility, one would have to know precisely what sort of psychological process produced each type of intuition and how much weight to accord to the output of each sort of process. We have begun the task of addressing these issues here, but clearly far more remains to be done.

Acknowledgments

Several people gave us great feedback on an early draft of this paper. We'd like to thank John Doris, Chris Hitchcock, Bob Kane, Neil Levy, Al Mele, Stephen Morris, Thomas Nadelhoffer, Eddy Nahmias, Derk Pereboom, Lynne Rudder-Baker, Tamler Sommers, Jason Turner, and Manuel Vargas.

Thanks also to John Fischer for posting a draft of this paper on the Garden of Forking Paths weblog (http://gfp.typepad.com/). Versions of this paper were delivered at the UNC/Duke workshop on Naturalized Ethics, the Society for Empirical Ethics, the Society for Philosophy and Psychology, Yale University, the University of Arizona, and the Inland Northwest Philosophy Conference. We thank the participants for their helpful comments.

Notes

1. Actually, compatibilists and incompatibilists argue both (1) about whether determinism is compatible with moral responsibility and (2) about whether determinism is compatible with *free will*. As Fischer (1999) has emphasized, these two questions are logically independent. One might maintain that determinism is compatible with moral responsibility but not with free will. Here, however, our concern lies entirely with the first of the two questions—whether determinism is compatible with moral responsibility.

2. We use the term 'theory' here loosely to refer to an internally represented body of information. Also, when we claim that the folk have an incompatibilist theory, we are not suggesting that this theory has a privileged status over the psychological systems that generate compatibilist intuitions. As will be apparent, we think that it remains an open question whether the system that generates incompatibilist intuitions has a privileged status.

3. One virtue of Nahmias and colleagues' question about moral responsibility is that the notion of 'moral responsibility' is supposed to be common between philosophers and the folk. That is, philosophers tend to assume that the notion of moral responsibility deployed in philosophy closely tracks the notion that people express when they attribute moral responsibility. Furthermore, incompatibilists often specify that the relevant incompatibilist notion of free will is precisely the notion of free will that is required for moral responsibility (e.g., Campbell 1951). Nahmias and colleagues also ask questions about whether the agent in the deterministic scenario "acts of his own free will," and they find that people give answers consonant with compatibilism. We find these results less compelling. For the expression 'free will' has become a term of philosophical art, and it's unclear how to interpret lay responses concerning such technical terms. Moreover, incompatibilists typically grant that there are compatibilist notions of freedom that get exploited by the folk. Incompatibilists just maintain that there is also a commonsense notion of freedom that is not compatibilist.

4. Although these results from Viney and colleagues are suggestive, the measure used for identifying determinists is too liberal, and as a result, the group of subjects coded as 'determinists' might well include indeterminists. (See McIntyre et al. 1984 for a detailed description of the measure.) It remains to be seen whether this result will hold up using better measures for identifying determinists.

5. A related problem for the incompatibilist concerns the history of philosophy—if incompatibilism is intuitive, why has compatibilism been so popular among the great philosophers in history? An incompatibilist-friendly explanation is given in Nichols (2007).

6. In our deterministic scenario, we say that given the past, each decision *has to happen* the way that it does. This scenario allows us to test folk intuitions about the type

of compatibilism most popular in contemporary philosophy. Most contemporary compatibilists argue, following Frankfurt (1969), that an agent can be morally responsible for her behavior even if she *had to* act the way she did. (As we shall see, most subjects in our concrete condition give responses that conform to this view.) However, it would also be possible for a compatibilist to maintain that (1) we can never be responsible for an event that had to occur the way it did but also that (2) even if a particular behavior is determined to occur by the laws of nature, the agent does not necessarily *have to* perform that behavior. Our experiment does not address the possibility that the folk subscribe to this type of compatibilism. With any luck, that possibility will be investigated in future research.

7. It will, of course, be important to investigate whether our results extend to other populations. However, as we will stress throughout, we are primarily looking at how subjects from the same population give different answers in the different conditions.

8. χ^2 (1, $N = 41$) = 6.034, $p < .05$, two-tailed.

9. We also ran an experiment that used a more real-world kind of case than the deterministic set up described in our main experiments. This was sparked by some perceptive comments from Daniel Batson, who also gave us extremely helpful suggestions in designing the study. Again, the idea was to test whether abstract conditions were more likely to generate incompatibilist responses than affect-laden concrete conditions. All subjects were told about a genetic condition that leads a person to perform horrible actions, but they were also told that there is now an inexpensive pill that counteracts the condition and that now everyone with the condition gets this pill. In the abstract condition, subjects were then asked to indicate whether the people who had this condition before the pill was created could be held morally responsible for their actions. In the concrete condition, subjects were told that Bill had this condition before the pill was invented, and Bill killed his wife and children to be with his secretary. Subjects were then asked to indicate whether Bill was morally responsible for his action. The results were quite clear, and they were in concert with all of our earlier findings. Subjects given the abstract question gave significantly lower ratings of responsibility than subjects given the concrete question. Thus, the basic effect can be obtained using quite different materials.

10. As far as we know, no prior research has posited a moral responsibility module, but there has been considerable enthusiasm for the more general idea that many basic cognitive capacities are driven by modules (Fodor 1983; Leslie 1994), and a number of authors have suggested that certain aspects of moral judgment might be subserved by module-like mechanisms (Dwyer 1999; Harman 1999; Hauser 2006).

11. We are grateful to Jesse Prinz for suggesting this possibility.

12. As in our previous experiments, the vast majority of subjects said that our universe was most similar to the indeterminist universe. We suspect that being a determinist might actually lead people to have more compatibilist views (see Nichols 2006), and as a result, we antecedently decided to exclude the minority who gave the determinist response from our statistical analyses. The statistical details are as follows. The contrast between high and low affect for the determinist condition was significant (χ^2 (1, $N = 44$) = 8.066, $p < .01$). That is, people were more likely to say that it's possible for the rapist to be fully morally responsible. The contrast between the two high affect conditions was also significant (χ^2 (1, $N = 45$) = 7.204, $p < .01$); that is, people were more likely to say that it's possible that the rapist is fully morally responsible in the indeterminist universe. The contrast between the two low affect conditions was very highly significant (χ^2 (1, $N = 45$) = 26.492,

$p < 0.0001$). Subjects were dramatically more likely to say that it's possible for the tax cheat to be fully morally responsible in the indeterminist universe.

13. The distinction between modularity hypotheses and affective hypotheses first entered the philosophical literature in the context of the debate about the role of moral considerations in intentional action (Knobe 2006; Malle and Nelson 2003; Nadelhoffer 2004; Young et al. 2006). In that context, modularity hypotheses are usually regarded as vindicating folk intuitions. However, there is a key difference between that context and the present one. The difference is that information about the moral status of the action might be accessible in an intentional action module, but information about determinism is unlikely to be accessible in a moral responsibility module.

14. The design of the pilot study was modeled on the initial experiments described in section 3. Participants were asked both the high affect (Bill stabbing his wife) and the abstract questions (counterbalanced for order). They then answered the reflective equilibrium question:

> Previous research indicates that when people are given question 3 above, they often say that Bill is fully morally responsible for killing his family. But when people are given question 2 above, most people say that it is not possible that people in Universe A are fully morally responsible for their actions. Clearly these claims are not consistent. Because if it is not possible to be fully morally responsible in Universe A, then Bill can't be fully morally responsible.

We are interested in how people will resolve this inconsistency. So, regardless of how you answered questions 2 and 3, please indicate which of the following you agree with most:

> i. In Universe A, it is *not* possible for people to be morally responsible for their actions.
>
> ii. Bill, who is in universe A, *is* fully morally responsible for killing his family.

15. There were 19 subjects. Of these, 10 gave incompatibilist response to the reflective equilibrium question; 9 gave compatibilist responses.

References

Blair, R. 1995. "A cognitive developmental approach to morality: investigating the psychopath," *Cognition* **57.1**: 1–29.

Blair, R., L. Jones, F. Clark, M. Smith, and L. Jones. 1997. "The psychopathic individual: a lack of responsiveness to distress cues?" *Psychophysiology* **34.2**: 192–198.

Campbell, C. A. 1951. "Is 'free will' a pseudo-problem?" *Journal of Philosophy* **60**: 446–465.

Dwyer, S. 1999. "Moral competence," in *Philosophy and Linguistics*, ed. K. Murasugi and R. Stainton. Boulder, CO: Westview Press.

Fischer, J. 1999. "Recent work on moral responsibility," *Ethics* **110**: 93–139.

Fodor, J. 1983. *Modularity of Mind*. Cambridge, MA: MIT Press.

Frankfurt, H. 1969. "Alternate possibilities and moral responsibility," *Journal of Philosophy* **66**.23: 829–839.

Frankfurt, H. 1988. *The Importance of What We Care About: Philosophical Essays.* Cambridge: Cambridge University Press.

Greene, J., R. Sommerville, L. Nystrom, J. Darley, and J. Cohen. 2001. "An fMRI investigation of emotional engagement in moral judgment," *Science* **293**.5537: 2105–2108.

Haidt, J. 2001. "The emotional dog and its rational tail: a social intuitionist approach to moral judgment," *Psychological Review* **108**.4: 814–834.

Haidt, J., S. H. Koller, and M. G. Dias. 1993. "Affect, culture, and morality, or is it wrong to eat your dog?" *Journal of Personality and Social Psychology* **65**.4: 613–628.

Harman, G. 1999. "Moral philosophy and linguistics," in *Proceedings of the 20th World Congress of Philosophy. Vol. 1, Ethics.* ed. K. Brinkmann. Philosophy Documentation Center.

Hauser, M. 2006. *Moral Minds: The Unconscious Voice of Right and Wrong.* New York: HarperCollins.

Hauser, M., L. Young, and F. Cushman. 2007. "Reviving Rawls' linguistic analogy: operative principles and the causal structure of moral actions," in *Moral Psychology*, ed. W. Sinnott-Armstrong. Cambridge, MA: MIT Press, 107–144.

Kane, R. 1999. "Responsibility, luck, and chance: reflections on free will and indeterminism," *Journal of Philosophy* **965**: 217–240.

Knobe, J. 2003a. "Intentional action and side-effects in ordinary language," *Analysis* **63**: 190–193.

Knobe, J. 2003b. "Intentional action in folk psychology: an experimental investigation," *Philosophical Psychology* **16**: 309–324.

Knobe, J. 2006. "The concept of intentional action: a case study in the uses of folk psychology," *Philosophical Studies* **130**.2: 203–231.

Kunda, Z. 1990. "The case for motivated reasoning," *Psychological Bulletin* **108**.3: 480–498.

Lerner, J., J. Goldberg, and P. Tetlock. 1998. "Sober second thought: the effects of accountability, anger, and authoritarianism on attributions of responsibility," *Personality and Social Psychology Bulletin* **24**: 563–574.

Leslie, A. 1994. "ToMM, ToBY and agency: core architecture and domain specificity," in *Mapping the Mind*, ed. L. Hirschfeld and S. Gelman, Cambridge: Cambridge University Press.

Malle, B. and Nelson, S. 2003. "Judging *mens rea*: the tension between folk concepts and legal concepts of intentionality," *Behavioral Sciences and the Law* **21**.5: 563–580.

McIntyre, R., D. Viney, and W. Viney. 1984. "Validity of a scale designed to measure beliefs in free will and determinism," *Psychological Reports* **54**.

Nadelhoffer, T. 2004. "Praise, side effects, and folk ascriptions of intentional action," *Journal of Theoretical and Philosophical Psychology* **24**.2: 196–213.

Nahmias, E., S. Morris, T. Nadelhoffer, and J. Turner. 2005. "Surveying freedom: folk intuitions about free will and moral responsibility," *Philosophical Psychology* **18**.5: 561–584.

Nichols, S. 2002. "Norms with feeling," *Cognition* **84**.2: 221–236.

Nichols, S. 2004a. "The folk psychology of free will: fits and starts," *Mind & Language* **19**.5: 473–502.

Nichols, S. 2004b. *Sentimental Rules: On the Natural Foundations of Moral Judgment.* Oxford: Oxford University Press.

Nichols, S. 2006. "Folk intuitions about free will," *Journal of Cognition and Culture* **6**: 57–86.

Nichols, S. 2007. "The rise of compatibilism: a case study in the quantitative history of philosophy," *Midwest Studies* **31**.1: 260–270.

Prinz, J. 2007. *The Emotional Construction of Morals*. Oxford: Oxford University Press.

Smart, D., and Loewenstein, G. 2005. "The devil you know: the effects of identifiability on punitiveness," *Journal of Behavioral Decision Making* **18**: 311–318.

Strawson, G. 1986. *Freedom and Belief*. Oxford: Oxford University Press.

Strawson, P. 1962. "Freedom and resentment," *Proceedings of the British Academy* 48, reprinted in *Free Will,* ed. G. Watson. Oxford: Oxford University Press, 1980. Page references are to the reprinted version.

Tversky, A., and D. Kahneman. 1981. "The framing of decisions and the psychology of choice," *Science* **211**.4481: 453–458.

Tversky, A., and D. Kahneman. 1983. "Extensional versus intuitive reasoning: the conjunction fallacy in probability judgments," *Psychological Review* **90**: 293–315.

Vargas, M. 2006. "On the importance of history for responsible agency," *Philosophical Studies* **127**.3: 351–382.

Viney, W., D. Waldman, and J. Barchilon. 1982. "Attitudes toward punishment in relation to beliefs in free will and determinism," *Human Relations* **35**.11: 939–949.

Viney, W., P. Parker-Martin, and S. D. H. Dotten. 1988. "Beliefs in free will and determinism and lack of relation to punishment rationale and magnitude," *Journal of General Psychology* **115**: 15–23.

Watson, G. 1987. "Responsibility and the limits of evil: variations on a Strawsonian theme," in *Responsibility, Character, and the Emotions: New Essays in Moral Psychology,* ed. F. Schoeman. Cambridge: Cambridge University Press, 256–286.

Weinberg, J., S. Nichols, and S. Stich. 2001. "Normativity and epistemic intuitions," *Philosophical Topics* **29**.1–2: 429–460.

Woolfolk, R., J. Doris, and J. Darley. 2006. "Identification, situational constraint, and social cognition," *Cognition* **100**.2: 283–301.

Young, L., F. Cushman, R. Adolphs, D. Tranel, and M. Hauser. 2006. "Does emotion mediate the effect of an action's moral status on its intentional status? Neuropsychological evidence," *Journal of Cognition and Culture* **6**.617: 291–304.

PART ELEVEN

Suggested Further Readings

XI. The Phenomenology of Agency and Experimental Philosophy

On the experience of agency:

Bayne, Tim. 2008. "The phenomenology of agency," *Philosophy Compass* 3.1: 182–202.

Bayne, Tim and Neil Levy. 2006. "The feeling of doing: deconstructing the phenomenology of agency," in N. Sebanz and W. Prinz, eds., *Disorders of Volition*. Cambridge, MA: MIT Press, 49–68.

Horgan, Terry. 2011. "The phenomenology of agency and freedom: lessons from introspection and lessons from its limits," *Humana.Mente* 15: 77–97.

Pacherie, Elizabeth. 2008. "The phenomenology of action: a conceptual framework," *Cognition* 107: 179–217.

On neuroscience and free will see:

Dennett, Daniel. 2003. *Freedom Evolves*. London: Penguin Books.

Gazzaniga, Michael S. 2011 *Who's in Charge?: Free Will and the Science of the Brain*. New York: Harper Collins.

Mele, Alfred, "Free will and science," in Robert Kane, ed., *The Oxford Handbook of Free Will*, 2nd ed. New York: Oxford University Press.

Walter, Henrik. 2009. *Neurophilosophy of Free Will: From Libertarian Illusions to a Concept of Natural Autonomy*. Cambridge, MA: MIT Press.

Wegner, Daniel. 2002. *The Illusion of Conscious Will*. Cambridge, MA: MIT Press.

For a survey article on experimental philosophy and free will see:

Sommers, Tamler. 2010. "Experimental philosophy and free will," *Philosophy Compass* 5.2: 199–212.

See also:

Deery, Oisín, Matt Bedke and Shaun Nichols. Forthcoming. "Phenomenal abilities: incompatibilism and the experience of agency," in David Shoemaker, ed., *Oxford Studies in Agency and Responsibility*. New York: Oxford University Press.

Knobe, Joshua and Shaun Nichols. 2011. "Free will and the bounds of the self," in Robert Kane, ed., *The Oxford Handbook of Free Will*, 2nd ed. New York: Oxford University Press.

Nahmias, Eddy and Dylan Murray. 2010. "Experimental philosophy on free will: an error theory for incompatibilist intuitions," in *New Waves in Philosophy of Action*, eds., J. Aguilar, A. Buckareff, and K. Frankish. London: Palgrave-Macmillan.

Roskies, A.L. 2010. "Why Libet's studies don't pose a threat to free will," in Sinnott-Armstrong, W. and L. Nadel (eds.). *Conscious Will and Responsibility*. New York: Oxford University Press.

Sinnott-Armstrong, Walter and Lynn Nadel, eds. 2010. *Conscious Will and Responsibility: A Tribute to Benjamin Libet*. New York: Oxford University Press.

A GUIDE TO FURTHER READING

This bibliography is not intended to be a comprehensive guide to the contemporary literature. We are including only books in the references below, apart from the online articles that we have cited. A number of these works contain extensive or substantial bibliographies, as indicated with an asterisk (*). The anthologies and collections cited are an appropriate place to find important and influential articles beyond the works included in this collection and our further readings suggestions at the end of each section.

A comprehensive review of the recent literature in this field can be found in:

* Levy, Neil and Michael McKenna. 2009. "Recent work on free will and moral responsibility." *Philosophy Compass* 4.1: 96–133.

Online Sources

STANFORD ENCYCLOPEDIA OF PHILOSOPHY:

An important source of various survey articles including:

*"Free Will" by Timothy O'Connor:
http://plato.stanford.edu/entries/freewill/
*"Compatibilism" by Michael McKenna:
http://plato.stanford.edu/entries/compatibilism/
*"Incompatibilist Theories of Free Will" by Randolph Clarke:
http://plato.stanford.edu/entries/incompatibilism-theories/
*"Arguments for Incompatibilism" by Kadri Vihvelin:
http://plato.stanford.edu/entries/incompatibilism-arguments/
*"Moral Responsibility" by Andrew Eshleman:
http://plato.stanford.edu/entries/moral-responsibility/

INTERNET ENCYCLOPEDIA OF PHILOSOPHY:

* "Free Will" by Kevin Timpe:
http://www.iep.utm.edu/freewill/
* "Responsibility" by Garrath Williams:
http://www.iep.utm.edu/responsi/

Anthologies and Collections

Aguilar, J., A. Buckareff, and K. Frankish, eds. 2010. *New Waves in Philosophy of Action*. London: Palgrave-Macmillan.
Baer, John, James C. Kaufman, and Roy F. Baumeister, eds. 2008. *Are We Free? Psychology and Free Will*. Oxford: Oxford University. Press.

Berofsky, Bernard. ed., 1966. *Free Will and Determinism*. New York: Harper & Row.

Campbell, Neil, ed. 2003. *Freedom, Determinism and Responsibility*. Upper Saddle River, NJ: Prentice Hall.

Ekstrom, Laura, ed. 2001. *Agency and Responsibility*. Boulder, CO: Westview Press.

Fischer, John Martin. ed. 1986. *Moral Responsibility*. Ithaca, NY: Cornell University. Press.

Fischer, John Martin, ed., 2005. *Free Will: Critical Concepts in Philosophy, Vols. 1–4*. London: Routledge.

Fischer, John M., and Mark Ravizza, eds. 1993. *Perspectives on Moral Responsibility*. Ithaca, NY: Cornell University Press.

Kane, Robert, ed. 2002. *Free Will*. Oxford: Blackwell.

McKenna, Michael, and Paul Russell, eds. 2008. *Free Will and Reactive Attitudes*. Aldershot, UK: Ashgate Press.

O'Connor, Timothy, ed. 1995. *Agents, Causes, and Events*. New York: Oxford University. Press.

Pereboom, Derk, ed. 2009. *Free Will*, 2d ed. Indianapolis: Hackett.

Schoeman, Ferdinand, ed. 1987. *Responsibility, Character, and the Emotions: New Essays on Moral Psychology*. Cambridge: Cambridge University Press.

David Shoemaker, ed., 2013. *Oxford Studies in Agency and Responsibility*. New York: Oxford University Press.

Swinburne, Richard. 2012. *Free Will and Modern Science*. New York: Oxford University Press.

Watson, Gary, ed. 2003. *Free Will*, 2d ed. New York: Oxford University Press.

Widerker, David, and Michael McKenna, eds. 2003. *Moral Responsibility and Alternative Possibilities*. Aldershot, UK: Ashgate Press.

Introductions and Surveys

Campbell, Joseph. 2011. *Free Will*. Cambridge: Polity Press.

Fischer, John Martin, Robert Kane, Derk Pereboom, and Manuel Vargas, 2007. *Four Views on Free Will*, Malden, MA: Blackwell Publishers.

Haji, Ishtiyaque, 2009. *Incompatibilism's Allure*. Peterborough, ON: Broadview Press.

Kane, Robert. 2005. *A Contemporary Introduction to Free Will*. New York: Oxford University Press.

*Kane, Robert, ed. *The Oxford Handbook of Free Will*, 2d ed. New York: Oxford University Press.

McFee, Graham. 2001. *Free Will*. Kingston/Montreal: McGill Queens Press.

Pink, Thomas. 2004. *Free Will: A Very Short Introduction*. Oxford: Oxford University Press.

Timpe, Kevin. 2008. *Free Will: Sourcehood and Alternatives*. London: Continuum.

Advanced and More Specialized Studies

Arpaly, Nomy, 2006. *Merit, Meaning, and Human Bondage*. Princeton, NJ: Princeton Univ. Press.

Arpaly, Nomy, 2003. *Unprincipled Virtue*. New York: Oxford University Press.

Balaguer, Mark. 2010. *Free Will as an Open Scientific Problem*. Cambridge, MA: MIT Press.

Berofsky, Bernard, 1995. *Liberation from Self.* Cambridge, UK: Cambridge University Press.

Bok, Hilary, 1998. *Freedom and Responsibility.* Princeton, NJ: Princeton University Press.

Bratman, Michael, 2007. *Structures of Agency.* New York: Oxford University Press.

Clarke, Randolph. 2003. *Libertarian Accounts of Free Will.* Oxford: Oxford University Press.

Darwall, Stephen. 2006. *The Second-Person Standpoint: Morality, Respect and Accountability.* Cambridge, Mass. Harvard University Press.

Dennett, Daniel, 1984. *Elbow Room: The Varieties of Free Will Worth Wanting.* Cambridge, MA: MIT Press.

Dennett, Daniel, 2003. *Freedom Evolves.* London: Penguin Books.

Dilman, Ilham. 1999. *Free Will: An Historical and Philosophical Introduction.* London: Routledge.

Doris, John. 2002. *Lack of Character: Personality and Moral Behavior.* Cambridge: Cambridge University Press.

Double, Richard. 1991. *The Non-Reality of Free Will.* New York: Oxford University Press.

Ekstrom, Laura Waddell. 2000. *Free Will: A Philosophical Study.* Boulder, CO: Westview Press.

Fischer, John Martin. 1994. *The Metaphysics of Free Will.* Oxford: Blackwell Publishers.

Fischer, John Martin. 2006. *My Way: Essays on Moral Responsibility.* New York: Oxford University Press.

Fischer, John Martin, and Mark Ravizza, 1998. *Responsibility and Control: An Essay on Moral Responsibility.* Cambridge, UK: Cambridge University Press.

Frankfurt, Harry. 1988. *The Importance of What We Care About.* Cambridge: Cambridge University Press.

Gazzaniga, Michael S. 2011. *Who's in Charge?: Free Will and the Science of the Brain.* New York: HarperCollins.

Haji, Ishtiyaque. 1998. *Moral Appraisability.* New York: Oxford University Press.

Harris, Sam 2012. *Free Will.* New York: Free Press.

Hodgson, David. 2012. *Rationality + Consciousness = Free Will.* Oxford: Oxford University Press.

Honderich, Ted. 2002. *How Free Are You?*, 2d ed. Oxford: Oxford University Press.

Kane, Robert. 1996. *The Significance of Free Will.* Oxford: Oxford University Press.

Kennett, Jeanette. 2003. *Agency and Responsibility.* New York: Oxford University Press.

Klein, Martha. 1990. *Determinism, Blameworthiness and Deprivation.* Oxford: Oxford University Press.

Levy, Neil. 2011. *Hard Luck.* New York: Oxford University Press.

McKenna, Michael. 2012. *Conversation & Responsibility.* New York: Oxford University Press.

Mele, Alfred. 2006. *Free Will and Luck.* New York: Oxford University Press.

Mele, Alfred, 1995. *Autonomous Agents.* New York: Oxford University Press.

Nagel, Thomas. 1986. *The View from Nowhere.* New York: Oxford University Press.

O'Connor, Timothy. 2000. *Persons and Causes: The Metaphysics of Free Will.* New York: Oxford University Press.

Nelkin, Dana. 2011. *Making Sense of Freedom and Responsibility.* New York: Oxford University Press.

Nozick, Robert. 1981. *Philosophical Explanations.* Cambridge, MA: Belknap Press of Harvard University Press.

Pereboom, Derk, 2001. *Living Without Free Will*. Cambridge: Cambridge University Press.

Pettit, Philip, 2001. *A Theory of Freedom: From the Psychology to the Politics of Agency*. New York: Oxford University Press.

Rowe, William, 1991. *Thomas Reid on Freedom and Morality*. Ithaca, NY: Cornell University Press.

Russell, Paul, 1995. *Freedom and Moral Sentiment: Hume's Way of Naturalizing Responsibility*. New York: Oxford University Press.

Scanlon, T.M., 2008. *Moral Dimensions: Permissibility, Meaning, Blame*. Cambridge, MA: Belknap Press of Harvard University Press.

Scanlon, T. M., 1998. *What We Owe to Each Other*. Cambridge, MA: Harvard University Press.

Sie, Maureen. 2005. *Justifying Blame: Why Free Will Matters and Why it Does Not*. Amsterdam: Rodolphi.

Sinnott-Armstrong, Walter and Lynn Nadel, eds. 2010. *Conscious Will and Responsibility: A Tribute to Benjamin Libet*. New York: Oxford University Press.

Sher, George. 2006. *In Praise of Blame*. New York: Oxford University Press.

Smilansky, Saul. 2000. *Free Will and Illusion*. Oxford: Oxford University Press.

Sorabji, Richard. 1980. *Necessity, Cause and Blame: Perspectives on Aristotle's Philosophy*. London: Duckworth.

Sommers, Tamler. 2012. *Relative Justice: Cultural Diversity, Free Will and Moral Responsibility*. Princeton, NJ: Princeton University Press.

Steward, Helen. 2012. *A Metaphysics of Freedom*. Oxford: Oxford University Press.

Strawson, Galen, 1986. *Freedom and Belief*. Oxford: Clarendon Press.

Van Inwagen, Peter. 1983. *An Essay on Free Will*. Oxford: Oxford University Press.

Wallace, R. Jay, 1994. *Responsibility and the Moral Sentiments*. Cambridge, MA: Harvard University Press.

Waller, Bruce. 2011. *Against Moral Responsibility*. Cambridge, MA: MIT Press.

Walter, Henrik. 2009. *Neurophilosophy of Free Will: From Libertarian Illusions to a Concept of Natural Autonomy*. Cambridge, MA: MIT Press.

Watson, Gary, 2004. *Agency and Answerability*. New York: Oxford University Press.

Wegner, Daniel 2002. *The Illusion of Conscious Will*. Cambridge, MA: MIT Press.

Williams, Bernard. 1993. *Shame and Necessity*. Berkeley: University of California Press.

Wolf, Susan. 1990. *Freedom Within Reason*. Oxford: Oxford University Press.

Woody, J. Melvin. 1998. *Freedom's Embrace*. Philadelphia: University of Pennsylvania Press.

Zimmerman, Michael. 1988. *An Essay on Moral Responsibility*. Totowa, N.J.: Rowman & Littlefield.

NAME INDEX

537

SUBJECT INDEX

Made in the USA
Monee, IL
06 January 2021